Middle School 3-2

학교시험 완벽대비

2학기 전과정

적중 100 plus

영어 기출문제집

중 3

천재 | 정사열

Best Collection

구성과 특징

교과서의 주요 학습 내용을 중심으로 학습 영역별 특성에 맞춰 단계별로 다양한 학습 기회를 제공하여
단원별 학습능력 평가는 물론 중간 및 기말고사 시험 등에 완벽하게 대비할 수 있도록 내용을 구성

Words & Expressions

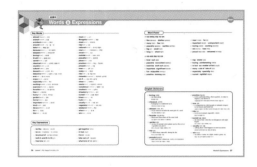

Step1 Key Words 단원별 핵심 단어 설명 및 풀이
Key Expression 단원별 핵심 숙어 및 관용어 설명
Word Power 반대 또는 비슷한 뜻 단어 배우기
English Dictionary 영어로 배우는 영어 단어

Step2 실력평가 단원별 수시평가 대비 주관식, 객관식 문제풀이

Step3 서술형 대비 학업성취도 및 수행능력평가 대비 서술형 문제풀이

Conversation

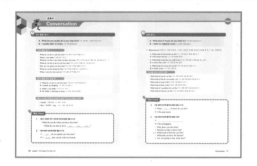

Step1 핵심 의사소통 소통에 필요한 주요 표현 방법 요약
핵심 Check 기본적인 표현 방법 및 활용능력 확인

Step2 대화문 익히기 교과서 대화문 심층 분석 및 확인

Step3 교과서 확인학습 빈칸 채우기를 통한 문장 완성 능력 확인

Step4 기본평가 시험대비 기초 학습 능력 평가

Step5 실력평가 단원별 수시평가 대비 주관식, 객관식 문제풀이

Step6 서술형 대비 학업성취도 및 수행능력평가 대비 서술형 문제풀이

Grammar

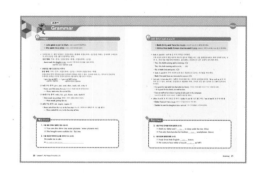

Step1 주요 문법 단원별 주요 문법 사항과 예문을 알기 쉽게 설명
핵심 Check 기본 문법사항에 대한 이해 여부 확인

Step2 기본평가 시험대비 기초 학습 능력 평가

Step3 실력평가 단원별 수시평가 대비 주관식, 객관식 문제풀이

Step4 서술형 대비 학업성취도 및 수행능력평가 대비 서술형 문제풀이

Reading

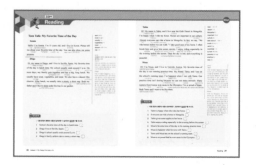

Step1 구문 분석 단원별로 제시된 문장에 대한 구문별 분석과 내용 설명
확인문제 문장에 대한 기본적인 이해와 인지능력 확인

Step2 확인학습A 빈칸 채우기를 통한 문장 완성 능력 확인

Step3 확인학습B 제시된 우리말을 영어로 완성하여 작문 능력 키우기

Step4 실력평가 단원별 수시평가 대비 주관식, 객관식 문제풀이

Step5 서술형 대비 학업성취도 및 수행능력평가 대비 서술형 문제풀이
교과서 구석구석 교과서에 나오는 기타 문장까지 완벽 학습

Composition

|영역별 핵심문제|

단어 및 어휘, 대화문, 문법, 독해 등 각 영역별 기출문제의 출제 유형을 분석하여 실전에 대비하고 연습할 수 있도록 문제를 배열

|단원별 예상문제|

기출문제를 분석한 후 새로운 시험 출제 경향을 더하여 새롭게 출제될 수 있는 문제를 포함하여 시험에 완벽하게 대비할 수 있도록 준비

|서술형 실전 및 창의사고력 문제|

학교 시험에서 점차 늘어나는 서술형 시험에 집중 대비하고 고득점을 취득하는데 만전을 기하기 위한 학습 코너

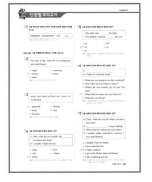

|단원별 모의고사|

영역별, 단계별 학습을 모두 마친 후 실전 연습을 위한 모의고사

on the textbook

교과서 파헤치기

- 단어Test1~3 영어 단어 우리말 쓰기, 우리말을 영어 단어로 쓰기, 영영풀이에 해당하는 단어와 우리말 쓰기
- 대화문Test1~2 대화문 빈칸 완성 및 전체 대화문 쓰기
- 본문Test1~5 빈칸 완성, 우리말 쓰기, 문장 배열연습, 영어 작문하기 복습 등 단계별 반복 학습을 통해 교과서 지문에 대한 완벽한 습득
- 구석구석지문Test1~2 지문 빈칸 완성 및 전문 영어로 쓰기

Lesson 5

Pictures Speak a Thousand Words

 의사소통 기능

- 궁금증 표현하기
  I'm curious about that balloon.

- 정의하기
  It means you must not enter.

 언어 형식

- 가정법 과거
  I **would** be so happy **if** you **were** with me.

- 관계대명사 whose
  It was written in 1973 by a woman **whose** husband was far away.

교과서
Words & Expressions

Key Words

- □ **ad(= advertisement)**[æd] 몡 광고
- □ **awesome**[ɔ́:səm] 혱 근사한, 멋진, 엄청난, 어마어마한
- □ **backpack**[bǽkpæk] 몡 배낭
- □ **balloon**[bəlúːn] 몡 풍선
- □ **battery**[bǽtəri] 몡 건전지
- □ **battle**[bǽtl] 몡 전쟁, 전투
- □ **bee**[biː] 몡 벌
- □ **board**[bɔːrd] 몡 넓은 판, 판자
- □ **border**[bɔ́ːrdər] 몡 국경, 경계
- □ **Braille**[breil] 몡 점자
- □ **cell phone** 휴대 전화
- □ **chimney**[tʃímni] 몡 굴뚝
- □ **close**[klous] 뷔 가까이, 근접하여
- □ **cross**[krɔːs] 동 건너다, 가로지르다
- □ **curious**[kjúəriəs] 혱 호기심이 많은, 궁금한
- □ **dead**[ded] 혱 죽은, 쓸모없는
- □ **discover**[diskʌ́vər] 동 발견하다
- □ **dot**[dɑt] 몡 점
- □ **enemy**[énəmi] 몡 적군, 적대자
- □ **exactly**[igzǽktli] 뷔 정확하게
- □ **expression**[ikspréʃən] 몡 표현
- □ **foreign**[fɔ́ːrən] 혱 외국의
- □ **gesture**[dʒéstʃər] 몡 몸짓, 몸동작
- □ **ground**[graund] 몡 땅, 지면
- □ **hidden**[hídn] 혱 숨은, 숨겨진
- □ **hire**[haiər] 동 고용하다
- □ **hug**[hʌg] 몡 포옹 동 포옹하다
- □ **hunter**[hʌ́ntər] 몡 사냥꾼
- □ **husband**[hʌ́zbənd] 몡 남편
- □ **ill**[il] 혱 아픈, 병든

- □ **knock**[nɑk] 동 치다, 두드리다
- □ **Latin**[lǽtən] 몡 라틴어 혱 라틴어의
- □ **letter**[létər] 몡 글자, 문자
- □ **light**[lait] 동 불을 붙이다, 불을 밝히다
- □ **loudly**[láudli] 뷔 큰 소리로, 시끄럽게
- □ **mean**[miːn] 동 의미하다
- □ **message**[mésidʒ] 몡 메시지, 전갈, 전언
- □ **misunderstanding**[misʌndərstǽndiŋ] 몡 오해
- □ **oil**[ɔil] 몡 기름
- □ **point**[pɔint] 동 가리키다, 지시하다
- □ **pond**[pɑnd] 몡 연못
- □ **powerful**[páuərfəl] 혱 강한, 강력한
- □ **prepare**[pripέər] 동 준비하다
- □ **product**[prɑ́dʌkt] 몡 상품, 제품
- □ **pull**[pul] 동 끌다, 잡아당기다
- □ **rather**[rǽðər] 뷔 다소, 약간
- □ **reply**[riplái] 몡 답장
- □ **ring**[riŋ] 몡 반지
- □ **seat**[siːt] 몡 좌석, 의석
- □ **seem**[siːm] 동 ~처럼 보이다
- □ **seriously**[síəriəsli] 뷔 진지하게, 심각하게
- □ **sign language** 수화
- □ **soldier**[sóuldʒər] 몡 군인
- □ **son**[sʌn] 몡 아들
- □ **system**[sístəm] 몡 체계, 시스템
- □ **toward**[tɔːrd] 전 ~을 향하여
- □ **traffic**[trǽfik] 몡 교통
- □ **translate**[trænsléit] 동 번역하다, 해석하다
- □ **vote**[vout] 동 투표하다, 선출하다
- □ **whether**[hwéðər] 접 ~이든지 아니든지

Key Expressions

- □ **at a price of** ~의 가격으로
- □ **be careful with** ~에 조심하다
- □ **be covered with** ~로 덮이다
- □ **be curious about** ~에 대하여 궁금해 하다
- □ **except for** ~을 제외하고
- □ **get over** 이겨내다, 극복하다
- □ **in good health** 건강하여
- □ **instead of** ~ 대신에
- □ **Let's see.** (= **Let me see.**) 글쎄.. 어디 보자.

- □ **look after** ~을 돌보다
- □ **pick up** 집어 올리다, 차에 태우다
- □ **right away** 즉시, 당장
- □ **step back** 물러서다
- □ **the rich** (= **rich people**) 부자들
- □ **turn off** ~을 끄다
- □ **vote for** ~에 (찬성하는) 투표를 하다
- □ **wait for** ~을 기다리다
- □ **win many seats** 많은 의석을 확보하다

Word Power

※ 서로 비슷한 뜻을 가진 어휘

- □ **ad** 광고 : **commercial** 광고
- □ **border** 국경, 경계 : **boundary** 경계
- □ **enemy** 적군, 적대자 : **foe** 적
- □ **hug** 포옹; 포옹하다 : **embrace** 끌어안다

- □ **battle** 전쟁, 전투 : **combat** 전투
- □ **curious** 궁금한 : **inquisitive** 탐구심이 많은
- □ **hire** 고용하다 : **employ** 고용하다
- □ **vote** 투표하다, 선출하다 : **elect** 선출하다

※ 서로 반대의 뜻을 가진 어휘

- □ **war** 전쟁 ↔ **peace** 평화
- □ **discover** 발견하다 ↔ **hide** 숨기다
- □ **hire** 고용하다 ↔ **fire** 해고하다

- □ **dead** 죽은, 쓸모없는 ↔ **alive** 살아 있는
- □ **enemy** 적군, 적대자 ↔ **friend** 친구
- □ **ill** 아픈, 병든 ↔ **healthy** 건강한

※ -ous = 형용사 어미

- □ **curious** 호기심이 많은
- □ **serious** 심각한
- □ **adventurous** 모험적인, 대담한

- □ **famous** 유명한
- □ **various** 다양한
- □ **dangerous** 위험한

- □ **delicious** 맛있는
- □ **nervous** 불안한

English Dictionary

- □ **dead** 죽은
  → no longer alive 더 이상 살아 있지 않은

- □ **discover** 발견하다
  → to find out something that you did not know before
  전에 알지 못했던 것을 찾아내다

- □ **foreign** 외국의
  → from another country 다른 나라로부터

- □ **ground** 땅, 지면
  → the surface of the Earth 지구의 표면

- □ **hire** 고용하다
  → to pay someone to work for you
  당신을 위해 일하도록 누군가에게 돈을 지급하다

- □ **hug** 포옹
  → the action of putting your arms around someone to show your love or friendship 당신의 애정이나 우정을 보여 주기 위하여 양팔로 다른 사람을 안는 행위

- □ **husband** 남편
  → the man that a woman is married to
  한 여자가 결혼한 남자

- □ **ill** 아픈, 병든
  → suffering from an illness or disease 질병으로 고통을 겪는

- □ **oil** 기름
  → a thick liquid made from plants or animals that is used in cooking
  요리를 위하여 사용되는 식물이나 동물로부터 만들어진 걸쭉한 액체

- □ **prepare** 준비하다
  → to make something ready for use
  어떤 것을 사용할 준비가 되도록 만들다

- □ **rather** 다소, 약간
  → in some degree 어느 정도로

- □ **reply** 답장
  → an answer to a letter 편지에 대한 답장

- □ **ring** 반지
  → a piece of jewelry in the form of a circle that you wear on a finger 손가락에 끼는 둥근 형태의 보석

- □ **seat** 의석
  → a position as a member of a committee, court, etc.
  위원회, 법정 등의 구성원으로서의 지위

- □ **son** 아들
  → someone's male child 누군가의 남자아이

- □ **toward** ~을 향하여
  → in the direction of ~ 방향으로

- □ **translate** 번역하다, 해석하다
  → to change spoken or written words into another language 구어 또는 문어를 다른 언어로 바꾸다

- □ **vote** 투표하다, 선출하다
  → to express one's preference for a candidate
  후보자에 대하여 선호를 표시하다

서답형

01 다음 문장의 빈칸에 〈영어 설명〉에 해당하는 단어를 주어진 철자로 시작하여 쓰시오.

> The child was very c_____ about the strange animal.
> 〈영어 설명〉 wanting to know or learn about something

02 다음 빈칸에 공통으로 들어갈 말로 가장 적절한 것은?

> • Traditional mail contains a special meaning because someone wrote a _____ by hand.
> • A long time ago, we didn't have our own _____s.

① border   ② letter
③ gesture   ④ product
⑤ reply

[03~04] 다음 설명에 해당하는 단어를 고르시오.

03

> to express one's preference for a candidate

① permit   ② hug
③ hire   ④ discover
⑤ vote

04

> the action of putting your arms around someone to show your love or friendship

① gesture   ② prepare
③ pull   ④ hug
⑤ hire

서답형

05 다음 우리말에 맞게 주어진 단어를 이용하여 쓰시오.

> 나무는 곧 푸른 잎으로 덮일 것입니다! (cover)

➡ Trees will _____ green leaves soon!

06 다음 빈칸에 들어갈 말로 알맞은 것은?

> (A) Niagara Falls is a truly _____ sight.
> (B) He showed his _____ talents as an actor.

① powerful – recognized
② curious – allowed
③ awesome – hidden
④ curious – hidden
⑤ awesome – allowed

07 다음 문장의 빈칸에 들어갈 단어를 〈보기〉에서 고르고, 각 단어의 첫 글자를 조합한 단어를 쓰시오.

> ┤ 보기 ├
> son   lit   except   crossing   oil

> 1. A woman was _____ the road toward me.
> 2. I _____ a candle.
> 3. You should put _____ at first in the frying pan to make a fried egg.
> 4. He has three daughters and two _____s.
> 5. I like to play every sport _____ for basketball.

➡ _____

01 〈보기〉에서 알맞은 단어를 찾아 빈칸을 완성하시오. (한 단어를 추가하고 필요하면 변형하여 쓰시오.)

┌─── 보기 ───┐
except   look   wait   lot
└──────────┘

(1) There are _____ great shoes in this store.

(2) We had to _____ him at the restaurant for twenty minutes.

(3) I am doing okay, and the weather is nice _____ the fine dust.

(4) My neighbor asked me to _____ her cat.

02 대화의 빈칸에 〈영영풀이〉에 해당하는 단어를 주어진 철자로 쓰시오.

┌──────────────────────────┐
G: What are these dots for? I'm curious about them.
B: Oh, they are _____. They are for blind people.
G: I see. Now I can guess what they mean.
└──────────────────────────┘

┌──────────────────────────┐
<영영풀이> a system of printing for blind people, using raised patterns that they read by touching
└──────────────────────────┘

➡ _____

03 다음 우리말과 같은 표현이 되도록 문장의 빈칸을 채우시오.

(1) 그들은 또한 감시를 위해 경비원을 고용할 수도 있다.
  ➡ They can also _____ a security guard to keep watch.

(2) 이건 나와 지나 사이에 오해가 있었기 때문이었어.
  ➡ This was because there was a _____ between Jina and me.

(3) 그는 다소 별나지만 그의 소설 속의 메시지는 우리에게 매우 친근하다.
  ➡ He is _____ strange, but his novels' messages are very familiar to us.

04 영영풀이에 해당하는 단어를 〈보기〉에서 찾아 첫 번째 빈칸에 쓰고, 두 번째 빈칸에는 우리말 뜻을 쓰시오.

┌──────────────────────────┐
oil   translate   ring   discover
└──────────────────────────┘

(1) _____ : a piece of jewelry in the form of a circle that you wear on a finger:
  _____

(2) _____ : to find out something that you did not know before: _____

(3) _____ : a thick liquid made from plants or animals that is used in cooking:
  _____

(4) _____ : to change spoken or written words into another language: _____

05 다음 빈칸에 주어진 철자로 시작하는 알맞은 단어를 쓰시오.

(A) Koreans use more water than other f_____ countries with large populations.

(B) Human beings are the greatest h_____ and have always eaten meat.

(C) He must be a s_____ because he is wearing the uniform.

Conversation

1 궁금증 표현하기

> • I'm curious about that balloon. 나는 저 풍선이 궁금해.

■ 궁금증을 표현할 때는 curious(궁금한, 호기심이 많은), wonder(궁금하다), want to know(알고 싶다) 등의 표현을 이용하여 'I'm curious about ~.(나는 ~이 궁금해.)', 'I wonder ~.(나는 ~이 궁금하다.)' 라고 말한다. 또한 궁금한 내용을 알고 싶다는 의미를 'I would like to know ~', 'I want to know ~.', 'I don't know why ~.'라고 표현할 수도 있다.

■ 궁금함을 나타내는 'I'm curious'와 명사구를 같이 쓸 때는 'I'm curious about+명사구'이고, 명사절과 함께 쓸 때는 'I'm curious if/whether ~.' 또는 'I'm curious 의문사 (주어)+동사 ~.'이다. 'I wonder ~.'를 사용할 때의 어순은 'I wonder+의문사+주어+동사 ~.', 'I wonder+if/whether+주어+동사 ~.'이고, 명사(구)와 함께 나타낼 때는 'I wonder about+명사(구)'이다.

■ 궁금한 점에 대하여 알고 싶을 때는 'Can you tell me about ~?(~에 대하여 이야기해 줄 수 있니?)', 'I'm interested to know ~.(나는 ~을 아는 것에 관심 있어.)'와 같이 표현할 수 있고, 'Can I ~?', 'Can/Could you ~?' 등과 같이 요구/요청을 나타내는 조동사 표현을 사용하여 'Can I ask you ~?' 또는 'Can you tell me ~?'와 같이 궁금한 점에 대하여 물어볼 수 있다. 그 외에 궁금증을 나타낼 때는 'Do you know ~?' 등을 사용할 수도 있다.

궁금증 표현하기

- I am curious about ~. 나는 ~이 궁금하다.
- I'm curious if/whether 주어+동사 ~. 나는 ~가 궁금하다.
- I'm wondering + if/whether/의문사 주어+동사 ~. 나는 ~인지 궁금하다.
- I would like/want to know ~. 나는 ~이 알고 싶다.
- I'd be very interested to know ~. 나는 ~이 알고 싶다.
- Can you tell me about ~? ~에 대해 말해 줄 수 있니?
- I want to know 명사구/명사절 ~. 나는 ~을 알고 싶다.

핵심 Check

1. 다음 밑줄 친 부분 대신 바꿔 쓰기에 적절하지 <u>않은</u> 것은?

G: I'm curious about that robot. Why is it standing there?

B: It's a kind of ad. It tells people their batteries are very powerful.

① I'm wondering about that robot.
② Can I tell you about that robot?
③ I would like to know about that robot.
④ Can you tell me about that robot?
⑤ I'd be very interested to know about that robot.

② 정의하기

• **It means you must not enter.** 그것은 네가 들어가지 말아야 한다는 것을 의미해.

■ 'I'm curious ∼.' 등으로 상대방이 궁금증을 표현하거나 의미를 물어보면 'This/It means ∼.(그것은 ∼을 의미한다.)' 또는 'It is ∼.(그것은 ∼이다.)' 등의 표현을 사용하여 상대방이 궁금해 하거나, 알고 싶어 하는 것의 의미나 정의를 설명하게 된다.

■ 정의를 말할 때는 'X means ∼.(X는 ∼을 의미한다.)' 또는 'The meaning of X is ∼.(X의 의미는 ∼이다.)'를 사용하고, 'X stands for ∼.(X는 ∼을 나타낸다.)'도 어떤 말이나 문자, 기호, 신호, 상징 등의 의미를 설명할 때 사용한다.

■ 보통 의미를 설명하거나 정의를 나타내는 말은 상대방이 궁금증을 표현하거나 설명을 요청할 때 그 대답으로 쓰인다. 설명을 요청할 때 쓰는 표현은 'What is X (exactly)?(X가 (정확하게) 무엇이니?)', 'What does that mean?(그것이 무슨 뜻입니까?)', 'What do you mean by X?(X가 무슨 뜻이니?)' 등이다.

■ 상대방에게 설명을 요청할 때는 'Could you explain the meaning of it?', 'Could you tell me more about them?' 등의 표현을 사용하거나, Could 대신 Would, Can, Will 등을 사용하기도 한다. 또한 'Do you mind if I ask you to explain ∼?'이라고 말할 수도 있다.

정의하기

• This means ∼. 이것은 ∼을 의미한다.

• The meaning of this is ∼. 이것의 의미는 ∼이다.

• X stands for ∼. X는 ∼을 나타낸다.

설명 요청하기

• What is X exactly? X가 정확하게 무엇이니?

• What does that mean? 그것이 무슨 뜻입니까?

• What do you mean by X? X가 무슨 뜻이니?

• What is the meaning of that exactly? 정확하게 그게 무슨 뜻입니까?

• Could you explain what it means? 그게 무엇을 의미하는지 설명 좀 해주시겠습니까?

핵심 Check

2. 주어진 어휘를 이용하여 밑줄 친 우리말에 해당하는 영어 문장을 쓰시오.

B: If there's no enemy, they don't smoke at all, do they?

G: Yes, they do. Smoke from one chimney means "No enemy."

B: Now smoke is rising from three chimneys. What does that mean?

G: 그것은 적이 국경선 근처에 접근하고 있다는 것을 의미해. (come close, the border)

➡ _____

Step Up – Real-life Scene

B: This painting has some hidden secrets in it.

G: Really? ❶I'm curious about them. Where are the secrets?

B: Find one yourself.

G: ❷Let's see. ... Oh, I see some letters here.

B: You found one! ❸It means "Jan van Eyck was here. 1434." It's Latin.

G: That's awesome! Any other secrets?

B: Okay. This dog tells us the man here was very rich.

G: I don't understand.

B: They had to spend lots of money ❹to buy a dog of that kind at that time.

G: I see. Only ❺the rich could have that kind of dog, right?

B: Exactly. Pictures speak a thousand words, you know.

B: 이 그림은 그 안에 숨겨진 비밀이 몇 개 있어.

G: 정말? 난 그것들이 궁금해. 그 비밀들은 어디에 있니?

B: 너 스스로 하나 찾아봐.

G: 어디 보자. … 오, 여기 글자들이 몇 개 보여.

B: 너 하나 찾았구나! 그것은 "Jan van Eyck가 여기 있었다. 1434."를 의미해. 그것은 라틴어야.

G: 멋지다! 다른 비밀들은?

B: 좋아. 이 개는 여기 있는 이 남자가 매우 부자였다는 것을 우리에게 말해 주지.

G: 나는 이해가 안 돼.

B: 당시에 저런 종류의 개를 사려면 많은 돈을 써야 했어.

G: 알겠다. 단지 부자들만 저런 종류의 개를 살 수 있었어, 맞지?

B: 정확해. 알다시피, 그림이 천 마디 말을 하지.

❶ 궁금증을 나타내는 표현으로 '~가 궁금해'로 해석한다.
❷ '글쎄.. 어디 보자.'의 의미로 'Let me see.'와 같은 의미로 사용된다.
❸ 상대방이 궁금증을 표현하거나 의미를 물어보면 'This/It means ~.(그것은 ~을 의미한다.)' 또는 'It is ~.(그것은 ~이다.)' 등의 표현을 사용해서 상대방이 궁금해 하거나 알고 싶어 하는 것의 의미나 정의를 설명하는 표현이다.
❹ 부정사의 부사적 용법 중 '목적'으로 '~하기 위해'로 해석한다.
❺ 'the+형용사'는 '복수명사'로 '~한 사람들'의 의미이다.

Check(√) True or False

(1) The girl found one secret in the painting. T ☐ F ☐

(2) The man in the picture wasn't very rich. T ☐ F ☐

Start Off – Listen & Talk A 1

B: What are the soldiers doing with the five chimneys on TV?

G: They are sending messages to the king ❶by using the chimneys.

B: Really? I'm curious about the system. Can you tell me more?

G: Well, do you see the two ❷smoking chimneys?

B: Yes. What do ❸they mean?

G: ❸They mean ❹they just saw an enemy.

B: TV에서 병사들이 5개의 굴뚝으로 무엇을 하고 있니?

G: 그들은 그 굴뚝을 이용하여 왕에게 메시지를 보내고 있어.

B: 정말? 난 그 체계가 궁금해. 좀 더 말해 줄 수 있어?

G: 음, 연기 나는 굴뚝 두 개가 보이지?

B: 그래. 그것들은 무엇을 의미하니?

G: 그것들은 그들이 방금 적을 봤다는 것을 의미해.

❶ 'by+ing'는 '~함으로써'로 해석한다.
❷ 'smoking'은 현재분사로 '연기 나는'의 의미이다.
❸ 'the two smoking chimneys'를 가리킨다.
❹ 'the soldiers'를 가리키는 대명사다.

Check(√) True or False

(3) The soldiers are sending messages to the king by using the chimneys. T ☐ F ☐

(4) The boy wants to know about the system. T ☐ F ☐

Get Ready 2

(1) G: I'm curious about that robot. Why is it standing there?
   B: It's a kind of ad. ❶It tells people their batteries are very powerful.

(2) G: What's this? I'm curious about it.
   B: It's a traffic sign. ❷It means "Do not enter."
   G: Oh, I see.

(3) G: ❸What are these dots for? I'm curious about them.
   B: Oh, they are Braille. They are for blind people.
   G: I see. Now I can guess what they mean.

(4) G: I'm curious about that balloon. Why is it hanging there?
   B: Oh, that. It's an ad. ❹It says the product is very powerful.

❶ people 뒤에 목적어를 이끄는 접속사 that이 생략되어 있다.
❷ '그것은 ~을 의미하다'라는 뜻으로 정의를 나타내는 표현이다.
❸ 'What ~ for?'는 '~은 무엇을 위한 것이니?'라는 의미이다.
❹ says 뒤에 목적어를 이끄는 접속사 that이 생략되어 있다.

Start Off – Listen & Talk A 2

B: If there's no enemy, they don't smoke at all, ❶do they?
G: Yes, they do. ❷Smoke from one chimney means "No enemy."
B: Now smoke is rising from three chimneys. What does that mean?
G: It means an enemy is coming ❸close to the border.

❶ 앞 문장이 일반동사 부정문일 때 사용하는 부가의문문으로 '그렇지?'의 의미로 사용된다.
❷ 주어가 단수명사 'Smoke'이므로 동사는 단수 'means'이다.
❸ 이 문장에서 'close'는 부사로 '가까이'란 의미이다.

Start Off – Listen & Talk B

B: Now the enemy is crossing the border in the dark. What are the soldiers going to do ❶to send messages? I'm curious about that.
G: They will ❷light four chimneys.

B: ❸When they light all five of the chimneys, what does that mean?
G: ❹It means the battle has started.

❶ 부정사의 부사적 용법 중 '목적'으로 '메시지를 보내기 위해'라고 해석한다.
❷ 여기서 'light'는 동사로 '불을 붙이다'의 의미이다.
❸ 'when'이 이끄는 문장은 시간의 부사절로 '~할 때'로 해석한다.
❹ 동사 'means'와 주어 'the battle' 사이에는 목적어를 이끄는 접속사 'that'이 생략되어 있다.

Start Off – Speak Up

B: I'm curious about sign language.
G: ❶Are you? ❷Let me show you one expression. Look.
B: What does it mean?
G: It means "Hello."

❶ Are you curious about sign language?를 줄여 쓴 표현이다.
❷ 'let(사역동사)+목적어+동사원형' 형태로 'Let me show ~'는 '내가 …에게 ~을 보여줄게'로 해석한다.

Express Yourself A

1. W: What does this woman's gesture mean? I'm curious about it.
   M: ❶I think it means "Jump into the pond."
   W: Why do you think so?
   M: The boy has lots of bees on his head. And the woman is pointing at the pond.

2. W: This woman doesn't want a dollar. So what does her gesture mean?
   M: It means she wants a chicken.
   W: Then the boy should bring a chicken ❷to get the fruit, right?
   M: I think so.

3. W: What does this man's gesture mean? I'm curious about it.
   M: It means "Turn it off."
   W: Really? ❸What makes you think so?
   M: ❹The other hunter there is coming close to an animal.
   W: Oh, I see.

❶ 상대방이 궁금해 하는 것의 의미나 정의를 설명하는 표현이다.
❷ 부정사의 부사적 용법 중 '목적'으로 '과일을 얻기 위해'라고 해석한다.
❸ 여기서 make는 사역동사로 '목적어+목적보어(동사원형)' 형태를 취한다. 그리고 '왜 그렇게 생각하니?'의 뜻으로 'Why do you think so?'와 같은 표현이다.
❹ 'The other+단수명사' 형태로 '나머지 사냥꾼 한 명'을 나타낸다.

다음 우리말과 일치하도록 빈칸에 알맞은 말을 쓰시오.

Get Ready 2

(1) G: I'm _____ _____ that robot. Why _____ _____ standing there?

　　B: It's _____ _____ _____ ad. It _____ people their _____ are very _____.

(2) G: What's this? I'_____ _____ _____ it.

　　B: It's a _____ _____. It _____ "Do not _____."

　　G: Oh, I see.

(3) G: What are these _____ _____? I'_____ _____ _____ them.

　　B: Oh, they are _____. They are for _____ people.

　　G: I see. Now I can _____ what they _____.

(4) G: I'm _____ about that _____. Why is it _____ there?

　　B: Oh, that. It's an _____. It says the _____ is very _____.

Start Off – Listen & Talk A

1. B: What are the _____ doing with the five _____ on TV?

　　G: They are sending _____ to the king _____ _____ the _____.

　　B: Really? I'_____ _____ _____ the _____. Can you tell me more?

　　G: Well, do you see the two _____ _____?

　　B: Yes. _____ do they _____?

　　G: They mean they just saw an _____.

2. B: If there's no _____, they don't _____ _____ _____, _____ they?

　　G: Yes, they do. _____ from one _____ means "No enemy."

　　B: Now smoke is _____ from three chimneys. _____ _____ that _____?

　　G: _____ an enemy is coming _____ to the _____.

Start Off B

B: Now the enemy _____ _____ the _____ in the _____. What are the _____ _____ _____ _____ to send _____? I'm curious _____ that.

G: They will _____ four _____.

B: When they _____ all five of the _____, what does that mean?

G: _____ _____ the _____ has started.

(1) G: 나는 저 로봇에 대해 알고 싶어. 그건 왜 저기에 서 있는 거니?
　　B: 그건 일종의 광고야. 그것은 그들의 건전지가 매우 강력하다는 것을 사람들에게 말하고 있어.
(2) G: 이것은 뭐지? 난 그게 궁금해.
　　B: 그것은 교통 표지판이야. 그것은 "들어오지 마시오."를 의미해.
　　G: 오, 알겠어.
(3) G: 이 점들은 무엇을 위한 거니? 난 그것들에 대해 알고 싶어.
　　B: 오, 그것들은 점자야. 그것들은 시각장애인을 위한 것이야.
　　G: 알겠어. 이제 그것들이 무엇을 의미하는지 추측할 수 있어.
(4) G: 나는 저 풍선이 궁금해. 그건 왜 저기에 매달려 있니?
　　B: 오, 저것. 그건 광고야. 그것은 그 상품이 매우 강력하다는 것을 말하고 있어.

1. B: TV에서 병사들이 5개의 굴뚝으로 무엇을 하고 있니?
　　G: 그들은 그 굴뚝을 이용하여 왕에게 메시지를 보내고 있어.
　　B: 정말? 난 그 체계가 궁금해. 좀 더 말해 줄 수 있어?
　　G: 음, 연기 나는 굴뚝 두 개가 보이지?
　　B: 그래. 그것들은 무엇을 의미하니?
　　G: 그것들은 그들이 방금 적을 봤다는 것을 의미해.
2. B: 만약 적이 없다면, 그들은 연기를 전혀 피우지 않아, 그렇지?
　　G: 아니, 연기를 피워. 굴뚝 한 곳에서 연기가 나오면 "적이 없음"을 의미해.
　　B: 이제 연기가 굴뚝 세 개에서 올라가고 있어. 그것은 무엇을 의미하니?
　　G: 그것은 적이 국경 가까이 접근하고 있음을 의미해.

B: 이제 적이 어둠 속에서 국경을 침입하고 있어. 메시지를 보내기 위해서 병사들은 무슨 일을 할까? 나는 그것이 궁금해.
G: 그들은 굴뚝 4개에 불을 붙일 거야.
B: 그들이 5개 굴뚝 모두에 불을 붙였을 때, 그것은 무엇을 의미하니?
G: 그것은 전투가 시작되었음을 의미해.

Start Off – Speak Up

B: I'_____ _____ _____ sign _____.
G: Are you? _____ me _____ you one _____. Look.
B: _____ does it _____?
G: _____ _____ "Hello."

Step Up– Real-life Scene

B: This painting has some _____ _____ in it.
G: Really? I'm _____ _____ them. Where are the _____?
B: Find one _____.
G: _____ _____. ... Oh, I see some _____ here.
B: You found _____! It _____ "Jan van Eyck was here. 1434." It's _____.
G: That's _____! _____ _____ secrets?
B: Okay. This dog _____ us the man here was very _____.
G: I don't _____.
B: They had to _____ _____ _____ money _____ a dog of that _____ at that time.
G: I see. Only _____ _____ could have _____ _____ of dog, right?
B: _____. Pictures _____ _____ _____ words, you know.

Express Yourself A

1. W: What does this woman's _____ mean? I'm _____ _____ it.
   M: I think _____ _____ "Jump into the _____."
   W: _____ do you _____ _____?
   M: The boy has _____ _____ bees on his head. And the woman is _____ at the _____.
2. W: This woman doesn't want a dollar. _____ what does her _____ _____?
   M: _____ _____ she wants a _____.
   W: Then the boy _____ _____ a chicken _____ _____ the fruit, _____?
   M: _____ _____ _____ _____.
3. W: _____ does this man's _____ _____? I'm curious about it.
   M: It means "_____ _____ ."
   W: Really? _____ _____ you think so?
   M: _____ _____ there is coming _____ to an animal.
   W: Oh, I _____.

해석

B: 난 수화가 궁금해.
G: 그러니? 내가 표현 하나를 알려줄게. 봐.
B: 그것은 무엇을 의미하니?
G: 그것은 "안녕하세요."를 의미해.

B: 이 그림은 그 안에 숨겨진 비밀이 몇 개 있어.
G: 정말? 난 그것들이 궁금해. 그 비밀들은 어디에 있니?
B: 너 스스로 하나 찾아봐.
G: 어디 보자. … 오, 여기 글자들이 몇 개 보여.
B: 너 하나 찾았구나! 그것은 "Jan van Eyck가 여기 있었다. 1434."를 의미해. 그것은 라틴어야.
G: 멋지다! 다른 비밀들은?
B: 좋아. 이 개는 여기 있는 이 남자가 매우 부자였다는 것을 우리에게 말해주지.
G: 나는 이해가 안 돼.
B: 당시에 저런 종류의 개를 사려면 많은 돈을 써야 했어.
G: 알겠다. 단지 부자들만 저런 종류의 개를 살 수 있었어, 맞지?
B: 정확해. 알다시피, 그림이 천 마디 말을 하지.

1. W: 이 여자의 몸짓은 무엇을 의미하니? 난 그것이 궁금해.
   M: 내 생각에 그것은 "연못으로 뛰어들어."를 의미해.
   W: 왜 그렇게 생각하니?
   M: 그 소년은 머리 위에 많은 벌이 있어. 그리고 그 여자는 연못을 가리키고 있어.
2. W: 이 여자는 1달러를 원하지 않아. 그렇다면 그녀의 몸짓은 무엇을 의미하니?
   M: 그것은 그녀가 닭 한 마리를 원한다는 것을 의미해.
   W: 그럼 그 소년은 과일을 얻기 위해 닭을 한 마리 가져와야 하는구나, 맞지?
   M: 난 그렇게 생각해.
3. W: 이 남자의 몸짓은 무엇을 의미하니? 난 그것이 궁금해.
   M: 그것은 "그것을 꺼."를 의미해.
   W: 정말? 왜 그렇게 생각하니?
   M: 거기 있는 나머지 다른 사냥꾼이 어떤 동물 가까이 접근하고 있어.
   W: 오, 알겠어.

01 우리말에 맞도록 주어진 단어를 활용하여 빈칸을 채우시오.

> 그것은 네가 들어가지 말아야 한다는 것을 의미해. (mean)

➡ _____ _____ you must _____ _____ .

02 다음 대화의 빈칸에 들어갈 말로 <u>어색한</u> 것은?

> G: What are these dots for? _____
> B: Oh, they are Braille. They are for blind people.
> G: I see. Now I can guess what they mean.

① I'm curious about them.
② I would like to know about them.
③ I'd be very interested to know about them.
④ Let me show you one expression
⑤ Can you tell me about them?

03 다음 대화의 빈칸에 들어갈 말로 적절한 것은?

> A: What does your name mean? I'm curious about it.
> B: _____
> A: That's beautiful.

① I know whose name it is. It's Hyeja's.
② What does it mean?   ③ It means "bright girl."
④ What does this letter mean?   ⑤ I don't care about it.

04 다음 대화의 밑줄 친 말의 의도로 알맞은 것은?

> G: <u>I'm curious about that balloon.</u> Why is it hanging there?
> B: Oh, that. It's an ad.

① 관심 표현하기   ② 충고 구하기
③ 가능성 묻기   ④ 유감 표현하기
⑤ 궁금증 표현하기

[01~02] 다음 대화를 읽고 물음에 답하시오.

W: What does this man's gesture (a)mean? I'm curious about (b)it.
M: It means "(c)Turn it off."
W: Really? _____(A)_____
M: (d)Other hunter there is coming (e)close to an animal.
W: Oh, I see.

01 위 대화의 빈칸 (A)에 들어갈 말로 알맞은 것을 모두 고르시오.

① How do you think so?
② What do you think about it?
③ What makes you think so?
④ Do you think I should turn it off?
⑤ Why do you think so?

서답형

02 위 대화의 (a)~(e)에서 어법상 틀린 곳을 찾아 바르게 고치시오. (1개)

➡ 틀린 것: _____
➡ 고치기: _____ ➡ _____

[03~04] 다음 대화를 읽고 물음에 답하시오.

B: Now the enemy is crossing the border in the dark. What are the soldiers going to do to send messages? _____(A)_____
G: They will light four chimneys.
B: When they light all five of the chimneys, _____(B)_____?
G: It means the battle has started.

03 위 대화의 빈칸 (A)에 들어갈 말로 알맞은 것은?

① I'm curious about who the soldiers are.
② Can you tell me how to light chimneys?

③ Do you think they should light chimneys?
④ I'm curious about that.
⑤ Can you tell me about the messages?

중요

04 위 대화의 흐름상 빈칸 (B)에 들어갈 알맞은 표현은?

① why did you say so
② what does that mean
③ do you think so
④ why not
⑤ do you mean the battle has started

[05~06] 다음 대화를 읽고 물음에 답하시오.

B: What are the soldiers doing with the five chimneys on TV?
G: They are sending (a)messages to the king by using the chimneys.
B: Really? I'm (b)curious about the system. Can you tell me more?
G: Well, do you see the two (c)smoking chimneys?
B: Yes. What do they mean?
G: They mean they just (d)saw an enemy.
B: If there's no enemy, they don't smoke at all, do they?
G: (A)Yes, they do. Smoke from one chimney means "(e)An enemy."
B: Now smoke is rising from three chimneys. What does that mean?
G: It means an enemy is coming close to the border.

05 위 대화의 흐름상 어휘의 쓰임이 어색한 것은?

① (a) ② (b) ③ (c) ④ (d) ⑤ (e)

06 위 대화의 밑줄 친 (A)의 우리말을 바르게 옮긴 것은?

① 응, 적이 와. ② 아니, 적이 오지 않아.

③ 응, 연기를 피워. ④ 아니, 연기를 피워.

⑤ 응, 연기를 피우지 않아.

서답형

07 다음 대화의 빈칸에 들어갈 단어를 주어진 영영풀이를 보고 '복수형'으로 쓰시오.

> G: I'm curious about that robot. Why is it standing there?
>
> B: It's a kind of ad. It tells people their _____ are very powerful.

> <영영풀이> an object that provides electricity for things such as radios, toys, or cars

➡ _____

[08~09] 다음 대화를 읽고 물음에 답하시오.

> G: What are these dots ___(a)___? ___(A)___ them.
>
> B: Oh, they are Braille. They are ___(b)___ blind people.
>
> G: I see. Now I can guess what they mean.
>
> G: ___(A)___ that balloon. Why is it hanging there?
>
> B: Oh, that. It's an ad. It says the product is very powerful.

08 위 대화의 빈칸 (A)에 공통으로 들어갈 말로 <u>어색한</u> 것은?

① I'm curious about

② I'm surprised about

③ I'd like to know about

④ I wonder about

⑤ I want to know about

서답형

09 위 대화의 빈칸 (a)와 (b)에 공통으로 들어갈 단어를 쓰시오.

➡ _____

[10~11] 다음 대화를 읽고 물음에 답하시오.

> B: This painting has some hidden secrets in (a)it.
>
> G: Really? I'm curious about them. Where are the secrets?
>
> B: Find one yourself. (A)
>
> G: Let's see. ... Oh, I see some letters here.
>
> B: You found one! (B) It means "Jan van Eyck was here. 1434." It's Latin.
>
> G: That's awesome! Any other secrets?
>
> B: Okay. (C)
>
> G: I don't understand. (D)
>
> B: They had to spend lots of money to buy a dog of that kind at that time.
>
> G: I see. (E) Only the rich could have that kind of dog, right?
>
> B: Exactly. Pictures speak a thousand words, you know.

10 위 대화의 (A)~(E) 중 주어진 문장이 들어갈 위치로 알맞은 것은?

> This dog tells us the man here was very rich.

① (A) ② (B) ③ (C) ④ (D) ⑤ (E)

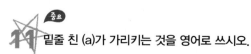

11 밑줄 친 (a)가 가리키는 것을 영어로 쓰시오.

➡ _____

[01~02] 다음 대화를 읽고 물음에 답하시오.

B: This painting has some hidden secrets in it.

G: Really? _____(A)_____ Where are the secrets?

B: Find one yourself.

G: Let's see. ... Oh, I see some letters here.

B: You found one! _____(B)_____ "Jan van Eyck was here. 1434." It's Latin.

G: That's awesome! Any other secrets?

B: Okay. This dog tells us the man here was very rich.

G: I don't understand.

B: They had to spend lots of money to buy a dog of that kind at that time.

G: I see. Only the rich could have that kind of dog, right?

B: Exactly. Pictures speak a thousand words, you know.

01 위 대화를 읽고 다음 물음에 영어로 답하시오.

Q: What do the letters the girl found mean?

➡ _____

02 위 대화의 빈칸 (A)와 (B)에 들어갈 말을 〈조건〉에 맞게 영어로 쓰시오.

┌─ 조건 ┐
(A) • 궁금증을 표현하는 말을 쓸 것.
   • '대명사'와 'curious'를 사용할 것.
(B) • 상대방이 알고 싶어 하는 것의 의미나 정의를 표현하는 말을 2단어로 쓸 것..
└─────┘

➡ (A) _____

   (B) _____

03 다음 대화의 밑줄 친 우리말 해석에 맞게 주어진 〈조건〉에 맞게 영어로 쓰시오.

W: What does this woman's gesture mean? I'm curious about it.

M: I think it means "Jump into the pond."

W: 왜 그렇게 생각하니?

M: The boy has lots of bees on his head. And the woman is pointing at the pond.

┌─ 조건 ┐
• 'make', 'think'를 이용할 것
└─────┘

➡ _____

[04~05] 다음 대화를 읽고 물음에 답하시오.

B: What are the soldiers doing with the five chimneys on TV?

G: (a)그들은 그 굴뚝을 이용하여 왕에게 메시지를 보내고 있어.

B: Really? I'm curious about the system. Can you tell me more?

G: Well, do you see the two smoking chimneys?

B: Yes. What do they mean?

G: _____(A)_____

04 위 대화의 흐름상 빈칸 (A)에 주어진 어구를 알맞은 순서로 배열하시오.

(saw / they / mean / just / an enemy / they)

➡ _____

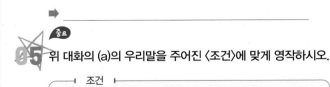

05 위 대화의 (a)의 우리말을 주어진 〈조건〉에 맞게 영작하시오.

┌─ 조건 ┐
• '진행형'과 'by ~ing'를 이용할 것.
└─────┘

➡ _____

_____

Grammar

① 가정법 과거

> • I **would** be so happy if you **were** with me. 당신이 나와 함께 있다면 난 정말 행복할 거예요.

- 형태: If+주어+동사 과거형, 주어+조동사 과거형(would/should/could/might)+동사원형
  의미: 만약 …한다면 ~할 텐데(현재 사실과 반대되는 상상이나 가정)

- 가정법 문장이라는 표시로 과거 동사를 사용할 뿐 의미상 과거를 나타내지 않고, 현재 말하는 사람의 느낌이나 감정을 표현한다.
  - If I **had** a car, I **could** give you a ride home. 만일 내가 차가 있다면, 너를 집까지 태워 줄 텐데.
  - = As I **don't have** a car, I **can't give** you a ride home.
    나는 차를 가지고 있지 않아서, 너를 집까지 태워줄 수 없다.

- if절에 쓰이는 be동사의 과거형은 'were'를 사용하지만, 구어체에서는 주어가 'I' 또는 3인칭 단수인 경우 'was'를 쓰기도 한다.
  - If I **were[was]** rich, I **would** help all the children in need.
    내가 부자라면, 도움이 필요한 모든 어린이들을 도와줄 텐데.

- 가정법 과거 문장을 현재시제의 직설법으로 바꿀 수 있다.
  - If he **knew** the answer, he **would** be very glad. 그가 정답을 안다면, 그는 매우 기쁠 텐데.
  - = As he **doesn't know** the answer, he **is not** very glad. 그는 정답을 모르기 때문에, 그는 별로 기쁘지 않다.

- if는 if절의 동사가 'were' 또는 'had'일 때 생략될 수 있으며, 이때는 주어와 동사가 도치된다.
  - If my family **were** at home, I **would** tell them everything about my school life.
    만일 가족들이 집에 있다면, 나는 그들에게 내 학교생활에 관한 모든 것을 말할 텐데.
  - = **Were** my family at home, I **would** tell them everything about my school life.
  - If Tom **had** a sister, he **could** play with her all day long.
    만일 Tom이 여동생이 있다면, 그는 하루 종일 그녀와 놀 수 있을 텐데.
  - = **Had** Tom a sister, he **could** play with her all day long

핵심 Check

1. 다음 괄호 안에서 알맞은 것을 고르시오.
   (1) If I (am / were) a fish, I would swim in the pond.
   (2) She (will / would) be very happy if she won the lottery.

❷ 관계대명사 whose

> • It was written in 1973 by a woman **whose** husband was far away.
> 그것은 남편이 멀리 떨어져 살았던 한 여자에 의해 1973년에 쓰여졌다.

■ 형태: 선행사+whose+명사

　의미: ~인, ~의

■ 소유격을 대신하고 두 문장을 이어주는 접속사 역할을 하는 관계대명사이다.

　• My brother has a girl friend. + He likes **her cat**.

　→ My brother has a girl friend **whose cat** he likes.
　　나의 남동생은 그녀의 고양이를 그가 좋아하는 여자 친구가 있다.

■ 선행사가 사물인 경우 'of which'를 쓰기도 한다.

　• I have a bag. + **Its handle** is made of bamboo.

　→ I have a bag **whose handle** is made of bamboo. 나는 손잡이가 대나무로 만들어진 가방을 가지고 있다.

　• I have a bag. + The handle **of it** is made of bamboo.

　→ I have a bag the handle **of which** is made of bamboo.

　→ I have a bag **of which** the handle is made of bamboo.

■ 소유격 관계대명사 다음의 동사는 소유격 관계대명사가 갖고 있는 명사의 수를 따른다.

　• I know a small girl whose **parents are** tall. 나는 부모님이 키가 큰 작은 소녀를 알고 있다.

■ 소유격과 한정사(a, an, the, this, that, some, any 등)는 함께 쓸 수 없으므로 소유격 관계사 다음에 한정사를 쓰지 않는다.

　• I have a dog whose the tail is long. (×)

　→ I have a dog **whose** tail is long. 또는 I have a dog **of which** the tail is long.

핵심 Check

2. 다음 괄호 안에서 알맞은 것을 고르시오.

　(1) He has a sister (of which / whose) eyes are brown.

　(2) The house (of which / whose) windows are very big is my father's.

　(3) I have a friend whose brothers (enjoy / enjoys) skateboarding.

Grammar 시험대비 기본평가

01 다음 우리말에 맞게 괄호 안에 주어진 단어를 이용하여 문장을 완성하시오.

(1) 내가 오리라면, 물속에서 수영할 수 있을 텐데. (if, be)

➡ _____, I could swim in the water.

(2) 날개를 가졌다면 너는 뭘 하겠니? (what, do)

➡ _____ if you had wings?

(3) Bubu는 그의 개가 인형을 가지고 다니는 소년이야. (be, carry)

➡ Bubu is the boy _____.

(4) Lala는 그녀의 개가 핫도그를 원하는 소녀야. (want, hot dog)

➡ Lala is the girl _____.

02 다음 문장에서 어법상 <u>어색한</u> 부분을 바르게 고쳐 쓰시오.

(1) If I had wings, I will fly in the sky.

➡ _____

(2) What would you do if you are a fish?

➡ _____

(3) Koko is the boy of which the bag is on a big cat.

➡ _____

(4) The girl who cat is dancing is Didi.

➡ _____

03 다음 〈보기〉의 문장을 참고하여 빈칸을 완성하시오.

┌─ 보기 ─

As she doesn't know the result, she is not happy.

= If she knew the result, she would be happy.

(1) As I don't have a lot of money, I can't travel around the world.

= _____

(2) As I am not tall, I can't be a basketball player.

= _____

01 다음 두 문장을 한 문장으로 고칠 때 빈칸에 알맞은 말은?

> • The movie attracted 10 million viewers.
> • The director of the movie won the Academy award.
> → The movie _____ the director won the Academy award attracted 10 million viewers.

① who ② whose ③ which
④ of which ⑤ what

02 중요 다음 빈칸에 들어갈 알맞은 것은?

> I have a ring _____ owner is unknown.

① whose ② who ③ that
④ of which ⑤ whom

서답형
03 관계대명사를 이용하여 두 문장을 한 문장으로 바꿔 쓰시오.

> • There was a queen.
> • Her daughter was cursed by an evil fairy.

➡ _____
_____

04 다음 중 어법상 올바른 문장을 고르시오.

① If I were him, I would buy the bag.
② If I had a car, I could drove her home.
③ Were I rich, I can help all of you.
④ She would be very happy if she wins the prize.
⑤ If your mom knew you passed the test, she will be very surprised.

05 중요 다음 문장의 뜻이 나머지 넷과 <u>다른</u> 것은?

① If I were in good physical condition, I could work out with you.
② Were I in good physical condition, I could work out with you.
③ With good physical condition, I can work out with you.
④ As I am not in good physical condition, I can't work out with you.
⑤ Because I am not in good physical condition, I can't work out with you.

06 빈칸에 공통으로 들어갈 말은? (대·소문자 무시)

> • If I _____ you, I would save some money for the future.
> • _____ I you, I would save some money for the future.

① am ② were ③ had
④ had been ⑤ weren't

서답형
07 다음 괄호 안에 주어진 단어들을 바르게 배열하여 문장을 완성하시오.

> Miso (a girl, jumping, dog, is, whose, rope, is).

➡ _____

서답형
08 다음 두 문장을 가정법을 이용하여 한 문장으로 쓰시오.

> • I don't have a lot of money.
> • I can't buy that car.

➡ _____
_____

09 다음 문장과 같은 뜻을 가진 문장을 <u>모두</u> 고르시오.

> As we don't have enough time, we can't stay longer.

① If we didn't have enough time, we couldn't stay longer.

② If we have enough time, we can stay longer.

③ If we had enough time, we could stay longer.

④ Without enough time, we could stay longer.

⑤ With enough time, we could stay longer.

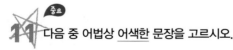
10 다음 문장에서 어법상 <u>어색한</u> 것을 바르게 고쳐 다시 쓰시오.

(1) If I have a monkey, I could play with it.

➡ _____

_____

(2) The boys whose mom is a lawyer lives next door.

➡ _____

_____

11 다음 중 어법상 <u>어색한</u> 문장을 고르시오.

① If he were here, he could help us.

② If I were a cheetah, I could run faster than you.

③ If I were not tired, I could go swimming.

④ If my brother were tall, he could play basketball better.

⑤ I lent it to you if I had the book.

서답형
12 다음 괄호 안에서 알맞은 말을 고르시오.

(1) If I were a millionaire, I (built / would build) a castle.

(2) I would call him if I (knew / had known) his phone number.

(3) I have a friend, (who / whose) family is from Germany.

(4) This is the student (who / whose) came from France.

(5) We need to help animals in Australia (which / whose) lives are in danger.

13 다음 우리말을 영어로 바르게 옮긴 것은?

> 내가 날개를 가졌다면, 내 친구를 만나러 부산으로 날아갈 텐데.

① If I have wings, I will fly to Busan to meet my friend.

② If I have wings, I would fly to Busan to meet my friend.

③ If I had wings, I will fly to Busan to meet my friend.

④ If I had wings, I would fly to Busan to meet my friend.

⑤ If I had had wings, I would fly to Busan to meet my friend.

서답형
14 주어진 어휘를 이용하여 다음 우리말을 영어로 쓰시오.

> 내가 새라면, 나는 산 너머로 날아갈 텐데. (a bird, fly, over)

➡ _____

서답형

15 다음 괄호 안에 주어진 단어들을 바르게 배열하여 문장을 완성하시오.

> The animal (begins, with z, whose, is, a zebra, name).

➡ _____

_____

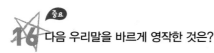

16 다음 우리말을 바르게 영작한 것은?

> 내 아들이 더 열심히 공부하면 나는 더 행복할 텐데.

① I will be happier if my son studied harder.
② I am happier if my son studied harder.
③ I would be happier if my son studies harder.
④ I would be happier if my son studied harder.
⑤ I would be happier if my son has studied harder.

17 다음 두 문장을 한 문장으로 바르게 옮긴 것은?

> • A girl is preparing for the audition.
> • Her dream is to be a movie star.

① A girl is preparing for the audition whose dream is to be a movie star.
② A girl is preparing for the audition who dream is to be a movie star.
③ A girl is preparing for the audition her dream is to be a movie star.
④ A girl whose dream is to be a movie star is preparing for the audition.
⑤ A girl of which the dream is to be a movie star is preparing for the audition.

18 빈칸에 들어갈 말을 순서대로 바르게 연결한 것은?

> • I like the candies _____ taste like apples.
> • I like the fresh baked bread _____ smell is so sweet.

① whose   – whose
② whose   – which
③ of which – which
④ which   – of which
⑤ which   – whose

서답형

19 주어진 어휘를 이용하여 다음 우리말을 영어로 쓰시오.

> 내가 대통령을 만난다면, 그와 악수를 할 텐데.
> (the President, shake)

➡ _____

_____

서답형

20 대화의 빈칸에 공통으로 들어갈 단어를 쓰시오.

(1) A: What _____ you do if you were a fish?
　　B: If I were a fish, I _____ swim in the pond.
(2) A: What would you do if you _____ a duck?
　　B: If I _____ a duck, I could swim in the water.

서답형

21 다음 두 문장이 같은 뜻이 되도록 빈칸에 알맞은 말을 쓰시오.

> If she worked with him, she would be very disappointed with him.
> = As _____,
> 　she _____.

01 관계대명사를 이용하여 두 문장을 한 문장으로 쓰시오.

(1) • I have a friend.
 • His brother enjoys skateboarding.

  ➡ _____
  _____

(2) • The boy is my brother.
 • He is dancing on the floor.

  ➡ _____
  _____

(3) • He wants to ride a bike.
 • I bought it yesterday.

  ➡ _____
  _____

(4) • Do you like the house?
 • Its roof looks like a hat.

  ➡ _____
  _____

(5) • The boy is Jeje.
 • His cat is spinning a hula hoop.

  ➡ _____
  _____

02 다음 우리말을 주어진 어휘를 이용하여 영어로 옮기시오.

(1) 내가 강한 팔을 가졌다면, 나는 나무에 오를 수 있을 텐데. (strong, climb)

  ➡ _____
  _____

(2) 내가 긴 코를 가졌다면, 나는 샤워하기 위해 그 것을 쓸 수 있을 텐데. (nose, shower)

  ➡ _____
  _____

(3) 내가 아름다운 목소리를 가졌다면, 나는 나무에 서 노래할 거야. (voice, on the tree)

  ➡ _____
  _____

03 주어진 문장을 가정법 문장으로 다시 쓰시오.

(1) As I am not an English teacher, I don't play word games every day.

  ➡ _____
  _____

(2) As I am not on the moon, I can't jump much higher.

  ➡ _____
  _____

04 잘못된 부분을 바르게 고쳐 문장을 다시 쓰시오.

(1) Did he rich, he could travel to Europe.

  ➡ _____
  _____

(2) The boy whose is talking to Mary is my cousin.

  ➡ _____
  _____

(3) He lent me the book of which I want to read.

  ➡ _____
  _____

(4) I stayed at the house which walls are white.

  ➡ _____
  _____

(5) If I were you, I took a swimming lesson.

  ➡ _____
  _____

05 다음 그림을 보고 빈칸에 알맞은 말을 써 넣으시오.

(1)

If I were the boy, I _____ the fruit to the monkey right away.

(2)

If I were the boy, I _____.

(3)

If I were the girl, I _____ out of the water right away.

06 다음 주어진 우리말에 맞게 빈칸에 들어갈 단어를 각각 쓰시오.

내가 만일 BTS 멤버라면, 나는 가난한 어린이들을 위해 춤추고 노래할 수 있을 텐데.
→ If I _____ a member of BTS, I _____ _____ _____ for poor children.

07 주어진 문장이 같은 뜻이 되도록 빈칸에 알맞은 말을 쓰시오.

(1) If he knew her, he would talk to her.
➡ As he doesn't know her, _____ _____.

(2) If he were at home, I would tell him the truth.
➡ _____, I would tell him the truth.

08 주어진 〈보기〉를 참고하여 두 문장을 하나의 문장으로 쓰시오.

┌── 보기 ──┐
The boy doesn't understand her gesture.
The woman doesn't want his money.
→ The boy whose money the woman doesn't want doesn't understand her gesture.

(1) The boy doesn't understand the man's gesture. His cell phone is ringing loudly.
➡ _____

(2) The girl doesn't understand the man's gesture. Her feet are in the water.
➡ _____

(3) The boy doesn't understand her gesture. The woman is pulling his hand.
➡ _____

(4) The boy doesn't understand its gesture. The monkey is pulling his bag.
➡ _____

A Picture Letter from a Mother of Three

Speaking to family members or friends in a foreign country is rather
동명사 주어
easy and simple today. But before the days of phones and the Internet,
시대
it was not that easy. People just sent a letter and waited for a reply for
= Speaking to family members or friends in a foreign country
weeks. And it was a lot harder if they couldn't read or write.
비교급을 강조하는 부사: a lot. much. far. still. even(훨씬)
This letter shows how people got over these difficulties. It was
관계부사 = the way. the way how(×)
written in 1973 by a woman whose husband was far away. She lived
소유격 관계대명사
in Sicily, an Italian island, while her husband worked in Germany. At
Sicily와 an Italian island는 동격
the time, more than 5% of the people in Italy could not read or write,
= over   illiterate: 글을 (읽거나 쓸 줄) 모르는, 문맹의
and she was one of them. This letter was discovered by Sicilian writer
→ 능동태: Sicilian writer Gesualdo Bufalino discovered this letter.
Gesualdo Bufalino.

Here's how he translated the pictures into words.
~가 여기 있다
My dear love, I miss you so much, and I reach my arms out toward
My dear love: 부부간의 호칭(여보, 당신)   reach ~ out: (손 등을) 내밀다, 뻗다
you, together with our three kids. We are all in good health except for
be in good health: 건강 상태가 좋다
the little one. He's a little sick, but not seriously.
= kid   = he's not seriously sick.

foreign 외국의

rather 다소, 약간

wait for ~을 기다리다

reply 답장

get over 이겨내다, 극복하다

husband 남편

discover 발견하다

translate 번역하다, 해석하다

toward ~을 향하여

in good health 건강하여

except for ~을 제외하고

seriously 진지하게, 심각하게

확인문제

● 다음 문장이 본문의 내용과 일치하면 T, 일치하지 <u>않으면</u> F를 쓰시오.

1 It is rather easy and simple today to speak to family members or friends in a foreign country. ☐

2 Before the days of phones and the Internet, people just sent a letter and waited for a reply for a few days. ☐

3 Speaking to family members or friends in a foreign country was a lot harder if people couldn't read or write. ☐

4 In 1973, more than 5% of the people in the world could not read or write ☐

5 Gesualdo Bufalino was a Sicilian writer. ☐

6 Gesualdo Bufalino translated words into the pictures. ☐

I already sent you a letter, but there was no reply, so I am sad about it.
there was no reply(편지를 보냈는데 답장이 없는 것)
If I got a letter from you, I would be very happy. Your mother fell ill,
가정법 과거 → 직설법: As I don't get a letter from you. I'm not very happy.　　　= became ill
and I'm going to visit her in the hospital with some money and food. I'll

go there with our middle son while the oldest looks after the youngest.
while: ~하는 동안에(접속사)　= the oldest kid　　= the youngest kid
I had two workers prepare our field and plant seeds for 150,000
사역동사 had로 목적어 다음에 동사원형(prepare. plant)을 쓴다.　　　　　~의 비용으로
lire. I voted for the DC. The PCI lost so many seats that it almost
너무 …해서 ~하다
seems dead. But whether one or the other wins, it's the same. Nothing
seem+형용사: ~해 보인다　　whether ~ or: ~이든지 아니든지
changes for us poor people. We worked yesterday, and we will work

again tomorrow.

We picked lots of olives from our olive trees this year. I hired a man

whose sons are good workers. He knocked the olives down, and his
소유격 관계대명사　　　　　　knock ~ down: ~을 두드려 떨어뜨리다
two sons helped him, picking them up from the ground. I paid him
'주우면서'라는 의미로 동시 동작을 표현
27,000 lire for the work. I spent 12,000 more for the olive press. I got
pay A B for C: A에게 C에 대한 대가로 B를 지불하다
enough oil to fill a large pot and a small one. I can sell it at a price of
enough … to ~: ~할 만큼 충분한 …　　　= pot　　~의 가격으로
1,300 lire a liter.
~당, ~에
My love, my heart thinks of you as Christmas is coming. I would be

so happy if you were with me. We all miss you so much. I'm sending
가정법 과거. → 직설법: As you are not with me. I'm not so happy.
you a big hug from me and our three little kids. Goodbye, dear love.

My heart is yours, joined to you as our two rings are.
과거분사(분사구문)　as: ~하듯이, ~하는 것처럼　are 뒤에 'joined'가 생략되었음.

ill 아픈. 병든
look after ~을 돌보다
prepare 준비하다
vote 투표하다. 선출하다
seat 의석
seem ~처럼 보이다
dead 죽은. 쓸모없는
whether ~이든지 아니든지
lots of 많은
hire 고용하다
knock 치다. 두드리다
ground 땅. 지면
oil 기름
at a price of ~의 가격으로
hug 포옹: 포옹하다
ring 반지

확인문제

● 다음 문장이 본문의 내용과 일치하면 T, 일치하지 않으면 F를 쓰시오.

1 The writer already sent her husband a letter, but there was no reply. ☐

2 The writer visited her mother-in-law in the hospital with some money and food. ☐

3 The writer got two workers to prepare their field and to plant seeds for 150,000 lire. ☐

4 The writer spent 27,000 lire for the olive press. ☐

5 The writer would be so happy if her husband were with her. ☐

6 The writer's husband is sending the writer and his three little kids a big hug. ☐

● 우리말을 참고하여 빈칸에 알맞은 말을 쓰시오.

1 _____ _____ _____ from a Mother of Three

2 _____ to family members or friends in a foreign country _____ _____ easy and simple today.

3 But before the days of phones and the Internet, it was not _____ _____.

4 People just sent a letter and _____ _____ a reply _____ _____.

5 And it was a lot harder if they _____ _____ _____ _____.

6 This letter shows how people _____ _____ these difficulties.

7 It was written in 1973 by a woman _____ husband was _____ _____.

8 She lived in Sicily, an Italian island, while her husband worked _____ _____.

9 At the time, _____ _____ _____ of the people in Italy could not read or write, and she was _____ _____ _____.

10 This letter _____ _____ _____ Sicilian writer Gesualdo Bufalino.

11 Here's how he _____ the pictures _____ words.

12 My dear love, I miss you so much, and I _____ my arms _____ toward you, together with our three kids.

13 We are _____ _____ _____ _____ except for the little _____.

14 He's a little sick, but _____ _____.

15 I already sent you a letter, but _____ _____ _____ _____, so I am sad about it.

16 If I _____ a letter from you, I _____ very happy.

1	세 아이의 엄마가 보낸 그림 편지
2	오늘날 외국에 있는 가족이나 친구와 대화하는 것은 다소 쉽고 간단하다.
3	하지만 전화와 인터넷 시대 이전에는 그것이 그렇게 쉽지 않았다.
4	사람들은 단지 편지를 보내고 답장을 몇 주 동안 기다렸다.
5	그리고 그들이 읽거나 쓸 수 없었다면 그건 훨씬 더 힘들었다.
6	이 편지는 사람들이 이런 어려움을 어떻게 극복했는지 보여 준다.
7	그것은 남편이 멀리 떨어져 살았던 한 여자에 의해 1973년에 쓰여졌다.
8	그녀의 남편은 독일에서 일한 반면, 그녀는 이탈리아의 섬인 시실리에서 살았다.
9	그 당시에는 5% 이상의 이탈리아 사람들이 읽거나 쓸 수 없었고, 그녀도 그들 중 한 명이었다.
10	이 편지는 시실리의 작가 Gesualdo Bufalino가 발견하였다.
11	그가 그림들을 어떻게 글로 번역했는지는 다음과 같다.
12	사랑하는 여보, 난 당신이 정말 그립고, 우리 세 아이와 함께 당신을 향해 내 팔을 쭉 뻗고 있어요.
13	막내를 제외하고는 우리 모두 건강해요.
14	그 아이는 약간 아프지만 심각하진 않아요.
15	난 당신에게 이미 편지를 보냈지만, 답장이 없어서 그것 때문에 나는 슬퍼요.
16	당신에게서 편지를 받는다면, 나는 정말 행복할 거예요.

17 Your mother _____ _____, and I'm going to visit her in the hospital with some money and food.

18 I'll go there with our middle son _____ the oldest _____ _____ the youngest.

19 I _____ two workers _____ our field and _____ seeds for 150,000 lire.

20 I _____ _____ the DC.

21 The PCI lost _____ many seats _____ it almost seems dead.

22 But _____ _____ _____ _____ wins, it's the same.

23 _____ _____ for us poor people.

24 We worked yesterday, and we _____ _____ _____ tomorrow.

25 We _____ lots of olives _____ our olive trees this year.

26 I _____ a man _____ sons are good workers.

27 He _____ the olives _____, and his two sons helped him, _____ them _____ from the ground.

28 I _____ him 27,000 lire _____ the work.

29 I _____ 12,000 more _____ the olive press.

30 I got _____ oil _____ _____ a large pot and a small _____.

31 I can sell it _____ _____ _____ _____ 1,300 lire a liter.

32 My love, my heart thinks of you _____ Christmas is coming.

33 I _____ _____ so happy if you _____ with me.

34 We all _____ you so much.

35 I'm sending you _____ _____ _____ from me and our three little kids.

36 Goodbye, _____ _____.

37 My heart is yours, _____ to you _____ our two rings are.

---

17 당신의 어머니께서는 병이 드셨고, 나는 약간의 돈과 음식을 가지고 병원에 있는 어머니를 방문할 예정이에요.

18 큰애가 막내를 돌보는 동안 둘째와 함께 그곳에 갈 거예요.

19 나는 150,000리라에 두 일꾼을 시켜 우리 밭을 준비하고 씨앗을 심게 했어요.

20 나는 DC에 투표했어요.

21 PCI는 매우 많은 의석을 잃어서 거의 죽은 것처럼 보여요.

22 하지만 이쪽이 이기건 저쪽이 이기건, 상황은 똑같아요.

23 우리 가난한 사람들에게는 아무것도 바뀌지 않지요.

24 우리는 어제도 일했고, 내일도 다시 일할 거예요.

25 우리는 올해 올리브나무에서 올리브를 많이 땄어요.

26 나는 아들들이 훌륭한 일꾼인 한 남자를 고용했어요.

27 그가 올리브를 쳐서 떨어뜨리면 그의 두 아들이 땅에서 올리브를 주우면서 그를 도왔어요.

28 나는 그 일을 위해 그에게 27,000리라를 지급했어요.

29 올리브 압착을 위해 12,000리라를 더 썼어요.

30 나는 큰 항아리 하나와 작은 항아리 하나를 채울 만큼 충분한 기름을 얻었어요.

31 리터당 1,300리라의 가격으로 팔 수 있을 것 같아요.

32 여보, 크리스마스가 다가오면서 내 마음은 당신을 떠올려요.

33 당신이 나와 함께 있다면 난 정말 행복할 거예요.

34 우리는 모두 당신을 매우 많이 그리워해요.

35 나와 우리 세 아이의 큰 포옹을 보내요.

36 잘 있어요, 여보.

37 내 마음은 당신의 것이에요, 우리들의 두 반지처럼 당신과 연결된 채로요.

● 우리말을 참고하여 본문을 영작하시오.

1 세 아이의 엄마가 보낸 그림 편지
➡ _____

2 오늘날 외국에 있는 가족이나 친구와 대화하는 것은 다소 쉽고 간단하다.
➡ _____

3 하지만 전화와 인터넷 시대 이전에는 그것이 그렇게 쉽지 않았다.
➡ _____

4 사람들은 단지 편지를 보내고 답장을 몇 주 동안 기다렸다.
➡ _____

5 그리고 그들이 읽거나 쓸 수 없었다면 그건 훨씬 더 힘들었다.
➡ _____

6 이 편지는 사람들이 이런 어려움을 어떻게 극복했는지 보여 준다.
➡ _____

7 그것은 남편이 멀리 떨어져 살았던 한 여자에 의해 1973년에 쓰여졌다.
➡ _____

8 그녀의 남편은 독일에서 일한 반면, 그녀는 이탈리아의 섬인 시실리에서 살았다.
➡ _____

9 그 당시에는 5% 이상의 이탈리아 사람들이 읽거나 쓸 수 없었고, 그녀도 그들 중 한 명이었다.
➡ _____

10 이 편지는 시실리의 작가 Gesualdo Bufalino가 발견하였다.
➡ _____

11 그가 그림들을 어떻게 글로 번역했는지는 다음과 같다.
➡ _____

12 사랑하는 여보, 난 당신이 정말 그립고, 우리 세 아이와 함께 당신을 향해 내 팔을 쭉 뻗고 있어요.
➡ _____

13 막내를 제외하고는 우리 모두 건강해요.
➡ _____

14 그 아이는 약간 아프지만 심각하진 않아요.
➡ _____

15 난 당신에게 이미 편지를 보냈지만, 답장이 없어서 그것 때문에 나는 슬퍼요.
➡ _____

16 당신에게서 편지를 받는다면, 나는 정말 행복할 거예요.
➡ _____

17 당신의 어머니께서는 병이 드셨고, 나는 약간의 돈과 음식을 가지고 병원에 있는 어머니를 방문할 예정이에요.
➡ _____

18 큰애가 막내를 돌보는 동안 둘째와 함께 그곳에 갈 거예요.
➡ _____

19 나는 150,000리라에 두 일꾼을 시켜 우리 밭을 준비하고 씨앗을 심게 했어요.
➡ _____

20 나는 DC에 투표했어요.
➡ _____

21 PCI는 매우 많은 의석을 잃어서 거의 죽은 것처럼 보여요.
➡ _____

22 하지만 이쪽이 이기건 저쪽이 이기건, 상황은 똑같아요.
➡ _____

23 우리 가난한 사람들에게는 아무 것도 바뀌지 않지요.
➡ _____

24 우리는 어제도 일했고, 내일도 다시 일할 거예요.
➡ _____

25 우리는 올해 올리브나무에서 올리브를 많이 땄어요.
➡ _____

26 나는 아들들이 훌륭한 일꾼인 한 남자를 고용했어요.
➡ _____

27 그가 올리브를 쳐서 떨어뜨리면 그의 두 아들이 땅에서 올리브를 주우면서 그를 도왔어요.
➡ _____

28 나는 그 일을 위해 그에게 27,000리라를 지급했어요.
➡ _____

29 올리브 압착을 위해 12,000리라를 더 썼어요.
➡ _____

30 나는 큰 항아리 하나와 작은 항아리 하나를 채울 만큼 충분한 기름을 얻었어요.
➡ _____

31 리터당 1,300리라의 가격으로 팔 수 있을 것 같아요.
➡ _____

32 여보, 크리스마스가 다가오면서 내 마음은 당신을 떠올려요.
➡ _____

33 당신이 나와 함께 있다면 난 정말 행복할 거예요.
➡ _____

34 우리는 모두 당신을 매우 많이 그리워해요.
➡ _____

35 나와 우리 세 아이의 큰 포옹을 보내요.
➡ _____

36 잘 있어요, 여보.
➡ _____

37 내 마음은 당신의 것이에요, 우리들의 두 반지처럼 당신과 연결된 채로요.
➡ _____

[01~03] 다음 글을 읽고 물음에 답하시오.

ⓐSpeaking to family members or friends in a foreign country is rather easy and simple today. But before the days of phones and the Internet, it was not that easy. People just sent a letter and waited for a reply for weeks. And it was a lot harder if they couldn't read or write.

01 위 글의 밑줄 친 ⓐSpeaking과 문법적 쓰임이 같은 것을 모두 고르시오.

① They were speaking in low voices.
② He went out without speaking to me.
③ Generally speaking, the more you pay, the more you get.
④ He is good at speaking English.
⑤ Be quiet! He hasn't finished speaking.

02 위 글의 제목으로 알맞은 것을 고르시오.

① How to Communicate with Family Members Who Couldn't Read or Write
② The Advantage of Phones and the Internet
③ The Development of the International Mail Service
④ The Difficulty of Speaking to People Abroad in Old Days
⑤ The Hard Lives of People Who Couldn't Read or Write

03 Which question CANNOT be answered after reading the passage?

① Today, is it difficult to speak to family members or friends in a foreign country?
② Before the days of phones and the Internet, was it easy to speak to family members or friends in a foreign country?
③ Before the days of phones and the Internet, how did people speak to people in a foreign country?
④ How long did it take to receive a reply after sending a letter to people in a foreign country?
⑤ How did people who couldn't read or write speak to people in a foreign country?

[04~06] 다음 글을 읽고 물음에 답하시오.

We picked lots of olives from our olive trees this year. I ____ⓐ____ a man whose sons are good workers. He knocked the olives down, and his two sons helped him, picking them up from the ground. I paid him 27,000 lire for ⓑthe work. I spent 12,000 more for the olive press. I got enough oil to fill a large pot and a small one. I can sell it at a price of 1,300 lire ⓒa liter.

서답형
04 주어진 영영풀이를 참고하여 빈칸 ⓐ에 철자 h로 시작하는 단어를 쓰시오.

| employed |

➡ _____

서답형
05 위 글의 밑줄 친 ⓑthe work가 가리키는 것을 우리말로 쓰시오.

➡ _____

_____

서답형

06 위 글의 밑줄 친 ⓒa와 바꿔 쓸 수 있는 말을 쓰시오.

➡ _____

[07~09] 다음 글을 읽고 물음에 답하시오.

This letter shows how people got over these difficulties. (①) She lived in Sicily, an Italian island, while her husband worked in Germany. (②) At the time, more than 5% of the people in Italy could not read or write, and she was one of them. (③) This letter was discovered ___ⓐ___ Sicilian writer Gesualdo Bufalino. (④)

Here's how he translated the pictures ___ⓑ___ words. (⑤)

07 위 글의 빈칸 ⓐ와 ⓑ에 들어갈 전치사가 바르게 짝지어진 것은?

	ⓐ	ⓑ		ⓐ	ⓑ
①	for	to	②	by	into
③	in	to	④	for	into
⑤	by	on			

08 위 글의 흐름으로 보아, 주어진 문장이 들어가기에 가장 적절한 곳은?

It was written in 1973 by a woman whose husband was far away.

① ② ③ ④ ⑤

중요

09 According to the passage, which is NOT true?

① A woman whose husband worked in Germany wrote this letter in 1973.

② She lived in Sicily, an Italian island, and she was illiterate.

③ At the time, over 5% of the Italians could not read or write.

④ Sicilian writer Gesualdo Bufalino discovered this letter.

⑤ Gesualdo Bufalino translated her words into pictures.

[10~12] 다음 글을 읽고 물음에 답하시오.

I had two workers ___ⓐ___ our field and plant seeds for (A)150,000 lire. I voted for the DC. (B)The PCI lost ___ⓑ___ many seats ___ⓒ___ it almost seems dead. But whether one or the other wins, it's the same. Nothing changes for us poor people. We worked yesterday, and we will work again tomorrow.

10 위 글의 빈칸 ⓐ에 들어갈 알맞은 말을 고르시오.

① prepare ② to prepare
③ prepared ④ to have prepared
⑤ had prepared

서답형

11 문장 (B)가 다음과 같은 뜻이 되도록, 빈칸 ⓑ와 ⓒ에 들어갈 알맞은 말을 쓰시오.

The PCI lost so many seats as to seem almost dead.

➡ ⓑ _____ ⓒ _____

서답형

12 위 글의 밑줄 친 (A)150,000을 영어로 읽는 법을 쓰시오.

➡ _____

[13~14] 다음 글을 읽고 물음에 답하시오.

My dear love, I miss you so much, and I reach my arms out toward you, together with our three kids. We are all in good health except for the little one. He's a little sick, but not seriously.

13 다음 중 위 글의 내용을 나타내는 그림 편지를 고르시오.

서답형

14 위 글의 내용을 다음과 같이 정리하고자 한다. 빈칸 (A)와 (B)에 들어갈 알맞은 단어를 쓰시오.

> A woman (A)_____ her husband who was far away and wrote a letter showing how she and their (B)_____ _____ were getting along.

[15~17] 다음 글을 읽고 물음에 답하시오.

> I'm sending you a big hug from me and our three little kids. Goodbye, dear love. My heart is yours, _____ⓐ_____ to you as our two rings (A)are.

서답형

15 위 글의 빈칸 ⓐ에 join을 알맞은 형태로 쓰시오.

➡ _____

16 다음 중 위 글의 내용을 나타내는 그림 편지를 고르시오.

서답형

17 위 글의 밑줄 친 (A)are 뒤에 생략된 말을 쓰시오.

➡ _____

[18~20] 다음 글을 읽고 물음에 답하시오.

> I already sent you a letter, but there was no reply, so I am sad about it. ⓐIf I got a letter from you, I would be very happy. Your mother fell ill, and I'm going to visit her in the hospital with some money and food. I'll go there with our middle son while the oldest ⓑlooks after the youngest.

서답형

18 위 글의 밑줄 친 ⓐ를 직설법 문장으로 고치시오.

➡ _____

또는 _____

19 위 글의 밑줄 친 ⓑlooks after와 바꿔 쓸 수 있는 말을 모두 고르시오.

① takes care of　　② takes after

③ cares for　　　　④ looks for

⑤ asks after

서답형

20 Why does the writer say that it is the same whether the DC or the PCI wins? Fill in the blanks (A)~(C) with suitable words.

> Because (A)_____ changes for poor people and they (B)_____ yesterday, and they (C)_____ _____ again tomorrow.

[21~23] 다음 글을 읽고 물음에 답하시오.

My dear love, I ⓐmiss you so much, and I reach my arms out toward you, together with our three kids. We are all in good health except for the little one. He's a little sick, but not seriously.

I already sent you a letter, but there was no reply, so I am sad about ⓑit. ⓒ당신에게서 편지를 받는다면, 나는 정말 행복할 거예요. Your mother fell ill, and I'm going to visit her in the hospital with some money and food. I'll go there with our middle son while the oldest looks after the youngest.

21 위 글의 밑줄 친 ⓐmiss와 같은 의미로 쓰인 것을 고르시오.

① The bullet did miss her by about six inches.
② I will miss her when she leaves.
③ You must not miss meals when you're training.
④ The sale prices were too good to miss.
⑤ She didn't want to miss a good party last night.

서답형

22 위 글의 밑줄 친 ⓑit이 가리키는 것을 본문에서 찾아 쓰시오.

➡ _____

서답형

23 위 글의 밑줄 친 ⓒ의 우리말에 맞게 주어진 어휘를 이용하여 12 단어로 영작하시오.

got, from, very happy

➡ _____

[24~26] 다음 글을 읽고 물음에 답하시오.

We picked lots of olives from our olive trees this year. I hired a man whose sons are good workers. He knocked the olives down, and his two sons helped him, picking them up from the ground. I paid him 27,000 lire ___ⓐ___ the work. I spent 12,000 more for the olive press. I got enough oil to fill a large pot and a small one. I can sell it ___ⓑ___ a price of 1,300 lire ⓒa liter.

24 위 글의 빈칸 ⓐ와 ⓑ에 들어갈 전치사가 바르게 짝지어진 것은?

	ⓐ	ⓑ			ⓐ	ⓑ
①	for	to		②	in	by
③	in	at		④	for	at
⑤	on	by				

25 위 글의 밑줄 친 ⓒa와 같은 의미로 쓰인 것을 모두 고르시오.

① There's a Mrs. Green to see you.
② They cost 7 dollars a kilo.
③ A lion is a dangerous animal.
④ I can type 50 words a minute.
⑤ There's a visitor for you.

26 위 글을 읽고 알 수 없는 것을 고르시오.

① Did they pick lots of olives from their olive trees this year?
② Whom did the writer hire?
③ How much did the writer pay the worker?
④ How much oil did the writer get?
⑤ How much did the writer earn by selling the olive oil?

[01~03] 다음 글을 읽고 물음에 답하시오.

ⓐ이 편지는 사람들이 이런 어려움을 어떻게 극복했는지 보여 준다. It was written in 1973 by a woman whose husband was far away. She lived in Sicily, an Italian island, while her husband worked in Germany. At the time, more than 5% of the people in Italy could not read or write, and she was one of them. ⓑ This letter was discovered by Sicilian writer Gesualdo Bufalino.

Here's how he translated the pictures into words.

★ **중요**
01 위 글의 밑줄 친 ⓐ의 우리말에 맞게 주어진 어휘를 알맞게 배열하시오.

> these difficulties / people / how / this letter / shows / got over

➡ _____

_____

02 위 글의 밑줄 친 ⓑ를 능동태로 고치시오.

➡ _____

_____

03 To whom did the woman write the letter? Fill in the blanks (A) and (B) with suitable words.

> She wrote it to (A)_____ _____
> who worked (B)_____ _____.

[04~06] 다음 글을 읽고 물음에 답하시오.

My dear love, I miss you so much, and I ⓐ reach my arms out toward you, together with

our three kids. ⓑ우리 모두 건강해요 except for the little ⓒone. He's a little sick, but not seriously.

고난이도
04 위 글의 밑줄 친 ⓐ와 바꿔 쓸 수 있는 단어를 철자 s로 시작하여 쓰시오.

➡ _____

05 위 글의 밑줄 친 ⓑ의 우리말에 맞게 6단어로 영작하시오.

➡ _____

★ **중요**
06 위 글의 밑줄 친 ⓒone이 가리키는 것을 본문에서 찾아 쓰시오.

➡ _____

[07~09] 다음 글을 읽고 물음에 답하시오.

We picked lots of olives from our olive trees this year. I hired a man whose sons are good workers. He knocked the olives down, and his two sons helped him, picking ⓐthem up from the ground. I paid him ___(A)___ lire for the work. I spent ___(B)___ more for the olive press. I got enough oil to fill a large pot and a small one. I can sell it at a price of ___(C)___ lire a liter.

07 다음 그림을 참조하여 위 글의 빈칸 (A)~(C)에 들어갈 알맞은 숫자를 쓰시오.

➡ (A) _____ (B) _____ (C) _____

08 위 글의 밑줄 친 ⓐthem이 가리키는 것을 본문에서 찾아 쓰시오.

➡ _____

09 How much did the writer spend picking the olives and pressing them? Answer in English in a full sentence. (4 words)

➡ _____

[10~12] 다음 글을 읽고 물음에 답하시오.

> ⓐI already sent you a letter, but there was no reply, so I am sad about it. ⓑIf I got a letter from you, I will be very happy. Your mother fell ill, and I'm going to visit her in the hospital with some money and food. I'll go there with our middle son while the oldest looks after the youngest.

10 위 글의 밑줄 친 ⓐ를 3형식 문장으로 고치시오.

➡ _____

11 위 글의 밑줄 친 ⓑ에서 어법상 틀린 부분을 찾아 고치시오.

_____ ➡ _____

12 Why is she going to the hospital and with what will she go there? Fill in the blanks (A) and (B) with suitable words.

> Because her mother-in-law (A)_____ _____ and is in the hospital, she is going to the hospital with (B)_____ _____ _____ _____.

[13~14] 다음 글을 읽고 물음에 답하시오.

> (A)I had two workers prepare our field and plant seeds ___ⓐ___ 150,000 lire. I voted ___ⓑ___ the DC. The PCI lost so many seats that it almost seems dead. But whether one or the other wins, it's the same. Nothing changes for us poor people. We worked yesterday, and we will work again tomorrow.

13 위 글의 빈칸 ⓐ와 ⓑ에 공통으로 들어갈 알맞은 전치사를 쓰시오.

➡ _____

14 위 글의 밑줄 친 (A)를 got을 사용하여 고칠 때, 빈칸에 들어갈 알맞은 말을 쓰시오.

➡ I got two workers _____ our field

[15~16] 다음 글을 읽고 물음에 답하시오.

> My love, my heart thinks of you ___ⓐ___ Christmas is coming. (A)I would be so happy if you were with me. We all miss you so much.
>
> I'm sending you a big hug from me and our three little kids. Goodbye, dear love. My heart is yours, joined to you ___ⓑ___ our two rings are.

15 위 글의 빈칸 ⓐ와 ⓑ에 공통으로 들어갈 알맞은 말을 쓰시오.

➡ _____

16 위 글의 밑줄 친 (A)를 직설법 문장으로 고치시오.

➡ _____

또는 _____

해석

Express Yourself C1

The boy <u>whose</u> head is covered with bees <u>doesn't</u> understand the woman's
소유격 관계대명사   don't(×)

gesture. I think <u>it</u> means "Jump into the pond." <u>If I were the boy, I would jump</u>
= the woman's gesture   = Were I

into the pond <u>right away</u>.
= right now = at once = immediately

구문해설 • **be covered with**: ～로 덮이다 • **gesture**: 몸짓 • **right away**: 즉시, 당장

머리가 벌로 덮인 소년은 그 여자의 몸짓을 이해하지 못합니다. 제 생각에 그것은 "연못으로 뛰어들어."를 의미합니다. 제가 그 소년이라면, 저는 당장 연못으로 뛰어들겠습니다.

Project Do it Yourself

"Climb up the mountain."

<u>If I had soldiers to lead, I would use kites to send my messages.</u> For example,
가정법 과거형으로 if절에 과거동사를, 주절에는 '조동사 과거형+동사원형'을 사용한다.

I would fly a kite <u>whose</u> face <u>looks like</u> a mountain to <u>make the soldiers climb</u>
소유격 관계대명사   look like+명사: ～처럼 보이다   사역동사+목적어+동사원형

up the mountain.

구문해설 • **kite**: 연

"산 위로 올라가라"
내가 병사를 지휘한다면, 나는 나의 메시지를 보내기 위해 연을 사용하겠다. 예를 들어, 나는 병사들이 산 위로 올라가게 하려고 앞면이 산처럼 보이는 연을 날리겠다.

Link to the World

Hangeul <u>was created</u> by King Sejong. At first, many people didn't want to
수동태

use this new writing system. However, King Sejong tried hard <u>to help</u> people
～하기 위해서

use Hangeul. Thanks to him, we can express anything with Hangeul now. If
목적보어(= to use)

we <u>didn't know</u> Hangeul, we <u>could not express</u> <u>ourselves</u> easily.
가정법 과거   조동사의 과거+동사원형   재귀대명사(주어 = 목적어)

구문해설 • **writing system**: 문자 체계 • **thanks to**: ～ 덕택에
• **express ourselves**: 자기 자신을 표현하다

한글은 세종대왕에 의해 창제되었다. 처음에는 많은 사람이 이 새로운 문자 체계를 사용하는 것을 원하지 않았다. 하지만, 세종대왕은 사람들이 한글을 사용하도록 돕기 위해 열심히 노력했다. 그분 덕택에, 우리는 지금 한글로 무엇이든 표현할 수 있다. 우리가 한글을 모른다면, 우리 자신을 쉽게 표현할 수 없을 것이다.

01 다음 주어진 두 단어의 관계가 같도록 빈칸에 알맞은 단어를 쓰시오.

> hire – employ : embrace – _____

02 다음 문장의 빈칸 (a)와 (b)에 들어갈 단어가 바르게 짝지어진 것은?

> • Do you have your own way to ___(a)___ the cold?
> • This is why it is important to ___(b)___ respectable politicians.

① break down – reject
② get over – vote for
③ stand up for – accept
④ pick up – vote for
⑤ get over – compete

[03~04] 다음 영영풀이에 해당하는 것을 고르시오.

03

> the man that a woman is married to

① son   ② hunter
③ manager   ④ reporter
⑤ husband

04

> a position as a member of a committee, court, etc.

① seat   ② permission
③ reply   ④ figure
⑤ vote

05 다음 대화의 빈칸에 들어갈 말을 〈영영풀이〉를 참고하여 주어진 철자로 시작하여 쓰시오.

> B: I'm curious about sign language.
> G: Are you? Let me show you one e_____. Look.
> B: What does it mean?
> G: It means "Hello."

> <영영풀이> a group of words that has a special meaning

➡ _____

06 다음 밑줄 친 부분의 뜻이 잘못된 것은?

① The little boy seemed very hungry. (~하게 보였다)
② The woman was so surprised to see the dead insects by the window. (죽은)
③ Whether or not you come to the party, you must call him. (~인지 아닌지)
④ I was asked to prepare a report for our next meeting. (준비하다)
⑤ He knocked me on the head. (쳤다)

07 다음 대화의 흐름상 단어의 쓰임이 어색한 부분을 찾아 바르게 고치시오. (1개)

> B: Now the enemy is crossing the (a)board in the dark. What are the soldiers going to do to send (b)messages? I'm curious about that.
> G: They will (c)light four chimneys.
> B: When they light all five of the (d)chimneys, what does that mean?
> G: It means the (e)battle has started.

_____ ➡ _____

[08~09] 다음 대화를 읽고 물음에 답하시오.

B: This painting has some hidden secrets in it.

G: Really? I'm curious about them. Where are the secrets?

B: Find one yourself.

G: Let's see. ... Oh, I see some letters here.

B: You found one! It means "Jan van Eyck was here. 1434." It's Latin.

G: That's awesome! Any other secrets?

B: Okay. This dog tells us the man here was very rich.

G: I don't understand.

B: They had to spend lots of money to buy a dog of that kind at that time.

G: I see. Only the rich could have that kind of dog, right?

B: Exactly. Pictures speak a thousand words, you know.

08 위 대화를 읽고 답할 수 <u>없는</u> 질문은?

① What does the painting have?

② What do the letters the girl found mean?

③ Are the letters the girl found English?

④ What kind of a dog did people at that time like to raise?

⑤ What makes people think the man in the picture was very rich?

09 위 대화의 제목으로 가장 적절한 것은?

① How to Hide the Secrets in the Painting

② Can You Read Jan van Eyck's Painting?

③ Different Hobbies in Different Times

④ Can You Appreciate the Painting Correctly?

⑤ Jan van Eyck's Genius for Drawing the Painting

10 다음 대화를 순서에 맞게 바르게 배열한 것은?

(A) I see. Now I can guess what they mean.

(B) Oh, they are Braille. They are for blind people.

(C) What are these dots for? I'm curious about them.

① (A) – (B) – (C)

② (B) – (A) – (C)

③ (C) – (B) – (A)

④ (A) – (C) – (B)

⑤ (C) – (A) – (B)

11 다음 짝지어진 대화 중 <u>어색한</u> 것은?

① A: What does his gesture mean? I'm curious about it.

B: It means "Step back from the pond."

② A: What would you do if you were a fish?

B: If I were a fish, I would swim in the pond.

③ A: What would you do if you had a beautiful voice?

B: If I had a beautiful voice, I would sing on the tree.

④ A: This woman doesn't want a dollar. So what does her gesture mean?

B: It means she wants a chicken.

⑤ A: I'm curious about sign language.

B: What is sign launguage? Let me show you one expression.

12 주어진 문장과 같은 뜻이 되도록 바꾼 것 중 올바르지 <u>않은</u> 것을 고르시오.

① As the bag is expensive, I can't buy it.
= If the bag were cheap, I could buy it.

② As I don't have a car, I can't give you a ride to school.
= If I had a car, I could give you a ride to school.

③ As he doesn't know how to open the door, he can't enter the house.
= If he knew how to open the door, he could enter the house.

④ If I had a bike, I would ride it to school.
= As I have no bike, I don't ride it to school.

⑤ If he were good at dancing, he could take part in the contest.
= As he is not poor at dancing, he can't take part in the contest.

13 다음 주어진 문장과 같은 의미의 문장을 가정법을 이용하여 쓰시오.

(1) As I know the singer, I can shake hands with him.
= If _____
_____.

(2) As he is not smart, he doesn't prepare for the game in advance.
= If _____
_____.

14 다음 빈칸에 들어갈 말이 다른 하나를 고르시오.

① I have speakers _____ sound loud.
② The girl _____ shirt is red is Emma's sister.

③ That is the shop _____ owner is not kind.
④ I know a boy _____ parents are both teachers.
⑤ My partner is the man _____ mother used to be an announcer.

15 다음 ⓐ~ⓔ 중 어법상 어색한 것을 찾아 바르게 고치시오.

Hangeul ⓐ<u>was created</u> by King Sejong. At first, many people didn't want ⓑ<u>to use</u> this new writing system. However, King Sejong tried hard ⓒ<u>to help</u> people use Hangeul. Thanks to him, we can express anything with Hangeul now. If we ⓓ<u>don't</u> know Hangeul, we could not express ⓔ<u>ourselves</u> easily.

_____ ➡ _____

16 다음 중 밑줄 친 부분의 쓰임이 나머지 넷과 <u>다른</u> 것은?

① Look at the car <u>whose</u> color is gold.
② I climbed the mountain <u>whose</u> top was covered with snow.
③ I'm not sure <u>whose</u> bag this is.
④ This is the backpack <u>whose</u> owner is unknown.
⑤ The girl <u>whose</u> dog has died is crying.

17 다음 중 어법상 어색한 문장의 개수로 알맞은 것은?

a. If I felt better, I could go shopping.
b. Were she you, she would never do that.
c. If I have more time, I could do it better.
d. If I were you, I won't go there.
e. If I knew her, I will introduce her to you.

① 1개 ② 2개 ③ 3개 ④ 4개 ⑤ 5개

18 우리말과 같은 뜻이 되도록 빈칸에 알맞은 말을 쓰시오.

> 그 소년이 키가 더 크다면, 그 장면을 볼 수 있을 텐데.
> → The boy _____ the scene if he _____.

19 다음 우리말을 주어진 어휘를 이용하여 영어로 옮기시오.

(1) 내가 병사들을 지휘한다면, 나는 나의 메시지를 보내기 위해 연을 사용하겠다.
➡ If I had soldiers to lead, I _____ _____. (kites, messages)

(2) 나는 앞면이 산처럼 보이는 연을 날리겠다.
➡ I would fly a kite _____ _____. (face, look like)

(3) 가방이 과일로 가득한 소년은 원숭이를 보는 중이다.
➡ The boy _____ is looking at the monkey. (full of, fruit)

Reading

[20~22] 다음 글을 읽고 물음에 답하시오.

This letter shows how people ①got over these difficulties. It was written in 1973 by a woman ②whose husband was far away. She lived in Sicily, an Italian island, while her husband worked in Germany. At the time, ③ more than 5% of ④the people in Italy could not read or write, and she was one of ⓐthem. This letter was discovered by Sicilian writer Gesualdo Bufalino.

Here's ⑤how he translated the pictures into words.

20 위 글의 밑줄 친 ①~⑤와 바꿔 쓸 수 있는 말로 옳지 않은 것을 고르시오.

① overcame   ② of which
③ over   ④ the Italians
⑤ the way

21 위 글의 밑줄 친 ⓐthem이 가리키는 것을 영어로 쓰시오.

➡ _____
_____

22 위 글의 뒤에 올 내용으로 가장 알맞은 것을 고르시오.

① Gesualdo Bufalino가 시실리 여인의 그림 편지를 발견한 상황
② 이탈리아 사람들의 높은 문맹률
③ Gesualdo Bufalino가 그림 편지들을 글로 번역한 내용
④ 여인의 남편이 보낸 답장의 내용
⑤ Gesualdo Bufalino가 시실리 여인의 말을 그림 편지로 옮겨준 내용

[23~25] 다음 글을 읽고 물음에 답하시오.

My dear love, I miss you so much, and I reach my arms out toward you, together with our three kids. We are all in good health except for the little ⓐone. He's a little sick, but not seriously.

I already sent you a letter, but there was no reply, so I am sad about it. If I got a ⓑletter from you, I would be very happy. Your mother fell ill, and I'm going to visit her in the hospital with some money and food. I'll go there with our middle son while the oldest looks after the youngest.

23 위 글의 밑줄 친 ⓐone과 문법적 쓰임이 같은 것을 고르시오.

① Do you want <u>one</u> biscuit or two?
② I saw her <u>one</u> afternoon last week.
③ They all went off in <u>one</u> direction.
④ <u>One</u> must observe the rules.
⑤ I have many bags, and this <u>one</u> is my favorite.

24 위 글의 밑줄 친 ⓑletter와 바꿔 쓸 수 있는 말을 본문에서 찾아 쓰시오.

➡ _____

25 According to the passage, which is NOT true?

① The writer misses her husband so much.
② The writer's little kid is a little sick.
③ The writer is sending a letter to her husband for the first time.
④ The writer's mother-in-law fell ill and is in the hospital now.
⑤ The writer's oldest kid will look after the youngest while their mom goes to visit their grandmother in the hospital.

[26~27] 다음 글을 읽고 물음에 답하시오.

We picked lots of olives from our olive trees this year. (①) He knocked the olives down, and his two sons helped him, ⓐ땅에서 그것들을 주우면서. (②) I paid him 27,000 lire for the work. (③) I spent 12,000 more for the olive press. (④) I got enough oil to fill a large pot and a small one. (⑤) I can sell it at a price of 1,300 lire a liter.

26 위 글의 흐름으로 보아, 주어진 문장이 들어가기에 가장 적절한 곳은?

| I hired a man whose sons are good workers. |

①   ②   ③   ④   ⑤

27 위 글의 밑줄 친 ⓐ의 우리말에 맞게 주어진 어휘를 이용하여 6 단어로 영작하시오.

| picking, ground |

➡ _____

[28~29] 다음 글을 읽고 물음에 답하시오.

The boy whose backpack the monkey is pulling doesn't understand its gesture. I think (A)it means "Give the fruit to me." If I ____ⓐ____ the boy, I would give the fruit to the monkey right away.

28 위 글의 빈칸 ⓐ에 be를 알맞은 형태로 쓰시오.

➡ _____

29 위 글의 밑줄 친 (A)it이 가리키는 것을 본문에서 찾아 쓰시오.

➡ _____

출제율 90%

01 다음 짝지어진 단어의 관계가 같도록 주어진 철자로 시작하는 단어를 쓰시오.

> ill – healthy : dead – a_____

출제율 95%

02 다음 영영풀이에 해당하는 단어는?

> to make something ready for use

① prefer   ② prepare

③ vote   ④ translate

⑤ encourage

출제율 90%

03 다음 대화를 읽고 빈칸에 들어갈 말을 〈조건〉에 맞게 쓰시오.

┤ 조건 ├
• 'It means'와 enter를 사용하여 정의를 나타내는 표현을 쓸 것.

G: What's this? I'm curious about it.
B: It's a traffic sign. _____
G: Oh, I see.

➡ _____
_____

[04~05] 다음 대화를 읽고 물음에 답하시오.

B: What are the soldiers doing with the five chimneys on TV?

(A) Really? I'm curious about the system. Can you tell me more?

(B) Well, do you see the two smoking chimneys?

(C) They are sending messages to the king by using the chimneys.

(D) Yes. What do they mean?

G: They mean they just saw an enemy.

출제율 100%

04 위 대화의 (A)~(D)를 순서대로 배열하시오.

➡ _____

출제율 95%

05 위 대화를 읽고 다음 질문에 영어로 답하시오. (be for를 이용하시오)

> Q: What do you think the chimneys are for?

➡ _____

출제율 90%

06 다음 대화의 빈칸 (A)에 들어갈 말로 알맞은 것은?

> B: If there's no enemy, they don't smoke at all, do they?
>
> G: _____(A)_____ Smoke from one chimney means "No enemy."
>
> B: Now smoke is rising from three chimneys. What does that mean?
>
> G: It means an enemy is coming close to the border.

① No, they don't.
② Yes, they don't.
③ Yes, they do.
④ No, they do.
⑤ Yes, they are.

07 다음 대화에서 주어진 문장이 들어갈 위치로 알맞은 것은?

> B: This painting has some hidden secrets in it.
> G: Really? I'm curious about them. Where are the secrets?
> B: Find one yourself. (A)
> G: Let's see. ... Oh, I see some letters here.
> B: You found one! (B) It's Latin.
> G: That's awesome! (C) Any other secrets?
> B: Okay. This dog tells us the man here was very rich.
> G: (D) I don't understand.
> B: They had to spend lots of money to buy a dog of that kind at that time.
> G: I see. (E) Only the rich could have that kind of dog, right?
> B: Exactly. Pictures speak a thousand words, you know.

> It means "Jan van Eyck was here. 1434."

① (A)　② (B)　③ (C)　④ (D)　⑤ (E)

08 다음 대화의 빈칸 (A)에 들어갈 말로 알맞은 것은?

> W: What does this woman's gesture mean? I'm curious about it.
> M: ＿＿＿＿＿＿＿ (A)
> W: Why do you think so?
> M: The boy has lots of bees on his head. And the woman is pointing at the pond.

① It means "You're welcome."
② It means "History repeats itself."
③ It means she wants a chicken.
④ I think it means "Jump into the pond."
⑤ It means "Turn it off."

09 다음 짝지어진 대화 중 어색한 것은?

① A: What does its gesture mean? I'm curious about it.
　B: It means "Give the fruit to me."
② A: What would you do if you had strong arms?
　B: If I had strong arms, I could climb trees.
③ A: Do you know what this means?
　B: Sure.
④ A: Do you know what this means?
　B: No, I don't. What does it mean?
⑤ A: This house is famous for having thousands of secrets in it.
　B: Really? It means you must find the secrets.

10 다음 대화의 빈칸에 들어갈 말로 알맞은 것은?

> W: This woman doesn't want a dollar. So what does her gesture mean?
> M: ＿＿＿＿＿＿＿＿＿＿＿＿
> W: Then the boy should bring a chicken to get the fruit, right?
> M: I think so.

① It means you must not ride a bike here.
② It means you must be careful with the animals.
③ It means she wants a chicken.
④ It means you must drive slowly here.
⑤ It means the battle has started.

11 다음 ①~⑤ 중 어법상 어색한 것은?

> The house ①which doors ②are painted ③red ④is ⑤my grandfather's.

출제율 90%

12 'whose'를 사용하여 〈보기〉와 같이 두 문장을 한 문장으로 연결하시오.

> ┤ 보기 ├
>
> Tom easily found the store.
> + Its address was on the Internet.
> → Tom easily found the store whose address was on the Internet.

(1) Is there any student?

　　+ His name was not called.

　　➡ _____

　　_____

(2) Mike is the boy.

　　+ His hair is very short.

　　➡ _____

　　_____

(3) The house is my uncle's.

　　+ Its windows are very big.

　　➡ _____

　　_____

(4) My sister is the girl.

　　+ Her cat is eating a fish.

　　➡ _____

　　_____

(5) Do you know the old man?

　　+ His shoes are red and blue.

　　➡ _____

　　_____

출제율 95%

13 잘못된 부분을 바르게 고쳐 문장을 다시 쓰시오.

(1) I know a boy who mother grows bananas.

　　➡ _____

(2) The boy of which dog is barking is my cousin.

　　➡ _____

(3) The girl whose hat is covered with flowers are a great dancer.

　　➡ _____

　　_____

(4) You were with me, I could show you my painting.

　　➡ _____

　　_____

(5) If I were a fish, I can swim in the water.

　　➡ _____

[14~16] 다음 글을 읽고 물음에 답하시오.

> Speaking to family members or friends in a foreign country is rather easy and simple today. But before the days of phones and the Internet, ⓐit was not ⓑthat easy. People just sent a letter and waited for a reply for weeks. And ⓒit was ⓓa lot harder if they couldn't read or write.

출제율 95%

14 위 글의 밑줄 친 ⓐit과 ⓒit이 공통으로 가리키는 것을 본문에서 찾아 쓰시오.

　　➡ _____

　　_____

출제율 100%

15 아래 〈보기〉에서 위 글의 밑줄 친 ⓑthat과 문법적 쓰임이 같은 것의 개수를 고르시오.

> ┤ 보기 ├
>
> ① I can't walk that far.
> ② Can you see that dog?
> ③ I know that you are busy.
> ④ This book is mine and that one is yours.
> ⑤ Are you sure she's that young?

① 1개　② 2개　③ 3개　④ 4개　⑤ 5개

16 위 글의 밑줄 친 ⓓa lot과 바꿔 쓸 수 없는 말을 고르시오. [출제율 95%]

① much ② even ③ still

④ rather ⑤ far

[17~19] 다음 글을 읽고 물음에 답하시오.

My dear love, I miss you so much, and ⓐI reach my arms out toward you, together with our three kids. (①) He's a little sick, but not seriously. (②)

I already sent you a letter, but there was no reply, so I am sad about it. (③) If I got a letter from you, I would be very happy. (④) Your mother fell ill, and I'm going to visit her in the hospital with some money and food. (⑤) I'll go there with our middle son while the oldest looks after the youngest.

17 위 글의 흐름으로 보아, 주어진 문장이 들어가기에 가장 적절한 곳은? [출제율 95%]

> We are all in good health except for the little one.

① ② ③ ④ ⑤

18 위 글의 밑줄 친 ⓐ를 다음과 같이 바꿔 쓸 때 빈칸에 들어갈 알맞은 단어를 쓰시오. [출제율 90%]

➡ I reach _____ my arms toward you

19 위 글을 읽고 알 수 없는 것을 고르시오. [출제율 100%]

① How many kids were there in the writer's family?

② Was the oldest kid sick?

③ Why was there no reply from her husband?

④ With whom will the writer visit the hospital?

⑤ Who will look after her youngest son while she goes to the hospital?

[20~21] 다음 글을 읽고 물음에 답하시오.

ⓐThe boy whose head is covered with bees don't understand the woman's gesture. I think it means "Jump into the pond." If I were the boy, I would jump into the pond ⓑright away.

20 위 글의 밑줄 친 ⓐ에서 어법상 틀린 부분을 찾아 고치시오. [출제율 90%]

_____ ➡ _____

21 위 글의 밑줄 친 ⓑright away와 바꿔 쓸 수 있는 말을 모두 고르시오. [출제율 95%]

① hesitatingly ② right now

③ at once ④ gradually

⑤ immediately

01 다음 대화의 우리말에 맞게 주어진 단어를 알맞은 순서로 배열하시오.

> G: I'm curious about that robot. Why is it standing there?
> B: It's a kind of ad. 그것은 그들의 건전지가 매우 강력하다는 것을 사람들에게 말하고 있어.

(their / it / people / tells / batteries / powerful / are / very)

➡ _____

[02~03] 다음 대화를 읽고 물음에 답하시오.

> B: This painting has some hidden secrets in it.
> G: Really? I'm curious about them. Where are the secrets?
> B: Find one yourself.
> G: Let's see. ... Oh, I see some letters here.
> B: You found one! It means "Jan van Eyck was here. 1434." It's Latin.
> G: That's awesome! Any other secrets?
> B: Okay. This dog tells us the man here was very rich.
> G: I don't understand.
> B: They had to spend lots of money to buy a dog of that kind at that time.
> G: I see. Only the rich could have that kind of dog, right?
> B: Exactly. _____, you know.

02 위 대화의 흐름상 빈칸은 글의 주제문에 해당한다. 〈조건〉에 맞게 쓰시오.

> ┌─ 조건 ─
> • 'pictures'와 'a thousand'를 이용하시오.

➡ _____

03 위 대화를 읽고 요약문을 완성하시오.

> The boy and the girl are talking about the _____ of Jan van Eyck's painting. The girl finds some _____ letters. It _____ "Jan van Eyck was here. 1434." The boy tells her about the dog. Only _____ could have that kind of dog at that time, so the man in the picture was very _____.

04 다음 글에서 어법상 틀린 곳의 기호를 쓰고 바르게 고치시오.

> Hangeul ㉠created by King Sejong. At first, many people didn't want to use this new writing system. However, King Sejong tried hard to help people ㉡using Hangeul. ㉢Thanks to him, we can express ㉣anything with Hangeul now. If we didn't know Hangeul, we ㉤can't express ourselves easily.

➡ (1) _____ (2) _____
　　(3) _____

05 다음 문장을 가정법을 이용하여 같은 의미의 문장으로 바꾸어 쓰시오.

(1) As I have some money, I can buy the new shoes.

➡ _____

_____

(2) As Suji is not here, I can't tell her the story.

➡ _____

_____

06 괄호 안에 주어진 표현을 사용하여 밑줄 친 우리말을 영어로 완성하시오.

(1) (the alarm clock)

A: I was late for school again today. I don't want to be late anymore.

B: 내가 너라면, 자명종을 맞춰 놓겠어.

➡ _____

(2) (by hand)

A: I can't finish my report. My computer is broken.

B: 내가 너라면, 그것을 손으로 쓰겠어.

➡ _____

(3) (search)

A: The music in the movie is so touching. I want to know the name of the song.

B: 내가 너라면, 인터넷에서 그것을 검색해 볼 텐데.

➡ _____

[07~08] 다음 글을 읽고 물음에 답하시오.

We picked lots of olives from our olive trees this year. I hired a man whose sons are good workers. ⓐHe knocked the olives down, and his two sons helped him, picking up them from the ground. I paid him 27,000 lire for the work. I spent 12,000 more for the olive press. I got enough oil to fill a large pot and a small one. I can sell ⓑit at a price of 1,300 lire a liter.

07 위 글의 밑줄 친 ⓐ에서 어법상 틀린 부분을 찾아 고치시오.

_____ ➡ _____

08 위 글의 밑줄 친 ⓑit이 가리키는 것을 영어로 쓰시오.

➡ _____

[09~11] 다음 글을 읽고 물음에 답하시오.

Speaking to family members or friends in a foreign country (A)[is / are] rather easy and simple today. But before the days of phones and the Internet, it was not that easy. People just sent a letter and waited for a reply for weeks. And (a)그들이 읽거나 쓸 수 없었다면 그건 훨씬 더 힘들었다.

This letter shows how people got over these difficulties. It was written in 1973 by a woman ___ⓐ___ husband was far away. She lived in Sicily, an Italian island, (B)[during / while] her husband worked in Germany. At the time, more than 5% of the people in Italy could not read or write, and she was one of them. This letter was discovered by Sicilian writer Gesualdo Bufalino.

Here's (C)[how / what] he translated the pictures into words.

09 Fill in the blank ⓐ with a suitable word.

➡ _____

10 위 글의 괄호 (A)~(C)에서 어법상 알맞은 낱말을 골라 쓰시오.

➡ (A) _____ (B) _____ (C) _____

11 위 글의 밑줄 친 (a)의 우리말에 맞게 주어진 어휘를 이용하여 11 단어로 영작하시오.

a lot

➡ _____

01 주어진 〈보기〉와 같이 표지판에 관한 의미를 묻고 답을 하시오.

보기
A: What does this sign mean?
B: It means you must be careful with the animals.

(1) _____

(2) _____

02 가정법 과거를 이용하여, 친구에게 충고하는 말을 써 보시오.

(1) If I were you, _____.

(2) Were I you, _____.

(3) If I were in your position, _____.

(4) If I were in your shoes, _____.

03 다음 내용과 대화를 바탕으로 기자의 방송 내용을 완성하시오.

> The girl's bag is in the pond. The girl is trying to pick up her bag, but she seems to be in danger.
>
> **A:** What does the man's gesture mean? I'm curious about it.
>
> **B:** It means "Step back from the pond."

> The girl whose bag is (A)_____ doesn't understand the man's (B)_____. I think it means "(C)_____." If I were the girl, I would step back from the pond.

단원별 모의고사

01 다음 단어에 대한 영어 설명이 <u>어색한</u> 것은?

① hidden: not easy to find
② reply: an answer to a letter
③ rather: in some degree
④ ill: in a way that is bad or dangerous enough to make you worried
⑤ toward: in the direction of

02 다음 짝지어진 단어의 관계가 같도록 빈칸에 알맞은 말을 쓰시오.

curious – inquisitive : boundary – _____

03 다음 영영풀이에 해당하는 단어를 고르시오.

the surface of the Earth

① disease   ② hospital   ③ climate
④ ground   ⑤ health

04 다음 중 짝지어진 대화가 <u>어색한</u> 것은?

① A: What does that mean?
   B: It means an enemy is coming close to the border.
② A: What does this man's gesture mean? I'm curious about it.
   B: It means "Turn it off."
③ A: I'm curious about sign language.
   B: Are you? Let me show you one expression. Look.
④ A: What does her name mean? I'm curious about it.
   B: It means "bright girl."
⑤ A: What does this letter mean?
   B: This letter was written in blue ink.

05 대화의 빈칸에 들어갈 말로 알맞은 것은?

B: Now the enemy is crossing the border in the dark. What are the soldiers going to do to send messages? I'm curious about that.
G: _____
B: When they light all five of the chimneys, what does that mean?
G: It means the battle has started.

① Can you tell me more?
② They will light four chimneys.
③ They're curious about that, too.
④ They mean they just saw an enemy.
⑤ It means you must not enter.

06 대화의 흐름상 빈칸에 들어갈 말을 본문에서 찾아 쓰시오. (2 단어)

B: If there's no enemy, they don't smoke at all, do they?
G: Yes, they do. Smoke from one chimney means "_____."
B: Now smoke is rising from three chimneys. What does that mean?
G: It means an enemy is coming close to the border.

➡ _____

07 다음 대화의 빈칸에 들어갈 말로 알맞은 것은?

G: What are these dots for? I'm curious _____ them.
B: Oh, they are Braille. They are for blind people.

① about   ② from   ③ with
④ for   ⑤ to

[08~09] 다음 대화를 읽고 물음에 답하시오.

B: This painting has _____ (A) _____ in it.
G: Really? I'm curious about them. Where are the secrets?
B: Find one yourself.
G: Let's see. ... Oh, I see some letters here.
B: You found one! It means "Jan van Eyck was here. 1434." It's Latin.
G: That's awesome! Any other secrets?
B: Okay. This dog tells us the man here was very rich.
G: I don't understand.
B: They had to spend lots of money to buy a dog of that kind at that time.
G: I see. Only the rich could have that kind of dog, right?
B: Exactly. Pictures speak a thousand words, you know.

08 위 대화의 빈칸 (A)에 들어갈 말로 알맞은 것은?

① some values
② several disappointing facts
③ some hidden secrets
④ wide gap between the rich and poor
⑤ some obvious facts

09 Why do people think the man in the picture was very rich?

➡ _____

_____

10 봉수대 신호에 관한 다음 대화의 빈칸 (A)~(C)에 들어갈 말을 〈보기〉에서 찾아 쓰시오.

B: What are the soldiers doing with the five chimneys on TV?
G: They are sending messages to the king by using the chimneys.

B: Really? I'm curious about the system. Can you tell me more?
G: Well, do you see the two smoking chimneys?
B: Yes. What do they mean?
G: _____ (A) _____
B: If there's no enemy, they don't smoke at all, do they?
G: Yes, they do. Smoke from one chimney means "No enemy."
B: Now smoke is rising from three chimneys. What does that mean?
G: It means an enemy is coming close to the border.
B: _____ (B) _____ What are the soldiers going to do to send messages? I'm curious about that.
G: They will light four chimneys.
B: When they light all five of the chimneys, what does that mean?
G: _____ (C) _____

┤ 보기 ├
• It means the battle has started.
• They mean they just saw an enemy.
• Now the enemy is crossing the border in the dark.

➡ (A) _____
(B) _____
(C) _____

11 빈칸 (A)에 들어갈 말로 알맞은 것은?

W: What does this man's gesture mean?
_____ (A) _____
M: It means "Turn it off."
W: Really? What makes you think so?
M: The other hunter there is coming close to an animal.
W: Oh, I see.

① It means " History repeats itself."

② I'm curious about it.

③ I'm curious about sign language.

④ I'm curious about the system.

⑤ I'm curious about that balloon.

12 다음 중 빈칸에 들어갈 단어가 <u>다른</u> 것은?

① If she _____ in Seoul now, she could see the parade.

② If it _____ not for your beautiful voice, people wouldn't listen to your song.

③ If you _____ on a desert island, what would you do first?

④ We couldn't live for a day if there _____ no water in the world.

⑤ I would fight bad guys if I _____ super powers.

13 다음 두 문장을 한 문장으로 바르게 옮긴 것은?

• The man is good at playing soccer.
• His son is a world-famous soccer player.

① The man is good at playing soccer whose son is a world-famous soccer player.

② The man whose son is a world-famous soccer player is good at playing soccer.

③ The man whose son is good at playing soccer is a world-famous soccer player.

④ The man his son is a world-famous soccer player is good at playing soccer.

⑤ The man is good at playing soccer his son is a world-famous soccer player.

14 다음 우리말을 영어로 바르게 옮긴 것은?

네가 좋아하는 아이돌이 너와 사랑에 빠지면, 너는 어떻게 하겠니?

① If your favorite idol star falls in love with you, what would you do?

② If your favorite idol star fell in love with you, what would you do?

③ If your favorite idol star fell in love with you, what will you do?

④ If your favorite idol star fell in love with you, what you would do?

⑤ If your favorite idol star were fallen in love with you, what would you do?

15 다음 우리말과 일치하도록 주어진 단어를 알맞게 배열하시오.

나는 직업이 소방관인 오빠가 있다.
(have, job, is, a, I, brother, a, fire fighter, whose)

➡ _____

16 다음 문장에서 밑줄 친 우리말을 영어로 옮기시오.

(1) <u>내가 신이라면</u>, I would help poor children.

➡ _____

(2) <u>내가 과거로 여행한다면</u>, I would tell people to protect our environment more.

➡ _____

[17~19] 다음 글을 읽고 물음에 답하시오.

Speaking to family members or friends in a foreign country is rather easy and simple today. But before the days of phones and the Internet, it was not that easy. People just sent a letter and waited for a reply for weeks. And it was a lot harder if they couldn't read or write.

This letter shows how people got over ⓐ these difficulties. It was written in 1973 by a woman whose husband was far away. She lived in Sicily, an Italian island, while her husband worked in Germany. At the time, more than 5% of the people in Italy could not read or write, and she was one of them. This letter was discovered by Sicilian writer Gesualdo Bufalino.

ⓑHere's the way how he translated the pictures into words.

17 위 글의 주제로 알맞은 것을 고르시오.

① the easy way to speak to people in a foreign country

② the difficulties that illiterate people experienced in the past

③ the high illiteracy rate of Italy in the past

④ a picture letter from a woman who couldn't read or write to her husband in a foreign country

⑤ the letter from Gesualdo Bufalino to a Sicilian woman

18 What do the underlined ⓐthese difficulties mean? Fill in the blanks (A) and (B) with suitable words.

> They mean the difficulties that people, especially the illiterate, experienced while trying to speak to family members or friends in (A)_____ _____ _____ before the days of (B)_____ _____ _____ _____.

19 위 글의 밑줄 친 ⓑ에서 어법상 틀린 부분을 찾아 고치시오.

_____ ➡ _____

[20~22] 다음 글을 읽고 물음에 답하시오.

We picked lots of olives from our olive trees this year. I hired a man whose sons are good workers. He knocked the olives down, and his two sons helped him, ⓐpicking them up from the ground. I paid him ⓑ27,000 lire for the work. I spent ⓒ12,000 more for the olive press. I got enough oil to fill a large pot and a small one. I can sell it at a price of ⓓ1,300 lire a liter.

20 아래 〈보기〉에서 위 글의 밑줄 친 ⓐpicking과 문법적 쓰임이 다른 것의 개수를 고르시오.

┤ 보기 ├
① I like to study, listening to pop music.
② They supported him, saying that he was right.
③ I punished him for being dishonest.
④ He extended his hand, smiling brightly.
⑤ My dream is traveling in Europe.

① 1개 ② 2개 ③ 3개 ④ 4개 ⑤ 5개

21 위 글의 밑줄 친 ⓑ27,000, ⓒ12,000, ⓓ1,300을 영어로 읽는 법을 쓰시오.

➡ ⓑ _____
  ⓒ _____
  ⓓ _____

22 According to the passage, which is NOT true?

① The writer employed a man whose sons are good workers.

② The worker's two sons helped him pick the olives up from the ground.

③ The writer paid the worker 27,000 lire for the work.

④ The writer spent 12,000 lire for the olive press.

⑤ The writer can sell the olive oil at a price of 1,300 lire a liter.

[23~25] 다음 글을 읽고 물음에 답하시오.

My dear love, I miss you so much, and I reach my arms out toward you, together with our three kids. We are all ___ⓐ___ good health except for the little one. He's a little sick, but not seriously.

I already sent you (A)_____ _____, but there was no reply, so I am sad about it. If I got a letter from you, I would be very happy. Your mother fell ill, and I'm going to visit her in (B)_____ _____ with some money and food. I'll go there with our middle son while the oldest looks ___ⓑ___ the youngest.

23 위 글의 빈칸 ⓐ와 ⓑ에 들어갈 전치사가 바르게 짝지어진 것은?

	ⓐ	ⓑ			ⓐ	ⓑ
①	on – for			②	in – for	
③	in – after			④	on – to	
⑤	for – after					

24 다음 그림을 참조하여 위 글의 빈칸 (A)와 (B)에 들어갈 알맞은 말을 쓰시오.

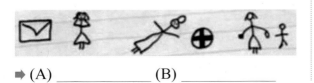

➡ (A) _____ (B) _____

25 다음 문장에서 위 글의 내용과 <u>다른</u> 부분을 찾아서 고치시오.

The writer will visit her husband's mother with her oldest son.

➡ _____ ➡ _____

[26~27] 다음 글을 읽고 물음에 답하시오.

We picked lots of olives from our olive trees this year. I hired a man whose sons are good workers. He knocked the olives down, and his two sons helped him, picking them up from the ground. I paid him 27,000 lire for the work. I spent 12,000 more for the olive press. I got enough oil ⓐto fill a large pot and a small ⓑone. I can sell it at a price of 1,300 lire a liter.

26 아래 〈보기〉에서 위 글의 밑줄 친 ⓐto fill과 to부정사의 용법이 같은 것의 개수를 고르시오.

보기
① It's time for you to go to bed.
② He went to the library to borrow books.
③ I have a pet to play with.
④ She has a special way to cook rice.
⑤ It is very good to get up early in the morning.

① 1개 ② 2개 ③ 3개 ④ 4개 ⑤ 5개

27 위 글의 밑줄 친 ⓑone이 가리키는 것을 본문에서 찾아 쓰시오.

➡ _____

MEMO

Lesson 6

We Are All Makers

🗣 의사소통 기능

- 선호에 대해 묻기
  Which do you prefer, pandas or cats?
- 싫어하는 것 표현하기
  I hate holding things in my hands.

🗣 언어 형식

- the + 비교급, the +비교급
  The more books we share, the more we learn.
- It ... that 강조구문
  It is this filtered water that you can drink.

Words & Expressions

교과서

Key Words

- [ ] **3D print** 3차원 인쇄를 하다
- [ ] **actually** [ǽktʃuəli] 分 사실, 실제로
- [ ] **artistic** [ɑ:rtístik] 阁 예술적인
- [ ] **artwork** [ά:rtwərk] 阁 예술품, 공예품
- [ ] **available** [əvéiləbl] 阁 이용할 수 있는
- [ ] **battery life** 건전지 수명
- [ ] **beat** [bi:t] 동 물리치다
- [ ] **bookstore** [búkstər] 阁 서점
- [ ] **check** [tʃek] 동 확인하다
- [ ] **cheerful** [tʃíərfəl] 阁 유쾌한, 기분 좋은
- [ ] **cloth** [klɔ:θ] 阁 천, 옷감
- [ ] **collect** [kəlékt] 동 모으다
- [ ] **colorful** [kʌ́lərfəl] 阁 화려한
- [ ] **company** [kʌ́mpəni] 阁 회사
- [ ] **connect** [kənékt] 동 연결하다
- [ ] **cute** [kju:t] 阁 귀여운
- [ ] **disease** [dizí:z] 阁 질병, 질환
- [ ] **display** [displéi] 阁 전시, 진열 동 전시하다, 진열하다
- [ ] **drinkable** [dríŋkəbl] 阁 마실 수 있는
- [ ] **enter** [éntər] 동 입력하다
- [ ] **facial** [féiʃəl] 阁 얼굴의
- [ ] **far** [fɑ:r] 阁 먼
- [ ] **figure** [fígjər] 阁 (사람, 동물의) 상, 모양, 숫자
- [ ] **filter** [fíltər] 동 ~을 거르다, 여과하다 阁 여과 장치
- [ ] **full moon** 보름달
- [ ] **impossible** [impάsəbl] 阁 불가능한
- [ ] **information** [ìnfərméiʃən] 阁 정보
- [ ] **jar** [dʒɑ:r] 阁 항아리, 병

- [ ] **leave** [li:v] 동 남겨 두다
- [ ] **length** [leŋkθ] 阁 길이
- [ ] **lovely** [lʌ́vli] 阁 사랑스러운, 아름다운
- [ ] **necessary** [nésəsèri] 阁 필요한
- [ ] **object** [άbdʒikt] 阁 물체
- [ ] **plant** [plænt] 동 심다
- [ ] **possible** [pάsəbl] 阁 가능한 (↔ impossible 불가능한)
- [ ] **potter** [pάtər] 阁 도공, 옹기장이, 도예가
- [ ] **pour** [pɔ:r] 동 붓다, 따르다
- [ ] **prefer** [prifə́:r] 동 선호하다, 더 좋아하다
- [ ] **print** [print] 동 인쇄하다, 출판하다
- [ ] **produce** [prədjú:s] 동 생산하다, 산출하다
- [ ] **proud** [praud] 阁 자랑으로 여기는
- [ ] **provide** [prəváid] 동 제공하다
- [ ] **public** [pʌ́blik] 阁 공공의, 공중의
- [ ] **publisher** [pʌ́bliʃər] 阁 출판업자, 출판사
- [ ] **register** [rédʒistər] 동 등록하다
- [ ] **relax** [rilǽks] 동 (마음의) 긴장을 풀다
- [ ] **report** [ripɔ́:rt] 동 알리다, 보고하다
- [ ] **round** [raund] 阁 둥근
- [ ] **seed** [si:d] 阁 씨앗
- [ ] **shoulder bag** 어깨에 메는 가방
- [ ] **tear** [tiər] 동 ~을 찢다, 뜯어내다(**tear-tore-torn**)
- [ ] **tiny** [táini] 阁 아주 작은
- [ ] **tired** [taiərd] 阁 지친
- [ ] **traditional** [trədíʃənl] 阁 전통적인
- [ ] **weight** [weit] 阁 무게, 중량
- [ ] **wonderful** [wʌ́ndərfəl] 阁 훌륭한

Key Expressions

- [ ] **both A and B** A와 B 둘 다
- [ ] **by hand** 손으로
- [ ] **find out** 알아내다
- [ ] **give away** 남에게 주다, 나누어 주다
- [ ] **hold ~ in hands** ~을 양손에 들다
- [ ] **How about -ing ~?** ~하는 것이 어떠니?
- [ ] **I can't wait for it!** 몹시 기다려진다!
- [ ] **not ~ anymore** 더 이상 ~ 않다

- [ ] **pick up** 집어들다
- [ ] **take a bath** 목욕하다
- [ ] **take a shower** 샤워하다
- [ ] **tear out** 찢다
- [ ] **think of ... as ~** …을 ~으로 생각하다
  (= **regard ... as ~, look upon ... as ~**)
- [ ] **this way** 이렇듯, 이런 식으로
- [ ] **Why don't we ~?** ~하는 게 어때?

Word Power

※ 서로 비슷한 뜻을 가진 어휘

- □ **actually** 사실, 실제로 – **really** 정말로
- □ **beat** 물리치다 – **defeat** 패배시키다, 물리치다
- □ **disease** 질병, 질환 – **illness** 질병
- □ **provide** 제공하다 – **furnish** 제공하다

- □ **artwork** 예술품, 공예품 – **craft** 공예품
- □ **company** 회사 – **corporation** 기업
- □ **proud** 자랑으로 여기는 – **boastful** 자랑하는
- □ **relax** (마음의) 긴장을 풀다 – **rest** 쉬다

※ 서로 반대의 뜻을 가진 어휘

- □ **beat** 물리치다 ↔ **surrender** 굴복하다
- □ **possible** 가능한 ↔ **impossible** 불가능한
- □ **public** 공공의 ↔ **private** 사적인

- □ **connect** 연결하다 ↔ **disconnect** 끊다
- □ **necessary** 필요한 ↔ **unnecessary** 불필요한
- □ **tiny** 아주 작은 ↔ **giant** 거대한

※ 명사 – 형용사

- □ **art** 예술 – **artistic** 예술적인
- □ **color** 색 – **colorful** 화려한
- □ **information** 정보 – **informative** 유용한 정보를 주는
- □ **love** 사랑 – **lovely** 사랑스러운, 아름다운
- □ **pride** 자랑 – **proud** 자랑으로 여기는

- □ **cheer** 환호성, 생기 – **cheerful** 유쾌한, 기분 좋은
- □ **face** 얼굴 – **facial** 얼굴의
- □ **length** 길이 – **long** 긴
- □ **necessity** 필요 – **necessary** 필요한
- □ **tradition** 전통 – **traditional** 전통적인

※ 동사 – 명사

- □ **collect** 모으다 – **collection** 수집
- □ **inform** 알려주다 – **information** 정보
- □ **produce** 생산하다 – **production** 생산
- □ **register** 등록하다 – **registration** 등록

- □ **connect** 연결하다 – **connection** 연결
- □ **prefer** 선호하다 – **preference** 선호
- □ **publish** 출판하다 – **publisher** 출판업자
- □ **weigh** 무게가 나가다 – **weight** 무게, 중량

English Dictionary

- □ **bookstore** 서점
  - → a store that sells books
    책을 파는 상점
- □ **drinkable** 마실 수 있는
  - → clean and safe to drink
    깨끗하고 마시기에 안전한
- □ **filter** ~을 거르다, 여과하다
  - → to remove unwanted substances from liquids or gases 액체나 기체에서 원치 않는 물질을 제거하다
- □ **leave** 남겨 두다
  - → to put something somewhere, especially in a place where it will stay
    어떤 것을 어떤 장소 특히 그것이 머무를 장소에 두다
- □ **pour** 붓다, 따르다
  - → to make a liquid flow out of a container
    용기 밖으로 액체가 흘러가도록 만들다

- □ **public** 공공의, 공중의
  - → relating to people in general
    일반 대중과 관련된
- □ **publisher** 출판업자, 출판사
  - → a person or company that prints books
    책을 출판하는 사람 또는 회사
- □ **register** 등록하다
  - → to put someone's or something's name on an official list 공식적인 명단에 누군가 또는 무엇인가의 이름을 올리다
- □ **tear** 찢다, 뜯어내다
  - → to pull apart or to pull pieces off
    잡아 찢거나 작은 조각으로 뜯어내다
- □ **tiny** 아주 작은
  - → extremely small
    매우 작은

서답형
01 다음 문장의 빈칸에 〈영어 설명〉에 해당하는 단어를 쓰시오.

> Most curtains are made of _____.
> 〈영어 설명〉 material used for making things such as clothes

02 다음 빈칸에 공통으로 들어갈 말로 가장 적절한 것은?

> • He made a bronze _____ of a horse.
> • The _____ is lower than the OECD average of $6,741.

① character   ② letter
③ figure   ④ product
⑤ statue

[03~04] 다음 설명에 해당하는 단어를 고르시오.

03

> to put someone's or something's name on an official list

① permit   ② hug
③ collect   ④ relax
⑤ register

04

> to remove unwanted substances from liquids or gases

① filter   ② print
③ prepare   ④ prefer
⑤ pour

서답형
05 다음 우리말에 맞게 주어진 단어를 이용하여 쓰시오.

> 그는 모든 음식을 가난한 사람들에게 나누어 주었다. (away)

➡ He _____ all the food to the poor.

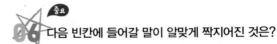
06 다음 빈칸에 들어갈 말이 알맞게 짝지어진 것은?

> (A) He stayed in the hospital because he had a serious _____.
> (B) She _____ her mom as her friend.

① illness – leaves
② secret – allows
③ project – hides
④ disease – thinks of
⑤ information – proves

07 다음 짝지어진 단어 중 성격이 <u>다른</u> 하나는?

① art – artistic   ② face – facial
③ color – colorful   ④ love – lovely
⑤ collect – collection

08 다음 빈칸에 공통으로 알맞은 것은?

> • _____: relating to all the people in a country
> • e.g. When we are outside, we have to use _____ restrooms.

① private   ② public
③ possible   ④ drinkable
⑤ human

01 〈보기〉에서 알맞은 단어를 찾아 빈칸을 완성하시오. (필요하면 변형하여 쓰시오.)

┤ 보기 ├

necessary   report   tear   drink

(1) Is this water _____?

(2) He was the first reporter to _____ the big story.

(3) Food and water are _____ for humans to live.

(4) My cat _____ the pages of the book yesterday.

02 다음 대화의 빈칸에 〈영영풀이〉에 해당하는 단어를 쓰시오.

A: Which do you _____, working with a plan or working without a plan?

B: I _____ working without a plan.

〈영영풀이〉 to like someone or something more than another person or thing

➡ _____

03 다음 우리말과 같은 표현이 되도록 문장의 빈칸을 채우시오. (철자가 주어진 것은 그 철자로 시작하는 단어를 쓸 것.)

(1) 그들의 밝은 미소와 유쾌한 춤이 많은 사람들에게 에너지를 주었습니다.

➡ Their bright smiles and c_____ dance gave many people energy.

(2) 믿기 힘들겠지만, 그것은 실제로 케이크입니다!

➡ It may be hard to believe, but it is a_____ a cake!

(3) 또 다른 장점은 그것들이 학생과 선생님 둘 다 보호한다는 것입니다.

➡ Another benefit is that they protect _____ students and teachers.

(4) 전자책은 종이책이 절대로 제공할 수 없는 다른 많은 서비스도 제공할 수 있다.

➡ E-books can also p_____ many other services paperback books can never p_____.

04 다음 영영풀이에 해당하는 단어를 〈보기〉에서 찾아 첫 번째 빈칸에 쓰고, 두 번째 빈칸에는 우리말 뜻을 쓰시오.

┤ 보기 ├

bookstore   leave   pour

(1) _____ : a store that sells books: _____

(2) _____ : to put something somewhere, especially in a place where it will stay:
_____

(3) _____ : to make a liquid flow out of a container: _____

05 두 문장의 뜻이 같도록 빈칸에 알맞은 말을 쓰시오.

• He worked for this company from the very beginning, so everyone regarded him as the real boss.

= He worked for this company from the very beginning, so everyone _____ him _____ the real boss.

➡ _____

Conversation

① 선호에 대해 묻기

> • **Which do you prefer, pandas or cats?** 너는 판다와 고양이 중에서 어떤 것을 더 좋아하니?

■ A와 B 둘 중에 어떤 것을 더 좋아하는지 상대방의 선호를 물을 때는 'prefer(더 좋아하다)'를 사용하여 'Which do you prefer, A or B?(너는 A와 B 중에서 어느 것을 더 좋아하니?)' 또는 'Do you prefer A or B?(너는 A를 더 좋아하니, B를 더 좋아하니?)'라고 표현한다. which는 정해진 범주 내에서 특정 대상의 선호도를 물을 때 사용하는 표현이다.

■ '더 좋아하다'에 해당하는 'like better'를 사용하여 'Which do you like better[more], A or B?' 또는 'Which one do you like better, A or B?'의 형태로 나타낼 수 있고, Which가 뒤에 오는 명사를 수식하는 의문형용사로 쓰이는 경우에는 'which+명사'로 쓰일 수 있으므로 'Which 명사+do you prefer, A or B?'라고 할 수도 있다.

■ prefer로 자신이 좋아하는 것을 나타낼 때는 전치사 to를 사용하여 'prefer A to B(B보다는 A를 더 좋아한다)'의 형태로 선호를 표현한다. 이는 'like A better than B'에 해당한다. 어떤 것을 더 좋아한다는 것은 상대적인 선택이므로, 다른 하나를 좋아할 수도 싫어할 수도 있다. 두 가지를 모두 좋아하지만 어느 하나를 더 좋아한다면, 'I like both, but I like … better.'나 'I like both, but I prefer ….'처럼 말한다.

선호에 대해 묻기

• Do you prefer A or B?	• Do you prefer A to B?
• Do you like A better than B?	• Which do you prefer, A or B?
• Which do you like better, A or B?	

선호를 표현할 때

• I prefer A (to B).	• I like A better (than B).

핵심 Check

1. 다음 밑줄 친 우리말에 맞게 영작하시오.

G: 너는 회화 작품(paper drawings)과 나무 블록으로 만든 모형 중에서 어떤 것을 더 좋아 하니?

B: I prefer wood block figures.

G: Me, too. Let's go to look at some of them.

➡ _____

② 싫어하는 것 표현하기

> • I hate holding things in my hands. 나는 손에 물건을 드는 것을 몹시 싫어해.

■ 자신이 좋아하는 것을 나타내는 말은 like, love, prefer 등을 사용하여 나타내지만, 싫어하는 것은 hate, dislike 등을 사용한다. 'I hate ~.(나는 ~하기를 싫어한다.)'는 자신이 하기 싫어하는 것을 강하게 표현하는 말이다.

■ '~를 싫어하다'라는 의미로 'hate' 뒤에 싫어하는 일을 나타내는 명사/동명사/to부정사를 사용하여 'hate+명사', 'hate+-ing', 'hate+to부정사' 형태로 나타내거나, 'hate+목적어(사람)+-ing', 'hate+목적어(사람)+for+명사'의 형태로 '~가 …하는 것을 싫어하다'의 의미로 사용하기도 한다.

■ 싫어하는 것을 나타낼 때는 hate, dislike 등을 사용하지만, 'don't like', 'don't love', 'don't want to ~' 등으로 자신이 좋아하지 않는 것, 즉 싫어하는 것을 표현할 수 있다. 싫어하는 정도가 매우 강할 때는 '~을 참을 수 없다'는 뜻으로 'can't stand', 'can't bear'를 쓰기도 한다. 'detest'는 '몹시 싫어하다, 혐오하다'의 뜻이다.

싫어하는 것 표현하기

- • I hate 명사/-ing /to ~.
- • I don't like 명사/-ing/to ~.
- • I dislike ~.
- • I don't want to ~.
- • I can't stand ~.
- • I can't bear ~.

핵심 Check

2. 다음 대화의 내용으로 보아, 빈칸에 들어가기에 적절하지 <u>않은</u> 것은?

B: Why don't we make a bag with old jeans?

G: Great! What kind of bag are we going to make?

B: Which do you prefer, a shoulder bag or a hand bag?

G: I prefer a shoulder bag. Actually, _____

B: Okay. Let's make a shoulder bag together.

① I don't want to hold things in my hands.

② I hate holding things in my hands.

③ I don't like to hold things in my hands.

④ I can stand holding things in my hands.

⑤ I dislike holding things in my hands.

Step Up - Real-life Scene

Minji: Seho, the book club day is just one week away.

Seho: Right, Minji. ❶I'm proud that we've collected so many interesting books ❷to give away.

Minji: Now, let's prepare some gifts for visitors. Do you have ❸any good ideas?

Seho: ❹How about making bookmarks?

Minji: Great idea! Let's write cheerful messages on them, too.

Seho: Okay. ❺Which do you prefer, making the bookmarks or writing the messages?

Minji: Actually, ❻I hate writing. I'd like to make the bookmarks.

Seho: No problem. I'll write the cheerful messages.

Minji: ❼I'm sure they will love our bookmarks.

민지: 세호야, 독서 동아리의 날이 겨우 한 주 남았어.

세호: 맞아, 민지야. 나는 우리가 나눠줄 재미있는 책을 많이 모아서 자랑스러워.

민지: 이제, 방문객들에게 줄 선물을 준비하자. 좋은 생각 있어?

세호: 책갈피를 만드는 게 어떨까?

민지: 좋은 생각이야! 거기에 기분 좋은 메시지도 쓰자.

세호: 그래. 너는 책갈피 만들기와 메시지 쓰기 중에서 어떤 것을 더 좋아하니?

민지: 사실, 나는 글쓰기를 몹시 싫어해. 나는 책갈피를 만들고 싶어.

세호: 문제없어. 내가 기분 좋은 메시지를 쓸게.

민지: 틀림없이 사람들이 우리가 만든 책갈피를 좋아할 거야.

❶ I'm proud that+주어+동사 ~: ~을 자랑스러워하다

❷ books를 수식하는 형용사 용법으로 '나누어줄'로 해석한다.

❸ '약간의, 어떤'의 의미로 의문문에서는 any를 사용한다.

❹ 'How about+동명사/명사?'는 '~하는 게 어때?'라는 제안을 하는 표현이다.

❺ 상대방의 선호를 물을 때는 'prefer(더 좋아하다)'를 사용하여 'Which do you prefer, A or B?(너는 A와 B 중에서 어느 것을 더 좋아하니?)' 또는 'Do you prefer A or B?'로 표현한다. 이때 A와 B는 문법적으로 병렬 관계가 되어야 한다.

❻ 'I hate ~(나는 ~하는 것을 싫어한다)'는 자신이 하기 싫어하는 것을 강하게 표현하는 말이다.

❼ 'I'm sure (that)+주어+동사 ~'는 '~할 것을 확신해. 틀림없이 ~할 거야'라는 확신을 나타내는 표현이다.

Check(√) True or False

(1) Minji and Seho are preparing for the book club day.　　　　T ☐ F ☐

(2) Minji hates making the bookmarks.　　　　T ☐ F ☐

Start Off - Listen & Talk A 1

G: ❶Why don't we make something with jean pockets?

B: Great! What shall we make?

G: Which do you prefer, a pocket board or a cell phone holder?

B: I prefer a cell phone holder. It'll be easier ❷to make. And I hate ❸ spending too much time making things.

G: Okay. Let's make a cute cell phone holder together.

G: 청바지 주머니로 뭔가 만들어 보는 게 어떨까?

B: 좋아! 뭘 만들까?

G: 너는 주머니를 붙인 판과 휴대 전화 주머니 중에서 어떤 것을 더 좋아하니?

B: 나는 휴대 전화 주머니가 더 좋아. 만들기가 더 쉬울 거야. 그리고 나는 뭔가를 만드는 데 시간을 너무 많이 들이는 걸 몹시 싫어해.

G: 좋아. 귀여운 휴대 전화 주머니를 함께 만들자.

❶ 'Why don't we+동사원형?'은 '~하는 게 어때?'라는 제안을 하는 표현으로 'How about+동명사/명사?'로 바꾸어 쓸 수 있다.

❷ 형용사 easier를 수식하는 부사적 용법으로 '만들기에'로 해석한다.

❸ 'spend+시간+-ing' 형태로 '~하는 데 시간을 보내다'라는 의미이다.

Check(√) True or False

(3) The girl wants to make something with a cell phone holder.　　　　T ☐ F ☐

(4) The boy wants to make a cell phone holder.　　　　T ☐ F ☐

Get Ready 2

(1) **G:** ❶Which do you like better, cloth dolls or digital artwork?
B: I like digital artwork better. Actually, I don't like dolls much.

(2) **G:** Which do you prefer, paper drawings or wood block figures?
B: I prefer wood block figures.
G: Me, too. ❷Let's go to look at some of them.

(3) **G:** Which do you prefer, folding paper or making clothes?
B: I prefer folding paper. It's fun and a great way ❸to relax.

❶ 상대방에게 선호를 묻는 표현이다.
❷ 'Let's+동사원형'은 '～하자'는 제안을 하는 표현이다.
❸ 명사 'way'를 수식하는 형용사 용법이다.

Start Off - Listen & Talk A 2

B: Why don't we make a bag with old jeans?
G: Great! ❶What kind of bag are we going to make?
B: Which do you prefer, a shoulder bag or a hand bag?
G: I prefer a shoulder bag. Actually, ❷I hate holding things in my hands.
B: Okay. Let's make a shoulder bag together.

❶ 'kind'는 명사로 '종류'라는 뜻이다.
❷ 'hate+동명사'로 싫어하는 것을 표현한다.

Start Off - Listen & Talk B

G: Junha, what are you doing with jeans?
B: I'm ❶making a pencil case for you.
G: That's great! What ❷are you going to draw on it?
B: Which do you prefer, pandas or cats?
G: I prefer cats. They're lovely.
B: Okay. Let me draw a lovely cat on this pencil case.
G: Thanks! ❸I can't wait for it!

❶ 'make+직접목적어+for+간접목적어' 형태로 '～에게 …을 만들어 주다'라는 뜻이다.
❷ 'be going to+동사원형'은 '～할 예정이다'라는 의미이다.
❸ 'I can't wait for+명사/동명사'는 '～이 몹시 기다려져'라는 의미로 기대를 나타내는 표현이다.

Start Off - Speak Up

A: Can I join your book-making project?
B: Sure. ❶Which do you prefer, paper books or digital books?
A: ❷I prefer digital books. Actually, I hate ❸ making paper books.
B: Okay. Let me introduce you to the digital book team.

❶ 'Which do you prefer, A or B?'는 상대방의 선호를 묻는 표현으로 A와 B는 병렬구조가 되어야 한다.
❷ 'I prefer digital books' 뒤에는 'to paper books'가 생략되어 있다.
❸ hate는 to부정사와 동명사를 목적어로 받을 수 있다.

Start Off - Your Turn

A: Which do you prefer, ❶taking the bus or taking the subway?
B: I prefer taking the subway. ❷Actually, I hate taking the bus.

❶ 상대방의 선호를 묻는 표현으로 'Which do you prefer, A or B?' 구문으로 A와 B는 병렬구조가 되어야 한다. 즉, 'taking ～ or taking …' 형태가 같아야 한다.
❷ 'actually'는 말하는 내용을 강조할 때 사용하는 표현이다.

Express Yourself A

1. **G:** Which do you prefer, ❶flying kites or flying drones?
B: I prefer flying kites.
G: Why is that?
B: I hate working with machines.

2. **B:** Which do you prefer, making masks or making food art?
G: I like ❷both, but ❸it is making food art that I prefer.
B: Why is that?
G: ❹I love making something delicious.

❶ 상대방의 선호를 묻는 표현으로 'Which do you prefer, A or B?' 구문으로 A와 B는 병렬구조가 되어야 한다.
❷ 'both'는 'making masks and making food art'를 가리킨다.
❸ 'it ～ that …' 강조구문으로 prefer의 목적어를 강조하는 문장이다.
❹ 자신이 좋아하는 것을 나타내는 말로 'like, love, prefer' 등을 사용하여 나타낸다.

● 다음 우리말과 일치하도록 빈칸에 알맞은 말을 쓰시오.

Get Ready 2

(1) G: _____ do you like _____, _____ dolls or digital _____?
B: I like digital artwork _____. _____, I don't like dolls much.

(2) G: _____ _____ _____ _____, paper _____ or _____ block figures?
B: I _____ wood block _____.
G: Me, too. _____ go to look at _____ _____ _____.

(3) G: _____ do you _____, _____ paper or making _____?
B: I prefer _____ _____. It's fun and a great way _____ _____.

Start Off - Listen & Talk A

1. G: _____ _____ _____ make something with jean _____?
B: Great! _____ _____ _____ make?
G: _____ do you prefer, a pocket _____ or a cell phone _____?
B: I _____ a cell phone _____. It'll be easier _____ _____. And I hate _____ too much time _____ things.
G: Okay. _____ make a cute cell phone holder _____.

2. B: _____ _____ _____ make a bag with old jeans?
G: Great! _____ _____ of bag are we going _____ _____?
B: Which do you _____, a shoulder bag or a hand bag?
G: I prefer a shoulder bag. Actually, I _____ _____ things _____ my hands.
B: Okay. _____ _____ a shoulder bag together.

Start Off - Listen & Talk B

G: Junha, what are you doing _____ _____?
B: I'm making a pencil case _____ you.
G: That's great! What are you going to _____ on it?
B: _____ _____ _____, pandas or cats?
G: I _____ cats. They're _____.
B: Okay. Let me _____ a lovely cat on this pencil case.
G: Thanks! _____ _____ _____ it!

해석

(1) G: 너는 헝겊 인형과 디지털 예술품 중에서 어떤 것을 더 좋아하니?
B: 나는 디지털 예술품이 더 좋아. 사실, 나는 인형을 별로 좋아하지 않아.
(2) G: 너는 회화 작품과 나무 블록으로 만든 모형 중에서 어떤 것을 더 좋아하니?
B: 나는 나무 블록으로 만든 모형이 더 좋아.
G: 나도 그래. 그것 중에서 몇 개를 보러 가자.
(3) G: 너는 종이접기와 옷 만들기 중에서 어떤 것을 더 좋아하니?
B: 나는 종이접기가 더 좋아. 재미있고 긴장을 풀 수 있는 좋은 방법이야.

1. G: 청바지 주머니로 뭔가 만들어 보는 게 어떨까?
B: 좋아! 뭘 만들까?
G: 너는 주머니를 붙인 판과 휴대 전화 주머니 중에서 어떤 것을 더 좋아하니?
B: 나는 휴대 전화 주머니가 더 좋아. 만들기가 더 쉬울 거야. 그리고 나는 뭔가를 만드는 데 시간을 너무 많이 들이는 걸 몹시 싫어해.
G: 좋아. 귀여운 휴대 전화 주머니를 함께 만들자.
2. B: 우리 낡은 청바지로 가방을 하나 만드는 게 어떨까?
G: 좋아! 어떤 종류의 가방을 만들 건데?
B: 너는 어깨에 메는 가방과 손에 드는 가방 중에서 어떤 것을 더 좋아하니?
G: 나는 어깨에 메는 가방이 더 좋아. 사실, 나는 손에 물건을 드는 것을 몹시 싫어해.
B: 좋아. 어깨에 메는 가방을 함께 만들자.

G: 준하야, 청바지로 뭐 해?
B: 너에게 줄 필통을 만들고 있어.
G: 멋지다! 그 위에 뭘 그릴 거야?
B: 너는 판다랑 고양이 중에서 어떤 것을 더 좋아하니?
G: 나는 고양이를 더 좋아해. 고양이는 사랑스러워.
B: 좋아. 내가 이 필통 위에 사랑스러운 고양이를 그려 줄게.
G: 고마워! 몹시 기다려진다!

Start Off - Speak Up

A: Can I join your book-making project?

B: _____. _____ do you _____, paper books _____ digital books?

A: I _____ digital books. Actually, I hate _____ paper books.

B: Okay. Let me _____ you _____ the digital book team.

Start Off - Your Turn

A: _____ do you prefer, _____ the bus or _____ the subway?

B: I _____ _____ the subway. Actually, I _____ _____ the bus.

Step Up - Real-life Scene

Minji: Seho, the book club day is just one week _____.

Seho: Right, Minji. I'm _____ _____ we've _____ so many _____ books _____ _____ _____.

Minji: Now, let's _____ some gifts for visitors. Do you have _____ good ideas?

Seho: How about _____ bookmarks?

Minji: Great idea! _____ write cheerful messages on them, too.

Seho: Okay. _____ do you _____, making the bookmarks or _____ the messages?

Minji: Actually, I hate _____. I'd like to make the bookmarks.

Seho: _____ _____. I'll write the _____ _____.

Minji: I'm _____ they will love our _____.

Express Yourself A

1. G: Which do you prefer, _____ kites or _____ _____?

   B: I prefer _____ kites.

   G: Why is that?

   B: I hate _____ with _____.

2. B: _____ do you prefer, _____ masks or _____ food art?

   G: I like _____, but _____ is making food art _____ I _____.

   B: Why is that?

   G: I love making _____ _____.

해석

A: 너희 책 만들기 프로젝트에 내가 함께 해도 될까?

B: 물론이지. 너는 종이책과 전자책 중에서 어떤 것을 더 좋아하니?

A: 나는 전자책을 더 좋아해. 사실, 나는 종이책 만들기를 몹시 싫어해.

B: 알았어. 전자책 팀에 너를 소개할게.

A: 너는 버스 타기와 지하철 타기 중에서 어떤 것을 더 좋아하니?

B: 나는 지하철 타기를 더 좋아해. 사실, 나는 버스 타기를 몹시 싫어해.

민지: 세호야. 독서 동아리의 날이 겨우 한 주 남았어.

세호: 맞아, 민지야. 나는 우리가 나눠 줄 재미있는 책을 많이 모아서 자랑스러워.

민지: 이제, 방문객들에게 줄 선물을 준비하자. 좋은 생각 있어?

세호: 책갈피를 만드는 게 어떨까?

민지: 좋은 생각이야! 거기에 기분 좋은 메시지도 쓰자.

세호: 그래. 너는 책갈피 만들기와 메시지 쓰기 중에서 어떤 것을 더 좋아하니?

민지: 사실, 나는 글쓰기를 몹시 싫어해. 나는 책갈피를 만들고 싶어.

세호: 문제없어. 내가 기분 좋은 메시지를 쓸게.

민지: 틀림없이 사람들이 우리가 만든 책갈피를 좋아할 거야.

1. G: 너는 연날리기와 드론 날리기 중에서 어떤 것을 더 좋아하니?
   B: 나는 연날리기를 더 좋아해.
   G: 왜 그런데?
   B: 나는 기계를 작동하는 것을 몹시 싫어해.

2. B: 너는 가면 만들기와 푸드 아트 만들기 중에서 어떤 것을 더 좋아하니?
   G: 나는 둘 다 좋지만, 내가 더 좋아하는 것은 푸드 아트 만들기야.
   B: 왜 그런데?
   G: 나는 맛있는 것을 만들기를 좋아해.

01 다음 대화의 빈칸에 들어갈 말로 알맞은 것은?

> A: Can I join your book-making project?
> B: Sure. Which do you prefer, paper books or digital books?
> A: I prefer digital books. Actually, _____
> B: Okay. Let me introduce you to the digital book team.

① I'm curious about making paper books.
② I would like to know how to make bookmarks.
③ I prefer working with numbers and texts.
④ I hate making paper books.
⑤ Actually, I hate working on a team.

02 다음 대화의 빈칸에 들어갈 말로 적절한 것은?

> B: Which do you prefer, making masks or making food art?
> G: I like both, but it is making food art that I prefer.
> B: Why is that?
> G: _____

① I hate working with machines.
② I love making something delicious.
③ I prefer working alone.
④ I love working with pictures and music.
⑤ I hate making food art.

03 다음 대화의 밑줄 친 말의 의도로 알맞은 것은?

> G: Which do you prefer, taking the bus or taking the subway?
> B: I prefer taking the subway. Actually, <u>I hate taking the bus.</u>

① 관심 표현하기   ② 선호에 대해 묻기
③ 요청하기   ④ 유감 표현하기
⑤ 싫어하는 것 표현하기

[01~02] 다음 대화를 읽고 물음에 답하시오.

G: Junha, what are you doing with jeans?
B: I'm making a pencil case for you.
G: That's great! What are you going to draw on it?
B: _____ (A) _____
G: I prefer cats. They're lovely.
B: Okay. (B)Let me to draw a lovely cat on this pencil case.
G: Thanks! I can't wait for it!

01 위 대화의 빈칸 (A)에 들어갈 말로 <u>어색한</u> 것은?

① Which do you prefer, pandas or cats?
② Do you prefer pandas or cats?
③ Which do you like better, pandas or cats?
④ Why do you like pandas better than cats?
⑤ Which do you like more, pandas or cats?

서답형

02 위 대화의 밑줄 친 (B)에서 어법상 <u>어색한</u> 부분을 찾아 고치시오.

_____ ➡ _____

[03~04] 다음 대화를 읽고 물음에 답하시오.

B: _____ (A) _____ a bag with old jeans?
G: Great! What kind of bag are we going to make?
B: Which do you prefer, a shoulder bag or a hand bag?
G: I prefer a shoulder bag. _____ (B) _____
B: Okay. Let's make a shoulder bag together.

03 위 대화의 빈칸 (A)에 들어갈 말로 알맞지 <u>않은</u> 것은?

① What about making
② Why don't we make
③ How do we make
④ How about making
⑤ Shall we make

04 위 대화의 흐름상 (B)에 들어갈 알맞은 표현은?

① Actually, I hate making photo books.
② Actually, I hate holding things in my hands.
③ Actually, I hate working with a plan.
④ Actually, I hate writing.
⑤ Actually, I hate taking a bus.

[05~07] 다음 대화를 읽고 물음에 답하시오.

Minji: Seho, (A)독서 동아리의 날이 겨우 한 주 남았어.
Seho: Right, Minji. I'm (a)proud that we've collected so many interesting books to (b)give away.
Minji: Now, let's _____ (B) _____ some gifts for visitors. Do you have any good ideas?
Seho: (c)How about making bookmarks?
Minji: Great idea! Let's write cheerful messages on them, too.
Seho: Okay. Which do you (d)prefer, making the bookmarks or writing the messages?
Minji: Actually, I (e)love writing. I'd like to make the bookmarks.
Seho: No problem. I'll write the cheerful messages.
Minji: I'm sure they will love our bookmarks.

서답형

05 위 대화의 우리말 (A)에 맞게 주어진 단어를 알맞게 배열하시오.

> (one / the / club / is / just / book / week / away / day)

➡ _____

서답형

06 위 대화의 빈칸 (B)에 들어갈 말을 주어진 영영풀이를 참고하여 한 단어로 쓰시오.

> <영영풀이> to make plans or arrangements for something that will happen in the future

➡ _____

07 위 대화의 (a)~(e) 중 흐름상 어휘의 쓰임이 <u>어색한</u> 것은?

① (a) ② (b) ③ (c) ④ (d) ⑤ (e)

[08~09] 다음 대화를 읽고 물음에 답하시오.

> G: Why don't we make something with jean pockets?
> B: Great! _____(A)_____
> G: Which do you prefer, a pocket board or a cell phone holder?
> B: I prefer a cell phone holder. It'll be easier to make. And _____(B)_____.
> G: Okay. Let's make a cute cell phone holder together.

중요

08 위 대화의 빈칸 (A)에 들어갈 말로 알맞은 것은?

① What are you going to draw on it?
② I prefer working alone.
③ What shall we make?
④ Can I join your book-making project?
⑤ Why is that?

09 위 대화의 (B)에 들어갈 말로 알맞은 것은?

① I hate holding things in my hands.
② I love spending too much time making things.
③ I prefer working on a team.
④ I hate spending too much time making things.
⑤ I hate working with a plan.

중요

10 대화의 빈칸 (A)에 공통으로 들어갈 말로 알맞은 것은?

> (1) G: _____(A)_____, cloth dolls or digital artwork?
>   B: I like digital artwork better. Actually, I don't like dolls much.
> (2) G: _____(A)_____, paper drawings or wood block figures?
>   B: I prefer wood block figures.
>   G: Me, too. Let's go to look at some of them.
> (3) G: _____(A)_____, folding paper or making clothes?
>   B: I prefer folding paper. It's fun and a great way to relax.

① Which do you like better
② Can I join
③ What are you going to make
④ Do you wonder
⑤ Why don't we make

서답형

11 다음 대화의 빈칸에 들어갈 알맞은 말을 쓰시오.

> A: Which do you prefer, taking the bus _____ taking the subway?
> B: I prefer taking the subway. Actually, I hate taking the bus.

➡ _____

[01~02] 다음 대화를 읽고 물음에 답하시오.

Minji: Seho, the book club day is just one week away.

Seho: Right, Minji. I'm proud that we've collected so many interesting books to give away.

Minji: Now, let's prepare some gifts for visitors. Do you have any good ideas?

Seho: How about making bookmarks?

Minji: Great idea! Let's write cheerful messages on them, too.

Seho: Okay. _____(A)_____

Minji: Actually, I hate writing. I'd like to make the bookmarks.

Seho: No problem. I'll write the cheerful messages.

Minji: I'm sure they will love our bookmarks.

01 위 대화의 빈칸 (A)에 들어갈 말을 〈조건〉에 맞게 영어로 쓰시오.

┌─ 조건 ┐
• 'which'와 'prefer'를 이용하여 선호를 묻는 말을 쓸 것.
• 'making the bookmarks', 'writing the messages'를 사용할 것.

➡ _____

_____

02 위 대화를 읽고 다음 물음에 영어로 답하시오.

Q: What is Minji going to make for the visitors?

➡ _____

03 다음 대화의 밑줄 친 우리말을 주어진 〈조건〉에 맞게 영어로 쓰시오.

B: Which do you prefer, making masks or making food art?

G: I like both, but it is making food art that I prefer.

B: Why is that?

G: 나는 맛있는 것을 만들기를 좋아해.

┌─ 조건 ┐
• 'love' 'delicious'를 이용할 것.
• 동명사를 사용할 것.

➡ _____

[04~05] 다음 대화를 읽고 물음에 답하시오.

G: _____(A)_____ (don't / make / with / pockets / why / we / something / jean)

B: Great! What shall we make?

G: Which do you prefer, a pocket board or a cell phone holder?

B: I prefer a cell phone holder. It'll be easier to make. And (B)나는 뭔가를 만드는 데 시간을 너무 많이 들이는 걸 몹시 싫어해.

G: Okay. Let's make a cute cell phone holder together.

04 위 대화의 흐름상 빈칸 (A)에 주어진 단어를 알맞게 배열하여 제안하는 표현을 완성하시오.

➡ _____

05 위 대화의 밑줄 친 (B)의 우리말을 주어진 〈조건〉에 맞게 영작하시오.

┌─ 조건 ┐
• hate, spend, too much, things와 동명사를 이용할 것.

➡ _____

Grammar

교과서

① the + 비교급, the + 비교급

• **The more** books we share, **the more** we learn.
우리가 더 많은 책을 공유할수록, 우리는 더 많이 배웁니다.

■ 형태: the+비교급(+주어+동사), the+비교급(+주어+동사)
의미: …하면 할수록, 더 ~하다

■ 비교급 자리에는 형용사, 부사 모두 올 수 있고, 그 구분은 뒤에 이어지는 동사에 따라 달라진다.

• **The colder** it is, **the more easily** you catch a cold.
날씨가 더 추워질수록, 더 쉽게 감기에 걸린다.

• **The more** money you have, **the more** money you want.
여러분은 더 많은 돈을 가질수록, 더 많은 돈을 원하게 된다.

■ '주어+동사'를 생략하고 간단히 'the+비교급, the+비교급'으로 나타낼 수 있다.

• The more, the better. 많으면 많을수록 더 좋다.

■ 접속사 'as' 또는 'if' 등을 사용하여 같은 의미의 문장을 쓸 수 있다.

• **The more** you eat, **the fatter** you will be. = If you eat more, you will be fatter.
당신이 더 많이 먹을수록, 더 살찌게 될 것이다.

• **The warmer** the weather gets, **the happier** I feel. = As the weather gets warmer, I feel happier.
날씨가 따뜻해질수록, 나는 더 행복하다.

핵심 Check

1. 다음 괄호 안의 단어를 이용하여 빈칸에 들어갈 알맞은 말을 쓰시오.

(1) The brighter the sun is, the _____ I feel. (happy)

(2) The harder you try, the _____ you learn. (well)

2 **It is[was] ⋯ that 강조구문**

> • **It is** this filtered water **that** you can drink. 여러분이 마실 수 있는 것은 이 여과된 물입니다.

■ 형태: It is[was]+강조할 부분+that+문장의 나머지 부분

  의미: ~하는 것은 바로 ⋯이다

■ 동사를 제외한 문장의 특정 부분을 강조할 때 사용하며, 강조하고자 하는 부분을 'It is[was]'와 'that' 사이에 넣고, 문장의 나머지 부분을 'that' 뒤에 원래 순서대로 쓴다.

■ 강조하는 대상을 마지막에 '바로 ⋯이다'에 넣어 해석한다.

■ 강조하는 대상이 사람이면 that 대신 who를 사용할 수 있으며, 강조하는 대상이 사물이면 that 대신 which를, 시간이나 장소일 경우에는 when이나 where를 사용할 수 있다.

  • Jack found Ted's dog in front of the shoe store yesterday.
    ①   ②   ③   ④

① 주어 강조

  = **It was** Jack **that[who]** found Ted's dog in front of the shoe store yesterday.
    어제 신발가게 앞에서 Ted의 개를 찾은 것은 바로 Jack이었다.

(2) 목적어 강조

  = **It was** Ted's dog **that[which]** Jack found in front of the shoe store yesterday.
    어제 신발가게 앞에서 Jack이 찾은 것은 바로 Ted의 개였다.

(3) 장소를 나타내는 부사구 in front of the shoe store 강조

  = **It was** in front of the shoe store **that[where]** Jack found Ted's dog yesterday.
    Jack이 어제 Ted의 개를 찾은 것은 바로 신발가게 앞에서였다.

(4) 때를 나타내는 부사 yesterday 강조

  = **It was** yesterday **that[when]** Jack found Ted's dog in front of the shoe store.
    Jack이 Ted의 개를 신발가게 앞에서 찾은 것은 바로 어제였다.

핵심 Check

2. 다음 밑줄 친 부분을 강조하는 문장으로 바꿀 때 빈칸에 알맞은 말을 쓰시오.

  (1) <u>My mother</u> made a chocolate cake last Saturday.

    = It ＿＿＿＿ ＿＿＿＿ ＿＿＿＿ ＿＿＿＿ made a chocolate cake last Saturday.

  (2) My mother made <u>a chocolate cake</u> last Saturday.

    = It ＿＿＿＿ ＿＿＿＿ ＿＿＿＿ ＿＿＿＿ ＿＿＿＿ my mother made last Saturday.

Grammar 시험대비 기본평가

01 다음 우리말에 맞게 괄호 안에 주어진 단어를 이용하여 문장을 완성하시오.

(1) 우리가 더 많은 책을 공유할수록, 우리는 더 많이 배웁니다. (book, share)

➡ _____, the more we learn.

(2) 우리가 바다 밑으로 더 깊이 갈수록, 더 어두워진다. (dark, get)

➡ The deeper we go under the sea, _____.

(3) 더 높이 올라갈수록, 우리는 더 멀리 봐. (far, see)

➡ The higher we go up, _____.

(4) 엄마가 크림파이를 만드신 것은 바로 지난 일요일이야. (it, that)

➡ _____ my mom made a cream pie.

02 다음 문장에서 어법상 어색한 부분을 바르게 고쳐 쓰시오.

(1) The longer I waited, the more angry I became.

➡ _____

(2) The hard you exercise, the stronger you will become.

➡ _____

(3) The earlier you register, the better you will get seat.

➡ _____

(4) The more books you read, the more wiser you become.

➡ _____

03 다음 〈보기〉의 문장을 참고하여 빈칸을 완성하시오.

┌─ 보기 ├─

A: Junha met Seho in the shopping mall.

B: No. It was in the park that Junha met Seho. (park)

(1) A: Seho likes New York the most.

B: No. _____ Seho likes the most. (Paris)

(2) A: Junha walks to school every day.

B: No. _____ walks to school every day. (Minji)

01 다음 빈칸에 들어갈 말로 알맞은 것은?

> The brighter the sun is, _____ I feel.

① the happy ② happier
③ the more happy ④ the happily
⑤ the happier

02 다음 빈칸에 들어갈 말로 적절하지 않은 것은?

> The harder you try, _____ you learn.

① the more ② the better
③ the more things ④ the best
⑤ the sooner

03 다음 빈칸에 들어갈 말로 알맞은 것을 모두 고르시오.

> It was Junha _____ bought a novel in the bookstore.

① that ② what ③ which
④ who ⑤ where

04 다음 중 밑줄 친 that의 쓰임이 다른 하나를 고르시오.

① It is Ms. Lee that keeps five dogs.
② It was on my birthday that I was given a toy car.
③ It was the museum that we visited yesterday.
④ It was Ted that won the contest.
⑤ It is clear that smartphones help students learn something new.

05 다음 기사의 내용과 일치하지 않는 것을 고르시오.

① It was Team Kim that beat the Canadian team in Gangneung in 2018.
② It was in 2018 that Team Kim beat the Canadian team in Gangneung.
③ It was by 2 points that Team Kim won the game.
④ It was Team Kim that the Canadian Team beat in Gangneung in 2018.
⑤ It was in Gangneung that Team Kim beat the Canadian team in 2018.

06 서답형 다음 문장에서 어법상 어색한 것을 바르게 고쳐 다시 쓰시오.

(1) It is Linda which doesn't like cheese cake.

➡ _____

(2) It is this old computer that give me a headache.

➡ _____

서답형

07 다음 괄호 안에 주어진 단어들을 바르게 배열하여 문장을 완성하시오.

> (you, more, the, make, mistakes), the more you will learn.

➡ _____, the more you will learn.

08 다음 문장과 같은 뜻을 가진 문장은?

> 시험이 어려울수록, 너는 더 열심히 공부해야 한다.

① The more the test is difficult, the harder you should try.
② The more the test is difficult, the hard you should try.
③ The more difficult the test is, the harder you should try.
④ The more difficult the test is, you should try harder.
⑤ The more test difficult is, the harder you should try.

서답형

09 다음 두 문장을 'the+비교급..., the+비교급 ~'을 사용하여 하나의 문장으로 완성하시오.

> • The wave rose higher.
> • We swam faster.

➡ _____

서답형

10 주어진 어휘를 이용하여 다음 우리말을 영어로 쓰시오.

> 더 일찍 떠날수록, 너는 더 빨리 도착할 것이다. (early, leave, soon, will arrive)

➡ _____

서답형

11 다음 〈보기〉와 같이 두 문장이 같은 뜻이 되도록 빈칸에 들어갈 알맞은 말을 쓰시오.

> ┌─ 조건 ─┐
> The harder you study, the more you will learn.
> = If you study harder, you will learn more.

(1) The brighter the sun shines, the happier I feel.
 ➡ As the sun _____.
(2) The longer I waited, the angrier I became.
 ➡ As I _____.
(3) The more books you read, the more things you will know.
 ➡ If _____
 _____.

서답형

12 ①~⑤ 중 that이 들어갈 곳으로 알맞은 것은?

> It ① was ② the chocolate cake ③ my sister ④ made ⑤ yesterday.

①   ②   ③   ④   ⑤

서답형

13 주어진 어휘를 이용하여 다음 우리말을 영어로 쓰시오. (11 글자)

> 사람들을 더 기분 좋게 만들 것은 이 아름다운 정원이다. (beautiful, better, that, make, feel)

➡ _____
 _____

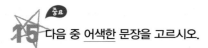

서답형

14 다음 괄호 안에 주어진 단어들을 바르게 배열하시오.

> The more trees I plant there, (come, birds, more, the, will).

➡ _____

15 다음 중 어색한 문장을 고르시오.

① The more you want, the more you will be disappointed.
② The younger you are, the harder you should work.
③ The more I learn English, the more I like it.
④ It was yesterday that I met Lean in the park.
⑤ It was five bottles of coke that Jack brought to the party.

16 빈칸에 공통으로 들어갈 수 있는 단어를 고르시오.

> • It was my dad _____ loved me most.
> • Jihun is the boy, _____ will have an audition this Friday.

① that   ② what   ③ which
④ who   ⑤ whom

17 빈칸에 들어갈 말을 순서대로 바르게 연결한 것은?

> In making food art, its display is important. It is an artistic display _____ _____ food look better. _____ _____ the food is, the more delicious it looks.

① which make – The pretty
② that make – The prettier
③ which makes – The pretty

④ that makes – More pretty
⑤ that makes – The prettier

18 다음 중 어법상 어색한 것을 고르시오.

> A: What happens ①when we go down ② faster?
> B: ③The more faster we go down, ④the more dangerous it ⑤gets.

①   ②   ③   ④   ⑤

서답형

19 대화의 빈칸에 쓰인 우리말 대답을 영어로 바꾸어 쓰시오.

(1) A: We went to Baker's Camp, right?
    B: No. 우리가 갔었던 것은 바로 Makers' Camp야.
    ➡ _____

(2) A: Van Gogh painted *I and the Village*, right?
    B: No. *I and the Village*를 그린 사람은 바로 Chagall이야.
    ➡ _____

20 다음 중 어법상 어색한 문장의 개수로 알맞은 것은?

> a. The better you know classical music, the more you will love it.
> b. It was the Internet that she bought her shirts.
> c. It is Kiyoung that love to write poems.
> d. The higher I climbed the mountain, the darker the sky is getting.
> e. The more you work out, the better you will feel.

① 1개   ② 2개   ③ 3개   ④ 4개   ⑤ 5개

01 다음 문장을 'the+비교급, the+비교급'을 이용하여 바꾸어 쓰시오.

(1) If you practice harder, you can type faster.

➡ _____

(2) As they tried more, they did better.

➡ _____

(3) If it gets colder, we need more clothes.

➡ _____

(4) As he got closer to the fire, he felt warmer.

➡ _____

(5) If you get up earlier, you can spend more time on makeup.

➡ _____

_____

02 밑줄 친 부분을 강조하는 문장으로 고쳐 쓰시오.

(1) Cats hate the smell of lemons.

➡ It is _____.

(2) My grandmother made me banana cakes.

➡ It was _____

_____.

(3) My grandfather told me the story.

➡ _____

_____

(4) We will attend a conference this Friday.

➡ _____

_____

(5) We saw the statue in front of the MBC building.

➡ _____

_____

03 다음 우리말에 맞게 주어진 어휘를 알맞게 배열하시오.

(1) 그가 서점에서 산 것은 똑같은 책 다섯 권이었어.
(he, at the bookstore, it, bought, was, five copies of the same books, that)

➡ _____

_____

(2) 내가 잊지 못할 것은 학급 현장 학습이야.
(that, forget, is, the class field trip, I, it, won't)

➡ _____

(3) 우리 모두를 깊게 연결해 준 것은 이 경험이었어.
(deeply, connected, it, this experience, is, all of us, that)

➡ _____

_____

04 다음 그림을 보고 빈칸에 알맞은 말을 써 넣으시오.

(1)

MAKING AND FLYING A DRONE

A light drone has a long battery life.

In making and flying a drone, its weight is important. It is _____ that has a long battery life. The _____ the drone is, the longer it flies.

(2)

The facial design makes a mask unique.

In making a mask, the design of its face is important. It is _____ that makes a mask unique. The funnier the face is, the _____ popular it is.

05 주어진 문장의 밑줄 친 부분을 괄호 안의 단어로 바꾸어 문장을 다시 쓰시오.

(1) It was yesterday that she sang the song. (tomorrow)

➡ _____

(2) It is my friends that cheer me up all the time. (Joan)

➡ _____

06 다음 대화에서 어법상 틀린 곳을 찾아 바르게 고치시오.

A: There are many cars, so the traffic is bad.

B: You're right. The more cars there are, the more worse the traffic becomes.

_____ ➡ _____

07 다음 문장의 밑줄 친 부분을 어법에 맞게 고쳐 쓰시오.

(1) It was her teddy bear that Cathy likes the best.

➡ _____

(2) It was from Junsu who I first heard the news.

➡ _____

(3) It is Minji that went to visit her aunt last Thursday.

➡ _____
_____

(4) It is the star watching experience in Yeongwol that Minjun can't forget it.

➡ _____
_____

(5) It was the bookstore that my dad first met my mom.

➡ _____
_____

This Book Is Amazing!

Most people think of books as traditional paper books to read.

<small>think of A as B: A를 B로 생각하다</small> <small>to부정사의 형용사적 용법</small>

However, there are many unique books around you. Let's learn about a

<small>앞에 나오는 내용과 상반되는 내용을 연결하는 연결사</small>

few of these books.

<small>many unique books around you</small>

Books Travel!

I found this old book on a park bench yesterday. A note on the cover

<small>↔ new</small>

read, "Free Book! Take me home and read me!" Actually, this book

<small>'~라고 쓰여 있다, ~로 해석되다'(자동사)</small> <small>= In fact. As a matter of fact: 사실</small>

had an ID number and was registered on a website. When I entered

<small>등위접속사 'and'가 동사구 'had ~ number'와 'was ~ website'를 연결</small>

the number online, I found out that the book had traveled to many

<small>과거의 특정 시점 이전에 일어난 일은 과거완료(had+과거분사)로 표현</small>

countries and that a number of readers in different countries had read it

<small>두 개의 that절이 등위접속사 'and'로 연결</small>

before me. How was that possible?

<small>'그 책이 여러 나라를 여행하고, 나보다 앞서 많은 다른 사람들이 그 책을 읽었다'는 앞 문장의 내용</small>

---

traditional 전통적인

unique 독특한

cover 커버, 표지

free 무료의

register 등록하다

a number of 많은

possible 가능한

확인문제

● 다음 문장이 본문의 내용과 일치하면 T, 일치하지 않으면 F를 쓰시오.

1 Most people consider books as traditional paper books to read. ☐

2 There are only a few unique books around you. ☐

3 The writer found an old book on a park bench yesterday. ☐

4 There was a note on the back cover of the book. ☐

5 The book which the writer found had an ID number and was registered on a website. ☐

6 The writer was the first reader of the book. ☐

There is a book-sharing project. First, <u>register your book online</u> and get an ID number. Next, leave <u>it</u> in a public place. When the next reader <u>finds</u> your book and <u>reports</u> back to the website, you can check <u>where your book is</u>. This way, the whole world can become a big library. <u>The more books we share, the more we learn.</u>

The Drinkable Book

This <u>tiny</u> book is really important to people in my town. It provides <u>both</u> the information <u>and</u> the tools necessary <u>to make</u> clean drinking water.

<u>It is called</u> the Drinkable Book. You cannot actually drink the book, but you can use it <u>as</u> a filter. Simply tear out a page and pour dirty water on it. As the water goes through the page, it changes into clean drinking water. <u>It is this filtered water that you can drink.</u> This is possible because the book is made of special filter paper. This <u>amazing</u> book saves the lives of many children from <u>diseases that come from</u> dirty water.

project 기획, 프로젝트
leave 남겨 두다
report 알리다, 보고하다
this way 이렇듯, 이런 식으로
tiny 아주 작은
provide 제공하다
both … and ~ …와 ~ 둘 다
necessary 필요한
simply 그냥, 그저, 간단히
tear ~을 찢다, 뜯어내다(tear-tore-torn)
pour 붓다, 따르다
disease 병, 질병

확인문제

● 다음 문장이 본문의 내용과 일치하면 T, 일치하지 <u>않으면</u> F를 쓰시오.

1 When we join a book-sharing project, we should register our book online and get an ID number. ☐

2 We should leave the book in a private place. ☐

3 As we share more books, we learn more. ☐

4 You can actually drink the Drinkable Book. ☐

5 You can use the book as a filter by simply tearing out a page and pouring dirty water on it. ☐

6 This amazing book saves the lives of many children from diseases that come from water shortage. ☐

The Tree-Book-Tree Project

This is the most amazing book that I have ever seen. After you
<small>that+주어+have ever+과거분사: 최상급 표현 뒤에서 '주어가 …해 본 중에서 가장 ~한'</small>

finish reading this book, plant it and water it. You will see new leaves
<small>finish는 목적어로 동명사를 취함.</small> <small>지각동사 see+목적어+현재분사: …가 ~하는 것을 보다</small>

growing on the book. In some bookstores in my town, you can see a
<small>지각동사 see+목적어+현재분사: …가 ~하는 것을 보다</small>

copy of this book producing new leaves.

The secret is that the book has seeds in each page. It is these tiny
<small>each+단수명사</small> <small>These tiny seeds change</small>

seeds that change the book into a tree. This book was made by a small
<small>the book into a tree.'에서 주어 'These tiny seeds'를 강조하기 위한 'It ~ that …' 강조구문   be made by: '~에 의해 만들어지다'</small>

children's book publisher in Argentina. Though the company does

not print this book anymore, this special project makes us think about
<small>not+anymore = no more</small> <small>사역동사 makes+목적어+동사원형</small>

where books come from.
<small>간접의문문('의문사+주어+동사'의 어순)</small>

These are just a few of the unique books you can find. What other
<small>books와 you 사이에 목적격 관계대명사 that[which] 생략</small>

unique books do you want to make? What special project would you
<small>want는 목적어로 to부정사를 취함</small>

like to do with the books? The bigger your imagination is, the more
<small>would like는 목적어로 to부정사를 취함   The+비교급+주어+동사 …, the+비교급+주어+동사 ~: …하면 할수록, 더 ~하다</small>

wonderful your books will become.

bookstore 서점
produce 생산하다, 산출하다
publisher 출판업자, 출판사
not ~ anymore 더 이상 ~ 않다
print 인쇄하다, 발행하다

📎 **확인문제**

● 다음 문장이 본문의 내용과 일치하면 T, 일치하지 <u>않으면</u> F를 쓰시오.

1 If you plant the book and water it after you finish reading it, you will see new leaves growing on the book. ☐

2 In many bookstores all around the world, you can see a copy of this book producing new leaves. ☐

3 This book has seeds in each page. ☐

4 A big children's book publisher in Argentina made this book. ☐

5 The Tree-Book-Tree Project makes us think about where books come from. ☐

6 As your imagination is bigger, your library will become more wonderful. ☐

• 우리말을 참고하여 빈칸에 알맞은 말을 쓰시오.

1 This Book Is _____!

2 Most people think of books as _____ _____ _____ to read.

3 However, there are many _____ books around you.

4 Let's learn about _____ _____ of these books.

5 Books _____!

6 I _____ this old book on a park bench yesterday.

7 A note on the cover _____, "_____ Book!

8 _____ _____ _____ and read me!"

9 Actually, this book had an _____ _____ and _____ _____ on a website.

10 When I entered the number online, I found out that the book _____ _____ to many countries and that a number of readers in different countries _____ _____ it before me.

11 _____ was that possible?

12 There is a _____ _____.

13 First, _____ your book online and _____ an ID number.

14 Next, _____ _____ in a public place.

---

1 이 책은 놀라워요!

2 대부분의 사람은 책을 읽기 위한 전통적인 종이책으로 생각합니다.

3 하지만, 여러분 주변에는 독특한 책이 많이 있습니다.

4 이러한 책 중 몇 가지에 대해 배워 봅시다.

5 책이 여행합니다!

6 저는 어제 공원 벤치에서 이 낡은 책을 발견했습니다.

7 표지 위의 쪽지에 "공짜 책이에요!

8 저를 집으로 데려가서 읽어 주세요!"라고 쓰여 있었습니다.

9 사실, 이 책은 ID 번호가 있고 웹사이트에 등록되어 있었어요.

10 제가 온라인으로 그 번호를 입력했을 때, 저는 그 책이 많은 나라를 여행하고 다른 나라의 많은 독자가 저보다 앞서 이 책을 읽었다는 것을 알아냈습니다.

11 그게 어떻게 가능했을까요?

12 책을 공유하는 프로젝트가 있습니다.

13 우선, 온라인에 여러분의 책을 등록하고 ID 번호를 얻으세요.

14 그다음, 그것을 공공장소에 놓아두세요.

15 When the next reader finds your book and _____ _____ to the website, you can check _____ _____ _____ _____.

16 This way, the whole world can become _____ _____ _____.

17 _____ _____ _____ we share, _____ _____ we learn.

18 The _____ Book

19 _____ _____ _____ is really important to people in my town.

20 It provides _____ _____ _____ _____ _____ _____ necessary to make clean drinking water.

21 It _____ _____ the Drinkable Book.

22 You cannot actually drink the book, but you can use it _____ _____ _____.

23 Simply _____ _____ a page and _____ dirty water _____ it.

24 _____ the water goes through the page, it _____ _____ clean drinking water.

25 _____ _____ this filtered water _____ you can drink.

26 This is possible because the book is made of _____ _____ _____.

27 This _____ book _____ the lives of many children _____ _____ that come from dirty water.

15 다음 독자가 여러분의 책을 발견해서 그 웹사이트에 다시 알릴 때, 여러분은 책이 어디 있는지 확인할 수 있습니다.

16 이런 식으로, 전 세계가 하나의 큰 도서관이 될 수 있습니다.

17 우리가 더 많은 책을 공유할수록, 우리는 더 많이 배웁니다.

18 마실 수 있는 책

19 이 작은 책은 우리 마을 사람들에게는 정말로 중요합니다.

20 그것은 깨끗한 마실 물을 만드는 데 필요한 정보와 도구 둘 다를 제공합니다.

21 그것은 '마실 수 있는 책'이라고 불립니다.

22 여러분은 실제로 그 책을 마실 수는 없지만, 그것을 필터로 사용할 수 있습니다.

23 그냥 한 페이지를 떼어 내서 그 위에 더러운 물을 부으세요.

24 물이 그 페이지를 통과하면서, 깨끗한 마실 물로 바뀝니다.

25 여러분이 마실 수 있는 것은 이 여과된 물입니다.

26 책이 특별한 여과지로 만들어졌기 때문에 이것이 가능합니다.

27 이 놀라운 책은 더러운 물로 생기는 질병으로부터 많은 어린이의 생명을 구합니다.

28 The _____ _____

29 This is _____ _____ _____ _____ that I have ever seen.

30 After you finish _____ this book, _____ it and _____ it.

31 You will see new leaves _____ on the book.

32 In some bookstores in my town, you can see _____ _____ _____ this book _____ new leaves.

33 The secret is that the book _____ _____ in each page.

34 It is _____ _____ _____ that change the book into a tree.

35 This book _____ _____ _____ a small children's book publisher in Argentina.

36 Though the company does _____ print this book _____, this special project makes us _____ about where books come from.

37 These are _____ _____ _____ of the unique books you can find.

38 _____ _____ _____ _____ do you want to make?

39 What special project _____ you _____ _____ _____ with the books?

40 _____ _____ your imagination is, _____ _____ _____ your books will become.

28	나무-책-나무 프로젝트
29	이것은 제가 지금까지 본 것 중에서 가장 놀라운 책입니다.
30	여러분이 이 책을 다 읽은 후에, 그것을 심고 물을 주세요.
31	여러분은 책에서 새잎이 자라는 것을 보게 될 거예요.
32	우리 마을의 몇몇 서점에서, 여러분은 이 책 한 권이 새잎을 내는 것을 볼 수 있습니다.
33	비밀은 책이 각 페이지 안에 씨앗을 갖고 있다는 것입니다.
34	책을 나무로 변화시키는 것은 이 아주 작은 씨앗들이에요.
35	이 책은 아르헨티나에 있는 한 작은 아동 도서 출판사에 의해 만들어졌습니다.
36	그 회사가 더는 이 책을 발행하지는 않지만, 이 특별한 프로젝트는 우리에게 책이 어디에서 오는지에 대해 생각하게 해 줍니다.
37	이것들은 여러분이 찾을 수 있는 독특한 책 중의 단지 몇 가지입니다.
38	여러분은 어떤 다른 독특한 책을 만들기 원하나요?
39	여러분은 책으로 어떤 특별한 프로젝트를 하고 싶나요?
40	여러분의 상상이 크면 클수록, 여러분의 책은 더 훌륭해질 것입니다.

● 우리말을 참고하여 본문을 영작하시오.

1 ▶ 이 책은 놀라워요!

　➡ _____

2 ▶ 대부분의 사람은 책을 읽기 위한 전통적인 종이책으로 생각합니다.

　➡ _____

3 ▶ 하지만, 여러분 주변에는 독특한 책이 많이 있습니다.

　➡ _____

4 ▶ 이러한 책 중 몇 가지에 대해 배워 봅시다.

　➡ _____

5 ▶ 책이 여행합니다!

　➡ _____

6 ▶ 저는 어제 공원 벤치에서 이 낡은 책을 발견했습니다.

　➡ _____

7 ▶ 표지 위의 쪽지에 "공짜 책이에요!

　➡ _____

8 ▶ 저를 집으로 데려가서 읽어 주세요!"라고 쓰여 있었습니다.

　➡ _____

9 ▶ 사실, 이 책은 ID 번호가 있고 웹사이트에 등록되어 있었어요.

　➡ _____

10 ▶ 제가 온라인으로 그 번호를 입력했을 때, 저는 그 책이 많은 나라를 여행하고 다른 나라의 많은 독자가 저보다 앞서 이 책을 읽었다는 것을 알아냈습니다.

　➡ _____

　_____

11 ▶ 그게 어떻게 가능했을까요?

　➡ _____

12 ▶ 책을 공유하는 프로젝트가 있습니다.

　➡ _____

13 ▶ 우선, 온라인에 여러분의 책을 등록하고 ID 번호를 얻으세요.

　➡ _____

14 그다음, 그것을 공공장소에 놓아두세요.

→ _____

15 다음 독자가 여러분의 책을 발견해서 그 웹사이트에 다시 알릴 때, 여러분은 책이 어디 있는지 확인할 수 있습니다.

→ _____

→ _____

16 이런 식으로, 전 세계가 하나의 큰 도서관이 될 수 있습니다.

→ _____

17 우리가 더 많은 책을 공유할수록, 우리는 더 많이 배웁니다.

→ _____

18 마실 수 있는 책

→ _____

19 이 작은 책은 우리 마을 사람들에게는 정말로 중요합니다.

→ _____

20 그것은 깨끗한 마실 물을 만드는 데 필요한 정보와 도구 둘 다를 제공합니다.

→ _____

21 그것은 '마실 수 있는 책'이라고 불립니다.

→ _____

22 여러분은 실제로 그 책을 마실 수는 없지만, 그것을 필터로 사용할 수 있습니다.

→ _____

23 그냥 한 페이지를 떼어 내서 그 위에 더러운 물을 부으세요.

→ _____

24 물이 그 페이지를 통과하면서, 깨끗한 마실 물로 바뀝니다.

→ _____

25 여러분이 마실 수 있는 것은 이 여과된 물입니다.

→ _____

26 책이 특별한 여과지로 만들어졌기 때문에 이것이 가능합니다.

→ _____

27 이 놀라운 책은 더러운 물로 생기는 질병으로부터 많은 어린이의 생명을 구합니다.

→ _____

28 나무-책-나무 프로젝트

➡ _____

29 이것은 제가 지금까지 본 것 중에서 가장 놀라운 책입니다.

➡ _____

30 여러분이 이 책을 다 읽은 후에, 그것을 심고 물을 주세요.

➡ _____

31 여러분은 책에서 새잎이 자라는 것을 보게 될 거예요.

➡ _____

32 우리 마을의 몇몇 서점에서, 여러분은 이 책 한 권이 새잎을 내는 것을 볼 수 있습니다.

➡ _____

33 비밀은 책이 각 페이지 안에 씨앗을 갖고 있다는 것입니다.

➡ _____

34 책을 나무로 변화시키는 것은 이 아주 작은 씨앗들이에요.

➡ _____

35 이 책은 아르헨티나에 있는 한 작은 아동 도서 출판사에 의해 만들어졌습니다.

➡ _____

36 그 회사가 더는 이 책을 발행하지는 않지만, 이 특별한 프로젝트는 우리에게 책이 어디에서 오는지에 대해 생각하게 해 줍니다.

➡ _____

_____

37 이것들은 여러분이 찾을 수 있는 독특한 책 중의 단지 몇 가지입니다.

➡ _____

38 여러분은 어떤 다른 독특한 책을 만들기 원하나요?

➡ _____

39 여러분은 책으로 어떤 특별한 프로젝트를 하고 싶나요?

➡ _____

40 여러분의 상상이 크면 클수록, 여러분의 책은 더 훌륭해질 것입니다.

➡ _____

[01~03] 다음 글을 읽고 물음에 답하시오.

Most people think of books as traditional paper books (A)to read. ⓐ , there are many unique books around you. Let's learn about a few of these books.

01 위 글의 빈칸 ⓐ에 들어갈 알맞은 말을 고르시오.

① That is
② Therefore
③ As a result
④ However
⑤ For example

02 위 글의 밑줄 친 (A)to read와 to부정사의 용법이 같은 것을 모두 고르시오.

① It's time for you to finish the work.
② This book was easy to read.
③ It was hard for me to solve the problem.
④ He was tall enough to play basketball.
⑤ She is the last person to do it.

03 위 글의 뒤에 올 내용으로 가장 알맞은 것을 고르시오.

① the decrease of traditional paper books
② the explanation of some unique books
③ various electronic books
④ the popularity of traditional paper books
⑤ the decrease of unique books

[04~06] 다음 글을 읽고 물음에 답하시오.

Books Travel!

I found this old book ⓐ a park bench yesterday. A note ⓑ the cover read, "Free Book! Take me home and read me!" Actually, this book had an ID number and was registered ⓒ a website. When I entered the number online, I found out that the book had traveled to many countries and that ⓓa number of readers in different countries had read it before me. How was that possible?

04 위 글의 빈칸 ⓐ~ⓒ에 공통으로 들어갈 알맞은 전치사를 고르시오.

① in
② on
③ to
④ at
⑤ from

서답형

05 위 글의 밑줄 친 ⓓa number of와 바꿔 쓸 수 있는 한 단어를 쓰시오.

➡ _____

중요

06 According to the passage, which is NOT true?

① The writer found a free old book yesterday.
② The writer could take the book home and read it.
③ The book had an ID number.
④ The writer found out that the book had traveled to many countries.
⑤ The writer was the first reader of the book.

[07~09] 다음 글을 읽고 물음에 답하시오.

There is a book-sharing project. First, register your book online and get an ID number. ⓐNext, leave it in a private place. When the next reader finds your book and reports back to the website, you can check where your book is. This way, the whole world can become a big library. The more books we share, the more we learn.

서답형

07 What is the first step in the book-sharing project? Fill in the blanks (A) and (B) with suitable words.

> The first step in the book-sharing project is to (A)_____ your book online and (B)_____ an ID number.

서답형

08 위 글의 밑줄 친 ⓐ에서 흐름상 어색한 부분을 찾아 고치시오.

_____ ➡ _____

중요

09 위 글의 주제로 알맞은 것을 고르시오.

① the way to register your book online
② the difficulty in getting an ID number
③ how to report back to the website on the book
④ the project to share books
⑤ the way to check where the book is

[10~11] 다음 글을 읽고 물음에 답하시오.

The Drinkable Book

This tiny book is really important to people in my town. It provides both the information and the tools necessary to make clean ⓐdrinking water.

It is called the Drinkable Book. You cannot actually drink the book, but you can use it as a filter. Simply tear out a page and pour dirty water on it. ⓑ물이 그 페이지를 통과하면서, 깨끗한 마실 물로 바뀝니다. It is this filtered water that you can drink. This is possible because the book is made of special filter paper. This amazing book saves the lives of many children from diseases that come from dirty water.

10 위 글의 밑줄 친 ⓐdrinking과 문법적 쓰임이 다른 것을 고르시오.

① She bought a swimming suit.
② He is in the waiting room now.
③ You can smoke only in a smoking room.
④ He is a walking dictionary.
⑤ He is wearing a hearing aid.

서답형

11 위 글의 밑줄 친 ⓑ의 우리말에 맞게 주어진 어휘를 이용하여 13 단어로 영작하시오.

> As, goes through, into

➡ _____

[12~14] 다음 글을 읽고 물음에 답하시오.

The Tree-Book-Tree Project

This is the most amazing book ___ⓐ___ I ⓑhave ever seen. ⓒAfter you finish to read this book, plant it and water it. You will see new leaves growing on the book. In some bookstores in my town, you can see a copy of this book producing new leaves.

12 위 글의 빈칸 ⓐ에 들어갈 알맞은 말을 고르시오.

① where   ② how   ③ what
④ that   ⑤ when

13 위 글의 밑줄 친 ⓑ의 현재완료와 용법이 같은 것을 **모두** 고르시오.

① I <u>have been</u> to Busan twice.
② <u>Have</u> you <u>been</u> to the bank yet?
③ I <u>have</u> never <u>read</u> this novel.
④ She <u>has been</u> sick since yesterday.
⑤ The train <u>has</u> just <u>arrived</u>.

서답형
14 위 글의 밑줄 친 ⓒ에서 어법상 **틀린** 부분을 찾아 고치시오.

━━━━━━━━━ ➡ ━━━━━━━━━

[15~18] 다음 글을 읽고 물음에 답하시오.

There is a book-sharing project. First, register your book online and get an ID number. Next, (A)<u>leave</u> it in a public place. When the next reader finds your book and reports back _____ⓐ_____ the website, you can check where your book is. This way, the whole world can become a big _____ⓑ_____. The more books we share, the more we learn.

15 위 글의 빈칸 ⓐ에 들어갈 알맞은 전치사를 고르시오.

① from   ② to
③ for   ④ of
⑤ on

16 위 글의 빈칸 ⓑ에 들어갈 알맞은 말을 고르시오.

① museum   ② publishing company
③ bookstore   ④ shopping center
⑤ library

17 위 글의 밑줄 친 (A)leave와 같은 의미로 쓰인 것을 고르시오.

① You can <u>leave</u> the cooking to me.
② When will the plane <u>leave</u> for Dallas?
③ <u>Leave</u> the key on the table.
④ She took a month's paid <u>leave</u>.
⑤ <u>Leave</u> the door open, please.

18 Which question CANNOT be answered after reading the passage?

① What is the first step to join the book-sharing project?
② Where should you leave your book after the first step?
③ What should the next reader do after finding your book?
④ How long does it usually take for the next reader to find your book?
⑤ When can you check where your book is?

[19~21] 다음 글을 읽고 물음에 답하시오.

Most people (A)<u>think of</u> books as traditional paper books to read. However, there are many unique books around you. Let's learn about a few of these books.
_____ⓐ_____
I found this old book on a park bench yesterday. (①) A note on the cover read, "Free Book! (②) Take me home and read me!" (③) Actually, this book had an ID number and was registered on a website. (④) When I entered the number online, I found out that the book had traveled to many countries and that a number of readers in different countries had read it before me. (⑤)

19 위 글의 빈칸 ⓐ에 들어갈 제목으로 알맞은 것을 고르시오.

① Register Your Book on a Website
② The Drinkable Book
③ Books Travel!
④ How to Get an ID Number for a Book
⑤ The Tree-Book-Tree Project

20 위 글의 밑줄 친 (A)think of와 바꿔 쓸 수 없는 말을 고르시오.

① regard   ② look upon
③ consider   ④ show
⑤ view

21 위 글의 흐름으로 보아, 주어진 문장이 들어가기에 가장 적절한 곳은?

> How was that possible?

①   ②   ③   ④   ⑤

[22~24] 다음 글을 읽고 물음에 답하시오.

The Drinkable Book

This tiny book is really important to people in my town. It provides both the information and the tools necessary to make clean drinking water.

It is called the Drinkable Book. You cannot actually drink the book, but you can use it ⓐas a filter. Simply tear out a page and pour dirty water on it. As the water goes through the page, ⓑit changes into clean drinking water. It is this filtered water that you can drink. This is possible because the book is made of special filter paper. This amazing book saves the lives of many children from diseases that come from dirty water.

22 위 글의 밑줄 친 ⓐas와 같은 의미로 쓰인 것을 고르시오.

① As I entered the room, they applauded.
② This plastic bag served as a hat.
③ Her anger grew as she talked.
④ She is as tall as you are.
⑤ Leave it as it is.

서답형

23 위 글의 밑줄 친 ⓑit이 가리키는 것을 본문에서 찾아 쓰시오.

➡ _____

24 위 글의 주제로 알맞은 것을 고르시오.

① the importance of a book which gives precious information
② the way to use tools necessary to make clean drinking water
③ how to make special filter paper
④ various ways to save the lives of many children from diseases
⑤ the book which provides the tools necessary to make clean drinking water

[25~26] 다음 글을 읽고 물음에 답하시오.

The secret is that the book has seeds in each page. (A)[It is / They are] these tiny seeds that change the book into a tree. This book was made by a small children's book publisher in Argentina. Though the company does not print this book anymore, this special project makes us (B)[think / to think] about where books come from.

These are just a few of the unique books you can find. What other unique books do you want to make? What special project would you like (C)[doing / to do] with the books? The bigger your imagination is, the more wonderful your books will become.

서답형

25 위 글의 괄호 (A)~(C)에서 문맥이나 어법상 알맞은 낱말을 골라 쓰시오.

➡ (A) _____ (B) _____ (C) _____

26 Which question CANNOT be answered after reading the passage?

① What does the book have in each page?
② Who made this book?
③ When was this book first published?
④ Is this book still printed?
⑤ Through this special project, what can we think about?

[27~28] 다음 글을 읽고 물음에 답하시오.

The Tree-Book-Tree Project

This is the most amazing book that I have ever seen. After you finish reading this book, plant it and water it. You will see new leaves growing on the book. In some bookstores in my town, you can see a copy of this book producing new leaves.

The secret is that the book has seeds in each page. It is these tiny seeds that change the book into a tree. (A)This book was made by a small children's book publisher in Argentina. Though the company does not print this book anymore, this special project makes us think about _____ ⓐ _____.

서답형

27 위 글의 빈칸 ⓐ에 다음 문장을 알맞은 형태로 쓰시오.

> Where does books come from?

➡ _____

28 위 글을 밑줄 친 (A)This book에 대한 설명으로 옳지 않은 것을 고르시오.

① It is the most amazing book that the writer has ever seen.
② If you plant it and water it, you will see new leaves growing on the book.
③ It has seeds in each page.
④ A small children's book publisher in Argentina made it.
⑤ Even now the publishing company prints this book.

[29~30] 다음 글을 읽고 물음에 답하시오.

These are just a few of the unique books you can find. What other unique books do you want to make? What special project would you like to do with the books? ⓐ The bigger your imagination is, the more wonderful your books will become.

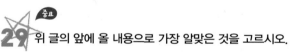

29 위 글의 앞에 올 내용으로 가장 알맞은 것을 고르시오.

① the history of books
② the explanation about a few unique books you can find
③ various kinds of books that people like most
④ a recent survey showing people's taste in books
⑤ the imagination about books

서답형

30 위 글의 밑줄 친 ⓐ를 다음과 같이 바꿔 쓸 때, 어법상 틀린 부분을 찾아 고치시오. (2 군데)

> As your imagination is the bigger, your books will become the more wonderful.

_____ ➡ _____

_____ ➡ _____

[01~03] 다음 글을 읽고 물음에 답하시오.

(A)[Almost / Most] people think of books as traditional paper books to read. However, there are many (B)[ordinary / unique] books around you. Let's learn about a few of these books.

Books Travel!

I found this old book on a park bench yesterday. A note on the cover read, "Free Book! Take me home and read me!" Actually, this book had an ID number and was registered on a website. When I entered the number online, I found out that the book had traveled to many countries and that (C)[a / the] number of readers in different countries had read it before me. How was ⓐthat possible?

01 위 글의 괄호 (A)~(C)에서 알맞은 낱말을 골라 쓰시오.

➡ (A) _____ (B) _____ (C) _____

02 위 글의 밑줄 친 ⓐthat이 가리키는 것을 영어로 쓰시오.

➡ _____

_____

_____

03 본문의 내용과 일치하도록 다음 빈칸 (A)~(C)에 알맞은 단어를 쓰시오.

The old book that the writer found on a park bench yesterday had (A)_____ _____ _____ and was registered (B)_____ _____ _____ . Anyone who found it could take it home and read it because it was a (C)_____ book.

[04~06] 다음 글을 읽고 물음에 답하시오.

There is a book-sharing project. First, ____ⓐ____ your book online and get an ID number. Next, leave it in a public place. When the next reader finds your book and reports back to the website, you can check where your book is. This way, the whole world can become a big library. ⓑThe more books we share, the more we learn.

04 주어진 영영풀이를 참고하여 빈칸 ⓐ에 철자 r로 시작하는 단어를 쓰시오.

to put your name on an official list, in order to be able to do something or to receive a service

➡ _____

05 위 글의 밑줄 친 ⓑ를 다음과 같이 바꿔 쓸 때 빈칸에 들어갈 알맞은 말을 쓰시오.

As we share _____ _____ , we learn _____ .

06 본문의 내용과 일치하도록 다음 빈칸 (A)~(D)에 알맞은 단어를 쓰시오.

1. Register your book and get (A)_____ _____ _____ .
2. Leave your book anywhere in (B)_____ _____ _____ .
3. Someone picks up your book and reports back to (C)_____ _____ .
4. Check (D)_____ your book goes and who reads it.

[07~09] 다음 글을 읽고 물음에 답하시오.

The Drinkable Book

This tiny book is really important to people in my town. It provides both the information and the tools necessary to make clean drinking water.

It is called the Drinkable Book. You cannot actually drink the book, but you can use it as a filter. Simply tear out a page and pour dirty water on it. As the water goes through the page, it changes into clean drinking water. ⓐ여러분이 마실 수 있는 것은 이 여과된 물입니다. This is possible because the book is made of special filter paper. This amazing book saves the lives of many children from diseases that come from dirty water.

07 다음 문장에서 위 글의 내용과 <u>다른</u> 부분을 찾아서 고치시오.

> As the Drinkable Book is made of special filter paper, you can not only drink the book but you can use it as a filter.

⟶ _____ ➡ _____

08 위 글의 밑줄 친 ⓐ의 우리말에 맞게 주어진 어휘를 알맞게 배열하시오.

> filtered water / can / is / you / this / that / drink / it

➡ _____

09 본문의 내용과 일치하도록 다음 빈칸에 알맞은 단어를 쓰시오.

> Thanks to the Drinkable Book, many children can protect themselves from diseases that come from _____ .

[10~12] 다음 글을 읽고 물음에 답하시오.

The Tree-Book-Tree Project

This is the most amazing book that I have ever seen. After you finish reading this book, plant it and water it. You will see new leaves growing on the book. In some bookstores in my town, you can see a copy of this book ___ⓐ___ new leaves.

The secret is that the book has seeds in each page. It is these tiny seeds that change the book into a tree. This book was made by a small children's book publisher in Argentina. ⓑThough the company does not print this book anymore, this special project makes us think about where books come from.

10 위 글의 빈칸 ⓐ에 produce를 알맞은 형태로 쓰시오.

➡ _____

11 위 글의 밑줄 친 ⓑ를 다음과 같이 바꿔 쓸 때 빈칸에 들어갈 알맞은 말을 두 단어로 쓰시오.

> Though the company prints this book _____ _____

12 What is the secret of the book on which new leaves grow? Answer in English beginning with "It's that ~". (9 words)

➡ _____

Express Yourself C

In making and flying a drone, its weight is important. It is a light drone that
= When you make and fly a drone. 'A light drone has a long battery life.'에서 주어 'A light drone'을 강조하기
has a long battery life. The lighter the drone is, the longer it flies.
위한 'It is … that ~' 강조구문   The+비교급+주어+동사 …, the+비교급+주어+동사 ~: …하면 할수록, 더 ~하다

구문해설) •drone: 드론, (무선 조종되는) 무인 비행 물체 •weight: 무게 •light: 가벼운 •battery
life: 건전지 수명

해석

드론을 만들어 날릴 때, 그것의 무게가 중요하다. 긴 건전지 수명을 가지는 것은 가벼운 드론이다. 드론이 가벼울수록, 더 오래 난다.

Link to the World

This is called Dalhang-ari, a moon jar, because it looks like a full moon. In the
수동태   ~처럼 생기다
past, it was impossible to make this large round jar by hand. The larger a jar
가주어   진주어   the 비교급
was, the more difficult it was to make. It was a potter that solved this problem.
the 비교급   It ~ that 강조구문
A smart potter put two large bowls together to make this moon jar.
                                                        부사적 용법(목적)

구문해설) •by hand: 손으로 •potter: 도공 •put ~ together: 합치다 •bowl: 사발

이것은 보름달처럼 생겨서 달항아리라고 불린다. 과거에는 손으로 이렇게 크고 둥근 항아리를 만드는 게 불가능했다. 항아리가 클수록, 만들기가 더 어려웠다. 이 문제를 해결한 것은 한 도공이었다. 현명한 도공은 두 개의 큰 사발을 합쳐서 이 달항아리를 만들었다.

Learning Diary – Listen & Speak 2

A: Which do you prefer, going camping or going swimming?
선호를 묻는 표현으로 prefer 대신 like better를 사용할 수 있다.
B: I prefer going camping. Actually, I hate going swimming. How about you?
                                              목적어로 사용된 동명사
A: Well, I prefer going swimming.

구문해설) •prefer: 선호하다 •actually: 사실 •hate: 싫어하다

A: 너는 캠핑 가기와 수영하러 가기 중에서 어떤 것을 더 좋아하니?
B: 나는 캠핑 가기를 더 좋아해. 사실, 나는 수영하러 가기를 몹시 싫어해. 너는 어때?
A: 음, 나는 수영하러 가기를 더 좋아해.

Words & Expressions

01 다음 주어진 두 단어의 관계가 같도록 빈칸에 알맞은 단어를 쓰시오.

> disease – illness : furnish – _____

02 다음 문장의 빈칸 (a)와 (b)에 들어갈 단어가 바르게 짝지어진 것은?

> • I'll ask my friend to ___(a)___ the score of the game.
> • The ___(b)___ ants worked together to lift the leaf.

① break down – useful
② find out – tiny
③ stand up for – necessary
④ give away – giant
⑤ get over – tiny

[03~04] 다음 영영풀이에 해당하는 것을 고르시오.

03

> to produce words, numbers, pictures, etc. on paper by using a machine

① bridge   ② hunt
③ publish   ④ production
⑤ print

04

> to pull apart or to pull pieces off

① tear   ② seat
③ reply   ④ pour
⑤ vote

05 다음 대화의 빈칸에 들어갈 말을 〈영영풀이〉를 참고하여 쓰시오.

> A: Can I join your book-making project?
> B: Sure. Which do you prefer, paper books or digital books?
> A: I prefer digital books. Actually, I hate making paper books.
> B: Okay. Let me _____ you to the digital book team.

> 〈영영풀이〉 to tell someone another person's name the first time that they meet

➡ _____

06 다음 밑줄 친 부분의 뜻이 잘못된 것은?

① I looked happy, but I was actually sad. (사실)
② The people are looking at the artwork in the museum. (예술품)
③ Most curtains are made of cloth. (천)
④ I was asked to prepare a report for our next meeting. (준비하다)
⑤ You must register on the Internet to join the club. (설치하다)

Conversation

07 다음 대화의 흐름상 밑줄 친 단어의 쓰임이 어색한 것을 찾아 바르게 고치시오.

> G: (a)Which do you prefer, flying kites (b)and flying drones?
> B: I prefer (c)flying kites.
> G: (d)Why is that?
> B: I (e)hate working with machines.

_____ ➡ _____

08 주어진 문장을 알맞은 대화 순서로 배열한 것은?

(A) I love making something delicious.
(B) I like both, but it is making food art that I prefer.
(C) Which do you prefer, making masks or making food art?
(D) Why is that?

① (B)-(A)-(C)-(D)
② (B)-(D)-(C)-(A)
③ (C)-(B)-(D)-(A)
④ (D)-(A)-(C)-(B)
⑤ (D)-(B)-(A)-(C)

09 다음 짝지어진 대화 중 어색한 것은?

① A: Which do you prefer, raising dogs or raising cats?
   B: I prefer raising dogs. Actually, I hate raising cats.
② A: Which do you prefer, watching sports or playing sports?
   B: I prefer watching sports. Actually, I hate playing sports.
③ A: Which do you prefer, climbing a mountain or going to the beach?
   B: I prefer climbing a mountain. Actually, I love going to the beach most.
④ A: Which do you prefer, riding a bike or riding a skateboard?
   B: I prefer riding a bike. Actually, I hate riding a skateboard.
⑤ A: We went to Bakers' Camp, right?
   B: No. It was Makers' Camp that we went to.

10 다음 대화의 흐름상 빈칸 (A)에 들어갈 말로 알맞은 것은?

B: Why don't we make a bag with old jeans?
G: Great! What kind of bag are we going to make?
B: Which do you prefer, a shoulder bag or a hand bag?
G: I prefer a shoulder bag. Actually, I hate holding things in my hands.
B: Okay. _____ (A)

① Who is going to make a shoulder bag?
② How about making a hand bag?
③ Actually I hate making a shoulder bag.
④ Let's make a shoulder bag together.
⑤ I prefer a hand bag.

11 대화의 제목으로 가장 적절한 것은?

Minji: Seho, the book club day is just one week away.
Seho: Right, Minji. I'm proud that we've collected so many interesting books to give away.
Minji: Now, let's prepare some gifts for visitors. Do you have any good ideas?
Seho: How about making bookmarks?
Minji: Great idea! Let's write cheerful messages on them, too.
Seho: Okay. Which do you prefer, making the bookmarks or writing the messages?
Minji: Actually, I hate writing. I'd like to make the bookmarks.
Seho: No problem. I'll write the cheerful messages.
Minji: I'm sure they will love our bookmarks.

① The Pleasure of Giving Away Gifts
② Preparing for Book Club Day
③ How to Make Bookmarks
④ The Reason Why Minji Hates Writing
⑤ Things That Book Club Does

Grammar

12 다음 중 어법상 어색한 문장을 고르시오.

① The more you have, the more you want.
② The higher I climbed, the colder I felt.
③ It is we that helped the stray dog.
④ It was in their car that Dave ate the hamburger by himself.
⑤ It is Ashley that go jogging every morning.

13 다음 글의 밑줄 친 단어를 알맞은 형태로 바꾸어 빈칸에 쓰시오.

> In making and flying a kite, its tail is important. It is the <u>length</u> of a tail that makes a kite fly <u>well</u>. The (a)_____ the tail is, the (b)_____ it flies.

14 다음 주어진 문장과 같은 뜻의 문장을 고르시오.

> As students are happier, they are more likely to enjoy their studies.

① The happier students are, the more they are likely to enjoy their studies.
② The happier students are, the more likely they are to enjoy their studies.
③ The more students are happy, the more likely they are to enjoy their studies.
④ The more happy students are, the more likely they are to enjoy their studies.
⑤ The happier students are, the likely they are more to enjoy their studies.

15 다음 중 어법상 어색한 문장의 개수로 알맞은 것은?

> a. It was Jack that he broke the vase.
> b. It was to the gym that the teacher went.
> c. It was Jessica that likes Korean dramas.
> d. The more information you provide, the well we can help you.
> e. The more money you make, the more you will buy things.
> f. The harder he practiced, the more beautiful he got to dance.

① 1개 ② 2개 ③ 3개 ④ 4개 ⑤ 5개

16 다음 우리말을 주어진 어휘를 이용하여 영어로 옮기시오.

(1) 그 불에 더 가까이 갈수록, 우리는 더 따뜻함을 느꼈다. (close, get, warm, feel)

➡ _____

_____

(2) 침대 아래에서 내가 찾은 것은 바로 그 잃어버린 열쇠야. (it, lost, found)

➡ _____

_____

(3) 그 아기가 토끼를 그린 곳은 바로 벽이야.
(it, wall, draw, rabbit)

➡ _____

_____

Reading

[17~19] 다음 글을 읽고 물음에 답하시오.

Most people think of books as traditional paper books to read. However, there are many ___ⓐ___ books around you. Let's learn about a few of these books.

Books Travel!
I found this old book on a park bench yesterday. A note on the cover read, "Free Book! Take me home and read me!" Actually, this book had an ID number and was registered on a website. When I ⓑentered the number online, I found out that the book had traveled to many countries and that a number of readers in different countries had read it before me. How was that possible?

17 위 글의 빈칸 ⓐ에 들어갈 알맞은 말을 고르시오.

① usual   ② normal
③ routine   ④ unique
⑤ typical

18 위 글의 밑줄 친 ⓑentered와 같은 의미로 쓰인 것을 고르시오.

① She knocked the door before she entered.
② The idea never entered his head.
③ He entered his name and address in the blanks.
④ Several new companies have now entered the market.
⑤ 1,000 children entered the competition.

19 위 글을 읽고 대답할 수 없는 것을 고르시오.

① Where did the writer find the old book?
② When did the writer find the old book?
③ What was written on a note on the book cover?
④ What was the ID number of the book?
⑤ When the writer entered the ID number online, what did the writer find out?

[20~22] 다음 글을 읽고 물음에 답하시오.

ⓐ
This tiny book is really important to people in my town. It provides both the information and the tools necessary ⓑto make clean drinking water.

It is called the Drinkable Book. You cannot actually drink the book, but you can use it as a filter. Simply tear out a page and pour dirty water on it. As the water goes through the page, it changes into clean drinking water. It is this filtered water that you can drink. ⓒThis is possible because the book is made of special filter paper. This amazing book saves the lives of many children from diseases that come from dirty water.

20 위 글의 빈칸 ⓐ에 들어갈 제목으로 알맞은 것을 고르시오.

① The Tree-Book-Tree Project
② All Drinking Water Must Be Filtered
③ The Drinkable Book
④ The Tools Necessary to Save Children's Lives
⑤ Books Travel!

21 다음 〈보기〉에서 위 글의 밑줄 친 ⓑto make와 to부정사의 용법이 다른 것의 개수를 고르시오.

┌─ 보기 ├─
① His fault is to talk too much.
② I hurried to the station only to miss the train.
③ He was the first man to land on the moon.
④ I make it a rule to take a walk early in the morning.
⑤ He must be a gentleman to behave like that.
└─────────

① 1개   ② 2개   ③ 3개   ④ 4개   ⑤ 5개

22 위 글의 밑줄 친 ⓒThis가 가리키는 내용을 우리말로 쓰시오.

➡ _____
_____
_____

[23~24] 다음 글을 읽고 물음에 답하시오.

The secret is that the book has seeds in each page. It is these tiny seeds that change the book into a tree. This book was made ⓐ____ a small children's book publisher in Argentina. Though the company does not print this book anymore, this special project makes us think about where books come from.

These are just a few of the unique books you can find. What other unique books do you want to make? What special project would you like to do with the books? ⓑThe bigger your imagination is, the more your books will become wonderful.

23 위 글의 빈칸 ⓐ에 들어갈 알맞은 말을 고르시오.

① from   ② for   ③ into
④ by   ⑤ of

24 위 글의 밑줄 친 ⓑ에서 어법상 틀린 부분을 찾아 고치시오.

➡ _____
_____

[25~26] 다음 글을 읽고 물음에 답하시오.

There is a book-sharing project. First, register your book online and get an ID number. Next, leave it in a public place. When the next reader finds your book and reports back to the website, ⓐ여러분은 책이 어디 있는지 확인할 수 있습니다. This way, the whole world can become a big library. The more books we share, the more we learn.

25 위 글의 밑줄 친 ⓐ의 우리말에 맞게 주어진 어휘를 알맞게 배열하시오.

┌─────────────────────┐
│ you, your, where, is, can, check, book │
└─────────────────────┘

➡ _____

26 According to the passage, which is NOT true?

① When you join a book-sharing project, you should register your book online and get an ID number first.
② You should leave your book in a public place.
③ The next reader should report back to the website when he or she finds your book.
④ After the next reader reports back to the website, you can locate your book.
⑤ As we have more big libraries, we share more books.

01 출제율 90%

다음 짝지어진 단어의 관계가 같도록 빈칸에 알맞은 단어를 쓰시오.

> collect – collection : connect – _____

02 출제율 95%

다음 영영풀이에 해당하는 단어는?

> feeling pleased about something that you have done or something that you own

① cheerful   ② proud   ③ actual
④ public   ⑤ necessary

03 출제율 90%

밑줄 친 부분의 표현을 이용하여 〈조건〉에 맞게 빈칸 (A)를 알맞게 채우시오.

> ┤ 조건 ├
> hate를 써서 싫어하는 것을 표현하는 문장을 쓰시오.

> A: Which do you prefer, working with a plan or working without a plan?
> B: I prefer working without a plan. Actually,
> _____(A)_____
> A: You and I prefer the same thing!

➡ _____

[04~05] 다음 대화를 읽고 물음에 답하시오.

> B: Why don't we make a bag with old jeans?
>
> (A) Which do you prefer, a shoulder bag or a hand bag?
>
> (B) I prefer a shoulder bag. Actually, I hate holding things in my hands.
>
> (C) Great! What kind of bag are we going to make?
>
> (D) Okay. Let's make a shoulder bag together.

04 출제율 100%

위 대화의 (A)~(D)를 알맞게 배열하시오.

➡ _____

05 출제율 90%

위 대화를 읽고 다음 질문에 영어로 답하시오.

> Q: What are the speakers going to make?

➡ _____

06 출제율 95%

다음 짝지어진 대화 중 어법상 어색한 것은?

① A: Which do you prefer, baseball or soccer?
  B: I prefer soccer.
② A: Which do you prefer, taking the bus or take the subway?
  B: I prefer taking the subway.
③ A: I prefer digital books. Actually, I hate making paper books.
  B: Okay. Let me introduce you to the digital book team.
④ A: I like both, but it is making food art that I prefer.
  B: Why is that?
⑤ A: Which do you like better, cloth dolls or digital artwork?
  B: I like digital artwork better. Actually, I don't like dolls much.

07 다음 대화의 빈칸에 알맞은 것은?

> B: _____, working with a plan or working without a plan?
> G: I like working with a plan better.
> B: Me, too! You and I prefer the same thing!

① What do you say to
② Do you think of
③ Which do you prefer
④ Would you like
⑤ Are you going to

08 다음 대화에서 주어진 문장이 들어갈 위치로 알맞은 것은?

> G: Why don't we make something with jean pockets? (A)
> B: Great! What shall we make? (B)
> G: Which do you prefer, a pocket board or a cell phone holder? (C)
> B: I prefer a cell phone holder. (D) And I hate spending too much time making things.
> G: Okay. (E) Let's make a cute cell phone holder together.

> It'll be easier to make.

① (A) ② (B) ③ (C) ④ (D) ⑤ (E)

09 다음 대화의 빈칸에 들어갈 말로 알맞은 것은?

> A: Can I join your book-making project?
> B: Sure. Which do you prefer, paper books _____ digital books?
> A: I prefer digital books. Actually, I hate making paper books.
> B: Okay. Let me introduce you to the digital book team.

① or ② of ③ and ④ for ⑤ so

10 다음 대화의 빈칸 (A)에 들어갈 말로 알맞은 것은?

> G: Junha, what are you doing with jeans?
> B: I'm making a pencil case for you.
> G: That's great! What are you going to draw on it?
> B: _____ (A)
> G: I prefer cats. They're lovely.
> B: Okay. Let me draw a lovely cat on this pencil case.
> G: Thanks! I can't wait for it!

① What animal are you drawing?
② Why don't we draw cats?
③ Do you like animals?
④ I think cats are smarter than pandas.
⑤ Which do you prefer, pandas or cats?

11 다음 밑줄 친 ①~⑤에서 어법상 어색한 부분을 모두 찾아 바르게 고치시오.

> This is ①called Dalhang-ari, a moon jar, because it ②looks a full moon. In the past, it was impossible to make this large round jar by hand. ③The large a jar was, the more difficult it was to make. It was a potter ④who solved this problem. A smart potter put two large bowls together ⑤to make this moon jar.

➡ _____

12 다음 중 밑줄 친 it의 쓰임이 나머지 넷과 다른 하나는?

① It is Ken that often fights with his brother.
② It is natural that kids like to run around and play.
③ It was Tom and Jack that we met on our way back home.
④ It was Woojin that broke my favorite mug.
⑤ It is iced Americano that my mom likes most.

13 다음 글에서 밑줄 친 우리말을 괄호 안에 주어진 단어를 활용하여 영어로 옮기시오.

> In 3D printing, the size of an object is important. (1)당신의 인쇄 시간에 영향을 주는 것은 크기이다.(size, influence, the time of your print) The larger the object is, (2)당신은 더 오래 기다려야 할 것이다.(long, will, wait)

(1) _____
(2) _____

[14~15] 다음 글을 읽고 물음에 답하시오.

> ⓐ_____
> This is the most amazing book that I have ever seen. After you finish reading this book, plant it and water it. You will see new leaves growing on the book. In some bookstores in my town, you can see a copy of this book producing new leaves.
> The secret is that the book has seeds in each page. It is these tiny seeds that change the book into a tree. ⓑThis book was made by a small children's book publisher in Argentina. Though the company does not print this book anymore, this special project makes us think about where books come from.

14 위 글의 빈칸 ⓐ에 들어갈 제목으로 알맞은 것을 고르시오.

① How to Recycle the Used Book
② The Tree-Book-Tree Project
③ Where Do Books Come from?
④ Books Travel!
⑤ The Drinkable Book

15 다음 빈칸 (A)와 (B)에 알맞은 단어를 넣어 밑줄 친 ⓑThis book에 대한 소개를 완성하시오.

> This book has (A)_____ in each page, so if you plant the book and water it, these tiny seeds change the book into (B)_____ _____.

[16~18] 다음 글을 읽고 물음에 답하시오.

> **Books Travel!**
> I found ①this old book on a park bench yesterday. A note on the cover ⓐread, "Free Book! Take ②me home and read me!" ⓑActually, this book had an ID number and was registered on a website. When I entered the number online, I found out that ③the book had traveled to many countries and that a number of readers in different countries had read ④it before ⑤me. How was that possible?

16 밑줄 친 ①~⑤ 중에서 가리키는 대상이 나머지 넷과 다른 것은?

①   ②   ③   ④   ⑤

17 위 글의 밑줄 친 ⓐread와 같은 의미로 쓰인 것을 고르시오.

① She's still learning to read.
② The sign read 'No admittance.'
③ A man came to read the gas meter.
④ I can't read your writing.
⑤ She read us a story.

18 위 글의 밑줄 친 ⓑActually와 바꿔 쓸 수 없는 말을 모두 고르시오.

① In reality　② In fact
③ Especially　④ In particular
⑤ As a matter of fact

[19~21] 다음 글을 읽고 물음에 답하시오.

The Drinkable Book

This tiny book is really important to people in my town. It provides both the information and the tools necessary to make clean drinking water.

It is called the Drinkable Book. (①) Simply tear out a page and pour dirty water on it. (②) As the water goes through the page, it changes ___ⓐ___ clean drinking water. (③) It is this filtered water that you can drink. (④) This is possible because the book is made of special filter paper. (⑤) This amazing book saves the lives of many children ___ⓑ___ diseases that come from dirty water.

19 위 글의 빈칸 ⓐ와 ⓑ에 들어갈 전치사가 바르게 짝지어진 것은?

ⓐ　ⓑ　　　ⓐ　ⓑ
① for – from　② into – for
③ into – from　④ for – to
⑤ on – for

20 위 글의 흐름으로 보아, 주어진 문장이 들어가기에 가장 적절한 곳은?

> You cannot actually drink the book, but you can use it as a filter.

① ② ③ ④ ⑤

21 How is it possible to make clean drinking water? Fill in the blanks with the suitable words.

> As the Drinkable Book is made of _____ _____ _____, it is possible to make clean drinking water simply by pouring dirty water on a page torn out from the Drinkable Book.

[22~23] 다음 글을 읽고 물음에 답하시오.

The Tree-Book-Tree Project

This is the most amazing book that I have ever seen. After you finish reading this book, plant it and water it. You will see new leaves growing on the book. In some bookstores in my town, you can see a copy of this book producing new leaves.

The secret is that the book has seeds in each page. It is these tiny seeds that change the book into a tree. ⓐThis book was made by a small children's book publisher in Argentina. Though the company does not print this book anymore, this special project makes us think about where books come from.

22 위 글의 밑줄 친 ⓐ를 능동태로 고치시오.

➡ _____

23 What does the Tree-Book-Tree Project make us think about? Answer in English in a full sentence. (9 words)

➡ _____

01 다음 대화를 읽고 질문에 영어로 답하시오.

> G: Why don't we make something with jean pockets?
>
> B: Great! What shall we make?
>
> G: Which do you prefer, a pocket board or a cell phone holder?
>
> B: I prefer a cell phone holder. It'll be easier to make. And I hate spending too much time making things.
>
> G: Okay. Let's make a cute cell phone holder together.

Q: Why does the boy prefer a cell phone holder? Write two things.

➡ _____

_____

_____

02 다음 대화의 밑줄 친 우리말을 〈조건〉에 맞게 쓰시오.

> B: Which do you prefer, making masks or making food art?
>
> G: I like both, but <u>내가 더 좋아하는 것은 푸드 아트 만들기야.</u>

┌─ 조건 ┐
• 강조구문과 동명사를 이용하시오.
• make / food art / prefer를 이용할 것.
└────────┘

➡ _____

03 다음 대화를 읽고 질문에 영어로 답하시오.

> Minji: Seho, the book club day is just one week away.
>
> Seho: Right, Minji. I'm proud that we've collected so many interesting books to give away.

> Minji: Now, let's prepare some gifts for visitors. Do you have any good ideas?
>
> Seho: How about making bookmarks?
>
> Minji: Great idea! Let's write cheerful messages on them, too.
>
> Seho: Okay. Which do you prefer, making the bookmarks or writing the messages?
>
> Minji: Actually, I hate writing. I'd like to make the bookmarks.
>
> Seho: No problem. I'll write the cheerful messages.
>
> Minji: I'm sure they will love our bookmarks.

Q: What is Seho going to do about making bookmarks?

➡ _____

_____

04 다음 문장에서 어법상 틀린 곳이 있으면 바르게 고치시오.

> (1) This called Dalhang-ari, a moon jar.
> (2) The larger a jar was, the more it was difficult to make.
> (3) It was a potter which solved this problem.

➡ (1) _____
　(2) _____
　(3) _____

05 다음 주어진 〈조건〉에 맞게 문장을 바꾸어 쓰시오.

> (1) <u>I</u> waited for him for a long time.
> (2) As my son grew bigger, I got more worried.

┌─ 조건 ┐
(1) 'It ... that' 강조구문으로 밑줄 친 부분을 강조
(2) 'the+비교급, the+비교급'을 사용
└────────┘

(1) _____
(2) _____

06 괄호 안에 주어진 표현을 사용하여 우리말을 영어로 옮기시오.

> (1) (*the Mona Lisa*)
> A: Leonardo da Vinci painted *The Starry Night*, right?
> B: No, Leonardo da Vinci가 그린 것은 바로 모나리자야.
> (2) (speak, can, well)
> A: English is still difficult for me. What should I do?
> B: The only way is to practice more. The more you practice, 너는 더 잘 말할 수 있어.

(1) _____

_____

(2) _____

[07~09] 다음 글을 읽고 물음에 답하시오.

> ⓐ대부분의 사람은 책을 읽기 위한 전통적인 종이 책으로만 생각합니다. However, there are many unique books around you. Let's learn about a few of ⓑthese books.
>
> **Books Travel!**
> I found this old book on a park bench yesterday. A note on the cover read, "Free Book! Take me home and read me!" Actually, this book had an ID number and was registered on a website. ⓒWhen I entered the number online, I found out that the book had traveled to many countries and that a number of readers in different countries read it before me. How was that possible?

07 위 글의 밑줄 친 ⓐ의 우리말에 맞게 주어진 어휘를 이용하여 11 단어로 영작하시오.

> think of

➡ _____

_____

08 위 글의 밑줄 친 ⓑthese books가 가리키는 것을 본문에서 찾아 쓰시오.

➡ _____

09 위 글의 밑줄 친 ⓒ에서 어법상 틀린 부분을 찾아 고치시오.

_____ ➡ _____

[10~12] 다음 글을 읽고 물음에 답하시오.

> **The Drinkable Book**
> This tiny book is really important to people in my town. It provides both the information and the tools necessary to make clean drinking water. ⓐIt is called the Drinkable Book. You cannot actually drink the book, but you can use it as a filter. Simply tear out a page and pour dirty water on it. As the water goes through the page, it changes into clean drinking water. It is this (A)[filtering / filtered] water that you can drink. This is possible because the book is made (B)[from / of] special filter paper. This (C)[amazing / amazed] book saves the lives of many children from diseases that come from dirty water.

10 위 글의 밑줄 친 ⓐ를 능동태로 고치시오.

➡ _____

11 위 글의 괄호 (A)~(C)에서 문맥이나 어법상 알맞은 낱말을 골라 쓰시오.

➡ (A) _____ (B) _____ (C) _____

12 본문의 내용과 일치하도록 다음 빈칸 (A)~(D)에 알맞은 단어를 쓰시오.

> The Drinkable Book provides (A)_____ _____ necessary to make clean drinking water. When you (B)_____ _____ a page of the book and (C)_____ dirty water on it, the water changes into (D)_____ drinking water.

창의사고력 서술형 문제

01 주어진 〈보기〉의 문장과 같이 선호를 묻는 말과 좋아하는 것과 싫어하는 것을 표현하는 대화를 완성하시오.

> 보기
>
> A: Which do you prefer, working alone or working on a team?
>
> B: I prefer working alone. Actually, I hate working on a team.

> □ working alone   □ working with a plan   □ working with numbers and texts
>
> □ working on a team   □ working without a plan   □ working with pictures and music

02 〈보기〉를 참고하여, 친구에게 옳은 답을 알려주는 문장을 완성하시오.

> 보기
>
> A: Edison invented the telephone, right?
>
> B: No, it was Bell that invented the telephone. (Bell)

(1) A: You can visit the Leaning Tower in Naples, right?

B: No, _____. (in Pisa)

(2) A: The Curies discovered the lasers, right?

B: No, _____. (radium)

(3) A: French is spoken all over the world, right?

B: No, _____. (English)

03 다음 내용을 바탕으로 작품 제작 과정에서 어떤 점이 중요한지 설명하는 글을 쓰시오.

> **MAKING AND FLYING A KITE**
> The length of a tail makes a kite fly well

> In making and flying (A)_____, its tail is important. It is (B)_____ of a tail that makes a kite fly well. The longer the tail is, (C)_____ it flies.

단원별 모의고사

01 다음 단어에 대한 영어 설명이 <u>어색한</u> 것은?

① drinkable: clean and safe to drink
② filter: to remove unwanted substances from liquids or gases
③ actually: used to refer to what is true or real
④ huge: extremely small
⑤ register: to put someone's or something's name on an official list

02 다음 짝지어진 단어의 관계가 같도록 주어진 철자로 시작하는 알맞은 말을 쓰시오.

necessary – unnecessary : like – d_____

03 다음 영영풀이에 해당하는 단어를 고르시오.

a person or company that prints books

① manager   ② bookstore
③ publisher   ④ disease
⑤ filter

04 다음 빈칸에 들어갈 말로 알맞은 것은?

A: Which do you prefer, taking the bus or taking the subway?
B: I prefer taking the subway. Actually, _____.

① taking the bus is not expensive
② I hate taking the bus
③ I prefer taking the bus
④ I don't like taking the subway
⑤ you had better take the bus

05 다음 대화의 밑줄 친 (A)를 'It ~ that ...' 강조구문을 이용하여 쓰시오.

G: Which do you prefer, flying kites or flying drones?
B: I prefer flying kites.
G: Why is that?
B: (A)I hate working with machines.

➡ _____

06 다음 대화의 빈칸에 들어갈 말로 알맞은 것은?

G: Why don't we make something with jean pockets?
B: Great! What shall we make?
G: Which do you prefer, a pocket board or a cell phone holder?
B: I prefer a cell phone holder. _____ And I hate spending too much time making things.
G: Okay. Let's make a cute cell phone holder together.

① The better the cell phone is, the more expensive it will be.
② I hate making a cell phone holder.
③ It'll be easier to make.
④ I hate making food art.
⑤ It'll be a bit expensive to buy.

07 대화의 밑줄 친 우리말에 맞게 주어진 단어를 이용하여 영어로 쓰시오.

> G: Junha, what are you doing with jeans?
> B: I'm making a pencil case for you.
> G: That's great! What are you going to draw on it?
> B: Which do you prefer, pandas or cats?
> G: I prefer cats. They're lovely.
> B: Okay. Let me draw a lovely cat on this pencil case.
> G: Thanks! <u>몹시 기다려진다</u>!(can / wait / it)

➡ _____

[08~09] 다음 대화를 읽고 물음에 답하시오.

> Minji: Seho, the book club day is just one week away.
> Seho: Right, Minji. I'm proud that we've collected so many interesting books to give away.
> Minji: Now, let's prepare some gifts for visitors. (A)_____
> Seho: How about making bookmarks?
> Minji: Great idea! Let's write cheerful messages on them, too.
> Seho: Okay. (B)_____
> Minji: Actually, (C)_____ I'd like to make the bookmarks.
> Seho: No problem. I'll write the cheerful messages.
> Minji: I'm sure they will love our bookmarks.

08 위 대화의 빈칸 (A)~(C)에 들어갈 말을 〈보기〉에서 찾아 쓰시오.

┌─ 보기 ─┐
- I hate writing.
- Do you have any good ideas?
- Which do you prefer, making the bookmarks or writing the messages?
└────────┘

➡ (A) _____
(B) _____
_____
(C) _____

09 What have Minji and Seho done?

➡ _____
_____

10 다음 중 어법상 어색한 문장을 고르시오.

① The more he gets, the more he wants.
② The faster you go up, the faster you go down.
③ The hotter it gets, the more people you will see near the sea.
④ The more foolish you are, the easier you believe what others say.
⑤ The longer he stayed there, the less he liked the people.

11 다음 주어진 문장과 같은 의미의 문장을 바르게 쓴 것을 고르시오.

> As you go farther, it is harder to come back.

① The more you go far, the harder it is to come back.
② The more you go far, the more hard it is to come back.
③ The farther you go, the harder it is to come back.
④ The farther you go, it is the harder to come back.
⑤ The farther you go, the more it is hard to come back.

12 다음 대화의 빈칸에 알맞은 것은?

> A: Did Mr. Kim buy shoes for his wife?
> B: No. It _____ for his wife. (a ring)

① is a ring that he buys
② is a ring what he bought
③ was a ring that he bought
④ was a ring that he buys
⑤ was a ring who he bought

13 다음 문장의 밑줄 친 부분을 강조하는 문장으로 다시 쓰시오.

(1) He became President in 2017.
　➡ It _____ .

(2) Dash chose what to eat at dinner.
　➡ It _____ .

14 다음 글에서 밑줄 친 우리말을 괄호 안의 단어를 활용하여 영어로 옮기시오.

> I'd like to make special cookies. (1)내가 설탕을 덜 사용할수록, 쿠키는 더 건강에 좋아진다.(little sugar, healthy) (2)모든 사람을 건강하게 만들 것은 이 건강에 좋은 쿠키이다.(these, will make, healthy, everyone)

(1) _____
(2) _____
　 _____

[15~17] 다음 글을 읽고 물음에 답하시오.

> **Books Travel!**
>   I found this old book on a park bench yesterday. A note on the cover read, "(A) Free Book! Take me home and read me!" Actually, this book had an ID number and was registered on a website. When I entered the number online, I found out that the book ⓐ _____ to many countries and that a number of readers in different countries had read it before me. How was that possible?

15 위 글의 빈칸 ⓐ에 travel을 알맞은 형태로 쓰시오.

➡ _____

16 위 글의 밑줄 친 (A)Free와 같은 의미로 쓰인 것을 고르시오.

① He held out his free hand and I took it.
② He lives free from care.
③ Admission is free.
④ Is this seat free?
⑤ You are free to come and go as you please.

17 위 글의 주제로 알맞은 것을 고르시오.

① the typical thoughts that many people have about books
② a unique book around you
③ a traditional place to borrow books
④ the cheapest way to buy a book
⑤ a traditional paper book to read

[18~19] 다음 글을 읽고 물음에 답하시오.

There is a book-sharing project. First, register your book online and get an ID number. Next, leave it in a public place. When the next reader finds your book and reports back to the website, you can check where your book is. This way, the whole world can become a big library. ⓐ우리가 더 많은 책을 공유할수록, 우리는 더 많이 배웁니다.

18 위 글의 밑줄 친 ⓐ의 우리말에 맞게 주어진 어휘를 이용하여 9 단어로 영작하시오.

the more

➡ _____

19 다음 중 전 세계가 하나의 큰 도서관이 될 수 있는 절차에 해당하지 않는 것을 고르시오.

① 책을 공유하는 프로젝트에 참가한다.
② 우선, 온라인에 여러분의 책을 등록한다.
③ 여러분의 책의 ID 번호를 얻는다.
④ 등록한 책을 공공장소에 놓아둔다.
⑤ 독자가 여러분의 책을 발견해서 가져가면, 여러분은 그 사실을 웹사이트에 다시 알려준다.

[20~22] 다음 글을 읽고 물음에 답하시오.

The Drinkable Book
①This tiny book is really important to people in my town. ②It provides both the information and the tools necessary to make clean drinking water. ③It is called the Drinkable Book. You cannot actually drink the book, but you can use ④it as a filter. Simply tear out a page and pour dirty water on ⑤it. As the water goes through the page, it changes into clean drinking water. It is this filtered water that you can drink. This is possible because the book is made of special filter paper. This ⓐamaze book saves the lives of many children from diseases that come from dirty water.

20 밑줄 친 ①~⑤ 중에서 가리키는 대상이 나머지 넷과 다른 것은?

①   ②   ③   ④   ⑤

21 위 글의 밑줄 친 ⓐamaze를 알맞은 형으로 고치시오.

➡ _____

22 According to the passage, which is NOT true?

① The Drinkable Book provides both the information and the tools necessary to make clean drinking water.
② You can use the Drinkable Book as a filter.
③ You can make clean drinking water simply by pouring dirty water on a page torn out from the Drinkable Book.
④ You can drink the water filtered through the page torn out from the Drinkable Book.
⑤ The Drinkable Book saves the lives of many children from diseases that come from malnutrition.

Lesson 7

Fact, Opinion or Fake

 의사소통 기능

- 의견 묻기
  How do you feel about this drama?

- 이의 제기하기
  I don't agree (with you).

 언어 형식

- 간접화법
  Garcia-Fuller **said** she was teaching her students how to tell fake news from real news.

- 명사절을 이끄는 접속사 if
  You also have to check **if** they are based on facts.

Key Words

- **actually**[ǽktʃuəli] 부 실제로, 사실
- **appear**[əpíər] 동 ~인 것 같다
- **artwork**[ɑ́:rtwərk] 명 예술 작품
- **attack**[ətǽk] 동 공격하다
- **boring**[bɔ́:riŋ] 형 지루한
- **check**[tʃek] 동 확인하다
- **cheer**[tʃiər] 동 환호하다
- **cleaner**[klí:nər] 명 세제, 청소기
- **clown**[klaun] 명 광대
- **comfortable**[kʌ́mfərtəbl] 형 편안한
- **complete**[kəmplí:t] 형 완전한
- **cool**[ku:l] 형 멋있는, 시원한
- **critically**[krítikəli] 부 비판적으로
- **cute**[kju:t] 형 귀여운
- **evidence**[évədəns] 명 증거
- **false**[fɔ:ls] 형 거짓의, 잘못된
- **friendly**[fréndli] 형 친절한
- **funny**[fʌ́ni] 형 우스운
- **healthy**[hélθi] 형 건강한
- **information**[ìnfərméiʃən] 명 정보
- **light**[lait] 형 가벼운
- **major**[méidʒər] 형 주요한, 주된
- **octopus**[ɑ́ktəpəs] 명 문어
- **offer**[ɔ́:fər] 동 제공하다
- **perfect**[pə́:rfikt] 형 완벽한

- **performance**[pərfɔ́:rməns] 명 공연, 수행
- **prefer**[prifə́:r] 동 선호하다
- **provide**[prəváid] 동 제공하다
- **recently**[rí:sntli] 부 최근에
- **save**[seiv] 동 구하다
- **scared**[skɛərd] 형 겁먹은
- **scary**[skɛ́əri] 형 무서운
- **search**[sə:rtʃ] 동 찾다, 검색하다
- **seem**[si:m] 동 ~인 것 같다
- **sink**[siŋk] 동 가라앉다
- **site**[sait] 명 장소
- **skill**[skil] 명 기술, 실력
- **smart**[smɑ:rt] 형 똑똑한
- **snake**[sneik] 명 뱀
- **source**[sɔ:rs] 명 근원, 출처
- **spread**[spred] 형 퍼진 동 퍼지다
- **support**[səpɔ́:rt] 동 지지하다, 후원하다
- **tooth**[tu:θ] 명 이, 치아
- **totally**[tóutəli] 부 전적으로
- **touching**[tʌ́tʃiŋ] 형 감동적인
- **unclear**[ənklíər] 형 불확실한
- **unique**[ju:ní:k] 형 독특한
- **untrue**[əntrú:] 형 사실이 아닌
- **wear**[wɛər] 동 착용하다

Key Expressions

- **along with** ~와 함께
- **be based on** ~에 바탕을 두다
- **be made out of** ~로부터 만들어지다
- **by the way** 그런데
- **get along well with** ~와 잘 지내다
- **get scared** 겁먹다
- **give up** 포기하다
- **laugh out loud** 큰 소리로 웃다
- **look like** ~처럼 보이다

- **made up** 꾸며낸, 지어낸
- **make sense** 의미가 통하다
- **pass away** 돌아가시다
- **pay attention to** ~에 주의를 기울이다
- **slow down** 속도를 줄이다
- **take a break** 휴식을 취하다
- **tell A from B** A와 B를 구별하다
- **too good to be true** 너무 좋아서 믿어지지 않는
- **turn out** 판명되다

Word Power

※ 서로 비슷한 뜻을 가진 어휘

- **appear** ~인 것 같다 – **seem** ~인 것 같다
- **attack** 공격하다 – **strike** 치다, 공격하다
- **evidence** 증거 – **proof** 증거
- **major** 주요한, 주된 – **principal** 주된
- **recently** 최근에 – **lately** 최근에
- **totally** 전적으로 – **wholly** 전적으로

- **artwork** 예술 작품 – **craft** 공예품
- **check** 확인하다 – **examine** 조사하다
- **false** 거짓의, 잘못된 – **fake** 거짓의
- **offer** 제공하다 – **provide** 제공하다, **supply** 공급하다
- **search** 찾다 – **investigate** 조사하다
- **unclear** 불확실한 – **uncertain** 불확실한

※ 서로 반대의 뜻을 가진 어휘

- **attack** 공격하다 ↔ **defend** 방어하다
- **comfortable** 편안한 ↔ **uncomfortable** 불편한
- **false** 거짓의 ↔ **true** 진실인
- **light** 가벼운 ↔ **heavy** 무거운
- **perfect** 완벽한 ↔ **imperfect** 불완전한
- **untrue** 사실이 아닌 ↔ **true** 사실인

- **boring** 지루한 ↔ **exciting** 흥미로운
- **complete** 완전한 ↔ **incomplete** 불완전한
- **friendly** 친절한 ↔ **unfriendly** 불친절한
- **major** 주요한, 주된 ↔ **minor** 사소한
- **sink** 가라앉다 ↔ **float** 떠오르다

※ 명사 – 형용사

- **comfort** 편안함 – **comfortable** 편안한
- **health** 건강 – **healthy** 건강한

- **evidence** 증거 – **evident** 명백한
- **skill** 기술, 실력 – **skillful** 능숙한

※ 동사 – 명사

- **inform** 알려주다 – **information** 정보

- **perform** 공연하다 – **performance** 공연, 수행

English Dictionary

- **attack** 공격하다
  → to try to hurt or damage someone or something using physical violence
  물리적인 폭력을 사용하여 다치게 하거나 손상을 주려고 하다

- **clown** 광대
  → a performer in a circus who wears funny clothes and bright make-up, and does silly things in order to make people laugh
  서커스에서 우스운 옷을 입고 밝은 화장을 하고 사람들을 웃게 하려고 어리석은 행동을 하는 공연자

- **critically** 비판적으로
  → in a way that expresses disapproval
  불찬성을 표현하는 방식으로

- **evidence** 증거
  → anything that causes you to believe that something is true
  당신이 어떤 것이 사실이라고 믿도록 만드는 어떤 것

- **false** 거짓의, 잘못된
  → incorrect, untrue, or mistaken
  정확하지 않거나 사실이 아닌, 또는 잘못된

- **lie** 거짓말
  → an untrue statement
  사실이 아닌 진술

- **major** 주된, 주요한
  → very important and serious
  매우 중요하고 진지한

- **octopus** 문어
  → a soft sea creature with eight long arms
  여덟 개의 긴 다리를 가진 연한 바다 생물

- **opinion** 의견
  → what you think or believe about something
  무엇에 관하여 생각하거나 믿고 있는 것

- **sink** 가라앉다
  → to disappear below the surface of the water
  수면 아래로 사라지다

- **spread** 퍼지다
  → to open it out or arrange it over a place or surface
  한 장소나 표면 위에 펼치거나 배열하다

- **support** 지지하다
  → to give assistance, approval, comfort, or encouragement to someone
  어떤 사람에게 도움, 동의, 위로, 격려 등을 주다

- **totally** 전적으로
  → completely, absolutely
  완전하게, 절대적으로

01 다음 문장의 빈칸에 〈영어 설명〉에 맞게 한 단어로 쓰시오.

In my _____, English is the most difficult subject.
<영어 설명> a thought or belief about something or someone

02 다음 빈칸에 공통으로 들어갈 말로 가장 적절한 것은?

- This new trend _____s to be continuing for a while.
- A new vending machine will _____ at a subway station in Tokyo.

① check   ② spread
③ report   ④ appear
⑤ provide

 중요

03 다음 빈칸에 들어갈 말이 알맞게 짝지어진 것은?

(A) My teacher got upset because my homework wasn't _____.
(B) We must find the _____ of the information first.

① false – source
② complete – resource
③ critical – impressed
④ complex – resource
⑤ complete – source

[04~05] 다음 설명에 해당하는 단어를 고르시오.

04

to try to hurt or damage someone or something using physical violence

① save   ② attack
③ support   ④ search
⑤ offer

05

a performer in a circus who wears funny clothes and bright make-up, and does silly things in order to make people

① snake   ② octopus
③ clown   ④ source
⑤ crown

 중요

06 짝지어진 단어의 관계가 나머지 넷과 다른 것은?

① inform – information
② evidence – evident
③ comfort – comfortable
④ skill – skillful
⑤ health – healthy

07 다음 우리말에 맞게 주어진 단어를 이용하여 두 단어로 쓰시오.

그의 이야기는 거짓으로 밝혀졌다. (turn)

➡ His story _____ to be a lie.

08 다음 짝지어진 단어의 관계가 같도록 알맞은 말을 쓰시오.

evidence – proof : fake – _____

중요

01 〈보기〉에서 알맞은 단어를 선택하여 문장의 빈칸을 완성하시오. (필요하면 변형하여 쓰시오.)

┌─ 보기 ┤
critical   scare   spread   sink
└─────────────

(1) The story quickly _____ to everyone.

(2) The workers must think _____ to solve problems.

(3) The little boy is _____ of monsters.

(4) If a boat has a hole in it, the boat will _____ .

02 대화의 빈칸에 〈영영풀이〉에 해당하는 단어를 주어진 철자로 쓰시오.

G: How do you feel about this drama?

B: I think it's very t_____ . The boy gave up his life to save his sister.

〈영영풀이〉 making you feel pity, sympathy, sadness, etc.

➡ _____

중요

03 다음 우리말과 같은 표현이 되도록 문장의 빈칸을 채우시오.

(1) 모든 승객들은 지하철에서 편안한 시간을 가질 권리가 있습니다.

➡ All passengers have a right to have a c_____ time in the subway.

(2) 매일 같은 것을 연습하는 것은 지루한 일입니다.

➡ Practicing the same thing every day is b_____ .

(3) 온실가스 배출은 지구 온난화의 주요한 원인들 중 하나입니다.

➡ Greenhouse gas emission is one of the m_____ causes of global warming.

(4) 신호등이 노란색으로 바뀌는 것을 볼 때는 속도를 낮춰라.

➡ S_____ down when you see the traffic light turn yellow.

04 영영풀이에 해당하는 단어를 〈보기〉에서 찾아 첫 번째 빈칸에 쓰고, 두 번째 빈칸에는 우리말 뜻을 쓰시오.

┌─ 보기 ┤
sink   support   octopus   spread
└─────────────

(1) _____ : to give assistance, approval, comfort, or encouragement to someone: _____

(2) _____ : to open it out or arrange it over a place or surface: _____

(3) _____ : to disappear below the surface of the water: _____

(4) _____ : a soft sea creature with eight long arms: _____

고난이도

05 다음 문장의 빈칸에 들어갈 말을 〈보기〉의 단어를 이용하여 완성하시오.

┌─ 보기 ┤
attention   tell   make up
└─────────────

(1) Students should _____ their teacher.

(2) His parents taught him how to _____ right _____ wrong.

(3) The story about the pink horse was _____ .

Conversation

① 의견 묻기

- **How do you feel about this drama?** 이 드라마에 대해서 어떻게 생각하니?

■ 'How do you feel about ~?'은 '~을[~에 대해] 어떻게 생각해?'라는 의미로 상대방에게 어떤 대상에 대한 의견을 물을 때 사용하는 표현이다. 'What do you think about ~?(~에 대하여 어떻게 생각하니?)', 'What's your opinion about ~?(~에 대한 의견이 무엇이니?)', 'What do you say about ~?(~에 대하여 어떻게 생각하십니까?)'와 같은 표현을 사용하여 의견을 물어볼 수 있다. 'How do you like ~?'는 '~가 마음에 드니?'의 의미로 상대방이 만족하는지 등의 의견을 물어보는 표현이다.

■ 경험한 일을 바탕으로 하여 상대방의 의견이나 감정을 물을 때는 'Do you find it ~?(너는 ~하다고 생각하니?)'를 사용할 수 있다. 주로 가목적어 it을 사용하여 'find it+형용사+to부정사'의 형태가 되고 목적격보어로 쓰이는 다양한 형용사 다음에 진목적어인 to부정사가 따라온다.

■ 상대방의 의견을 물어보는 표현으로 'Would you find it easy/hard to ~ if you had the chance to ~?(만약 네가 ~할 기회가 있다면 너는 ~하는 것이 쉽다고/어렵다고 생각하니?)'를 사용할 수 있고, think를 사용하여 'Do you think it is easy/hard to ~?(너는 ~하는 것이 쉽다고/어렵다고 생각하니?)'와 같이 물어볼 수 있다.

상대방의 의견 묻기

- How do you feel about ~? ~에 대하여 어떻게 생각하니?
- What do you think about ~? ~에 대하여 어떻게 생각하니?
- What's your opinion about ~? ~에 대한 의견이 무엇이니?
- What do you say about ~? ~에 대하여 어떻게 생각하십니까?
- Do you find it ~? 너는 ~하다고 생각하니?
- Do you think it is easy/hard to ~? 너는 ~을 쉽다고/어렵다고 생각하니?

핵심 Check

1. 다음 우리말을 주어진 단어를 포함하여 영작하시오.

   G: Look at those shoes the girl is wearing. I think they're great. <u>그것에 대하여 어떻게 생각하니?</u> (feel, how)

   B: I think they look light and comfortable.

   G: Right. I want to buy them for the school field trip.

   ➡ _____

② 이의 제기하기

• I don't agree (with you). 저는 동의하지 않아요.

- 'I don't agree with you.(나는 동의하지 않아요.)'는 상대와 의견이 달라서 동의하지 않고 상대의 의견에 이의를 제기하는 말이다. 'I have a different idea.(나는 생각이 달라.)', 'I don't think so.(나는 그렇게 생각하지 않아.)', 'I don't believe so.(그렇게 생각하지 않습니다.)', 'I disagree with you.(저는 반대합니다.)'도 이의를 제기하는 표현이다.

- 상대방의 말이나 의견에 동의할 때는 'You can say that again.'이라고 한다. 'I agree with you.'라고 할 수도 있다. 상대방에게 자신의 말에 대하여 동의를 구할 때 간단하게는 부가의문문을 덧붙여서 나타낼 수 있고, 구체적으로 'Don't you agree (with me)?'라고 하거나 '제 생각에 동의하지 않으세요?'의 의미로 'Don't you think so?'라고 할 수도 있다.

- 상대방의 표현에 동의할 때는 '나도 그래.'의 의미로 'Me, too.' 또는 'So+동사+주어.'의 형태를 쓴다. 이때 사용하는 동사는 be동사, do, does, did를 포함하는 조동사들이다. 부정문에 이어지는 경우에는 so 대신 neither를 사용하여 'Neither+동사+주어.'라고 하거나 'Me neither.'라고 할 수 있다.

이의 제기하기

- I don't agree with you. 나는 동의하지 않아.
- I don't think so. 나는 그렇게 생각하지 않아.
- I disagree with you. 저는 반대합니다.
- I have a different idea. 나는 생각이 달라.
- I don't believe so. 저는 그렇게 생각하지 않습니다.

동의하기

- You can say that again. 네 말이 맞아.
- So am/do I. 나도 마찬가지야.
- Me, neither. 나도 그래. (부정의 대답)
- I agree with you. 네 말에 동의해
- Me, too. 나도 그래. (긍정의 대답)

핵심 Check

2. 다음 대화의 내용으로 보아, 밑줄 친 말 대신 쓰기에 <u>어색한</u> 것은?

G: I like the coat the boy is wearing. I think it's warm and light.

B: Well, <u>I don't agree with you.</u> Actually, I bought one last week. It's not so warm, and it's much heavier than it looks.

G: Really? I don't believe it.

① I don't think so.
② I have a different idea.
③ You can say that again.
④ I don't believe so.
⑤ I disagree with you.

Step UP - Real-life Scene

Alex: Big Mouth's show is really cool. ❶How do you feel about it?

Somi: Well, ❷I don't think it's that great.

Alex: Come on. I love Mr. Big Mouth. He always ❸makes me laugh out loud.

Somi: He's funny, but ❹don't believe everything he says.

Alex: All right. Oh, look at his photo of an octopus. ❺He said it lives in a tree.

Somi: It doesn't make sense.

Alex: He took the photo when it was climbing the tree. I don't think he's lying. It's a great photo.

Somi: ❻I don't agree with you. It's a fake photo. An octopus can't live out of the sea.

Alex: Big Mouth 쇼는 정말 굉장해. 너는 어떻게 생각하니?

소미: 글쎄, 나는 그렇게 대단한 것 같지 않아.

Alex: 왜 그래. 나는 Big Mouth 씨를 진짜 좋아해. 그는 언제나 나를 큰 소리로 웃게 해 줘.

소미: 웃기긴 하지만, 그가 하는 모든 말을 믿지는 마.

Alex: 알았어. 오, 그가 찍은 문어 사진을 봐. 그가 말하기를 그건 나무에 산대.

소미: 말도 안 돼.

Alex: 그는 문어가 나무에 기어 올라갈 때 사진을 찍었대. 그가 거짓말하고 있는 것 같지는 않아. 대단한 사진이야.

소미: 나는 네 말에 동의하지 않아. 그건 가짜 사진이야. 문어는 바다 밖에서는 살 수 없대.

❶ 'How do you feel about ~?(~에 대해 어떻게 생각하니?)'의 뜻으로 상대방의 의견이나 느낌을 묻는 표현이다.
❷ 'I don't think (that)+주어+동사 ~.'는 '~하지 않다고 생각해.'라는 의미로 목적어를 이끄는 접속사 'that'이 생략되어 있다.
❸ 'make'는 사역동사로 'make+목적어(me)+목적격보어(동사원형: laugh)' 형태를 가진다. '~가 …하도록 하게 하다[시키다]'로 해석한다. 'out loud'는 '큰 소리로'의 뜻으로 'aloud'로 바꾸어 사용할 수 있다.
❹ '~하지 마'라는 의미로 명령문을 부정할 때 'Don't'나 'Never'를 사용한다. 'everything'과 'he says' 사이에는 목적격 관계대명사 'that'이 생략되어 있다.
❺ 동사 'said' 뒤에는 목적어를 이끄는 접속사 'that'이 생략되어 있다.
❻ 상대방의 말에 동의하지 않을 때 사용하는 표현으로 'I don't think so.'로 바꾸어 표현할 수 있다.

Check(√) True or False

(1) Alex thinks that Mr. Big Mouth's photo is real.   T ☐ F ☐

(2) Alex said the octopus in the photo lives in a tree.   T ☐ F ☐

Start Off - Listen & Talk A 1

G: ❶Look at those shoes the girl is wearing. I think they're great. How do you feel about them?

B: I think they ❷look light and comfortable.

G: Right. I ❸want to buy them for the school field trip.

G: 저 여자애가 신고 있는 신발 좀 봐. 멋있는 것 같아. 너는 저 신발을 어떻게 생각해?

B: 가볍고 편안해 보여.

G: 맞아. 난 학교 체험 학습 때 신으려고 저걸 사고 싶어.

❶ 'the girl is wearing'은 선행사 'those shoes'를 수식하는 목적격 관계대명사절로 관계대명사 'that' 또는 'which'가 생략되어 있다.
❷ 'look+형용사' 형태로 '~하게 보인다'라는 의미이다.
❸ 'want'는 목적어로 to부정사를 취하는 동사이다.

Check(√) True or False

(3) The girl thinks those shoes the girl is wearing are great.   T ☐ F ☐

(4) The boy agrees with the girl.   T ☐ F ☐

Get Ready 2

(1) **G:** ❶There's no monkey like this in the world. Its nose is too big. I think it's fake.
B: I don't agree. I saw that kind of monkey on TV. It's real.

(2) **G:** This animal has a long nose and two long, sharp teeth. ❷What do you think of it? Is it real?
B: Well, let's search the Internet and check it together.
G: That's a good idea.

(3) **B:** What do you think of this animal?
G: It doesn't have legs, but it doesn't ❸look like a snake. It's very strange.
B: I think so, too.

(4) **B:** This monkey is very small. Is it real?
G: I don't know. Let's visit some animal fact sites and check it together.
B: That's a good idea.

❶ 'There is+단수명사'로 '~가 있다'는 의미이고, 'no'는 'not ~ any'의 의미로 명사를 부정할 때 사용한다.
❷ What do you think of[about] ~?: '~에 대해 어떻게 생각하니?'의 의미로 상대방의 생각을 물어볼 때 사용한다.
❸ 'look like+명사'는 '~처럼 보인다'라는 의미이다.

Start Off - Listen & Talk A 2

G: I like the coat the boy is wearing. I think it's warm and light.
B: Well, I don't agree with you. ❷Actually, I bought one last week. It's not so warm, and it's ❸much heavier than it looks.
G: Really? I don't believe it.

❶ 'the coat'와 'the boy' 사이에 목적격 관계대명사 'that/which'가 생략되어 있다.
❷ 'Actually'는 앞 문장의 말에 대해 강조하여 말할 때 사용하는 부사로 '사실'의 뜻이다.
❸ 'much'는 비교급을 강조하는 말로 '훨씬, 한층'의 의미로 해석한다. 'much' 대신에 'still, even, far, a lot'을 사용할 수 있다.

Start Off - Listen & Talk B

G: ❶How do you feel about this drama?
B: I think it's very touching. The boy gave up his life to save his sister. It's the best drama of this year.
G: I don't agree. It's not a good drama.
B: Come on. ❷Why do you think so?
G: It doesn't ❸seem real. And it's ❹a little boring.

❶ How do you feel about ~?: '~에 대해 어떻게 생각하니?'의 뜻으로 상대방의 의견이나 느낌을 묻는 표현이다.
❷ '왜 그렇게 생각하니?'의 의미로 'What makes you think so?'와 같은 표현이다.
❸ 'seem+형용사' 형태로 '~하게 보이다'로 해석한다.
❹ 'a little'은 부사구로 형용사 'boring'을 수식하고 '약간, 조금'의 뜻이다.

Start Off - Speak Up

A: How do you feel about this ad?
B: I think it's great. ❶It shows the phone is strong.
A: I don't agree. We should not believe every ad.

❶ 동사 'shows' 뒤에는 목적절을 이끄는 접속사 'that'이 생략되어 있다.

Start Off - Express Yourself A

1. **G:** How do you feel about these animals?
B: They are very cute, but ❶I think cats don't get along well with dogs.
G: I don't agree. And these two are good friends. They are enjoying the trip together.

2. **G:** How do you feel about this kid here?
B: I think she is very pretty. ❷By the way, why did she cut her hair?
G: Can you guess?
B: Well, girls these days prefer short hair.
G: I don't agree with that. Most girls like long hair better than short hair. And this kid here is not a girl. In fact, he is a boy.
B: Really?
G: Yes. He grew his hair ❸to help sick children.

3. **G:** How do you feel about the teddy bears?
B: They are cute. Is there ❹anything special about them?
G: They were made out of a police officer's uniform.
B: Oh, I see.
G: This police officer made them for the kids. Their dad was a police officer, and he ❺passed away recently.
B: That's very touching.

❶ 동사 'think' 뒤에는 목적절을 이끄는 접속사 'that'이 생략되어 있다. 'get along with ~'는 '~와 사이좋게 지내다, 잘 지내다'라는 뜻이다.
❷ 'By the way'는 대화나 글의 화제를 전환할 때 사용하는 표현으로 '그런데'의 의미이다.
❸ 'to help'는 부정사의 부사적 용법의 '목적'으로 '~하기 위해'의 의미. 'so as to'나 'in order to'로 바꾸어 쓸 수 있다.
❹ 부정대명사 'anything'은 형용사가 뒤에서 수식을 한다. '-thing, -one, -body'로 끝나는 부정대명사는 형용사가 반드시 뒤에서 수식을 해야 한다.
❺ 'pass away'는 '돌아가시다'라는 의미이다.

다음 우리말과 일치하도록 빈칸에 알맞은 말을 쓰시오.

Get Ready 2

(1) **G:** There's no monkey _____ this in the world. Its nose is too big. _____ _____ it's _____.

B: I don't _____. I saw that _____ of monkey on TV. It's _____.

(2) **G:** This animal has a long nose and two long, _____ _____. _____ _____ _____ _____ _____ it? Is it _____?

B: Well, let's _____ the Internet and _____ it together.

G: That's a good idea.

(3) **B:** _____ do you think of this animal?

G: It doesn't have legs, but it doesn't _____ _____ a snake. It's very _____.

B: I think so, _____.

(4) **B:** _____ monkey is very small. Is it _____?

G: I don't know. _____ visit some animal _____ sites and check it together.

B: That's a good idea.

Start Off - Listen & Talk A

1. **G:** Look at those shoes the girl is wearing. I think they're great. _____ _____ _____ _____ _____ them?

B: I think they look _____ and _____.

G: Right. I want _____ _____ them for the _____ _____.

2. **G:** I like the coat the boy _____ _____. I think it's warm and light.

B: Well, I don't _____ _____ you. _____, I bought one last week. It's not so warm, and it's _____ _____ than it looks.

G: Really? I don't _____ it.

Start Off - Listen & Talk B

G: _____ do you _____ about this drama?

B: I think it's very _____. The boy _____ _____ his life _____ _____ his sister. It's the best drama of this year.

G: I don't agree. It's not a good drama.

B: Come on. _____ do you think so?

G: It doesn't _____ _____. And it's _____ _____ _____.

(1) **G:** 세상에 이런 원숭이는 없어. 코가 너무 크잖아. 나는 그것이 가짜라고 생각해.

B: 나는 동의하지 않아. 저런 종류의 원숭이를 TV에서 본 적이 있어. 그건 진짜야.

(2) **G:** 이 동물은 긴 코와 두 개의 길고 날카로운 이빨을 가지고 있어. 그것을 어떻게 생각해? 진짜일까?

B: 음, 인터넷을 찾아보고 함께 확인해 보자.

G: 좋은 생각이야.

(3) **B:** 이 동물을 어떻게 생각해?

G: 그것은 다리가 없지만 뱀처럼 보이지는 않아. 정말 이상하네.

B: 나도 그렇게 생각해.

(4) **B:** 이 원숭이는 정말 작다. 진짜일까?

G: 모르겠어. 동물 사실 확인 사이트를 방문해서 함께 확인해 보자.

B: 좋은 생각이야.

1. **G:** 저 여자애가 신고 있는 신발 좀 봐. 멋있는 것 같아. 너는 저 신발을 어떻게 생각해?

B: 가볍고 편안해 보여.

G: 맞아. 난 학교 체험 학습 때 신으려고 저걸 사고 싶어.

2. **G:** 저 남자애가 입고 있는 코트가 마음에 들어. 따뜻하고 가벼울 것 같아.

B: 글쎄, 나는 동의하지 않아. 사실 나는 지난주에 저것을 샀어. 그렇게 따뜻하지도 않고 보기보다 훨씬 더 무거워.

G: 정말로? 믿을 수가 없어.

G: 이 드라마를 어떻게 생각하니?

B: 난 아주 감동적이라고 생각해. 소년이 그의 여동생을 구하기 위해 자신의 생명을 포기했잖아. 올해 최고의 드라마야.

G: 난 동의하지 않아. 그건 좋은 드라마가 아니야.

B: 이런. 왜 그렇게 생각해?

G: 현실적으로 보이지 않아. 그리고 약간 지루해.

Start Off - Speak Up

A: _____ do you feel _____ this _____?
B: I think it's great. It _____ the phone is strong.
A: I don't agree. We _____ _____ believe every ad.

Step Up - Real-life Scene

Alex: Big Mouth's show is really _____. _____ _____
_____ _____ it?
Somi: Well, I don't think it's _____ great.
Alex: Come on. I love Mr. Big Mouth. He always _____ me
_____ out _____.
Somi: He's funny, but don't believe everything he says.
Alex: All right. Oh, look at his photo of an _____. He said it lives
in a tree.
Somi: It doesn't _____ _____.
Alex: He took the photo _____ it was _____ the tree. I don't
think he's _____. It's a great photo.
Somi: I don't _____ _____ you. It's a _____ photo. An octopus
can't live _____ _____ the sea.

Express Yourself A

1. G: _____ do you feel _____ these animals?
   B: They are very cute, but I think cats don't _____ _____ well
   _____ dogs.
   G: I don't agree. And _____ _____ are good friends. They
   are _____ the trip _____.
2. G: How do you feel about this kid here?
   B: I think she is very pretty. _____ _____ _____, why did
   she cut her hair?
   G: Can you _____?
   B: Well, girls these days _____ short hair.
   G: I don't agree _____ that. Most girls like long hair _____
   _____ short hair. And this kid here is not a girl. _____
   _____, he is a boy.
   B: Really?
   G: Yes. He grew his hair _____ _____ sick children.
3. G: How do you _____ _____ the teddy bears?
   B: They are cute. Is there _____ _____ about them?
   G: They _____ _____ out of a police officer's _____.
   B: Oh, I see.
   G: This police officer made them for the kids. Their dad was a
   police officer, and he _____ _____ recently.
   B: That's very _____.

해석

A: 이 광고를 어떻게 생각하니?
B: 굉장하다고 생각해. 그건 그 전화기가 튼튼하다는 것을 보여주고 있어.
A: 나는 동의하지 않아. 우리는 모든 광고를 믿어서는 안 돼.

Alex: Big Mouth 쇼는 정말 굉장해. 너는 어떻게 생각하니?
소미: 글쎄, 나는 그렇게 대단한 것 같지 않아.
Alex: 왜 그래. 나는 Big Mouth 씨를 진짜 좋아해. 그는 언제나 나를 큰 소리로 웃게 해 줘.
소미: 웃기긴 하지만, 그가 하는 모든 말을 믿지는 마.
Alex: 알았어. 오, 그가 찍은 문어 사진을 봐. 그가 말하기를 그건 나무에 산대.
소미: 말도 안 돼.
Alex: 그는 문어가 나무에 기어 올라갈 때 사진을 찍었대. 그가 거짓말하고 있는 것 같지는 않아. 대단한 사진이야.
소미: 나는 네 말에 동의하지 않아. 그건 가짜 사진이야. 문어는 바다 밖에서는 살 수 없다고.

1. G: 이 동물들을 어떻게 생각해?
   B: 아주 귀엽지만, 고양이는 개와 잘 어울리지 못한다고 생각해.
   G: 나는 동의하지 않아. 그리고 이 둘은 좋은 친구야. 그들은 함께 즐겁게 여행하고 있어.
2. G: 여기 이 아이를 어떻게 생각해?
   B: 매우 예쁘다고 생각해. 그런데 그녀는 왜 머리카락을 잘랐니?
   G: 짐작할 수 있어?
   B: 음, 요새 여자아이들은 짧은 머리를 더 좋아하더라.
   G: 난 그것에 동의하지 않아. 대부분의 여자아이는 짧은 머리보다 긴 머리를 좋아해. 그리고 여기 이 아이는 여자아이가 아니야. 사실, 이 아이는 남자아이야.
   B: 정말이니?
   G: 응. 그는 아픈 아이들을 돕기 위해 머리를 길렀어.
3. G: 곰 인형들을 어떻게 생각해?
   B: 귀여워. 뭔가 특별한 점이 있니?
   G: 그것들은 한 경찰관의 제복으로 만들어졌어.
   B: 아, 그렇구나.
   G: 이 경찰이 아이들을 위해 그것들을 만들어 줬어. 그들의 아빠는 경찰관이었고, 최근에 세상을 떠나셨어.
   B: 아주 감동적이야.

01 우리말에 맞도록 주어진 단어를 활용하여 빈칸을 채우시오.

> 이 동물을 어떻게 생각해? (think)

➡ _____ do you _____ _____ this animal?

02 다음 대화의 빈칸에 들어갈 말로 <u>어색한</u> 것은?

> A: _____ classical music?
> B: I love it. It makes me calm down and feel happy.

① How do you feel about
② What do you think about
③ What do you say about
④ What do you know about
⑤ What's your opinion about

03 다음 대화의 빈칸에 들어갈 말로 알맞지 <u>않은</u> 것은?

> A: What do you think of listening to music while studying math?
> B: I think it's very helpful.
> A: _____

① I agree with you.
② I don't think so.
③ I've never done that.
④ I couldn't agree more.
⑤ I can't agree with you more.

04 다음 대화의 밑줄 친 말의 의도로 알맞은 것은?

> G: I like the coat the boy is wearing. I think it's warm and light.
> B: <u>Well, I don't agree with you.</u> Actually, I bought one last week. It's not so warm, and it's much heavier than it looks.

① 관심 표현하기　　　　② 이의 제기하기
③ 동의하기　　　　　　④ 의견 표현하기
⑤ 의도 표현하기

[01~02] 다음 대화를 읽고 물음에 답하시오.

G: How do you feel about this drama?
B: I think it's very (a)(touch). The boy gave up his life to save his sister. It's the best drama of this year.
G: _____(A)_____ It's not a good drama.
B: Come on. Why do you think so?
G: It doesn't seem real. And it's a little (b)(bore).

01 위 대화의 빈칸 (A)에 들어갈 말로 알맞은 것은?

① I couldn't agree more.
② I think so, too.
③ I can't agree with you more.
④ I don't agree.
⑤ You can say that again.

서답형

02 위 대화의 (a)와 (b)의 단어를 알맞은 형태로 고쳐 쓰시오.

(a) _____ (b) _____

[03~04] 다음 대화를 읽고 물음에 답하시오.

Alex: Big Mouth's show is really cool. How do you feel about it?
Somi: Well, I don't think it's that great.
Alex: Come on. I love Mr. Big Mouth. He always makes me laugh out loud.
Somi: He's funny, but don't believe everything he says.
Alex: All right. Oh, look at his photo of (a)an octopus. He said (b)it lives in a tree.
Somi: (c)It doesn't make sense.
Alex: He took the photo when (d)it was climbing

the tree. I don't think he's lying. It's a great photo.
Somi: I don't agree with you. It's a fake photo. (e)It can't live out of the sea.

03 위 대화를 읽고 답할 수 <u>없는</u> 질문은?

① What are they talking about?
② What are they watching now?
③ Why does Alex like Mr. Big Mouth?
④ Does Somi agree with Alex about the photo?
⑤ Does Alex know a lot about an octopus?

04 위 대화의 (a)~(e) 중 가리키는 대상이 <u>다른</u> 하나는?

① (a)   ② (b)   ③ (c)   ④ (d)   ⑤ (e)

[05~06] 다음 대화를 읽고 물음에 답하시오.

G: I like the coat the boy is wearing. I think it's warm and light.
B: Well, I don't agree with you. ___(A)___, I bought one last week. It's not so warm, and it's ___(B)___ heavier than it looks.
G: Really? I don't believe it.

05 위 대화의 빈칸 (A)에 들어갈 말로 알맞은 것은?

① Therefore   ② For example
③ Actually   ④ However
⑤ On the other hand

06 위 대화의 흐름상 (B)에 들어갈 말로 알맞지 <u>않은</u> 것은?

① much   ② very
③ even   ④ still
⑤ a lot

07 다음 대화의 빈칸에 들어갈 단어를 주어진 영영풀이를 보고 3 단어로 쓰시오.

> G: How do you feel about these animals?
> B: They are very cute, but I think cats don't _____ _____ well _____ dogs.
> G: I don't agree. And these two are good friends. They are enjoying the trip together.

> <영영풀이> If two or more people get along, they have a friendly relationship.

➡ _____

[08~09] 다음 대화를 읽고 물음에 답하시오.

> G: (A)How do you feel about this kid here?
> B: I think she is very pretty. By the way, why did she cut her hair?
> G: Can you guess?
> B: Well, girls these days prefer short hair.
> G: I don't agree with that. Most girls like long hair better than short hair. And this kid here is not a girl. In fact, he is a boy.
> B: Really?
> G: Yes. He grew his hair to help sick children.

08 위 대화의 밑줄 친 (A)와 바꾸어 쓸 수 있는 말은?

① What do you know about this kid here?
② Have you ever met this kid here?
③ Why do you think so about this kid here?
④ What did you say to this kid here?
⑤ What's your opinion about this kid here?

09 위 대화를 읽고 Fact에 해당하는 문장을 고르시오.

① Girls these days prefer short hair.
② This kid is very pretty.
③ Every girl likes long hair better than short hair.
④ This kid grew his hair to help sick children.
⑤ This kid here is a girl.

[10~11] 다음 대화를 읽고 물음에 답하시오.

> (1) G: This animal has a long nose and two long, sharp teeth. _____(A)_____ it? Is it _____(a)_____?
> B: Well, let's search the Internet and check it together.
> G: That's a good idea.
> (2) B: _____(A)_____ this animal?
> G: It doesn't have legs, but it doesn't look like a snake. It's very _____(b)_____.
> B: I think so, too.

10 위 대화의 빈칸 (A)에 공통으로 들어갈 말은?

① What do you think of
② Have you ever heard of
③ How did you like
④ How about seeing
⑤ Why did you feel so about

11 위 대화의 흐름상 빈칸 (a)와 (b)에 들어갈 말로 알맞은 것은?

① fake – real ② interesting – real
③ real – strange ④ real – boring
⑤ fake – disappointing

[01~02] 다음 대화를 읽고 물음에 답하시오.

Alex: (A)Big Mouth's show is really cool.
_____(A)_____

Somi: Well, I don't think it's that great.

Alex: Come on. I love Mr. Big Mouth. He always makes me laugh out loud.

Somi: He's funny, but don't believe everything he says.

Alex: All right. Oh, look at his photo of an octopus. He said it lives in a tree.

Somi: It doesn't make sense.

Alex: He took the photo when it was climbing the tree. I don't think he's lying. It's a great photo.

Somi: _____(B)_____ It's a fake photo. An octopus can't live out of the sea.

01 위 대화의 빈칸 (A)와 (B)에 들어갈 말을 〈조건〉에 맞게 영어로 쓰시오.

┤ 조건 ├
(A) • Big Mouth's show에 대한 의견을 묻는 표현을 사용할 것.
    • 'feel'과 'it'을 사용할 것.
(B) • 'agree'를 이용하여 상대방의 의견에 동의하지 않는 표현을 사용할 것. (5 words)

(A) _____
(B) _____

02 위 대화를 읽고 다음 물음에 영어로 답하시오. (Because를 사용할 것.)

Q: Why does Alex like Mr. Big Mouth?

➡ _____

03 다음 대화의 빈칸 (A)와 (B)에 아래의 〈조건〉에 맞게 알맞은 표현을 쓰시오.

B: _____(A)_____ these animals?

G: They are very cute, but ____(B)____.

B: I don't agree. And these two are good friends. They are enjoying the trip together.

┤ 조건 ├
(A) 'about', 'think'를 이용하여 상대방의 의견을 묻는 표현을 쓸 것.
(B) '고양이는 개와 잘 어울리지 못한다고 생각해.'라는 의견을 말하는 표현을 쓸 것.

(A) _____
(B) _____

04 대화의 흐름상 빈칸 (A)에 들어갈 말을 〈조건〉에 맞게 쓰시오.

G: I like the coat the boy is wearing. I think it's warm and light.

B: Well, _____(A)_____. Actually, I bought one last week. It's not so warm, and it's much heavier than it looks.

G: Really? I don't believe it.

┤ 조건 ├
'agree'를 이용할 것 (5 words)

➡ _____

Conversation **129**

Grammar

① 간접화법

> • Garcia-Fuller **said** she was teaching her students how to tell fake news from real news.
>
> Garcia-Fuller는 그녀가 자신의 학생들에게 가짜 뉴스와 진짜 뉴스를 구분하는 방법을 가르치고 있다고 말했다.

■ 직접화법: 다른 사람의 말을 따옴표(" ")로 묶어 그대로 되풀이하여 전달한다.

　직접화법: 따옴표 없이 전하는 이의 입장에서 시제나 인칭을 바꿔 내용을 전달한다.

■ 직접화법의 간접화법으로의 전환

(1) 평서문
- 전달동사를 바꾼다. say → say, say to 사람 → tell 사람
- 전달하는 내용의 콤마(,)와 따옴표(" ")를 없애고 접속사 'that'을 넣는다. (단, 생략 가능)
- 전달동사가 현재이면 시제를 그대로 사용하고 전달동사가 과거라면, 시제의 일치 법칙에 맞게 시제를 바꾼다. (현재 → 과거, 현재완료 또는 과거 → 과거완료)

※ 시제의 일치의 예외: 전할 말이 전하는 시점에서도 여전히 사실일 경우에는 현재 시제를 과거로 바꾸는 것이 필수적인 것은 아니며, 현재 시제를 그대로 사용할 수도 있다. 또한 전할 말이 역사적인 사실일 경우 과거시제를 유지한다.
- 인칭대명사를 전달자의 입장에 맞게 바꾼다.
  ex) 따옴표 속 'I'는 문장의 주어, 따옴표 속 'you'는 듣는 이로 바꾼다.
- 지시대명사와 부사를 전달자의 입장에 맞게 바꾼다.

　　here → there　　this → that　　　now → then　　today → that day
　　tonight → that night　　　　yesterday → the day before, the previous day
　　tomorrow → the next day, the following day

(2) 의문문
- 전달동사를 바꾼다. say 또는 say to → ask
- 전달하는 내용의 콤마(,)와 따옴표(" ")를 없애고 간접의문문으로 전환한다. 물음표(?)는 마침표로 바꾼다.
- 시제, 인칭대명사, 지시대명사, 부사 등을 적절하게 바꾼다.

(3) 명령문
- 전달동사를 어조에 따라 tell, ask, order, advise 등으로 바꾼다.
- 명령문의 동사원형을 긍정은 to부정사로, 부정은 not to 또는 never to부정사로 바꾼다.

핵심 Check

1. 다음 괄호 안에서 알맞은 것을 고르시오.
　(1) Tom (said to / told) her that he wanted to play soccer then.
　(2) My mom said that dinner (is / was) ready.

② 명사절을 이끄는 접속사 if

> • You also have to check **if** they are based on facts.
> 여러분은 그것들이 사실에 기반을 둔 것인지를 확인해 보아야 합니다.

- 형태: if 주어+동사

  의미: ~인지 아닌지

- 명사절을 이끌며 주로 동사의 목적어로 쓰인다.

  • I don't know **if** she works for the company. 나는 그녀가 그 회사에서 일하는지 아닌지 모르겠다.

- 명사절을 이끄는 접속사 'if'는 좀 더 격식을 갖춘 표현인 'whether'로 대체할 수 있다. 단, 'whether'는 주어, 보어, 동사의 목적어, 전치사의 목적어 자리에 모두 쓰일 수 있고, 'if'는 동사의 목적어 자리에 주로 쓰인다.

  • He asked **if** I could speak English. = He asked **whether** I could speak English.
  그는 내가 영어를 말할 수 있는지 물었다.

  • If it will snow or not doesn't matter. (×) → **Whether** it will snow or not doesn't matter. (○)
  눈이 올지 안 올지는 중요하지 않다.

- 'if'는 'or not'을 함께 사용할 때 문장 끝에만 사용 가능하며, 'whether'는 바로 다음이나 문장 끝에 'or not'을 붙여 쓸 수도 있다.

  • Tell me **if** or not she is married. (×)

  • Tell me **if** she is married or not. (○)

  • Tell me **whether** or not she is married. (○)

  • Tell me **whether** she is married or not. (○)

- '만일 ~라면'의 뜻으로 쓰인 'if'는 조건을 나타내는 부사절의 접속사이고 미래시제를 현재시제로 나타내는 반면, 명사절의 'if'는 정해진 시제를 그대로 쓴다.

  • **If** you do well on the next exam, I will buy you the latest smart phone.
  만일 다음 시험을 잘 본다면, 나는 너에게 최신식 스마트폰을 사줄 거야.

  • I'm not sure **if** you will do well on the next exam. 나는 네가 다음 시험을 잘 볼지 확신하지 못한다.

핵심 Check

2. 다음 괄호 안에서 알맞은 것을 고르시오.

(1) (If / Whether) you succeed or fail depends on your effort.

(2) I'm not sure (if / whether) or not he will come.

01 〈보기〉를 참고하여 A의 질문에 대한 B의 응답을 따옴표 안에 주어진 문장을 사용하여 빈칸에 알맞은 형태로 써 넣으시오.

> ┤ 보기 ├
>
> "You have blue eyes like me."
> A: What did the man say to his sister?
> B: He told her that <u>she had blue eyes like him.</u>

(1) "You are very tall."

   A: What did the woman say to her brother?

   B: She told him that _____.

(2) "I'm very happy to meet you."

   A: What did the woman say to her brother?

   B: She told him that _____.

(3) "I'm not crying."

   A: What did the woman say to her brother?

   B: She told him that _____.

(4) "You look great."

   A: What did the man say to his sister?

   B: He told her that _____.

02 다음 문장에서 어법상 어색한 부분을 바르게 고쳐 쓰시오.

(1) I wonder that she will like my present.

   ➡ _____

(2) I don't know if or not he will give me flowers.

   ➡ _____

(3) I want to know if will he throw the ball.

   ➡ _____

(4) The question is if they believe what I said or not.

   ➡ _____

중요

01 다음 중 간접화법으로의 전환이 올바르지 <u>않은</u> 것을 고르시오.

① Sarah said, "I am so happy."
   = Sarah said that she was so happy.
② Suji said, "I will be back in ten minutes."
   = Suji said that she would be back in ten minutes.
③ Minsu said to her, "You look tired today."
   = Minsu told her that she looked tired that day.
④ Jason said to me, "I ate lunch."
   = Jason told me that he has eaten lunch.
⑤ She said to him, "You are very tall."
   = She told him that he was very tall.

서답형

02 다음 괄호 안에 주어진 어구를 바르게 배열하여 문장을 완성하시오.

(if, will, I, he, my ball, wonder, catch).

➡ _____

03 다음 중 밑줄 친 <u>if</u>의 뜻이 나머지 넷과 <u>다른</u> 것은?

① I'm not sure <u>if</u> he is single.
② I don't know <u>if</u> he will come back from his long journey.
③ Mom doesn't remember <u>if</u> she turned off the gas or not.
④ What he has to do is to see <u>if</u> anyone is in the building.
⑤ You can see the animal <u>if</u> it is in a good mood.

중요

04 다음 중 내용상 어색한 문장을 고르시오.

① He told me that he wanted to help me.
② She told me that she had gone on a picnic the day before.
③ He told me that my mom would come.
④ Jaeho said that he would be busy tomorrow.
⑤ Jenny said that she had already read that book.

05 다음 빈칸에 들어갈 말로 적절한 것을 고르시오.

He asked me _____ or not I could help him.

① if   ② what   ③ that
④ whether   ⑤ how

서답형

06 다음 직접화법을 간접화법으로 바꾼 문장에서 어법상 <u>어색</u>한 것을 바르게 고쳐 다시 쓰시오.

(1) I said to Amy, "I want to play with you now."
   ➡ I told Amy that I wanted to play with her now.
   ➡ _____
(2) Mom said to me, "Are you finished with your homework?"
   ➡ Mom told me if I was finished with my homework.
   ➡ _____

07 다음 중 빈칸에 들어갈 단어가 <u>다른</u> 하나를 고르시오.

① _____ you aren't busy, we will watch the TV show.

② Do you know _____ the news is true?

③ I knew _____ it rained yesterday as the road was wet this morning.

④ I can help you _____ you want.

⑤ He wondered _____ he could get the diamond ring.

08 다음 주어진 화법 전환에서 <u>어색한</u> 부분을 바르게 고친 것은?

She said to me, "What do you want to buy?"
→ She ①said to me ②what ③I ④wanted ⑤to buy.

① said to → asked

② what → that

③ I → she

④ wanted → did I want

⑤ to buy → buy

09 빈칸에 들어갈 말을 순서대로 바르게 연결한 것은?

• I wonder _____ you made this reusable tote bag.

• What I want to know is _____ she remembers my name.

① that – if   ② that – whether

③ if – whether   ④ whether – if

⑤ if – that

서답형

10 다음 괄호 안에 주어진 어구를 바르게 배열하여 문장을 완성하시오.

I am (if, do, on, not, I, well, the test, sure)

➡ _____

중요

11 다음 문장과 같은 뜻을 가진 것은?

She said to him, "I want to stay with you forever."

① She said to him that she wanted to stay with me forever.

② She asked him that she wanted to stay with him forever.

③ She told him that she wanted to stay with him forever.

④ She said to him that she wanted to stay with you forever.

⑤ She told him that I wanted to stay with you forever.

서답형

12 다음 두 문장을 접속사를 사용하여 한 문장으로 연결하시오.

• Will they give me a big hand?

• I'm not sure.

➡ _____

_____

서답형

13 주어진 어휘를 이용하여 다음 우리말을 영어로 쓰시오.

나의 언니는 내가 그 시험에서 부정행위를 했는지 안 했는지 의심한다. (if, doubt, cheat, the test)

➡ _____

14 다음 중 어법상 <u>어색한</u> 문장을 고르시오.

① Tom says that he likes Amy.
② My sister told me that she meets Tom by chance the day before.
③ She told me that she had received the gift that day.
④ She advised me to take the medicine regularly.
⑤ My brother asked me where I had put his glasses.

15 빈칸에 들어갈 말을 순서대로 바르게 연결한 것은?

> • _____ he will come or not is another matter.
> • The detective must find out _____ the document is fake or not.

① That – if
② Whether – that
③ If – whether
④ That – whether
⑤ Whether – if

16 다음 빈칸에 들어갈 수 <u>없는</u> 것은?

> The old lady _____ me to keep an eye on her dog.

① asked
② told
③ ordered
④ got
⑤ made

17 다음 우리말을 영어로 바르게 옮긴 것은?

> 그녀가 지금 회의 중인지 내가 확인할게.

① Let me check that she's in the meeting now.
② Let me check if she's in the meeting now.
③ Let me to check if she's in the meeting now.
④ Let me check if or not she's in the meeting now.
⑤ Let me check that she's in the meeting or not now.

18 다음 중 어법상 <u>어색한</u> 문장의 개수로 알맞은 것은?

> a. Mom ordered me to brush my teeth before breakfast.
> b. She told that she was not ready for the race.
> c. The doctor said me that I should take a rest for a few days.
> d. I told my father to not smoke indoors.
> e. They wanted to know if I was satisfied with the result.

① 1개   ② 2개   ③ 3개   ④ 4개   ⑤ 5개

서답형
19 다음 괄호 안에서 알맞은 말을 고르시오.

(1) She (said to / asked) me where I was going.
(2) John (says / tells) that he has a dream of being a musical actor.
(3) My teacher asked me (if / that) I could lend him a pen.
(4) Tom said that he (feels / felt) sick that day.
(5) Our science teacher said that the Earth (is / was) round.

01 명사절의 접속사(if, whether, that)를 사용하여 두 문장을 한 문장으로 쓰시오.

(1) • I wonder.
   • Did the plane arrive on time?
   ➡ _____

(2) • I asked.
   • Was she married?
   ➡ _____

(3) • Is the meeting ready?
   • The question is this.
   ➡ _____

(4) • I think.
   • He is very honest.
   ➡ _____

(5) • Will she attend the audition?
   • It depends on her physical condition.
   ➡ _____
   _____

02 다음 문장을 간접화법으로 바꾸어 쓰시오.

(1) He said to me, "I really appreciate your help."
   ➡ _____

(2) My roommate said to me, "I will be late tonight."
   ➡ _____
   _____

03 다음 빈칸에 알맞은 말을 쓰시오.

(1) He said, "I know the answer."
   ➡ He said that _____ _____ the answer.

(2) Jane said, "_____ _____ to be a teacher."
   ➡ Jane said that she wanted to be a teacher.

(3) He said to me, "I will help you."
   ➡ He told me that _____ _____ _____ _____.

04 잘못된 부분을 바르게 고쳐 문장을 다시 쓰시오.

(1) John said Mary, "I love you."
   ➡ _____

(2) She told him that she is sorry.
   ➡ _____

(3) I told my dad that I would call you later.
   ➡ _____

(4) Mr. Brown said me that he wanted me to study more.
   ➡ _____
   _____

(5) My mom said this dish tasted good.
   ➡ _____

05 다음 두 문장을 간접화법을 이용하여 하나의 문장으로 바꾸어 쓰시오.

> • He said to her.
> • What is the weather like in New York today?

➡ _____

_____

06 다음 문장을 어법에 맞게 고쳐 쓰시오.

(1) I understand if you don't want to talk about it.

➡ _____

(2) Whether you are a boy or a girl make no difference to me.

➡ _____

(3) If you will succeed or not depends on your efforts.

➡ _____

_____

(4) I am not sure that there is life on other planets.

➡ _____

_____

(5) Tell me that you have any plans for your future.

➡ _____

_____

07 〈보기〉에 주어진 문장과 접속사 'if, that, whether'를 각각 한번만 써서 문장의 빈칸을 완성하시오.

> ┤ 보기 ├
> • He had lied to his family.
> • She will have a garage sale in her backyard.
> • We have enough money to buy the new car.

(1) Our question is _____

_____ .

(2) He admitted _____ .

(3) I asked my grandmother _____

_____ .

08 다음 그림 속 내용을 다른 사람에게 전달하는 문장으로 완성하시오.

(1)

> The man asked if the cat _____ and he wondered _____ .

(2)

> The man said the cat _____ and he wondered _____ .

Reading

How to Be a Smart News Reader

In October 2016, stories about scary clowns shook schools across the Washington area, but Danina Garcia-Fuller's students didn't believe them a bit.

"Some people were getting scared because they saw things on social media," said Patricia Visoso, one of Garcia-Fuller's students. "But they never checked up on who was saying this." The stories were actually made by teenagers, not by major newspapers or TV stations. They offered no hard evidence that clowns really were trying to attack students. The story turned out to be a complete lie.

"I think a lot of people just look at one thing and believe it's true," Patricia's classmate Ivy-Brooks said. "It's really important to look at the right sources and to pay attention to what is real and what is fake."

Like Garcia-Fuller's students, many teenagers in America are learning to think critically about information they're seeing in the news and on the Internet. This skill is getting more important these days as stories can spread very fast, and anyone can make a website full of false information.

scary 무서운	
clown 광대	
area 지역, 구역	
a bit 조금, 약간	
scared 무서워하는	
social media 소셜 미디어	
check up on ～을 확인하다	
major 주요한, 중대한	
hard 명백한	
evidence 증거	
attack 공격하다	
turn out ～인 것으로 드러나다, 밝혀지다	
complete 완벽한, 완전한	
lie 거짓말	
source 자료, 출처	
pay attention to ～에 주목하다, 유의하다	
critically 비판적으로	
spread 퍼지다	
false 틀린, 거짓의	

 확인문제

● 다음 문장이 본문의 내용과 일치하면 T, 일치하지 않으면 F를 쓰시오.

1 Danina Garcia-Fuller's students didn't believe stories about scary clowns a bit. ☐

2 The stories about scary clowns were actually made by major newspapers or TV stations. ☐

3 Ivy-Brooks said a lot of people just looked at one thing and believed it was true. ☐

4 These days, anyone can make a website full of true information. ☐

Garcia-Fuller said she was teaching her students how to tell fake
직접화법: Garcia-Fuller said. "I am teaching my students how to tell fake news from real news."
news from real news.

↓ If: '만약 ~한다면'이라는 조건의 의미를 지니는 부사절을 이끎.
"One of the first steps is to slow down. If a story or a photo seems
one of+복수명사: '~ 중 하나'라는 뜻   to slow down: to부정사의 명사적 용법

too good to be true, stop and think: Is there any evidence that supports
너무 좋아서 믿어지지 않는, too+형용사/부사+to부정사: 너무 …해서 ~할 수 없다   주격 관계대명사

what the writer says? And where is this coming from?"
what: 선행사를 포함한 관계대명사, '~한 것'

Garcia-Fuller's students also learn how to tell fact from opinion in
how+to부정사: ~하는 방법   tell A from B: A와 B를 구분하다

the news. "Opinions are good to read," said 15-year-old McKenzie
형용사 'good'을 수식하는 to부정사의 부사적 용법

Campbell, "but you also have to check if they are based on facts."
= whether. if: ~인지 아닌지 (명사절을 이끎)

Garcia-Fuller also said sometimes it can be very hard to be a smart
said 다음에 접속사 'that' 생략   가주어   진주어

news reader. She tests her students with a website that appears to
주격 관계대명사(= which)

provide information on an animal called a tree octopus. The site is full of
appear to+동사원형: ~인 것 같다   'an animal' 뒤에 'which is' 생략

information on this animal, along with a few unclear photos of octopuses
~와 함께

in trees. But like the story of scary clowns, it's totally made up.

The lesson, Garcia-Fuller tells her students, is to "check the
to부정사의 명사적 용법

information you're seeing once more carefully" and to "question
ormation' 다음에 목적격 관계대명사 'that[which]' 생략   to부정사의 명사적 용법

everything, even things that I say."
목적격 관계대명사, 생략가능.

tell ... from ~ …를 ~와 구분하다
slow down (속도, 활동을) 늦추다
support 지지하다, 지원하다
be based on ~에 기초하다, 근거하다
appear 나타나다, ~인 것 같다
octopus 문어
site 사이트, 현장, 위치
unclear 불확실한, 불분명한
totally 완전히
be made up ~로 꾸며지다
question 의심하다, 의문을 갖다

🖇 확인문제

● 다음 문장이 본문의 내용과 일치하면 T, 일치하지 <u>않으면</u> F를 쓰시오.

1 Garcia-Fuller said she was teaching her students how to distinguish fake news from real news. ☐

2 Garcia-Fuller's students also learn how to tell fake news from opinion in the news. ☐

3 Garcia-Fuller said sometimes it can be very hard to be a smart news reader. ☐

4 Unlike the story of scary clowns, the information on a tree octopus is true. ☐

● 우리말을 참고하여 빈칸에 알맞은 말을 쓰시오.

1 How to Be a _____ _____ _____

2 In October 2016, stories about scary clowns _____ across the Washington area, but Danina Garcia-Fuller's students _____ _____ them _____ _____.

3 "Some people were _____ _____ because they saw things on social media," said Patricia Visoso, one of Garcia-Fuller's students.

4 "But they never _____ _____ _____ who was saying this."

5 The stories _____ _____ _____ by teenagers, not by major newspapers or TV stations.

6 They offered _____ _____ _____ that clowns really were trying to attack students.

7 The story _____ _____ _____ _____ a complete lie.

8 "I think a lot of people _____ _____ _____ _____ _____ and believe it's true," Patricia's classmate Ivy-Brooks said.

9 "It's really important _____ _____ _____ _____ _____ _____ and to pay attention to _____ _____ _____ and _____ _____ _____."

10 _____ Garcia-Fuller's students, many teenagers in America are learning _____ _____ _____ about information they're seeing in the news and _____ _____ _____.

11 This skill is _____ _____ _____ these days as stories can spread very fast, and anyone can make a website full of false information.

1 현명한 뉴스 독자가 되는 방법

2 2016년 10월, 무서운 광대들에 관한 이야기가 워싱턴 지역 전역의 학교에 충격을 안겼지만, Danina Garcia-Fuller의 학생들은 조금도 그 이야기들을 믿지 않았다.

3 "몇몇 사람들은 그들이 소셜 미디어에 올라온 것들을 봤기 때문에 무서워했어요."라고 Garcia-Fuller의 학생 중 한 명인 Patricia Visoso가 말했다.

4 "하지만 그들은 이것을 누가 말하고 있는지를 전혀 확인하지 않았어요."

5 그 이야기들은 실제로 주요 신문사나 TV 방송국이 아닌 10대들이 지어냈다.

6 그들은 광대들이 정말로 학생들을 공격하려고 한다는 명백한 증거를 하나도 제공하지 않았다.

7 그 이야기는 결국 완벽한 거짓말인 것으로 드러났다.

8 "많은 사람이 단지 한 가지만을 보고 그것이 사실이라고 믿는 것 같아요.라고 Patricia의 반 친구인 Ivy-Brooks가 말했다.

9 올바른 출처를 살펴보고, 무엇이 진짜이고 무엇이 가짜인지에 주의를 기울이는 것은 정말 중요해요."

10 Garcia-Fuller의 학생들처럼, 많은 미국의 10대들은 뉴스 속 그리고 인터넷상에서 보고 있는 정보에 관해 비판적으로 생각하는 것을 배워 나가고 있다.

11 이 기능은 최근 더 중요해지고 있는데, 이야기들은 아주 빠른 속도로 퍼져 나갈 수 있고 누구나 허위 정보로 가득 찬 웹사이트를 만들어 낼 수 있기 때문이다.

12 Garcia-Fuller said she was teaching her students _____
_____ _____ fake news _____ real news.

13 "_____ _____ _____ _____ _____ _____ is to slow down.

14 If a story or a photo seems _____ _____ _____ _____
_____, stop and think.

15 Is there any evidence that supports _____ _____
_____?

16 And where is this _____ _____?"

17 Garcia-Fuller's students also learn _____ _____ _____
fact _____ opinion in the news.

18 "Opinions are good to read," said 15-year-old McKenzie
Campbell, "but you also have to check _____ they _____
_____ _____ facts."

19 Garcia-Fuller also said sometimes it can be very hard to be
_____ _____ _____ _____.

20 She tests her students with a website that _____ _____
_____information on an animal called a tree octopus.

21 The site is full of information on this animal, _____ _____ a
few unclear photos of octopuses in trees.

22 But _____ the story of scary clowns, it's totally _____
_____.

23 The lesson, Garcia-Fuller tells her students, is to "check the
information you're seeing _____ _____ _____" and to
"_____ _____, even things that I say."

12 Garcia-Fuller는 그녀가 자신의 학생들에게 가짜 뉴스를 진짜 뉴스로부터 구분하는 방법을 가르치고 있다고 말했다.

13 "첫 단계 중 하나는 속도를 늦추는 것(천천히 생각하는 것)입니다.

14 만약 어떤 이야기나 어떤 사진이 진짜라고 하기엔 너무 좋아 보인다면, 멈춰서 생각해 보세요.

15 글쓴이가 말하고 있는 것을 뒷받침하는 어떠한 증거라도 있나요?

16 그리고 이 정보가 어디서 온 것인가요?"

17 Garcia-Fuller의 학생들은 또한 뉴스에서 사실을 의견과 구분하는 방법에 대해서도 배운다.

18 "의견들은 읽을 만한 가치가 있습니다."라고 15살인 McKenzie Campbell이 말했다. "하지만 여러분은 그것들이 사실에 기반을 둔 것인지를 확인해 보아야 합니다."

19 Garcia-Fuller는 또한 때때로 현명한 뉴스 독자가 되는 것이 아주 어려울 수도 있다고 말했다.

20 그녀는 자신의 학생들을 '나무 문어'라는 이름의 동물에 대한 정보를 제공하는 것처럼 보이는 웹사이트로 시험한다.

21 그 사이트는 나무 위에 있는 문어들의 몇몇 불확실한 사진과 함께, 이 동물에 대한 정보로 가득 차 있다.

22 하지만 무서운 광대들의 이야기와 마찬가지로, 그것은 완전히 꾸며진 것이다.

23 Garcia-Fuller가 그녀의 학생들에게 말하는 교훈은 '당신이 보고 있는 정보를 한 번만 더 신중하게 확인해 보라'는 것과 '모든 것, 심지어 내가 말하는 것에도 의문을 가져 보라'는 것이다.

● 우리말을 참고하여 본문을 영작하시오.

1 현명한 뉴스 독자가 되는 방법

➡ _____

2 2016년 10월, 무서운 광대들에 관한 이야기가 워싱턴 지역 전역의 학교에 충격을 안겼지만, Danina Garcia-Fuller의 학생들은 조금도 그 이야기들을 믿지 않았다.

➡ _____

3 "몇몇 사람들은 그들이 소셜 미디어에 올라온 것들을 봤기 때문에 무서워했어요."라고 Garcia-Fuller의 학생 중 한 명인 Patricia Visoso가 말했다.

➡ _____

_____

4 "하지만 그들은 이것을 누가 말하고 있는지를 전혀 확인하지 않았어요."

➡ _____

5 그 이야기들은 실제로 주요 신문사나 TV 방송국이 아닌 10대들이 지어냈다.

➡ _____

6 그들은 광대들이 정말로 학생들을 공격하려고 한다는 명백한 증거를 하나도 제공하지 않았다.

➡ _____

7 그 이야기는 결국 완벽한 거짓말인 것으로 드러났다.

➡ _____

8 "많은 사람이 단지 한 가지만을 보고 그것이 사실이라고 믿는 것 같아요."라고 Patricia의 반 친구인 Ivy-Brooks가 말했다.

➡ _____

9 "올바른 출처를 살펴보고, 무엇이 진짜이고 무엇이 가짜인지에 주의를 기울이는 것은 정말 중요해요."

➡ _____

10 Garcia-Fuller의 학생들처럼, 많은 미국의 10대들은 뉴스 속 그리고 인터넷상에서 보고 있는 정보에 관해 비판적으로 생각하는 것을 배워 나가고 있다.

➡ _____

11 이 기능은 최근 더 중요해지고 있는데, 이야기들은 아주 빠른 속도로 퍼져 나갈 수 있고 누구나 허위 정보로 가득 찬 웹사이트를 만들어 낼 수 있기 때문이다.

➡ _____

_____

12 Garcia-Fuller는 그녀가 자신의 학생들에게 가짜 뉴스를 진짜 뉴스로부터 구분하는 방법을 가르치고 있다고 말했다.

➡ _____

13 "첫 단계 중 하나는 속도를 늦추는 것(천천히 생각하는 것)입니다.

➡ _____

14 만약 어떤 이야기나 어떤 사진이 진짜라고 하기엔 너무 좋아 보인다면, 멈춰서 생각해 보세요.

➡ _____

15 글쓴이가 말하고 있는 것을 뒷받침하는 어떠한 증거라도 있나요?

➡ _____

16 그리고 이 정보가 어디서 온 것인가요?"

➡ _____

17 Garcia-Fuller의 학생들은 또한 뉴스에서 사실을 의견과 구분하는 방법에 대해서도 배운다.

➡ _____

18 "의견들은 읽을 만한 가치가 있습니다,"라고 15살인 McKenzie Campbell이 말했다. "하지만 여러분은 그것들이 사실에 기반을 둔 것인지를 확인해 보아야 합니다."

➡ _____
_____

19 Garcia-Fuller는 또한 때때로 현명한 뉴스 독자가 되는 것이 아주 어려울 수도 있다고 말했다.

➡ _____

20 그녀는 자신의 학생들을 '나무 문어'라는 이름의 동물에 대한 정보를 제공하는 것처럼 보이는 웹사이트로 시험한다.

➡ _____

21 그 사이트는 나무 위에 있는 문어들의 몇몇 불확실한 사진과 함께, 이 동물에 대한 정보로 가득 차 있다.

➡ _____

22 하지만 무서운 광대들의 이야기와 마찬가지로, 그것은 완전히 꾸며진 것이다.

➡ _____

23 Garcia-Fuller가 그녀의 학생들에게 말하는 교훈은 '당신이 보고 있는 정보를 한 번만 더 신중하게 확인해 보라'는 것과 '모든 것, 심지어 내가 말하는 것에도 의문을 가져 보라'는 것이다.

➡ _____
_____

[01~03] 다음 글을 읽고 물음에 답하시오.

In October 2016, stories about scary clowns shook schools across the Washington area, but Danina Garcia-Fuller's students didn't believe them a bit.

"Some people were getting scared because they saw things ___ⓐ___ social media," said Patricia Visoso, one of Garcia-Fuller's students. "But they never checked up ___ⓑ___ who was saying this." The stories were actually made by teenagers, not by major newspapers or TV stations. ⓒThey offered no hard evidence that clowns really were trying to attack students. The story turned out to be a complete lie.

01 위 글의 빈칸 ⓐ와 ⓑ에 들어갈 전치사가 바르게 짝지어진 것은?

ⓐ   ⓑ   ⓐ   ⓑ
① to – on   ② on – in
③ to – in   ④ in – to
⑤ on – on

서답형

02 위 글의 밑줄 친 ⓒThey가 가리키는 것을 본문에서 찾아 쓰시오.

➡ _____

03 **중요**
According to the passage, which is NOT true?

① In October 2016, schools across the Washington area were shocked at stories about scary clowns.

② Danina Garcia-Fuller's students didn't believe the stories about scary clowns a bit.

③ Some people who were getting scared because they saw things on social media never found out who was saying this.

④ The stories about scary clowns were not made by teenagers but by major newspapers or TV stations.

⑤ The story about scary clowns proved to be a complete lie.

[04~06] 다음 글을 읽고 물음에 답하시오.

"I think a lot of people just look at one thing and believe it's true," Patricia's classmate Ivy-Brooks said. "It's really important to look at the right (A)[sources / resources] and to pay attention to what is real and what is fake."

(B)[Alike / Like] Garcia-Fuller's students, many teenagers in America are learning to think ___ⓐ___ about information they're seeing in the news and on the Internet. This skill is getting more important these days as stories can spread very fast, and anyone can make a website full of (C)[false / true] information.

04 위 글의 빈칸 ⓐ에 들어갈 알맞은 말을 고르시오.

① unquestioningly
② conformingly
③ adaptationally
④ critically
⑤ unconditionally

서답형

05 위 글의 괄호 (A)~(C)에서 문맥이나 어법상 알맞은 낱말을 골라 쓰시오.

➡ (A) _____ (B) _____ (C) _____

서답형

06 다음 문장에서 위 글의 내용과 <u>다른</u> 부분을 찾아서 고치시오.

> Patricia's classmate Ivy-Brooks thinks many people look at everything and believe it's true.

_____ ➡ _____

[07~09] 다음 글을 읽고 물음에 답하시오.

Garcia-Fuller also said sometimes it can be very hard to be a smart news reader. ⓐ <u>She tests her students with a website that is appeared to provide information on an animal called a tree octopus.</u> The site is full of information on this animal, ⓑ<u>along with</u> a few unclear photos of octopuses in trees. But like the story of scary clowns, it's totally made up.

The lesson, Garcia-Fuller tells her students, is to "check the information you're seeing once more carefully" and to "question everything, even things that I say."

서답형

07 위 글의 밑줄 친 ⓐ에서 어법상 틀린 부분을 찾아 고치시오.

_____ ➡ _____

서답형

08 위 글의 밑줄 친 ⓑalong with와 바꿔 쓸 수 있는 단어를 쓰시오. (two words)

➡ _____

중요

09 위 글을 읽고 알 수 <u>없는</u> 것을 고르시오.

① According to Garcia-Fuller, sometimes what can be very hard?
② Is it always easy to be a smart news reader?
③ What does the website with which Garcia-Fuller tests her students seem to provide?
④ What is the website with which Garcia-Fuller tests her students full of?
⑤ Who made up the information on the tree octopus?

[10~12] 다음 글을 읽고 물음에 답하시오.

Garcia-Fuller said she was teaching her students how to ⓐ<u>tell</u> fake news from real news.

"One of the first steps is to slow down. If a story or a photo seems too good to be true, stop and think: Is there any evidence ⓑ<u>that</u> supports what the writer says? And where is this coming from?"

Garcia-Fuller's students also learn how to tell fact from opinion in the news. "Opinions are good to read," said 15-year-old McKenzie Campbell, "but you also have to check if they are based on facts."

10 위 글의 밑줄 친 ⓐtell과 바꿔 쓸 수 있는 말을 <u>모두</u> 고르시오.

① know   ② protect
③ talk   ④ distinguish
⑤ keep

중요

11 위 글의 밑줄 친 ⓑthat과 문법적 쓰임이 같은 것을 <u>모두</u> 고르시오.

① She was so tired <u>that</u> she couldn't think properly.
② This is all <u>that</u> matters.
③ The rumor <u>that</u> he married Kate is not true.
④ She said <u>that</u> the story was true.
⑤ Where's the letter <u>that</u> came yesterday?

12 위 글의 주제로 알맞은 것을 고르시오.

① the best way to teach students the importance of real news

② the reason to stop and think when a story seems too good to be true

③ how to tell fake news from real news and fact from opinion in the news

④ how to find out the evidence that supports what the writer says

⑤ the opinions which are based on facts

[13~14] 다음 글을 읽고 물음에 답하시오.

"I think a lot of people just look at one thing and believe it's true," Patricia's classmate Ivy-Brooks said. "It's really important to look at the right sources and to pay attention to what is real and what is fake."

Like Garcia-Fuller's students, many teenagers in America are learning to think critically about information they're seeing in the news and on the Internet. This skill is getting more important these days as stories can spread very fast, and anyone can make a website ⓐfull of false information.

서답형

13 위 글의 밑줄 친 ⓐfull of false information 앞에 생략된 말을 쓰시오.

➡ _____

14 Which question CANNOT be answered after reading the passage?

① According to Ivy-Brooks, what do many people look at when they believe it's true?

② What are many teenagers in America learning?

③ Where are many teenagers in America seeing information?

④ Are many teenagers in America learning to think critically about information?

⑤ Why do people make a website full of false information?

[15~16] 다음 글을 읽고 물음에 답하시오.

Garcia-Fuller said she was teaching her students how to tell fake news from real news.

"One of the first steps is to slow down. If a story or a photo seems too good to be true, stop and think: ⓐ글쓴이가 말하고 있는 것을 뒷받침하는 어떠한 증거라도 있나요? And where is this coming from?"

Garcia-Fuller's students also learn how to tell fact from opinion in the news. "Opinions are good to read," said 15-year-old McKenzie Campbell, "but you also have to check if ⓑ they are based on facts."

서답형

15 위 글의 밑줄 친 ⓐ의 우리말에 맞게 주어진 어휘를 알맞게 배열하시오.

the writer / that / there / supports / any evidence / is / says / what / ?

➡ _____
_____

서답형

16 위 글의 밑줄 친 ⓑthey가 가리키는 것을 본문에서 찾아 쓰시오.

➡ _____

[17~19] 다음 글을 읽고 물음에 답하시오.

In October 2016, stories about scary clowns shook schools across the Washington area, but Danina Garcia-Fuller's students didn't believe them a bit. (①)

"Some people were getting scared because they saw things on social media," said Patricia Visoso, one of Garcia-Fuller's students. (②) The stories were actually made by teenagers, not by major newspapers or TV stations. (③) They offered no hard evidence ⓐthat clowns really were trying to attack students. (④) The story turned out to be a complete lie. (⑤)

17 위 글의 흐름으로 보아, 주어진 문장이 들어가기에 가장 적절한 곳은?

> "But they never checked up on who was saying this."

①　　②　　③　　④　　⑤

18 위 글의 밑줄 친 ⓐthat과 문법적 쓰임이 같은 것을 모두 고르시오.

① There was no hope that she would recover her health.
② She said that the story was true.
③ No one can deny the fact that you are guilty.
④ It's true that we were a little late.
⑤ The trouble is that we are short of money.

19 위 글의 제목으로 알맞은 것을 고르시오.

① Scary Clowns Shook Schools across the Washington Area
② Danina Garcia-Fuller's Smart Students
③ Hey, Be Careful in Believing Things on Social Media!
④ Stories on Social Media Made by Teenagers
⑤ Why Don't You Believe Things on Social Media?

[20~21] 다음 글을 읽고 물음에 답하시오.

Garcia-Fuller also said sometimes it can be very hard to be a smart news reader. She tests her students with a website that appears to provide information on an animal ___ⓐ___ a tree octopus. The site is full of information on this animal, along with a few unclear photos of octopuses in trees. But like the story of scary clowns, it's totally made up.

The ⓑlesson, Garcia-Fuller tells her students, is to "check the information you're seeing once more carefully" and to "question everything, even things that I say."

서답형

20 위 글의 빈칸 ⓐ에 call을 알맞은 형태로 쓰시오.

➡ _____

21 위 글의 밑줄 친 ⓑlesson과 같은 의미로 쓰인 것을 고르시오.

① What did we do last lesson?
② Let her fate be a valuable lesson to you.
③ We studied lesson Five today.
④ She was preparing a lesson plan for a class she was teaching.
⑤ No talking was allowed during the lesson.

[01~04] 다음 글을 읽고 물음에 답하시오.

In October 2016, stories about scary clowns shook schools across the Washington area, but Danina Garcia-Fuller's students didn't believe them a bit.

ⓐ"Some people were getting scared because they saw things on social media," said Patricia Visoso, one of Garcia-Fuller's student. "But they never checked up on who was saying this." ⓑThe stories were actually made by teenagers, not by major newspapers or TV stations. They offered no hard evidence that clowns really were trying to attack students. ⓒThe story turned out to be a complete lie.

01 위 글의 밑줄 친 ⓐ에서 어법상 틀린 부분을 찾아 고치시오.

_____ ➡ _____

02 위 글의 밑줄 친 ⓑ를 다음과 같이 바꿔 쓸 때 빈칸에 들어갈 알맞은 단어를 쓰시오.

> The stories were actually made _____ by major newspapers or TV stations _____ by teenagers.

03 위 글의 밑줄 친 ⓒ를 복문으로 바꾸시오.

➡ _____

04 본문의 내용과 일치하도록 다음 빈칸 (A)와 (B)에 알맞은 단어를 쓰시오.

> Some people were getting scared of the stories about scary clowns because they saw things (A)_____ _____ _____, but they never checked up on who was saying the story, which turned out to be (B)_____ _____.

[05~07] 다음 글을 읽고 물음에 답하시오.

"I think a lot of people just look at one thing and believe it's true," Patricia's classmate Ivy-Brooks said. "It's really important to look at the right sources and to pay attention to what is real and what is fake."

Like Garcia-Fuller's students, many teenagers in America are learning to think critically about information they're seeing in the news and on the Internet. ⓐThis skill is getting more important these days as stories can spread very fast, and anyone can make a website ⓑfull of false information.

05 위 글의 밑줄 친 ⓐThis skill이 가리키는 것을 본문에서 찾아 쓰시오.

➡ _____

_____

06 위 글의 밑줄 친 ⓑfull of와 바꿔 쓸 수 있는 말을 쓰시오.

➡ _____

07 According to Patricia's classmate Ivy-Brooks, what is really important? Answer in English in a full sentence beginning with "It".

➡ _____

_____

_____

[08~11] 다음 글을 읽고 물음에 답하시오.

ⓐGarcia-Fuller said she was teaching her students how to tell fake news from real news.

"One of the first steps (A)[are / is] to slow down. If a story or a photo seems (B)[good enough / too good] to be true, stop and think: Is there any evidence that (C)[denies / supports] what the writer says? And where is this coming from?"

ⓑGarcia-Fuller's students also learn how to tell fact from opinion in the news. "Opinions are good to read," said 15-year-old McKenzie Campbell, "but you also have to check if they are based on facts."

08 위 글의 밑줄 친 ⓐ를 직접화법으로 고칠 때, 빈칸 (A)와 (B)에 들어갈 알맞은 말을 쓰시오.

Garcia-Fuller said, "(A)_____ _____ teaching (B)_____ students how to tell fake news from real news."

09 위 글의 괄호 (A)~(C)에서 문맥이나 어법상 알맞은 낱말을 골라 쓰시오.

➡ (A) _____ (B) _____ (C) _____

10 위 글의 밑줄 친 ⓑ를 다음과 같이 바꿔 쓸 때 빈칸에 들어갈 알맞은 말을 두 단어로 쓰시오.

Garcia-Fuller's students also learn how _____ _____ tell fact from opinion in the news.

11 What's one of the first steps to tell fake news from real news? Fill in the blanks (A)~(C) with suitable words.

It's to (A)_____ _____. When it seems that a story or a photo is so good that it can't be true, you must (B)_____ and think if there is (C)_____ _____ that supports the writer's word and the source of this.

[12~14] 다음 글을 읽고 물음에 답하시오.

Garcia-Fuller also said sometimes it can be very hard to be a smart news reader. She tests her students with a website that appears to provide information on an animal called a tree octopus. The site is full of information on ⓐthis animal, along with a few unclear photos of octopuses in trees. But like the story of scary clowns, it's totally made up.

The lesson, Garcia-Fuller tells her students, is to "check the information you're seeing once more carefully" and to "question everything, even ⓑthings that I say."

12 위 글의 밑줄 친 ⓐthis animal이 가리키는 것을 본문에서 찾아 쓰시오.

➡ _____

13 위 글의 밑줄 친 ⓑthings that과 바꿔 쓸 수 있는 한 단어를 쓰시오.

➡ _____

14 What is the lesson that Garcia-Fuller gives to her students? Fill in the blanks (A) and (B) with suitable words.

It's to "check the information you're seeing (A)_____ _____ _____" and to "(B)_____ _____, even things that she says."

해석

After You Read A

• In October 2016, stories about scary clowns shook schools across the

in: 시간과 함께 쓰여 '(특정 기간)에'   about: 주제와 연관성의 의미로 '···에 관한'   across: 장소와 함께 쓰여 '~에 걸쳐, 온 ···에'

Washington area.

↓ how+to부정사: '···하는 방법'

• Garcia-Fuller's students also learn how to tell fact from opinion in the news.

tell A from B: A와 B를 구분하다

• The site is full of information on this animal, along with a few unclear

be full of: ~로 가득 차 있다   = together with

photos of octopuses in trees.

구문해설 • scary: 무서운 • clown: 광대 • area: 지역, 구역 • tell … from ~: ···를 ~와 구분하다
• site: 사이트, 현장, 위치 • unclear: 불확실한, 불분명한 • octopus: 문어

- 2016년 10월, 무서운 광대들에 관한 이야기가 워싱턴 지역 전역의 학교에 충격을 안겼다.
- Garcia-Fuller의 학생들은 또한 뉴스에서 사실을 의견과 구분하는 방법에 대해서도 배운다.
- 그 사이트는 나무 위에 있는 문어들의 몇몇 불확실한 사진과 함께, 이 동물에 대한 정보로 가득 차 있다.

Do It Yourself

Team NW danced on the stage during the school festival. They wondered if

전치사 '~ 동안'   'wonder'의 목적어를 이끄는 접속사로 '~인지 아닌지' = whether

the students and teachers would like their dancing. But they performed much

비교급 강조(훨씬)

better than any other team. A lot of students stood up and cheered loudly when

비교급 than any other+단수명사   = Many   부사로 동사 'cheered'를 수식

the team danced. Ms. Yu, the P.E. teacher, said it was the performance of the year.

Ms. Yu를 설명하는 동격어구

구문해설 • stage: 무대 • festival: 축제 • wonder: 궁금해 하다 • perform: 공연하다
• cheer: 환호하다 • performance: 공연

NW 팀은 학교 축제 기간에 무대에서 춤을 선보였다. 그들은 학생들과 선생님들이 그들의 춤을 좋아할지 확신이 서지 않았다. 하지만 그들은 다른 어떠한 팀보다 훨씬 더 멋지게 공연을 해냈다. 그 팀이 춤출 때 많은 학생이 일어서서 크게 환호했다. 체육 선생님인 유 선생님은 그해 최고의 공연이라고 말씀하셨다.

Link to the World

Fact

• This drawing, *Don Quixote*, is one of Picasso's works.

one of 복수명사

• Picasso drew it in 1955 with black lines against a white background.

Opinion

• I don't know if the man on the horse is brave, but he looks very tired and

~인지 아닌지

hungry. I think he needs some food and water.

• I think this artwork shows the most interesting part of Cervantes' novel *Don*

뒤에 접속사 that 생략

Quixote.

구문해설 • drawing: 그림 • work: 작품 • artwork: 미술작품 • novel: 소설

사실
- 이 그림 '돈키호테'는 피카소의 작품 중 하나이다.
- 피카소는 이 그림을 1955년에 흰 배경과 대비를 이루는 검은 선들로 그렸다.
의견
- 말 위에 올라탄 남자가 용감한지는 잘 모르겠지만, 그는 매우 피곤하고 굶주려 보인다. 내 생각에는 그에게 약간의 음식과 물이 필요한 것 같다.
- 나는 이 미술품이 세르반테스의 소설인 '돈키호테'의 가장 흥미로운 부분을 보여 주고 있다고 생각한다.

영역별 핵심문제

01 다음 주어진 두 단어의 관계가 같도록 빈칸에 알맞은 단어를 쓰시오.

> boring – exciting : defend – _____

02 다음 문장의 빈칸 (a)와 (b)에 들어갈 단어로 바르게 짝지어진 것은?

> • This book _____ (a) _____ a true story.
> • The story about the pink horse _____ (b) _____.

① gets along with – was slowed down
② gives up – was got over
③ is based on – was made up
④ stands up for – got scared
⑤ looks like – passed away

03 다음 밑줄 친 부분의 뜻이 잘못된 것은?

① You look pretty <u>cool</u> with that new haircut. (멋진)
② This sentence doesn't <u>make sense</u>. (타당하다, 말이 되다)
③ The roller coaster looked so <u>scary</u> that we didn't ride it. (무서운)
④ My teacher got upset because my homework wasn't <u>complete</u>. (완료하다)
⑤ The <u>major</u> roads in this city are always busy. (주요한)

[04~05] 다음 영영풀이에 해당하는 것을 고르시오.

04
> anything that causes you to believe that something is true

① performance
② source
③ skill
④ evidence
⑤ site

05
> in a way that expresses disapproval

① critically
② friendly
③ totally
④ recently
⑤ unclearly

06 다음 대화의 빈칸에 들어갈 말을 〈영영풀이〉를 참고하여 네 글자(four letters)로 된 한 단어를 쓰시오.

> G: There's no monkey like this in the world. Its nose is too big. I think it's _____.
> B: I don't agree. I saw that kind of monkey on TV. It's real.

> <영영풀이> not real, but made to look or seem real

➡ _____

Conversation

07 다음 대화의 밑줄 친 단어를 알맞은 형으로 고치시오.

> G: Look at those shoes the girl is wearing. I think they're great. How do you feel about them?
> B: I think they look light and <u>comfort</u>.

➡ _____

08 다음 대화의 빈칸에 'B'의 입장에서 할 말로 알맞은 것은?

> G: There's no monkey like this in the world. Its nose is too big. I think it's fake.
> B: I don't agree. I saw that kind of monkey on TV. It's _____.

① fake
② exciting
③ real
④ an opinion
⑤ a lie

09 다음 짝지어진 대화 중 어색한 것은?

① A: Let's take a lunch break. I want to eat some healthy food.
　 B: Sounds great! I'm ready to eat anything.
② A: How do you feel about this bird?
　 B: I think it looks clean. It's a perfect pet for us.
③ A: What do you think of this dog?
　 B: I think it looks friendly.
④ A: This monkey is a perfect pet for us. Don't you agree?
　 B: Yes, I agree.
⑤ A: How do you feel about this ad?
　 B: I think it's great. We should not believe every ad.

[10~12] 다음 대화를 읽고 물음에 답하시오.

> Alex: Big Mouth's show is really cool. How do you feel about it?
> Somi: Well, (a)<u>I don't think it's that great.</u>
> Alex: Come on. I love Mr. Big Mouth. He always (b)<u>makes me laugh out loud.</u>
> Somi: He's funny, but (c)<u>don't believe everything he says.</u>
> Alex: All right. Oh, look at his photo of an octopus. He said it lives in a tree.
> Somi: (d)<u>It makes sense.</u>
> Alex: He took the photo when it was climbing the tree. I don't think he's lying. It's a great photo.
> Somi: (e)<u>I don't agree with you.</u> It's a fake photo. An octopus can't live out of the sea.

10 위 대화의 흐름상 밑줄 친 (a)~(e) 중 어휘의 쓰임이 어색한 것은?

① (a)　② (b)　③ (c)　④ (d)　⑤ (e)

11 위 대화의 제목으로 가장 적절한 것은?

① How to Make a Popular Show
② Big Mouth's Show: Real or Fake?
③ Truth Becoming Falsehood
④ Where an Octopus Lives
⑤ Big Mouth's Show Alex Really Likes

12 위 대화의 내용과 일치하지 않는 것을 고르시오.

① Alex and Somi are looking at a photo of an octopus.
② Alex likes Mr. Big Mouth because he makes him laugh out loud.
③ Somi warns Alex not to trust Mr. Big Mouth.
④ Alex doesn't think a picture of an octopus climbing a tree is real.
⑤ Somi doesn't agree with Alex because an octopus can't live out of the sea.

13 주어진 문장의 밑줄 친 if와 용법이 같은 것은?

> This test tells if a student understands what she learned.

① You don't have to come if you don't want to.

② I am worrying if I can receive the support fund.

③ We will leave if everyone is ready.

④ You can see this movie if you are over 18 years old.

⑤ I won't go there if you don't come.

14 다음 글에서 어법상 어색한 부분을 찾아 바르게 고치시오.

> Opinion
> • I don't know ①that the man on the horse ②is brave, but he looks very ③tired and hungry. I think he ④needs some food and water.
> • I think this artwork shows ⑤the most interesting part of Cervantes' novel *Don Quixote*.

_____ ➡ _____

15 다음 두 문장이 같은 뜻이 되도록 빈칸에 들어갈 알맞은 것은?

> He said to me, "Who brought this gecko home?"
> = He asked me _____.

① who brought that gecko home

② who had brought this gecko home

③ who that gecko had brought home

④ who had brought that gecko home

⑤ who that gecko brought home

16 다음 중 어법상 어색한 문장의 개수로 알맞은 것은?

> a. Do you know if will it be rainy tomorrow?
> b. I am not sure that he can finish his project.
> c. Jenny told me that she was sleepy then.
> d. Tell me do you have the time.
> e. He asked me if I want something to eat.
> f. Mom asked me not to lose my umbrella again.

① 1개 　② 2개 　③ 3개 　④ 4개 　⑤ 5개

17 다음 두 문장이 같은 뜻이 되도록 빈칸에 들어갈 알맞은 것은?

> Mr. Hong said to me, "You can come to my house for dinner tomorrow."
> = Mr. Hong told me that _____.

① you could come to my house for dinner the following day

② he could come to my house for dinner the following day

③ I could come to his house for dinner the following day

④ I could come to his house for dinner the previous day

⑤ you could come to my house for dinner the previous day

18 다음 직접화법 문장들을 간접화법으로 바꿀 때 잘못된 곳을 바르게 고치시오.

(1) He asked her what she was doing there.

　➡ He said to her, "What you are doing here?"

　➡ _____

(2) She told him that she had met her sister the day before.

➡ She said to him, "I meet my sister yesterday."

➡ _____

(3) She said that she was very happy then.

➡ She said, "I am very happy then."

➡ _____

Reading

[19~21] 다음 글을 읽고 물음에 답하시오.

In October 2016, stories about scary clowns shook schools across the Washington area, but Danina Garcia-Fuller's students didn't believe them a bit.

"Some people were getting scared because they saw things on social media," said Patricia Visoso, one of Garcia-Fuller's students. "But they never checked up on who was saying (A)this." The stories were actually made by teenagers, not by major newspapers or TV stations. (B)그들은 광대들이 정말로 학생들을 공격하려고 한다는 명백한 증거를 하나도 제공하지 않았다. The story turned out to be ____ⓐ____ .

19 위 글의 빈칸 ⓐ에 들어갈 알맞은 말을 고르시오.

① a reliable rumor   ② a complete lie
③ a valid story   ④ a complete truth
⑤ a suspicious column

20 위 글의 밑줄 친 (A)가 가리키는 것을 우리말로 쓰시오.

➡ _____

21 위 글의 밑줄 친 (B)의 우리말에 맞게 주어진 어휘를 알맞게 배열하시오.

to attack / no / clowns / offered / trying / really / students / hard evidence / they / were / that

➡ _____
_____

[22~24] 다음 글을 읽고 물음에 답하시오.

"I think a lot of people just look at one thing and believe it's true," Patricia's classmate Ivy-Brooks said. "It's really important to look at the right sources and to pay attention to what is real and what is fake."

Like Garcia-Fuller's students, many teenagers in America are learning to think critically about information they're seeing in the news and on the Internet. This skill is getting more important these days ⓐas stories can spread very fast, and anyone can make a website full of false information.

22 위 글의 밑줄 친 ⓐas와 문법적 쓰임이 같은 것을 고르시오.

① Leave the papers as they are.
② As you know, Julia is leaving soon.
③ As we go up, the air grows colder.
④ As I was tired, I soon fell asleep.
⑤ He came up to me as I was speaking.

23 위 글의 주제로 알맞은 것을 고르시오.

① the situation where people look at just one thing and believe it's true
② the importance of thinking critically about information you're seeing in the news and on the Internet

③ how to look at the right sources

④ the way you can pay attention to what is real and what is fake

⑤ the skill to make a website full of false information

24 According to the passage, which is NOT true?

① Ivy-Brooks thinks many people just look at one thing and believe it's true.

② Ivy-Brooks said that it was really important to look at the right sources.

③ Many teenagers in America are learning to think critically about information they're seeing only on the SNS.

④ These days, stories can spread very fast.

⑤ These days, it is possible for anyone to make a website full of false information.

[25~26] 다음 글을 읽고 물음에 답하시오.

Garcia-Fuller also said sometimes it can be very hard to be a smart news reader. She tests her students with a website that appears to provide information on an animal called a tree octopus. The site is full of information on this animal, along with a few unclear photos of octopuses in trees. But like the story of scary clowns, it's totally ⓐmade up.

The lesson, Garcia-Fuller tells her students, is to "check the information you're seeing once more carefully" and to "question everything, even things that I say."

25 위 글의 밑줄 친 ⓐmade up과 같은 뜻을 가지는 단어를 철자 i로 시작하여 쓰시오.

➡ _____

26 위 글의 제목으로 알맞은 것을 고르시오.

① Who Is a Smart News Reader?

② To Test Students with a Website

③ Information on an Animal Called a Tree Octopus

④ Can You Believe the Information on the Tree Octopus?

⑤ Check the Information Carefully and Question Everything

[27~28] 다음 글을 읽고 물음에 답하시오.

The reporter says the ducks jumped down on the road by themselves. ____ⓐ____, it's not a fact. ⓑA man took the ducks and put down them safely on the road one by one. I wonder if the reporter saw the scene himself.

27 위 글의 빈칸 ⓐ에 들어갈 알맞은 말을 고르시오.

① For example   ② In addition

③ In other words   ④ However

⑤ Therefore

28 위 글의 밑줄 친 ⓑ에서 어법상 틀린 부분을 찾아 고치시오.

_____ ➡ _____

01 다음 짝지어진 단어의 관계가 같도록 빈칸에 알맞은 말을 쓰시오.

| information – inform : performance – _____ |

02 다음 영영풀이에 해당하는 단어는?

| very important and serious |

① minor　　② noisy　　③ false

④ total　　⑤ major

[03~04] 다음 대화를 읽고 물음에 답하시오.

G: How do you feel about the teddy bears?
B: They are cute. (A)뭔가 특별한 점이 있니?
G: They were made out of a police officer's uniform.
B: Oh, I see.
G: This police officer made them for the kids. Their dad was a police officer, and he passed away recently.
B: That's very touching.

03 위 대화의 'Teddy Bears'에 관한 내용 중에서 'Fact'에 해당하는 문장을 모두 찾아 그대로 쓰시오.

➡ _____

_____

04 위 대화의 우리말 (A)에 맞게 주어진 단어를 알맞은 순서로 배열하시오.

| (special / there / anything / them / about / is / ?) |

➡ _____

05 다음 대화의 빈칸에 들어갈 말로 알맞은 것은?

G: There's no monkey like this in the world. Its nose is too big. I think it's fake.
B: _____ I saw that kind of monkey on TV. It's real.

① I think so, too.
② I don't agree.
③ I agree with you.
④ You can say that again.
⑤ I couldn't agree with you more.

[06~07] 다음 대화를 읽고 물음에 답하시오.

G: How do you feel about this kid here?
B: (A) I think she is very pretty. ___(a)___ , why did she cut her hair? (B)
G: Can you guess?
B: Well, girls these days prefer short hair. (C)
G: I don't agree with that. (D) And this kid here is not a girl. ___(b)___ , he is a boy. (E)
B: Really?
G: Yes. He grew his hair to help sick children.

06 위 대화의 (A)~(E) 중 주어진 문장이 들어갈 위치로 알맞은 것은?

| Most girls like long hair better than short hair. |

① (A)　　② (B)　　③ (C)　　④ (D)　　⑤ (E)

07 위 대화의 빈칸 ⓐ와 ⓑ에 들어갈 말로 알맞은 것은?

① By the way – Moreover
② In addition – On the other hand
③ By the way – In fact
④ However – Actually
⑤ Therefore – For example

08 다음 빈칸에 들어갈 말로 적절한 것을 <u>모두</u> 고르시오.

> Team A and Team B will debate _____ teenagers should work part-time job.

① that ② if ③ what
④ though ⑤ whether

09 다음 화법 전환 문장들에서 빈칸에 알맞은 말을 쓰시오.

(1) She said to me, "How do you know the answer of this question?"
  ➡ She asked me how I knew _____
  _____.

(2) He said, "I was in trouble."
  ➡ He said that he _____.

(3) Eric told me that he was happy with his new house then.
  ➡ Eric said to me, "I'm happy with
  _____."

(4) He told me he liked the job.
  ➡ He _____ me, "I like the job."

(5) He asked me if I was hungry then.
  ➡ He said to me, "_____?"

10 다음 우리말을 참고하여 괄호 안에 주어진 단어로 빈칸에 알맞은 말을 써 넣으시오.

> 선생님은 학생들에게 수업 중에 밖에 나가지 말라고 말씀하셨다. (go out, during)
> (1) The teacher said to students, "_____
> _____."
> (2) The teacher _____
> _____

11 주어진 어휘를 이용하여 다음 우리말을 영어로 쓰시오.

> 나는 그들이 우리에게 부채춤을 보여 줄 것인지 궁금해. (wonder, the fan dance)

➡ _____
_____

12 다음 대화의 빈칸에 밑줄 친 문장을 알맞은 형태로 바꾸어 써 넣으시오.

> (1) A: She said, "_____."
>   B: She said what?
>   A: She said that <u>she was so tired then</u>.
> (2) A: He said to me, "<u>You are right</u>."
>   B: What did he say?
>   A: He told me that _____.

[13~15] 다음 글을 읽고 물음에 답하시오.

In October 2016, stories about scary clowns shook schools across the Washington area, but Danina Garcia-Fuller's students didn't believe them a bit.

"Some people were getting scared because they saw things on social media," said Patricia Visoso, one of Garcia-Fuller's students. "But they never checked up on who was saying this." The stories were actually made by teenagers, not by major newspapers or TV stations. They offered no ⓐhard evidence that clowns really were trying to attack students. The story ⓑturned out to be a complete lie.

출제율 95%

13 위 글의 밑줄 친 ⓐhard와 같은 의미로 쓰인 것을 고르시오.

① Wait for the concrete to go hard.
② You must try hard.
③ It is hard to believe that she's only nine.
④ The newspaper story is based on hard facts.
⑤ She's a very hard worker.

출제율 90%

14 위 글의 밑줄 친 ⓑturned out과 바꿔 쓸 수 있는 한 단어를 쓰시오.

➡ _____

출제율 95%

15 By whom were the stories about scary clowns made? Answer in English in a full sentence. (5 words)

➡ _____

[16~17] 다음 글을 읽고 물음에 답하시오.

"I think a lot of people just look at one thing and believe it's true," Patricia's classmate Ivy-Brooks said. "It's really important to look at the right sources and ⓐto pay attention to what is real and what is fake."

Like Garcia-Fuller's students, many teenagers in America are learning to think critically about information ⓑthey're seeing in the news and on the Internet. This skill is getting more important these days as stories can spread very fast, and anyone can make a website full of false information.

출제율 100%

16 아래 〈보기〉에서 위 글의 밑줄 친 ⓐto pay와 to부정사의 용법이 같은 것의 개수를 고르시오.

┌─ 보기 ─┐

① I turned on the computer to surf the Internet.
② I don't know where to go.
③ Do you have something interesting to read?
④ Everybody was surprised to see him.
⑤ His wish is to have good eyesight.

① 1개 ② 2개 ③ 3개 ④ 4개 ⑤ 5개

출제율 90%

17 위 글의 밑줄 친 ⓑthey가 가리키는 것을 본문에서 찾아 쓰시오.

➡ _____

[18~20] 다음 글을 읽고 물음에 답하시오.

Garcia-Fuller said she was teaching her students how to tell fake news from real news.

"(①) If a story or a photo seems too good to be true, stop and think: Is there any evidence that supports what the writer says? (②) And where is this coming from? (③)"

Garcia-Fuller's students also learn how to tell fact from opinion in the news. (④) "Opinions are good ⓐto read," said 15-year-old McKenzie Campbell, "but you also have to check if they are based on facts." (⑤)

18 위 글의 흐름으로 보아, 주어진 문장이 들어가기에 가장 적절한 곳은?

출제율 95%

> One of the first steps is to slow down.

①   ②   ③   ④   ⑤

19 위 글의 밑줄 친 ⓐto read와 to부정사의 용법이 다른 것을 모두 고르시오.

출제율 95%

① I'm sorry to hear the bad news.
② It's about time to go for a walk.
③ I think it wrong to tell a lie.
④ Jenny grew up to be a pianist.
⑤ Mom told me to stop watching TV.

20 According to the passage, which is NOT true?

출제율 100%

① Garcia-Fuller was teaching her students how to tell fake news from real news.
② One of the first steps to tell fake news from real news is to slow down.
③ Garcia-Fuller's students also learn how to distinguish fact from opinion in the news.
④ 15-year-old McKenzie Campbell said that opinions are good to speak.
⑤ 15-year-old McKenzie Campbell said that we also had to check if the opinions were based on facts.

[21~23] 다음 글을 읽고 물음에 답하시오.

> ⓐTeam NW danced on the stage while the school festival. They wondered ⓑif the students and teachers would like their dancing. ⓒBut they performed much better than any other team. A lot of students stood up and cheered loudly when the team danced. Ms. Yu, the P.E. teacher, said it was the performance of the year.

21 위 글의 밑줄 친 ⓐ에서 어법상 틀린 부분을 찾아 고치시오.

출제율 90%

_____ ➡ _____

22 위 글의 밑줄 친 ⓑif와 문법적 쓰임이 같은 것을 모두 고르시오.

출제율 95%

① I asked her if she knew Mr. White.
② If you see him, give him this note.
③ I'll work here if you offer me more money.
④ He couldn't tell if she was laughing or crying.
⑤ If necessary, I can come at once.

23 위 글의 밑줄 친 ⓒ를 다음과 같이 바꿔 쓸 때 빈칸에 들어갈 알맞은 한 단어를 쓰시오.

출제율 95%

> But they performed _____ of all the teams.

01 다음 대화를 읽고 질문에 영어로 답하시오.

> Alex: Big Mouth's show is really cool. How do you feel about it?
>
> Somi: Well, I don't think it's that great.
>
> Alex: Come on. I love Mr. Big Mouth. He always makes me laugh out loud.
>
> Somi: He's funny, but don't believe everything he says.
>
> Alex: All right. Oh, look at his photo of an octopus. He said it lives in a tree.
>
> Somi: It doesn't make sense
>
> Alex: He took the photo when it was climbing the tree. I don't think he's lying. It's a great photo.
>
> Somi: I don't agree with you. It's a fake photo. An octopus can't live out of the sea.

Q: Why did Somi say it was a fake photo?

➡ _____

02 접속사 'if', 'that', 'whether' 중 적절한 것을 한 번씩만 골라 주어진 단어와 함께 알맞게 배열하시오.

(1) I am wondering (fit, these, feet, shoes, his).

➡ _____

(2) I am sure (is, the, crying, baby, now).

➡ _____

(3) (a boy, kid, this, is, a girl, or) doesn't matter to me at all.

➡ _____

03 다음 주어진 문장들을 간접화법으로 바꿔 쓰시오.

(1) She said, "I like Tony."

➡ She said that _____.

(2) The old man said, "I want some water."

➡ The old man said that _____ _____.

(3) Bob said, "My sister looks happy."

➡ Bob said that _____.

04 대화의 흐름에 맞게 빈칸에 들어갈 말을 영어로 쓰시오.

(1) A: She said to me, "Where are you living now?"

B: Pardon me? Can you repeat that again?

A: She asked me where _____.

(2) A: He said to me, "Do you like to study in this library?"

B: I can't hear what you are saying.

A: He asked me _____ _____.

05 다음 그림 속 내용을 다른 사람에게 전달하는 문장으로 완성하시오.

The boy said _____ _____ and he wondered _____.

"I think a lot of people just look at one thing and believe it's true," Patricia's classmate Ivy-Brooks said. "It's really important to look at the right sources and to pay attention to what is real and what is fake."

Like Garcia-Fuller's students, many teenagers in America are learning to think critically ⓐ뉴스에서 그리고 인터넷상에서 보고 있는 정보에 관해. This skill is getting more important these days as stories can spread very fast, and anyone can make a website full of false information.

06 위 글의 밑줄 친 ⓐ의 우리말에 맞게 주어진 어휘를 이용하여 11 단어로 영작하시오.

about, seeing

➡ _____

_____

07 주어진 영영풀이에 해당하는 단어를 본문에서 찾아 쓰시오.

not genuine or real; being an imitation of the genuine article

➡ _____

08 본문의 내용과 일치하도록 다음 빈칸 (A)와 (B)에 알맞은 단어를 쓰시오.

According to Patricia's classmate Ivy-Brooks, looking at (A)_____ _____ _____ and paying attention to (B)_____ _____ _____ and what is fake are really important.

Garcia-Fuller said she was teaching her students how to tell fake news from real news.

"One of the first steps is to slow down. ⓐIf a story or a photo seems too good to be true, stop and think: Is there any evidence that supports what the writer says? And where is this coming from?"

Garcia-Fuller's students also learn how to tell fact from opinion in the news. "Opinions are good to read," said 15-year-old McKenzie Campbell, "ⓑbut you also have to check that they are based on facts."

09 위 글의 밑줄 친 ⓐ를 다음과 같이 바꿔 쓸 때 빈칸에 들어갈 알맞은 단어를 쓰시오.

If a story or a photo seems _____ good _____ it _____ be true

10 위 글의 밑줄 친 ⓑ에서 어법상 틀린 부분을 찾아 고치시오.

_____ ➡ _____

11 According to McKenzie Campbell, when we read opinions in the news, what do we have to check? Answer in English in a full sentence.

➡ _____

창의사고력 서술형 문제

01 아래 표의 (A)의 과일이나 야채에 대해 (B)는 좋아하거나 싫어하는 것을 나타낸 것이다. 〈보기〉처럼 상대방의 의견을 묻는 말과 그 대답을 쓰시오.

보기

A: How do you feel about apples?
B: I really love them.

(A)	(B)
• apples • persimmons • cucumbers • pears	• I really love them. • I like them. • I hate them. • I don't like them.

02 다음은 야구선수 Kelly와의 인터뷰를 정리한 내용이다. 인터뷰를 읽고, 조건에 맞게 정리한 내용의 빈칸에 알맞은 말을 쓰시오. (The reporter is a woman and Kelly is a man. Complete the sentence using pronouns.)

보기

Reporter: Kelly, our readers want to know all about you. (1)Can you tell me about your day?
Kelly: (2)I always get up at 6 and go to the stadium at 7.
Reporter: You get up so early. (3)How long were your training hours today?
Kelly: (4)It took 5 hours and was really hard.
Reporter: (5)What will you do in your spare time today?
Kelly: (6)After this interview, I will go swimming or watch a movie.
Reporter: It's been really nice talking to you. Thank you for letting us take time for the interview.

---

(1) The reporter asked Kelly _____.

(2) Kelly said that _____.

(3) The reporter asked Kelly _____.

(4) Kelly said that _____.

(5) The reporter asked Kelly _____.

(6) Kelly said that _____.

단원별 모의고사

01 다음 단어에 대한 영어 설명이 <u>어색한</u> 것은?

① false: incorrect, untrue, or mistaken
② fact: what you think or believe about something
③ lie: an untrue statement
④ totally: completely, absolutely
⑤ octopus: a soft sea creature with eight long arms

02 다음 짝지어진 단어의 관계가 같도록 빈칸에 알맞은 말을 주어진 글자로 시작하여 쓰시오.

search – investigate : supply – p_____

03 다음 영영풀이에 해당하는 단어를 고르시오.

a particular part of a town, a country, or the world

① clown   ② social media
③ evidence   ④ source
⑤ area

04 다음 중 짝지어진 대화가 <u>어색한</u> 것은?

① A: What did the woman say to her brother?
  B: She told him that she was very happy to meet him.
② A: How do you feel about the girl?
  B: I think she's pretty.
③ A: How do you feel about the dog?
  B: I think it's cute.
④ A: How do you feel about the ducks?
  B: I don't agree with you.
⑤ A: How do you feel about this ad?
  B: I think it's great. It shows the phone is strong.

[05~06] 다음 대화를 읽고 물음에 답하시오.

G: How do you feel about this drama?
B: _____(A)_____ The boy gave up his life to save his sister. It's the best drama of this year.
G: I don't agree. It's not a good drama.
B: Come on. Why do you think so?
G: It doesn't seem real. And it's a little boring.

05 위 대화의 빈칸 (A)에 들어갈 말로 알맞은 것은?

① I think it's very boring.
② That's a good idea.
③ I think it's very touching.
④ I don't believe it.
⑤ It's not a good drama.

06 위 대화를 읽고 다음 물음에 대한 대답을 완성하시오.

> G: Why doesn't the girl think it's a good drama?

> Because _____ and _____.

07 다음 대화의 흐름상 밑줄 친 (1)~(5) 중 어색한 것은?

> G: How do you feel about this kid here?
> B: (1)I think she is very pretty. By the way, why did she cut her hair?
> G: (2)Can you guess?
> B: Well, girls these days prefer short hair.
> G: (3)I agree with that. Most girls like long hair better than short hair. And this kid here is not a girl. (4)In fact, he is a boy.
> B: Really?
> G: Yes. (5)He grew his hair to help sick children.

① (1) ② (2) ③ (3) ④ (4) ⑤ (5)

08 다음 대화의 밑줄 친 우리말에 맞게 주어진 단어를 알맞은 순서로 배열하시오.

> G: 저 여자애가 신고 있는 신발 좀 봐. (the girl / those / is / look / wearing / at / shoes) I think they're great. How do you feel about them?
> B: I think they look light and comfortable.
> G: Right. I want to buy them for the school field trip.

➡ _____

09 다음 대화를 읽고, 아래의 〈Criticism〉에 해당하는 문장의 빈칸을 완성하시오.

> G: How do you feel about the teddy bears?
> B: They are cute. Is there anything special about them?
> G: They were made out of a police officer's uniform.
> B: Oh, I see.
> G: This police officer made them for the kids. Their dad was a police officer, and he passed away recently.
> B: That's very touching.

> The reporter says the police officer bought teddy bears for the kids. However, it's not a (1)_____. The police officer made them out of the kids' dad's (2)_____ for the kids. I wonder (3)_____ the reporter met them himself.

[10~11] 다음 대화를 읽고 물음에 답하시오.

> Alex: Big Mouth's show is really cool. How do you feel about it?
> Somi: Well, I don't think it's (A)that great.
> Alex: Come on. I love Mr. Big Mouth. He always makes me laugh out loud.
> Somi: He's funny, but don't believe everything he says.
> Alex: All right. Oh, look at his photo of an octopus. He said it lives in a tree.
> Somi: It doesn't make sense.
> Alex: He took the photo when it was climbing the tree. I don't think he's lying. It's a great photo.
> Somi: I don't agree with you. It's a fake photo. An octopus can't live out of the sea.

10 위 대화를 읽고 다음 질문에 영어로 답하시오.

> G: What is the octopus in the photo doing?

➡ _____

11 위 대화의 밑줄 친 (A)that과 같은 의미로 사용된 것은?

① This book is much thicker than that one.
② My arm doesn't reach that far.
③ The point is that you are still responsible.
④ It was yesterday that the accident happened.
⑤ That was the best time.

12 다음 중 밑줄 친 if의 의미가 다른 하나를 고르시오.

① We will discuss if this has a positive impact on our society.
② I will help you if you are busy now.
③ Any student will fail if he or she cheats on the test.
④ You can't come on board if you don't have your passport.
⑤ I will be angry if you tell a lie.

13 다음 문장을 간접화법으로 바꿔 쓰시오.

> Mr. Kim said to his daughter, "Can I ask you a few questions?"

➡ _____
_____

14 다음 각 문장에서 어법상 **틀린** 부분을 찾아 바르게 고쳐 쓰시오.

(1) He says her, "Where do you work now?"
➡ _____

(2) She told me that she hasn't been at school the day before.
➡ _____
_____

15 다음 두 문장을 한 문장으로 바르게 옮긴 것은?

> • Was this song composed by him?
> • That is unknown.

① Whether was this song composed by him is unknown.
② If was this song composed by him is unknown.
③ Whether this song was composed by him is unknown.
④ If this song was composed by him is unknown.
⑤ It is unknown that this song was composed by him

16 다음 우리말을 주어진 단어를 사용하여 영어로 옮기시오.

> (1) 나는 그녀가 내 선물을 좋아할지 궁금해. (if, present)
> (2) 너는 그녀가 결혼했는지 알고 있니? (if, is)

(1) _____
(2) _____

[17~18] 다음 글을 읽고 물음에 답하시오.

In October 2016, stories about (A)[scared / scary] clowns shook schools across the Washington area, but Danina Garcia-Fuller's students didn't believe ⓐthem a bit.

"Some people were getting (B)[scared / scary] because they saw things on social media," said Patricia Visoso, one of Garcia-Fuller's students. "But they never checked up on who was saying this." The stories were actually made by teenagers, not by major newspapers or TV stations. They (C)[offered / were offered] no hard evidence that clowns really were trying to attack students. The story turned out to be a complete lie.

17 위 글의 괄호 (A)~(C)에서 문맥이나 어법상 알맞은 낱말을 골라 쓰시오.

➡ (A) _____ (B) _____ (C) _____

18 위 글의 밑줄 친 ⓐthem이 가리키는 것을 본문에서 찾아 쓰시오.

➡ _____

[19~20] 다음 글을 읽고 물음에 답하시오.

"I think a lot of people just look at one thing and believe it's true," Patricia's classmate Ivy-Brooks said. "It's really important to look at the right sources and to pay attention ___ⓐ___ what is real and what is fake."

(A)Like Garcia-Fuller's students, many teenagers in America are learning to think critically about information they're seeing in the news and ___ⓑ___ the Internet. This skill is getting more important these days as stories can spread very fast, and anyone can make a website full of false information.

19 위 글의 빈칸 ⓐ와 ⓑ에 들어갈 전치사가 바르게 짝지어진 것은?

	ⓐ	ⓑ		ⓐ	ⓑ
①	for	to	②	to	by
③	to	on	④	for	on
⑤	on	to			

20 위 글의 밑줄 친 (A)Like와 같은 의미로 쓰인 것을 고르시오.

① I had a chance to meet people of like mind.

② There are many hobbies like photography or painting.

③ At weekends I like to sleep late.

④ He likes jazz, rock and the like.

⑤ Students were angry at being treated like children.

[21~22] 다음 글을 읽고 물음에 답하시오.

Garcia-Fuller said she was teaching her students how to tell fake news from real news. "One of the first steps is to slow down. If a story or a photo seems too good to be true, stop and think: Is there any evidence that supports what the writer says? And where is this coming from?"

Garcia-Fuller's students also learn how to tell fact from opinion in the news. "Opinions are good to read," said 15-year-old McKenzie Campbell, "but you also have to check if they are based on facts."

21 다음 문장에서 위 글의 내용과 <u>다른</u> 부분을 찾아서 고치시오.

> Garcia-Fuller was teaching her students how to tell fake news from opinion in the news.

➡ _____

22 만약 어떤 이야기나 어떤 사진이 진짜라고 하기엔 너무 좋아 보일 때 생각해 보아야 할 두 가지를 우리말로 쓰시오.

① _____

_____

② _____

[23~24] 다음 글을 읽고 물음에 답하시오.

(①) Garcia-Fuller also said sometimes it can be very hard to be a smart news reader. (②) She tests her students with a website that appears to provide information on an animal called a tree octopus. (③) But like the story of scary clowns, it's totally made up. (④)

The lesson, Garcia-Fuller tells her students, is to "check the information you're seeing once more carefully" and to "question everything, even things that I say." (⑤)

23 위 글의 흐름으로 보아, 주어진 문장이 들어가기에 가장 적절한 곳은?

> The site is full of information on this animal, along with a few unclear photos of octopuses in trees.

①   ②   ③   ④   ⑤

24 According to the passage, which is NOT true?

① According to Garcia-Fuller, sometimes it can be very hard to be a smart news reader.

② Garcia-Fuller tests her students with a website that appears to provide information on a tree octopus.

③ The website is full of information on a tree octopus, together with a few unclear photos of octopuses in trees.

④ Unlike the story of scary clowns, the information on a tree octopus is true.

⑤ Garcia-Fuller tells her students to check the information carefully and to question everything.

MEMO

Lesson 8

Make Peace with Others

 의사소통 기능

- 화냄 표현하기
  I can't stand it.

- 화냄에 응대하기
  Calm down!

 언어 형식

- 부정대명사
  Some gave him angry looks, and **others** shouted at him.

- 5형식(동사 + 목적어 + to부정사)
  The king **ordered** him **to go** to a famous military school.

Words & Expressions

Key Words

- **above** [əbʌ́v] 전 ~보다 위에
- **anymore** [ènimɔ́:r] 부 더 이상
- **approach** [əpróutʃ] 동 다가가다
- **army** [á:rmi] 명 군대, 육군
- **bark** [bɑ:rk] 동 (개가) 짖다
- **during** [djúəriŋ] 전 ~ 동안
- **fast** [fæst] 동 단식하다
- **finally** [fáinəli] 부 마침내
- **fix** [fiks] 동 수리하다
- **follow** [fálou] 동 따르다, 따라가다
- **forget** [fərgét] 동 잊다
- **gate** [geit] 명 정문, 대문
- **general** [dʒénərəl] 명 장군
- **grass** [græs] 명 풀, 잔디
- **happen** [hǽpən] 동 일어나다, 발생하다
- **heater** [hí:tər] 명 난방기, 히터
- **injured** [índʒərd] 형 부상당한
- **instead** [instéd] 부 대신에
- **knowing** [nóuiŋ] 형 다 안다는 듯한
- **look** [luk] 명 표정
- **might** [mait] 조 ~일지도 모른다

- **military** [mílitèri] 명 군대 형 군대의
- **movement** [mú:vmənt] 명 (사람들이 조직적으로 벌이는) 운동
- **noise** [nɔiz] 명 소음
- **order** [ɔ́:rdər] 동 명령하다
- **palace** [pǽlis] 명 궁, 궁전
- **patience** [péiʃəns] 명 인내심, 참을성
- **pole** [poul] 명 기둥, 막대, 장대
- **powerful** [páuərfəl] 형 강력한
- **push** [puʃ] 동 밀다
- **reason** [rí:zn] 명 이유
- **situation** [sitʃuéiʃən] 명 상황
- **stand** [stænd] 동 참다, 견디다
- **suddenly** [sʌ́dnli] 부 갑자기
- **sword** [sɔ:rd] 명 검, 칼
- **tie** [tai] 동 묶다
- **war** [wɔ:r] 명 전쟁
- **warrior** [wɔ́:riər] 명 전사
- **weapon** [wépən] 명 무기
- **winner** [wínər] 명 승리자, 우승자
- **wise** [waiz] 형 현명한
- **yell** [jel] 동 소리 지르다

Key Expressions

- **at that moment** 그 순간에
- **be in trouble** 곤경에 처하다
- **calm down** 진정하다
- **focus on** ~에 집중하다
- **give up** 포기하다
- **harder and harder** 점점 더 심하게
- **I can't stand** ~을 참을 수가 없다
- **in all possible ways** 모든 가능한 방법으로
- **in the middle** 중간에서
- **keep -ing** 계속해서 ~하다
- **let ~ go** ~을 풀어주다, 석방하다
- **on the side of** ~을 편들어, ~의 면에

- **pass by** 옆을 지나가다
- **return to** ~로 돌아가다
- **set free** 자유의 몸이 되게 하다, 석방하다
- **should have been** ~이었어야 했다
- **sooner or later** 조만간, 머지않아
- **stand against** ~에 기대다
- **stand in line** 줄을 서다
- **step on** ~을 밟다
- **take care of** ~을 돌보다
- **wait for** ~을 기다리다
- **wait in line** 줄 서서 기다리다
- **win a war** 전쟁에서 이기다

Word Power

※ 서로 비슷한 뜻을 가진 어휘

- **above** ~보다 위에 – **over** ~을 넘어
- **injured** 부상당한 – **wounded** 부상당한
- **powerful** 강력한 – **mighty** 강력한, 강대한
- **sword** 검, 칼 – **knife** (짧은) 칼
- **let ~ go** ~를 풀어주다, 석방하다 – **set free** 자유의 몸이 되게 하다, 석방하다

- **gate** 정문, 대문 – **gateway** 출입구, 통로
- **pass by** 옆을 지나가다 – **go by** 지나가다
- **suddenly** 갑자기 – **unexpectedly** 갑자기, 예상 외로
- **warrior** 전사 – **fighter** 전사, 투사

※ 서로 반대의 뜻을 가진 어휘

- **above** ~보다 위에 ↔ **under** ~의 아래에
- **follow** 따르다, 따라가다 ↔ **avoid** 피하다, 비키다
- **knowing** 다 안다는 듯한 ↔ **unknowing** 자신도 모르는
- **patience** 인내심, 참을성 ↔ **impatience** 성급함, 조급함
- **push** 밀다 ↔ **pull** 당기다
- **winner** 승리자, 우승자 ↔ **loser** 실패자

- **approach** 다가가다 ↔ **withdraw** 물러나다
- **injured** 부상당한 ↔ **uninjured** 부상당하지 않은
- **tie** 묶다 ↔ **untie** 풀다
- **powerful** 강력한 ↔ **powerless** 무능한, 무력한
- **war** 전쟁 ↔ **peace** 평화
- **wise** 현명한 ↔ **unwise** 현명하지 못한

※ 접미사 -er/-or

- **win** + **-er** → **winner** 승리자
- **lead** + **-er** → **leader** 지도자, 대표
- **work** + **-er** → **worker** 노동자
- **war** + **-or** → **warrior** 전사
- **protect** + **-or** → **protector** 보호자, 보호기관
- **sculpt** + **-or** → **sculptor** 조각가

- **care** + **-er** → **carer** 간병인
- **drive** + **-er** → **driver** 운전기사
- **sing** + **-er** → **singer** 가수
- **project** + **-or** → **projector** 영사기
- **direct** + **-or** → **director** 감독, 책임자

English Dictionary

- **finally** 결국, 마침내
  → after a long period of time
  기나긴 시간 후에

- **injured** 부상당한
  → having physical damage to a part of the body
  신체의 일부분에 물리적인 상처를 입은

- **military** 군대
  → the armed forces of a country
  한 국가의 무장한 세력

- **order** 명령하다
  → to tell someone to do something
  어떤 일을 하라고 누군가에게 말하다

- **patience** 인내심
  → being able to stay calm and not get annoyed
  화내지 않고 침착하게 있을 수 있는 것

- **powerful** 강력한
  → having a lot of power to control people and events
  사람과 사건을 통제할 수 있는 많은 힘을 갖고 있는

- **reason** 이유
  → a fact or situation which explains why something happens
  어떤 일이 왜 일어나는지 설명하는 사실이나 상황

- **realize** 깨닫다
  → to become aware of a fact or to understand it
  어떤 사실을 알게 되거나 이해하다

- **warrior** 전사
  → a fighter or soldier, especially one in old times who was very brave and experienced in fighting
  특히 옛날에 존재하던 매우 용감하고 싸움에 숙련된 군인 또는 투사

- **yell** 소리 지르다
  → to shout loudly 큰 소리로 고함지르다

서답형

01 다음 문장의 빈칸에 〈영어 설명〉에 맞게 한 단어로 쓰시오.

> Even if someone is _____ing at you, do not respond in the same way.
> 〈영어 설명〉 to shout loudly

➡ _____

중요

02 다음 빈칸에 공통으로 들어갈 말로 가장 적절한 것은?

> • The cello is still considered an unfamiliar instrument to the _____ public.
> • Kim Yu-sin was a great _____ in Korean history.

① common
② traditional
③ general
④ powerful
⑤ soldier

[03~04] 다음 설명에 해당하는 단어를 고르시오.

03

> a fighter or soldier, especially one in old times who was very brave and experienced in fighting

① attack
② weapon
③ army
④ sword
⑤ warrior

중요

04

> to become aware of a fact or to understand it

① follow
② realize
③ pass
④ happen
⑤ remember

서답형

05 다음 우리말에 맞게 두 단어로 쓰시오.

> 나는 길 위의 마른 낙엽을 밟을 때 나는 소리를 좋아해.
> ➡ I like the sound when I _____ _____ the dry fallen leaves on the street.

중요

06 다음 빈칸에 들어갈 말로 알맞은 것은?

> (1) These voters _____ for hours because they are passionate about trying to change the society they live in.
> (2) It wasn't easy for him, but he didn't _____.

① stand against – set free
② take care of – give up
③ pass by – focus on
④ stand in line – give up
⑤ wait in line – wait for

서답형

07 다음 짝지어진 단어의 관계가 같도록 빈칸에 알맞은 말을 쓰시오.

> war – peace : patience – _____

08 다음 중 주어진 단어의 관계가 나머지와 다른 것은?

① cook – cooker
② sing – singer
③ lead – leader
④ drive – driver
⑤ win – winner

01 다음 〈보기〉에서 알맞은 단어를 선택하여 문장의 빈칸을 완성하시오. (필요하면 변형하거나 단어를 추가하시오.)

> ┤ 보기 ├
> army　　reason　　above　　set

(1) His picture was placed on the shelf _____ the desk.

(2) My brother joined the _____ last year.

(3) The king ordered his men to _____ the prisoner _____.

(4) There are two _____ why I want to be a doctor.

02 다음 문장의 빈칸에 알맞은 단어를 쓰시오. (2)번은 주어진 영영 풀이에 어울리는 단어를 쓰시오.

> <영영 풀이> a long thin piece of wood or metal

(1) People must not bring any _____s, such as knives or guns, on an airplane.

(2) We saw the country's flag at the top of the _____.

03 다음 우리말과 같은 표현이 되도록 문장의 빈칸을 채우시오.

(1) 우리가 크게 웃자 한 선생님은 화난 표정을 지었다.
　➡ Ms. Han gave us an angry _____ when we laughed out loud.

(2) 위험한 상황에 처해 있다면, 경찰에 전화해야 한다.
　➡ If you are in a dangerous _____, you should call the police.

(3) 올해, 사람들은 경복궁에서 한복 패션쇼를 즐겼습니다.
　➡ This year, people enjoyed a hanbok fashion show at Gyeongbokgung _____.

04 영영풀이에 해당하는 단어를 〈보기〉에서 찾아 첫 번째 빈칸에 쓰고, 두 번째 빈칸에는 우리말 뜻을 쓰시오.

> ┤ 보기 ├
> injured　　wise　　push　　powerful

(1) _____ : having a lot of power to control people and events: _____

(2) _____ : having the power to judge properly what is true or right: _____

(3) _____ : having physical damage to a part of the body : _____

(4) _____ : to make someone or something move by pressing them with your hands: _____

05 다음 문장의 빈칸에 들어갈 말을 〈보기〉의 단어를 이용하여 완성하시오.

> ┤ 보기 ├
> pass　　decrease　　soon

(1) The number of elementary school students keeps _____.

(2) The vacation will begin and _____ _____, whether you do something or not.

(3) _____ _____ _____, he will realize she really loved him.

Conversation 교과서

1 화냄 표현하기

> **A** Smoke is coming from the lower floor. I can't stand it.
> 아래층에서 담배 연기가 올라와. 참을 수 없어.
>
> **B** Me, too. Let's go downstairs and ask them to close the window.
> 나도 그래. 아래층에 가서 창문 닫아달라고 말하자.

■ 화난 감정을 표현하는 문장으로 'I can't stand it.(참을 수 없어.)'을 사용할 수 있다. 이외에도 'I'm very angry.', 'I'm very upset.', 'I'm very annoyed.', 'How irritating!', 'I'm tired of it.', 'I'm fed up with it.', 'I'm disgusted with it.' 등을 대신 사용할 수 있다.

화난 상태 표현 정리 1

- angry (보편적 의미에서) 화가 난
- annoyed 짜증난
- irritated 짜증난
- upset 속상한, 섭섭한
- mad 성난

화난 상태 표현 정리 2

- I'm tired of it. 난 그게 지긋지긋해.
- I'm fed up with it. 난 그게 넌더리가 나.
- I'm disgusted with it. 난 그게 정말 역겨워.

핵심 Check

1. 다음 대화에서 밑줄 친 부분을 대체할 수 <u>없는</u> 표현은?

A: Children upstairs are running around all day. <u>I can't stand it.</u>

B: Calm down. They're having a birthday party.

① How annoying!
② How irritating!
③ I'm irritated.
④ I can't be tired of it.
⑤ I'm fed up with it.

2 화냄에 응대하기

> **A** I can't stand this place. It's too crowded. 이 장소를 견딜 수가 없어. 너무 사람이 많아.
>
> **B** Calm down! We're at the festival. Let's enjoy it. 진정해! 우리 축제에 와 있잖아. 축제를 즐기자.

■ 화낸 상대방에 응대할 때, 'Calm down!(진정해!)'이라는 표현을 쓸 수 있다. 이와 같은 표현으로는 'Relax.', 'Take it easy.', 'It's going to be okay. Take a deep breath and try to relax.', 'Chill out!', 'Don't stress yourself.', 'Control yourself.' 등이 있다.

화냄에 응대하는 표현 정리

- Relax. 진정해.
- Take it easy. 진정해
- It's going to be okay. Take a deep breath and try to relax. 괜찮아질 거야. 심호흡하고 진정해 봐.
- Chill out! 진정해!
- Don't stress yourself. 스트레스 받지 마.
- Control yourself. (화를) 자제해.

핵심 Check

2. 다음 대화의 빈칸에 들어갈 수 없는 표현은?

A: Ouch! He stepped on my foot again.

B: Are you okay?

A: No. This is the third time he did that today. I can't stand it. I'll go and talk to him.

B: _____ He's not wearing glasses today, so he can't see well.

① Calm down!　　　　　　　② Cool down!

③ Don't stress yourself.　　　④ Don't control yourself.

⑤ It's going to be okay. Take a deep breath and try to relax.

Step Up - Real-life Scene

Minji: Minsu, there is no cup ❶I can use. Why didn't you do the dishes?

Minsu: Sorry, but ❷I forgot to do them.

Minji: What? You always forget ❸what you have to do. ❹I can't stand it. I cleaned the living room all morning.

Minsu: Calm down! ❺I'm busy doing my homework.

Minji: Do the dishes first, and then do your homework.

Minsu: I can't. I don't think I can finish my homework today. Science is too difficult for me.

Minji: Science? ❻You know I'm good at science. ❼Let me help you.

Minsu: Great. Thanks. I'll wash your cup right now and I'll do ❽the rest of the dishes after finishing this.

민지: 민수야, 내가 사용할 컵이 없어. 왜 설거지를 안 했니?
민수: 미안하지만, 설거지하는 걸 잊었어.
민지: 뭐라고? 너는 항상 해야 할 일을 잊어버리는구나. 참을 수가 없어. 나는 아침 내내 거실 청소를 했어.
민수: 진정해! 나는 숙제하느라 바빠.
민지: 설거지를 먼저 하고 난 뒤에 숙제해.
민수: 안 돼! 오늘 숙제를 끝낼 수가 없을 것 같아. 과학은 나에게 너무 어려워.
민지: 과학이라고? 너도 알겠지만 내가 과학을 잘하잖아. 내가 도와줄게.
민수: 잘됐다. 고마워. 당장 누나 컵부터 씻을게. 그리고 나머지 설거지는 숙제 끝낸 후에 할게.

❶ 'I can use'는 선행사 'cup'을 수식하는 목적격 관계대명사절로 목적격 관계대명사 'that/which'가 생략되어 있다.
❷ 'forget to+동사원형'은 '~할 것을 잊다'라는 의미이다. 'them'은 'the dishes'를 가리키는 대명사다.
❸ 동사 'forget'의 목적어 역할을 하는 명사절로 'what'은 관계대명사로 '~하는 것'의 뜻이다. 'what'은 'the thing that[which]'으로 바꾸어 사용할 수 있다.
❹ 'I can't stand it.(참을 수 없어.)'은 화난 감정을 표현하는 문장이다.
❺ 'be busy -ing'는 '~하느라 바쁘다'라는 의미이다.
❻ 동사 'know' 뒤에는 목적어를 이끄는 접속사 'that'이 생략되어 있다.
❼ '사역동사(let)+목적어(me)+동사원형(help)' 형태로 '…가 ~하게 하다'라는 의미이다.
❽ 'the rest'는 '나머지'라는 뜻이다. 'rest'는 '휴식'의 의미이다.

Check(√) True or False

(1) Minsu hates doing the dishes.   T ☐ F ☐

(2) Minji will help Minsu do his homework.   T ☐ F ☐

Start Off - Listen & Talk A 1

B: What's ❶that noise outside?

G: They're fixing the heaters.

B: ❷I can't focus on my studies at all. I can't stand it.

G: ❸Calm down! They will finish it soon.

B: 밖에서 나는 저 소음은 뭐지?
G: 히터를 고치고 있어.
B: 공부에 전혀 집중할 수가 없잖아. 참을 수가 없어.
G: 진정해! 곧 끝날 거야.

❶ 'that'은 명사 'noise'를 수식하는 '지시형용사'로 '저'로 해석한다.
❷ 'not ~ at all'은 '전혀 ~ 않다'라는 뜻으로 부정문을 강조할 때 사용한다.
❸ 화낸 상대방에 응대할 때, 'Calm down!(진정해!)'이라는 표현을 쓸 수 있다. 같은 의미의 표현인 'Relax.', 'Take it easy.' 등으로 바꾸어 쓸 수 있다.

Check(√) True or False

(3) The boy can't concentrate on his studies because of noise outside.   T ☐ F ☐

(4) The girl is going to finish fixing the heaters.   T ☐ F ☐

Get Ready 2

(1) **M:** We've waited ❶for more than one hour, and we're still waiting.

W: Calm down! We're almost there.

(2) **G:** Brrr…. ❷What a cold day! I hate standing in line in cold weather.

B: Calm down! Drink this hot milk.

G: Oh, thank you so much.

(3) **G:** Look! That man didn't wait in line! I'm very angry.

B: Calm down! He works here.

(4) **B:** The boy behind me ❸keeps pushing me. I can't stand it.

G: Calm down. He's just a child.

❶ 'for+숫자 기간'은 '～ 동안'의 의미이다.
❷ 'What+a+형용사+명사!' 어순의 감탄문이다.
❸ 'keep+-ing'는 '계속해서 ～하다'라는 의미이다.

Start Off - Listen & Talk A 2

G: I can't find my pencil case. Have you seen it?

B: No, I haven't. Where did you put it?

G: I put it on my desk, but now ❶it's gone. I'm really upset.

B: Calm down! I'll ❷help you find it.

❶ 'it's gone'은 '사라지다'라는 의미이다.
❷ 'help+목적어+목적보어(동사원형/to부정사)'로 '…가 ～하는 것을 돕다'라는 의미이다.

Start Off - Listen & Talk B

B: Ouch! He stepped on my foot again.

G: Are you okay?

B: No. This is the third time ❶he did that today. I can't stand it. I'll go and talk to him.

G: Calm down! He's not wearing his glasses today, so he can't see well.

B: What happened to his glasses?

G: He broke his glasses ❷during a soccer game this morning.

B: I see, but he ❸should have been more careful.

❶ 'he did that today'는 'time'을 수식하는 관계부사절로 'time'과 'he' 사이에는 관계부사 'when'이 생략되어 있다. 'that'은 'stepping on my foot'을 가리키는 지시대명사다.
❷ 'during'은 전치사로 '～ 동안'의 의미이고, 뒤에는 특정 기간을 나타내는 명사가 온다.
❸ 'should have+과거분사'는 '～했어야 했는데'의 의미로 과거의 유감이나 후회를 나타내는 표현이다.

Start Off - Speak Up

A: I can't ❶stand this place. It's too crowded.

B: Calm down! We're at the festival. Let's enjoy it.

❶ 'stand'는 '참다, 견디다'의 의미로 사용되었다. 'bear'의 의미와 같다.

Express Yourself A

1. **M1:** The king sent me here. Open the door.

   M2: Wait there. The door will open ❶in a hundred days.

   M1: What? A hundred days? I can't ❷spend a hundred days doing nothing. I can't stand it.

   M2: Calm down! It is an important rule ❸to get in this school.

2. **M1:** Why did you ❹tie me up here? Please ❺set me free.

   M2: How can you ❻get free? Think.

   M1: I can't stand this sign. I'm not dangerous or bad.

   M2: Calm down. I'm sure you'll find a way.

❶ 전치사 'in'은 '～ 후에'라는 의미이다.
❷ 'spend+시간+-ing' 구문으로 '～하면서 시간을 보내다'라는 의미이다.
❸ 'to get'은 명사 'rule'을 꾸며주는 형용사 용법이다.
❹ '동사+인칭대명사+부사' 어순의 이어 동사로 인칭대명사는 반드시 동사와 부사 사이에 위치해야 한다. 즉, 'tie up me'로 쓸 수 없다.
❺ 'set+목적어+free'는 '～를 자유롭게 하다, 풀어주다'라는 뜻이다.
❻ 'get free'는 '풀려나다, 자유의 몸이 되다'라는 뜻이다.

Check yourself

G: What's that noise outside?

B: A dog is barking.

G: I ❶can't focus on my studies at all. I can't stand it.

B: Calm down! He will be quiet soon.

❶ 'not ～ at all'은 '전혀 ～ 않다'라는 의미로 부정문을 강조하는 말이다. 'never'와 같은 의미이다.

다음 우리말과 일치하도록 빈칸에 알맞은 말을 쓰시오.

Get Ready 2

(1) M: We'_____ _____ for more than one hour, and we're still waiting.

    W: _____ down! We're _____ there.

(2) G: Brrr.... _____ a cold day! I _____ standing _____ _____ in cold weather.

    B: _____ _____! Drink this hot milk.

    G: Oh, thank you so much.

(3) G: Look! That man didn't _____ _____ _____! I'm very angry.

    B: _____ _____! He works here.

(4) B: The boy _____ me _____ _____ me. I _____ _____ it.

    G: _____ _____. He's _____ a child.

Start Off - Listen & Talk A

1. B: What's that _____ outside?

    G: They're _____ the _____.

    B: I can't _____ _____ my studies _____ _____. I _____ _____ _____.

    G: Calm down! They will finish it soon.

2. G: I _____ _____ my pencil case. Have you _____ it?

    B: No, I haven't. Where did you _____ it?

    G: I put it on my desk, but now it's _____. I'm really _____.

    B: _____ down! I'll help you _____ it.

Start Off - Listen & Talk B

B: Ouch! He stepped _____ my _____ again.

G: Are you _____?

B: No. This is the _____ time he _____ _____ today. I _____ _____ it. I'll go and talk to him.

G: _____ _____! He's not _____ his _____ today, so he can't see well.

B: What _____ to his glasses?

G: He _____ his glasses _____ a soccer game this morning.

B: I see, but he _____ _____ _____ more careful.

해석

(1) M: 우리 한 시간 이상 기다렸는데 아직도 기다리고 있네.
    W: 진정해! 거의 다 되어 가.

(2) G: 부르르…. 정말 추운 날이네! 나는 추운 날씨에 줄 서는 게 싫어.
    B: 진정해! 이 뜨거운 우유를 마셔 봐.
    G: 와, 정말 고마워.

(3) G: 저것 봐! 저 남자가 줄을 서지 않았어! 정말 화가 나.
    B: 진정해! 저 사람은 여기서 일하는 사람이야.

(4) B: 내 뒤에 있는 남자아이가 자꾸 밀어. 참을 수가 없어.
    G: 진정해. 아직 어린아이야.

1. B: 밖에서 나는 저 소음은 뭐지?
    G: 히터를 고치고 있어.
    B: 공부에 전혀 집중할 수가 없잖아. 참을 수가 없어.
    G: 진정해! 곧 끝날 거야.

2. G: 내 필통을 찾을 수가 없어. 내 필통 봤니?
    B: 아니, 못 봤어. 어디에 뒀어?
    G: 내 책상 위에 뒀는데 사라졌어. 정말 화가 나.
    B: 진정해! 내가 그걸 찾는 걸 도와줄게.

B: 아! 그 애가 또 내 발을 밟았어.
G: 괜찮니?
B: 아니. 이번이 오늘 그 애가 내 발을 세 번째로 밟은 거야. 참을 수가 없어. 가서 말해야겠어.
G: 진정해! 그 애는 오늘 안경을 안 쓰고 있어서 잘 볼 수가 없어.
B: 안경이 어떻게 됐는데?
G: 오늘 아침에 축구 경기를 하다가 안경을 깨뜨렸어.
B: 그렇구나. 하지만 그 애는 더 조심했어야 했어.

Start Off - Speak Up

A: I _____ _____ this place. It's too _____.

B: _____ _____! We're at the _____. Let's _____ it.

Step Up - Real-life Scene

Minji: Minsu, there is no cup _____ _____ _____. _____ _____ _____ do the _____?

Minho: Sorry, but I _____ _____ _____ them.

Minji: What? You always forget _____ you _____ _____ _____. _____ _____ _____ it. I _____ the living room all morning.

Minho: Calm down! I'm _____ _____ my homework.

Minji: _____ the dishes first, and then do your homework.

Minho: I can't. I don't think I can _____ my homework today. Science is _____ _____ for me.

Minji: Science? You know I'_____ _____ _____ science. _____ _____ _____ you.

Minho: Great. Thanks. I'll wash your cup _____ _____ and I'll do _____ _____ of the dishes after _____ this.

Express Yourself A

1. M1: The king _____ me here. Open the door.
   M2: Wait there. The door will open _____ a _____ days.
   M1: What? A hundred days? I can't _____ a hundred days _____ _____. I _____ _____ _____.
   M2: _____ _____! It is an important _____ _____ _____ in this school.

2. M1: Why did you _____ _____ _____ here? Please _____ _____ _____.
   M2: How can you _____ _____? Think.
   M1: I _____ _____ this _____. I'm not _____ or bad.
   M2: Calm down. _____ _____ _____ you'll find a _____.

Check yourself

G: What's that noise _____?

B: A dog is _____.

G: I _____ _____ _____ my studies at all. I can't _____ _____.

B: _____ _____! He will be _____ soon.

A: 나는 이 장소를 참을 수가 없어. 너무 사람이 많아.
B: 진정해! 우리는 축제에 와 있잖아. 축제를 즐기자.

민지: 민수야, 내가 사용할 컵이 없어. 왜 설거지를 안 했니?
민수: 미안하지만, 설거지하는 걸 잊었어.
민지: 뭐라고? 너는 항상 해야 할 일을 잊어버리는구나. 참을 수가 없어. 나는 아침 내내 거실 청소를 했어.
민수: 진정해! 나는 숙제하느라 바빠.
민지: 설거지를 먼저 하고 난 뒤에 숙제해.
민수: 안 돼! 오늘 숙제를 끝낼 수가 없을 것 같아. 과학은 나에게 너무 어려워.
민지: 과학이라고? 너도 알겠지만 내가 과학을 잘하잖아. 내가 도와줄게.
민수: 잘됐다. 고마워. 당장 누나 컵부터 씻을게. 그리고 나머지 설거지는 숙제 끝낸 후에 할게.

1. M1: 왕이 나를 여기에 보냈소. 문을 여시오.
   M2: 거기서 기다리시오. 100일 후 문이 열릴 것이오.
   M1: 뭐라고요? 100일이라고요? 아무것도 하지 않고 100일을 보낼 수는 없소. 참을 수가 없소.
   M2: 진정하시오! 그것이 이 학교에 들어오기 위한 중요한 규칙이오.

2. M1: 저를 왜 여기에 묶어 두셨습니까? 저를 풀어 주십시오.
   M2: 어떻게 풀려날 수 있겠느냐? 생각해 보아라.
   M1: 저는 이 굇말을 참을 수가 없습니다. 저는 위험하지도 나쁘지도 않습니다.
   M2: 진정하거라. 나는 네가 방법을 찾을 것이라고 확신한다.

G: 밖에서 나는 저 소음은 뭐지?
B: 개가 짖고 있는 거야.
G: 공부에 전혀 집중할 수가 없어. 참을 수가 없어.
B: 진정해! 곧 조용해질 거야.

01 다음 우리말에 맞도록 주어진 단어를 활용하여 빈칸을 채우시오.

> 나는 이 장소를 참을 수가 없어. 너무 사람이 많아. (stand / crowd)
> ➡ I _____ _____ this place. It's too _____.

02 다음 대화의 빈칸에 들어갈 말로 어색한 것은?

> G: Look! That man didn't wait in line! I'm very angry.
> B: _____ He works here.

① Calm down!   ② Relax.
③ Take it easy.   ④ Take care of yourself.
⑤ Take a deep breath and try to relax.

03 다음 대화의 빈칸에 들어갈 말로 알맞지 않은 것은?

> G: I can't find my pencil case. Have you seen it?
> B: No, I haven't. Where did you put it?
> G: I put it on my desk, but now it's gone. _____
> B: Calm down! I'll help you find it.

① I'm really upset.   ② I can't stand it.
③ I'm very annoying.   ④ I'm very angry.
⑤ How irritating!

04 다음 대화의 밑줄 친 말의 의도로 알맞은 것은?

> M: We've waited for more than one hour, and we're still waiting.
> W: <u>Calm down!</u> We're almost there.

① 감사하기   ② 이의 제기하기
③ 기원하기   ④ 화냄에 응대하기
⑤ 화냄 표현하기

[01~02] 다음 대화를 읽고 물음에 답하시오.

Ben: Ouch! He stepped on my foot again.

Gary: Are you okay?

Ben: No. This is the third time he did that today. I can't stand it. I'll go and talk to him.

Gary: Calm down! He's not wearing his glasses today, so he can't see well.

Ben: What happened to his glasses?

Gary: He broke his glasses during a soccer game this morning.

Ben: I see, but _____(A)_____.

01 위 대화의 빈칸 (A)에 들어갈 말로 적절한 것은?

① he must have been more careful
② he may have been more careful
③ he should have been more careful
④ he needn't have been more careful
⑤ he shouldn't have been more careful

서답형

02 Write the reason why Ben is angry.

Because a boy _____ _____
foot _____ times.

[03~04] 다음 대화의 빈칸에 들어갈 말로 알맞은 것은?

03

B: What's that noise outside?

G: They're fixing the heaters.

B: I can't focus on my studies at all. I can't stand it.

G: _____ They will finish it soon.

① I'll help you.
② Is it okay if they are fixing the heaters?

③ Calm down!
④ I'm fed up with it.
⑤ I'm disgusted with it.

04

G: Brrr.... What a cold day! _____
B: Calm down! Drink this hot milk.
G: Oh, thank you so much.

① I like winter.
② I hate standing in line in cold weather.
③ Take a deep breath and try to relax.
④ Don't stress yourself.
⑤ I didn't wait in line.

서답형

05 위 대화의 빈칸에 들어갈 단어를 주어진 영영풀이를 보고 쓰시오.

M1: Why did you tie me up here? Please _____ me _____.

M2: How can you get free? Think.

M1: I can't stand this sign. I'm not dangerous or bad.

M2: Calm down. I'm sure you'll find a way.

<영영풀이> to allow someone to leave prison

➡ _____

[06~07] 다음 대화를 읽고 물음에 답하시오.

M1: The king sent me here. Open the door.

M2: Wait there. The door will open in a hundred days.

M1: What? A hundred days? (A)아무것도 하지 않고 100일을 보낼 수는 없소. I can't stand it.

M2: Calm down! (B)It is an important rule to get in this school.

서답형

06 위 대화의 밑줄 친 (A)의 우리말에 맞게 주어진 어구를 알맞은 순서로 배열하시오.

> (I / a hundred / can't / spend / doing nothing / days)

➡ _____

07 위 대화의 밑줄 친 (B)It에 대한 설명으로 올바른 것은?

① 가주어로 사용된 'It'이다.
② 앞 문장의 'I can't stand it'을 가리키는 대명사이다.
③ 비인칭 주어로 사용된 'It'이다.
④ 'Waiting there for 100 days'를 가리키는 대명사이다.
⑤ 'the door'를 가리키는 대명사이다.

[08~09] 다음 대화를 읽고 물음에 답하시오.

Minji: Minsu, there is no cup I can use. Why didn't you do the dishes?

Minsu: Sorry, but I forgot (a)doing them.

Minji: What? You always forget (b)what you have to do. I can't stand it. I cleaned the living room all morning.

Minsu: Calm down! I'm busy (c)doing my homework.

Minji: Do the dishes first, and then do your homework.

Minsu: I can't. I don't think I can finish my homework today. Science is too difficult for me.

Minji: Science? You know I'm good at science. (d)Let me help you.

Minsu: Great. Thanks. I'll wash your cup right now and I'll do the rest of the dishes (e)after finishing this.

중요

08 위 대화를 읽고 답할 수 없는 질문은?

① Does Minsu feel sorry to his sister?
② Why is Minsu's sister angry at Minsu?
③ Why didn't Minsu do the dishes?
④ Does Minsu find science homework easy?
⑤ What is Minsu's sister's favorite subject?

09 위 대화의 (a)~(e) 중 문법적으로 잘못된 것은?

① (a)   ② (b)   ③ (c)   ④ (d)   ⑤ (e)

[10~11] 다음 대화를 읽고 물음에 답하시오.

(1) G: Look! That man didn't wait in line!
_____(A)_____
B: Calm down! He works here.

(2) B: 내 뒤에 있는 남자아이가 자꾸 밀어.
_____(A)_____
G: Calm down. He's just a child.

10 위 대화의 빈칸 (A)에 공통으로 들어갈 말로 적절하지 않은 것은?

① I'm very angry.   ② I can't stand it.
③ I'm really upset.   ④ Chill out!
⑤ I'm very annoyed.

서답형

11 위 대화 (2)의 밑줄 친 우리말에 맞게 주어진 단어를 활용하여 영어로 문장을 완성하시오.

> (behind / keep / push)

➡ _____

[01~02] 다음 대화를 읽고 물음에 답하시오.

Minji: Minsu, there is no cup I can use. Why didn't you do the dishes?

Minsu: Sorry, but I forgot to do them.

Minji: What? You always forget what you have to do. I can't stand it. I cleaned the living room all morning.

Minsu: Calm down! I'm busy doing my homework.

Minji: Do the dishes first, and then do your homework.

Minsu: I can't. I don't think I can finish my homework today. Science is too difficult for me.

Minji: Science? You know I'm good at science. Let me help you.

Minsu: Great. Thanks. I'll wash your cup right now and I'll do the rest of the dishes after finishing this.

01 위 대화를 읽고 다음 물음에 영어로 답하시오.

> Q: When will Minsu do the dishes?

➡ _____

02 다음은 위 대화의 요약문이다. 빈칸에 알맞은 말을 쓰시오.

Minsu and his sister are talking about Minsu's forgetting _____ _____ _____ _____. Minsu's sister is angry because he always forgets _____ _____ _____ _____ _____. Minsu's excuse is his _____ science homework. His sister will _____ him _____ his homework, and he will do the dishes _____ finishing his homework.

03 Look at the picture and make a dialogue about getting angry and calming an angry woman.

Woman: Smoke is coming from the lower floor. _____ _____ _____ _____.

Man: _____ _____! They're having a birthday party.

04 다음 그림을 보고 대화의 빈칸을 완성하시오. (주어진 철자로 단어를 쓰시오.)

M1: Why did you t_____ _____ _____ here? Please s_____ _____ _____.

M2: How can you get free? Think.

M1: I _____ s_____ this sign. I'm not dangerous or bad.

M2: C_____ _____. I'm sure you'll find a way.

Grammar
교과서

① 부정대명사

> • **Some** gave him angry looks, and **others** shouted at him.
> 몇몇은 그를 화난 표정으로 쳐다봤고, 다른 몇몇은 그에게 소리를 질렀다.

■ 부정대명사란 불특정한 사람, 사물 또는 일정하지 않은 수량을 나타내는 대명사이다.

■ one, the other 둘 중 하나, 나머지 하나

  • We have two computers in the office. **One** is new and **the other** is 3 years old.
  사무실에 컴퓨터 두 대가 있습니다. 하나는 새 것이고, 나머지 하나는 (구매한지) 3년이 되었습니다.

■ some, others 몇몇, 다른 몇몇

  • **Some** scientists think we should focus on renewable energy to prevent global warming but **others** disagree. 몇몇 과학자들은 지구 온난화를 예방하기 위해 재생 가능 에너지에 집중해야 한다고 생각하지만, 다른 몇몇은 동의하지 않는다.

■ some, the others 몇몇, 나머지 전부

  • Here are many boxes. **Some** are for clothes and **the others** are for books.
  여기 많은 상자가 있어. 몇몇은 옷을 담기 위한 것이고, 나머지는 모두 책을 담기 위한 것이야.

핵심 Check

1. 다음 괄호 안에서 알맞은 것을 고르시오.

   (1) Here are two books. One is yours, and (another / the other) is mine.

   (2) There are many candies in the dish. Some are for Ann, and (the others / the other) are for me.

   (3) Among various kinds of movies, (one / some) like to see comedies. Others like to see horror movies.

② 5형식(동사 + 목적어 + to부정사)

> • The king **ordered** him **to go** to a famous military school.
> 왕은 그에게 유명한 군사학교에 갈 것을 명령했다.

■ 'order'는 목적격보어 자리에 to부정사가 오는 동사이다. 이와 같은 종류의 동사로는 'want, ask, tell, allow, teach, advise, expect' 등이 있다.

  • The king **ordered** his servants **to bring** the wizard to his court.
  왕은 그의 신하들에게 그 마법사를 그의 궁정으로 데려오라고 명령했다.

■ 목적격보어에 원형부정사를 쓰는 동사들도 있다. 이와 같은 종류의 동사로는 'let, make, have, see, watch, hear, feel' 등이 있다.

  • The king was surprised to **see** the wizard **destroy** his palace.
  왕은 그 마법사가 그의 궁전을 파괴하는 것을 보고 놀랐습니다.

■ 'see, watch, hear, feel' 등은 목적격보어로 현재분사를 쓸 수 있다.

  • I **watched** the dog **waiting** for her owner under the bridge.
  나는 그 개가 다리 밑에서 주인을 기다리는 것을 지켜보았습니다.

■ 목적어와 목적격보어의 관계가 수동이면 목적격보어로 과거분사를 쓴다.

  • Maybe we could go to an amusement park and **have** our faces **painted**.
  어쩌면 우리는 놀이동산에 가서 얼굴에 그림을 그릴 수 있을 거야.

핵심 Check

2. 다음 괄호 안에서 알맞은 것을 고르시오.

  (1) My mother wants me (being / to be) a doctor.

  (2) My father allowed me (go / to go) camping with friends.

  (3) My teacher (told / made) her to be quiet.

01 다음 우리말에 맞게 괄호 안에 주어진 단어를 이용하여 문장을 완성하시오.

(1) 몇몇은 눈사람을 만들고 있고, 다른 몇몇은 눈싸움을 하고 있다.
(other, play, snowballs)
➡ Some are making snowmen, and _____.

(2) 새 두 마리가 있어. 한 마리는 날고 있고 나머지 한 마리는 나무 위에 앉아 있어.
(other, sit, tree)
➡ There are two birds. One is flying, and _____.

(3) 남자는 그 개에게 공을 가져오라고 명령했다. (dog, get)
➡ The man ordered _____.

(4) 여자는 그 소년에게 조심하라고 말했다. (boy, careful)
➡ The woman told _____.

02 다음 문장에서 어법상 <u>어색한</u> 부분을 바르게 고치시오.

(1) Here are two shapes. One is a star and another is a circle.

_____ ➡ _____

(2) Some went on foot, and the others went by bike, and the others went by bus.

_____ ➡ _____

(3) I don't want you tell anybody this secret.

_____ ➡ _____

(4) My uncle advised me studying hard.

_____ ➡ _____

03 다음 〈보기〉와 같이 주어진 어구를 이용하여 빈칸을 완성하시오.

┌─ 보기 ─
(jump up and down)
A: What are the two dogs doing?
B: One is eating snow, and <u>the other is jumping up and down</u>

(1) (dance)
A: What are the five singers doing?
B: One is singing, and _____.

(2) (wave their hands, the singer)
A: What are the seven people doing?
B: Some are taking pictures, and _____
_____.

01 다음 빈칸에 'help'를 적절한 형태로 넣을 때 다른 하나를 고르시오.

① The girl asked the boy _____ her.
② The girl told the boy _____ her.
③ The girl ordered the boy _____ her.
④ The girl wanted the boy _____ her.
⑤ The girl made the boy _____ her.

02 다음 주어진 우리말을 영어로 바르게 쓴 것을 고르시오.

> 선생님은 나에게 사전을 사라고 조언하셨다.

① My teacher advises me to buy a dictionary.
② My teacher advises me buy a dictionary.
③ My teacher advised me buying a dictionary.
④ My teacher advised me to buy a dictionary.
⑤ My teacher advised me buy a dictionary.

03 다음 빈칸에 들어갈 말로 적절한 것을 고르시오.

> Some went on foot, and _____ went by bike, and the others went by bus.

① one　　② the other　　③ other
④ others　　⑤ the others

04 다음 중 어법상 어색한 문장을 고르시오.

① Here are two hats. One is yours, and the other is mine.
② Here are two dogs. One is black, and the other is white.
③ He ordered the girl to wait there.
④ What did the woman tell the boy to do?
⑤ The woman asked the boy to feeding the ducks.

05 다음 빈칸에 'go'를 적절한 형태로 넣을 때 다른 하나를 고르시오.

① My father allowed me _____ to the concert with my girlfriend.
② My teacher told us _____ outside.
③ You should keep the hula hoop _____ around your waist.
④ Don't order the dog _____ out of the house.
⑤ The doctor advised Tom _____ hiking at least once a week.

06 다음 밑줄 친 우리말을 영어로 바르게 옮긴 것은?

> 아버지는 내가 용돈을 아끼기를 원하신다.

① Dad wants me saved my allowance.
② Dad wants me save my allowance.
③ Dad wants me to save my allowance.
④ Dad wants me saving my allowance.
⑤ Dad wants me to saving my allowance.

서답형

07 다음 괄호 안에 주어진 단어들을 바르게 배열하여 문장을 완성하시오.

> help / to / us / peace / each / other / tells

➡ _____

08 다음 빈칸에 들어갈 말을 순서대로 바르게 연결한 것은?

> • My friend Eunah has two strong points. One is that she sings well. _____ is that she is fun.
> • Many teenagers like idol groups. Some love TTS and _____ like Wanna Love.

① The others – others
② The other – other
③ The other – others
④ Another – the other
⑤ Another – the others

서답형
09 다음 문장에서 어법상 어색한 것을 바르게 고쳐 다시 쓰시오.

(1) He ordered his robot done his homework.

➡ _____

_____

(2) She told him locking the door.

➡ _____

_____

서답형
10 다음 빈칸에 주어진 단어 중 필요한 것만 골라 문장을 완성하시오.

> get, getting, got, gotten, to, up

> My mom told me _____ early in the morning. (엄마는 나에게 아침에 일찍 일어나라고 말씀하셨다.)

11 다음 중 어법상 어색한 문장을 고르시오.

① Ms. Green told him to wait in her office.
② I saw some children to play chess.
③ My boss asked me to send this book by parcel post.
④ The members want Jane to be their leader.
⑤ His word encouraged me to restart my life.

서답형
12 다음 괄호 안에서 알맞은 말을 고르시오.

(1) Two boys are singing. One is singing well and (another / the other) is not.

(2) Students in the classroom are taking a test. Some finished it, but (others / the others) do not yet.

(3) Mom has five brothers. One lives in Japan, and (the other / the others) live in Korea.

(4) Two people are talking. One is holding pizza, and (the other / the others) is holding balloons.

(5) In the park, there are many people. (One / Some) are taking picturers, and others are lying on the grass.

서답형
13 다음 그림을 보고 문장을 완성하시오.

> ★★★★○○ : Here are 6 shapes. _____ _____ and the others are circles.

➡ _____

서답형

14 다음 주어진 단어들을 바르게 배열하여 문장을 완성하시오.

> to / him / the / I / truth / want / know

➡ _____

15 다음 우리말을 바르게 영작한 것은?

> 나는 내 아들이 내 휴대전화를 사용하는 것을 허락하지 않는다.

① I don't allow my son use my cell phone.
② I don't let my son to use my cell phone.
③ I don't allow my son to use my cell phone.
④ I don't let my son using my cell phone.
⑤ I don't allow my son using my cell phone.

서답형

16 다음 문장의 밑줄 친 부분을 괄호 안의 단어로 바꾸어 문장을 다시 쓰시오.

(1) Can you <u>make</u> your brothers stop fighting? (force)

➡ _____
_____

(2) My parents <u>allowed</u> me to buy a new tablet PC. (let)

➡ _____
_____

중요

17 다음 빈칸에 들어갈 말을 순서대로 바르게 연결한 것은?

> • My friend Minsu has two good points. _____ is that he plays soccer well. The other is that he is handsome.
> • I like summer because I can swim. _____ reason I like summer is that I can enjoy a lot of fruits.

① One – Another
② One – Other
③ Some – The other
④ Some – Another
⑤ Another – Other

서답형

18 주어진 어휘를 이용하여 다음 우리말을 영어로 쓰시오.

> 엄마는 내가 캠핑을 가도록 허락하셨다.
> (allow, camping)

➡ _____

19 다음 우리말을 바르게 영작한 것은?

> 엄마는 나에게 설거지를 하라고 시키셨다.

① My mom had me wash the dishes.
② My mom got me wash the dishes.
③ My mom had me to wash the dishes.
④ My mom got me washed the dishes.
⑤ My mom had me washed the dishes.

중요

20 다음 중 어법상 <u>어색한</u> 문장을 고르시오.

① Mom wants me to become a golfer.
② I asked the students to answer the survey.
③ Let me know your address and phone number.
④ The English teacher got us write an essay.
⑤ We saw the sun rise over the sea.

Grammar **189**

01 다음 문장의 **틀린** 곳을 바르게 고쳐 다시 쓰시오.

(1) Here are two birds. One is flying, and other is sitting on the tree.

　➡ _____

　_____

(2) The woman told the boy be careful.

　➡ _____

(3) She has a lot of pens. Some are yellow, and other are red.

　➡ _____

　_____

(4) Jane asks me teach math.

　➡ _____

(5) The farmer wanted me feeding the pigs.

　➡ _____

02 다음 우리말을 주어진 어휘를 이용하여 영어로 옮기시오.

(1) 어머니는 나에게 일찍 일어나라고 말씀하셨다. (my, tell, get up)

　➡ _____

(2) 나는 네가 어느 누구에게도 이 비밀을 말하는 것을 원하지 않는다. (tell, anybody, secret)

　➡ _____

(3) 아버지는 삼촌이 차를 사용하는 것을 허락하셨다. (my, allow, uncle, use)

　➡ _____

03 주어진 문장의 밑줄 친 부분을 괄호 안의 단어로 바꾸어 문장을 다시 쓰시오.

(1) Mr. Kim <u>let</u> us bring what we wanted to eat. (allow)

　➡ _____

　_____

(2) Dr. Wang <u>advised</u> her patients to work out regularly during the day. (see)

　➡ _____

　_____

04 다음 그림을 보고 괄호 안의 단어를 사용하여 빈칸에 알맞은 말을 써 넣으시오.

(1) (other, curly)

There are two children. One has short hair and _____.

(2) (other, boy)

There are five children. Some are girls and _____.

(3) (roll, the snow)

There are three children. One is holding branches, _____ into a ball, the other is carrying a large snowball.

05 다음 우리말을 괄호 안의 단어를 사용하여 영어로 바르게 옮기시오.

(1) 그 남자는 소년이 잔디에 들어가는 것을 허락했다. (allow, enter)

➡ _____

_____

(2) 그녀는 세 명의 아들이 있다. 한 명은 가수이고 나머지는 댄서이다. (singer, dancer)

➡ _____

_____

06 주어진 어휘를 바르게 배열하여 영작하시오.

(1) (his / peacefully / He / people / fight / asked / to)

➡ _____

(2) (ordered / man / The police officer / come / out / the / to)

➡ _____

(3) (help / to / her / the boy / asked / The girl)

➡ _____

(4) (the boy / The teacher / hard / told / study / to)

➡ _____

07 다음 잘못된 부분을 바르게 고쳐 문장을 다시 쓰시오.

(1) I want everyone came here.

➡ _____

(2) I'd like you listen carefully.

➡ _____

(3) They allow people fishing here.

➡ _____

(4) I advise you to not walk home alone.

➡ _____

(5) The dentist told Daniel given up eating sweets.

➡ _____

08 〈보기〉에 주어진 부정대명사를 빈칸에 적절하게 찾아 넣으시오.

┤ 보기 ├
some, one, another, others, the other, the others

• There are five people in the room. (1)_____ is a man. The others are women.
• Four people are walking on the street. (2)_____ have long hair. The others have short hair.
• There are three desks in the classroom. One is big, and (3)_____ _____ are small.

Corky, the Best Warrior

Corky was a brave young man. He wanted to be a general, but the
king said, "You're the strongest man in my army, but you have much
to learn." He ordered Corky to go to a famous military school.

"Wait there. In a hundred days, your training will start," a voice said
from inside the school gate. Corky got angry. But then he thought there
might be a reason, so he waited. On the hundred and first day, the gate
opened. An old man said, "You have learned to use your first weapon:
patience. Patience is the most important thing to win a war."

Then, the teacher told Corky to stand against a pole. Suddenly, he tied
Corky to the pole. Above his head, he put a sign that read "Dangerous
and Bad." Many people passed by. Some gave Corky angry looks, and
others shouted at him. Corky shouted back. He yelled, "Set me free, or
you all will be in big trouble!" That made the situation worse.

---

warrior 전사

patience 인내심, 참을성

war 전쟁

military 군대; 군대의

general 장군

army 군대

order 명령하다

gate 정문, 대문

might ∼일지도 모른다

reason 이유

weapon 무기

pole 기둥, 막대, 장대

tie 묶다

above ∼보다 위에

look 표정

yell 소리 지르다

📎 확인문제

● 다음 문장이 본문의 내용과 일치하면 T, 일치하지 않으면 F를 쓰시오.

1 Corky wanted to be a general. ☐

2 The teacher ordered Corky to go to a famous military school. ☐

3 Corky has learned to use his first weapon: patience. ☐

4 The general told Corky to stand against a pole. ☐

5 Corky yelled, "Set me free, or you all will be in big trouble!" ☐

6 Corky made the situation better. ☐

"I need to try another way," he thought. Then, Corky began to speak softly. He said he was <u>not</u> dangerous or bad <u>but</u> was a good man. He
not A but B: A가 아니라 B
kept saying this in all possible ways. Finally, the people <u>let him go</u>.
let(사역동사)+목적어+동사원형(목적격 보어): ···가 ~하도록 허락하다

"Now you control the most powerful weapon: words. Soft words are stronger than sharp swords," said the teacher.

Next, the teacher <u>took Corky to a large hall</u> with a chair in the
take A to B: A를 B로 데려가다
middle. There were 19 <u>other</u> warriors <u>who</u> <u>had passed</u> their tests. "The
other: (그 밖의) 다른 who: 주격 관계대명사 과거완료: 과거보다 앞선 시제를 나타냄.
first one to sit in the chair will be the winner," the teacher said.

Corky and <u>the others</u> began fighting. They pushed, pulled, ran, and
나머지 사람들 모두
jumped. They fought <u>harder and harder</u>, so Corky became tired.
비교급 and 비교급: 점점 더 ~한[하게]

Finally, he said, "I will not fight anymore. Instead, I will take care of <u>the injured</u>." The other warriors saw this and fought even harder. <u>As</u>
부상자들(the+과거분사 = 복수 보통명사) ~함에 따라(접속사)
they fought, more warriors became tired and hurt. Corky took good care of them, so they followed him. Soon, all the warriors except Thunder were following Corky.

set free 석방하다, 풀어 주다
situation 상황
powerful 강력한
sword 검, 칼
in the middle ~의 가운데에
winner 승리자, 우승자
push 밀다
finally 결국, 마침내
take care of ~을 돌보다
injured 부상당한

확인문제

● 다음 문장이 본문의 내용과 일치하면 T, 일치하지 <u>않으면</u> F를 쓰시오.

1 Corky said he was not dangerous or bad but was a good man. ☐

2 "Sharp swords are stronger than soft words," said the teacher. ☐

3 The teacher took Corky to a large hall with a chair in the middle. ☐

4 The first one to lift the chair will be the winner. ☐

5 As Corky and the others fought harder and harder, Corky became tired. ☐

6 Soon, all the warriors including Thunder were following Corky. ☐

Reading **193**

Thunder walked toward the chair to sit in it. Then, he <u>saw Corky</u>
지각동사+목적어+현재분사/동사원형(목적격 보어): …가 ~하는 것을 보다
<u>standing</u> with his 18 followers. Thunder realized he was all alone. "I
give up. You're the real winner," Thunder said to Corky.

At that moment, the teacher appeared and said. "Of all the great
weapons, peace is my favorite. Sooner or later, everyone wants to
stand on the side of peace."

Corky returned to the palace after his training ended. When the king
saw him approach, he <u>gave Corky a wise and knowing smile</u> and said,
수여동사+간접목적어+직접목적어(4형식)
"What's up, General?"

realize 깨닫다
give up 포기하다
favorite 특히 좋아하는 것(사람)
sooner or later 조만간, 머잖아
on the side of ~ 편에
palace 궁, 궁전
approach 다가가다
wise 현명한

📎 **확인문제**

● 다음 문장이 본문의 내용과 일치하면 T, 일치하지 <u>않으면</u> F를 쓰시오.

1 Thunder walked toward the chair in order to sit in it. ☐

2 Corky saw Thunder standing with his 18 followers. ☐

3 Thunder realized he was all by himself. ☐

4 Corky said that of all the great weapons, peace was his favorite. ☐

5 Sooner or later, everyone wants to stand on the side of peace. ☐

6 Corky returned to the palace before his training ended. ☐

우리말을 참고하여 빈칸에 알맞은 말을 쓰시오.

1 Corky, _____ _____ _____

2 Corky was a _____ _____ man.

3 He wanted to be a general, but the king said, "You're the _____ man in my army, but you _____ _____ _____ _____."

4 He ordered Corky _____ _____ to a famous military school.

5 "Wait there. _____ _____ _____ _____, your training will start," a voice said from inside the school gate.

6 Corky _____ _____.

7 But then he thought there _____ _____ _____ _____, so he waited.

8 _____ _____ _____ _____ _____ _____ _____, the gate opened.

9 An old man said, "You have learned to use your _____ _____: _____.

10 Patience is the most important thing _____ _____ _____ _____."

11 Then, the teacher told Corky to _____ _____ a pole.

12 Suddenly, he _____ Corky _____ the pole.

13 Above his head, he put a sign _____ _____ "Dangerous and Bad."

14 Many people _____.

1   최고의 전사, Corky

2   Corky는 용감한 청년이었다.

3   그는 장군이 되기를 원했지만 왕은 이렇게 말했다. "자네는 우리 군대에서 가장 강한 전사이네. 하지만 자네는 아직도 배울 게 많아."

4   왕은 Corky에게 유명한 군사 학교에 갈 것을 명령했다.

5   "거기서 기다려라. 훈련은 100일 후에 시작할 것이다." 군사 학교 안에서 이렇게 외치는 목소리가 들렸다.

6   Corky는 화가 났다.

7   하지만 이유가 있을 것으로 생각하고 기다렸다.

8   101일째 되던 날, 문이 열렸다.

9   한 노인이 이렇게 말했다. "너는 첫 번째 무기인 '인내'를 사용하는 법을 배운 것이다.

10 인내는 전쟁에서 이기기 위해 가장 중요한 것이다."

11 그리고 난 뒤, 스승은 Corky에게 기둥 앞에 서라고 말했다.

12 갑자기 그는 Corky를 기둥에 묶었다.

13 그의 머리 위에는 '위험하고 나쁨'이라는 푯말을 붙였다.

14 많은 사람이 지나갔다.

15 _____ gave Corky angry looks, and _____ shouted at him.

16 Corky _____ _____.

17 He yelled, "_____ _____ _____, _____ you all will be in big trouble!"

18 That _____ the situation _____.

19 "I need to try _____ way," he thought.

20 Then, Corky began to speak _____.

21 He said he was _____ dangerous or bad _____ was a good man.

22 He _____ _____ this in all possible ways.

23 Finally, the people _____ _____ _____.

24 "Now you control _____ _____ _____ _____ : words.

25 Soft words are _____ _____ sharp swords," said the teacher.

26 Next, the teacher _____ Corky _____ a large hall with a chair in the middle.

27 There were 19 other warriors who _____ _____ their tests.

28 "_____ _____ _____ _____ sit in the chair will be the winner," the teacher said.

29 Corky and _____ _____ began fighting.

30 They _____, _____, ran, and jumped.

---

15 몇몇은 Corky를 화난 표정으로 쳐다봤고, 다른 몇몇은 그에게 소리를 질렀다.

16 Corky도 그들에게 소리를 질렀다.

17 그는 "나를 풀어 줘. 그러지 않으면 모두 혼쭐날 줄 알아!"라고 외쳤다.

18 그것은 상황을 더 악화시켰다.

19 그는 '다른 방법을 써야겠어.'라고 생각했다.

20 그러고 나서 Corky는 부드럽게 말하기 시작했다.

21 그는 자신이 위험하거나 나쁘지 않고 좋은 사람이라고 말했다.

22 그는 모든 방법을 동원해 계속해서 이렇게 말했다.

23 마침내 사람들은 그를 풀어 주었다.

24 "이제 너는 가장 강력한 무기인 '말'을 통제하게 되었다.

25 부드러운 말은 날카로운 칼보다 강하니라."라고 스승은 말했다.

26 다음 단계로 스승은 Corky를 중앙에 의자가 놓여 있는 커다란 홀로 데리고 갔다.

27 그곳에는 시험에 통과한 19명의 다른 전사들이 있었다.

28 "저 의자에 가장 먼저 앉는 사람이 승자가 될 것이다."라고 스승이 말했다.

29 Corky와 나머지 전사들은 싸우기 시작했다.

30 그들은 밀고 당기고 달리고 뛰어올랐다.

31 They fought _____ _____ _____, so Corky became tired.

32 Finally, he said, "I will not fight _____.

33 Instead, I will take care of _____ _____."

34 The other warriors saw this and fought _____ _____.

35 _____ they fought, more warriors became tired and hurt.

36 Corky _____ _____ _____ _____ them, so they followed him.

37 Soon, all the warriors _____ Thunder were _____ Corky.

38 Thunder walked toward the chair _____ _____ _____ _____.

39 Then, he saw Corky _____ _____ his 18 followers.

40 Thunder realized he was _____ _____.

41 "I give up. You're _____ _____ _____," Thunder said to Corky.

42 _____ _____ _____, the teacher appeared and said. "Of all the great weapons, peace is _____ _____.

43 _____ _____ _____, everyone wants to stand on the side of peace."

44 Corky _____ _____ the palace after his training ended.

45 When the king saw him _____, he gave Corky a wise and _____ smile and said, "_____ _____, General?"

---

31 그들은 점점 더 격렬히 싸웠고, Corky는 지쳤다.

32 마침내 그가 말했다. "나는 더는 싸움을 하지 않겠다.

33 대신에 부상당한 자들을 돌볼 것이다."

34 나머지 전사들은 이것을 보고 더 심하게 싸움을 했다.

35 그들이 싸움을 할수록 더 많은 전사들이 지치고 다쳤다.

36 Corky는 그들을 잘 돌봐 주었고, 그들은 Corky를 따르게 되었다.

37 곧 Thunder를 제외한 모든 전사들이 Corky를 따르고 있었다.

38 Thunder는 의자로 걸어가 그곳에 앉으려 했다.

39 그러다 그는 Corky가 18명의 추종자들과 함께 서 있는 것을 봤다.

40 Thunder는 자신이 혼자라는 사실을 깨달았다.

41 "나는 포기하겠다. 네가 진정한 승자다."라고 Thunder가 Corky에게 말했다.

42 그때 스승이 나타나 말했다. "모든 훌륭한 무기 중에서 평화는 내가 가장 좋아하는 것이다.

43 조만간 모든 사람은 평화의 편에 서기를 원한다."

44 Corky는 훈련을 마친 후 성으로 돌아갔다.

45 Corky가 다가오는 것을 본 왕은 그에게 이미 모든 것을 알고 있다는 듯한 현명한 미소를 띠며 말했다. "안녕하시오, 장군?"

● 우리말을 참고하여 본문을 영작하시오.

1 최고의 전사, Corky

➡ _____

2 Corky는 용감한 청년이었다.

➡ _____

3 그는 장군이 되기를 원했지만 왕은 이렇게 말했다. "자네는 우리 군대에서 가장 강한 전사이네.
하지만 자네는 아직도 배울 게 많아."

➡ _____

➡ _____

4 왕은 Corky에게 유명한 군사 학교에 갈 것을 명령했다.

➡ _____

5 "거기서 기다려라. 훈련은 100일 후에 시작할 것이다." 군사 학교 안에서 이렇게 외치는 목소리가 들렸다.

➡ _____

6 Corky는 화가 났다.

➡ _____

7 하지만 이유가 있을 것으로 생각하고 기다렸다.

➡ _____

8 101일째 되던 날, 문이 열렸다.

➡ _____

9 한 노인이 이렇게 말했다. "너는 첫 번째 무기인 '인내'를 사용하는 법을 배운 것이다.

➡ _____

10 인내는 전쟁에서 이기기 위해 가장 중요한 것이다."

➡ _____

11 그리고 난 뒤, 스승은 Corky에게 기둥 앞에 서라고 말했다.

➡ _____

12 갑자기 그는 Corky를 기둥에 묶었다.

➡ _____

13 그의 머리 위에는 '위험하고 나쁨'이라는 푯말을 붙였다.

➡ _____

14 많은 사람이 지나갔다.

➡ _____

15 몇몇은 Corky를 화난 표정으로 쳐다봤고, 다른 몇몇은 그에게 소리를 질렀다.

➡ _____

16 Corky도 그들에게 소리를 질렀다.

➡ _____

17 그는 "나를 풀어 줘. 그러지 않으면 모두 혼쭐날 줄 알아!"라고 외쳤다.

➡ _____

18 그것은 상황을 더 악화시켰다.

➡ _____

19 그는 '다른 방법을 써야겠어.'라고 생각했다.

➡ _____

20 그러고 나서 Corky는 부드럽게 말하기 시작했다.

➡ _____

21 그는 자신이 위험하거나 나쁘지 않고 좋은 사람이라고 말했다.

➡ _____

22 그는 모든 방법을 동원해 계속해서 이렇게 말했다.

➡ _____

23 마침내 사람들은 그를 풀어 주었다.

➡ _____

24 "이제 너는 가장 강력한 무기인 '말'을 통제하게 되었다.

➡ _____

25 부드러운 말은 날카로운 칼보다 강하니라."라고 스승은 말했다.

➡ _____

26 다음 단계로 스승은 Corky를 중앙에 의자가 놓여 있는 커다란 홀로 데리고 갔다.

➡ _____

27 그곳에는 시험에 통과한 19명의 다른 전사들이 있었다.

➡ _____

28 "저 의자에 가장 먼저 앉는 사람이 승자가 될 것이다."라고 스승이 말했다.

➡ _____

29 Corky와 나머지 전사들은 싸우기 시작했다.

➡ _____

30 그들은 밀고 당기고 달리고 뛰어올랐다.

➡ _____

31 그들은 점점 더 격렬히 싸웠고, Corky는 지쳤다.

➡ _____

32 마침내 그가 말했다. "나는 더는 싸움을 하지 않겠다.

➡ _____

33 대신에 부상당한 자들을 돌볼 것이다."

➡ _____

34 나머지 전사들은 이것을 보고 더 심하게 싸움을 했다.

➡ _____

35 그들이 싸움을 할수록 더 많은 전사들이 지치고 다쳤다.

➡ _____

36 Corky는 그들을 잘 돌봐 주었고, 그들은 Corky를 따르게 되었다.

➡ _____

37 곧 Thunder를 제외한 모든 전사들이 Corky를 따르고 있었다.

➡ _____

38 Thunder는 의자로 걸어가 그곳에 앉으려 했다.

➡ _____

39 그러다 그는 Corky가 18명의 추종자들과 함께 서 있는 것을 봤다.

➡ _____

40 Thunder는 자신이 혼자라는 사실을 깨달았다.

➡ _____

41 "나는 포기하겠다. 네가 진정한 승자다."라고 Thunder가 Corky에게 말했다.

➡ _____

42 그때 스승이 나타나 말했다. "모든 훌륭한 무기 중에서 평화는 내가 가장 좋아하는 것이다.

➡ _____

_____

43 조만간 모든 사람은 평화의 편에 서기를 원한다."

➡ _____

44 Corky는 훈련을 마친 후 성으로 돌아갔다.

➡ _____

45 Corky가 다가오는 것을 본 왕은 그에게 이미 모든 것을 알고 있다는 듯한 현명한 미소를 띠며 말했다. "안녕하시오, 장군?"

➡ _____

_____

[01~03] 다음 글을 읽고 물음에 답하시오.

Corky was a brave young man. ①He wanted to be a general, but the king said, "You're the strongest man in my army, but you have much ⓐto learn." ②He ordered Corky to go to a famous military school.

"Wait there. In a hundred days, your training will start," a voice said from inside the school gate. Corky got angry. But then ③he thought there might be a reason, so ④he waited. On the hundred and first day, the gate opened. An old man said, "⑤You have learned to use your first weapon: patience. Patience is the most important thing to win a war."

01 밑줄 친 ①~⑤ 중에서 가리키는 대상이 나머지 넷과 다른 것은?

①   ②   ③   ④   ⑤

02 위 글의 밑줄 친 ⓐto learn과 to부정사의 용법이 같은 것을 모두 고르시오.

① There is no one to do it.
② She must be a fool to say like that.
③ I want a chair to sit on.
④ I think it wrong to tell a lie.
⑤ He is the last man to tell a lie.

03 According to the passage, which is NOT true?

① The king said that Corky was the strongest man in his army.
② The king ordered Corky to go to a famous military school.
③ Corky got angry when he heard a voice from inside the school gate.

④ On the hundredth day, the gate opened.
⑤ An old man said, "You have learned to use your first weapon: patience. Patience is the most important thing to win a war."

[04~06] 다음 글을 읽고 물음에 답하시오.

Then, the teacher told Corky to stand against a pole. Suddenly, he tied Corky to the pole. Above his head, he put a sign that read "Dangerous and Bad." Many people passed by. Some gave Corky angry looks, and others shouted at him. Corky shouted back. He yelled, "Set me free, or you all will be in big trouble!" That made the situation worse.

"I need to try another way," he thought. Then, Corky began to speak softly. He said he was not dangerous or bad but was a good man. He kept saying this in all possible ways. Finally, the people ___ⓐ___ him go.

"Now you control the most powerful weapon: words. ⓑ부드러운 말은 날카로운 칼보다 강하니라," said the teacher.

04 위 글의 빈칸 ⓐ에 들어갈 알맞은 말을 고르시오.

① wanted   ② let
③ ordered   ④ told
⑤ allowed

서답형

05 위 글의 밑줄 친 ⓑ의 우리말에 맞게 주어진 어휘를 이용하여 7 단어로 영작하시오.

sharp swords

➡ _____

06 Which question CANNOT be answered after reading the passage?

① What did the teacher tell Corky to do?

② What did people do when they passed by the pole?

③ Why did Corky begin to speak softly though people shouted at him?

④ How long was Corky tied to the pole?

⑤ What weapon did Corky come to control?

[07~09] 다음 글을 읽고 물음에 답하시오.

Next, the teacher took Corky to a large hall with a chair in the middle. There were 19 other warriors who had passed their tests. "The first one to sit in the chair will be the winner," the teacher said.

Corky and the others began fighting. They pushed, pulled, ran, and jumped. They fought harder and harder, so Corky became tired.

Finally, he said, "I will not fight anymore. _____ⓐ_____ , I will take care of the injured." The other warriors saw this and fought ⓑeven harder. As they fought, more warriors became tired and hurt. Corky took good care of them, so they followed him. Soon, all the warriors except Thunder were following Corky.

07 위 글의 빈칸 ⓐ에 들어갈 알맞은 말을 고르시오.

① Still
② Instead
③ In fact
④ For example
⑤ Therefore

08 위 글의 밑줄 친 ⓑeven과 바꿔 쓸 수 없는 말을 고르시오.

① much
② still
③ more
④ far
⑤ a lot

09 위 글을 읽고 스승의 시험에 대한 Corky의 행동 변화를 우리말로 쓰시오.

➡ _____

[10~11] 다음 글을 읽고 물음에 답하시오.

Thunder walked toward the chair to sit in it. Then, ①he saw Corky standing with ② his 18 followers. Thunder realized he was all alone. "I give up. ③You're the real winner," Thunder said to Corky.

At that moment, the teacher appeared and said. "Of all the great weapons, peace is my favorite. Sooner or later, everyone wants to stand on the side of peace."

Corky returned to the palace after ④his training ended. When the king saw ⑤him approach, he gave Corky a wise and knowing smile and said, "What's up, General?"

10 밑줄 친 ①~⑤ 중에서 가리키는 대상이 나머지 넷과 다른 것은?

①   ②   ③   ④   ⑤

11 위 글의 교훈으로 알맞은 것을 고르시오.

① It is difficult to fight with others without any help.

② Sometimes it is wise to give up.

③ There are various ways to be the real winner.

④ There are no winners in the battle of life.

⑤ Everyone wants to stand on the side of peace.

[12~14] 다음 글을 읽고 물음에 답하시오.

Then, the teacher told Corky to stand against a pole. Suddenly, he tied Corky to the pole. Above his head, he put a sign that (A)read "Dangerous and Bad." Many people passed by. Some gave Corky angry looks, and others shouted at him. Corky shouted back. He yelled, "Set me free, or you all will be in big trouble!" That made the situation worse.

"I need to try another way," he thought. Then, Corky began to speak softly. He said he was not dangerous or bad but was a good man. He kept _____ⓐ_____ this in all possible ways. Finally, the people let him go.

"Now you control the most powerful weapon: words. Soft words are stronger than sharp swords," said the teacher.

서답형

12 위 글의 빈칸 ⓐ에 say를 알맞은 형태로 쓰시오.

➡ _____

13 위 글의 밑줄 친 (A)read와 같은 의미로 쓰인 것을 고르시오.

① I read about the accident in the local paper.

② How do you read the present situation?

③ A man came to read the gas meter.

④ The sign read 'No admittance.'

⑤ My computer can't read the disk you sent.

서답형

14 위 글을 읽고 스승의 시험에 대한 Corky의 행동 변화를 우리말로 쓰시오.

첫 번째 반응: _____

_____

두 번째 반응: _____

_____

[15~17] 다음 글을 읽고 물음에 답하시오.

Next, the teacher took Corky to a large hall with a chair in the middle. There were 19 other warriors who had passed their tests. "The first one to sit in the chair will be the winner," the teacher said.

Corky and ⓐthe others began fighting. They pushed, pulled, ran, and jumped. They fought harder and harder, so Corky became tired.

Finally, he said, "I will not fight anymore. Instead, I will take care of ⓑthe injured." The other warriors saw this and fought even harder. As they fought, more warriors became tired and hurt. Corky took good care of them, so they followed him. Soon, all the warriors except Thunder were following Corky.

서답형

15 위 글의 밑줄 친 ⓐthe others가 가리키는 것을 본문에서 찾아 쓰시오.

➡ _____

서답형

16 위 글의 밑줄 친 ⓑthe injured와 바꿔 쓸 수 있는 말을 두 단어로 쓰시오.

➡ _____

17 위 글의 주제로 알맞은 것을 고르시오.

① The teacher made the warriors fight with each other to sit first in the chair.
② The warriors fought harder and harder.
③ Corky became tired, so he gave up fighting.
④ All the warriors except Corky fought even harder.
⑤ Corky got many followers by taking care of the injured.

[18~20] 다음 글을 읽고 물음에 답하시오.

Thunder walked toward the chair to sit in it. ⓐThen, he saw Corky to stand with his 18 followers. Thunder realized he was all alone. "I give up. You're the real winner," Thunder said to Corky.

At that moment, the teacher appeared and said. "Of all the great weapons, peace is my favorite. ⓑ조만간 모든 사람은 평화의 편에 서기를 원한다."

Corky returned to the palace after his training ended. When the king saw him approach, he gave Corky a wise and knowing smile and said, "What's up, General?"

서답형

18 위 글의 밑줄 친 ⓐ에서 어법상 틀린 부분을 찾아 고치시오.

_____ ➡ _____

서답형

19 위 글의 밑줄 친 ⓑ의 우리말에 맞게 주어진 어휘를 이용하여 12 단어로 영작하시오.

sooner, on the side of

➡ _____

_____

20 위 글의 제목으로 가장 알맞은 것을 고르시오.

① Thunder Saw Corky Standing with His 18 Followers
② Corky, the Real Winner, Got the Last Weapon, Peace
③ Thunder Realized He Was All Alone
④ Peace Is My Favorite of All the Great Weapons
⑤ The King Gave Corky a Wise and Knowing Smile

[21~23] 다음 글을 읽고 물음에 답하시오.

Corky was a brave young man. He wanted to be a general, but the king said, "You're the strongest man in my army, but (A)you have much to learn." He ordered Corky to go to a famous military school.

(①) "Wait there. ____ⓐ____ a hundred days, your training will start," a voice said from inside the school gate. (②) But then he thought there might be a reason, so he waited. (③) ____ⓑ____ the hundred and first day, the gate opened. (④) An old man said, "You have learned to use your first weapon: patience. Patience is the most important thing to win a war." (⑤)

21 위 글의 빈칸 ⓐ와 ⓑ에 들어갈 전치사가 바르게 짝지어진 것은?

ⓐ ⓑ	ⓐ ⓑ
① For – In	② In – By
③ In – On	④ On – In
⑤ For – On	

서답형

22 위 글의 밑줄 친 (A)를 다음과 같이 바꿔 쓸 때 빈칸에 들어갈 알맞은 말을 두 단어로 쓰시오.

> you have much _____ _____ learn

23 위 글의 흐름으로 보아, 주어진 문장이 들어가기에 가장 적절한 곳은?

> Corky got angry.

①   ②   ③   ④   ⑤

[24~26] 다음 글을 읽고 물음에 답하시오.

Then, the teacher told Corky to stand against a pole. Suddenly, he tied Corky to the pole. Above his head, he put a sign ___ⓐ___ read "Dangerous and Bad." Many people passed by. Some gave Corky angry looks, and others shouted at him. Corky shouted back. He yelled, "Set me free, or you all will be in big trouble!" ⓑThat made the situation better. "I need to try another way," he thought. Then, Corky began to speak softly. He said he was not dangerous or bad but was a good man. He kept saying this in all possible ways. ⓒFinally, the people let him go. "Now you control the most powerful weapon: words. Soft words are stronger than sharp swords," said the teacher.

서답형

24 위 글의 빈칸 ⓐ에 들어갈 알맞은 말을 쓰시오.

➡ _____

서답형

25 위 글의 밑줄 친 ⓑ에서 흐름상 어색한 부분을 찾아 고치시오.

_____ ➡ _____

26 위 글의 밑줄 친 ⓒFinally와 바꿔 쓸 수 없는 단어를 고르시오.

① At last   ② In the end
③ After all   ④ Immediately
⑤ Eventually

[27~28] 다음 글을 읽고 물음에 답하시오.

Next, the teacher took Corky to a large hall with a chair in the middle. There were 19 other warriors who had passed their tests. "The first one to sit in the chair will be the winner," the teacher said.

Corky and the others began fighting. They pushed, pulled, ran, and jumped. They fought harder and harder, so Corky became tired. Finally, he said, "I will not fight anymore. Instead, I will ⓐtake care of the injured." The other warriors saw this and fought even harder. As they fought, more warriors became tired and hurt. Corky took good care of them, so they followed him. Soon, all the warriors except Thunder were following Corky.

27 위 글의 밑줄 친 ⓐtake care of와 바꿔 쓸 수 있는 말을 모두 고르시오.

① look after   ② take off
③ deal in   ④ care for
⑤ look for

중요

28 위 글을 읽고 알 수 없는 것을 고르시오.

① Where did the teacher take Corky?
② How many warriors were there in the large hall except Corky?
③ Who will be the winner?
④ How long did the warriors fight?
⑤ Why did the warriors except Thunder follow Corky?

[01~03] 다음 글을 읽고 물음에 답하시오.

Corky was a brave young man. He wanted to be a general, but the king said, "You're the strongest man in my army, but you have much to learn." He ordered Corky to go to a famous military school.

"Wait there. In a hundred days, your training will start," a voice said from inside the school gate. Corky got angry. ⓐBut then he thought there might be a reason, so he waited. On the hundred and first day, the gate opened. An old man said, "You have learned to use your first weapon: patience. Patience is the most important thing to win a war."

01 Why did the king order Corky to go to a famous military school? Fill in the blanks (A) and (B) with suitable words.

Because he thought that though Corky was (A)_____ _____ _____ in his army, he had much (B)_____ _____.

02 다음 빈칸 (A)와 (B)에 알맞은 단어를 넣어, 위 글의 밑줄 친 문장 ⓐ 뒤에 생략된 부분을 완성하시오.

But then he thought there might be a reason for making him (A)_____ _____ for (B)_____ _____ days.

03 본문의 내용과 일치하도록 다음 빈칸 (A)와 (B)에 알맞은 단어를 쓰시오.

Corky went to a famous military school but had to wait (A)_____ _____ _____ its gate for a hundred days. On the hundred and first day, an old man said that Corky had learned to use his first weapon, (B)_____, for the past one hundred days.

[04~05] 다음 글을 읽고 물음에 답하시오.

Then, the teacher told Corky to stand against a pole. Suddenly, he tied Corky to the pole. Above his head, he put a sign that read "Dangerous and Bad." Many people passed by. Some gave Corky angry looks, and others shouted at him. Corky shouted back. He yelled, "ⓐSet me free, or you all will be in big trouble!" That made the situation worse.

"I need to try ⓑanother way," he thought. Then, Corky began to speak softly. He said he was not dangerous or bad but was a good man. He kept saying this in all possible ways. Finally, the people let him go.

"Now you control the most powerful weapon: words. Soft words are stronger than sharp swords," said the teacher.

04 위 글의 밑줄 친 ⓐ를 다음과 같이 바꿔 쓸 때 빈칸에 들어갈 알맞은 말을 쓰시오.

(1) _____ _____ _____ set me free, you all will be in big trouble!

(2) _____ _____ set me free, you all will be in big trouble!

05 위 글의 밑줄 친 ⓑ가 가리키는 구체적인 방법 두 가지를 우리말로 쓰시오.

(1) _____

(2) _____

_____

[06~08] 다음 글을 읽고 물음에 답하시오.

Next, the teacher took Corky to a large hall with a chair in the middle. There were 19 other warriors who had passed their tests. "ⓐ저 의자에 가장 먼저 앉는 사람이 승자가 될 것이다," the teacher said.

Corky and the others began fighting. They pushed, pulled, ran, and jumped. They fought harder and harder, so Corky became (A)[tiring / tired].

Finally, he said, "I will not fight anymore. Instead, I will take care of the (B)[injured / victims]." The other warriors saw this and fought even harder. As they fought, more warriors became tired and hurt. Corky took good care of them, so they followed him. Soon, all the warriors except Thunder were (C)[following / followed] Corky.

06 위 글의 밑줄 친 ⓐ의 우리말에 맞게 주어진 어휘를 이용하여 12 단어로 영작하시오.

first one, in, will be

➡ _____

07 위 글의 괄호 (A)~(C)에서 문맥이나 어법상 알맞은 낱말을 골라 쓰시오.

➡ (A) _____ (B) _____ (C) _____

08 본문의 내용과 일치하도록 다음 빈칸 (A)와 (B)에 알맞은 단어를 쓰시오.

Corky got many followers by (A)_____ _____ _____ the injured instead of (B)_____ with other warriors.

[09~11] 다음 글을 읽고 물음에 답하시오.

Thunder walked toward the chair to sit in it. Then, he saw Corky standing with his 18 followers. Thunder realized he was all alone. "I give up. You're the real winner," Thunder said to Corky.

At that moment, the teacher appeared and said. "Of all the great weapons, peace is my favorite. Sooner or later, everyone wants to stand on the side of peace."

Corky returned to the palace after his training ended. When the king saw him approach, ⓐ he gave Corky a wise and knowing smile and said, "What's up, General?"

09 위 글의 밑줄 친 ⓐ를 3형식 문장으로 고치시오.

➡ _____

10 What's the last weapon that Corky got? Answer in English beginning with "It". (3 words)

➡ _____

11 본문의 내용과 일치하도록 다음 빈칸 (A)와 (B)에 알맞은 단어를 쓰시오.

Thunder said that Corky was the (A)_____ _____. Finally, Corky got the last (B)_____ which was also his teacher's favorite weapon. After all the training, Corky returned and became a general.

구석구석

After You Read A

1. Corky wanted to be a general in the army.
   want는 to부정사를 목적어로 취함.
2. Corky went to the military school and waited for a hundred days.
   for+숫자: ~ 동안
3. Corky kept saying he was not dangerous[bad], so people finally set him free.
   keep ~ing: 계속해서 ~하다   set free: 석방하다, 풀어 주다
4. Corky stopped fighting and took care of the injured.
   stop ~ing: ~을 그만두다   the injured: 부상자들(the+과거분사 = 복수 보통명사)

구문해설 · general: 장군 · army: 군대 · military: 군대; 군대의 · set free: 석방하다, 풀어 주다
· take care of: ~을 돌보다 · injured: 부상당한

1. Corky는 군대에서 장군이 되기를 원했다.
2. Corky는 군사 학교에 가서 100일 동안 기다렸다.
3. Corky는 계속해서 자신이 위험하지[나쁘지] 않다고 말해서, 사람들이 마침내 그를 풀어 주었다.
4. Corky는 싸움을 멈추고 부상당한 자들을 돌보아주었다.

Inside the Story

Two people are talking in the hall. One is the king, and the other is Corky.

The king orders Corky to go to the military school. Many people are standing
orders의 목적격보어
around Corky. One is talking to Corky, the others are listening. The teacher
나머지 모두
tells Corky to be quiet and stay there.
tell의 목적격보어 ①   tell의 목적격보어 ②
Two men are standing inside the gate. One is holding a sword, and the other
둘 중 하나   둘 중 나머지 하나
is holding a stick. The man holding a sword tells Corky to wait there for 100
tells의 목적격보어
days.

Many warriors are listening to the teacher. Some are standing, and the others
나머지 모두
are kneeling. The teacher wants them to keep fighting to sit in the chair.
want의 목적격보어

구문해설 · military: 군사의 · sword: 칼 · kneel: 무릎을 꿇다

두 사람이 홀에서 말하고 있다. 한 사람은 왕이고 나머지 한 사람은 Corky이다. 왕은 Corky에게 군사 학교로 가라고 명령한다. 많은 사람이 Corky 주변에 서 있다. 한 사람은 Corky에게 말하고 있고 나머지 사람들은 듣고 있다. 스승은 Corky에게 조용히 하고 거기 있으라고 말한다. 두 남자가 문 안에 서 있다. 한 명은 칼을 들고 있고 나머지 한 명은 곤봉을 들고 있다. 칼을 들고 있는 남자는 Corky에게 100일 동안 거기서 기다리라고 말한다. 많은 전사가 스승의 말을 듣고 있다. 몇몇은 서 있고 나머지는 무릎을 꿇고 있다. 스승은 그들이 의자에 앉기 위해 계속 싸우기를 원한다.

Link to the World

· Mahatma Gandhi led a peaceful movement to free India.
                                        'movement'를 수식하는 형용사적 용법
· He asked his people to fight peacefully against England.
   ask+목적어+to부정사: …가 ~하도록 요청하다   'fight'를 수식하는 부사
· He fasted for a long time instead of fighting with weapons.
                              전치사 of 뒤에 명사를 사용한다.
· "An eye for an eye will only make the whole world blind," he said.
   눈에는 눈이라는 식의 복수(같은 방법에 의한 보복)   make+목적어+목적보어(형용사)

구문해설 · lead(-led-led): 이끌다 · movement: 운동 · free: 해방시키다 · against: ~에 대항하여
· fast: 단식하다, 굶다 · instead of: ~ 대신에 · weapon: 무기 · blind: 눈 먼

· 마하트마 간디는 인도를 해방하기 위한 평화 운동을 이끌었다.
· 그는 그의 국민들에게 영국에 대항하여 평화롭게 싸울 것을 요청했다.
· 그는 무기를 들고 싸우는 대신 오랫동안 단식 투쟁을 했다.
· "눈에는 눈이라는 식의 복수는 오직 전 세계를 눈멀게 할 뿐이다."라고 그는 말했다.

영역별 핵심문제

01 다음 짝지어진 두 단어의 관계가 같도록 빈칸에 알맞은 단어를 쓰시오.

> fighter – warrior : wounded – _____

02 다음 문장의 빈칸 (a)와 (b)에 들어갈 어구가 바르게 짝지어진 것은?

> • (a)_____ you will have to make a decision.
> • She hoped to (b)_____ her native land.

① In all possible ways – step on
② In all possible ways – wait for
③ Sooner or later – should have been
④ Sooner or later – return to
⑤ Sooner or later – pass by

[03~04] 다음 영영풀이에 해당하는 것을 고르시오.

03

> to tell someone to do something

① order   ② insist
③ yell   ④ stand
⑤ forget

04

> the person that wins a competition

① grass   ② winner
③ general   ④ situation
⑤ patience

05 다음 대화의 빈칸에 들어갈 말을 〈영영풀이〉를 참고하여 두 단어로 쓰시오.

> G: I can't find my pencil case. Have you seen it?
> B: No, I haven't. Where did you put it?
> G: I put it on my desk, but now it's gone. I'm really upset.
> B: _____! I'll help you find it.

> 〈영영풀이〉 to stop feeling angry, upset, or excited

06 다음 밑줄 친 부분의 뜻이 잘못된 것은?

① He drank too much, and that <u>finally</u> made him sick. (마침내)
② The children learned how to <u>take care of</u> the hamster. (돌보다)
③ I didn't <u>realize</u> how late it was. (깨닫다)
④ Ms. Han gave us an angry <u>look</u> when we laughed out loud. (바라보다)
⑤ The couple <u>approached</u> the woman to ask her a question. (다가갔다)

07 다음 대화의 빈칸에 알맞은 것은?

> A: I can't stand this place. _____
> B: Calm down! We're at the festival. Let's enjoy it.

① It's very fantastic.
② It's exciting.
③ The music sounds great.
④ They are enjoying themselves.
⑤ It's too crowded.

08 다음 대화의 순서를 바르게 배열한 것은?

(A) I can't focus on my studies at all. I can't stand it.
(B) What's that noise outside?
(C) They're fixing the heaters.
(D) Calm down! They will finish it soon.

① (B) – (A) – (C) – (D)
② (B) – (C) – (A) – (D)
③ (C) – (A) – (D) – (B)
④ (C) – (B) – (D) – (A)
⑤ (D) – (B) – (A) – (C)

09 다음 짝지어진 대화 중 어색한 것은?

① A: Wait here for 100 days? I can't stand it.
  B: Calm down! If you get through this situation, you'll be a great general.
② A: Keep fighting to sit in the chair? I can't stand it.
  B: Take it easy!
③ A: Be quiet and stay here? I can't stand it.
  B: Don't stress yourself.
④ A: What are the singers doing?
  B: One is singing, and another are dancing.
⑤ A: The baby keeps crying. I can't stand it.
  B: Calm down! He must be sick.

[10~11] 다음 대화를 읽고 물음에 답하시오.

B: Ouch! He (a)stepped on my foot again.
G: Are you okay?
B: No. This is the third time he did that today. I (b)can't stand it. I'll go and talk to him.
G: (c)Calm down! He's not wearing his glasses today, so he (d)can see well.
B: What happened to his glasses?
G: He (e)broke his glasses during a soccer game this morning.
B: I see, but (A)he should be more careful.

10 위 대화의 밑줄 친 (a)~(e) 중 어휘의 쓰임이 어색한 것은?

① (a)   ② (b)   ③ (c)   ④ (d)   ⑤ (e)

11 위 대화의 밑줄 친 (A)를 어법이나 문맥상 알맞게 고쳐 쓰시오.

➡ _____

12 다음 대화의 빈칸에 들어갈 말로 알맞은 것은?

B: The boy behind me keeps pushing me. I can't stand it.
G: _____

① Calm down! I don't know him.
② Calm down! He's waiting for you.
③ Calm down. He's just a child.
④ Calm down! They're having a birthday party.
⑤ Calm down! I'll help you find him.

Grammar

13 다음 빈칸에 들어갈 말로 적절한 것을 모두 고르시오.

The color green _____ us feel relaxed and refreshed.

① makes   ② helps   ③ keeps
④ allows   ⑤ leaves

14 다음 중 어법상 <u>어색한</u> 문장의 개수로 알맞은 것은?

> a. The woman advised the boy to be careful.
> b. Look at the two dogs. One is eating meat, and another is jumping up and down.
> c. Josh heard Olly to talk about his new car.
> d. I saw you getting on the bus this morning.
> e. The man ordered us to go out.
> f. Here are five singers on the stage. One is singing, and others are dancing.

① 1개　② 2개　③ 3개　④ 4개　⑤ 5개

15 다음 빈칸 (A)와 (B)에 들어갈 말로 적절한 것은?

> Two men are standing inside the gate. One is holding a sword, and (A)_____ is holding a stick. The man holding a sword tells Corky (B)_____ there for 100 days.

① the other–wait　② another–to wait
③ the other–to wait　④ another– wait
⑤ the other–waiting

16 다음 글에서 어법상 <u>어색한</u> 부분을 찾아 바르게 고치시오.

> Many people are ①standing around Corky. ②One is talking to Corky, ③the others are listening. The teacher tells Corky ④be quiet and ⑤stay there.

_____ ➡ _____

17 다음 우리말을 주어진 어휘를 이용하여 영어로 옮기시오.

(1) 우리는 평화를 위해 두 가지가 필요하다. 하나는 사랑, 나머지 하나는 희망이다.
(things, peace, love, and, hope)

➡ _____

_____

(2) 우리는 당신이 평화를 위해 우리와 함께하기를 요청한다. (ask, join, peace)

➡ _____

(3) 나는 네가 싸움을 그만두기를 원한다. (want, stop, fight)

➡ _____

18 다음 빈칸에 들어갈 말로 알맞지 <u>않은</u> 것은?

> Dad _____ me to set the table.

① got　② helped
③ ordered　④ told
⑤ had

19 다음 중 어법상 <u>어색한</u> 문장의 개수로 알맞은 것은?

> a. This skirt is too small. Show me another, please.
> b. There are fifty patients in the hospital. Some are emergency patients and the others are non-emergency patients.
> c. I have four foreign friends. One is from France, and the other are from China.
> d. He has quadruplet daughters. Some like Pengsoo, and others like Pororo.
> e. Jack has six cats. One is yellow, other is black, and the others are white.
>
> *quadruplet: 네쌍둥이

① 1개　② 2개　③ 3개　④ 4개　⑤ 5개

Reading

20 주어진 문장 다음에 이어질 글의 순서로 가장 적절한 것은?

> Then, the teacher told Corky to stand against a pole.

> (A) "I need to try another way," he thought. Then, Corky began to speak softly. He said he was not dangerous or bad but was a good man. He kept saying this in all possible ways. Finally, the people let him go.
> (B) Suddenly, he tied Corky to the pole. Above his head, he put a sign that read "Dangerous and Bad." Many people passed by. Some gave Corky angry looks, and others shouted at him. Corky shouted back. He yelled, "Set me free, or you all will be in big trouble!" That made the situation worse.
> (C) "Now you control the most powerful weapon: words. Soft words are stronger than sharp swords," said the teacher.

① (A) – (C) – (B) ② (B) – (A) – (C)
③ (B) – (C) – (A) ④ (C) – (A) – (B)
⑤ (C) – (B) – (A)

[21~23] 다음 글을 읽고 물음에 답하시오.

> Corky was a brave young man. He wanted to be a general, but the king said, "You're the strongest man in my army, but you have much to learn." ⓐHe ordered Corky to go to a famous military school.
> "Wait there. In a hundred days, your training will start," a voice said from inside the school gate. Corky got angry. But then he thought there might be a reason, so he waited. On the hundred and first day, the gate opened. An old

man said, "You have learned to use your first weapon: patience. ⓑ인내는 전쟁에서 이기기 위해 가장 중요한 것이다."

21 위 글의 밑줄 친 ⓐ를 복문으로 고칠 때, 빈칸에 들어갈 알맞은 말을 두 단어로 쓰시오.

> He ordered Corky _____ _____ to a famous military school.

22 위 글의 밑줄 친 ⓑ의 우리말에 맞게 주어진 어휘를 알맞게 배열하시오.

> a war / the / thing / patience / to win / most important / is

➡ _____

23 위 글의 제목으로 가장 알맞은 것을 고르시오.

① Corky, a Brave Young Man
② Corky, You Have Much to Learn!
③ Finally, Corky Got the First Weapon, Patience!
④ Wait in Front of the Gate!
⑤ Corky's Training Will Start in a Hundred Days.

[24~25] 다음 글을 읽고 물음에 답하시오.

> Finally, he said, "I will not fight anymore. (①) Instead, I will take care of the injured." (②) The other warriors saw this and fought ⓐeven harder. (③) As they fought, more warriors became tired and hurt. (④) Soon, all the warriors except Thunder were following Corky. (⑤)

24 위 글의 흐름으로 보아, 주어진 문장이 들어가기에 가장 적절한 곳은?

> Corky took good care of them, so they followed him.

①   ②   ③   ④   ⑤

25 위 글의 밑줄 친 ⓐeven과 같은 의미로 쓰인 것을 고르시오.

① 4, 6, 8, 10 are all even numbers.
② She's even more intelligent than her sister.
③ You need an even surface to work on.
④ It was cold there even in summer.
⑤ Our scores are now even.

[26~28] 다음 글을 읽고 물음에 답하시오.

　Then, the teacher told Corky to stand against a pole. Suddenly, he tied Corky ___ⓐ___ the pole. Above his head, he put a sign that read "Dangerous and Bad." Many people passed by. Some gave Corky angry looks, and others shouted at him. Corky shouted back. He yelled, "Set me free, or you all will be ___ⓑ___ big trouble!" That made the situation worse.

　"I need to try another way," he thought. Then, Corky began to speak softly. He said he was not dangerous or bad but was a good man. He kept saying ⓒthis in all possible ways. Finally, the people let him go.

　"Now you control the most powerful weapon: words. Soft words are stronger than sharp swords," said the teacher.

26 위 글의 빈칸 ⓐ와 ⓑ에 들어갈 전치사가 바르게 짝지어진 것은?

① to – in   ② in – at   ③ to – at
④ for – in   ⑤ in – to

27 위 글의 밑줄 친 ⓒthis가 가리키는 것을 본문에서 찾아 쓰시오.

➡ _____

28 According to the passage, which is NOT true?

① The teacher put a sign that read "Dangerous and Bad" above Corky's head.
② Some gave angry looks to Corky, and others shouted at him.
③ Corky began to speak softly when the situation got worse.
④ The people allowed Corky to go.
⑤ According to the teacher, the most important weapon is courage.

[29~30] 다음 글을 읽고 물음에 답하시오.

　Two men are standing inside the gate. One is holding a sword, and ___ⓐ___ is holding a stick. The man ⓑholding a sword tells Corky to wait there for 100 days.

29 위 글의 빈칸 ⓐ에 들어갈 알맞은 말을 쓰시오.

➡ _____

30 위 글의 밑줄 친 ⓑholding과 문법적 쓰임이 같은 것을 모두 고르시오.

① He's saving money to buy a bike.
② Taking a walk every day is very good for you.
③ Who is the girl playing the piano?
④ My hobby is reading books.
⑤ I enjoyed playing soccer.

01 다음 짝지어진 단어의 관계가 같도록 빈칸에 알맞은 말을 쓰시오.

> push – pull : tie – _____

02 다음 영영풀이에 해당하는 단어는?

> a fact or situation which explains why something happens

① thought   ② search

③ situation   ④ pole

⑤ reason

[03~04] 다음 대화를 읽고 물음에 답하시오.

> B: Ouch! He stepped on my foot again.
>
> G: Are you okay?
>
> B: No. (a)이번이 오늘 그 애가 내 발을 세 번째로 밟은 거야. I can't stand it. I'll go and talk to him.
>
> G: Calm down! He's not wearing his glasses today, so he can't see well.
>
> B: _____(A)_____
>
> G: He broke his glasses during a soccer game this morning.
>
> B: I see, but he should have been more careful.

03 위 대화의 빈칸 (A)에 들어갈 말로 알맞은 것은?

① How come he played soccer?

② When was he playing soccer?

③ What happened to his glasses?

④ Without his glasses, could he play soccer?

⑤ How long has he been wearing glasses?

04 위 대화의 우리말 (a)에 맞게 주어진 단어를 알맞은 순서로 배열하시오.

> (he / did / this / the / is / time / that / today / third)

➡ _____

05 다음 대화의 빈칸에 들어갈 말로 어색한 것은?

> G: I can't find my pencil case. Have you seen it?
>
> B: No, I haven't. Where did you put it?
>
> G: I put it on my desk, but now it's gone. _____
>
> B: Calm down! I'll help you find it.

① I'm really upset.

② How irritating!

③ I'm very refreshed.

④ I'm very angry.

⑤ I'm fed up with it.

06 다음 대화의 빈칸에 들어갈 말로 알맞은 것은?

> G: Look! _____ I'm very angry.
>
> B: Calm down! He works here.

① He can't stand it.

② The boy behind me keeps pushing me.

③ That man didn't wait in line!

④ I hate standing in line in cold weather.

⑤ They're playing music too loud.

07 다음 짝지어진 대화 중 <u>어색한</u> 것은?

① A: That baby keeps crying. I can't stand it.
   B: Chill out! He must be sick.

② A: Children upstairs are running around. I can't stand it.
   B: It's going to be okay. Take a deep breath and try to relax.

③ A: Look! That man didn't wait in line! I'm very angry.
   B: Calm down! He works here.

④ A: His head keeps hitting me on my shoulder.
   B: Calm down! He is very old. He can't hear well.

⑤ A: I can't stand this place. It's too crowded.
   B: Calm down! We're at the festival.

[08~09] 다음 대화를 읽고 물음에 답하시오.

Minji: Minsu, there is no cup I can use. Why didn't you do the dishes?

Minsu: Sorry, but I forgot to do them.

Minji: What? (A)<u>너는 항상 해야 할 일을 잊어버리는 구나</u>. I can't stand it. I cleaned the living room all morning.

Minsu: Calm down! I'm busy doing my homework.

Minji: Do the dishes first, and then do your homework.

Minsu: I can't. I don't think I can finish my homework today. Science is too difficult for me.

Minji: Science? You know I'm good at science. Let me help you.

Minsu: Great. Thanks. I'll wash your cup right now and I'll do the rest of the dishes after finishing this.

08 위 대화의 밑줄 친 우리말 (A)에 맞게 주어진 단어를 활용하여 영작하시오.

(always / what / have)

➡ _____

09 위 대화의 내용과 일치하지 <u>않는</u> 것은?

① Because Minsu didn't wash the dishes, he feels sorry to his sister.
② Minsu's sister thinks Minsu always forgets what he has to do.
③ Minsu says he was busy doing his homework.
④ Minsu thinks science is so easy for him.
⑤ Minsu's sister thinks she is good at science.

10 다음 빈칸에 들어갈 말로 적절한 것을 고르시오.

He has five daughters. One is a teacher, and _____ are doctors.

① another   ② the one   ③ other
④ others   ⑤ the others

11 다음 우리말에 맞게 주어진 단어를 활용하여 영어로 문장을 완성하시오. (중복 사용 가능)

> 홍 선생님은 그녀의 학생들에게 대화를 들으라고 말씀하셨다. (tell, listen, dialog)

➡ Ms. Hong _____

_____ .

12 다음 문장에서 <u>잘못된</u> 부분을 바르게 고쳐 문장을 다시 쓰시오.

(1) She told him locked the door.

➡ _____

(2) She wouldn't allow him used her phone.

➡ _____

(3) The grapes on the dish look very delicious. Some are green, and others are purple.

➡ _____

_____

(4) Many children are big fans of animals. Some like monkeys, and the others like lions.

➡ _____

_____

(5) I bought two pens. Another is for me, and the other is for you.

➡ _____

_____

13 다음 우리말에 맞게 주어진 단어를 배열하시오.

> 그는 그의 국민들에게 영국에 대항하여 평화롭게 싸울 것을 요청했다.
> (people / asked / He / England / fight / to / his / against / peacefully)

➡ _____

_____

[14~16] 다음 글을 읽고 물음에 답하시오.

Corky was a brave young man. He wanted to be a general, but the king said, "You're the strongest man in my army, but you have much to learn." He ordered Corky to go to a famous military school.

"Wait there. In a hundred days, your training will start," a voice said from inside the school gate. Corky got angry. But then he thought there might be a reason, so he waited. ⓐ <u>101일째 되던 날, 문이 열렸다.</u> An old man said, "You have learned to use your first weapon: patience. Patience is the most important thing to win a war."

14 위 글의 밑줄 친 ⓐ의 우리말에 맞게 주어진 어휘를 이용하여 9 단어로 영작하시오.

> the hundred and first

➡ _____

15 위 글의 종류로 알맞은 것을 고르시오.

① essay　　　　② short story

③ article　　　　④ review

⑤ book report

16 What is the most important thing to win a war? Answer in English in a full sentence.

➡ _____

[17~19] 다음 글을 읽고 물음에 답하시오.

Then, the teacher told Corky to stand against a pole. Suddenly, he tied Corky to the pole. Above his head, he put a sign that read "Dangerous and Bad." (①) Many people passed by. (②) Some gave Corky angry looks, and others shouted at him. (③) Corky shouted back. (④) He yelled, "Set me free, or you all will be in big trouble!" (⑤)

"I need to try another way," he thought. Then, Corky began to speak softly. He said he was not dangerous or bad but was a good man. He kept saying this in all possible ways. Finally, the people let him go.

"Now you control the most powerful weapon: words. Soft words are stronger than sharp swords," said the teacher.

17 위 글의 흐름으로 보아, 주어진 문장이 들어가기에 가장 적절한 곳은?

That made the situation worse.

① ② ③ ④ ⑤

18 위 글의 주제로 알맞은 것을 고르시오.

① The teacher made Corky stand against a pole.
② Many people blamed Corky for being dangerous and bad.
③ Corky came to control the most powerful weapon: words.
④ Corky reacted to people's blame in two ways.
⑤ The people finally let Corky go.

19 본문의 내용과 일치하도록 다음 빈칸 (A)와 (B)에 알맞은 단어를 쓰시오.

The teacher tied Corky to the pole and put a sign that read "Dangerous and Bad" above Corky's head in order to teach Corky how to (A)_____ the most powerful weapon: (B)_____.

[20~21] 다음 글을 읽고 물음에 답하시오.

Next, the teacher took Corky to a large hall with a chair in the middle. There were 19 other warriors who had passed their tests. "The first one ⓐto sit in the chair will be the winner," the teacher said.

Corky and the others began fighting. They pushed, pulled, ran, and jumped. They fought harder and harder, so Corky became tired.

Finally, he said, "I will not fight anymore. Instead, I will take care of the injured." The other warriors saw ⓑthis and fought even harder. As they fought, more warriors became tired and hurt. Corky took good care of them, so they followed him. Soon, all the warriors except Thunder were following Corky.

20 위 글의 밑줄 친 ⓐto sit과 to부정사의 용법이 다른 것을 모두 고르시오.

① They came here to ask me a question.
② It is not difficult to read this book.
③ Do you have anything to eat?
④ It's time to go home.
⑤ I use a computer to draw a picture.

21 위 글의 밑줄 친 ⓑthis가 가리키는 내용을 우리말로 쓰시오.

➡ _____
_____

01 다음 대화의 빈칸 (A)와 (B)에 들어갈 말을 주어진 단어를 이용하여 완성하시오.

> A: You're late again. (A)_____
>   (stand)
> B: (B)_____ (take) I woke up late.
> A: You always wake up late when you meet me.
> B: I'm really sorry.

02 대화의 빈칸 (A)에 들어갈 말을 제시된 〈조건〉을 만족하는 문장으로 쓰시오.

> B: Ouch! He stepped on my foot again.
> G: Are you okay?
> B: No. This is the third time he did that today. I can't stand it. I'll go and talk to him.
> G: Calm down! He's not wearing his glasses today, so he can't see well.
> B: What happened to his glasses?
> G: He broke his glasses during a soccer game this morning.
> B: I see, but _____(A)_____.

> (1) He ought to have been more careful.
> (2) I'm sorry that he wasn't more careful.

┤ 조건 ├
조동사를 사용하여 위 (1)~(2)의 의미와 같은 문장을 한 문장으로 영작하시오.

➡ _____

03 대화를 읽고 질문에 영어로 답하시오.

> Minji: Minsu, there is no cup I can use. Why didn't you do the dishes?
> Minsu: Sorry, but I forgot to do them.
> Minji: What? You always forget what you have to do. I can't stand it. I cleaned the living room all morning.
> Minsu: Calm down! I'm busy doing my homework.
> Minji: Do the dishes first, and then do your homework.
> Minsu: I can't. I don't think I can finish my homework today. Science is too difficult for me.
> Minji: Science? You know I'm good at science. Let me help you.
> Minsu: Great. Thanks. I'll wash your cup right now and I'll do the rest of the dishes after finishing this.

> Q: What's Minsu's excuse for forgetting to do the dishes?
> ➡ His excuse is that _____
>   _____.

04 다음 문장에서 어법상 틀린 곳을 찾아 바르게 다시 쓰시오.

(1) Three of six people came to the party. The other didn't.

➡ _____

_____

(2) Amy wants Brian tell her about his problem.

➡ _____

05 우리말과 같은 의미가 되도록 문장을 완성하시오.

(1) 그것들 중 어떤 것들은 빨간색이다; others are brown.

➡ _____

(2) 내가 남기를 원한다면, say you want me to stay.

➡ _____

06 괄호 안에 주어진 표현을 사용하여 우리말로 된 대화를 영어로 쓰시오.

(1) (order, get down, on the ground)

A: What did the man order his dog to do?

B: 그는 그의 개에게 바닥에 엎드리라고 명령했어.

➡ _____

(2) (tell, close the door)

A: What did the girl say to the boy?

B: 그녀는 그에게 문을 닫지 말라고 말했어.

➡ _____

(3) (allow, go there)

A: Will you go to Eighteen's concert next month?

B: I'm not sure. 나의 엄마는 내가 거기 가는 것을 허락해 주시지 않을 거야.

➡ _____

[07~09] 다음 글을 읽고 물음에 답하시오.

Then, the teacher told Corky to stand against a pole. Suddenly, he tied Corky to the pole. Above his head, he put a sign that read "Dangerous and Bad." Many people passed by. (A)[One / Some] gave Corky angry looks, and (B)[others / the other] shouted at him. Corky shouted back. He yelled, "Set me free, or you all will be in big trouble!" ⓐThat made the situation worse.

"I need to try (C)[another / the other] way," he thought. Then, Corky began to speak softly. He said he was not dangerous or bad but was a good man. He kept saying this in all possible ways. Finally, the people let him go.

"Now you control the most powerful weapon: words. Soft words are stronger than sharp swords," said the teacher.

07 위 글의 괄호 (A)~(C)에서 어법상 알맞은 낱말을 골라 쓰시오.

➡ (A) _____ (B) _____ (C) _____

08 위 글의 밑줄 친 ⓐThat이 가리키는 것을 본문에서 찾아 쓰시오.

➡ _____

_____

09 본문의 내용과 일치하도록 다음 빈칸 (A)와 (B)에 알맞은 단어를 쓰시오.

Corky was tied to a pole under a sign saying "Dangerous and Bad." He made the situation (A)_____ by yelling, "Set me free, or you all will be in big trouble!" But when he (B)_____ _____ that he was not dangerous or bad but was a good man, he was set (C)_____ and got the second (D)_____, words.

창의사고력 서술형 문제

01 지하철에서 화가 나는 상황들을 나타낸 다음 그림을 보고, 화를 진정시키는 대화를 〈보기〉처럼 완성하시오.

> 보기
>
> A: That baby keeps crying. I can't stand it.
> B: Calm down! He must be sick.

02 다음 내용을 바탕으로 그림 속의 장면을 설명하는 글을 쓰시오.

There is a chair in the middle. The teacher is talking to the warriors, and the warriors are listening.
The teacher: Keep fighting to sit in the chair.

Many (A)_____ are listening to (B)_____. Some are (C)_____, and the others are kneeling. The teacher wants them to keep fighting (D)_____.

단원별 모의고사

01 다음 단어에 대한 영어 설명이 <u>어색한</u> 것은?

① military: the armed forces of a country

② finally: after a long period of time

③ impatience: being able to stay calm and not get annoyed

④ war: fighting using soldiers and weapons between two or more countries

⑤ general: a high-ranking officer in the army

02 다음 짝지어진 단어의 관계가 같도록 빈칸에 알맞은 말을 쓰시오.

pass by – go by : mighty – _____

03 다음 영영풀이에 해당하는 단어를 고르시오.

a door in a fence or outside a wall

① gate ② goat ③ pole
④ gather ⑤ sword

04 다음 중 짝지어진 대화가 <u>어색한</u> 것은?

① A: What are the birds doing?
   B: One is flying, and the other is sitting on the tree.

② A: There are two dogs over there. What are the dogs doing?
   B: One is playing with a ball, and the other is jumping up and down.

③ A: What are the people doing?
   B: Some are playing soccer, and the others are playing badminton.

④ A: Go to the military school? I can't stand it.
   B: Control yourself! If you get through this situation, you'll be a great general.

⑤ A: A dog is barking. I can't focus on my studies at all. I can't stand it.
   B: That's great! He'll keep barking all the way.

05 다음 그림에 맞게 대화의 빈칸에 주어진 철자로 시작하는 단어를 써서 대화를 완성하시오.

B: What's that n_____ outside?
G: They're f_____ the heaters.
B: I can't f_____ _____ my studies at all. I can't s_____ _____.
G: C_____ _____! They will finish it soon.

06 대화의 밑줄 친 (a)~(e)에 관한 설명으로 <u>잘못된</u> 것은?

B: Ouch! He stepped on my foot again.
G: Are you okay?
B: No. This is the third time (a)he did that today. (b)I can't stand it. I'll go and talk to him.
G: (c)Calm down! He's not wearing his glasses today, so he can't see well.
B: What happened to his glasses?
G: He broke his glasses (d)during a soccer game this morning.
B: I see, but he (e)should have been more careful.

① (a) 'the third time'을 수식하는 역할을 하고, 관계부사 'when'이 생략되어 있다.

② (b) 화난 감정을 표현하는 문장으로 'I'm very annoyed.'로 바꾸어 말할 수 있다.

③ (c) 화낸 상대방에 응대하여 진정시키는 표현으로 'Relax.'로 바꾸어 말할 수 있다.

④ (d) 전치사로 '~ 동안'의 의미를 가지고 있고 'for'로 바꾸어 쓸 수 있다.

⑤ (e) 과거의 유감을 나타내는 표현으로 'ought to have been'으로 바꾸어 쓸 수 있다.

07 대화의 흐름상 밑줄 친 ①~⑤ 중 어색한 것은?

> M1: ①The king sent me here. Open the door.
>
> M2: Wait there. ②The door will open in a hundred days.
>
> M1: What? A hundred days? ③I can't spend a hundred days doing nothing. I can't stand it.
>
> M2: ④Calm down! It is an important rule to get in this school. ⑤However, how can you get free? Think.

①   ②   ③   ④   ⑤

08 다음 대화의 밑줄 친 우리말에 맞게 주어진 단어를 이용하여 영작하시오. (동명사 형태를 쓸 것.)

> G: Brrr.... What a cold day! 나는 추운 날씨에 줄 서는 게 싫어.
>
> B: Calm down! Drink this hot milk.

(hate / stand / line / in)

➡ _____

[09~11] 다음 대화를 읽고 물음에 답하시오.

> Minji: Minsu, there is no cup I can use. Why didn't you do the dishes?
>
> Minsu: Sorry, but I forgot (A)(do) them.
>
> Minji: What? You always forget what you have to do. I can't stand it. I cleaned the living room all morning.
>
> Minsu: Calm down! I'm busy (B)(do) my homework.
>
> Minji: Do the dishes first, and then do your homework.
>
> Minsu: I can't. I don't think I can finish my homework today. Science is too difficult for me.
>
> Minji: Science? You know I'm good at science. Let me help you.
>
> Minsu: Great. Thanks. I'll wash your cup right now and I'll do the (C)rest of the dishes after finishing this.

09 위 대화의 괄호 (A)와 (B)의 단어를 알맞은 형태로 고치시오.

(A) _____ (B) _____

10 Why is Minsu's sister angry at Minsu?

> Because she thinks _____
> _____.

11 위 대화의 밑줄 친 (C)rest와 같은 의미로 사용된 것은?

① Now I see why taking a rest is so important!

② I will devote the rest of my life to making people happy.

③ When we're adults, we won't have much time to rest and relax.

④ Can you feel your brain taking a rest when you blink?

⑤ I just wanted to take a rest while watching my favorite TV show.

12 다음 빈칸 (A)~(C)에 들어갈 말이 바르게 짝지어진 것은?

> The guys keep five dogs. (A)_____ is white, (B)_____ is brown, and (C)_____ are spotted.

① One – another – the other
② One – another – the others
③ Some – other – the other
④ Some – other – the others
⑤ Another – other – the other

13 다음 대화를 읽고 빈칸에 적절한 것은?

> Minsu: Will you help me?
> Kelly: Sure.
> ➡ Minsu asked _____.

① Kelly help him
② Kelly to help him
③ Kelly helped him
④ Kelly helps him
⑤ Kelly helping him

14 다음 대화의 내용을 영어로 바르게 옮긴 것은?

> Mom: Go to bed.
> Son: OK.

① She told her son to go to bed.
② She made her son to go to bed.
③ She told her son go to bed.
④ She made her son going to bed.
⑤ She ordered her son going to bed.

15 다음 대화를 읽고 빈칸을 완성하시오.

> (1) Mina: Can I use your pen?
>   Aaron: Sure.
>   ➡ Aaron allowed _____.
> (2) The lawyer: Don't say anything to the police.
>   The man: OK. I won't.
>   ➡ The lawyer advised _____
>   _____.

16 다음 밑줄 친 우리말을 영어로 옮기시오.

> (1) I have a lot of friends. 몇몇은 친절하고, and others aren't.
>   ➡ _____
> (2) I have two bags. One is black, and 나머지 하나는 갈색이다.
>   ➡ _____

[17~18] 다음 글을 읽고 물음에 답하시오.

> Corky was a brave young man. He wanted to be a general, but the king said, "You're the strongest man in my army, but you have much to learn." He ordered Corky to go to a famous military school.
> "Wait ⓐthere. In a hundred days, your training will start," a voice said from inside the school gate. Corky got angry. But then he thought there might be a reason, so he waited. On the hundred and first day, the gate opened. An old man said, "You have learned ⓑto use your first weapon: patience. Patience is the most important thing to win a war."

17 위 글의 밑줄 친 ⓐthere가 가리키는 것을 우리말로 쓰시오.

➡ _____

18 아래 〈보기〉에서 위 글의 밑줄 친 ⓑ와 to부정사의 용법이 다른 것의 개수를 고르시오.

> ┌── 보기 ──
> ① It is important to use your time well.
> ② He went to the store to buy some fruit.
> ③ I don't have any friends to talk with.
> ④ He promised me to work hard.
> ⑤ He can't be rich to ask me for some money.

① 1개　② 2개　③ 3개　④ 4개　⑤ 5개

[19~20] 다음 글을 읽고 물음에 답하시오.

Then, the teacher told Corky to stand against a pole. Suddenly, he tied Corky to the pole. Above his head, he put a sign that read "Dangerous and Bad." Many people passed by. Some gave Corky angry looks, and others shouted at him. Corky shouted back. He yelled, "ⓐ나를 풀어 줘. 그러지 않으면 모두 혼쭐날 줄 알아!" That made the situation worse.

"I need to try another way," he thought. Then, Corky began to speak softly. He said he was not dangerous or bad but was a good man. He kept saying this in all possible ways. Finally, the people let him go.

"Now you control the most powerful weapon: words. ⓑSoft words are stronger than sharp swords," said the teacher.

19 위 글의 밑줄 친 ⓐ의 우리말에 맞게 한 단어를 보충하여, 주어진 어휘를 알맞게 배열하시오.

> you / big / free / will / trouble / be / all / set / in / me / , /

➡ _____

20 위 글의 밑줄 친 ⓑ를 다음과 같이 바꿔 쓸 때 빈칸에 들어갈 알맞은 말을 4 단어로 쓰시오.

> Sharps words are _____ _____ _____ _____ soft words

[21~22] 다음 글을 읽고 물음에 답하시오.

Next, the teacher took Corky to a large hall with a chair in the middle. There were 19 other warriors who ___ⓐ___ their tests. "The first one to sit in the chair will be the winner," the teacher said.

Corky and the others began fighting. They pushed, pulled, ran, and jumped. They fought harder and harder, so Corky became tired.

Finally, he said, "I will not fight anymore. Instead, I will take care of the injured." The other warriors saw this and fought even harder. ⓑAs they fought, more warriors became tired and hurt. Corky took good care of them, so they followed him. Soon, all the warriors except Thunder were following Corky.

21 위 글의 빈칸 ⓐ에 pass를 알맞은 형태로 쓰시오.

➡ _____

22 위 글의 밑줄 친 ⓑAs와 같은 의미로 쓰인 것을 고르시오.

① I respect him as a lawyer.
② Leave the papers as they are.
③ As you were out, I left a message.
④ As we go up, the air grows colder.
⑤ As you know, Julia is leaving soon.

Lesson

Special

Teen's Magazine

Words & Expressions

Key Words

- **about** [əbáut] 튀 대략
- **average** [ǽvəridʒ] 몡 평균 혱 평균의
- **backward** [bǽkwərd] 튀 뒤에서부터, 역방향으로
- **bookmark** [búkmàːrk] 몡 책갈피
- **case** [keis] 몡 사건
- **control** [kəntróul] 동 통제하다, 조종하다
- **cook** [kuk] 몡 요리사 동 요리하다
- **create** [kriéit] 동 창조하다, 만들어 내다
- **critic** [krítik] 몡 비평가
- **dog ear, dog-ear** 동 책장의 모서리를 접어 표시하다 몡 책장의 모서리가 접힌 부분
- **effort** [éfərt] 몡 노력
- **fake** [feik] 혱 가짜의
- **fold** [fould] 동 접다
- **forest** [fɔ́ːrist] 몡 숲, 삼림
- **hate** [heit] 동 싫어하다
- **hold** [hould] 동 잡다
- **imagine** [imǽdʒin] 동 상상하다
- **instead** [instéd] 튀 대신에
- **invite** [inváit] 동 초대하다
- **joke** [dʒouk] 몡 농담
- **mean** [miːn] 동 의미하다
- **million** [míljən] 몡 백만
- **neighbor** [néibər] 몡 이웃, 옆집 사람
- **officer** [ɔ́ːfisər] 몡 관리, 관료
- **once** [wʌns] 접 일단 ~하기만 하면
- **own** [oun] 혱 (주로 소유격 뒤에서) ~ 자신의
- **peace** [piːs] 몡 평화
- **piece** [piːs] 몡 조각
- **public** [pʌ́blik] 혱 공공의
- **public officer** 공무원
- **quickly** [kwíkli] 튀 빨리
- **race car** 경주용 차
- **realize** [ríːəlàiz] 동 깨닫다
- **save** [seiv] 동 구하다, 절약하다
- **shape** [ʃeip] 몡 모양, 형태
- **share** [ʃɛər] 동 공유하다, 나누다
- **shout** [ʃaut] 동 소리치다
- **solve** [sɑlv] 동 해결하다
- **square feet** 평방 피트
- **stone** [stoun] 몡 돌멩이
- **tiny** [táini] 혱 작은
- **tip** [tip] 몡 조언, 도움말

Key Expressions

- **cut ~ into small pieces** ~를 잘게 썰다
- **don't forget to** 잊지 않고 ~하다
- **dream of** ~에 관해 꿈꾸다
- **end up -ing** 결국 ~가 되다
- **every second letter** 두 번째 글자마다
- **get closer to** ~와 가까워지다
- **had better+동사원형** ~하는 게 좋다
- **keep ~ away** ~를 멀리하게 하다
- **laugh out loud** 큰 소리로 웃다
- **make sure** 틀림없이 ~하다
- **need to+동사원형** ~할 필요가 있다
- **rain cats and dogs** 비가 억수같이 오다
- **say hello to** ~에게 인사하다
- **stop+-ing** ~하는 것을 멈추다
- **would rather A than B** B하느니 A하겠다

Word Power

※ 서로 반대의 뜻을 가진 어휘

- □ **hate** (싫어하다) ↔ **like** (좋아하다)
- □ **quickly** (빨리) ↔ **slowly** (느리게)
- □ **backward** (위로, 거꾸로) ↔ **forward** (앞으로)
- □ **fake** (가짜의) ↔ **genuine** (진짜의)

- □ **public** (공공의) ↔ **private** (사적인)
- □ **fold** (접다) ↔ **unfold** (펼치다)
- □ **tiny** (작은) ↔ **huge** (거대한)

※ 서로 비슷한 뜻을 가진 어휘

- □ **save** : **rescue** (구하다)
- □ **secret** : **confidential** (비밀의)
- □ **imagine** : **visualize** (상상하다)

- □ **solve** : **resolve** (해결하다)
- □ **piece** : **bit** (조각)
- □ **shout** : **yell** (외치다)

English Dictionary

- □ **backward** 뒤로
  → in the direction behind you
  당신 뒤의 방향으로

- □ **critic** 비평가
  → someone whose job is to give their opinion of a book, play, movie, etc.
  책, 연극, 영화 등에 대한 의견을 말하는 것이 직업인 사람

- □ **delicious** 맛있는
  → very good to eat or drink   먹거나 마시기에 매우 좋은

- □ **effort** 노력
  → an attempt to do something
  무언가를 하려는 시도

- □ **fold** 접다
  → to bend something so that one part of it lies flat on top of another part
  어떤 것의 일부분이 다른 부분 위에 평평하게 놓이도록 어떤 것을 구부리다

- □ **forest** 숲
  → a large area of trees growing close together
  가까이 함께 자라는 나무들의 넓은 지역

- □ **imagine** 상상하다
  → to make an idea or picture of something in your mind
  당신의 마음속에 어떤 생각이나 그림을 만들다

- □ **instead** 대신에
  → in the place of someone or something else
  다른 사람 또는 다른 어떤 것을 대신하여

- □ **invite** 초대하다
  → to ask someone to come to your house, to a party, etc.
  누군가에게 당신의 집이나 파티에 오라고 부탁하다

- □ **make sure** 틀림없이 ~하다
  → to take action so that you are certain that something happens, is true, etc.
  어떤 일이 일어나거나, 사실이거나, 기타 등등일 거라고 확신하도록 조치를 취하다

- □ **neighbor** 이웃 사람
  → someone who lives near you
  당신 근처에 사는 사람

- □ **peace** 평화
  → a situation in which there is no war, violence, or arguing
  전쟁, 폭력 또는 논쟁이 없는 상황

- □ **rain cats and dogs** 비가 억수같이 오다
  → to rain very heavily   비가 심하게 내리다

- □ **realize** 깨닫다
  → to notice or understand something that you did not notice or understand before
  이전에는 알아차리지 못하거나 이해하지 못했던 것을 알아차리거나 이해하다

- □ **share** 공유하다
  → to have or use something at the same time as someone else
  다른 사람과 동시에 무언가를 가지거나 사용하다

Teens' Magazine

Ways to Make Your Town Better
형용사적 용법의 to부정사

Doing something nice for your neighbors can change your town.
동명사 주어   'something'을 형용사가 수식할 때는 뒤에서 수식
Start small. Here are some tips.

1. Say hello to your neighbors and smile.

2. Don't forget to say, "Thank you."
   forget+to부정사: (미래에) ~해야 할 것을 잊다

3. Share your umbrella on a rainy day.

4. Laugh out loud when your neighbor tells a joke.

5. Make something for your neighbors.

6. Hold the door for the person behind you.
   형용사구

7. Invite your neighbors to your party.

If you just do one thing each day, you can make your town better.

Messages for Peace

On World Peace Day, we put our peace messages on the board.

Peace means having friends around the world. - Kim Jimin
동명사

I'd rather have peace on Earth than pieces of Earth. - Seo Eunji

I want peace every place I go because there is always someone

fighting or shouting. - Park Hansol
'someone'을 꾸며 주는 현재분사
Peace makes everyone smile. - Yang Miran

Peace is inside all of us. We just need to share it. - Jang Jaehee

LET'S LAUGH

An apple a day

Jake came in to see his dad. "Dad!" he said, "Is it true that an apple a
'it'은 가주어, 'that' 이하의 명사절이 진주어
day keeps the doctor away?"

"That's what they say," said his dad.
관계대명사(~하는 것)
"Well, give me an apple quickly! I just broke the doctor's window!"
과거형이 'just'와 함께 쓰여 '바로 전에 ~했다'

neighbor 이웃, 옆집 사람

say hello to ~에게 인사하다

don't forget to 잊지 않고 ~하다

share 공유하다, 나누다

hold 잡다

invite 초대하다

peace 평화

would rather … than ~하느니 …하겠다

piece 조각

need to+동사원형 ~할 필요가 있다

keep … away …를 멀리하게 하다

quickly 빨리

Be Kind to Books!

Do you know what books hate? They hate water, the sun, and dog
간접의문문(의문사+주어+동사)

ears. Why dog ears?

Water is bad for WITCHES and BOOKS! / The SUN also TURNs

Books YELLOW / Don't DOG-EAR! Use a bookmark! / Be Kind to

Books!

Stop folding dog ears in books. Use a bookmark instead. It is a
'a bookmark'를 강조하는 'It is … that ~' 강조구문

bookmark that can save your books. Be kind to your books. The more
The+비교급+주어+동사, the+비교급+주어+동사: …하면 할수록 더 ~하다

you love your books, the happier your books will be. How about

making your own?

Facts That Sound Fake
주격 관계대명사로 'Facts'를 수식

1. About 7% of all people who have ever lived are living on the Earth
   약

   today. About 108,200 million people have ever been born in the
   millions(✗)

   history of the world. And about 7,442 million are living on the

   Earth today.

2. Bangladesh has more people than Russia. Russia is the world's

   largest country, but tiny Bangladesh has 166.3 million people in
   large의 최상급

   2018. Russia has 143.9 million people.

3. A banyan tree near Kolkata, India, is bigger than the average
   big의 비교급

   Walmart. The average Walmart store covers about 104,000 square
   약   *평방피트*

   feet. The Great Banyan Tree in Kolkata, India, is about the size of a

   forest, covering 155,000 square feet.

4. Baby carrots were invented in 1986. Baby carrots are not actually
   과거 수동태

   baby carrots. Big ugly carrots are cut into small pieces that have
   선행사 'pieces'를 수식하는 주격 관계대명사

   the shape of a baby carrot. Farmer Mike Yurosek invented them in

   1986 as a way to use ugly carrots that weren't sold.
   주격 관계대명사 'that'의 선행사는 'ugly carrots'

---

hate 싫어하다

dog ear. dog-ear 귀 모양으로 책장
의 모서리를 접어 표시하다. 귀 모양으로
책장 모서리가 접힌 부분

fold 접다

instead 대신에

save 구하다

about 대략

million 백만

average 평균; 평균의

square feet 평방피트

forest 숲

cut … into small pieces …를 잘게
썰다

shape 모양, 형태

Jobs in the Movies

Zootopia (2016) It's the greatest movie ever!
지금까지

Flash is a public officer. He is very slow but works hard. You will be surprised to see what he does in his free time. It's driving a race car!
간접의문문(의문사+주어+동사)

Nick is a fox with a big mouth. Helping Judy, he gets closer to her. He
동시동작을 나타내는 분사구문, 'Judy를 도우면서'
later becomes a police officer like Judy. Judy is a small rabbit, but she's smart and strong. After a lot of effort, she becomes a police officer and solves many cases.

Ratatouille (2007) Everyone will love this movie.

Anton Ego is a food critic. After he eats the food Remy cooked, he realizes that anyone can cook.
접속사

Remy, a little mouse, dreams of becoming a cook. He goes into a restaurant and meets a boy named Linguini. Controlling Linguini, he
동시동작을 나타내는 분사구문, Linguini를 통제하면서
makes delicious food and ends up becoming a great cook.
end up ~ing: 결국 ~하다

Say It with Emojis

Do you know what these emojis mean? Killing two birds with one
동명사(주어)
stone. / The apple of your eyes. / Don't play games with fire. / Once in a blue moon. / Let's call it a day. / Money does not grow on trees. / It's raining cats and dogs. / A piece of cake.

Emoji Song

Now, let's sing a Christmas song together! The louder, the happier!
The+비교급, the+비교급: …하면 할수록 더 ~하다!

---

public 공공의
officer 관리, 관료
public officer 공무원
race car 경주용 차
get closer to ~와 가까워지다
effort 노력
critic 비평가
realize 깨닫다
control 통제하다, 조종하다
stone 돌멩이
rain cats and dogs 비가 억수같이 오다
You better = You'd better 너는 ~하는 게 좋다

Secret Messages

Imagine you can send messages to your friend that no one else can read! It's not so difficult for you to learn how to read and write your own secret messages.

1. Read Backward

This is easy to solve. Just read the words backward! It seems simple once you know the secret, but it can be a hard one when you don't.

2. Read Every Second Letter

Read every second letter starting with the first letter, and when you finish, start again on the letters you missed.

3. Pig-pen

The Pig-pen is easier than it looks. The lines around each letter mean the letter inside the lines.

Now create your own set of secret letters and write secret messages to send to your friends. Make sure you send along a key so your friends can understand your messages!

imagine 상상하다
backward 뒤에서부터, 역방향으로
once 일단 ~하기만 하면
every second letter 두 번째 글자마다
create 창조하다, 만들어 내다
make sure 틀림없이 ~하다

● 우리말을 참고하여 빈칸에 알맞은 말을 쓰시오.

1 _____ Magazine

2 Ways to _____ Your Town _____

3 Doing _____ _____ for your neighbors can change your town. Start small. Here are some tips.

4 1. _____ _____ _____ your neighbors and smile.

5 2. Don't forget _____ _____, "Thank you."

6 3. Share your umbrella _____ _____ _____ _____.

7 4. _____ _____ _____ when your neighbor tells a joke.

8 5. Make something _____ your neighbors.

9 6. Hold the door for the person _____ _____.

10 7. _____ your neighbors _____ your party.

11 If you just do one thing each day, you can _____ your town _____.

12 Messages for _____

13 On World Peace Day, we _____ our peace messages _____ the board.

14 Peace means _____ _____ around the world. - Kim Jimin

15 _____ _____ have peace on Earth than pieces of Earth. - Seo Eunji

16 I want peace every place I go because there is always someone _____ or _____. - Park Hansol

17 Peace makes everyone _____.- Yang Miran

18 Peace is _____ all of us. We just need to share it. - Jang Jaehee

19 LET'S _____

20 An apple _____

1	십대들의 잡지
2	마을을 더 좋게 만드는 방법들
3	이웃들을 위해 뭔가 좋은 일을 하면 여러분의 마을을 변화시킬 수 있다. 작은 것부터 시작하라. 여기 몇 가지 도움말이 있다.
4	1. 이웃들에게 인사를 하고 미소를 지어라.
5	2. 잊지 말고 "고맙습니다."라고 말해라.
6	3. 비 오는 날에 당신의 우산을 함께 써라.
7	4. 이웃이 농담하면 크게 소리 내어 웃어라.
8	5. 이웃들을 위해 뭔가를 만들어라.
9	6. 뒤에 오는 사람을 위해 문을 잡아 줘라.
10	7. 이웃을 당신의 파티에 초대해라.
11	만약 당신이 매일 한 가지씩 하기만 하면, 당신의 마을을 더 좋게 만들 수 있다.
12	평화 메시지
13	우리는 세계 평화의 날에 게시판에 평화 메시지를 붙였다.
14	평화는 세상 어디에서나 친구가 있다는 것을 의미한다. – 김지민
15	나는 지구의 조각들을 갖느니 지구 위의 평화를 갖겠다. – 서은지
16	항상 싸우거나 소리치는 누군가가 있으므로 나는 내가 가는 모든 곳에서 평화를 원한다. – 박한솔
17	평화는 모든 사람을 미소 짓게 만든다. – 양미란
18	평화는 우리 모두의 내면에 있다. 우리는 단지 그것을 공유할 필요가 있을 뿐이다. – 장재희
19	웃읍시다
20	하루에 사과 한 개

21 Jake came in to see his dad. "Dad!" he said, "Is it true that an apple a day _____ the doctor _____?"

22 "That's _____ _____ _____," said his dad.

23 "Well, give me an apple quickly! I _____ _____ the doctor's window!"

24 _____ _____ to Books!

25 Do you know _____ _____ _____? They hate water, the sun, and dog ears. _____ dog ears?

26 Water is bad for WITCHES and BOOKS! / The SUN also TURNs Books YELLOW / Don't DOG-EAR! Use a _____! / Be Kind to Books!

27 Stop _____ dog ears in books. Use a bookmark instead.

28 _____ _____ a bookmark _____ can save your books. Be kind to your books.

29 _____ _____ you love your books, _____ _____ your books will be. _____ _____ making your own?

30 _____ That Sound _____

31 1. About 7% of all people who _____ _____ are living on the Earth today.

32 About 108,200 million people _____ _____ _____ _____ in the history of the world. And about 7,442 million are living on the Earth today.

33 2. Bangladesh has _____ people _____ Russia.

34 Russia is the world's _____ country, but tiny Bangladesh has 166.3 million people in 2018. Russia has 143.9 million people.

35 3. A banyan tree near Kolkata, India, is _____ the average Walmart.

36 The average Walmart store _____ about 104,000 square feet. The Great Banyan Tree in Kolkata, India, is about _____ _____ _____ a forest, _____ 155,000 square feet.

37 4. Baby carrots _____ _____ in 1986.

38 Baby carrots are not actually baby carrots. Big ugly carrots _____ _____ small _____ that have the shape of a baby carrot. Farmer Mike Yurosek invented them in 1986 as a way to use ugly carrots that weren't sold.

39 _____ in the Movies

40 Zootopia (2016) It's _____ _____ _____ ever!

---

21 Jake가 아빠를 보러 들어왔다. "아빠!" 그는 "하루에 사과 한 개가 의사를 멀리하게 만든다는 것이 사실이에요?"라고 말했다.

22 "사람들이 그렇게 말하지," 아빠가 말했다.

23 "자, 저에게 빨리 사과 한 개를 주세요! 제가 방금 의사 선생님의 유리창을 깨뜨렸어요!"

24 책들을 친절하게 대해 주세요!

25 여러분은 책들이 무엇을 싫어하는지 아나요? 그들은 물, 햇빛, 그리고 강아지 귀를 싫어합니다. 왜 강아지 귀일까요?

26 물은 마녀와 책에 해롭다! / 햇빛도 책을 누렇게 뜨게 한다. / 강아지 귀처럼 책을 접지 마라! 책갈피를 사용해라! / 책들을 친절하게 대해 주세요!

27 강아지 귀 모양으로 책을 접는 것을 멈춰 주세요. 대신에 책갈피를 이용하세요.

28 여러분의 책을 구해 주는 것은 바로 책갈피입니다. 여러분의 책들을 친절하게 대해 주세요.

29 여러분이 책을 더 많이 사랑하면 할수록 여러분의 책들은 더 행복해질 겁니다. 여러분 자신의 책갈피를 만들어 보는 게 어떨까요?

30 가짜 같은 사실

31 1 지금까지 살아온 모든 사람의 약 7%가 오늘날 지구상에 살고 있다.

32 세계 역사에서 약 1천8십2억 명의 사람들이 지금까지 태어났다. 그리고 약 7십4억 4천2백만 명이 오늘날 지구상에 살고 있다.

33 2 방글라데시는 러시아보다 인구가 더 많다.

34 러시아는 세계에서 가장 큰 나라이지만, 아주 작은 방글라데시에는 2018년 기준으로 1억 6천6백3십만 명의 인구가 있다. 러시아는 1억 4천3백9십만 명의 인구가 있다.

35 3 인도 Kolkata 부근의 한 바니안(banyan) 나무는 평균적인 월마트보다 크다.

36 평균적인 월마트 상점은 약 10만4천 평방피트의 넓이이다. 인도 Kolkata에 있는 그레이트 바니안 나무는 대략 숲 하나의 크기로 15만5천 평방피트를 차지한다.

37 4 베이비 당근은 1986년 발명되었다.

38 베이비 당근은 실제로 아기처럼 작은 당근이 아니다. 크고 못생긴 당근들이 베이비 당근 모양을 가진 작은 조각으로 잘린다. 농부 Mike Yurosek이 팔리지 않는 못생긴 당근을 사용할 하나의 방편으로 1986년에 그것을 발명하였다.

39 영화 속 직업들

40 주토피아(2016) 그것은 이제까지 가장 대단한 영화이다!

41 Flash is a public officer. He is very slow but works hard. You will be surprised to see _____ _____ _____ in his free time. It's driving a race car!

42 Nick is a fox _____ a big mouth. _____ _____, he gets closer to her. He later becomes a police officer like Judy.

43 Judy is a small rabbit, but she's smart and strong. After a lot of effort, she becomes a police officer and _____ _____ _____.

44 Ratatouille (2007) _____ will love this movie.

45 Anton Ego is a food critic. After he eats the food Remy cooked, he realizes that _____ can cook.

46 Remy, a little mouse, dreams of becoming a cook. He goes into a restaurant and meets a boy _____ Linguini. _____ Linguini, he makes delicious food and _____ _____ _____ a great cook.

47 Say It _____ Emojis

48 Do you know _____ _____ _____ _____?

49 Killing two birds with one stone. / The apple of your eyes. / Don't play games with fire. / _____ _____ _____ blue moon. / Let's call it a day. / Money does not grow on trees. / It's raining cats and dogs. / _____ _____ _____ cake.

50 Emoji Song

51 Now, let's sing a Christmas song together! _____ _____, _____ _____!

52 _____ Messages

53 Imagine you can send messages to your friend that _____ _____ _____ _____ _____! It's not so difficult for you to learn how to read and write your own secret messages.

54 1. Read _____

55 This is _____ _____ _____. Just read the words _____! It seems simple once you know the secret, but it can be a hard one when you don't.

56 2. Read _____ Second Letter

57 Read every second letter _____ _____ the first letter, and when you finish, start again on the letters you missed.

58 3. Pig-pen

59 The Pig-pen is _____ _____ _____ _____. The lines around each letter mean the letter inside the lines.

60 Now create your own set of secret letters and write secret messages _____ _____ _____ your friends. _____ _____ you _____ _____ a key so your friends can understand your messages!

41 Flash는 공무원이다. 그는 아주 느리지만 열심히 일한다. 여러분은 그가 여가 시간에 무엇을 하는지 알게 되면 놀랄 것이다. 그것은 경주용 자동차를 운전하는 것이다!

42 Nick은 커다란 입을 가진 여우이다. Judy를 도우면서 그녀와 가까워진다. 나중에 Judy처럼 경찰관이 된다.

43 Judy는 작은 토끼지만, 영리하고 강하다. 많은 노력을 한 후에, 그녀는 경찰관이 되었고 많은 사건을 해결한다.

44 라따뚜이(2007) 누구라도 이 영화를 사랑할 것이다.

45 Anton Ego는 음식 비평가이다. Remy가 요리한 음식을 먹은 후에, 그는 "누구라도 요리할 수 있다."라는 것을 깨닫는다.

46 작은 쥐 Remy는 요리사가 되기를 꿈꾼다. 그는 식당에 들어가서 Linguini라는 이름의 소년을 만난다. Linguini를 통제하면서 그는 맛있는 음식을 만들고 결국에는 훌륭한 요리사가 된다.

47 이모지로 말하자

48 이 이모지들이 무엇을 의미하는지 아니?

49 돌 하나로 새 두 마리 잡기. (일석이조.) / 당신이 가장 사랑하는 사람. (눈에 넣어도 안 아플 사람.) / 불을 가지고 장난치지 마라. / 극히 드물게. / 오늘은 이만하자. / 돈이 나무에서 자라는 것은 아니다. (돈이 그냥 생기는 건 아니다.) / 비가 억수같이 온다. / 케이크 한 조각. (누워서 떡 먹기.)

50 이모지 노래

51 자, 함께 크리스마스 노래를 불러 봅시다! 더 크게 부를수록, 더 행복해집니다!

52 비밀 메시지

53 다른 어떤 사람도 읽을 수 없는 메시지를 친구에게 보낼 수 있다고 상상해 봐라! 여러분 자신의 비밀 메시지를 읽고 쓰는 법을 배우는 것이 그렇게 어렵지는 않다.

54 1. 거꾸로 읽어라

55 이것은 풀기 쉽다 – 그냥 단어들을 거꾸로 읽어라! 일단 여러분이 비밀을 알면 간단하지만, 그렇지 못하면 어려울 수 있다.

56 2. 두 번째 글자마다 읽어라

57 첫 번째 글자에서 시작해서 두 번째 글자마다 읽어라. 그리고 끝나면 여러분이 빠뜨린 글자로 다시 시작하라.

58 3. 피그펜

59 피그펜(돼지우리)은 보기보다 쉽다. 각 글자 주변의 선들은 그 선들 안에 있는 글자를 의미한다.

60 이제 여러분은 자신만의 비밀 문자 세트를 만들어서 친구들에게 보낼 비밀 메시지를 써 보아라. 친구들이 메시지를 이해할 수 있도록 해결의 열쇠도 함께 보내도록 해라.

● 우리말을 참고하여 본문을 영작하시오.

1 십대들의 잡지
➡ _____

2 마을을 더 좋게 만드는 방법들
➡ _____

3 이웃들을 위해 뭔가 좋은 일을 하면 여러분의 마을을 변화시킬 수 있다. 작은 것부터 시작하라.
여기 몇 가지 도움말이 있다.
➡ _____

4 1. 이웃들에게 인사를 하고 미소를 지어라.
➡ _____

5 2. 잊지 말고 "고맙습니다."라고 말해라.
➡ _____

6 3. 비 오는 날에 당신의 우산을 함께 써라.
➡ _____

7 4. 이웃이 농담하면 크게 소리 내어 웃어라.
➡ _____

8 5. 이웃들을 위해 뭔가를 만들어라.
➡ _____

9 6. 뒤에 오는 사람을 위해 문을 잡아 줘라.
➡ _____

10 7. 이웃을 당신의 파티에 초대해라.
➡ _____

11 만약 당신이 매일 한 가지씩 하기만 하면, 당신의 마을을 더 좋게 만들 수 있다.
➡ _____

12 평화 메시지
➡ _____

13 우리는 세계 평화의 날에 게시판에 평화 메시지를 붙였다.
➡ _____

14 평화는 세상 어디에서나 친구가 있다는 것을 의미한다. – 김지민
➡ _____

15 나는 지구의 조각들을 갖느니 지구 위의 평화를 갖겠다. – 서은지
➡ _____

16 항상 싸우거나 소리치는 누군가가 있으므로 나는 내가 가는 모든 곳에서 평화를 원한다. – 박한솔
➡ _____

17 평화는 모든 사람을 미소 짓게 만든다. – 양미란
➡ _____

18 평화는 우리 모두의 내면에 있다. 우리는 단지 그것을 공유할 필요가 있을 뿐이다. – 장재희
➡ _____

19 웃읍시다
➡ _____

20 하루에 사과 한 개
➡ _____

21 Jake가 아빠를 보러 들어왔다. "아빠!" 그는 "하루에 사과 한 개가 의사를 멀리하게 만든다는 것이 사실이에요?"라고 말했다.
➡ _____

22 "사람들이 그렇게 말하지," 아빠가 말했다.
➡ _____

23 "자, 저에게 빨리 사과 한 개를 주세요! 제가 방금 의사 선생님의 유리창을 깨뜨렸어요!"
➡ _____

24 책들을 친절하게 대해 주세요!
➡ _____

25 여러분은 책들이 무엇을 싫어하는지 아나요? 그들은 물, 햇빛, 그리고 강아지 귀를 싫어합니다. 왜 강아지 귀일까요?
➡ _____

26 물은 마녀와 책에 해롭다! / 햇빛도 책을 누렇게 뜨게 한다. / 강아지 귀처럼 책을 접지 마라! 책갈피를 사용해라! / 책들을 친절하게 대해 주세요!
➡ _____

27 강아지 귀 모양으로 책을 접는 것을 멈춰 주세요. 대신에 책갈피를 이용하세요.
➡ _____

28 여러분의 책을 구해 주는 것은 바로 책갈피입니다. 여러분의 책들을 친절하게 대해 주세요.
➡ _____

29 여러분이 책을 더 많이 사랑하면 할수록 여러분의 책들은 더 행복해질 겁니다. 여러분 자신의 책갈피를 만들어 보는 게 어떨까요?
➡ _____

30 가짜 같은 사실
➡ _____

31 1. 지금까지 살아온 모든 사람의 약 7%가 오늘날 지구상에 살고 있다.
➡ _____

32 세계 역사에서 약 1천8십2억 명의 사람들이 지금까지 태어났다. 그리고 약 7십4억 4천2백만 명이 오늘날 지구상에 살고 있다.
➡ _____

33 2. 방글라데시는 러시아보다 인구가 더 많다.
➡ _____

34 러시아는 세계에서 가장 큰 나라이지만, 아주 작은 방글라데시에는 2018년 기준으로 1억 6천6백3십만 명의 인구가 있다. 러시아는 1억 4천3백9십만 명의 인구가 있다.
➡ _____

35 3. 인도 Kolkata 부근의 한 바니안(banyan) 나무는 평균적인 월마트보다 크다.
➡ _____

36 평균적인 월마트 상점은 약 10만4천 평방피트의 넓이이다. 인도 Kolkata에 있는 그레이트 바니안 나무는 대략 숲 하나의 크기로 15만5천 평방피트를 차지한다.
➡ _____

37 4. 베이비 당근은 1986년 발명되었다.
➡ _____

38 베이비 당근은 실제로 아기처럼 작은 당근이 아니다. 크고 못생긴 당근들이 베이비 당근 모양을 가진 작은 조각으로 잘린다. 농부 Mike Yurosek이 팔리지 않는 못생긴 당근을 사용할 하나의 방편으로 1986년에 그것을 발명하였다.
➡ _____
_____

39 영화 속 직업들
➡ _____

40 주토피아(2016) 그것은 이제까지 가장 대단한 영화이다!
➡ _____

41 Flash는 공무원이다. 그는 아주 느리지만 열심히 일한다. 여러분은 그가 여가 시간에 무엇을 하는지 알게 되면 놀랄 것이다. 그것은 경주용 자동차를 운전하는 것이다!

➡ _____

42 Nick은 커다란 입을 가진 여우이다. Judy를 도우면서 그녀와 가까워진다. 나중에 Judy처럼 경찰관이 된다.

➡ _____

43 Judy는 작은 토끼지만, 영리하고 강하다. 많은 노력을 한 후에, 그녀는 경찰관이 되었고 많은 사건을 해결한다.

➡ _____

44 라따뚜이(2007) 누구라도 이 영화를 사랑할 것이다.

45 Anton Ego는 음식 비평가이다. Remy가 요리한 음식을 먹은 후에, 그는 "누구라도 요리할 수 있다." 라는 것을 깨닫는다.

46 작은 쥐 Remy는 요리사가 되기를 꿈꾼다. 그는 식당에 들어가서 Linguini라는 이름의 소년을 만난다. Linguini를 통제하면서 그는 맛있는 음식을 만들고 결국에는 훌륭한 요리사가 된다.

➡ _____

47 이모지로 말하자

➡ _____

48 이 이모지들이 무엇을 의미하는지 아니?

➡ _____

49 돌 하나로 새 두 마리 잡기. (일석이조.) / 당신이 가장 사랑하는 사람. (눈에 넣어도 안 아플 사람.) / 불을 가지고 장난치지 마라. / 극히 드물게. / 오늘은 이만하자. / 돈이 나무에서 자라는 것은 아니다. (돈이 그냥 생기는 건 아니다.) / 비가 억수같이 온다. / 케이크 한 조각. (누워서 떡 먹기.)

➡ _____

50 이모지 노래

➡ _____

51 자, 함께 크리스마스 노래를 불러 봅시다! 더 크게 부를수록, 더 행복해집니다!

52 비밀 메시지

53 다른 어떤 사람도 읽을 수 없는 메시지를 친구에게 보낼 수 있다고 상상해 봐라! 여러분 자신의 비밀 메시지를 읽고 쓰는 법을 배우는 것이 그렇게 어렵지는 않다.

➡ _____

54 1. 거꾸로 읽어라

➡ _____

55 이것은 풀기 쉽다 - 그냥 단어들을 거꾸로 읽어라! 일단 여러분이 비밀을 알면 간단하지만, 그렇지 못하면 어려울 수 있다.

➡ _____

56 2. 두 번째 글자마다 읽어라

➡ _____

57 첫 번째 글자에서 시작해서 두 번째 글자마다 읽어라. 그리고 끝나면 여러분이 빠뜨린 글자로 다시 시작하라.

➡ _____

58 3. 피그펜

59 피그펜(돼지우리)은 보기보다 쉽다. 각 글자 주변의 선들은 그 선들 안에 있는 글자를 의미한다.

60 이제 여러분은 자신만의 비밀 문자 세트를 만들어서 친구들에게 보낼 비밀 메시지를 써 보아라. 친구들이 메시지를 이해할 수 있도록 해결의 열쇠도 함께 보내도록 해라.

➡ _____

01 다음 문장에 공통으로 들어갈 말을 쓰시오.

> (1) In some _____s people had to wait several weeks for an appointment.
>
> (2) The police have decided to reopen the _____.

02 다음 빈칸에 들어갈 말을 〈보기〉에서 찾아 쓰시오. (필요하면 변형하거나 단어를 추가하여 쓰시오.)

> ┤ 보기 ├
>
> end   better   keep   sure

(1) You _____ _____ do the dishes before you go out.

(2) An apple a day _____ the doctor _____.

(3) Schools should focus on _____ _____ that students are learning.

03 우리말과 같은 뜻이 되도록 주어진 단어를 활용하여 빈칸을 채우시오.

(1) 당신은 결국 주변 사람들과 논쟁하거나 싸우게 된다.
   ➡ You _____ _____ _____ or fighting with people around you. (argue)

(2) 딸꾹질을 할 때 설탕을 한 숟가락 먹으면 멈추게 할 수 있습니다.
   ➡ You can usually _____ _____ by eating a spoonful of sugar. (hiccup)

(3) 여기엔 비가 억수같이 쏟아졌어.
   ➡ It _____ here. (cat, dog)

04 다음 문장을 간접화법으로 바꾸어 쓰시오.

(1) Jake said, "I just broke the doctor's window!"
   ➡ Jake _____
   _____.

(2) Jake said to his dad, "Give me an apple quickly"
   ➡ Jake _____
   _____.

05 다음 첫 번째 문장의 it 대신 두 번째 문장의 의문문을 넣어 문장을 다시 쓰시오.

> • You will be surprised to see it.
> • What does he do in his free time?

➡ _____
_____

06 주어진 문장에서 어법상 틀린 곳을 찾아 고치고 이유를 쓰시오.

> Big ugly carrots cut into small pieces that has the shape of a baby carrot.

(1) _____ ➡ _____
➡ 이유: _____
_____

(2) _____ ➡ _____
➡ 이유: _____
_____

[07~09] 다음 글을 읽고 물음에 답하시오.

Be Kind to Books!

Do you know what books hate? They hate water, the sun, and dog ears. ⓐWhy dog ears?

Water is bad for WITCHES and BOOKS! / The SUN also TURNs Books YELLOW / Don't DOG-EAR! Use a bookmark! / Be Kind to Books!

ⓑStop to fold dog ears in books. Use a bookmark instead. It is a bookmark that can save your books. Be kind to your books. ⓒ The more you love your books, the happier your books will be. How about making your own?

07 위 글의 밑줄 친 문장 ⓐ에 생략된 말을 넣어 문장을 다시 쓰시오.

➡ _____

08 위 글의 밑줄 친 ⓑ에서 어법상 틀린 부분을 찾아 고치시오.

_____ ➡ _____

09 위 글의 밑줄 친 ⓒ를 접속사 As를 사용하여 고칠 때, 빈칸에 들어갈 알맞은 말을 쓰시오.

As you love your books _____, your books will be _____.

[10~12] 다음 글을 읽고 물음에 답하시오.

Secret Messages

• ⓐ**YEOAUTLTOOODKAGYR**

Read ⓑ매 두 번째 글자 starting with the first letter, and when you finish, start again on the letters you missed.

• Pig-pen

ⓒ
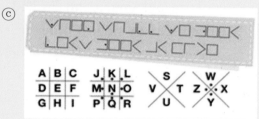

The Pig-pen is easier than it looks. The lines around each letter mean the letter inside the lines.

10 위 글의 밑줄 친 비밀 메시지 ⓐ의 내용을 영어로 쓰시오.

➡ _____

11 위 글의 밑줄 친 ⓑ의 우리말에 맞게 3 단어로 영작하시오.

➡ _____

12 위 글의 비밀 메시지 ⓒ의 내용을 영어로 쓰시오.

➡ _____

01 출제율 95%

다음 단어에 대한 영어 설명이 <u>어색한</u> 것은?

① effort: an attempt to do something

② forest: a large area of trees growing close together

③ playwriter: someone whose job is to give their opinion of a book, play, movie, etc.

④ delicious: very good to eat or drink

⑤ wave: to put your hand up and move it from side to side in order to attract someone's attention or to say goodbye

02 출제율 90%

다음 짝지어진 단어의 관계가 같도록 빈칸에 알맞은 말을 쓰시오.

save : rescue – yell : _____

03 출제율 95%

다음 영영풀이에 해당하는 단어를 고르시오.

to ask someone to come to your house, to a party, etc.

① invite   ② stop by

③ cook   ④ visit

⑤ worry

04 출제율 95%

다음 문장의 빈칸에 공통으로 들어갈 단어를 쓰시오.

• Today I _____d the importance of energy for the first time.

• He recently _____d his dream.

➡ _____

05 출제율 95%

다음 주어진 문장과 같은 의미를 가진 문장을 쓰시오.
(would를 사용할 것.)

• I prefer staying home to going there.

• I prefer to stay home rather than to go there.

➡ _____

06 출제율 100%

다음 빈칸에 들어갈 말이 알맞게 짝지어진 것은?

• Many actors dream _____ performing at Broadway theaters in New York.

• I can chat more with my friends and get closer _____ them.

• So, who knows? You may end _____ becoming a wonderful chef!

① on – with – down   ② into – of – up

③ by – of – up   ④ of – to – up

⑤ by – of – down

07 출제율 90%

다음 중 짝지어진 단어의 관계가 <u>다른</u> 것은?

① quickly : slowly

② hate : like

③ backward : forward

④ tiny : huge

⑤ imagine : visualize

08 다음 영영풀이에 해당하는 단어를 〈보기〉에서 찾아 첫 번째 빈칸에 쓰고, 두 번째 빈칸에는 우리말 뜻을 쓰시오.

┌─── 보기 ───┐
share   fold   instead   realize
└───────────┘

(1) _____ : in the place of someone or something else: _____

(2) _____ : to have or use something at the same time as someone else: _____

(3) _____ : to bend something so that one part of it lies flat on top of another part: _____

(4) _____ : to notice or understand something that you did not notice or understand before: _____

09 다음 밑줄 친 that의 쓰임이 다른 하나를 고르시오.

① It is a bookmark that can save your books.
② It was last Sunday that I visited my uncle's house.
③ It is my dog that makes me happy.
④ It was in front of the Eiffel Tower that I took this selfie.
⑤ It was so hot and humid that we couldn't walk anymore.

10 다음 우리말에 맞게 주어진 어휘를 배열하시오.

(1) 너의 책을 네가 더 많이 사랑할수록, 너의 책은 더 행복해질 것이다.
(your / the / books / be / love / you / books / happier / more / the / your / will)
➡ _____
_____

(2) 너는 더 많이 운동할수록, 더 열심히 공부할 수 있다.
(out / you / can / the / you / study / harder / work / the / more)
➡ _____
_____

(3) 날씨가 더워질수록, 우리의 바지가 더 짧아진다.
(shorter / the / it / our / the / gets / hotter / pants / get)
➡ _____
_____

11 다음 두 문장을 한 문장으로 바르게 옮긴 것은?

┌─────────────────────┐
• Do you know?
• What do books hate?
└─────────────────────┘

① Do you know what do books hate?
② Do you know what books hate?
③ Do you know what books do hate?
④ What do you know books hate?
⑤ What books do you know hate?

12 다음 문장의 틀린 곳을 바르게 고치지 않은 것은?

┌─────────────────────────────┐
It's not so ①difficultly ②of you to ③ learning how ④read and write ⑤yours own secret messages.
└─────────────────────────────┘

① difficultly → difficult
② of → for
③ learning → learn
④ read → reading
⑤ yours → your

13 다음 우리말을 영어로 바르게 옮긴 것을 <u>모두</u> 고르시오.

> 우리가 더 크게 노래할수록, 우리는 더 행복해진다.

① The loud we sing, the happy we become.
② The more loud we sing, the more happy we become.
③ The louder we sing, the happier we become.
④ As we sing more loudly, we become more happily.
⑤ As we sing louder, we become happier.

14 다음 밑줄 친 <u>it</u>의 쓰임이 나머지 넷과 <u>다른</u> 하나를 고르시오.

① Is <u>it</u> okay to go out without anything to eat?
② <u>It</u> is a bad idea to go there alone.
③ <u>It</u> must be dark in the cave.
④ Is <u>it</u> true that an apple a day keeps the doctor away?
⑤ <u>It</u> is impossible for me to hate cats.

15 다음 중 의미가 <u>다른</u> 하나를 고르시오.

① Make sure to send along a key.
② Make sure you send along a key.
③ Be sure you send along a key.
④ Don't forget to send along a key.
⑤ Remember sending along a key.

[16~18] 다음 글을 읽고 물음에 답하시오.

Jobs in the Movies

Ratatouille (2007) Everyone will love this movie.,

Anton Ego is a food critic. After he eats the food Remy cooked, he realizes that anyone can cook.

Remy, a little mouse, dreams of becoming a cook. He goes into a restaurant and meets a boy named Linguini. Controlling Linguini, (A)<u>he</u> makes delicious food and ends up ___ⓐ___ a great cook.

16 위 글의 빈칸 ⓐ에 become을 알맞은 형태로 쓰시오.

➡ _____

17 주어진 영영풀이에 해당하는 단어를 본문에서 찾아 쓰시오.

> a person who writes about and expresses opinions about things such as books, films, music, or art

➡ _____

18 위 글의 밑줄 친 (A)he가 가리키는 것을 본문에서 찾아 쓰시오.

➡ _____

[19~21] 다음 글을 읽고 물음에 답하시오.

Ways to Make Your Town Better

Doing something nice for your neighbors can change your town. Start small. Here are some tips.

1. Say hello to your neighbors and smile.
2. (A)<u>Don't forget saying, "Thank you."</u>
3. Share your umbrella on a rainy day.

4. Laugh out loud when your neighbor tells a joke.

5. Make something for your neighbors.

6. Hold the door ____ⓐ____ the person behind you.

7. Invite your neighbors ____ⓑ____ your party.

If you just do one thing each day, you can make your town better.

출제율 95%

19 위 글의 빈칸 ⓐ와 ⓑ에 들어갈 전치사가 바르게 짝지어진 것은?

　　　ⓐ　ⓑ　　　　　　　ⓐ　ⓑ
① for – in　　　　　② by – at
③ to – at　　　　　④ for – to
⑤ by – to

출제율 90%

20 위 글의 밑줄 친 (A)에서 어법상 틀린 부분을 찾아 고치시오.

_____ ➡ _____

출제율 100%

21 위 글을 읽고 다음 중 마을을 더 좋게 만드는 방법에 해당하지 않는 것을 고르시오.

① 큰 실천 사항부터 시작하라.
② 이웃들에게 인사를 하고 미소를 지어라.
③ 비 오는 날에 당신의 우산을 함께 써라.
④ 이웃이 농담하면 크게 소리 내어 웃어라.
⑤ 이웃들을 위해 뭔가를 만들어라.

[22~24] 다음 글을 읽고 물음에 답하시오.

Be Kind to Books!

Do you know what books hate? They hate water, the sun, and dog ears. Why dog ears?

Water is bad for WITCHES and BOOKS! / The SUN also TURNs Books YELLOW / Don't DOG-EAR! Use a bookmark! / Be Kind to Books!

Stop folding dog ears in books. Use a bookmark instead. ⓐ여러분의 책을 구해 주는 것은 바로 책갈피입니다. Be kind to your books. The more you love your books, the happier your books will be. ⓑHow about making your own?

출제율 90%

22 위 글의 밑줄 친 ⓐ의 우리말에 맞게 주어진 어휘를 이용하여 9 단어로 영작하시오.

| it, that, save |

➡ _____

출제율 95%

23 위 글의 밑줄 친 ⓑ와 바꿔 쓸 수 있는 말을 모두 고르시오.

① Why don't you make your own?
② How do you like your own?
③ What about making your own?
④ Why don't we make your own?
⑤ Why not make your own?

출제율 100%

24 According to the passage, which is NOT true?

① The things which books hate are water, the sun, and dog ears.
② You should use dog ears instead of a bookmark.
③ A bookmark can save your books.
④ You should be kind to your books.
⑤ As you love your books more, your books will be happier.

[25~27] 다음 글을 읽고 물음에 답하시오.

Secret Messages

ⓐ다른 어떤 사람도 읽을 수 없는 메시지를 친구에게 보낼 수 있다고 상상해 봐라! It's not so difficult for you to learn how to read and write your own secret messages.

1. Read Backward

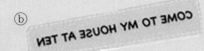
ⓑ

This is easy ⓒto solve. Just read the words backward! It seems simple once you know the secret, but it can be a hard one when you don't.

✏️ 출제율 90%

25 위 글의 밑줄 친 ⓐ의 우리말에 맞게 주어진 어휘를 알맞게 배열하시오.

> your friend / else / messages / imagine / to / can / you / read / that / send / can / no one

➡️ _____

_____

_____

_____

✏️ 출제율 95%

26 위 글의 비밀 메시지 ⓑ의 내용을 영어로 쓰시오.

➡️ _____

✏️ 출제율 95%

27 아래 〈보기〉에서 위 글의 밑줄 친 ⓒto solve와 to부정사의 용법이 같은 것의 개수를 고르시오.

> ┤ 보기 ├
> ① I need a pencil to write with.
> ② She stood up to go out.
> ③ It is very important to study English hard.
> ④ His job is to sing a song.
> ⑤ This water is not good to drink.

① 1개　② 2개　③ 3개　④ 4개　⑤ 5개

[28~30] 다음 글을 읽고 물음에 답하시오.

Jobs in the Movies

Zootopia (2016) It's the greatest movie ever!

Flash is a public officer. He is very slow but works hard. You will be surprised to see what he does in his free time. ⓐIt's ⓑdriving a race car!

Nick is a fox with a big mouth. ⓒHelping Judy, he gets closer to her. He later becomes a police officer like Judy.

Judy is a small rabbit, but she's smart and strong. After a lot of effort, she becomes a police officer and solves many cases.

✏️ 출제율 90%

28 위 글의 밑줄 친 ⓐIt이 가리키는 것을 본문에서 찾아 쓰시오.

➡️ _____

✏️ 출제율 100%

29 위 글의 밑줄 친 ⓑdriving과 문법적 쓰임이 같은 것을 모두 고르시오.

① He is good at playing tennis.
② Seeing is believing.
③ Do you know that boy playing the piano?
④ His job is selling cars.
⑤ She is writing a letter.

✏️ 출제율 95%

30 위 글의 밑줄 친 ⓒ를 다음과 같이 고칠 때, 빈칸에 들어갈 알맞은 접속사를 모두 고르시오.

> _____ he helps Judy, he gets closer to her.

① Though　② As
③ If　④ Until
⑤ While

중간 + 기말

적중100 plus

영어 기출문제집

영어 중 3

천재 | 정사열

Best Collection

내용문의 중등영어발전소 적중100 편집부 TEL 070-7707-0457

INSIGHT
on the textbook

교과서 파헤치기

영어 기출 문제집

적중100 plus
2학기 전과정

영어 중 3

천재 | 정사열

INSIGHT
on the textbook
교과서 파헤치기

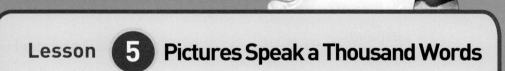

※ 다음 영어를 우리말로 쓰시오.

01	awesome	
02	battle	
03	ground	
04	toward	
05	traffic	
06	chimney	
07	ad(= advertisement)	
08	powerful	
09	close	
10	translate	
11	prepare	
12	curious	
13	rather	
14	reply	
15	husband	
16	dead	
17	knock	
18	discover	
19	hidden	
20	hug	
21	misunderstanding	

22	seriously	
23	loudly	
24	seem	
25	enemy	
26	seat	
27	soldier	
28	exactly	
29	vote	
30	border	
31	Braille	
32	expression	
33	hire	
34	product	
35	get over	
36	look after	
37	be covered with	
38	at a price of	
39	except for	
40	vote for	
41	be careful with	
42	right away	
43	instead of	

※ 다음 우리말을 영어로 쓰시오.

01 교통

02 근사한, 멋진,
엄청난, 어마어마한

03 글자, 문자

04 전쟁, 전투

05 번역하다, 해석하다

06 죽은, 쓸모없는

07 적군, 적대자

08 발견하다

09 불을 붙이다, 불을 밝히다

10 큰 소리로, 시끄럽게

11 정확하게

12 호기심이 많은, 궁금한

13 표현

14 남편

15 ~을 향하여

16 굴뚝

17 진지하게, 심각하게

18 다소, 약간

19 준비하다

20 숨은, 숨겨진

21 군인

22 국경, 경계

23 상품, 제품

24 수화

25 고용하다

26 오해

27 포옹; 포옹하다

28 치다, 두드리다

29 좌석, 의석

30 연못

31 외국의

32 몸짓, 몸동작

33 끌다, 잡아당기다

34 투표하다, 선출하다

35 ~ 대신에

36 ~을 제외하고

37 ~을 돌보다

38 ~에 조심하다

39 물러서다

40 즉시, 당장

41 ~로 덮이다

42 ~의 가격으로

43 이겨내다, 극복하다

※ 다음 영영풀이에 알맞은 단어를 <보기>에서 골라 쓴 후, 우리말 뜻을 쓰시오.

1 _____ : no longer alive: _____

2 _____ : in the direction of: _____

3 _____ : an answer to a letter: _____

4 _____ : from another country: _____

5 _____ : the surface of the Earth: _____

6 _____ : to pay someone to work for you: _____

7 _____ : the man that a woman is married to: _____

8 _____ : suffering from an illness or disease:: _____

9 _____ : to make something ready for use: _____

10 _____ : a position as a member of a committee, court, etc.: _____

11 _____ : to express one's preference for a candidate: _____

12 _____ : a thick liquid made from plants or animals that is used in cooking:
_____

13 _____ : a piece of jewelry in the form of a circle that you wear on a finger:
_____

14 _____ : to change spoken or written words into another language: _____

15 _____ : to find out something that you did not know before: _____

16 _____ : the action of putting your arms around someone to show your love or
friendship: _____

보기			
oil	vote	hire	foreign
hug	translate	dead	ill
seat	prepare	toward	reply
discover	ring	husband	ground

※ 다음 우리말과 일치하도록 빈칸에 알맞은 말을 쓰시오.

Get Ready 2

(1) G: I'm _____ _____ that robot. Why _____ _____ _____ there?

B: It's _____ _____ _____ ad. It _____ people their _____ are very _____.

(2) G: What's this? I'_____ _____ _____ it.

B: It's a _____ _____. It _____ "Do not _____."

G: Oh, I see.

(3) G: What are these _____ _____? I'_____ _____ _____ them.

B: Oh, they are _____. They are for _____ people.

G: I see. Now I can _____ _____ they _____.

(4) G: I'm _____ about that _____. Why is it _____ there?

B: Oh, that. It's an _____. It says the _____ is very _____.

Start Off – Listen & Talk A

1. B: What are the _____ doing _____ the five _____ on TV?

G: They are sending _____ to the king _____ _____ the _____.

B: Really? I'_____ _____ the _____. Can you tell me more?

G: Well, do you see the two _____ _____?

B: Yes. _____ do they _____?

G: They mean they just _____ an _____.

2. B: If there's no _____, they don't _____ _____ _____, _____ they?

G: Yes, they do. _____ from one _____ means "No _____."

B: Now smoke is _____ from three chimneys. _____ that _____?

G: _____ _____ an enemy is coming _____ to the _____.

Start Off B

B: Now the enemy _____ _____ the _____ in the _____. What are the _____ _____ _____ _____ _____ to send _____? I'_____ _____ _____ that.

G: They will _____ four _____.

B: When they _____ all five of the _____, what does that mean?

G: _____ the _____ has _____.

(1) G: 나는 저 로봇에 대해 알고 싶어. 그건 왜 저기에 서 있는 거니?

B: 그건 일종의 광고야. 그것은 그들의 건전지가 매우 강력하다는 것을 사람들에게 말하고 있어.

(2) G: 이것은 뭐지? 난 그게 궁금해.

B: 그것은 교통 표지판이야. 그것은 "들어오지 마시오."를 의미해.

G: 오, 알겠어.

(3) G: 이 점들은 무엇을 위한 거니? 난 그것들에 대해 알고 싶어.

B: 오, 그것들은 점자야. 그것들은 시각장애인을 위한 것이야.

G: 알겠어. 이제 그것들이 무엇을 의미하는지 추측할 수 있어.

(4) G: 나는 저 풍선이 궁금해. 그건 왜 저기에 매달려 있니?

B: 오, 저것. 그건 광고야. 그것은 그 상품이 매우 강력하다는 것을 말하고 있어.

1. B: TV에서 병사들이 5개의 굴뚝으로 무엇을 하고 있니?

G: 그들은 그 굴뚝을 이용하여 왕에게 메시지를 보내고 있어.

B: 정말? 난 그 체계가 궁금해. 좀 더 말해 줄 수 있어?

G: 음, 연기 나는 굴뚝 두 개가 보이지?

B: 그래. 그것들은 무엇을 의미하니?

G: 그것들은 그들이 방금 적을 봤다는 것을 의미해.

2. B: 만약 적이 없다면, 그들은 연기를 전혀 피우지 않아, 그렇지?

G: 아니, 연기를 피워. 굴뚝 한 곳에서 연기가 나오면 "적이 없음"을 의미해.

B: 이제 연기가 굴뚝 세 개에서 올라가고 있어. 그것은 무엇을 의미하니?

G: 그것은 적이 국경 가까이 접근하고 있음을 의미해.

B: 이제 적이 어둠 속에서 국경을 침입하고 있어. 메시지를 보내기 위해서 병사들은 무슨 일을 할까? 나는 그것이 궁금해.

G: 그들은 굴뚝 4개에 불을 붙일 거야.

B: 그들이 5개 굴뚝 모두에 불을 붙였을 때, 그것은 무엇을 의미하니?

G: 그것은 전투가 시작되었음을 의미해.

Start Off – Speak Up

B: I'_____ _____ _____ sign _____.
G: Are you? _____ me _____ you one _____. Look.
B: _____ does it _____?
G: _____ _____ "Hello."

Step Up – Real-life Scene

B: This painting has some _____ _____ in it.
G: Really? I'm _____ _____ them. Where are the _____?
B: _____ one _____.
G: _____ _____. ... Oh, I see some _____ here.
B: You found _____! It _____ "Jan van Eyck was here. 1434." It's _____.
G: That's _____! _____ _____ _____?
B: Okay. This dog _____ us the man here was very _____.
G: I don't _____.
B: They had to _____ _____ _____ money _____ _____ a dog of that _____ _____ _____ _____ _____.
G: I see. Only _____ _____ could have _____ _____ of _____ dog, _____?
B: _____. Pictures _____ _____ _____ words, you know.

Express Yourself A

1. **W:** What does this woman's _____ mean? I'm _____ _____ it.
   M: I think _____ _____ "Jump _____ the _____."
   W: _____ do you _____ _____?
   M: The boy has _____ _____ _____ on his head. And the woman is _____ at the _____.
2. **W:** This woman doesn't want a dollar. _____ what does her _____ _____?
   M: _____ _____ she wants a _____.
   W: Then the boy _____ _____ a chicken _____ _____ the fruit, _____?
   M: _____ _____ _____.
3. **W:** _____ does this man's _____ _____? I'm _____ _____ it.
   M: It means "_____ _____ _____."
   W: Really? _____ _____ you think _____?
   M: _____ _____ _____ there is coming _____ to an animal.
   W: Oh, I _____.

B: 난 수화가 궁금해.
G: 그러니? 내가 표현 하나를 알려줄게. 봐.
B: 그것은 무엇을 의미하니?
G: 그것은 "안녕하세요."를 의미해.

B: 이 그림은 그 안에 숨겨진 비밀이 몇 개 있어.
G: 정말? 난 그것들이 궁금해. 그 비밀들은 어디에 있니?
B: 너 스스로 하나 찾아봐.
G: 어디 보자. … 오, 여기 글자들이 몇 개 보여.
B: 너 하나 찾았구나! 그것은 "Jan van Eyck가 여기 있었다. 1434."를 의미해. 그것은 라틴어야.
G: 멋지다! 다른 비밀들은?
B: 좋아. 이 개는 여기 있는 이 남자가 매우 부자였다는 것을 우리에게 말해주지.
G: 나는 이해가 안 돼.
B: 당시에 저런 종류의 개를 사려면 많은 돈을 써야 했어.
G: 알겠다. 단지 부자들만 저런 종류의 개를 살 수 있었어, 맞지?
B: 정확해. 알다시피, 그림이 천 마디 말을 하지.

1. **W:** 이 여자의 몸짓은 무엇을 의미하니? 난 그것이 궁금해.
   M: 내 생각에 그것은 "연못으로 뛰어들어."를 의미해.
   W: 왜 그렇게 생각하니?
   M: 그 소년은 머리 위에 많은 벌이 있어. 그리고 그 여자는 연못을 가리키고 있어.
2. **W:** 이 여자는 1달러를 원하지 않아. 그렇다면 그녀의 몸짓은 무엇을 의미하니?
   M: 그것은 그녀가 닭 한 마리를 원한다는 것을 의미해.
   W: 그럼 그 소년은 과일을 얻기 위해 닭을 한 마리 가져와야 하는구나, 맞지?
   M: 난 그렇게 생각해.
3. **W:** 이 남자의 몸짓은 무엇을 의미하니? 난 그것이 궁금해.
   M: 그것은 "그것을 꺼."를 의미해.
   W: 정말? 왜 그렇게 생각하니?
   M: 거기 있는 나머지 다른 사냥꾼이 어떤 동물 가까이 접근하고 있어.
   W: 오, 알겠어.

※ 다음 우리말에 맞도록 대화를 영어로 쓰시오.

해석

Get Ready 2

(1) G: _____

　　 B: _____

(2) G: _____

　　 B: _____

　　 G: _____

(3) G: _____

　　 B: _____

　　 G: _____

(4) G: _____

　　 B: _____

Start Off – Listen & Talk A

1. B: _____

　 G: _____

　 B: _____

　 G: _____

　 B: _____

　 G: _____

2. B: _____

　 G: _____

　 B: _____

　 G: _____

Start Off B

B: _____

_____

G: _____

B: _____

G: _____

(1) G: 나는 저 로봇에 대해 알고 싶어. 그건 왜 저기에 서 있는 거니?
　 B: 그건 일종의 광고야. 그것은 그들의 건전지가 매우 강력하다는 것을 사람들에게 말하고 있어.
(2) G: 이것은 뭐지? 난 그게 궁금해.
　 B: 그것은 교통 표지판이야. 그것은 "들어오지 마시오."를 의미해.
　 G: 오, 알겠어.
(3) G: 이 점들은 무엇을 위한 거니? 난 그것들에 대해 알고 싶어.
　 B: 오, 그것들은 점자야. 그것들은 시각장애인을 위한 것이야.
　 G: 알겠어. 이제 그것들이 무엇을 의미하는지 추측할 수 있어.
(4) G: 나는 저 풍선이 궁금해. 그건 왜 저기에 매달려 있니?
　 B: 오, 저것. 그건 광고야. 그것은 그 상품이 매우 강력하다는 것을 말하고 있어.

1. B: TV에서 병사들이 5개의 굴뚝으로 무엇을 하고 있니?
　 G: 그들은 그 굴뚝을 이용하여 왕에게 메시지를 보내고 있어.
　 B: 정말? 난 그 체계가 궁금해. 좀 더 말해 줄 수 있어?
　 G: 음, 연기 나는 굴뚝 두 개가 보이지?
　 B: 그래. 그것들은 무엇을 의미하니?
　 G: 그것들은 그들이 방금 적을 봤다는 것을 의미해.
2. B: 만약 적이 없다면, 그들은 연기를 전혀 피우지 않아, 그렇지?
　 G: 아니, 연기를 피워. 굴뚝 한 곳에서 연기가 나오면 "적이 없음"을 의미해.
　 B: 이제 연기가 굴뚝 세 개에서 올라가고 있어. 그것은 무엇을 의미하니?
　 G: 그것은 적이 국경 가까이 접근하고 있음을 의미해.

B: 이제 적이 어둠 속에서 국경을 침입하고 있어. 메시지를 보내기 위해서 병사들은 무슨 일을 할까? 나는 그것이 궁금해.
G: 그들은 굴뚝 4개에 불을 붙일 거야.
B: 그들이 5개 굴뚝 모두에 불을 붙였을 때, 그것은 무엇을 의미하니?
G: 그것은 전투가 시작되었음을 의미해.

Start Off – Speak Up

B: _____

G: _____

B: _____

G: _____

Step Up – Real-life Scene

B: _____

G: _____

B: _____

G: _____

B: _____

G: _____

B: _____

G: _____

B: _____

G: _____

B: _____

Express Yourself A

1. W: _____

   M: _____

   W: _____

   M: _____

2. W: _____

   M: _____

   W: _____

   M: _____

3. W: _____

   M: _____

   W: _____

   M: _____

   W: _____

B: 난 수화가 궁금해.

G: 그러니? 내가 표현 하나를 알려줄게. 봐.

B: 그것은 무엇을 의미하니?

G: 그것은 "안녕하세요."를 의미해.

B: 이 그림은 그 안에 숨겨진 비밀이 몇 개 있어.

G: 정말? 난 그것들이 궁금해. 그 비밀들은 어디에 있니?

B: 너 스스로 하나 찾아봐.

G: 어디 보자. … 오, 여기 글자들이 몇 개 보여.

B: 너 하나 찾았구나! 그것은 "Jan van Eyck가 여기 있었다. 1434."를 의미해. 그것은 라틴어야.

G: 멋지다! 다른 비밀들은?

B: 좋아. 이 개는 여기 있는 이 남자가 매우 부자였다는 것을 우리에게 말해주지.

G: 나는 이해가 안 돼.

B: 당시에 저런 종류의 개를 사려면 많은 돈을 써야 했어.

G: 알겠다. 단지 부자들만 저런 종류의 개를 살 수 있었어, 맞지?

B: 정확해. 알다시피, 그림이 천 마디 말을 하지.

1. W: 이 여자의 몸짓은 무엇을 의미하니? 난 그것이 궁금해.

   M: 내 생각에 그것은 "연못으로 뛰어들어."를 의미해.

   W: 왜 그렇게 생각하니?

   M: 그 소년은 머리 위에 많은 벌이 있어. 그리고 그 여자는 연못을 가리키고 있어.

2. W: 이 여자는 1달러를 원하지 않아. 그렇다면 그녀의 몸짓은 무엇을 의미하니?

   M: 그것은 그녀가 닭 한 마리를 원한다는 것을 의미해.

   W: 그럼 그 소년은 과일을 얻기 위해 닭을 한 마리 가져와야 하는구나, 맞지?

   M: 난 그렇게 생각해.

3. W: 이 남자의 몸짓은 무엇을 의미하니? 난 그것이 궁금해.

   M: 그것은 "그것을 꺼."를 의미해.

   W: 정말? 왜 그렇게 생각하니?

   M: 거기 있는 나머지 다른 사냥꾼이 어떤 동물 가까이 접근하고 있어.

   W: 오, 알겠어.

※ 다음 우리말과 일치하도록 빈칸에 알맞은 것을 골라 쓰시오.

1 A _____ _____ _____ a Mother _____ Three
     A. from   B. Picture   C. Letter   D. of

2 _____ to family members or friends in a _____ country is
     _____ easy and _____ today.
     A. rather   B. speaking   C. simple   D. foreign

3 But _____ the _____ of phones and the Internet, it was not
     _____ _____ .
     A. easy   B. before   C. that   D. days

4 People just _____ a letter and _____ _____ a _____
     for weeks.
     A. reply   B. for   C. sent   D. waited

5 And it was a _____ _____ if they _____ read or _____ .
     A. harder   B. write   C. lot   D. couldn't

6 This letter shows _____ people _____ these _____ .
     A. difficulties   B. got   C. how   D. over

7 It was written in 1973 _____ a woman _____ husband was
     _____ _____ .
     A. away   B. by   C. whose   D. far

8 She lived in Sicily, an Italian _____ , _____ her husband
     _____ _____ Germany.
     A. while   B. in   C. island   D. worked

9 At the time, _____ _____ 5% of the people in Italy could not
     read or write, and she was _____ _____ them.
     A. than   B. one   C. more   D. of

10 This letter _____ _____ _____ Sicilian _____ Gesualdo
     Bufalino.
     A. by   B. discovered   C. was   D. writer

11 Here's _____ he _____ the pictures _____ _____ .
     A. into   B. how   C. translated   D. words

12 My dear love, I _____ you so much, and I _____ my arms
     _____ you, together with our three kids.
     A. toward   B. out   C. reach   D. miss

13 We are all _____ good health _____ _____ the _____
     one.
     A. for   B. little   C. except   D. in

14 He's a _____ _____ , but _____ _____ .
     A. little   B. seriously   C. not   D. sick

15 I already _____ you a letter, but _____ was no _____ ,
     _____ I am sad about it.
     A. reply   B. sent   C. there   D. so

16 If I _____ a letter _____ you, I _____ _____ very
     happy.
     A. be   B. got   C. would   D. from

---

1 세 아이의 엄마가 보낸 그림 편지

2 오늘날 외국에 있는 가족이나 친구와 대화하는 것은 다소 쉽고 간단하다.

3 하지만 전화와 인터넷 시대 이전에는 그것이 그렇게 쉽지 않았다.

4 사람들은 단지 편지를 보내고 답장을 몇 주 동안 기다렸다.

5 그리고 그들이 읽거나 쓸 수 없었다면 그건 훨씬 더 힘들었다.

6 이 편지는 사람들이 이런 어려움을 어떻게 극복했는지 보여준다.

7 그것은 남편이 멀리 떨어져 살았던 한 여자에 의해 1973년에 쓰여졌다.

8 그녀의 남편은 독일에서 일한 반면, 그녀는 이탈리아의 섬인 시실리에서 살았다.

9 그 당시에는 5% 이상의 이탈리아 사람들이 읽거나 쓸 수 없었고, 그녀도 그들 중 한 명이었다.

10 이 편지는 시실리의 작가 *Gesualdo Bufalino*가 발견하였다.

11 그가 그림들을 어떻게 글로 번역했는지는 다음과 같다.

12 사랑하는 여보, 난 당신이 정말 그립고, 우리 세 아이와 함께 당신을 향해 내 팔을 쭉 뻗고 있어요.

13 막내를 제외하고는 우리 모두 건강해요.

14 그 아이는 약간 아프지만 심각하진 않아요.

15 난 당신에게 이미 편지를 보냈지만, 답장이 없어서 그것 때문에 나는 슬퍼요.

16 당신에게서 편지를 받는다면, 나는 정말 행복할 거예요.

17 Your mother _____ _____, and I'm _____ to visit her in the hospital _____ some money and food.
　A. ill　　　　　　B. with　　　　　C. fell　　　　　D. going

18 I'll go there _____ our middle son _____ the oldest _____ after the _____.
　A. looks　　　　　B. while　　　　C. with　　　　　D. youngest

19 I _____ two workers _____ our field and _____ for 150,000 lire.
　A. plant　　　　　B. had　　　　　C. seeds　　　　D. prepare

20 I _____ _____ the DC.
　A. for　　　　　　B. voted

21 The PCI lost _____ many seats _____ it _____ _____ dead.
　A. that　　　　　B. seems　　　　C. almost　　　D. so

22 But _____ one or the _____, it's the _____.
　A. other　　　　　B. whether　　　C. same　　　D. wins

23 _____ _____ for us _____ people.
　A. changes　　　　B. poor　　　　C. nothing

24 We _____ yesterday, and we _____ _____ tomorrow.
　A. will　　　　　　B. again　　　　C. worked　　D. work

25 We _____ _____ of olives _____ our olive trees _____ year.
　A. this　　　　　　B. lots　　　　　C. from　　　D. picked

26 I _____ a man _____ sons are good _____.
　A. workers　　　　B. whose　　　　C. hired

27 He _____ the olives _____, and his two sons helped him, _____ them _____ from the ground.
　A. up　　　　　　　B. down　　　　C. picking　　D. knocked

28 I _____ him 27,000 lire _____ the _____.
　A. for　　　　　　　B. paid　　　　C. work

29 I _____ 12,000 more _____ the olive _____.
　A. for　　　　　　　B. press　　　　C. spent

30 I got _____ oil _____ _____ a large _____ and a small one.
　A. fill　　　　　　　B. enough　　　C. to　　　　D. pot

31 I can _____ it _____ a _____ of 1,300 _____ a liter.
　A. lire　　　　　　　B. sell　　　　　C. at　　　　D. price

32 My love, my _____ thinks _____ you _____ Christmas is _____.
　A. as　　　　　　　B. heart　　　　C. coming　　D. of

33 I _____ so happy _____ you _____ with me.
　A. if　　　　　　　　B. be　　　　　C. were　　　D. would

34 We _____ _____ you _____ much.
　A. miss　　　　　　B. all　　　　　C. so

35 I'm _____ you a _____ _____ from me and our three _____ kids.
　A. hug　　　　　　　B. sending　　C. little　　　D. big

36 Goodbye, _____.
　A. love　　　　　　B. dear

37 My _____ is _____, _____ to you _____ our two rings are.
　A. as　　　　　　　B. yours　　　　C. joined　　D. heart

---

17 당신의 어머니께서는 병이 드셨고, 나는 약간의 돈과 음식을 가지고 병원에 있는 어머니를 방문할 예정이에요.

18 큰애가 막내를 돌보는 동안 둘째와 함께 그곳에 갈 거예요.

19 나는 150,000리라에 두 일꾼을 시켜 우리 밭을 준비하고 씨앗을 심게 했어요.

20 나는 DC에 투표했어요.

21 PCI는 매우 많은 의석을 잃어서 거의 죽은 것처럼 보여요.

22 하지만 이쪽이 이기건 저쪽이 이기건, 상황은 똑같아요.

23 우리 가난한 사람들에게는 아무것도 바뀌지 않지요.

24 우리는 어제도 일했고, 내일도 다시 일할 거예요.

25 우리는 올해 올리브나무에서 올리브를 많이 땄어요.

26 나는 아들들이 훌륭한 일꾼인 한 남자를 고용했어요.

27 그가 올리브를 쳐서 떨어뜨리면 그의 두 아들이 땅에서 올리브를 주우면서 그를 도왔어요.

28 나는 그 일을 위해 그에게 27,000리라를 지급했어요.

29 올리브 압착을 위해 12,000리라를 더 썼어요.

30 나는 큰 항아리 하나와 작은 항아리 하나를 채울 만큼 충분한 기름을 얻었어요.

31 리터당 1,300리라의 가격으로 팔 수 있을 것 같아요.

32 여보, 크리스마스가 다가오면서 내 마음은 당신을 떠올려요.

33 당신이 나와 함께 있다면 난 정말 행복할 거예요.

34 우리는 모두 당신을 매우 많이 그리워해요.

35 나와 우리 세 아이의 큰 포옹을 보내요.

36 잘 있어요, 여보.

37 내 마음은 당신의 것이에요. 우리들의 두 반지처럼 당신과 연결된 채로요.

※ 다음 우리말과 일치하도록 빈칸에 알맞은 것을 골라 쓰시오.

1 _____ _____ _____ from a Mother of Three

2 _____ to family members or friends in a _____ _____ _____ _____ easy and _____ today.

3 But _____ the days of phones and the Internet, it was not _____ _____ .

4 People just _____ a letter and _____ _____ a reply _____ _____ .

5 And it was _____ _____ _____ if they _____ _____ _____ _____ .

6 This letter shows how people _____ _____ these difficulties.

7 It _____ _____ _____ 1973 by a woman _____ husband was _____ _____ .

8 She lived in Sicily, an Italian island, _____ her husband _____ _____ _____ .

9 At the time, _____ _____ _____ of the people in Italy could not read or write, and she was _____ _____ _____ .

10 This letter _____ _____ _____ Sicilian _____ Gesualdo Bufalino.

11 Here's _____ he _____ the pictures _____ words.

12 My dear love, I _____ you so much, and I _____ my arms _____ _____ you, together with our three kids.

13 We are _____ _____ _____ _____ the little _____ .

14 He's _____ _____ sick, but _____ _____ .

15 I _____ sent you a letter, but _____ _____ _____ , so I am sad about it.

16 If I _____ a letter from you, I _____ _____ very happy.

1 세 아이의 엄마가 보낸 그림 편지

2 오늘날 외국에 있는 가족이나 친구와 대화하는 것은 다소 쉽고 간단하다.

3 하지만 전화와 인터넷 시대 이전에는 그것이 그렇게 쉽지 않았다.

4 사람들은 단지 편지를 보내고 답장을 몇 주 동안 기다렸다.

5 그리고 그들이 읽거나 쓸 수 없었다면 그건 훨씬 더 힘들었다.

6 이 편지는 사람들이 이런 어려움을 어떻게 극복했는지 보여준다.

7 그것은 남편이 멀리 떨어져 살았던 한 여자에 의해 1973년에 쓰여졌다.

8 그녀의 남편은 독일에서 일한 반면, 그녀는 이탈리아의 섬인 시실리에서 살았다.

9 그 당시에는 5% 이상의 이탈리아 사람들이 읽거나 쓸 수 없었고, 그녀도 그들 중 한 명이었다.

10 이 편지는 시실리의 작가 Gesualdo Bufalino가 발견하였다.

11 그가 그림들을 어떻게 글로 번역했는지는 다음과 같다.

12 사랑하는 여보, 난 당신이 정말 그립고, 우리 세 아이와 함께 당신을 향해 내 팔을 쭉 뻗고 있어요.

13 막내를 제외하고는 우리 모두 건강해요.

14 그 아이는 약간 아프지만 심각하진 않아요.

15 난 당신에게 이미 편지를 보냈지만, 답장이 없어서 그것 때문에 나는 슬퍼요.

16 당신에게서 편지를 받는다면, 나는 정말 행복할 거예요.

17 Your mother _____ _____, and I'm going to visit her in the hospital _____ some money and food.

18 I'll go there with our middle son _____ the oldest _____ _____ the _____.

19 I _____ two workers _____ our field and _____ _____ for 150,000 lire.

20 I _____ _____ the DC.

21 The PCI lost _____ many seats _____ it almost seems dead.

22 But _____ _____ _____ _____ _____ wins, it's _____ _____.

23 _____ _____ for us poor people.

24 We worked yesterday, and we _____ _____ _____ tomorrow.

25 We _____ lots of olives _____ our olive trees this year.

26 I _____ a man _____ sons are good _____.

27 He _____ the olives _____, and his two sons helped him, _____ them _____ _____ the ground.

28 I _____ him 27,000 lire _____ the work.

29 I _____ 12,000 more _____ the olive _____.

30 I got _____ oil _____ _____ a large pot and a small _____.

31 I can sell it _____ _____ _____ _____ 1,300 lire a liter.

32 My love, my heart thinks of you _____ Christmas is coming.

33 I _____ _____ so happy if you _____ _____ me.

34 We all _____ you so much.

35 I'm sending you _____ _____ _____ from me and our three _____ _____.

36 Goodbye, _____ _____.

37 My heart is yours, _____ to you _____ our two rings are.

17 당신의 어머니께서는 병이 드셨고, 나는 약간의 돈과 음식을 가지고 병원에 있는 어머니를 방문할 예정이에요.

18 큰애가 막내를 돌보는 동안 둘째와 함께 그곳에 갈 거예요.

19 나는 150,000리라에 두 일꾼을 시켜 우리 밭을 준비하고 씨앗을 심게 했어요.

20 나는 DC에 투표했어요.

21 PCI는 매우 많은 의석을 잃어서 거의 죽은 것처럼 보여요.

22 하지만 이쪽이 이기건 저쪽이 이기건, 상황은 똑같아요.

23 우리 가난한 사람들에게는 아무 것도 바뀌지 않지요.

24 우리는 어제도 일했고, 내일도 다시 일할 거예요.

25 우리는 올해 올리브나무에서 올리브를 많이 땄어요.

26 나는 아들들이 훌륭한 일꾼인 한 남자를 고용했어요.

27 그가 올리브를 쳐서 떨어뜨리면 그의 두 아들이 땅에서 올리브를 주우면서 그를 도왔어요.

28 나는 그 일을 위해 그에게 27,000리라를 지급했어요.

29 올리브 압착을 위해 12,000리라를 더 썼어요.

30 나는 큰 항아리 하나와 작은 항아리 하나를 채울 만큼 충분한 기름을 얻었어요.

31 리터당 1,300리라의 가격으로 팔 수 있을 것 같아요.

32 여보, 크리스마스가 다가오면서 내 마음은 당신을 떠올려요.

33 당신이 나와 함께 있다면 난 정말 행복할 거예요.

34 우리는 모두 당신을 매우 많이 그리워해요.

35 나와 우리 세 아이의 큰 포옹을 보내요.

36 잘 있어요, 여보.

37 내 마음은 당신의 것이에요, 우리들의 두 반지처럼 당신과 연결된 채로요.

※ 다음 문장을 우리말로 쓰시오.

1 A Picture Letter from a Mother of Three

➡ _____

2 Speaking to family members or friends in a foreign country is rather easy and simple today.

➡ _____

3 But before the days of phones and the Internet, it was not that easy.

➡ _____

4 People just sent a letter and waited for a reply for weeks.

➡ _____

5 And it was a lot harder if they couldn't read or write.

➡ _____

6 This letter shows how people got over these difficulties.

➡ _____

7 It was written in 1973 by a woman whose husband was far away.

➡ _____

8 She lived in Sicily, an Italian island, while her husband worked in Germany.

➡ _____

9 At the time, more than 5% of the people in Italy could not read or write, and she was one of them.

➡ _____

10 This letter was discovered by Sicilian writer Gesualdo Bufalino.

➡ _____

11 Here's how he translated the pictures into words.

➡ _____

12 My dear love, I miss you so much, and I reach my arms out toward you, together with our three kids.

➡ _____

13 We are all in good health except for the little one.

➡ _____

14 He's a little sick, but not seriously.

➡ _____

15 I already sent you a letter, but there was no reply, so I am sad about it.

➡ _____

16 If I got a letter from you, I would be very happy.

➡ _____

17 Your mother fell ill, and I'm going to visit her in the hospital with some money and food.

➡ _____

18 ⟩ I'll go there with our middle son while the oldest looks after the youngest.

➡ _____

19 ⟩ I had two workers prepare our field and plant seeds for 150,000 lire.

➡ _____

20 ⟩ I voted for the DC.

➡ _____

21 ⟩ The PCI lost so many seats that it almost seems dead.

➡ _____

22 ⟩ But whether one or the other wins, it's the same.

➡ _____

23 ⟩ Nothing changes for us poor people.

➡ _____

24 ⟩ We worked yesterday, and we will work again tomorrow.

➡ _____

25 ⟩ We picked lots of olives from our olive trees this year.

➡ _____

26 ⟩ I hired a man whose sons are good workers.

➡ _____

27 ⟩ He knocked the olives down, and his two sons helped him, picking them up from the ground.

➡ _____

28 ⟩ I paid him 27,000 lire for the work.

➡ _____

29 ⟩ I spent 12,000 more for the olive press.

➡ _____

30 ⟩ I got enough oil to fill a large pot and a small one.

➡ _____

31 ⟩ I can sell it at a price of 1,300 lire a liter.

➡ _____

32 ⟩ My love, my heart thinks of you as Christmas is coming.

➡ _____

33 ⟩ I would be so happy if you were with me.

➡ _____

34 ⟩ We all miss you so much.

➡ _____

35 ⟩ I'm sending you a big hug from me and our three little kids.

➡ _____

36 ⟩ Goodbye, dear love.

➡ _____

37 ⟩ My heart is yours, joined to you as our two rings are.

➡ _____

※ 다음 괄호 안의 단어들을 우리말에 맞도록 바르게 배열하시오.

1 (Picture / A / from / Letter / a / Three / of / Mother)
➡ _____

2 (to / speaking / members / family / or / in / friends / a / country / foreign / easy / is / rather / and / today. / simple)
➡ _____

3 (before / but / days / the / phones / of / and / Internet, / the / was / it / that / not / easy.)
➡ _____

4 (just / people / sent / letter / a / and / for / waited / reply / a / weeks. / for)
➡ _____

5 (it / and / was / lot / a / harder / they / if / read / couldn't / write. / or)
➡ _____

6 (letter / this / shows / people / how / over / got / difficulties. / these)
➡ _____

7 (was / it / in / written / 1973 / a / by / whose / woman / was / husband / away. / far)
➡ _____

8 (lived / she / Sicily, / in / Italian / an / island, / her / while / worked / husband / Germany. / in)
➡ _____

9 (the / at / time, / than / more / 5% / the / of / people / Italy / in / not / could / write, / or / read / and / was / she / of / one / them.)
➡ _____

10 (letter / this / discovered / was / Sicilian / by / writer / Bufalino. / Gesualdo)
➡ _____

11 (how / here's / translated / he / pictures / the / words. / into)
➡ _____

12 (dear / my / love, / miss / I / so / you / much, / and / reach / I / arms / my / toward / out / you, / with / together / three / our / kids.)
➡ _____

13 (are / we / in / all / health / good / for / except / little / the / one.)
➡ _____

14 (a / he's / little / sick, / not / but / seriously.)
➡ _____

15 (already / I / sent / a / you / letter, / there / but / no / was / reply, / I / so / am / about / sad / it.)
➡ _____

16 (I / if / got / letter / a / you, / from / would / I / very / be / happy.)
➡ _____

17 (mother / your / ill, / fell / and / going / I'm / visit / to / in / her / hospital / the / with / money / some / food. / and)
➡ _____

18 (go / I'll / with / there / our / son / middle / the / while / looks / oldest / the / after / youngest.)
➡ _____

1 세 아이의 엄마가 보낸 그림 편지

2 오늘날 외국에 있는 가족이나 친구와 대화하는 것은 다소 쉽고 간단하다.

3 하지만 전화와 인터넷 시대 이전에는 그것이 그렇게 쉽지 않았다.

4 사람들은 단지 편지를 보내고 답장을 몇 주 동안 기다렸다.

5 그리고 그들이 읽거나 쓸 수 없었다면 그건 훨씬 더 힘들었다.

6 이 편지는 사람들이 이런 어려움을 어떻게 극복했는지 보여 준다.

7 그것은 남편이 멀리 떨어져 살았던 한 여자에 의해 1973년에 쓰여졌다.

8 그녀의 남편은 독일에서 일한 반면, 그녀는 이탈리아의 섬인 시실리에서 살았다.

9 그 당시에는 5% 이상의 이탈리아 사람들이 읽거나 쓸 수 없었고, 그녀도 그들 중 한 명이었다.

10 이 편지는 시실리의 작가 Gesualdo Bufalino가 발견하였다.

11 그가 그림들을 어떻게 글로 번역했는지는 다음과 같다.

12 사랑하는 여보, 난 당신이 정말 그립고, 우리 세 아이와 함께 당신을 향해 내 팔을 쭉 뻗고 있어요.

13 막내를 제외하고는 우리 모두 건강해요.

14 그 아이는 약간 아프지만 심각하진 않아요.

15 난 당신에게 이미 편지를 보냈지만, 답장이 없어서 그것 때문에 나는 슬퍼요.

16 당신에게서 편지를 받는다면, 나는 정말 행복할 거예요.

17 당신의 어머니께서는 병이 드셨고, 나는 약간의 돈과 음식을 가지고 병원에 있는 어머니를 방문할 예정이에요.

18 큰애가 막내를 돌보는 동안 둘째와 함께 그곳에 갈 거예요.

19 (had / I / two / prepare / workers / field / our / and / seeds / plant / for / lire. / 150,000)
➡ _____

20 (voted / I / the / for / DC.)
➡ _____

21 (PCI / the / so / lost / seats / many / that / almost / it / dead. / seems)
➡ _____

22 (whether / but / or / one / other / the / wins, / the / it's / same.)
➡ _____

23 (changes / nothing / us / for / people. / poor)
➡ _____

24 (worked / we / yesterday, / we / and / will / again / work / tomorrow.)
➡ _____

25 (picked / we / of / lots / olives / our / from / olive / this / trees / year.)
➡ _____

26 (hired / I / man / a / whose / are / sons / workers. / good)
➡ _____

27 (knocked / he / olives / the / down, / and / two / his / helped / sons / him, / them / picking / up / the / from / ground.)
➡ _____

28 (paid / I / him / lire / 27,000 / for / work. / the)
➡ _____

29 (spent / I / 12,000 / for / more / olive / the / press.)
➡ _____

30 (got / I / enough / to / oil / fill / large / a / pot / and / a / one. / small)
➡ _____

31 (can / I / sell / at / it / price / a / of / lire / 1,300 / liter. / a)
➡ _____

32 (love, / my / heart / my / thinks / of / as / you / is / Christmas / coming.)
➡ _____

33 (would / I / so / be / happy / you / if / with / were / me.)
➡ _____

34 (all / we / you / miss / much. / so)
➡ _____

35 (sending / I'm / a / you / big / from / hug / and / me / our / little / three / kids.)
➡ _____

36 (dear / goodbye, / love.)
➡ _____

37 (heart / my / yours, / is / to / joined / you / our / as / rings / two / are.)
➡ _____

19 나는 150,000리라에 두 일꾼을 시켜 우리 밭을 준비하고 씨앗을 심게 했어요.

20 나는 DC에 투표했어요.

21 PCI는 매우 많은 의석을 잃어서 거의 죽은 것처럼 보여요.

22 하지만 이쪽이 이기건 저쪽이 이기건, 상황은 똑같아요.

23 우리 가난한 사람들에게는 아무 것도 바뀌지 않지요.

24 우리는 어제도 일했고, 내일도 다시 일할 거예요.

25 우리는 올해 올리브나무에서 올리브를 많이 땄어요.

26 나는 아들들이 훌륭한 일꾼인 한 남자를 고용했어요.

27 그가 올리브를 쳐서 떨어뜨리면 그의 두 아들이 땅에서 올리브를 주우면서 그를 도왔어요.

28 나는 그 일을 위해 그에게 27,000리라를 지급했어요.

29 올리브 압착을 위해 12,000리라를 더 썼어요.

30 나는 큰 항아리 하나와 작은 항아리 하나를 채울 만큼 충분한 기름을 얻었어요.

31 리터당 1,300리라의 가격으로 팔 수 있을 것 같아요.

32 여보, 크리스마스가 다가오면서 내 마음은 당신을 떠올려요.

33 당신이 나와 함께 있다면 난 정말 행복할 거예요.

34 우리는 모두 당신을 매우 많이 그리워해요.

35 나와 우리 세 아이의 큰 포옹을 보내요.

36 잘 있어요, 여보.

37 내 마음은 당신의 것이에요, 우리들의 두 반지처럼 당신과 연결된 채로요.

※ 다음 우리말을 영어로 쓰시오.

1 세 아이의 엄마가 보낸 그림 편지

➡ _____

2 오늘날 외국에 있는 가족이나 친구와 대화하는 것은 다소 쉽고 간단하다.

➡ _____

3 하지만 전화와 인터넷 시대 이전에는 그것이 그렇게 쉽지 않았다.

➡ _____

4 사람들은 단지 편지를 보내고 답장을 몇 주 동안 기다렸다.

➡ _____

5 그리고 그들이 읽거나 쓸 수 없었다면 그건 훨씬 더 힘들었다.

➡ _____

6 이 편지는 사람들이 이런 어려움을 어떻게 극복했는지 보여 준다.

➡ _____

7 그것은 남편이 멀리 떨어져 살았던 한 여자에 의해 1973년에 쓰여졌다.

➡ _____

8 그녀의 남편은 독일에서 일한 반면, 그녀는 이탈리아의 섬인 시실리에서 살았다.

➡ _____

9 그 당시에는 5% 이상의 이탈리아 사람들이 읽거나 쓸 수 없었고, 그녀도 그들 중 한 명이었다.

➡ _____

10 이 편지는 시실리의 작가 Gesualdo Bufalino가 발견하였다.

➡ _____

11 그가 그림들을 어떻게 글로 번역했는지는 다음과 같다.

➡ _____

12 사랑하는 여보, 난 당신이 정말 그립고, 우리 세 아이와 함께 당신을 향해 내 팔을 쭉 뻗고 있어요.

➡ _____

13 막내를 제외하고는 우리 모두 건강해요.

➡ _____

14 그 아이는 약간 아프지만 심각하진 않아요.

➡ _____

15 난 당신에게 이미 편지를 보냈지만, 답장이 없어서 그것 때문에 나는 슬퍼요.

➡ _____

16 당신에게서 편지를 받는다면, 나는 정말 행복할 거예요.

➡ _____

17 당신의 어머니께서는 병이 드셨고, 나는 약간의 돈과 음식을 가지고 병원에 있는 어머니를 방문할 예정이에요.

➡ _____

18 큰애가 막내를 돌보는 동안 둘째와 함께 그곳에 갈 거예요.
➡ _____

19 나는 150,000리라에 두 일꾼을 시켜 우리 밭을 준비하고 씨앗을 심게 했어요.
➡ _____

20 나는 DC에 투표했어요.
➡ _____

21 PCI는 매우 많은 의석을 잃어서 거의 죽은 것처럼 보여요.
➡ _____

22 하지만 이쪽이 이기건 저쪽이 이기건, 상황은 똑같아요.
➡ _____

23 우리 가난한 사람들에게는 아무 것도 바뀌지 않지요.
➡ _____

24 우리는 어제도 일했고, 내일도 다시 일할 거예요.
➡ _____

25 우리는 올해 올리브나무에서 올리브를 많이 땄어요.
➡ _____

26 나는 아들들이 훌륭한 일꾼인 한 남자를 고용했어요.
➡ _____

27 그가 올리브를 쳐서 떨어뜨리면 그의 두 아들이 땅에서 올리브를 주우면서 그를 도왔어요.
➡ _____

28 나는 그 일을 위해 그에게 27,000리라를 지급했어요.
➡ _____

29 올리브 압착을 위해 12,000리라를 더 썼어요.
➡ _____

30 나는 큰 항아리 하나와 작은 항아리 하나를 채울 만큼 충분한 기름을 얻었어요.
➡ _____

31 리터당 1,300리라의 가격으로 팔 수 있을 것 같아요.
➡ _____

32 여보, 크리스마스가 다가오면서 내 마음은 당신을 떠올려요.
➡ _____

33 당신이 나와 함께 있다면 난 정말 행복할 거예요.
➡ _____

34 우리는 모두 당신을 매우 많이 그리워해요.
➡ _____

35 나와 우리 세 아이의 큰 포옹을 보내요.
➡ _____

36 잘 있어요, 여보.
➡ _____

37 내 마음은 당신의 것이에요, 우리들의 두 반지처럼 당신과 연결된 채로요.
➡ _____

※ 다음 우리말과 일치하도록 빈칸에 알맞은 말을 쓰시오.

Express Yourself C1

1. The boy _____ head _____ _____ _____ bees _____ _____ the woman's gesture.

2. I think it _____ "_____ _____ the pond."

3. If I _____ the boy, I _____ _____ _____ the pond _____ _____.

1. 머리가 벌로 덮인 소년은 그 여자의 몸짓을 이해하지 못합니다.
2. 제 생각에 그것은 "연못으로 뛰어들어."를 의미합니다.
3. 제가 그 소년이라면, 저는 당장 연못으로 뛰어들겠습니다.

Project Do It Yourself

1. "_____ _____ the mountain."

2. If I _____ soldiers to lead, I _____ _____ _____ _____ my messages.

3. For example, I _____ _____ a kite _____ face _____ _____ a mountain to _____ _____ _____ _____ up the mountain.

1. "산 위로 올라가라."
2. 내가 병사를 지휘한다면, 나는 나의 메시지를 보내기 위해 연을 사용하겠다.
3. 예를 들어, 나는 병사들이 산 위로 올라가게 하려고 앞면이 산처럼 보이는 연을 날리겠다.

Link to the World

1. Hangeul _____ _____ _____ King Sejong.

2. _____ _____, many people _____ _____ _____ this new _____ _____.

3. _____, King Sejong _____ _____ _____ _____ _____ people _____ Hangeul.

4. _____ _____ him, we _____ _____ _____ Hangeul now.

5. If we _____ _____ Hangeul, we _____ _____ _____ _____ easily.

1. 한글은 세종대왕에 의해 창제되었다.
2. 처음에는 많은 사람이 이 새로운 문자 체계를 사용하는 것을 원하지 않았다.
3. 하지만, 세종대왕은 사람들이 한글을 사용하도록 돕기 위해 열심히 노력했다.
4. 그분 덕택에, 우리는 지금 한글로 무엇이든 표현할 수 있다.
5. 우리가 한글을 모른다면, 우리 자신을 쉽게 표현할 수 없을 것이다.

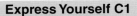

※ 다음 우리말을 영어로 쓰시오.

Express Yourself C1

1. 머리가 벌로 덮인 소년은 그 여자의 몸짓을 이해하지 못합니다.

   ➡ _____

2. 제 생각에 그것은 "연못으로 뛰어들어."를 의미합니다.

   ➡ _____

3. 제가 그 소년이라면, 저는 당장 연못으로 뛰어들겠습니다.

   ➡ _____

Project Do It Yourself

1. "산 위로 올라가라."

   ➡ _____

2. 내가 병사를 지휘한다면, 나는 나의 메시지를 보내기 위해 연을 사용하겠다.

   ➡ _____

3. 예를 들어, 나는 병사들이 산 위로 올라가게 하려고 앞면이 산처럼 보이는 연을 날리겠다.

   ➡ _____

Link to the World

1. 한글은 세종대왕에 의해 창제되었다.

   ➡ _____

2. 처음에는 많은 사람이 이 새로운 문자 체계를 사용하는 것을 원하지 않았다.

   ➡ _____

3. 하지만, 세종대왕은 사람들이 한글을 사용하도록 돕기 위해 열심히 노력했다.

   ➡ _____

4. 그분 덕택에, 우리는 지금 한글로 무엇이든 표현할 수 있다.

   ➡ _____

5. 우리가 한글을 모른다면, 우리 자신을 쉽게 표현할 수 없을 것이다.

   ➡ _____

※ 다음 영어를 우리말로 쓰시오.

01	produce		22	seed
02	available		23	length
03	filter		24	tear
04	disease		25	tiny
05	facial		26	cheerful
06	artwork		27	display
07	public		28	drinkable
08	potter		29	proud
09	connect		30	beat
10	publisher		31	figure
11	artistic		32	impossible
12	register		33	necessary
13	actually		34	object
14	relax		35	by hand
15	3D print		36	tear out
16	collect		37	pick up
17	traditional		38	take a bath
18	provide		39	find out
19	weight		40	both A and B
20	colorful		41	give away
21	company		42	not ~ anymore
			43	think of … as ~

※ 다음 우리말을 영어로 쓰시오.

01	전통적인	
02	이용할 수 있는	
03	생산하다, 산출하다	
04	예술적인	
05	물리치다	
06	모으다	
07	~을 찢다, 뜯어내다	
08	(마음의) 긴장을 풀다	
09	화려한	
10	자랑으로 여기는	
11	연결하다	
12	질병, 질환	
13	회사	
14	무게, 중량	
15	제공하다	
16	사실, 실제로	
17	유쾌한, 기분 좋은	
18	전시, 진열	
19	공공의, 공중의	
20	마실 수 있는	
21	(사람, 동물의) 상; 모양	

22	~을 거르다, 여과하다	
23	얼굴의	
24	예술품, 공예품	
25	가능한	
26	붓다, 따르다	
27	출판업자, 출판사	
28	등록하다	
29	필요한	
30	물체	
31	길이	
32	씨앗	
33	3차원 인쇄를 하다	
34	아주 작은	
35	알아내다	
36	집어들다	
37	찢다	
38	손으로	
39	목욕하다	
40	…을 ~으로 생각하다	
41	A와 B 둘 다	
42	남에게 주다, 나누어 주다	
43	더 이상 ~ 않다	

※ 다음 영영풀이에 알맞은 단어를 <보기>에서 골라 쓴 후, 우리말 뜻을 쓰시오.

1 _____ : extremely small: _____

2 _____ : a store that sells books: _____

3 _____ : clean and safe to drink: _____

4 _____ : relating to people in general: _____

5 _____ : a measurement of how long something is: _____

6 _____ : to make a liquid flow out of a container: _____

7 _____ : to pull apart or to pull pieces off: _____

8 _____ : to remove unwanted substances from liquids or gases: _____

9 _____ : a person or company that prints books: _____

10 _____ : a person who makes pottery by hand: _____

11 _____ : to put someone's or something's name on an official list: _____

12 _____ : a measurement that indicates how heavy a person or thing is: _____

13 _____ : to put something somewhere, especially in a place where it will stay: _____

14 _____ : to put something in a place where people can see it easily: _____

15 _____ : the small hard part produced by a plant, from which a new plant can grow: _____

16 _____ : to produce words, numbers, pictures, etc. on paper by using a machine: _____

보기			
print	pour	seed	filter
weight	drinkable	publisher	bookstore
leave	length	display	tear
register	tiny	potter	public

※ 다음 우리말과 일치하도록 빈칸에 알맞은 말을 쓰시오.

Get Ready 2

(1) G: _____ do you like _____, _____ dolls or digital _____?
   B: I like digital artwork _____. _____, I don't like dolls much.

(2) G: _____ _____ _____ _____, paper _____ or _____ block _____?
   B: I _____ wood block _____.
   G: Me, too. _____ go to look at _____ _____ _____.

(3) G: _____ do you _____, _____ paper or making _____?
   B: I _____ _____ _____. It's fun and a great _____ _____ _____.

Start Off - Listen & Talk A

1. G: _____ _____ _____ make something with jean _____?
   B: Great! _____ _____ _____ make?
   G: _____ do you prefer, a pocket _____ or a cell phone _____?
   B: I _____ a cell phone _____. It'll be easier _____ _____.
      And I _____ _____ too much time _____ things.
   G: Okay. _____ make a cute cell phone holder _____.

2. B: _____ _____ _____ make a bag _____ old jeans?
   G: Great! _____ _____ of bag are we going _____ _____?
   B: _____ do you _____, a shoulder bag or a hand bag?
   G: I prefer a shoulder bag. _____, I _____ _____ things _____ my hands.
   B: Okay. _____ _____ a shoulder bag _____.

Start Off - Listen & Talk B

G: Junha, what are you doing _____ _____?
B: I'm making a _____ _____ _____ you.
G: That's great! What are you _____ _____ _____ on it?
B: _____ _____ _____ _____, pandas or cats?
G: I _____ cats. They're _____.
B: Okay. Let me _____ a _____ cat on this pencil case.
G: Thanks! _____ _____ _____ _____ it!

해석

(1) G: 너는 헝겊 인형과 디지털 예술품 중에서 어떤 것을 더 좋아하니?
   B: 나는 디지털 예술품이 더 좋아. 사실, 나는 인형을 별로 좋아하지 않아.
(2) G: 너는 회화 작품과 나무 블록으로 만든 모형 중에서 어떤 것을 더 좋아하니?
   B: 나는 나무 블록으로 만든 모형이 더 좋아.
   G: 나도 그래. 그것 중에서 몇 개를 보러 가자.
(3) G: 너는 종이접기와 옷 만들기 중에서 어떤 것을 더 좋아하니?
   B: 나는 종이접기가 더 좋아. 재미있고 긴장을 풀 수 있는 좋은 방법이야.

1. G: 청바지 주머니로 뭔가 만들어 보는 게 어떨까?
   B: 좋아! 뭘 만들까?
   G: 너는 주머니를 붙인 판과 휴대 전화 주머니 중에서 어떤 것을 더 좋아하니?
   B: 나는 휴대 전화 주머니가 더 좋아. 만들기가 더 쉬울 거야. 그리고 나는 뭔가를 만드는 데 시간을 너무 많이 들이는 걸 몹시 싫어해.
   G: 좋아. 귀여운 휴대 전화 주머니를 함께 만들자.
2. B: 우리 낡은 청바지로 가방을 하나 만드는 게 어떨까?
   G: 좋아! 어떤 종류의 가방을 만들 건데?
   B: 너는 어깨에 메는 가방과 손에 드는 가방 중에서 어떤 것을 더 좋아하니?
   G: 나는 어깨에 메는 가방이 더 좋아. 사실, 나는 손에 물건을 드는 것을 몹시 싫어해.
   B: 좋아. 어깨에 메는 가방을 함께 만들자.

G: 준하야, 청바지로 뭐 해?
B: 너에게 줄 필통을 만들고 있어.
G: 멋지다! 그 위에 뭘 그릴 거야?
B: 너는 판다랑 고양이 중에서 어떤 것을 더 좋아하니?
G: 나는 고양이를 더 좋아해. 고양이는 사랑스러워.
B: 좋아. 내가 이 필통 위에 사랑스러운 고양이를 그려 줄게.
G: 고마워! 몹시 기다려진다!

Start Off - Speak Up

A: Can I _____ your book-making project?

B: _____. _____ do you _____, paper books _____ digital books?

A: I _____ digital books. Actually, I hate _____ paper books.

B: Okay. _____ me _____ you _____ the digital book team.

Start Off - Your Turn

A: _____ do you prefer, _____ the bus or _____ the subway?

B: I _____ _____ _____ _____ _____. Actually, I _____ _____ the bus.

Step Up - Real-life Scene

Minji: Seho, the book club day is _____ one week _____.

Seho: Right, Minji. I'm _____ _____ we've _____ so many _____ books _____ _____ _____.

Minji: Now, _____ _____ some gifts for visitors. Do you have _____ good ideas?

Seho: How about _____ _____?

Minji: Great idea! _____ write cheerful messages on them, too.

Seho: Okay. _____ do you _____, making the bookmarks or _____ the messages?

Minji: _____, I hate _____. I'd like to make the bookmarks.

Seho: _____ _____. I'll write the _____ _____.

Minji: I'm _____ they will love our _____.

Express Yourself A

1. G: Which do you prefer, _____ kites or _____ _____?

   B: I _____ _____ kites.

   G: Why is that?

   B: I hate _____ with _____.

2. B: _____ do you prefer, _____ masks or _____ food art?

   G: I like _____, but _____ is _____ food art _____ I _____.

   B: Why is that?

   G: I love making _____ _____.

A: 너희 책 만들기 프로젝트에 내가 함께 해도 될까?
B: 물론이지. 너는 종이책과 전자책 중에서 어떤 것을 더 좋아하니?
A: 나는 전자책을 더 좋아해. 사실, 나는 종이책 만들기를 몹시 싫어해.
B: 알았어. 전자책 팀에 너를 소개할게.

A: 너는 버스 타기와 지하철 타기 중에서 어떤 것을 더 좋아하니?
B: 나는 지하철 타기를 더 좋아해. 사실, 나는 버스 타기를 몹시 싫어해.

민지: 세호야, 독서 동아리의 날이 겨우 한 주 남았어.
세호: 맞아, 민지야. 나는 우리가 나눠 줄 재미있는 책을 많이 모아서 자랑스러워.
민지: 이제, 방문객들에게 줄 선물을 준비하자. 좋은 생각 있어?
세호: 책갈피를 만드는 게 어떨까?
민지: 좋은 생각이야! 거기에 기분 좋은 메시지도 쓰자.
세호: 그래. 너는 책갈피 만들기와 메시지 쓰기 중에서 어떤 것을 더 좋아하니?
민지: 사실, 나는 글쓰기를 몹시 싫어해. 나는 책갈피를 만들고 싶어.
세호: 문제없어. 내가 기분 좋은 메시지를 쓸게.
민지: 틀림없이 사람들이 우리가 만든 책갈피를 좋아할 거야.

1. G: 너는 연날리기와 드론 날리기 중에서 어떤 것을 더 좋아하니?
   B: 나는 연날리기를 더 좋아해.
   G: 왜 그런데?
   B: 나는 기계를 작동하는 것을 몹시 싫어해.
2. B: 너는 가면 만들기와 푸드 아트 만들기 중에서 어떤 것을 더 좋아하니?
   G: 나는 둘 다 좋지만, 내가 더 좋아하는 것은 푸드 아트 만들기야.
   B: 왜 그런데?
   G: 나는 맛있는 것을 만들기를 좋아해.

※ 다음 우리말에 맞도록 대화를 영어로 쓰시오.

Get Ready 2

(1) G: _____

    B: _____

(2) G: _____

    B: _____

    G: _____

(3) G: _____

    B: _____

(1) G: 너는 헝겊 인형과 디지털 예술품 중에서 어떤 것을 더 좋아하니?
   B: 나는 디지털 예술품이 더 좋아. 사실, 나는 인형을 별로 좋아하지 않아.
(2) G: 너는 회화 작품과 나무 블록으로 만든 모형 중에서 어떤 것을 더 좋아하니?
   B: 나는 나무 블록으로 만든 모형이 더 좋아.
   G: 나도 그래. 그것 중에서 몇 개를 보러 가자.
(3) G: 너는 종이접기와 옷 만들기 중에서 어떤 것을 더 좋아하니?
   B: 나는 종이접기가 더 좋아. 재미있고 긴장을 풀 수 있는 좋은 방법이야.

Start Off - Listen & Talk A

1. G: _____

    B: _____

    G: _____

    B: _____

    G: _____

2. B: _____

    G: _____

    B: _____

    G: _____

    B: _____

1. G: 청바지 주머니로 뭔가 만들어 보는 게 어떨까?
   B: 좋아! 뭘 만들까?
   G: 너는 주머니를 붙인 판과 휴대 전화 주머니 중에서 어떤 것을 더 좋아하니?
   B: 나는 휴대 전화 주머니가 더 좋아. 만들기가 더 쉬울 거야. 그리고 나는 뭔가를 만드는 데 시간을 너무 많이 들이는 걸 몹시 싫어해.
   G: 좋아. 귀여운 휴대 전화 주머니를 함께 만들자.
2. B: 우리 낡은 청바지로 가방을 하나 만드는 게 어떨까?
   G: 좋아! 어떤 종류의 가방을 만들 건데?
   B: 너는 어깨에 메는 가방과 손에 드는 가방 중에서 어떤 것을 더 좋아하니?
   G: 나는 어깨에 메는 가방이 더 좋아. 사실, 나는 손에 물건을 드는 것을 몹시 싫어해.
   B: 좋아. 어깨에 메는 가방을 함께 만들자.

Start Off - Listen & Talk B

G: _____

B: _____

G: _____

B: _____

G: _____

B: _____

G: _____

G: 준하야, 청바지로 뭐 해?
B: 너에게 줄 필통을 만들고 있어.
G: 멋지다! 그 위에 뭘 그릴 거야?
B: 너는 판다랑 고양이 중에서 어떤 것을 더 좋아하니?
G: 나는 고양이를 더 좋아해. 고양이는 사랑스러워.
B: 좋아. 내가 이 필통 위에 사랑스러운 고양이를 그려 줄게.
G: 고마워! 몹시 기다려진다!

Start Off - Speak Up

A: _____

B: _____

A: _____

B: _____

A: 너희 책 만들기 프로젝트에 내가 함께 해도 될까?
B: 물론이지. 너는 종이책과 전자책 중에서 어떤 것을 더 좋아하니?
A: 나는 전자책을 더 좋아해. 사실, 나는 종이책 만들기를 몹시 싫어해.
B: 알았어. 전자책 팀에 너를 소개할게.

Start Off - Your Turn

A: _____

B: _____

A: 너는 버스 타기와 지하철 타기 중에서 어떤 것을 더 좋아하니?
B: 나는 지하철 타기를 더 좋아해. 사실, 나는 버스 타기를 몹시 싫어해.

Step Up - Real-life Scene

Minji: _____

Seho: _____

_____

Minji: _____

Seho: _____

Minji: _____

Seho: _____

Minji: _____

Seho: _____

Minji: _____

민지: 세호야, 독서 동아리의 날이 겨우 한 주 남았어.
세호: 맞아, 민지야. 나는 우리가 나눠 줄 재미있는 책을 많이 모아서 자랑스러워.
민지: 이제, 방문객들에게 줄 선물을 준비하자. 좋은 생각 있어?
세호: 책갈피를 만드는 게 어떨까?
민지: 좋은 생각이야! 거기에 기분 좋은 메시지도 쓰자.
세호: 그래. 너는 책갈피 만들기와 메시지 쓰기 중에서 어떤 것을 더 좋아하니?
민지: 사실, 나는 글쓰기를 몹시 싫어해. 나는 책갈피를 만들고 싶어.
세호: 문제없어. 내가 기분 좋은 메시지를 쓸게.
민지: 틀림없이 사람들이 우리가 만든 책갈피를 좋아할 거야.

Express Yourself A

1. G: _____
   B: _____
   G: _____
   B: _____
2. B: _____
   G: _____
   B: _____
   G: _____

1. G: 너는 연날리기와 드론 날리기 중에서 어떤 것을 더 좋아하니?
   B: 나는 연날리기를 더 좋아해.
   G: 왜 그런데?
   B: 나는 기계를 작동하는 것을 몹시 싫어해.
2. B: 너는 가면 만들기와 푸드 아트 만들기 중에서 어떤 것을 더 좋아하니?
   G: 나는 둘 다 좋지만, 내가 더 좋아하는 것은 푸드 아트 만들기야.
   B: 왜 그런데?
   G: 나는 맛있는 것을 만들기를 좋아해.

※ 다음 우리말과 일치하도록 빈칸에 알맞은 것을 골라 쓰시오.

1 _____ Book Is _____!
A. Amazing   B. This

2 Most people _____ of books as _____ paper _____ to _____.
A. read   B. think   C. books   D. traditional

3 _____, _____ are many _____ books _____ you.
A. around   B. there   C. unique   D. however

4 _____ _____ about _____ _____ of these books.
A. few   B. let's   C. a   D. learn

5 _____ _____!
A. Travel   B. Books

6 I _____ this _____ book _____ a park bench yesterday.
A. on   B. found   C. old

7 A _____ on the cover _____, " _____ Book!
A. read   B. free   C. note

8 _____ _____ _____ and read me!"
A. home   B. take   C. me

9 _____, this book _____ an ID number and _____ _____ on a website.
A. registered   B. actually   C. had   D. was

10 When I entered the number online, I found _____ that the book had _____ to many countries and that a _____ of readers in _____ countries had read it before me.
A. different   B. out   C. traveled   D. number

11 _____ was _____ _____?
A. that   B. how   C. possible

12 _____ is a _____ _____.
A. project   B. there   C. book-sharing

13 First, _____ your book _____ and _____ an ID number.
A. register   B. get   C. online

14 Next, _____ it in a _____ _____.
A. public   B. leave   C. place

1 이 책은 놀라워요!

2 대부분의 사람은 책을 읽기 위한 전통적인 종이책으로 생각합니다.

3 하지만, 여러분 주변에는 독특한 책이 많이 있습니다.

4 이러한 책 중 몇 가지에 대해 배워 봅시다.

5 책이 여행합니다!

6 저는 어제 공원 벤치에서 이 낡은 책을 발견했습니다.

7 표지 위의 쪽지에 "공짜 책이에요!

8 저를 집으로 데려가서 읽어 주세요!"라고 쓰여 있었습니다.

9 사실, 이 책은 ID 번호가 있고 웹사이트에 등록되어 있었어요.

10 제가 온라인으로 그 번호를 입력했을 때, 저는 그 책이 많은 나라를 여행하고 다른 나라의 많은 독자가 저보다 앞서 이 책을 읽었다는 것을 알아냈습니다.

11 그게 어떻게 가능했을까요?

12 책을 공유하는 프로젝트가 있습니다.

13 우선, 온라인에 여러분의 책을 등록하고 ID 번호를 얻으세요.

14 그다음, 그것을 공공장소에 놓아두세요.

15 When the next _____ finds your book and _____ _____ to the website, you can _____ where your book is.

    A. back   B. check   C. reports   D. reader

16 This _____, the _____ world can _____ a big _____.

    A. whole   B. become   C. way   D. library

17 The _____ books we _____, _____ more we _____.

    A. share   B. more   C. learn   D. the

18 The _____ _____

    A. Book   B. Drinkable

19 This _____ book is really _____ to people _____ my _____.

    A. tiny   B. town   C. important   D. in

20 It _____ _____ the _____ and the _____ necessary to make clean drinking water.

    A. both   B. tools   C. information   D. provides

21 It _____ _____ the _____ Book.

    A. called   B. is   C. Drinkable

22 You cannot _____ drink the book, but you can _____ it _____ a _____.

    A. filter   B. actually   C. as   D. use

23 Simply _____ _____ a page and _____ dirty water _____ it.

    A. pour   B. tear   C. on   D. out

24 _____ the water goes _____ the page, it _____ _____ clean drinking water.

    A. into   B. as   C. through   D. changes

25 _____ is this _____ water _____ you can _____.

    A. filtered   B. drink   C. that   D. it

26 This is _____ _____ the book is _____ of _____ filter paper.

    A. because   B. made   C. special   D. possible

27 This _____ book _____ the lives of many children _____ _____ that come from dirty water.

    A. diseases   B. saves   C. from   D. amazing

15 다음 독자가 여러분의 책을 발견해서 그 웹사이트에 다시 알릴 때, 여러분은 책이 어디 있는지 확인할 수 있습니다.

16 이런 식으로, 전 세계가 하나의 큰 도서관이 될 수 있습니다.

17 우리가 더 많은 책을 공유할수록, 우리는 더 많이 배웁니다.

18 마실 수 있는 책

19 이 작은 책은 우리 마을 사람들에게는 정말로 중요합니다.

20 그것은 깨끗한 마실 물을 만드는 데 필요한 정보와 도구 둘 다를 제공합니다.

21 그것은 '마실 수 있는 책'이라고 불립니다.

22 여러분은 실제로 그 책을 마실 수는 없지만, 그것을 필터로 사용할 수 있습니다.

23 그냥 한 페이지를 떼어 내서 그 위에 더러운 물을 부으세요.

24 물이 그 페이지를 통과하면서, 깨끗한 마실 물로 바뀝니다.

25 여러분이 마실 수 있는 것은 이 여과된 물입니다.

26 책이 특별한 여과지로 만들어졌기 때문에 이것이 가능합니다.

27 이 놀라운 책은 더러운 물로 생기는 질병으로부터 많은 어린이의 생명을 구합니다.

28 The _____ _____

    A. Project   B. Tree-Book-Tree

29 This is the _____ _____ book that I _____ ever _____.

    A. seen   B. amazing   C. have   D. most

30 After you _____ _____ this book, _____ it and _____ it.

    A. plant   B. water   C. reading   D. finish

31 You will _____ _____ _____ _____ on the book.

    A. growing   B. new   C. see   D. leaves

32 In _____ bookstores in my town, you can see a _____ of this book _____ new _____.

    A. copy   B. leaves   C. producing   D. some

33 The _____ is that the book _____ _____ in _____ page.

    A. each   B. secret   C. seeds   D. has

34 It is these _____ _____ that _____ the book _____ a tree.

    A. into   B. seeds   C. change   D. tiny

35 This book was _____ _____ a small _____ book _____ in Argentina.

    A. publisher   B. by   C. children's   D. made

36 Though the company does _____ print this book _____, this special project makes us _____ about where books come _____.

    A. anymore   B. from   C. not   D. think

37 These are _____ _____ _____ of the _____ books you can find.

    A. unique   B. few   C. a   D. just

38 _____ _____ _____ _____ do you want to make?

    A. unique   B. what   C. books   D. other

39 What special project _____ you _____ _____ _____ with the books?

    A. to   B. would   C. do   D. like

40 The _____ your _____ is, the _____ _____ your books will become.

    A. imagination B. wonderful C. bigger   D. more

---

28 나무-책-나무 프로젝트

29 이것은 제가 지금까지 본 것 중에서 가장 놀라운 책입니다.

30 여러분이 이 책을 다 읽은 후에, 그것을 심고 물을 주세요.

31 여러분은 책에서 새잎이 자라는 것을 보게 될 거예요.

32 우리 마을의 몇몇 서점에서, 여러분은 이 책 한 권이 새잎을 내는 것을 볼 수 있습니다.

33 비밀은 책이 각 페이지 안에 씨앗을 갖고 있다는 것입니다.

34 책을 나무로 변화시키는 것은 이 아주 작은 씨앗들이에요.

35 이 책은 아르헨티나에 있는 한 작은 아동 도서 출판사에 의해 만들어졌습니다.

36 그 회사가 더는 이 책을 발행하지는 않지만, 이 특별한 프로젝트는 우리에게 책이 어디에서 오는지에 대해 생각하게 해 줍니다.

37 이것들은 여러분이 찾을 수 있는 독특한 책 중의 단지 몇 가지입니다.

38 여러분은 어떤 다른 독특한 책을 만들기 원하나요?

39 여러분은 책으로 어떤 특별한 프로젝트를 하고 싶나요?

40 여러분의 상상이 크면 클수록, 여러분의 책은 더 훌륭해질 것입니다.

※ 다음 우리말과 일치하도록 빈칸에 알맞은 것을 골라 쓰시오.

1 _____ Book Is _____ !

2 Most people _____ _____ books _____ _____ _____ _____ to read.

3 However, there _____ many _____ books _____ you.

4 _____ learn about _____ _____ of these books.

5 Books _____ !

6 I _____ this _____ _____ on a park bench yesterday.

7 A _____ on the cover _____ , " _____ Book!

8 _____ _____ _____ and read me!"

9 _____ , this book had an _____ _____ and _____ _____ on a website.

10 When I entered the number online, I _____ _____ that the book _____ _____ to many countries and that a number of readers in different countries _____ _____ it before me.

11 _____ was that _____ ?

12 There is a _____ _____ .

13 First, _____ your book online and _____ an ID number.

14 Next, _____ _____ in a _____ _____ .

1 이 책은 놀라워요!

2 대부분의 사람은 책을 읽기 위한 전통적인 종이책으로 생각합니다.

3 하지만, 여러분 주변에는 독특한 책이 많이 있습니다.

4 이러한 책 중 몇 가지에 대해 배워 봅시다.

5 책이 여행합니다!

6 저는 어제 공원 벤치에서 이 낡은 책을 발견했습니다.

7 표지 위의 쪽지에 "공짜 책이에요!

8 저를 집으로 데려가서 읽어 주세요!"라고 쓰여 있었습니다.

9 사실, 이 책은 ID 번호가 있고 웹사이트에 등록되어 있었어요.

10 제가 온라인으로 그 번호를 입력했을 때, 저는 그 책이 많은 나라를 여행하고 다른 나라의 많은 독자가 저보다 앞서 이 책을 읽었다는 것을 알아냈습니다.

11 그게 어떻게 가능했을까요?

12 책을 공유하는 프로젝트가 있습니다.

13 우선, 온라인에 여러분의 책을 등록하고 ID 번호를 얻으세요.

14 그다음, 그것을 공공장소에 놓아두세요.

15 When the next reader finds your book and _____ _____ to the website, you can check _____ _____ _____ _____.

16 This way, the _____ _____ can become _____ _____ _____.

17 _____ _____ _____ we share, _____ _____ we learn.

18 The _____ Book

19 _____ _____ _____ is really important to people in my town.

20 It provides _____ _____ _____ _____ _____ _____ _____ _____ clean drinking water.

21 It _____ _____ the _____ Book.

22 You cannot actually drink the book, but you can use it _____ _____ _____.

23 Simply _____ _____ a page and _____ dirty water _____ it.

24 _____ the water _____ _____ the page, it _____ _____ clean drinking water.

25 _____ _____ this filtered water _____ you can drink.

26 This is possible because the book _____ _____ _____ _____ _____ _____.

27 This _____ book _____ the lives of many children _____ _____ that _____ _____ dirty water.

15 다음 독자가 여러분의 책을 발견해서 그 웹사이트에 다시 알릴 때, 여러분은 책이 어디 있는지 확인할 수 있습니다.

16 이런 식으로, 전 세계가 하나의 큰 도서관이 될 수 있습니다.

17 우리가 더 많은 책을 공유할수록, 우리는 더 많이 배웁니다.

18 마실 수 있는 책

19 이 작은 책은 우리 마을 사람들에게는 정말로 중요합니다.

20 그것은 깨끗한 마실 물을 만드는 데 필요한 정보와 도구 둘 다를 제공합니다.

21 그것은 '마실 수 있는 책'이라고 불립니다.

22 여러분은 실제로 그 책을 마실 수는 없지만, 그것을 필터로 사용할 수 있습니다.

23 그냥 한 페이지를 떼어 내서 그 위에 더러운 물을 부으세요.

24 물이 그 페이지를 통과하면서, 깨끗한 마실 물로 바뀝니다.

25 여러분이 마실 수 있는 것은 이 여과된 물입니다.

26 책이 특별한 여과지로 만들어졌기 때문에 이것이 가능합니다.

27 이 놀라운 책은 더러운 물로 생기는 질병으로부터 많은 어린이의 생명을 구합니다.

28 The _____ _____

29 This is _____ _____ _____ _____ that I have ever _____.

30 After you finish _____ this book, _____ it and _____ it.

31 You will _____ _____ _____ _____ on the book.

32 In some bookstores in my town, you can see _____ _____ _____ this book _____ _____ _____.

33 The secret is that the book _____ _____ in each page.

34 It is _____ _____ _____ that _____ the book _____ a tree.

35 This book _____ _____ _____ a small children's book _____ in Argentina.

36 _____ the company does _____ print this book _____, this special project _____ us _____ about where books come from.

37 These are _____ _____ _____ of the _____ _____ you can find.

38 _____ _____ _____ _____ _____ do you want to make?

39 What special project _____ you _____ _____ _____ _____ the books?

40 _____ _____ your _____ is, _____ _____ _____ _____ your books will become.

28 나무-책-나무 프로젝트

29 이것은 제가 지금까지 본 것 중에서 가장 놀라운 책입니다.

30 여러분이 이 책을 다 읽은 후에, 그것을 심고 물을 주세요.

31 여러분은 책에서 새잎이 자라는 것을 보게 될 거예요.

32 우리 마을의 몇몇 서점에서, 여러분은 이 책 한 권이 새잎을 내는 것을 볼 수 있습니다.

33 비밀은 책이 각 페이지 안에 씨앗을 갖고 있다는 것입니다.

34 책을 나무로 변화시키는 것은 이 아주 작은 씨앗들이에요.

35 이 책은 아르헨티나에 있는 한 작은 아동 도서 출판사에 의해 만들어졌습니다.

36 그 회사가 더는 이 책을 발행하지는 않지만, 이 특별한 프로젝트는 우리에게 책이 어디에서 오는지에 대해 생각하게 해 줍니다.

37 이것들은 여러분이 찾을 수 있는 독특한 책 중의 단지 몇 가지입니다.

38 여러분은 어떤 다른 독특한 책을 만들기 원하나요?

39 여러분은 책으로 어떤 특별한 프로젝트를 하고 싶나요?

40 여러분의 상상이 크면 클수록, 여러분의 책은 더 훌륭해질 것입니다.

※ 다음 문장을 우리말로 쓰시오.

1 This Book Is Amazing!

➡ _____

2 Most people think of books as traditional paper books to read.

➡ _____

3 However, there are many unique books around you.

➡ _____

4 Let's learn about a few of these books.

➡ _____

5 Books Travel!

➡ _____

6 I found this old book on a park bench yesterday.

➡ _____

7 A note on the cover read, "Free Book!

➡ _____

8 Take me home and read me!"

➡ _____

9 Actually, this book had an ID number and was registered on a website.

➡ _____

10 When I entered the number online, I found out that the book had traveled to many countries and that a number of readers in different countries had read it before me.

➡ _____

_____

11 How was that possible?

➡ _____

12 There is a book-sharing project.

➡ _____

13 First, register your book online and get an ID number.

➡ _____

14 Next, leave it in a public place.

➡ _____

15 When the next reader finds your book and reports back to the website, you can check where your book is.

➡ _____

16 This way, the whole world can become a big library.

➡ _____

17 The more books we share, the more we learn.

➡ _____

18 The Drinkable Book

➡ _____

19 This tiny book is really important to people in my town.

➡ _____

20 It provides both the information and the tools necessary to make clean drinking water.

➡ _____

21 It is called the Drinkable Book.

➡ _____

22 You cannot actually drink the book, but you can use it as a filter.

➡ _____

23 Simply tear out a page and pour dirty water on it.

➡ _____

24 As the water goes through the page, it changes into clean drinking water.

➡ _____

25 It is this filtered water that you can drink.

➡ _____

26 This is possible because the book is made of special filter paper.

➡ _____

27 This amazing book saves the lives of many children from diseases that come from dirty water.

➡ _____

28 The Tree-Book-Tree Project

➡ _____

29 This is the most amazing book that I have ever seen.

➡ _____

30 After you finish reading this book, plant it and water it.

➡ _____

31 You will see new leaves growing on the book.

➡ _____

32 In some bookstores in my town, you can see a copy of this book producing new leaves.

➡ _____

33 The secret is that the book has seeds in each page.

➡ _____

34 It is these tiny seeds that change the book into a tree.

➡ _____

35 This book was made by a small children's book publisher in Argentina.

➡ _____

36 Though the company does not print this book anymore, this special project makes us think about where books come from.

➡ _____

37 These are just a few of the unique books you can find.

➡ _____

38 What other unique books do you want to make?

➡ _____

39 What special project would you like to do with the books?

➡ _____

40 The bigger your imagination is, the more wonderful your books will become.

➡ _____

※ 다음 괄호 안의 단어들을 우리말에 맞도록 바르게 배열하시오.

1 (Book / This / Amazing! / Is)
➡ _____

2 (people / most / of / think / as / books / paper / traditional / books / read. / to)
➡ _____

3 (there / however, / many / are / books / unique / you. / around)
➡ _____

4 (learn / let's / a / about / few / of / books. / these)
➡ _____

5 (Travel! / Books)
➡ _____

6 (found / I / old / this / book / a / on / park / yesterday. / bench)
➡ _____

7 (note / a / the / on / read, / cover / Book! / "Free)
➡ _____

8 (me / take / and / home / me!" / read)
➡ _____

9 (this / actually, / book / an / had / number / ID / and / registered / was / a / on / website.)
➡ _____

10 (I / when / the / entered / number / I / online, / found / that / out / book / the / traveled / had / many / to / countries / that / and / number / a / of / readers / different / in / countries / read / had / before / it / me.)
➡ _____
_____
_____

11 (was / how / possible? / that)
➡ _____

12 (is / there / a / project. / book-sharing)
➡ _____

13 (register / first, / book / your / and / online / get / ID / an / number.)
➡ _____

14 (leave / next, / in / it / a / place. / public)
➡ _____

1 이 책은 놀라워요!

2 대부분의 사람은 책을 읽기 위한 전통적인 종이책으로 생각합니다.

3 하지만, 여러분 주변에는 독특한 책이 많이 있습니다.

4 이러한 책 중 몇 가지에 대해 배워 봅시다.

5 책이 여행합니다!

6 저는 어제 공원 벤치에서 이 낡은 책을 발견했습니다.

7 표지 위의 쪽지에 "공짜 책이에요!

8 저를 집으로 데려가서 읽어 주세요!"라고 쓰여 있었습니다.

9 사실, 이 책은 ID 번호가 있고 웹사이트에 등록되어 있었어요.

10 제가 온라인으로 그 번호를 입력했을 때, 저는 그 책이 많은 나라를 여행하고 다른 나라의 많은 독자가 저보다 앞서 이 책을 읽었다는 것을 알아냈습니다.

11 그게 어떻게 가능했을까요?

12 책을 공유하는 프로젝트가 있습니다.

13 우선, 온라인에 여러분의 책을 등록하고 ID 번호를 얻으세요.

14 그다음, 그것을 공공장소에 놓아두세요.

15 (the / when / reader / next / your / finds / book / and / back / reports / to / the / website, / can / you / where / check / book / your / is.)

➡ _____

_____

16 (way, / this / whole / the / can / world / a / become / library. / big)

➡ _____

17 (more / the / we / books / share, / more / the / learn. / we)

➡ _____

18 (Book / Drinkable / The)

➡ _____

19 (tiny / this / is / book / important / really / people / to / my / in / town.)

➡ _____

20 (provides / it / the / both / information / and / tools / the / to / necessary / clean / make / water. / drinking)

➡ _____

_____

21 (is / it / the / called / Book. / Drinkable)

➡ _____

22 (cannot / you / drink / actually / book, / the / you / but / use / can / it / a / as / filter.)

➡ _____

23 (tear / simply / a / out / and / page / dirty / pour / on / water / it.)

➡ _____

24 (the / as / goes / water / the / through / page, / changes / it / clean / into / water. / drinking)

➡ _____

_____

25 (is / it / filtered / this / that / water / can / you / drink.)

➡ _____

26 (is / this / because / possible / book / the / is / of / made / filter / special / paper.)

➡ _____

_____

27 (amazing / this / saves / book / lives / the / of / children / many / diseases / from / come / that / dirty / from / water.)

➡ _____

_____

15 다음 독자가 여러분의 책을 발견해서 그 웹사이트에 다시 알릴 때, 여러분은 책이 어디 있는지 확인할 수 있습니다.

16 이런 식으로, 전 세계가 하나의 큰 도서관이 될 수 있습니다.

17 우리가 더 많은 책을 공유할수록, 우리는 더 많이 배웁니다.

18 마실 수 있는 책

19 이 작은 책은 우리 마을 사람들에게는 정말로 중요합니다.

20 그것은 깨끗한 마실 물을 만드는 데 필요한 정보와 도구 둘 다를 제공합니다.

21 그것은 '마실 수 있는 책'이라고 불립니다.

22 여러분은 실제로 그 책을 마실 수는 없지만, 그것을 필터로 사용할 수 있습니다.

23 그냥 한 페이지를 떼어 내서 그 위에 더러운 물을 부으세요.

24 물이 그 페이지를 통과하면서, 깨끗한 마실 물로 바뀝니다.

25 여러분이 마실 수 있는 것은 이 여과된 물입니다.

26 책이 특별한 여과지로 만들어졌기 때문에 이것이 가능합니다.

27 이 놀라운 책은 더러운 물로 생기는 질병으로부터 많은 어린이의 생명을 구합니다.

28 (Project / Tree-Book-Tree / The)

➡ _____

29 (is / this / most / the / book / amazing / I / that / ever / have / seen.)

➡ _____

30 (you / after / reading / finish / book, / this / it / plant / and / it. / water)

➡ _____

31 (will / you / new / see / growing / leaves / the / on / book.)

➡ _____

32 (some / in / bookstores / my / in / town, / can / you / a / see / of / copy / book / this / new / producing / leaves.)

➡ _____

➡ _____

33 (secret / the / that / is / the / has / book / in / seeds / page. / each)

➡ _____

34 (is / it / tiny / these / seeds / change / that / book / the / a / into / tree.)

➡ _____

35 (book / this / made / was / a / by / children's / small / book / publisher / Argentina. / in)

➡ _____

36 (the / though / does / company / print / not / book / this / anymore, / special / this / makes / project / us / think / where / about / come / from. / books)

➡ _____

➡ _____

37 (are / these / a / just / of / few / unique / the / you / books / find. / can)

➡ _____

38 (other / what / books / unique / you / do / want / make? / to)

➡ _____

39 (special / what / would / project / like / you / do / to / the / with / books?)

➡ _____

40 (bigger / the / imagination / your / is, / more / the / your / wonderful / books / become. / will)

➡ _____

28 나무-책-나무 프로젝트

29 이것은 제가 지금까지 본 것 중에서 가장 놀라운 책입니다.

30 여러분이 이 책을 다 읽은 후에, 그것을 심고 물을 주세요.

31 여러분은 책에서 새잎이 자라는 것을 보게 될 거예요.

32 우리 마을의 몇몇 서점에서, 여러분은 이 책 한 권이 새잎을 내는 것을 볼 수 있습니다.

33 비밀은 책이 각 페이지 안에 씨앗을 갖고 있다는 것입니다.

34 책을 나무로 변화시키는 것은 이 아주 작은 씨앗들이에요.

35 이 책은 아르헨티나에 있는 한 작은 아동 도서 출판사에 의해 만들어졌습니다.

36 그 회사가 더는 이 책을 발행하지는 않지만, 이 특별한 프로젝트는 우리에게 책이 어디에서 오는지에 대해 생각하게 해 줍니다.

37 이것들은 여러분이 찾을 수 있는 독특한 책 중의 단지 몇 가지입니다.

38 여러분은 어떤 다른 독특한 책을 만들기 원하나요?

39 여러분은 책으로 어떤 특별한 프로젝트를 하고 싶나요?

40 여러분의 상상이 크면 클수록, 여러분의 책은 더 훌륭해질 것입니다.

※ 다음 우리말을 영어로 쓰시오.

1 이 책은 놀라워요!

➡ _____

2 대부분의 사람은 책을 읽기 위한 전통적인 종이책으로 생각합니다.

➡ _____

3 하지만, 여러분 주변에는 독특한 책이 많이 있습니다.

➡ _____

4 이러한 책 중 몇 가지에 대해 배워 봅시다.

➡ _____

5 책이 여행합니다!

➡ _____

6 저는 어제 공원 벤치에서 이 낡은 책을 발견했습니다.

➡ _____

7 표지 위의 쪽지에 "공짜 책이에요!

➡ _____

8 저를 집으로 데려가서 읽어 주세요!"라고 쓰여 있었습니다.

➡ _____

9 사실, 이 책은 ID 번호가 있고 웹사이트에 등록되어 있었어요.

➡ _____

10 제가 온라인으로 그 번호를 입력했을 때, 저는 그 책이 많은 나라를 여행하고 다른 나라의 많은 독자가 저보다 앞서 이 책을 읽었다는 것을 알아냈습니다.

➡ _____

_____

11 그게 어떻게 가능했을까요?

➡ _____

12 책을 공유하는 프로젝트가 있습니다.

➡ _____

13 우선, 온라인에 여러분의 책을 등록하고 ID 번호를 얻으세요.

➡ _____

14 그다음, 그것을 공공장소에 놓아두세요.

➡ _____

15 다음 독자가 여러분의 책을 발견해서 그 웹사이트에 다시 알릴 때, 여러분은 책이 어디 있는지
확인할 수 있습니다.

➡ _____

_____

16 이런 식으로, 전 세계가 하나의 큰 도서관이 될 수 있습니다.

➡ _____

17 우리가 더 많은 책을 공유할수록, 우리는 더 많이 배웁니다.

➡ _____

18 마실 수 있는 책

➡ _____

19 이 작은 책은 우리 마을 사람들에게는 정말로 중요합니다.

➡ _____

20 그것은 깨끗한 마실 물을 만드는 데 필요한 정보와 도구 둘 다를 제공합니다.

➡ _____

21 그것은 '마실 수 있는 책'이라고 불립니다.

➡ _____

22 여러분은 실제로 그 책을 마실 수는 없지만, 그것을 필터로 사용할 수 있습니다.

➡ _____

23 그냥 한 페이지를 떼어 내서 그 위에 더러운 물을 부으세요.

➡ _____

24 물이 그 페이지를 통과하면서, 깨끗한 마실 물로 바뀝니다.

➡ _____

25 여러분이 마실 수 있는 것은 이 여과된 물입니다.

➡ _____

26 책이 특별한 여과지로 만들어졌기 때문에 이것이 가능합니다.

➡ _____

27 이 놀라운 책은 더러운 물로 생기는 질병으로부터 많은 어린이의 생명을 구합니다.

➡ _____

28 나무–책–나무 프로젝트

➡ _____

29 이것은 제가 지금까지 본 것 중에서 가장 놀라운 책입니다.

➡ _____

30 여러분이 이 책을 다 읽은 후에, 그것을 심고 물을 주세요.

➡ _____

31 여러분은 책에서 새잎이 자라는 것을 보게 될 거예요.

➡ _____

32 우리 마을의 몇몇 서점에서, 여러분은 이 책 한 권이 새잎을 내는 것을 볼 수 있습니다.

➡ _____

33 비밀은 책이 각 페이지 안에 씨앗을 갖고 있다는 것입니다.

➡ _____

34 책을 나무로 변화시키는 것은 이 아주 작은 씨앗들이에요.

➡ _____

35 이 책은 아르헨티나에 있는 한 작은 아동 도서 출판사에 의해 만들어졌습니다.

➡ _____

36 그 회사가 더는 이 책을 발행하지는 않지만, 이 특별한 프로젝트는 우리에게 책이 어디에서 오는지에 대해 생각하게 해 줍니다.

➡ _____

_____

37 이것들은 여러분이 찾을 수 있는 독특한 책 중의 단지 몇 가지입니다.

➡ _____

38 여러분은 어떤 다른 독특한 책을 만들기 원하나요?

➡ _____

39 여러분은 책으로 어떤 특별한 프로젝트를 하고 싶나요?

➡ _____

40 여러분의 상상이 크면 클수록, 여러분의 책은 더 훌륭해질 것입니다.

➡ _____

※ 다음 우리말과 일치하도록 빈칸에 알맞은 말을 쓰시오.

Express Yourself C

1. In _____ and _____ a drone, _____ _____ is important.
2. It is a _____ _____ that has a _____ _____ _____.
3. _____ _____ the drone is, _____ _____ it flies.

1. 드론을 만들어 날릴 때, 그것의 무게가 중요하다.
2. 긴 건전지 수명을 가지는 것은 가벼운 드론이다.
3. 드론이 가벼울수록, 더 오래 난다.

Link to the World

1. This _____ _____ Dalhang-ari, a moon jar, _____ it _____ _____ _____ _____ _____ _____.
2. In the past, _____ was _____ _____ _____ _____ this large round jar _____ _____.
3. _____ _____ a jar was, _____ _____ _____ it was to make.
4. _____ was _____ _____ _____ solved this problem.
5. A smart potter _____ two large bowls together _____ _____ _____ _____ _____.

1. 이것은 보름달처럼 생겨서 달항아리라고 불린다.
2. 과거에는 손으로 이렇게 크고 둥근 항아리를 만드는 게 불가능했다.
3. 항아리가 클수록, 만들기가 더 어려웠다.
4. 이 문제를 해결한 것은 도공이었다.
5. 현명한 도공은 두 개의 큰 사발을 합쳐서 이 달항아리를 만들었다.

Learning Diary – Listen & Speak 2

1. A: _____ do you _____, going camping _____ going swimming?
2. B: I _____ _____ _____. Actually, I _____ _____ _____. How about you?
3. A: Well, I _____ _____ _____.

1. A: 너는 캠핑 가기와 수영하러 가기 중에서 어떤 것을 더 좋아하니?
2. B: 나는 캠핑 가기를 더 좋아해. 사실, 나는 수영하러 가기를 몹시 싫어해. 너는 어때?
3. A: 음, 나는 수영하러 가기를 더 좋아해.

구석구석 지문 Test

※ 다음 우리말을 영어로 쓰시오.

Express Yourself C

1. 드론을 만들어 날릴 때, 그것의 무게가 중요하다.

   ➡ _____

2. 긴 건전지 수명을 가지는 것은 가벼운 드론이다.

   ➡ _____

3. 드론이 가벼울수록, 더 오래 난다.

   ➡ _____

Link to the World

1. 이것은 보름달처럼 생겨서 달항아리라고 불린다.

   ➡ _____

2. 과거에는 손으로 이렇게 크고 둥근 항아리를 만드는 게 불가능했다.

   ➡ _____

3. 항아리가 클수록, 만들기가 더 어려웠다.

   ➡ _____

4. 이 문제를 해결한 것은 도공이었다.

   ➡ _____

5. 현명한 도공은 두 개의 큰 사발을 합쳐서 이 달항아리를 만들었다.

   ➡ _____

Learning Diary – Listen & Speak 2

1. A: 너는 캠핑 가기와 수영하러 가기 중에서 어떤 것을 더 좋아하니?

   ➡ _____

2. B: 나는 캠핑 가기를 더 좋아해. 사실, 나는 수영하러 가기를 몹시 싫어해. 너는 어때?

   ➡ _____

3. A: 음, 나는 수영하러 가기를 더 좋아해.

   ➡ _____

※ 다음 영어를 우리말로 쓰시오.

01	provide		22	clown
02	recently		23	offer
03	healthy		24	unique
04	search		25	comfortable
05	evidence		26	untrue
06	false		27	cleaner
07	source		28	perfect
08	actually		29	performance
09	artwork		30	spread
10	support		31	unclear
11	seem		32	complete
12	totally		33	snake
13	sink		34	prefer
14	critically		35	turn out
15	funny		36	give up
16	light		37	tell A from B
17	major		38	make sense
18	octopus		39	be based on
19	touching		40	pass away
20	site		41	pay attention to
21	attack		42	made up
			43	laugh out loud

※ 다음 우리말을 영어로 쓰시오.

01 구하다	
02 완벽한	
03 가라앉다	
04 선호하다	
05 세제, 청소기	
06 비판적으로	
07 공격하다	
08 최근에	
09 거짓의, 잘못된	
10 공연, 수행	
11 편안한	
12 실제로, 사실	
13 전적으로	
14 근원, 출처	
15 증거	
16 지지하다, 후원하다	
17 완전한	
18 제공하다	
19 무서운	
20 장소	
21 광대	

22 퍼진; 퍼지다	
23 건강한	
24 환호하다	
25 사실이 아닌	
26 가벼운	
27 주요한, 주된	
28 감동적인	
29 문어	
30 예술 작품	
31 독특한	
32 착용하다	
33 지루한	
34 찾다, 검색하다	
35 포기하다	
36 돌아가시다	
37 ~에 바탕을 두다	
38 의미가 통하다	
39 큰 소리로 웃다	
40 ~로부터 만들어지다	
41 판명되다	
42 ~에 주의를 기울이다	
43 A와 B를 구별하다	

※ 다음 영영풀이에 알맞은 단어를 <보기>에서 골라 쓴 후, 우리말 뜻을 쓰시오.

1 _____ : completely, absolutely: _____

2 _____ : an untrue statement: _____

3 _____ : having a strong emotional effect: _____

4 _____ : very important and serious: _____

5 _____ : incorrect, untrue, or mistaken: _____

6 _____ : to shout with joy, approval, or enthusiasm: _____

7 _____ : what you think or believe about something: _____

8 _____ : to supply something that is wanted or needed: _____

9 _____ : in a way that expresses disapproval: _____

10 _____ : to disappear below the surface of the water: _____

11 _____ : a soft sea creature with eight long arms: _____

12 _____ : anything that causes you to believe that something is true: _____

13 _____ : to open it out or arrange it over a place or surface: _____

14 _____ : to try to hurt or damage someone or something using physical violence:
_____

15 _____ : to give assistance, approval, comfort, or encouragement to someone:
_____

16 _____ : a performer in a circus who wears funny clothes and bright make-up,
and does silly things in order to make people laugh: _____

보기			
sink	cheer	attack	octopus
clown	touching	opinion	support
critically	false	totally	evidence
provide	lie	major	spread

※ 다음 우리말과 일치하도록 빈칸에 알맞은 말을 쓰시오.

Get Ready 2

(1) **G:** There's no monkey _____ this in the world. Its nose is too big. _____ _____ it's _____.

   B: I don't _____. I saw that _____ of monkey on TV. It's _____.

(2) **G:** This animal has a long nose and two long, _____ _____. _____ _____ _____ _____ _____ it? Is it _____?

   B: Well, _____ _____ the Internet and _____ it together.

   G: That's a good idea.

(3) **B:** _____ do you _____ _____ this animal?

   G: It doesn't have legs, but it doesn't _____ _____ a snake. It's very _____.

   B: I think so, _____.

(4) **B:** _____ monkey is very small. Is it _____?

   G: I don't know. _____ visit some animal _____ _____ and _____ it _____.

   B: That's a good idea.

Start Off - Listen & Talk A

1. **G:** Look at those shoes the girl is wearing. I think they're great. _____ _____ _____ _____ _____ them?

   B: I think they look _____ and _____.

   G: Right. I want _____ _____ them for the _____ _____ _____.

2. **G:** I like the coat the boy _____ _____. I think it's _____ and _____.

   B: Well, I don't _____ _____ you. _____, I bought one last week. It's not so warm, and it's _____ _____ than it looks.

   G: Really? I don't _____ it.

Start Off - Listen & Talk B

G: _____ do you _____ about this drama?

B: I think it's very _____. The boy _____ _____ his life _____ _____ his sister. It's _____ _____ of this year.

G: I _____ _____. It's not a good drama.

B: Come on. _____ do you _____ _____ ?

G: It doesn't _____ _____. And it's _____ _____ _____.

Start Off - Speak Up

A: _____ do you feel _____ this _____?
B: I think it's great. It _____ the phone is strong.
A: I don't agree. We _____ _____ _____ every ad.

Step Up - Real-life Scene

Alex: Big Mouth's show is really _____. _____ _____ _____ _____ _____ it?
Somi: Well, I don't think it's _____ great.
Alex: Come on. I love Mr. Big Mouth. He always _____ me _____ _____ _____.
Somi: He's funny, but don't believe _____ he _____.
Alex: All right. Oh, look at his photo of an _____. He said it lives in a tree.
Somi: It doesn't _____ _____.
Alex: He took the photo _____ it was _____ the tree. I don't think he's _____. It's a great photo.
Somi: I don't _____ _____ you. It's a _____ photo. An octopus can't live _____ _____ the sea.

Express Yourself A

1. **G:** _____ do you _____ _____ these animals?
   B: They are very cute, but I think cats don't _____ _____ well _____ dogs.
   G: I don't agree. And _____ _____ are good friends. They are _____ the trip _____.
2. **G:** _____ do you _____ about this kid here?
   B: I think she is very pretty. _____ _____ _____, why did she cut her hair?
   G: Can you _____?
   B: Well, girls these days _____ short hair.
   G: I don't agree _____ that. Most girls like long hair _____ _____ short hair. And this kid here is not a girl. _____ _____, he is a boy.
   B: Really?
   G: Yes. He grew his hair _____ _____ sick children.
3. **G:** How do you _____ _____ the teddy bears?
   B: They are cute. Is there _____ _____ about them?
   G: They _____ _____ _____ of a police officer's _____.
   B: Oh, I see.
   G: This police officer made them for the kids. Their dad was a police officer, and he _____ _____ _____.
   B: That's very _____.

A: 이 광고를 어떻게 생각하니?
B: 굉장하다고 생각해. 그건 그 전화기가 튼튼하다는 것을 보여주고 있어.
A: 나는 동의하지 않아. 우리는 모든 광고를 믿어서는 안 돼.

Alex: Big Mouth 쇼는 정말 굉장해. 너는 어떻게 생각하니?
소미: 글쎄, 나는 그렇게 대단한 것 같지 않아.
Alex: 왜 그래. 나는 Big Mouth 씨를 진짜 좋아해. 그는 언제나 나를 큰 소리로 웃게 해 줘.
소미: 웃기긴 하지만, 그가 하는 모든 말을 믿지는 마.
Alex: 알았어. 오, 그가 찍은 문어 사진을 봐. 그가 말하기를 그건 나무에 산대.
소미: 말도 안 돼.
Alex: 그는 문어가 나무에 기어 올라갈 때 사진을 찍었대. 그가 거짓말하고 있는 것 같지는 않아. 대단한 사진이야.
소미: 나는 네 말에 동의하지 않아. 그건 가짜 사진이야. 문어는 바다 밖에서는 살 수 없다고.

1. **G:** 이 동물들을 어떻게 생각해?
   B: 아주 귀엽지만, 고양이는 개와 잘 어울리지 못한다고 생각해.
   G: 나는 동의하지 않아. 그리고 이 둘은 좋은 친구야. 그들은 함께 즐겁게 여행하고 있어.
2. **G:** 여기 이 아이를 어떻게 생각해?
   B: 매우 예쁘다고 생각해. 그런데 그녀는 왜 머리카락을 잘랐니?
   G: 짐작할 수 있어?
   B: 음, 요새 여자아이들은 짧은 머리를 더 좋아하더라.
   G: 난 그것에 동의하지 않아. 대부분의 여자아이는 짧은 머리보다 긴 머리를 좋아해. 그리고 여기 이 아이는 여자아이가 아니야. 사실, 이 아이는 남자아이야.
   B: 정말이니?
   G: 응. 그는 아픈 아이들을 돕기 위해 머리를 길렀어.
3. **G:** 곰 인형들을 어떻게 생각해?
   B: 귀여워. 뭔가 특별한 점이 있니?
   G: 그것들은 한 경찰관의 제복으로 만들어졌어.
   B: 아, 그렇구나.
   G: 이 경찰이 아이들을 위해 그것들을 만들어 줬어. 그들의 아빠는 경찰관이었고, 최근에 세상을 떠나셨어.
   B: 아주 감동적이야.

※ 다음 우리말에 맞도록 대화를 영어로 쓰시오.

Get Ready 2

(1) G: _____

    B: _____

(2) G: _____

    B: _____

    G: _____

(3) B: _____

    G: _____

    B: _____

(4) B: _____

    G: _____

    B: _____

Start Off - Listen & Talk A

1. G: _____
      _____

    B: _____

    G: _____

2. G: _____

    B: _____
      _____

    G: _____

Start Off - Listen & Talk B

G: _____

B: _____
   _____

G: _____

B: _____

G: _____

---

(1) G: 세상에 이런 원숭이는 없어. 코가 너무 크잖아. 나는 그것이 가짜라고 생각해.
    B: 나는 동의하지 않아. 저런 종류의 원숭이를 TV에서 본 적이 있어. 그건 진짜야.

(2) G: 이 동물은 긴 코와 두 개의 길고 날카로운 이빨을 가지고 있어. 그것을 어떻게 생각해? 진짜일까?
    B: 음, 인터넷을 찾아보고 함께 확인해 보자.
    G: 좋은 생각이야.

(3) B: 이 동물을 어떻게 생각해?
    G: 그것은 다리가 없지만 뱀처럼 보이지는 않아. 정말 이상하네.
    B: 나도 그렇게 생각해.

(4) B: 이 원숭이는 정말 작다. 진짜일까?
    G: 모르겠어. 동물 사실 확인 사이트를 방문해서 함께 확인해 보자.
    B: 좋은 생각이야.

1. G: 저 여자애가 신고 있는 신발 좀 봐. 멋있는 것 같아. 너는 저 신발을 어떻게 생각해?
    B: 가볍고 편안해 보여.
    G: 맞아. 난 학교 체험 학습 때 신으려고 저걸 사고 싶어.

2. G: 저 남자애가 입고 있는 코트가 마음에 들어. 따뜻하고 가벼울 것 같아.
    B: 글쎄, 나는 동의하지 않아. 사실 나는 지난주에 저것을 샀어. 그렇게 따뜻하지도 않고 보기보다 훨씬 더 무거워.
    G: 정말로? 믿을 수가 없어.

G: 이 드라마를 어떻게 생각하니?
B: 난 아주 감동적이라고 생각해. 소년이 그의 여동생을 구하기 위해 자신의 생명을 포기했잖아. 올해 최고의 드라마야.
G: 난 동의하지 않아. 그건 좋은 드라마가 아니야.
B: 이런. 왜 그렇게 생각해?
G: 현실적으로 보이지 않아. 그리고 약간 지루해.

Start Off - Speak Up

A: _____

B: _____

A: _____

Step Up - Real-life Scene

Alex: _____

Somi: _____

Alex: _____

Somi: _____

Alex: _____

Somi: _____

Alex: _____

_____

Somi: _____

Express Yourself A

1. G: _____

   B: _____

   G: _____

2. G: _____

   B: _____

   G: _____

   B: _____

   G: _____

   B: _____

   G: _____

3. G: _____

   B: _____

   G: _____

   B: _____

   G: _____

   B: _____

A: 이 광고를 어떻게 생각하니?
B: 굉장하다고 생각해. 그건 그 전화기가 튼튼하다는 것을 보여주고 있어.
A: 나는 동의하지 않아. 우리는 모든 광고를 믿어서는 안 돼.

Alex: Big Mouth 쇼는 정말 굉장해. 너는 어떻게 생각하니?
소미: 글쎄, 나는 그렇게 대단한 것 같지 않아.
Alex: 왜 그래. 나는 Big Mouth 씨를 진짜 좋아해. 그는 언제나 나를 큰 소리로 웃게 해 줘.
소미: 웃기긴 하지만, 그가 하는 모든 말을 믿지는 마.
Alex: 알았어. 오, 그가 찍은 문어 사진을 봐. 그가 말하기를 그건 나무에 산대.
소미: 말도 안 돼.
Alex: 그는 문어가 나무에 기어 올라갈 때 사진을 찍었대. 그가 거짓말하고 있는 것 같지는 않아. 대단한 사진이야.
소미: 나는 네 말에 동의하지 않아. 그건 가짜 사진이야. 문어는 바다 밖에서는 살 수 없다고.

1. G: 이 동물들을 어떻게 생각해?
   B: 아주 귀엽지만, 고양이는 개와 잘 어울리지 못한다고 생각해.
   G: 나는 동의하지 않아. 그리고 이 둘은 좋은 친구야. 그들은 함께 즐겁게 여행하고 있어.

2. G: 여기 이 아이를 어떻게 생각해?
   B: 매우 예쁘다고 생각해. 그런데 그녀는 왜 머리카락을 잘랐니?
   G: 짐작할 수 있어?
   B: 음, 요새 여자아이들은 짧은 머리를 더 좋아하더라.
   G: 난 그것에 동의하지 않아. 대부분의 여자아이는 짧은 머리보다 긴 머리를 좋아해. 그리고 여기 이 아이는 여자아이가 아니야. 사실, 이 아이는 남자아이야.
   B: 정말이니?
   G: 응. 그는 아픈 아이들을 돕기 위해 머리를 길렀어.

3. G: 곰 인형들을 어떻게 생각해?
   B: 귀여워. 뭔가 특별한 점이 있니?
   G: 그것들은 한 경찰관의 제복으로 만들어졌어.
   B: 아, 그렇구나.
   G: 이 경찰이 아이들을 위해 그것들을 만들어 줬어. 그들의 아빠는 경찰관이었고, 최근에 세상을 떠나셨어.
   B: 아주 감동적이야.

※ 다음 우리말과 일치하도록 빈칸에 알맞은 것을 골라 쓰시오.

1 How to Be a _____ _____ _____

   A. News   B. Smart   C. Reader

2 In October 2016, stories about _____ clowns _____ schools _____ the Washington area, but Danina Garcia-Fuller's students didn't believe them a _____.

   A. shook   B. bit   C. scary   D. across

3 "Some people were _____ _____ because they saw _____ on social media," said Patricia Visoso, _____ of Garcia-Fuller's students.

   A. scared   B. one   C. things   D. getting

4 "But they never _____ _____ _____ who was _____ this."

   A. saying   B. checked   C. on   D. up

5 The stories were _____ _____ _____ teenagers, not by major newspapers or TV _____.

   A. by   B. made   C. stations   D. actually

6 They offered no _____ _____ that clowns really were _____ to _____ students.

   A. attack   B. hard   C. trying   D. evidence

7 The story _____ _____ to be a _____ _____.

   A. out   B. turned   C. lie   D. complete

8 "I think a _____ of people just look _____ one _____ and believe it's _____," Patricia's classmate Ivy-Brooks said.

   A. true   B. thing   C. at   D. lot

9 "It's really important to look at the _____ _____ and to pay attention to what is _____ and what is _____."

   A. sources   B. real   C. right   D. fake

10 _____ Garcia-Fuller's students, many _____ in America are learning to _____ _____ about information they're seeing in the news and on the Internet.

   A. critically   B. like   C. teenagers   D. think

11 This skill is _____ more important these days as stories can _____ very fast, and anyone can make a website _____ of _____ information.

   A. spread   B. false   C. getting   D. full

---

1 현명한 뉴스 독자가 되는 방법

2 2016년 10월, 무서운 광대들에 관한 이야기가 워싱턴 지역 전역의 학교에 충격을 안겼지만, Danina Garcia-Fuller의 학생들은 조금도 그 이야기들을 믿지 않았다.

3 "몇몇 사람들은 그들이 소셜 미디어에 올라온 것들을 봤기 때문에 무서워했어요."라고 Garcia-Fuller의 학생 중 한 명인 Patricia Visoso가 말했다.

4 "하지만 그들은 이것을 누가 말하고 있는지를 전혀 확인하지 않았어요."

5 그 이야기들은 실제로 주요 신문사나 TV 방송국이 아닌 10대들이 지어냈다.

6 그들은 광대들이 정말로 학생들을 공격하려고 한다는 명백한 증거를 하나도 제공하지 않았다.

7 그 이야기는 결국 완벽한 거짓말인 것으로 드러났다.

8 "많은 사람이 단지 한 가지만을 보고 그것이 사실이라고 믿는 것 같아요."라고 Patricia의 반 친구인 Ivy-Brooks가 말했다.

9 올바른 출처를 살펴보고, 무엇이 진짜이고 무엇이 가짜인지에 주의를 기울이는 것은 정말 중요해요."

10 Garcia-Fuller의 학생들처럼, 많은 미국의 10대들은 뉴스 속 그리고 인터넷상에서 보고 있는 정보에 관해 비판적으로 생각하는 것을 배워 나가고 있다.

11 이 기능은 최근 더 중요해지고 있는데, 이야기들은 아주 빠른 속도로 퍼져 나갈 수 있고 누구나 허위 정보로 가득 찬 웹사이트를 만들어 낼 수 있기 때문이다.

12 Garcia-Fuller said she was teaching her students _____ _____ _____ fake news _____ real news.

    A. tell   B. how   C. from   D. to

13 "_____ of the first _____ is to _____ _____.

    A. steps   B. down   C. one   D. slow

14 If a story or a photo seems _____ good _____ be _____, stop and _____.

    A. to   B. think   C. too   D. true

15 Is there any _____ that _____ _____ the writer _____?

    A. supports   B. evidence   C. what   D. says

16 And _____ is this _____ _____?"

    A. coming   B. where   C. from

17 Garcia-Fuller's students also learn how to _____ _____ _____ _____ in the news.

    A. fact   B. from   C. opinion   D. tell

18 "Opinions are good to read," said 15-year-old McKenzie Campbell, "but you also have to _____ if they are _____ _____ _____."

    A. based   B. facts   C. check   D. on

19 Garcia-Fuller also said sometimes it can be very _____ to be a _____ _____ _____.

    A. hard   B. reader   C. smart   D. news

20 She tests her students with a website that _____ to _____ information on an animal _____ a tree _____.

    A. called   B. appears   C. octopus   D. provide

21 The _____ is _____ of information on this animal, _____ with a few _____ photos of octopuses in trees.

    A. unclear   B. full   C. along   D. site

22 But like the story of _____ _____, it's totally _____.

    A. made   B. scary   C. up   D. clowns

23 The lesson, Garcia-Fuller tells her students, is to "check the information you're seeing _____ more _____" and to "question _____, _____ things that I say."

    A. carefully   B. even   C. everything   D. once

---

12 Garcia-Fuller는 그녀가 자신의 학생들에게 가짜 뉴스를 진짜 뉴스로부터 구분하는 방법을 가르치고 있다고 말했다.

13 "첫 단계 중 하나는 속도를 늦추는 것(천천히 생각하는 것)입니다.

14 만약 어떤 이야기나 어떤 사진이 진짜라고 하기엔 너무 좋아 보인다면, 멈춰서 생각해 보세요.

15 글쓴이가 말하고 있는 것을 뒷받침하는 어떠한 증거라도 있나요?

16 그리고 이 정보가 어디서 온 것인가요?"

17 Garcia-Fuller의 학생들은 또한 뉴스에서 사실을 의견과 구분하는 방법에 대해서도 배운다.

18 "의견들은 읽을 만한 가치가 있습니다."라고 15살인 McKenzie Campbell이 말했다. "하지만 여러분은 그것들이 사실에 기반을 둔 것인지를 확인해 보아야 합니다."

19 Garcia-Fuller는 또한 때때로 현명한 뉴스 독자가 되는 것이 아주 어려울 수도 있다고 말했다.

20 그녀는 자신의 학생들을 '나무 문어'라는 이름의 동물에 대한 정보를 제공하는 것처럼 보이는 웹사이트로 시험한다.

21 그 사이트는 나무 위에 있는 문어들의 몇몇 불확실한 사진과 함께, 이 동물에 대한 정보로 가득 차 있다.

22 하지만 무서운 광대들의 이야기와 마찬가지로, 그것은 완전히 꾸며진 것이다.

23 Garcia-Fuller가 그녀의 학생들에게 말하는 교훈은 '당신이 보고 있는 정보를 한 번만 더 신중하게 확인해 보라'는 것과 '모든 것, 심지어 내가 말하는 것에도 의문을 가져 보라'는 것이다.

※ 다음 우리말과 일치하도록 빈칸에 알맞은 것을 골라 쓰시오.

1 _____ _____ Be a _____ _____ _____

2 In October 2016, stories about scary clowns _____ _____ _____ the Washington area, but Danina Garcia-Fuller's students _____ _____ them _____ _____.

3 "Some people were _____ _____ because they saw things on social media," said Patricia Visoso, _____ _____ Garcia-Fuller's students.

4 "But they never _____ _____ _____ who _____ _____ this."

5 The stories _____ _____ _____ _____ teenagers, not by _____ _____ or TV stations.

6 They offered _____ _____ _____ that clowns really were _____ _____ _____ students.

7 The story _____ _____ _____ _____ a _____ _____.

8 "I think a lot of people _____ _____ _____ _____ and believe it's true," Patricia's classmate Ivy-Brooks said.

9 "It's really important _____ _____ _____ _____ _____ and to _____ _____ _____ _____ _____ _____ and _____ _____ _____ _____."

10 _____ Garcia-Fuller's students, many teenagers in America are learning _____ _____ _____ about information they're seeing in the news and _____ _____ _____.

11 This skill is _____ _____ _____ these days as stories can _____ very fast, and anyone can make a website _____ _____ _____ _____.

12 Garcia-Fuller said she was teaching her students _____ _____ _____ fake news _____ _____ _____.

13 "_____ _____ _____ _____ _____ is to _____ _____."

14 If a story or a photo seems _____ _____ _____, stop and think.

15 Is there any _____ that supports _____ _____ _____?

16 And where is this _____ _____?"

17 Garcia-Fuller's students also learn _____ _____ _____ fact _____ opinion in the news.

18 "Opinions are good to read," said 15-year-old McKenzie Campbell, "but you also _____ _____ check _____ they _____ _____ _____ _____."

19 Garcia-Fuller also said sometimes it can be very hard to be _____ _____ _____ _____.

20 She tests her students with a website that _____ _____ _____ information on an animal called a tree octopus.

21 The site _____ _____ _____ information on this animal, _____ _____ a few _____ _____ of octopuses in trees.

22 But _____ the story of _____ _____, it's totally _____ _____.

23 The lesson, Garcia-Fuller tells her students, is to "check the information you're seeing _____ _____ _____" and to "_____ _____, even things that I say."

12 Garcia-Fuller는 그녀가 자신의 학생들에게 가짜 뉴스를 진짜 뉴스로부터 구분하는 방법을 가르치고 있다고 말했다.

13 "첫 단계 중 하나는 속도를 늦추는 것(천천히 생각하는 것)입니다.

14 만약 어떤 이야기나 어떤 사진이 진짜라고 하기엔 너무 좋아 보인다면, 멈춰서 생각해 보세요.

15 글쓴이가 말하고 있는 것을 뒷받침하는 어떠한 증거라도 있나요?

16 그리고 이 정보가 어디서 온 것인가요?"

17 Garcia-Fuller의 학생들은 또한 뉴스에서 사실을 의견과 구분하는 방법에 대해서도 배운다.

18 "의견들은 읽을 만한 가치가 있습니다,"라고 15살인 McKenzie Campbell이 말했다. "하지만 여러분은 그것들이 사실에 기반을 둔 것인지를 확인해 보아야 합니다."

19 Garcia-Fuller는 또한 때때로 현명한 뉴스 독자가 되는 것이 아주 어려울 수도 있다고 말했다.

20 그녀는 자신의 학생들을 '나무 문어'라는 이름의 동물에 대한 정보를 제공하는 것처럼 보이는 웹사이트로 시험한다.

21 그 사이트는 나무 위에 있는 문어들의 몇몇 불확실한 사진과 함께, 이 동물에 대한 정보로 가득 차 있다.

22 하지만 무서운 광대들의 이야기와 마찬가지로, 그것은 완전히 꾸며진 것이다.

23 Garcia-Fuller가 그녀의 학생들에게 말하는 교훈은 '당신이 보고 있는 정보를 한 번만 더 신중하게 확인해 보라'는 것과 '모든 것, 심지어 내가 말하는 것에도 의문을 가져 보라'는 것이다.

본문 Test **55**

※ 다음 문장을 우리말로 쓰시오.

1 How to Be a Smart News Reader

➡ _____

2 In October 2016, stories about scary clowns shook schools across the Washington area, but Danina Garcia-Fuller's students didn't believe them a bit.

➡ _____

3 "Some people were getting scared because they saw things on social media," said Patricia Visoso, one of Garcia-Fuller's students.

➡ _____
_____

4 "But they never checked up on who was saying this."

➡ _____

5 The stories were actually made by teenagers, not by major newspapers or TV stations.

➡ _____

6 They offered no hard evidence that clowns really were trying to attack students.

➡ _____

7 The story turned out to be a complete lie.

➡ _____

8 "I think a lot of people just look at one thing and believe it's true," Patricia's classmate Ivy-Brooks said.

➡ _____
_____

9 "It's really important to look at the right sources and to pay attention to what is real and what is fake."

➡ _____

10 Like Garcia-Fuller's students, many teenagers in America are learning to think critically about information they're seeing in the news and on the Internet.

➡ _____
_____

11 This skill is getting more important these days as stories can spread very fast, and anyone can make a website full of false information.

➡ _____
_____

12 Garcia-Fuller said she was teaching her students how to tell fake news from real news.

➡ _____

13 "One of the first steps is to slow down.

➡ _____

14 If a story or a photo seems too good to be true, stop and think.

➡ _____

15 Is there any evidence that supports what the writer says?

➡ _____

16 And where is this coming from?"

➡ _____

17 Garcia-Fuller's students also learn how to tell fact from opinion in the news.

➡ _____

18 "Opinions are good to read," said 15-year-old McKenzie Campbell, "but you also have to check if they are based on facts."

➡ _____

_____

19 Garcia-Fuller also said sometimes it can be very hard to be a smart news reader.

➡ _____

20 She tests her students with a website that appears to provide information on an animal called a tree octopus.

➡ _____

21 The site is full of information on this animal, along with a few unclear photos of octopuses in trees.

➡ _____

22 But like the story of scary clowns, it's totally made up.

➡ _____

23 The lesson, Garcia-Fuller tells her students, is to "check the information you're seeing once more carefully" and to "question everything, even things that I say."

➡ _____

_____

※ 다음 괄호 안의 단어들을 우리말에 맞도록 바르게 배열하시오.

1 (to / How / a / Be / News / Smart / Reader)
➡ _____

2 (October / in / 2016, / about / stories / clowns / scary / schools / shook / the / across / area, / Washington / but / Garcia-Fuller's / Danina / students / believe / didn't / them / bit. / a)
➡ _____
_____
_____

3 (people / "some / were / scared / getting / because / saw / they / things / social / on / media, / Patricia / said / one / Visoso, / of / students. / Garcia-Fuller's)
➡ _____
_____

4 ("but / never / they / up / checked / who / on / was / this." / saying)
➡ _____

5 (stories / the / actually / were / by / made / teenagers, / by / not / newspapers / major / TV / or / stations.)
➡ _____

6 (offered / they / hard / no / that / evidence / clowns / were / really / trying / were / attack / to / students.)
➡ _____

7 (story / the / out / turned / be / to / a / lie. / complete)
➡ _____

8 (think / "I / lot / a / people / of / look / just / one / at / and / thing / it's / believe / true," / classmate / Paricia's / said. / Ivy-Brooks)
➡ _____

9 (really / "it's / to / important / look / at / right / the / and / sources / to / attention / pay / to / is / what / and / real / is / what / fake.")
➡ _____

10 (Gracia-Fuller's / like / students, / teenagers / many / in / are / America / to / learning / critically / think / information / about / seeing / they're / the / in / and / news / on / Internet. / the)
➡ _____

11 (skill / this / getting / is / important / more / days / these / stories / as / spread / can / fast, / very / anyone / and / make / can / website / a / of / full / information. / false)
➡ _____

1 현명한 뉴스 독자가 되는 방법

2 2016년 10월, 무서운 광대들에 관한 이야기가 워싱턴 지역 전역의 학교에 충격을 안겼지만, Danina Garcia-Fuller의 학생들은 조금도 그 이야기들을 믿지 않았다.

3 "몇몇 사람들은 그들이 소셜 미디어에 올라온 것들을 봤기 때문에 무서워했어요."라고 Garcia-Fuller의 학생 중 한 명인 Patricia Visoso가 말했다.

4 "하지만 그들은 이것을 누가 말하고 있는지를 전혀 확인하지 않았어요."

5 그 이야기들은 실제로 주요 신문사나 TV 방송국이 아닌 10대들이 지어냈다.

6 그들은 광대들이 정말로 학생들을 공격하려고 한다는 명백한 증거를 하나도 제공하지 않았다.

7 그 이야기는 결국 완벽한 거짓말인 것으로 드러났다.

8 "많은 사람이 단지 한 가지만을 보고 그것이 사실이라고 믿는 것 같아요."라고 Patricia의 반 친구인 Ivy-Brooks가 말했다.

9 올바른 출처를 살펴보고, 무엇이 진짜이고 무엇이 가짜인지에 주의를 기울이는 것은 정말 중요해요."

10 Garcia-Fuller의 학생들처럼, 많은 미국의 10대들은 뉴스 속 그리고 인터넷상에서 보고 있는 정보에 관해 비판적으로 생각하는 것을 배워 나가고 있다.

11 이 기능은 최근 더 중요해지고 있는데, 이야기들은 아주 빠른 속도로 퍼져 나갈 수 있고 누구나 허위 정보로 가득 찬 웹사이트를 만들어 낼 수 있기 때문이다.

12 (said / Garcia-Fuller / was / she / her / teaching / how / students / to / fake / tell / news / real / from / news.)

➡ _____

_____

13 (of / "one / first / the / is / steps / slow / to / down.)

➡ _____

14 (a / if / or / story / photo / a / too / seems / to / good / true, / be / and / think. / stop)

➡ _____

15 (there / is / evidence / any / supports / that / the / what / says? / writer)

➡ _____

16 (where / and / this / is / from?" / coming)

➡ _____

17 (students / Garcia-Fuller's / learn / also / to / how / fact / tell / from / in / opinion / news. / the)

➡ _____

_____

18 (are / "opinions / to / good / read," / 15-year-old / said / Campbell, / McKenzie / you / "but / also / you / to / have / if / check / are / they / on / based / facts.")

➡ _____

_____

19 (Garcia-Fuller / said / also / it / sometimes / be / can / hard / very / be / to / a / news / smart / reader.)

➡ _____

_____

20 (tests / she / students / her / a / with / that / website / to / appears / information / provide / an / on / called / animal / tree / octopus. / a)

➡ _____

_____

21 (site / the / full / is / information / of / this / on / animal, / with / along / few / a / photos / unclear / octopuses / of / trees. / in)

➡ _____

_____

22 (like / but / story / the / scary / of / clowns, / totally / it's / up. / made)

➡ _____

23 (lesson, / the / Garcia-Fuller / her / tells / students, / to / is / the / "check / information / seeing / you're / more / once / carefully" / to / and / everything / "question / even / that / things / say." / I)

➡ _____

_____

_____

12 Garcia-Fuller는 그녀가 자신의 학생들에게 가짜 뉴스를 진짜 뉴스로부터 구분하는 방법을 가르치고 있다고 말했다.

13 "첫 단계 중 하나는 속도를 늦추는 것(천천히 생각하는 것)입니다.

14 만약 어떤 이야기나 어떤 사진이 진짜라고 하기엔 너무 좋아 보인다면, 멈춰서 생각해 보세요.

15 글쓴이가 말하고 있는 것을 뒷받침하는 어떠한 증거라도 있나요?

16 그리고 이 정보가 어디서 온 것인가요?"

17 Garcia-Fuller의 학생들은 또한 뉴스에서 사실을 의견과 구분하는 방법에 대해서도 배운다.

18 "의견들은 읽을 만한 가치가 있습니다."라고 15살인 McKenzie Campbell이 말했다. "하지만 여러분은 그것들이 사실에 기반을 둔 것인지를 확인해 보아야 합니다."

19 Garcia-Fuller는 또한 때때로 현명한 뉴스 독자가 되는 것이 아주 어려울 수도 있다고 말했다.

20 그녀는 자신의 학생들을 '나무 문어'라는 이름의 동물에 대한 정보를 제공하는 것처럼 보이는 웹사이트로 시험한다.

21 그 사이트는 나무 위에 있는 문어들의 몇몇 불확실한 사진과 함께, 이 동물에 대한 정보로 가득 차 있다.

22 하지만 무서운 광대들의 이야기와 마찬가지로, 그것은 완전히 꾸며진 것이다.

23 Garcia-Fuller가 그녀의 학생들에게 말하는 교훈은 '당신이 보고 있는 정보를 한 번만 더 신중하게 확인해 보라'는 것과 '모든 것, 심지어 내가 말하는 것에도 의문을 가져 보라'는 것이다.

※ 다음 우리말을 영어로 쓰시오.

1 현명한 뉴스 독자가 되는 방법

➡ _____

2 2016년 10월, 무서운 광대들에 관한 이야기가 워싱턴 지역 전역의 학교에 충격을 안겼지만,
Danina Garcia-Fuller의 학생들은 조금도 그 이야기들을 믿지 않았다.

➡ _____

_____

3 "몇몇 사람들은 그들이 소셜 미디어에 올라온 것들을 봤기 때문에 무서워했어요."라고 Garcia-Fuller의
학생 중 한 명인 Patricia Visoso가 말했다.

➡ _____

_____

4 "하지만 그들은 이것을 누가 말하고 있는지를 전혀 확인하지 않았어요."

➡ _____

5 그 이야기들은 실제로 주요 신문사나 TV 방송국이 아닌 10대들이 지어냈다.

➡ _____

6 그들은 광대들이 정말로 학생들을 공격하려고 한다는 명백한 증거를 하나도 제공하지 않았다.

➡ _____

7 그 이야기는 결국 완벽한 거짓말인 것으로 드러났다.

➡ _____

8 "많은 사람이 단지 한 가지만을 보고 그것이 사실이라고 믿는 것 같아요."라고 Patricia의
반 친구인 Ivy-Brooks가 말했다.

➡ _____

9 "올바른 출처를 살펴보고, 무엇이 진짜이고 무엇이 가짜인지에 주의를 기울이는 것은 정말 중요해요."

➡ _____

10 Garcia-Fuller의 학생들처럼, 많은 미국의 10대들은 뉴스 속 그리고 인터넷상에서 보고 있는 정보에 관해
비판적으로 생각하는 것을 배워 나가고 있다.

➡ _____

_____

11 이 기능은 최근 더 중요해지고 있는데, 이야기들은 아주 빠른 속도로 퍼져 나갈 수 있고 누구나 허위 정보로
가득 찬 웹사이트를 만들어 낼 수 있기 때문이다.

➡ _____

_____

12 Garcia-Fuller는 그녀가 자신의 학생들에게 가짜 뉴스를 진짜 뉴스로부터 구분하는 방법을 가르치고 있다고 말했다.

➡ _____

13 "첫 단계 중 하나는 속도를 늦추는 것(천천히 생각하는 것)입니다.

➡ _____

14 만약 어떤 이야기나 어떤 사진이 진짜라고 하기엔 너무 좋아 보인다면, 멈춰서 생각해 보세요.

➡ _____

15 글쓴이가 말하고 있는 것을 뒷받침하는 어떠한 증거라도 있나요?

➡ _____

16 그리고 이 정보가 어디서 온 것인가요?"

➡ _____

17 Garcia-Fuller의 학생들은 또한 뉴스에서 사실을 의견과 구분하는 방법에 대해서도 배운다.

➡ _____

18 "의견들은 읽을 만한 가치가 있습니다."라고 15살인 McKenzie Campbell이 말했다. "하지만 여러분은 그것들이 사실에 기반을 둔 것인지를 확인해 보아야 합니다."

➡ _____
_____

19 Garcia-Fuller는 또한 때때로 현명한 뉴스 독자가 되는 것이 아주 어려울 수도 있다고 말했다.

➡ _____

20 그녀는 자신의 학생들을 '나무 문어'라는 이름의 동물에 대한 정보를 제공하는 것처럼 보이는 웹사이트로 시험한다.

➡ _____

21 그 사이트는 나무 위에 있는 문어들의 몇몇 불확실한 사진과 함께, 이 동물에 대한 정보로 가득 차 있다.

➡ _____
_____

22 하지만 무서운 광대들의 이야기와 마찬가지로, 그것은 완전히 꾸며진 것이다.

➡ _____

23 Garcia-Fuller가 그녀의 학생들에게 말하는 교훈은 '당신이 보고 있는 정보를 한 번만 더 신중하게 확인해 보라'는 것과 '모든 것, 심지어 내가 말하는 것에도 의문을 가져 보라'는 것이다.

➡ _____
_____

※ 다음 우리말과 일치하도록 빈칸에 알맞은 말을 쓰시오.

After You Read A

1. In October 2016, stories about scary clowns _____ schools _____ _____ _____ _____.

2. Garcia-Fuller's students also learn _____ _____ _____ _____ _____ _____ in the news.

3. The site _____ _____ _____ information on this animal, _____ _____ a few _____ _____ _____ _____ in trees.

> 1. 2016년 10월, 무서운 광대들에 관한 이야기가 워싱턴 지역 전역의 학교에 충격을 안겼다.
> 2. Garcia-Fuller의 학생들은 또한 뉴스에서 사실을 의견과 구분하는 방법에 대해서도 배운다.
> 3. 그 사이트는 나무 위에 있는 문어들의 몇몇 불확실한 사진과 함께, 이 동물에 대한 정보로 가득 차 있다.

Do It Yourself

1. Team NW _____ _____ _____ _____ _____ the school festival.

2. They _____ _____ the students and teachers _____ _____ _____ _____.

3. But they performed _____ _____ _____ _____ _____ team.

4. A lot of students _____ _____ and _____ _____ when the team danced.

5. Ms. Yu, the P.E. teacher, said it was _____ _____ _____ _____ _____.

> 1. NW 팀은 학교 축제 기간에 무대에서 춤을 선보였다.
> 2. 그들은 학생들과 선생님들이 그들의 춤을 좋아할지 확신이 서지 않았다.
> 3. 하지만 그들은 다른 어떠한 팀보다 훨씬 더 멋지게 공연을 해냈다.
> 4. 그 팀이 춤출 때 많은 학생이 일어서서 크게 환호했다.
> 5. 체육 선생님인 유 선생님은 그해 최고의 공연이라고 말씀하셨다.

Link to the World

Fact

1. This drawing, *Don Quixote*, is _____ _____ _____ _____.

2. Picasso _____ it in 1955 _____ black lines _____ _____ _____.

Opinion

3. I don't know _____ the man on the horse is _____, but he _____ _____ _____ and _____.

4. I think he _____ _____ _____ and _____.

5. I think this _____ _____ _____ _____ _____ _____ of Cervantes' novel *Don Quixote*.

> 사실
> 1. 이 그림 '돈키호테'는 피카소의 작품 중 하나이다.
> 2. 피카소는 이 그림을 1955년에 흰 배경과 대비를 이루는 검은 선들로 그렸다.
> 의견
> 3. 말 위에 올라탄 남자가 용감한지는 잘 모르겠지만, 그는 매우 피곤하고 굶주려 보인다.
> 4. 내 생각에는 그에게 약간의 음식과 물이 필요한 것 같다.
> 5. 나는 이 미술품이 세르반테스의 소설인 '돈키호테'의 가장 흥미로운 부분을 보여 주고 있다고 생각한다.

※ **다음 우리말을 영어로 쓰시오.**

After You Read A

1. 2016년 10월, 무서운 광대들에 관한 이야기가 워싱턴 지역 전역의 학교에 충격을 안겼다.

   ➡ _____

2. Garcia-Fuller의 학생들은 또한 뉴스에서 사실을 의견과 구분하는 방법에 대해서도 배운다.

   ➡ _____

3. 그 사이트는 나무 위에 있는 문어들의 몇몇 불확실한 사진과 함께, 이 동물에 대한 정보로 가득 차 있다.

   ➡ _____

Do It Yourself

1. NW 팀은 학교 축제 기간에 무대에서 춤을 선보였다.

   ➡ _____

2. 그들은 학생들과 선생님들이 그들의 춤을 좋아할지 확신이 서지 않았다.

   ➡ _____

3. 하지만 그들은 다른 어떠한 팀보다 훨씬 더 멋지게 공연을 해냈다.

   ➡ _____

4. 그 팀이 춤출 때 많은 학생이 일어서서 크게 환호했다.

   ➡ _____

5. 체육 선생님인 유 선생님은 그해 최고의 공연이라고 말씀하셨다.

   ➡ _____

Link to the World

사실

1. 이 그림 '돈키호테'는 피카소의 작품 중 하나이다.

   ➡ _____

2. 피카소는 이 그림을 1955년에 흰 배경과 대비를 이루는 검은 선들로 그렸다.

   ➡ _____

의견

3. 말 위에 올라탄 남자가 용감한지는 잘 모르겠지만, 그는 매우 피곤하고 굶주려 보인다.

   ➡ _____

4. 내 생각에는 그에게 약간의 음식과 물이 필요한 것 같다.

   ➡ _____

5. 나는 이 미술품이 세르반테스의 소설인 '돈키호테'의 가장 흥미로운 부분을 보여 주고 있다고 생각한다.

   ➡ _____

※ 다음 영어를 우리말로 쓰시오.

01 pole	22 look
02 fix	23 heater
03 weapon	24 order
04 reason	25 palace
05 situation	26 army
06 instead	27 bark
07 knowing	28 powerful
08 approach	29 gate
09 military	30 push
10 warrior	31 sword
11 injured	32 tie
12 movement	33 finally
13 patience	34 noise
14 follow	35 give up
15 stand	36 stand against
16 suddenly	37 let ~ go
17 general	38 focus on
18 above	39 calm down
19 anymore	40 sooner or later
20 happen	41 stand in line
21 yell	42 at that moment
	43 in all possible ways

※ 다음 우리말을 영어로 쓰시오.

01 정문, 대문	_____
02 군대, 군대의	_____
03 ~보다 위에	_____
04 검, 칼	_____
05 인내심, 참을성	_____
06 수리하다	_____
07 상황	_____
08 명령하다	_____
09 마침내	_____
10 더 이상	_____
11 부상당한	_____
12 장군	_____
13 기둥, 막대, 장대	_____
14 일어나다, 발생하다	_____
15 대신에	_____
16 다가가다	_____
17 참다, 견디다	_____
18 단식하다	_____
19 따르다, 따라가다	_____
20 전사	_____
21 군대, 육군	_____

22 궁, 궁전	_____
23 (개가) 짖다	_____
24 다 안다는 듯한	_____
25 표정	_____
26 승리자, 우승자	_____
27 이유	_____
28 (사람들이 조직적으로 벌이는) 운동	_____
29 소음	_____
30 무기	_____
31 소리 지르다	_____
32 강력한	_____
33 갑자기	_____
34 묶다	_____
35 곤경에 처하다	_____
36 ~에 집중하다	_____
37 조만간, 머지않아	_____
38 ~을 풀어주다, 석방하다	_____
39 그 순간에	_____
40 진정하다	_____
41 포기하다	_____
42 ~을 돌보다	_____
43 ~을 편들어, ~의 면에	_____

※ 다음 영영풀이에 알맞은 단어를 <보기>에서 골라 쓴 후, 우리말 뜻을 쓰시오.

1 _____ : to shout loudly: _____

2 _____ : to repair or correct something: _____

3 _____ : a military officer of very high rank: _____

4 _____ : to eat no food for a period of time: _____

5 _____ : the armed forces of a country: _____

6 _____ : after a long period of time: _____

7 _____ : to tell someone to do something: _____

8 _____ : to become aware of a fact or to understand it: _____

9 _____ : having physical damage to a part of the body: _____

10 _____ : being able to stay calm and not get annoyed: _____

11 _____ : having a lot of power to control people and events: _____

12 _____ : someone or something that wins a contest, prize, etc.: _____

13 _____ : to make the short loud sound that a dog makes: _____

14 _____ : the emotions and feelings that can be seen in a person's face or eyes:
    _____

15 _____ : a fact or situation which explains why something happens: _____

16 _____ : a fighter or soldier, especially one in old times who was very brave and
    experienced in fighting: _____

보기			
reason	finally	patience	order
injured	fix	powerful	yell
bark	military	look	realize
warrior	general	winner	fast

※ 다음 우리말과 일치하도록 빈칸에 알맞은 말을 쓰시오.

Get Ready 2

(1) M: We'_____ _____ _____ _____ _____ one hour, and we're still waiting.

W: _____ down! We're _____ there.

(2) G: Brrr.... _____ a cold day! I _____ standing _____ _____ in _____ _____.

B: _____ _____! Drink this _____ _____.

G: Oh, thank you so much.

(3) G: Look! That man didn't _____ _____ _____! I'm very angry.

B: _____ _____! He _____ here.

(4) B: The boy _____ me _____ _____ me. I _____ it.

G: _____ _____. He's _____ a child.

(1) M: 우리 한 시간 이상 기다렸는데 아직도 기다리고 있네.
W: 진정해! 거의 다 되어 가.

(2) G: 부르르…. 정말 추운 날이네! 나는 추운 날씨에 줄 서는 게 싫어.
B: 진정해! 이 뜨거운 우유를 마셔 봐.
G: 와, 정말 고마워.

(3) G: 저것 봐! 저 남자가 줄을 서지 않았어! 정말 화가 나.
B: 진정해! 저 사람은 여기서 일하는 사람이야.

(4) B: 내 뒤에 있는 남자아이가 자꾸 밀어. 참을 수가 없어.
G: 진정해. 아직 어린아이야.

Start Off - Listen & Talk A

1. B: What's that _____ _____?

G: They're _____ the _____.

B: I can't _____ _____ my studies _____ _____. I _____ _____ _____.

G: Calm _____! They will finish it soon.

2. G: I _____ _____ my pencil case. Have you _____ it?

B: No, I _____. Where did you _____ it?

G: I put it on my desk, but now it's _____. I'm really _____.

B: _____ down! I'll help you _____ it.

1. B: 밖에서 나는 저 소음은 뭐지?
G: 히터를 고치고 있어.
B: 공부에 전혀 집중할 수가 없잖아. 참을 수가 없어.
G: 진정해! 곧 끝날 거야.

2. G: 내 필통을 찾을 수가 없어. 내 필통 봤니?
B: 아니, 못 봤어. 어디에 뒀어?
G: 내 책상 위에 뒀는데 사라졌어. 정말 화가 나.
B: 진정해! 내가 그걸 찾는 걸 도와줄게.

Start Off - Listen & Talk B

B: Ouch! He _____ _____ my _____ again.

G: Are you _____?

B: No. This is the _____ time he _____ _____ today. I _____ _____ it. I'll go and talk to him.

G: _____ _____! He's not _____ his _____ today, so he can't see well.

B: What _____ _____ his glasses?

G: He _____ his glasses _____ a soccer game this morning.

B: I see, but he _____ _____ _____ more careful.

B: 아! 그 애가 또 내 발을 밟았어.
G: 괜찮니?
B: 아니. 이번이 오늘 그 애가 내 발을 세 번째로 밟은 거야. 참을 수가 없어. 가서 말해야겠어.
G: 진정해! 그 애는 오늘 안경을 안 쓰고 있어서 잘 볼 수가 없어.
B: 안경이 어떻게 됐는데?
G: 오늘 아침에 축구 경기를 하다가 안경을 깨뜨렸어.
B: 그렇구나. 하지만 그 애는 더 조심했어야 했어.

Start Off - Speak Up

A: I _____ _____ this place. It's too _____.

B: _____ _____! We're at the _____. Let's _____ it.

A: 나는 이 장소를 참을 수가 없어. 너무 사람이 많아.
B: 진정해! 우리는 축제에 와 있잖아. 축제를 즐기자.

Step Up - Real-life Scene

Minji: Minsu, there is no cup _____ _____ _____. _____ _____ _____ do the _____?

Minho: Sorry, but I _____ _____ _____ them.

Minji: What? You always forget _____ you _____ _____ _____. _____ it. I _____ the living room all morning.

Minho: Calm down! I'm _____ _____ my homework.

Minji: _____ the _____ first, and then do your homework.

Minho: I can't. I don't think I can _____ my homework today. Science is _____ _____ for me.

Minji: Science? You know I'_____ _____ _____ science. _____ _____ _____ you.

Minho: Great. Thanks. I'll wash your cup _____ _____ and I'll do _____ of the dishes _____ _____ this.

민지: 민수야, 내가 사용할 컵이 없어. 왜 설거지를 안 했니?
민수: 미안하지만, 설거지하는 걸 잊었어.
민지: 뭐라고? 너는 항상 해야 할 일을 잊어버리는구나. 참을 수가 없어. 나는 아침 내내 거실 청소를 했어.
민수: 진정해! 나는 숙제하느라 바빠.
민지: 설거지를 먼저 하고 난 뒤에 숙제해.
민수: 안 돼! 오늘 숙제를 끝낼 수가 없을 것 같아. 과학은 나에게 너무 어려워.
민지: 과학이라고? 너도 알겠지만 내가 과학을 잘하잖아. 내가 도와줄게.
민수: 잘됐다. 고마워. 당장 누나 컵부터 씻을게. 그리고 나머지 설거지는 숙제 끝낸 후에 할게.

Express Yourself A

1. M1: The king _____ me here. Open the door.

   M2: Wait there. The door will open _____ a _____ days.

   M1: What? A hundred days? I can't _____ a hundred days _____ _____. I _____ _____ _____.

   M2: _____ _____! _____ is an important _____ _____ in this school.

2. M1: Why did you _____ _____ _____ here? Please _____ _____ _____.

   M2: How can you _____ _____? Think.

   M1: I _____ _____ this _____. I'm not _____ or bad.

   M2: Calm down. _____ _____ you'll find a _____.

1. M1: 왕이 나를 여기에 보냈소. 문을 여시오.
   M2: 거기서 기다리시오. 100일 후 문이 열릴 것이오.
   M1: 뭐라고요? 100일이라고요? 아무것도 하지 않고 100일을 보낼 수는 없소. 참을 수가 없소.
   M2: 진정하시오! 그것이 이 학교에 들어오기 위한 중요한 규칙이오.

2. M1: 저를 왜 여기에 묶어 두셨습니까? 저를 풀어 주십시오.
   M2: 어떻게 풀려날 수 있겠느냐? 생각해 보아라.
   M1: 저는 이 푯말을 참을 수가 없습니다. 저는 위험하지도 나쁘지도 않습니다.
   M2: 진정하거라. 나는 네가 방법을 찾을 것이라고 확신한다.

Check yourself

G: What's that _____ _____?

B: A dog is _____.

G: I _____ _____ _____ my studies at all. I can't _____ _____.

B: _____ _____! He will be _____ soon.

G: 밖에서 나는 저 소음은 뭐지?
B: 개가 짖고 있는 거야.
G: 공부에 전혀 집중할 수가 없어. 참을 수가 없어.
B: 진정해! 곧 조용해질 거야.

※ 다음 우리말에 맞도록 대화를 영어로 쓰시오.

Get Ready 2

(1) M: _____
　　 W: _____

(2) G: _____
　　 B: _____
　　 G: _____

(3) G: _____
　　 B: _____

(4) B: _____
　　 G: _____

(1) M: 우리 한 시간 이상 기다렸는데 아직도 기다리고 있네.
　　 W: 진정해! 거의 다 되어 가.

(2) G: 부르르…. 정말 추운 날이네! 나는 추운 날씨에 줄 서는 게 싫어.
　　 B: 진정해! 이 뜨거운 우유를 마셔 봐.
　　 G: 와, 정말 고마워.

(3) G: 저것 봐! 저 남자가 줄을 서지 않았어! 정말 화가 나.
　　 B: 진정해! 저 사람은 여기서 일하는 사람이야.

(4) B: 내 뒤에 있는 남자아이가 자꾸 밀어. 참을 수가 없어.
　　 G: 진정해. 아직 어린아이야.

Start Off - Listen & Talk A

1. B: _____
　 G: _____
　 B: _____
　 G: _____

2. G: _____
　 B: _____
　 G: _____
　 B: _____

1. B: 밖에서 나는 저 소음은 뭐지?
　 G: 히터를 고치고 있어.
　 B: 공부에 전혀 집중할 수가 없잖아. 참을 수가 없어.
　 G: 진정해! 곧 끝날 거야.

2. G: 내 필통을 찾을 수가 없어. 내 필통 봤니?
　 B: 아니, 못 봤어. 어디에 뒀어?
　 G: 내 책상 위에 뒀는데 사라졌어. 정말 화가 나.
　 B: 진정해! 내가 그걸 찾는 걸 도와줄게.

Start Off - Listen & Talk B

B: _____
G: _____
B: _____
G: _____
B: _____
G: _____
B: _____

B: 아! 그 애가 또 내 발을 밟았어.
G: 괜찮니?
B: 아니. 이번이 오늘 그 애가 내 발을 세 번째로 밟은 거야. 참을 수가 없어. 가서 말해야겠어.
G: 진정해! 그 애는 오늘 안경을 안 쓰고 있어서 잘 볼 수가 없어.
B: 안경이 어떻게 됐는데?
G: 오늘 아침에 축구 경기를 하다가 안경을 깨뜨렸어.
B: 그렇구나. 하지만 그 애는 더 조심했어야 했어.

Start Off - Speak Up

A: _____

B: _____

A: 나는 이 장소를 참을 수가 없어. 너무 사람이 많아.
B: 진정해! 우리는 축제에 와 있잖아. 축제를 즐기자.

Step Up - Real-life Scene

Minji: _____

Minho: _____

Minji: _____

_____

Minho: _____

Minji: _____

Minho: _____

_____

Minji: _____

Minho: _____

_____

민지: 민수야, 내가 사용할 컵이 없어. 왜 설거지를 안 했니?
민수: 미안하지만, 설거지하는 걸 잊었어.
민지: 뭐라고? 너는 항상 해야 할 일을 잊어버리는구나. 참을 수가 없어. 나는 아침 내내 거실 청소를 했어.
민수: 진정해! 나는 숙제하느라 바빠.
민지: 설거지를 먼저 하고 난 뒤에 숙제해.
민수: 안 돼! 오늘 숙제를 끝낼 수가 없을 것 같아. 과학은 나에게 너무 어려워.
민지: 과학이라고? 너도 알겠지만 내가 과학을 잘하잖아. 내가 도와줄게.
민수: 잘됐다. 고마워. 당장 누나 컵부터 씻을게. 그리고 나머지 설거지는 숙제 끝낸 후에 할게.

Express Yourself A

1. M1: _____

   M2: _____

   M1: _____

   _____

   M2: _____

2. M1: _____

   M2: _____

   M1: _____

   M2: _____

1. M1: 왕이 나를 여기에 보냈소. 문을 여시오.
   M2: 거기서 기다리시오. 100일 후 문이 열릴 것이오.
   M1: 뭐라고요? 100일이라고요? 아무것도 하지 않고 100일을 보낼 수는 없소. 참을 수가 없소.
   M2: 진정하시오! 그것이 이 학교에 들어오기 위한 중요한 규칙이오.

2. M1: 저를 왜 여기에 묶어 두셨습니까? 저를 풀어 주십시오.
   M2: 어떻게 풀려날 수 있겠느냐? 생각해 보아라.
   M1: 저는 이 푯말을 참을 수가 없습니다. 저는 위험하지도 나쁘지도 않습니다.
   M2: 진정하거라. 나는 네가 방법을 찾을 것이라고 확신한다.

Check yourself

G: _____

B: _____

G: _____

B: _____

G: 밖에서 나는 저 소음은 뭐지?
B: 개가 짖고 있는 거야.
G: 공부에 전혀 집중할 수가 없어. 참을 수가 없어.
B: 진정해! 곧 조용해질 거야.

※ 다음 우리말과 일치하도록 빈칸에 알맞은 것을 골라 쓰시오.

1 Corky, _____ _____ _____

　　A. Warrior　　　　B. Best　　　　C. the

2 Corky was a _____ _____ _____.

　　A. young　　　　B. brave　　　　C. man

3 He wanted to be a _____, but the king said, "You're the _____ man in my _____, but you have _____ to learn."

　　A. strongest　　B. general　　C. army　　D. much

4 He _____ Corky _____ go to a _____ _____ school.

　　A. military　　B. ordered　　C. famous　　D. to

5 "Wait there. in a _____ days, your _____ will start," a _____ said from inside the school _____.

　　A. training　　B. gate　　C. hundred　　D. voice

6 Corky _____ _____.

　　A. angry　　　　B. got

7 But then he _____ there _____ be a _____, so he _____.

　　A. reason　　B. thought　　C. might　　D. waited

8 On the _____ and _____ day, the _____ _____.

　　A. first　　B. opened　　C. hundred　　D. gate

9 An old man said, "You have _____ to _____ your first _____: _____.

　　A. patience　　B. learned　　C. weapon　　D. use

10 _____ is the _____ important _____ to _____ a war."

　　A. win　　B. patience　　C. thing　　D. most

11 _____, the teacher told Corky to _____ _____ a _____.

　　A. against　　B. then　　C. pole　　D. stand

12 _____, he _____ Corky _____ the _____.

　　A. pole　　B. suddenly　　C. to　　D. tied

13 _____ his head, he _____ a sign that _____ " _____ and Bad."

　　A. dangerous　　B. above　　C. read　　D. put

14 Many people _____ _____.

　　A. by　　　　B. passed

1　최고의 전사, Corky

2　Corky는 용감한 청년이었다.

3　그는 장군이 되기를 원했지만 왕은 이렇게 말했다. "자네는 우리 군대에서 가장 강한 전사이네. 하지만 자네는 아직도 배울 게 많아."

4　왕은 Corky에게 유명한 군사 학교에 갈 것을 명령했다.

5　"거기서 기다려라. 훈련은 100일 후에 시작할 것이다." 군사 학교 안에서 이렇게 외치는 목소리가 들렸다.

6　Corky는 화가 났다.

7　하지만 이유가 있을 것으로 생각하고 기다렸다.

8　101일째 되던 날, 문이 열렸다.

9　한 노인이 이렇게 말했다. "너는 첫 번째 무기인 '인내'를 사용하는 법을 배운 것이다.

10　인내는 전쟁에서 이기기 위해 가장 중요한 것이다."

11　그리고 난 뒤, 스승은 Corky에게 기둥 앞에 서라고 말했다.

12　갑자기 그는 Corky를 기둥에 묶었다.

13　그의 머리 위에는 '위험하고 나쁨'이라는 푯말을 붙였다.

14　많은 사람이 지나갔다.

15 _____ gave Corky angry _____, and _____ _____ at him.

A. others   B. some   C. looks   D. shouted

16 Corky _____ _____.

A. back   B. shouted

17 He _____, "_____ me _____, or you all will be in big _____!"

A. trouble   B. yelled   C. free   D. set

18 That _____ the _____ _____.

A. worse   B. made   C. situation

19 "I need to _____ _____ _____," he _____.

A. thought   B. another   C. try   D. way

20 _____, Corky began to _____ _____.

A. speak   B. then   C. softly

21 He said he was _____ or _____ _____ was a good man.

A. but   B. bad   C. dangerous   D. not

22 He _____ _____ this in all _____ _____.

A. possible   B. kept   C. ways   D. saying

23 Finally, the people _____ _____ _____.

A. let   B. go   C. him

24 "Now you control _____ _____ _____ _____: words.

A. weapon   B. most   C. the   D. powerful

25 Soft _____ are _____ sharp _____," said the teacher.

A. swords   B. words   C. than   D. stronger

26 Next, the teacher _____ Corky _____ a large hall _____ a chair in the _____.

A. with   B. took   C. middle   D. to

27 There were 19 _____ _____ who _____ _____ their tests.

A. warriors   B. passed   C. other   D. had

28 "The _____ _____ _____ _____ in the chair will be the winner," the teacher said.

A. to   B. one   C. sit   D. first

29 Corky and _____ _____ began _____.

A. fighting   B. others   C. the

30 They _____, _____, ran, and _____.

A. jumped   B. pulled   C. pushed

15 몇몇은 Corky를 화난 표정으로 쳐다봤고, 다른 몇몇은 그에게 소리를 질렀다.

16 Corky도 그들에게 소리를 질렀다.

17 그는 "나를 풀어 줘. 그러지 않으면 모두 혼쭐날 줄 알아!"라고 외쳤다.

18 그것은 상황을 더 악화시켰다.

19 그는 '다른 방법을 써야겠어.'라고 생각했다.

20 그러고 나서 Corky는 부드럽게 말하기 시작했다.

21 그는 자신이 위험하거나 나쁘지 않고 좋은 사람이라고 말했다.

22 그는 모든 방법을 동원해 계속해서 이렇게 말했다.

23 마침내 사람들은 그를 풀어 주었다.

24 "이제 너는 가장 강력한 무기인 '말'을 통제하게 되었다.

25 부드러운 말은 날카로운 칼보다 강하니라."라고 스승은 말했다.

26 다음 단계로 스승은 Corky를 중앙에 의자가 놓여 있는 커다란 홀로 데리고 갔다.

27 그곳에는 시험에 통과한 19명의 다른 전사들이 있었다.

28 "저 의자에 가장 먼저 앉는 사람이 승자가 될 것이다."라고 스승이 말했다.

29 Corky와 나머지 전사들은 싸우기 시작했다.

30 그들은 밀고 당기고 달리고 뛰어올랐다.

31 They _____ harder and _____, so Corky _____ _____.

    A. harder   B. tired   C. fought   D. became

32 _____, he said, "I will not _____ _____.

    A. anymore   B. finally   C. fight

33 _____, I will _____ _____ of the _____."

    A. injured   B. instead   C. care   D. take

34 The _____ _____ saw this and fought _____ _____.

    A. harder   B. warriors   C. even   D. other

35 _____ they _____, more _____ became tired and _____.

    A. warriors   B. fought   C. as   D. hurt

36 Corky took good _____ _____ them, _____ they _____ him.

    A. followed   B. care   C. so   D. of

37 Soon, _____ the _____ _____ Thunder were _____ Corky.

    A. following   B. all   C. except   D. warriors

38 Thunder _____ _____ the chair to _____ _____ it.

    A. toward   B. sit   C. walked   D. in

39 Then, he _____ Corky _____ _____ his 18 _____.

    A. followers   B. saw   C. with   D. standing

40 Thunder _____ he was _____ _____.

    A. all   B. realized   C. alone

41 "I _____ _____. You're the _____ _____," Thunder said to Corky.

    A. winner   B. up   C. real   D. give

42 At that _____, the teacher _____ and said. "Of all the great _____, peace is my _____.

    A. appeared   B. weapons   C. moment   D. favorite

43 _____ or _____, everyone wants to stand on the _____ of _____."

    A. side   B. later   C. sooner   D. peace

44 Corky _____ to the _____ after his _____ _____.

    A. palace   B. ended   C. returned   D. training

45 When the king saw him _____, he gave Corky a _____ and _____ smile and said, "What's _____, General?"

    A. knowing   B. up   C. approach   D. wise

31 그들은 점점 더 격렬히 싸웠고, Corky는 지쳤다.

32 마침내 그가 말했다. "나는 더는 싸움을 하지 않겠다.

33 대신에 부상당한 자들을 돌볼 것이다."

34 나머지 전사들은 이것을 보고 더 심하게 싸움을 했다.

35 그들이 싸움을 할수록 더 많은 전사들이 지치고 다쳤다.

36 Corky는 그들을 잘 돌봐 주었고, 그들은 Corky를 따르게 되었다.

37 곧 Thunder를 제외한 모든 전사들이 Corky를 따르고 있었다.

38 Thunder는 의자로 걸어가 그곳에 앉으려 했다.

39 그러다 그는 Corky가 18명의 추종자들과 함께 서 있는 것을 봤다.

40 Thunder는 자신이 혼자라는 사실을 깨달았다.

41 "나는 포기하겠다. 네가 진정한 승자다."라고 Thunder가 Corky에게 말했다.

42 그때 스승이 나타나 말했다. "모든 훌륭한 무기 중에서 평화는 내가 가장 좋아하는 것이다.

43 조만간 모든 사람은 평화의 편에 서기를 원한다."

44 Corky는 훈련을 마친 후 성으로 돌아갔다.

45 Corky가 다가오는 것을 본 왕은 그에게 이미 모든 것을 알고 있다는 듯한 현명한 미소를 띠며 말했다. "안녕하시오, 장군?"

※ 다음 우리말과 일치하도록 빈칸에 알맞은 것을 골라 쓰시오.

1 Corky, _____ _____ _____

2 Corky was a _____ _____ _____ .

3 He wanted to be a _____ , but the king said, "You're _____ _____ _____ in my army, but you _____ _____ _____ _____ ."

4 He _____ Corky _____ _____ to a famous military school.

5 "Wait there. _____ _____ _____ _____ , your training will start," a _____ _____ from inside the school gate.

6 Corky _____ _____ .

7 But then he thought there _____ _____ _____ _____ , _____ he _____ .

8 _____ _____ _____ _____ _____ , the gate opened.

9 An old man said, "You _____ _____ to use your _____ _____ : _____ .

10 Patience is the most important thing _____ _____ _____ ."

11 Then, the teacher told Corky _____ _____ _____ a pole.

12 _____ , he _____ Corky _____ the pole.

13 _____ his head, he put a sign _____ _____ "Dangerous and Bad."

14 Many people _____ _____ .

---

1 최고의 전사, Corky

2 Corky는 용감한 청년이었다.

3 그는 장군이 되기를 원했지만 왕은 이렇게 말했다. "자네는 우리 군대에서 가장 강한 전사이네. 하지만 자네는 아직도 배울 게 많아."

4 왕은 Corky에게 유명한 군사 학교에 갈 것을 명령했다.

5 "거기서 기다려라. 훈련은 100일 후에 시작할 것이다." 군사 학교 안에서 이렇게 외치는 목소리가 들렸다.

6 Corky는 화가 났다.

7 하지만 이유가 있을 것으로 생각하고 기다렸다.

8 101일째 되던 날, 문이 열렸다.

9 한 노인이 이렇게 말했다. "너는 첫 번째 무기인 '인내'를 사용하는 법을 배운 것이다.

10 인내는 전쟁에서 이기기 위해 가장 중요한 것이다."

11 그리고 난 뒤, 스승은 Corky에게 기둥 앞에 서라고 말했다.

12 갑자기 그는 Corky를 기둥에 묶었다.

13 그의 머리 위에는 '위험하고 나쁨'이라는 푯말을 붙였다.

14 많은 사람이 지나갔다.

15 _____ gave Corky _____ _____, and _____ shouted at him.

16 Corky _____ _____.

17 He yelled, "_____ _____ _____, _____ you all will be _____ _____ _____!"

18 That _____ the situation _____.

19 "I need to try _____ way," he _____.

20 Then, Corky _____ _____ _____ _____.

21 He said he was _____ dangerous or bad _____ was a good man.

22 He _____ _____ this in _____ _____ _____.

23 _____, the people _____ _____ _____ _____.

24 "Now you control _____ _____ _____ _____: words.

25 Soft words are _____ _____ _____ _____," said the teacher.

26 Next, the teacher _____ Corky _____ a large hall with a chair _____ _____ _____.

27 There were 19 _____ warriors who _____ _____ their tests.

28 "_____ _____ _____ _____ sit in the chair will be the _____," the teacher said.

29 Corky and _____ _____ _____ _____ _____.

30 They _____, _____, ran, and _____.

15 몇몇은 Corky를 화난 표정으로 쳐다봤고, 다른 몇몇은 그에게 소리를 질렀다.

16 Corky도 그들에게 소리를 질렀다.

17 그는 "나를 풀어 줘. 그러지 않으면 모두 혼쭐날 줄 알아!"라고 외쳤다.

18 그것은 상황을 더 악화시켰다.

19 그는 '다른 방법을 써야겠어.'라고 생각했다.

20 그러고 나서 Corky는 부드럽게 말하기 시작했다.

21 그는 자신이 위험하거나 나쁘지 않고 좋은 사람이라고 말했다.

22 그는 모든 방법을 동원해 계속해서 이렇게 말했다.

23 마침내 사람들은 그를 풀어 주었다.

24 "이제 너는 가장 강력한 무기인 '말'을 통제하게 되었다.

25 부드러운 말은 날카로운 칼보다 강하니라."라고 스승은 말했다.

26 다음 단계로 스승은 Corky를 중앙에 의자가 놓여 있는 커다란 홀로 데리고 갔다.

27 그곳에는 시험에 통과한 19명의 다른 전사들이 있었다.

28 "저 의자에 가장 먼저 앉는 사람이 승자가 될 것이다."라고 스승이 말했다.

29 Corky와 나머지 전사들은 싸우기 시작했다.

30 그들은 밀고 당기고 달리고 뛰어올랐다.

31 They fought _____ _____ _____, so Corky _____ _____.

32 Finally, he said, "I will not fight _____.

33 Instead, I will _____ _____ _____ _____ _____."

34 The _____ _____ saw this and fought _____ _____.

35 _____ they fought, more warriors _____ _____ and _____.

36 Corky _____ _____ _____ them, so they followed him.

37 Soon, all the warriors _____ Thunder were _____ Corky.

38 Thunder _____ _____ the chair _____ _____ _____ _____.

39 Then, he saw Corky _____ _____ his 18 followers.

40 Thunder realized he was _____ _____.

41 "I _____ _____. You're _____ _____ _____," Thunder said to Corky.

42 _____ _____ _____, the teacher _____ and said. "Of all the great weapons, peace is _____ _____.

43 _____ _____ _____, everyone wants to stand _____ _____ _____ _____ peace."

44 Corky _____ _____ the palace after his training ended.

45 When the king saw him _____, he gave Corky a wise and _____ smile and said, "_____ _____, General?"

---

31 그들은 점점 더 격렬히 싸웠고, Corky는 지쳤다.

32 마침내 그가 말했다. "나는 더는 싸움을 하지 않겠다.

33 대신에 부상당한 자들을 돌볼 것이다."

34 나머지 전사들은 이것을 보고 더 심하게 싸움을 했다.

35 그들이 싸움을 할수록 더 많은 전사들이 지치고 다쳤다.

36 Corky는 그들을 잘 돌봐 주었고, 그들은 Corky를 따르게 되었다.

37 곧 Thunder를 제외한 모든 전사들이 Corky를 따르고 있었다.

38 Thunder는 의자로 걸어가 그곳에 앉으려 했다.

39 그러다 그는 Corky가 18명의 추종자들과 함께 서 있는 것을 봤다.

40 Thunder는 자신이 혼자라는 사실을 깨달았다.

41 "나는 포기하겠다. 네가 진정한 승자다."라고 Thunder가 Corky에게 말했다.

42 그때 스승이 나타나 말했다. "모든 훌륭한 무기 중에서 평화는 내가 가장 좋아하는 것이다.

43 조만간 모든 사람은 평화의 편에 서기를 원한다."

44 Corky는 훈련을 마친 후 성으로 돌아갔다.

45 Corky가 다가오는 것을 본 왕은 그에게 이미 모든 것을 알고 있다는 듯한 현명한 미소를 띠며 말했다. "안녕하시오, 장군?"

※ 다음 문장을 우리말로 쓰시오.

1 Corky, the Best Warrior

➡ _____

2 Corky was a brave young man.

➡ _____

3 He wanted to be a general, but the king said, "You're the strongest man in my army, but you

have much to learn."

➡ _____

_____

4 He ordered Corky to go to a famous military school.

➡ _____

5 "Wait there. In a hundred days, your training will start," a voice said from inside the school gate.

➡ _____

6 Corky got angry.

➡ _____

7 But then he thought there might be a reason, so he waited.

➡ _____

8 On the hundred and first day, the gate opened.

➡ _____

9 An old man said, "You have learned to use your first weapon: patience.

➡ _____

10 Patience is the most important thing to win a war."

➡ _____

11 Then, the teacher told Corky to stand against a pole.

➡ _____

12 Suddenly, he tied Corky to the pole.

➡ _____

13 Above his head, he put a sign that read "Dangerous and Bad."

➡ _____

14 ▸ Many people passed by.

➡ _____

15 ▸ Some gave Corky angry looks, and others shouted at him.

➡ _____

16 ▸ Corky shouted back.

➡ _____

17 ▸ He yelled, "Set me free, or you all will be in big trouble!"

➡ _____

18 ▸ That made the situation worse.

➡ _____

19 ▸ "I need to try another way," he thought.

➡ _____

20 ▸ Then, Corky began to speak softly.

➡ _____

21 ▸ He said he was not dangerous or bad but was a good man.

➡ _____

22 ▸ He kept saying this in all possible ways.

➡ _____

23 ▸ Finally, the people let him go.

➡ _____

24 ▸ "Now you control the most powerful weapon: words.

➡ _____

25 ▸ Soft words are stronger than sharp swords," said the teacher.

➡ _____

26 ▸ Next, the teacher took Corky to a large hall with a chair in the middle.

➡ _____

27 ▸ There were 19 other warriors who had passed their tests.

➡ _____

28 ▸ "The first one to sit in the chair will be the winner," the teacher said.

➡ _____

29 ▸ Corky and the others began fighting.

➡ _____

30 ▸ They pushed, pulled, ran, and jumped.

➡ _____

31 They fought harder and harder, so Corky became tired.

➡ _____

32 Finally, he said, "I will not fight anymore.

➡ _____

33 Instead, I will take care of the injured."

➡ _____

34 The other warriors saw this and fought even harder.

➡ _____

35 As they fought, more warriors became tired and hurt.

➡ _____

36 Corky took good care of them, so they followed him.

➡ _____

37 Soon, all the warriors except Thunder were following Corky.

➡ _____

38 Thunder walked toward the chair to sit in it.

➡ _____

39 Then, he saw Corky standing with his 18 followers.

➡ _____

40 Thunder realized he was all alone.

➡ _____

41 "I give up. You're the real winner," Thunder said to Corky.

➡ _____

42 At that moment, the teacher appeared and said. "Of all the great weapons, peace is my favorite.

➡ _____

43 Sooner or later, everyone wants to stand on the side of peace."

➡ _____

44 Corky returned to the palace after his training ended.

➡ _____

45 When the king saw him approach, he gave Corky a wise and knowing smile and said, "What's up, General?"

➡ _____

※ 다음 괄호 안의 단어들을 우리말에 맞도록 바르게 배열하시오.

1 (the / Corky, / Warrior / Best)
➡ _____

2 (was / Corky / brave / a / man. / young)
➡ _____

3 (wanted / he / be / to / general, / a / the / but / said, / king / the / "you're / man / strongest / my / in / army, / you / but / much / have / learn." / to)
➡ _____

4 (ordered / he / to / Corky / to / go / famous / a / school. / military)
➡ _____

5 (there. / "wait // a / in / days, / hundred / training / your / start," / will / voice / a / from / said / inside / school / the / gate.)
➡ _____
_____

6 (got / Corky / angry.)
➡ _____

7 (then / but / thought / he / might / there / a / be / reason, / he / so / waited.)
➡ _____

8 (the / on / hundred / first / and / day, / gate / the / opened.)
➡ _____

9 (old / an / said, / man / have / "you / learned / use / to / first / your / patience. / weapon:)
➡ _____

10 (is / patience / most / the / thing / important / win / to / war." / a)
➡ _____

11 (the / then, / told / teacher / to / Corky / against / stand / pole. / a)
➡ _____

12 (he / suddenly, / Corky / tied / to / pole. / the)
➡ _____

13 (his / above / head, / put / he / sign / a / read / that / Bad." / and / "Dangerous)
➡ _____

14 (people / many / by. / passed)
➡ _____

---

1 최고의 전사, Corky

2 Corky는 용감한 청년이었다.

3 그는 장군이 되기를 원했지만 왕은 이렇게 말했다. "자네는 우리 군대에서 가장 강한 전사이네. 하지만 자네는 아직도 배울 게 많아."

4 왕은 Corky에게 유명한 군사 학교에 갈 것을 명령했다.

5 "거기서 기다려라. 훈련은 100일 후에 시작할 것이다." 군사 학교 안에서 이렇게 외치는 목소리가 들렸다.

6 Corky는 화가 났다.

7 하지만 이유가 있을 것으로 생각하고 기다렸다.

8 101일째 되던 날, 문이 열렸다.

9 한 노인이 이렇게 말했다. "너는 첫 번째 무기인 '인내'를 사용하는 법을 배운 것이다.

10 인내는 전쟁에서 이기기 위해 가장 중요한 것이다."

11 그리고 난 뒤, 스승은 Corky에게 기둥 앞에 서라고 말했다.

12 갑자기 그는 Corky를 기둥에 묶었다.

13 그의 머리 위에는 '위험하고 나쁨'이라는 푯말을 붙였다.

14 많은 사람이 지나갔다.

15 (gave / some / angry / Corky / looks, / others / and / at / shouted / him.)

➡ _____

16 (shouted / Corky / back.)

➡ _____

17 (yelled, / he / me / "set / or / free, / all / you / be / will / big / in / trouble!")

➡ _____

18 (made / that / situation / the / worse.)

➡ _____

19 (need / "I / to / another / try / way," / thought. / he)

➡ _____

20 (Corky / then, / to / began / softly. / speak)

➡ _____

21 (said / he / was / he / not / or / dangerous / but / bad / a / was / man. / good)

➡ _____

22 (kept / he / this / saying / all / in / ways. / possible)

➡ _____

23 (the / finally, / let / people / go. / him)

➡ _____

24 (you / "now / the / control / powerful / most / words. / weapon:)

➡ _____

25 (words / soft / stronger / are / sharp / than / said / swords," / teacher. / the)

➡ _____

26 (the / next, / took / teacher / to / Corky / a / hall / large / with / chair / a / the / in / middle.)

➡ _____

27 (were / there / other / 19 / who / warriors / passed / had / tests. / their)

➡ _____

28 (first / "the / to / one / in / sit / chair / the / be / will / winner," / the / teacher / the / said.)

➡ _____

29 (Corky / the / and / others / fighting. / began)

➡ _____

30 (pushed, / they / ran, / pulled, / jumped. / and)

➡ _____

15 몇몇은 Corky를 화난 표정으로 쳐다봤고, 다른 몇몇은 그에게 소리를 질렀다.

16 Corky도 그들에게 소리를 질렀다.

17 그는 "나를 풀어 줘. 그러지 않으면 모두 혼쭐날 줄 알아!"라고 외쳤다.

18 그것은 상황을 더 악화시켰다.

19 그는 '다른 방법을 써야겠어.'라고 생각했다.

20 그러고 나서 Corky는 부드럽게 말하기 시작했다.

21 그는 자신이 위험하거나 나쁘지 않고 좋은 사람이라고 말했다.

22 그는 모든 방법을 동원해 계속해서 이렇게 말했다.

23 마침내 사람들은 그를 풀어 주었다.

24 "이제 너는 가장 강력한 무기인 '말'을 통제하게 되었다.

25 부드러운 말은 날카로운 칼보다 강하니라."라고 스승은 말했다.

26 다음 단계로 스승은 Corky를 중앙에 의자가 놓여 있는 커다란 홀로 데리고 갔다.

27 그곳에는 시험에 통과한 19명의 다른 전사들이 있었다.

28 "저 의자에 가장 먼저 앉는 사람이 승자가 될 것이다."라고 스승이 말했다.

29 Corky와 나머지 전사들은 싸우기 시작했다.

30 그들은 밀고 당기고 달리고 뛰어올랐다.

31 (fought / they / and / harder / so / harder, / became / Corky / tired.)

➡ _____

32 (he / finally, / said, / will / "I / fight / not / anymore.)

➡ _____

33 (I / instead, / take / will / of / care / injured." / the)

➡ _____

34 (other / the / saw / warriors / this / and / even / fought / harder.)

➡ _____

35 (they / as / fought, / warriors / more / tired / became / hurt. / and)

➡ _____

36 (took / Corky / care / good / them, / of / they / so / him. / followed)

➡ _____

37 (all / soon, / the / except / warriors / were / Thunder / Corky. / following)

➡ _____

38 (walked / Thunder / the / toward / to / chair / sit / it. / in)

➡ _____

39 (he / then, / Corky / saw / with / standing / 18 / his / followers.)

➡ _____

40 (realized / Thunder / was / he / alone. / all)

➡ _____

41 (give / "I / up. // the / you're / winner," / real / said / Thunder / Corky. / to)

➡ _____

42 (that / at / moment, / teacher / the / and / appeared / said. // "of / the / all / weapons, / great / is / peace / favorite. / my)

➡ _____

43 (later, / or / sooner / wants / everyone / stand / to / the / on / of / side / peace.")

➡ _____

44 (returned / Corky / the / to / after / palace / training / his / ended.)

➡ _____

45 (the / when / saw / king / approach, / him / gave / he / Corky / wise / a / knowing / and / and / smile / said, / up, / General?" / "what's)

➡ _____

31 그들은 점점 더 격렬히 싸웠고, Corky는 지쳤다.
32 마침내 그가 말했다. "나는 더는 싸움을 하지 않겠다.
33 대신에 부상당한 자들을 돌볼 것이다."
34 나머지 전사들은 이것을 보고 더 심하게 싸움을 했다.
35 그들이 싸움을 할수록 더 많은 전사들이 지치고 다쳤다.
36 Corky는 그들을 잘 돌봐 주었고, 그들은 Corky를 따르게 되었다.
37 곧 Thunder를 제외한 모든 전사들이 Corky를 따르고 있었다.
38 Thunder는 의자로 걸어가 그곳에 앉으려 했다.
39 그러다 그는 Corky가 18명의 추종자들과 함께 서 있는 것을 봤다.
40 Thunder는 자신이 혼자라는 사실을 깨달았다.
41 "나는 포기하겠다. 네가 진정한 승자다."라고 Thunder가 Corky에게 말했다.
42 그때 스승이 나타나 말했다. "모든 훌륭한 무기 중에서 평화는 내가 가장 좋아하는 것이다.
43 조만간 모든 사람은 평화의 편에 서기를 원한다."
44 Corky는 훈련을 마친 후 성으로 돌아갔다.
45 Corky가 다가오는 것을 본 왕은 그에게 이미 모든 것을 알고 있다는 듯한 현명한 미소를 띠며 말했다. "안녕하시오, 장군?"

※ 다음 우리말을 영어로 쓰시오.

1 최고의 전사, Corky

➡ _____

2 Corky는 용감한 청년이었다.

➡ _____

3 그는 장군이 되기를 원했지만 왕은 이렇게 말했다. "자네는 우리 군대에서 가장 강한 전사이네. 하지만 자네는 아직도 배울 게 많아."

➡ _____

_____

4 왕은 Corky에게 유명한 군사 학교에 갈 것을 명령했다.

➡ _____

5 "거기서 기다려라. 훈련은 100일 후에 시작할 것이다." 군사 학교 안에서 이렇게 외치는 목소리가 들렸다.

➡ _____

6 Corky는 화가 났다.

➡ _____

7 하지만 이유가 있을 것으로 생각하고 기다렸다.

➡ _____

8 101일째 되던 날, 문이 열렸다.

➡ _____

9 한 노인이 이렇게 말했다. "너는 첫 번째 무기인 '인내'를 사용하는 법을 배운 것이다.

➡ _____

10 인내는 전쟁에서 이기기 위해 가장 중요한 것이다."

➡ _____

11 그리고 난 뒤, 스승은 Corky에게 기둥 앞에 서라고 말했다.

➡ _____

12 갑자기 그는 Corky를 기둥에 묶었다.

➡ _____

13 그의 머리 위에는 '위험하고 나쁨'이라는 푯말을 붙였다.

➡ _____

14 많은 사람이 지나갔다.

➡ _____

15 몇몇은 Corky를 화난 표정으로 쳐다봤고, 다른 몇몇은 그에게 소리를 질렀다.

➡ _____

16 Corky도 그들에게 소리를 질렀다.

➡ _____

17 그는 "나를 풀어 줘. 그러지 않으면 모두 혼쭐날 줄 알아!"라고 외쳤다.

➡ _____

18 그것은 상황을 더 악화시켰다.

➡ _____

19 그는 '다른 방법을 써야겠어.'라고 생각했다.

➡ _____

20 그러고 나서 Corky는 부드럽게 말하기 시작했다.

➡ _____

21 그는 자신이 위험하거나 나쁘지 않고 좋은 사람이라고 말했다.

➡ _____

22 그는 모든 방법을 동원해 계속해서 이렇게 말했다.

➡ _____

23 마침내 사람들은 그를 풀어 주었다.

➡ _____

24 "이제 너는 가장 강력한 무기인 '말'을 통제하게 되었다.

➡ _____

25 부드러운 말은 날카로운 칼보다 강하니라."라고 스승은 말했다.

➡ _____

26 다음 단계로 스승은 Corky를 중앙에 의자가 놓여 있는 커다란 홀로 데리고 갔다.

➡ _____

27 그곳에는 시험에 통과한 19명의 다른 전사들이 있었다.

➡ _____

28 "저 의자에 가장 먼저 앉는 사람이 승자가 될 것이다."라고 스승이 말했다.

➡ _____

29 Corky와 나머지 전사들은 싸우기 시작했다.

➡ _____

30 그들은 밀고 당기고 달리고 뛰어올랐다.

➡ _____

31 그들은 점점 더 격렬히 싸웠고, Corky는 지쳤다.

➡ _____

32 마침내 그가 말했다. "나는 더는 싸움을 하지 않겠다.

➡ _____

33 대신에 부상당한 자들을 돌볼 것이다."

➡ _____

34 나머지 전사들은 이것을 보고 더 심하게 싸움을 했다.

➡ _____

35 그들이 싸움을 할수록 더 많은 전사들이 지치고 다쳤다.

➡ _____

36 Corky는 그들을 잘 돌봐 주었고, 그들은 Corky를 따르게 되었다.

➡ _____

37 곧 Thunder를 제외한 모든 전사들이 Corky를 따르고 있었다.

➡ _____

38 Thunder는 의자로 걸어가 그곳에 앉으려 했다.

➡ _____

39 그러다 그는 Corky가 18명의 추종자들과 함께 서 있는 것을 봤다.

➡ _____

40 Thunder는 자신이 혼자라는 사실을 깨달았다.

➡ _____

41 "나는 포기하겠다. 네가 진정한 승자다."라고 Thunder가 Corky에게 말했다.

➡ _____

42 그때 스승이 나타나 말했다. "모든 훌륭한 무기 중에서 평화는 내가 가장 좋아하는 것이다.

➡ _____

_____

43 조만간 모든 사람은 평화의 편에 서기를 원한다."

➡ _____

44 Corky는 훈련을 마친 후 성으로 돌아갔다.

➡ _____

45 Corky가 다가오는 것을 본 왕은 그에게 이미 모든 것을 알고 있다는 듯한 현명한 미소를 띠며 말했다.
"안녕하시오, 장군?"

➡ _____

_____

※ 다음 우리말과 일치하도록 빈칸에 알맞은 말을 쓰시오.

After You Read A

1. Corky _____ _____ _____ _____ _____ in the army.

2. Corky went to _____ _____ _____ and waited _____ _____ _____ _____.

3. Corky _____ _____ he was not _____, so people finally _____ him _____.

4. Corky _____ _____ and took care of _____ _____.

1. Corky는 군대에서 장군이 되기를 원했다.
2. Corky는 군사 학교에 가서 100일 동안 기다렸다.
3. Corky는 계속해서 자신이 위험하지 [나쁘지] 않다고 말해서, 사람들이 마침내 그를 풀어 주었다.
4. Corky는 싸움을 멈추고 부상당한 자들을 돌보아주었다.

Inside the Story

1. Two people _____ _____ in the hall. _____ is the king, and _____ _____ is Corky.

2. The king _____ Corky _____ _____ _____ _____ _____.

3. Many people are standing around Corky. _____ is talking to Corky, _____ _____ _____ _____.

4. The teacher _____ _____ _____ _____ _____ and _____ there.

5. Two men are standing inside the gate. _____ is holding a _____, and _____ _____ _____ _____ _____ _____ _____.

6. _____ _____ _____ _____ _____ tells Corky _____ _____ there for 100 days.

7. Many warriors are listening to the teacher. _____ are standing, and _____ _____ _____ _____.

8. The teacher wants them _____ _____ _____ _____ _____ _____ the chair.

1. 두 사람이 홀에서 말하고 있다. 한 사람은 왕이고 나머지 한 사람은 Corky이다.
2. 왕은 Corky에게 군사 학교로 가라고 명령한다.
3. 많은 사람이 Corky 주변에 서 있다. 한 사람은 Corky에게 말하고 있고 나머지 사람들은 듣고 있다.
4. 스승은 Corky에게 조용히 하고 거기 있으라고 말한다.
5. 두 남자가 문 안에 서 있다. 한 명은 칼을 들고 있고 나머지 한 명은 곤봉을 들고 있다.
6. 칼을 들고 있는 남자는 Corky에게 100일 동안 거기서 기다리라고 말한다.
7. 많은 전사가 스승의 말을 듣고 있다. 몇몇은 서 있고 나머지는 무릎을 꿇고 있다.
8. 스승은 그들이 의자에 앉기 위해 계속 싸우기를 원한다.

Link to the World

1. Mahatma Gandhi led a _____ _____ _____ _____ _____.

2. He _____ his people _____ _____ _____ England.

3. He _____ for a long time _____ _____ _____ _____ with weapons.

4. "_____ _____ _____ _____ _____ will only _____ the whole world _____," he said.

1. 마하트마 간디는 인도를 해방하기 위한 평화 운동을 이끌었다.
2. 그는 그의 국민들에게 영국에 대항하여 평화롭게 싸울 것을 요청했다.
3. 그는 무기를 들고 싸우는 대신 오랫동안 단식 투쟁을 했다.
4. "눈에는 눈이라는 식의 복수는 오직 전 세계를 눈멀게 할 뿐이다."라고 그는 말했다.

※ 다음 우리말을 영어로 쓰시오.

After You Read A

1. Corky는 군대에서 장군이 되기를 원했다.
   ➡ _____

2. Corky는 군사 학교에 가서 100일 동안 기다렸다.
   ➡ _____

3. Corky는 계속해서 자신이 위험하지[나쁘지] 않다고 말해서, 사람들이 마침내 그를 풀어 주었다.
   ➡ _____

4. Corky는 싸움을 멈추고 부상당한 자들을 돌보아주었다.
   ➡ _____

Inside the Story

1. 두 사람이 홀에서 말하고 있다. 한 사람은 왕이고 나머지 한 사람은 Corky이다.
   ➡ _____

2. 왕은 Corky에게 군사 학교로 가라고 명령한다.
   ➡ _____

3. 많은 사람이 Corky 주변에 서 있다. 한 사람은 Corky에게 말하고 있고 나머지 사람들은 듣고 있다.
   ➡ _____

4. 스승은 Corky에게 조용히 하고 거기 있으라고 말한다.
   ➡ _____

5. 두 남자가 문 안에 서 있다. 한 명은 칼을 들고 있고 나머지 한 명은 곤봉을 들고 있다.
   ➡ _____

6. 칼을 들고 있는 남자는 Corky에게 100일 동안 거기서 기다리라고 말한다.
   ➡ _____

7. 많은 전사가 스승의 말을 듣고 있다. 몇몇은 서 있고 나머지는 무릎을 꿇고 있다.
   ➡ _____

8. 스승은 그들이 의자에 앉기 위해 계속 싸우기를 원한다.
   ➡ _____

Link to the World

1. 마하트마 간디는 인도를 해방하기 위한 평화 운동을 이끌었다.
   ➡ _____

2. 그는 그의 국민들에게 영국에 대항하여 평화롭게 싸울 것을 요청했다.
   ➡ _____

3. 그는 무기를 들고 싸우는 대신 오랫동안 단식 투쟁을 했다.
   ➡ _____

4. "눈에는 눈이라는 식의 복수는 오직 전 세계를 눈멀게 할 뿐이다."라고 그는 말했다.
   ➡ _____

※ 다음 영어를 우리말로 쓰시오.

01 instead

02 average

03 control

04 tip

05 critic

06 effort

07 public

08 realize

09 about

10 fake

11 fold

12 forest

13 shape

14 million

15 backward

16 case

17 hold

18 imagine

19 share

20 tiny

21 joke

22 neighbor

23 shout

24 once

25 own

26 peace

27 public officer

28 save

29 hate

30 bookmark

31 officer

32 piece

33 solve

34 race car

35 end up -ing

36 would rather A than B

37 get closer to

38 keep ~ away

39 laugh out loud

40 cut ~ into small pieces

41 stop+-ing

42 say hello to

43 rain cats and dogs

※ 다음 우리말을 영어로 쓰시오.

01 비평가 _____

02 노력 _____

03 평균; 평균의 _____

04 가짜의 _____

05 조언, 도움말 _____

06 접다 _____

07 통제하다, 조종하다 _____

08 공유하다, 나누다 _____

09 대략 _____

10 농담 _____

11 공공의 _____

12 숲 _____

13 해결하다 _____

14 일단 ~하기만 하면 _____

15 경주용 차 _____

16 깨닫다 _____

17 구하다 _____

18 소리치다 _____

19 작은 _____

20 뒤에서부터, 역방향으로 _____

(주로 소유격 뒤에서)
21 ~ 자신의 _____

22 평화 _____

23 사건 _____

24 백만 _____

25 창조하다, 만들어 내다 _____

26 모양, 형태 _____

27 책갈피 _____

28 공무원 _____

29 잡다 _____

30 이웃, 옆집 사람 _____

31 관리, 관료 _____

32 대신에 _____

33 조각 _____

34 상상하다 _____

35 큰 소리로 웃다 _____

36 ~하는 것을 멈추다 _____

37 틀림없이 ~하다 _____

38 B하느니 A하겠다 _____

39 결국 ~가 되다 _____

40 ~와 가까워지다 _____

41 ~를 멀리하게 하다 _____

42 ~에게 인사하다 _____

43 비가 억수같이 오다 _____

※ 다음 영영풀이에 알맞은 단어를 <보기>에서 골라 쓴 후, 우리말 뜻을 쓰시오.

1 _____ : an attempt to do something: _____

2 _____ : someone who lives near you: _____

3 _____ : in the direction behind you: _____

4 _____ : very good to eat or drink: _____

5 _____ : a large area of trees growing close together: _____

6 _____ : to rain very heavily: _____

7 _____ : in the place of someone or something else: _____

8 _____ : to ask someone to come to your house, to a party, etc.: _____

9 _____ : to make an idea or picture of something in your mind: _____

10 _____ : a situation in which there is no war, violence, or arguing: _____

11 _____ : to have or use something at the same time as someone else: _____

12 _____ : to bend something so that one part of it lies flat on top of another part:

_____

13 _____ : to keep someone or something safe from death, harm, loss, etc.: _____

14 _____ : someone whose job is to give their opinion of a book, play, movie, etc.:

_____

15 _____ : to notice or understand something that you did not notice or understand

before: _____

16 _____ : to take action so that you are certain that something happens, is true, etc.:

_____

보기	fold	neighbor	imagine	backward
	make sure	instead	realize	invite
	share	delicious	peace	effort
	save	forest	critic	rain cats and dogs

※ 다음 우리말과 일치하도록 빈칸에 알맞은 것을 골라 쓰시오.

1 _____ _____
　　A. Magazine　　　B. Teens'

2 _____ to _____ Your Town _____
　　A. Make　　　B. Ways　　　C. Better

3 Doing _____ _____ for your neighbors can _____ your town. Start small. Here are some _____ .
　　A. change　　　B. something　　　C. tips　　　D. nice

4 1. _____ _____ to your _____ and _____ .
　　A. smile　　　B. hello　　　C. neighbors　　　D. say

5 2. Don't _____ _____ _____ , "Thank you."
　　A. forget　　　B. say　　　C. to

6 3. Share your umbrella _____ _____ _____ _____ .
　　A. rainy　　　B. on　　　C. day　　　D. a

7 4. _____ _____ _____ when your neighbor tells a _____ .
　　A. joke　　　B. out　　　C. laugh　　　D. loud

8 5. Make _____ _____ your _____ .
　　A. for　　　B. something　　　C. neighbors

9 6. _____ the _____ for the _____ _____ you.
　　A. behind　　　B. hold　　　C. person　　　D. door

10 7. _____ your _____ _____ your party.
　　A. to　　　B. invite　　　C. neighbors

11 If you just do one thing _____ day, you can _____ your _____ _____ .
　　A. better　　　B. each　　　C. make　　　D. town

12 _____ for _____
　　A. Peace　　　B. Messages

13 On World Peace Day, we _____ our peace _____ the _____ .
　　A. on　　　B. put　　　C. board　　　D. messages

14 Peace means _____ _____ _____ the world. - Kim Jimin
　　A. around　　　B. having　　　C. friends

15 I'd _____ have _____ on Earth _____ _____ of Earth. - Seo Eunji
　　A. pieces　　　B. rather　　　C. than　　　D. peace

16 I want peace every _____ I go _____ there is always someone _____ or _____ . - Park Hansol
　　A. shouting　　　B. fighting　　　C. because　　　D. place

17 Peace _____ _____ _____ .- Yang Miran
　　A. everyone　　　B. makes　　　C. smile

1 십대들의 잡지

2 마을을 더 좋게 만드는 방법들

3 이웃들을 위해 뭔가 좋은 일을 하면 여러분의 마을을 변화시킬 수 있다. 작은 것부터 시작하라. 여기 몇 가지 도움말이 있다.

4 1. 이웃들에게 인사를 하고 미소를 지어라.

5 2. 잊지 말고 "고맙습니다."라고 말해라.

6 3. 비 오는 날에 당신의 우산을 함께 써라.

7 4. 이웃이 농담하면 크게 소리 내어 웃어라.

8 5. 이웃들을 위해 뭔가를 만들어라.

9 6. 뒤에 오는 사람을 위해 문을 잡아 줘라.

10 7. 이웃을 당신의 파티에 초대해라.

11 만약 당신이 매일 한 가지씩 하기만 하면, 당신의 마을을 더 좋게 만들 수 있다.

12 평화 메시지

13 우리는 세계 평화의 날에 게시판에 평화 메시지를 붙였다.

14 평화는 세상 어디에서나 친구가 있다는 것을 의미한다. – 김지민

15 나는 지구의 조각들을 갖느니 지구 위의 평화를 갖겠다. – 서은지

16 항상 싸우거나 소리치는 누군가가 있으므로 나는 내가 가는 모든 곳에서 평화를 원한다. – 박한솔

17 평화는 모든 사람을 미소 짓게 만든다. – 양미란

18 Peace is _____ all of us. We just _____ _____ _____ it. - Jang Jaehee

A. share   B. inside   C. to   D. need

19 _____

A. LAUGH   B. LET'S

20 _____ apple _____ _____

A. a   B. an   C. day

21 Jake came in to see his dad. "Dad!" he said, "Is it _____ _____ an apple a day _____ the doctor _____?"

A. keeps   B. true   C. away   D. that

22 "That's _____ _____ _____," said his dad.

A. say   B. they   C. what

23 "Well, give me an _____ quickly! I _____ _____ the doctor's _____!"

A. apple   B. window   C. broke   D. just

24 _____ _____ _____ Books!

A. to   B. Be   C. Kind

25 Do you know _____ _____ _____? They hate water, the sun, and dog ears. _____ dog ears?

A. what   B. hate   C. why   D. books

26 Water is _____ for _____ and BOOKS! / The SUN also _____ Books YELLOW / Don't DOG-EAR! Use a _____! / Be Kind to Books!

A. bookmark   B. bad   C. TURNs   D. WITCHES

27 _____ _____ dog ears in books. Use a _____ _____.

A. instead   B. folding   C. stop   D. bookmark

28 _____ is a bookmark _____ can _____ your books. _____ kind to your books.

A. save   B. that   C. be   D. it

29 The _____ you love your books, the _____ your books will be. _____ _____ making your own?

A. about   B. more   C. happier   D. how

30 _____ That Sound _____

A. Fake   B. Facts

31 1. _____ 7% of all people who _____ _____ _____ are living on the Earth today.

A. lived   B. about   C. ever   D. have

32 About 108,200 million people _____ _____ _____ in the history of the world. And about 7,442 million are living on the Earth today.

A. ever   B. born   C. been   D. have

33 2. Bangladesh _____ _____ _____ Russia.

A. than   B. has   C. people   D. more

---

18 평화는 우리 모두의 내면에 있다. 우리는 단지 그것을 공유할 필요가 있을 뿐이다. – 장재희

19 웃읍시다

20 하루에 사과 한 개

21 Jake가 아빠를 보러 들어왔다. "아빠!" 그는 "하루에 사과 한 개가 의사를 멀리하게 만든다는 것이 사실이에요?"라고 말했다.

22 "사람들이 그렇게 말하지," 아빠가 말했다.

23 "자, 저에게 빨리 사과 한 개를 주세요! 제가 방금 의사 선생님의 유리창을 깨뜨렸어요!"

24 책들을 친절하게 대해 주세요!

25 여러분은 책들이 무엇을 싫어하는지 아나요? 그들은 물, 햇빛, 그리고 강아지 귀를 싫어합니다. 왜 강아지 귀일까요?

26 물은 마녀와 책에 해롭다! / 햇빛도 책을 누렇게 뜨게 한다. / 강아지 귀처럼 책을 접지 마라! 책갈피를 사용해라! / 책들을 친절하게 대해 주세요!

27 강아지 귀 모양으로 책을 접는 것을 멈춰 주세요. 대신에 책갈피를 이용하세요.

28 여러분의 책을 구해 주는 것은 바로 책갈피입니다. 여러분의 책들을 친절하게 대해 주세요.

29 여러분이 책을 더 많이 사랑하면 할수록 여러분의 책들은 더 행복해질 겁니다. 여러분 자신의 책갈피를 만들어 보는 게 어떨까요?

30 가짜 같은 사실

31 1 지금까지 살아온 모든 사람의 약 7%가 오늘날 지구상에 살고 있다.

32 세계 역사에서 약 1천8십2억 명의 사람들이 지금까지 태어났다. 그리고 약 7십4억 4천2백만 명이 오늘날 지구상에 살고 있다.

33 2 방글라데시는 러시아보다 인구가 더 많다.

34 Russia is the world's _____ _____, but _____ Bangladesh has 166.3 million people _____ 2018. Russia has 143.9 million people.

    A. tiny   B. in   C. country   D. largest

35 3. A banyan tree _____ Kolkata, India, is _____ the _____ Walmart.

    A. average   B. near   C. than   D. bigger

36 The average Walmart store _____ about 104,000 _____ feet. The Great Banyan Tree in Kolkata, India, is about the _____ of a forest, _____ 155,000 square feet.

    A. covering   B. covers   C. size   D. square

37 4. Baby carrots _____ _____ 1986.

    A. invented   B. in   C. were

38 Baby carrots are not actually baby carrots. Big ugly carrots are cut _____ small _____ that have the _____ of a baby carrot. Farmer Mike Yurosek invented them in 1986 as a way to use ugly carrots that weren't _____.

    A. into   B. sold   C. shape   D. pieces

39 _____ _____ the _____

    A. Movies   B. in   C. Jobs

40 Zootopia (2016) It's _____ _____ _____ _____ !

    A. movie   B. the   C. ever   D. greatest

41 Flash is a _____ officer. He is very slow but works hard. You will be _____ to see _____ he does in his _____ time. It's driving a race car!

    A. free   B. surprised   C. public   D. what

42 Nick is a fox _____ a big mouth. Helping Judy, he _____ _____ to her. He _____ becomes a police officer like Judy.

    A. closer   B. with   C. later   D. gets

43 Judy is a small rabbit, but she's smart and strong. After a _____ of _____, she becomes a police officer and _____ many _____.

    A. cases   B. effort   C. solves   D. lot

44 Ratatouille (2007) Everyone _____ _____ _____ movie.

    A. love   B. will   C. this

45 Anton Ego is a food _____. After he eats the food Remy _____, he _____ that _____ can cook.

    A. critic   B. cooked   C. anyone   D. realizes

34 러시아는 세계에서 가장 큰 나라이지만, 아주 작은 방글라데시에는 2018년 기준으로 1억 6천6백3십만 명의 인구가 있다. 러시아는 1억 4천3백9십만 명의 인구가 있다.

35 3 인도 Kolkata 부근의 한 바니안(banyan) 나무는 평균적인 월마트보다 크다.

36 평균적인 월마트 상점은 약 10만4천 평방피트의 넓이이다. 인도 Kolkata에 있는 그레이트 바니안 나무는 대략 숲 하나의 크기로 15만5천 평방피트를 차지한다.

37 4 베이비 당근은 1986년 발명되었다.

38 베이비 당근은 실제로 아기처럼 작은 당근이 아니다. 크고 못생긴 당근들이 베이비 당근 모양을 가진 작은 조각으로 잘린다. 농부 Mike Yurosek이 팔리지 않는 못생긴 당근을 사용할 하나의 방편으로 1986년에 그것을 발명하였다.

39 영화 속 직업들

40 주토피아(2016) 그것은 이제까지 가장 대단한 영화이다!

41 Flash는 공무원이다. 그는 아주 느리지만 열심히 일한다. 여러분은 그가 여가 시간에 무엇을 하는지 알게 되면 놀랄 것이다. 그것은 경주용 자동차를 운전하는 것이다!

42 Nick은 커다란 입을 가진 여우이다. Judy를 도우면서 그녀와 가까워진다. 나중에 Judy처럼 경찰관이 된다.

43 Judy는 작은 토끼지만, 영리하고 강하다. 많은 노력을 한 후에, 그녀는 경찰관이 되었고 많은 사건을 해결한다.

44 라따뚜이(2007) 누구라도 이 영화를 사랑할 것이다.

45 Anton Ego는 음식 비평가이다. Remy가 요리한 음식을 먹은 후에, 그는 "누구라도 요리할 수 있다."라는 것을 깨닫는다.

46 Remy, a little mouse, dreams of becoming a cook. He goes into a restaurant and meets a boy _____ Linguini. _____ Linguini, he makes delicious food and _____ up _____ a great cook.

    A. ends   B. named   C. becoming   D. controlling

47 _____ _____ _____ Emojis

    A. with   B. Say   C. It

48 Do you know _____ _____ _____ _____?

    A. mean   B. these   C. emojis   D. what

49 Killing two birds with one _____. / The apple of your eyes. / Don't play games with fire. / Once in a blue moon. / Let's call it a day. / Money does not _____ on trees. / It's raining _____ and dogs. / A _____ of cake.

    A. grow   B. stone   C. cats   D. piece

50 _____ _____

    A. Songe   B. Emoji

51 Now, _____ _____ a Christmas song together! The _____, the _____!

    A. louder   B. sing   C. happier   D. let's

52 _____ _____

    A. Messages   B. Secret

53 _____ you can send messages to your friend that no one _____ can read! It's not so _____ for you to learn how to read and write your own _____ messages.

    A. else   B. secret   C. imagine   D. difficult

54 1. _____ _____

    A. Backward   B. Read

55 This is easy to _____. Just read the words _____! It seems _____ once you know the secret, but it can be a _____ one when you don't.

    A. backward   B. hard   C. simple   D. solve

56 2. Read _____ _____ _____

    A. Letter   B. Second   C. Every

57 Read _____ second letter _____ with the first letter, and when you _____, start again on the letters you _____.

    A. finish   B. missed   C. starting   D. every

58 3. Pig-pen

59 The Pig-pen is _____ than it _____. The lines _____ each letter mean the letter _____ the lines.

    A. looks   B. around   C. inside   D. easier

60 Now create your own set of secret letters and write secret messages to send to your friends. _____ _____ you _____ a key so your friends can understand your messages!

    A. sure   B. along   C. make   D. send

46 작은 쥐 Remy는 요리사가 되기를 꿈꾼다. 그는 식당에 들어가서 Linguini라는 이름의 소년을 만난다. Linguini를 통제하면서 그는 맛있는 음식을 만들고 결국에는 훌륭한 요리사가 된다.

47 이모지로 말하자

48 이 이모지들이 무엇을 의미하는지 아니?

49 돌 하나로 새 두 마리 잡기. (일석이조.) / 당신이 가장 사랑하는 사람. (눈에 넣어도 안 아플 사람.) / 불을 가지고 장난치지 마라. / 극히 드물게. / 오늘은 이만하자. / 돈이 나무에서 자라는 것은 아니다. (돈이 그냥 생기는 건 아니다.) / 비가 억수같이 온다. / 케이크 한 조각. (누워서 떡 먹기.)

50 이모지 노래

51 자, 함께 크리스마스 노래를 불러 봅시다! 더 크게 부를수록, 더 행복해집니다!

52 비밀 메시지

53 다른 어떤 사람도 읽을 수 없는 메시지를 친구에게 보낼 수 있다고 상상해 봐라! 여러분 자신의 비밀 메시지를 읽고 쓰는 법을 배우는 것이 그렇게 어렵지는 않다.

54 1. 거꾸로 읽어라

55 이것은 풀기 쉽다 – 그냥 단어들을 거꾸로 읽어라! 일단 여러분이 비밀을 알면 간단하지만, 그렇지 못하면 어려울 수 있다.

56 2. 두 번째 글자마다 읽어라

57 첫 번째 글자에서 시작해서 두 번째 글자마다 읽어라. 그리고 끝나면 여러분이 빠뜨린 글자로 다시 시작하라.

58 3. 피그펜

59 피그펜(돼지우리)은 보기보다 쉽다. 각 글자 주변의 선들은 그 선들 안에 있는 글자를 의미한다.

60 이제 여러분은 자신만의 비밀 문자 세트를 만들어서 친구들에게 보낼 비밀 메시지를 써 보아라. 친구들이 메시지를 이해할 수 있도록 해결의 열쇠도 함께 보내도록 해라.

※ 다음 우리말과 일치하도록 빈칸에 알맞은 것을 골라 쓰시오.

1　_____ Magazine

2　_____ _____ _____ Your Town _____

3　Doing _____ _____ for your neighbors can change your town. Start small. Here are _____ _____.

4　1. _____ _____ your neighbors and _____.

5　2. Don't _____ _____ _____, "Thank you."

6　3. Share your umbrella _____ _____ _____ _____.

7　4. _____ _____ _____ when your neighbor tells a joke.

8　5. Make something _____ your neighbors.

9　6. _____ the door for the person _____ _____.

10　7. _____ your neighbors _____ your party.

11　If you just do one thing _____ _____, you can _____ your town _____.

12　Messages for _____

13　On World Peace Day, we _____ our peace messages _____ the board.

14　Peace means _____ _____ around the world. - Kim Jimin

15　_____ _____ have peace on Earth _____ _____ of Earth. - Seo Eunji

16　I want peace _____ _____ I go because there is always someone _____ or _____. - Park Hansol

17　Peace _____ everyone _____.- Yang Miran

18　Peace is _____ all of us. We just need to share it. - Jang Jaehee

19　LET'S _____

20　An apple _____ _____

1	십대들의 잡지
2	마을을 더 좋게 만드는 방법들
3	이웃들을 위해 뭔가 좋은 일을 하면 여러분의 마을을 변화시킬 수 있다. 작은 것부터 시작하라. 여기 몇 가지 도움말이 있다.
4	1. 이웃들에게 인사를 하고 미소를 지어라.
5	2. 잊지 말고 "고맙습니다."라고 말해라.
6	3. 비 오는 날에 당신의 우산을 함께 써라.
7	4. 이웃이 농담하면 크게 소리 내어 웃어라.
8	5. 이웃들을 위해 뭔가를 만들어라.
9	6. 뒤에 오는 사람을 위해 문을 잡아 줘라.
10	7. 이웃을 당신의 파티에 초대해라.
11	만약 당신이 매일 한 가지씩 하기만 하면. 당신의 마을을 더 좋게 만들 수 있다.
12	평화 메시지
13	우리는 세계 평화의 날에 게시판에 평화 메시지를 붙였다.
14	평화는 세상 어디에서나 친구가 있다는 것을 의미한다. – 김지민
15	나는 지구의 조각들을 갖으니 지구 위의 평화를 갖겠다. – 서은지
16	항상 싸우거나 소리치는 누군가가 있으므로 나는 내가 가는 모든 곳에서 평화를 원한다. – 박한솔
17	평화는 모든 사람을 미소 짓게 만든다. – 양미란
18	평화는 우리 모두의 내면에 있다. 우리는 단지 그것을 공유할 필요가 있을 뿐이다. – 장재희
19	웃읍시다
20	하루에 사과 한 개

21 Jake came in to see his dad. "Dad!" he said, "Is _____ true _____ an apple a day _____ the doctor _____?"

22 "That's _____ _____ _____," said his dad.

23 "Well, give me an apple quickly! I _____ _____ the doctor's window!"

24 _____ _____ to Books!

25 Do you know _____ _____ _____? They hate water, the sun, and dog ears. _____ dog ears?

26 Water is bad for _____ and BOOKS! / The SUN also _____ Books YELLOW / _____ DOG-EAR! Use a _____! / _____ _____ to Books!

27 Stop _____ dog ears in books. Use a bookmark _____.

28 _____ _____ a bookmark _____ _____ _____ your books. Be kind to your books.

29 _____ _____ you love your books, _____ _____ your books will be. _____ _____ making _____ _____?

30 _____ That _____ _____

31 1. About 7% of all people who _____ _____ _____ are _____ _____ the Earth today.

32 About 108,200 million people _____ _____ _____ _____ in the history of the world. And _____ 7,442 million are living on the Earth today.

33 2. Bangladesh has _____ people _____ Russia.

34 Russia is the world's _____ country, but tiny Bangladesh has 166.3 million people in 2018. Russia has 143.9 million people.

35 3. A banyan tree near Kolkata, India, is _____ the _____ Walmart.

36 The average Walmart store _____ about 104,000 square feet. The Great Banyan Tree in Kolkata, India, is about _____ _____ a forest, _____ 155,000 square feet.

37 4. Baby carrots _____ _____ _____ 1986.

38 Baby carrots are not actually baby carrots. Big ugly carrots _____ _____ _____ small _____ that have the shape of a baby carrot. Farmer Mike Yurosek invented them in 1986 as a _____ _____ _____ ugly carrots that _____ _____.

39 _____ in the Movies

40 Zootopia (2016) It's _____ _____ _____ ever!

21 Jake가 아빠를 보러 들어왔다. "아빠!" 그는 "하루에 사과 한 개가 의사를 멀리하게 만든다는 것이 사실이에요?"라고 말했다.

22 "사람들이 그렇게 말하지." 아빠가 말했다.

23 "자, 저에게 빨리 사과 한 개를 주세요! 제가 방금 의사 선생님의 유리창을 깨뜨렸어요!"

24 책들을 친절하게 대해 주세요!

25 여러분은 책들이 무엇을 싫어하는지 아나요? 그들은 물, 햇빛, 그리고 강아지 귀를 싫어합니다. 왜 강아지 귀일까요?

26 물은 마녀와 책에 해롭다! / 햇빛도 책을 누렇게 뜨게 한다. / 강아지 귀처럼 책을 접지 마라! 책갈피를 사용해라! / 책들을 친절하게 대해 주세요!

27 강아지 귀 모양으로 책을 접는 것을 멈춰 주세요. 대신에 책갈피를 이용하세요.

28 여러분의 책을 구해 주는 것은 바로 책갈피입니다. 여러분의 책들을 친절하게 대해 주세요.

29 여러분이 책을 더 많이 사랑하면 할수록 여러분의 책들은 더 행복해질 겁니다. 여러분 자신의 책갈피를 만들어 보는 게 어떨까요?

30 가짜 같은 사실

31 1 지금까지 살아온 모든 사람의 약 7%가 오늘날 지구상에 살고 있다.

32 세계 역사에서 약 1천8십2억 명의 사람들이 지금까지 태어났다. 그리고 약 7십4억 4천2백만 명이 오늘날 지구상에 살고 있다.

33 2 방글라데시는 러시아보다 인구가 더 많다.

34 러시아는 세계에서 가장 큰 나라이지만, 아주 작은 방글라데시에는 2018년 기준으로 1억 6천6백3십만 명의 인구가 있다. 러시아는 1억 4천3백9십 명의 인구가 있다.

35 3 인도 Kolkata 부근의 한 바니안(banyan) 나무는 평균적인 월마트보다 크다.

36 평균적인 월마트 상점은 약 10만4천 평방피트의 넓이이다. 인도 Kolkata에 있는 그레이트 바니안 나무는 대략 숲 하나의 크기로 15만5천 평방피트를 차지한다.

37 4 베이비 당근은 1986년 발명되었다.

38 베이비 당근은 실제로 아기처럼 작은 당근이 아니다. 크고 못생긴 당근들이 베이비 당근 모양을 가진 작은 조각으로 잘린다. 농부 Mike Yurosek이 팔리지 않는 못생긴 당근을 사용할 하나의 방편으로 1986년에 그것을 발명하였다.

39 영화 속 직업들

40 주토피아(2016) 그것은 이제까지 가장 대단한 영화이다!

41 Flash is a _____ _____. He is very slow but works hard. You will be _____ _____ _____ _____ _____ _____ in his free time. It's driving a race car!

42 Nick is a fox _____ a big mouth. _____ _____, he gets closer to her. He _____ becomes a police officer like Judy.

43 Judy is a small rabbit, but she's smart and strong. After _____ _____ _____ _____, she becomes a police officer and _____ _____ _____.

44 Ratatouille (2007) _____ _____ _____ this movie.

45 Anton Ego is a _____ _____. After he eats the food Remy cooked, he _____ that _____ can cook.

46 Remy, a little mouse, _____ _____ _____ a cook. He goes into a restaurant and meets a boy _____ Linguini. _____ Linguini, he makes delicious food and _____ _____ _____ a great cook.

47 Say It _____ Emojis

48 Do you know _____ _____ _____ _____ _____?

49 Killing two birds with one stone. / The apple of your eyes. / Don't play games with fire. / _____ _____ _____ blue moon. / Let's call it a day. / Money does not grow on trees. / It's raining _____ and _____. / _____ _____ _____ cake.

50 Emoji Song

51 Now, _____ _____ a Christmas song together! _____ _____, _____ _____!

52 _____ Messages

53 Imagine you can send messages to your friend that _____ _____ _____ _____ _____! It's not so difficult for you to learn how to read and write your own secret messages.

54 1. Read _____

55 This is _____ _____ _____. Just read the words _____! It seems simple _____ you know the secret, but it can be a hard one when you don't.

56 2. Read _____ Second Letter

57 Read every second letter _____ _____ the first letter, and when you finish, start again on the letters you _____.

58 3. Pig-pen

59 The Pig-pen is _____ _____ _____ _____. The lines around _____ _____ mean the letter inside the lines.

60 Now create your own set of _____ _____ and write secret messages _____ _____ _____ your friends. _____ _____ you _____ _____ a key so your friends can understand your messages!

※ 다음 문장을 우리말로 쓰시오.

1 Teens' Magazine
➡ _____

2 Ways to Make Your Town Better
➡ _____

3 Doing something nice for your neighbors can change your town. Start small. Here are some tips.
➡ _____

4 1. Say hello to your neighbors and smile.
➡ _____

5 2. Don't forget to say, "Thank you."
➡ _____

6 3. Share your umbrella on a rainy day.
➡ _____

7 4. Laugh out loud when your neighbor tells a joke.
➡ _____

8 5. Make something for your neighbors.
➡ _____

9 6. Hold the door for the person behind you.
➡ _____

10 7. Invite your neighbors to your party.
➡ _____

11 If you just do one thing each day, you can make your town better.
➡ _____

12 Messages for Peace
➡ _____

13 On World Peace Day, we put our peace messages on the board.
➡ _____

14 Peace means having friends around the world. - Kim Jimin
➡ _____

15 I'd rather have peace on Earth than pieces of Earth. - Seo Eunji
➡ _____

16 I want peace every place I go because there is always someone fighting or shouting. - Park Hansol
➡ _____

17 Peace makes everyone smile.- Yang Miran
➡ _____

18 Peace is inside all of us. We just need to share it. - Jang Jaehee
➡ _____

19 LET'S LAUGH
➡ _____

20 An apple a day
➡ _____

21 Jake came in to see his dad. "Dad!" he said, "Is it true that an apple a day keeps the doctor away?"
➡ _____

22 "That's what they say," said his dad.
➡ _____

23 "Well, give me an apple quickly! I just broke the doctor's window!"
➡ _____

24 Be Kind to Books!
➡ _____

25 Do you know what books hate? They hate water, the sun, and dog ears. Why dog ears?
➡ _____

26 Water is bad for WITCHES and BOOKS! / The SUN also TURNs Books YELLOW / Don't DOG-EAR! Use a bookmark! / Be Kind to Books!
➡ _____

27 Stop folding dog ears in books. Use a bookmark instead.
➡ _____

28 It is a bookmark that can save your books. Be kind to your books.
➡ _____

29 The more you love your books, the happier your books will be. How about making your own?
➡ _____

30 Facts That Sound Fake
➡ _____

31 1. About 7% of all people who have ever lived are living on the Earth today.
➡ _____

32 About 108,200 million people have ever been born in the history of the world. And about 7,442 million are living on the Earth today.
➡ _____

33 2. Bangladesh has more people than Russia.
➡ _____

34 Russia is the world's largest country, but tiny Bangladesh has 166.3 million people in 2018. Russia has 143.9 million people.
➡ _____

35 3. A banyan tree near Kolkata, India, is bigger than the average Walmart.
➡ _____

36 The average Walmart store covers about 104,000 square feet. The Great Banyan Tree in Kolkata, India, is about the size of a forest, covering 155,000 square feet.
➡ _____

37 4. Baby carrots were invented in 1986.
➡ _____

38 Baby carrots are not actually baby carrots. Big ugly carrots are cut into small pieces that have the shape of a baby carrot. Farmer Mike Yurosek invented them in 1986 as a way to use ugly carrots that weren't sold.
➡ _____

39 Jobs in the Movies
➡ _____

40 Zootopia (2016) It's the greatest movie ever!
➡ _____

41 Flash is a public officer. He is very slow but works hard. You will be surprised to see what he does in his free time. It's driving a race car!
➡ _____

42 Nick is a fox with a big mouth. Helping Judy, he gets closer to her. He later becomes a police officer like Judy.
➡ _____

43 Judy is a small rabbit, but she's smart and strong. After a lot of effort, she becomes a police officer and solves many cases.
➡ _____

44 Ratatouille (2007) Everyone will love this movie.
➡ _____

45 Anton Ego is a food critic. After he eats the food Remy cooked, he realizes that anyone can cook.
➡ _____

46 Remy, a little mouse, dreams of becoming a cook. He goes into a restaurant and meets a boy named Linguini. Controlling Linguini, he makes delicious food and ends up becoming a great cook.
➡ _____

47 Say It with Emojis
➡ _____

48 Do you know what these emojis mean?
➡ _____

49 Killing two birds with one stone. / The apple of your eyes. / Don't play games with fire. / Once in a blue moon. / Let's call it a day. / Money does not grow on trees. / It's raining cats and dogs. / A piece of cake.
➡ _____
_____
_____

50 Emoji Song
➡ _____

51 Now, let's sing a Christmas song together! The louder, the happier!
➡ _____

52 Secret Messages
➡ _____

53 Imagine you can send messages to your friend that no one else can read! It's not so difficult for you to learn how to read and write your own secret messages.
➡ _____

54 1. Read Backward
➡ _____

55 This is easy to solve. Just read the words backward! It seems simple once you know the secret, but it can be a hard one when you don't.
➡ _____

56 2. Read Every Second Letter
➡ _____

57 Read every second letter starting with the first letter, and when you finish, start again on the letters you missed.
➡ _____

58 3. Pig-pen
➡ _____

59 The Pig-pen is easier than it looks. The lines around each letter mean the letter inside the lines.
➡ _____

60 Now create your own set of secret letters and write secret messages to send to your friends. Make sure you send along a key so your friends can understand your messages!
➡ _____
_____

※ 다음 괄호 안의 단어들을 우리말에 맞도록 바르게 배열하시오.

1 (Magazine / Teens')
➡ _____

2 (to / Ways / Your / Make / Better / Town)
➡ _____

3 (something / doing / for / nice / neighbors / your / change / can / town. / your // small. / start // are / here / tips. / some)
➡ _____
_____

4 (1. / hello / say / your / to / and / smile. / neighbors)
➡ _____

5 (2. / forget / don't / say, / to / you." / "thank)
➡ _____

6 (3. / your / share / on / umbrella / day. / rainy / a)
➡ _____

7 (4. / out / laugh / when / loud / neighbor / your / a / joke. / tells)
➡ _____

8 (5. / something / make / your / for / neighbors.)
➡ _____

9 (6. / the / hold / for / door / person / the / you. / behind)
➡ _____

10 (7. / your / invite / neighbors / to / party. / your)
➡ _____

11 (you / if / do / just / thing / one / day, / each / can / you / make / town / your / better.)
➡ _____

12 (for / Messages / Peace)
➡ _____

13 (World / On / Day, / Peace / put / we / peace / our / on / messages / board. / the)
➡ _____

14 (means / peace / friends / having / the / around / world. / - / Jimin / Kim)
➡ _____

15 (rather / I'd / peace / have / Earth / on / pieces / than / Earth. / of / - / Eunji / Seo)
➡ _____

16 (want / I / every / peace / I / place / because / go / is / there / someone / always / shouting. / or / fighting / - / Hansol / Park)
➡ _____

17 (peace / everyone / smile. / makes / - / Miran / Yang)
➡ _____

1 십대들의 잡지

2 마을을 더 좋게 만드는 방법들

3 이웃들을 위해 뭔가 좋은 일을 하면 여러분의 마을을 변화시킬 수 있다. 작은 것부터 시작하라. 여기 몇 가지 도움말이 있다.

4 1. 이웃들에게 인사를 하고 미소를 지어라.

5 2. 잊지 말고 "고맙습니다."라고 말해라.

6 3. 비 오는 날에 당신의 우산을 함께 써라.

7 4. 이웃이 농담하면 크게 소리 내어 웃어라.

8 5. 이웃들을 위해 뭔가를 만들어라.

9 6. 뒤에 오는 사람을 위해 문을 잡아 줘라.

10 7. 이웃을 당신의 파티에 초대해라.

11 만약 당신이 매일 한 가지씩 하기만 하면, 당신의 마을을 더 좋게 만들 수 있다.

12 평화 메시지

13 우리는 세계 평화의 날에 게시판에 평화 메시지를 붙였다.

14 평화는 세상 어디에서나 친구가 있다는 것을 의미한다. - 김지민

15 나는 지구의 조각들을 갖느니 지구 위의 평화를 갖겠다. - 서은지

16 항상 싸우거나 소리치는 누군가가 있으므로 나는 내가 가는 모든 곳에서 평화를 원한다. - 박한솔

17 평화는 모든 사람을 미소 짓게 만든다. - 양미란

18 (is / peace / all / inside / us. / of // we / need / just / share / to / it. / Jaehee / Jang)
➡ _____

19 (LAUGH / LET'S)
➡ _____

20 (apple / an / day / a)
➡ _____

21 (came / Jake / to / in / his / see / dad. // he / "dad!" / said, / it / "is / that / true / apple / an / day / a / keeps / doctor / the / away?")
➡ _____

22 ("that's / they / what / say," / his / said / dad.)
➡ _____

23 (give / "well, / me / apple / an / quickly! // just / I / the / broke / window!" / doctor's)
➡ _____

24 (Kind / Be / Books! / to)
➡ _____

25 (you / do / what / know / hate? / books // hate / they / water, / sun, / the / and / ears. / dog // dog / why / ears?)
➡ _____

26 (is / water / for / bad / BOOKS! / and / WITCHES // SUN / the / also / Books / TURNs / YELLOW // DOG-EAR! / Don't / a / use / bookmark! // Kind / Be / Books! / to)
➡ _____

27 (folding / stop / ears / dog / books. / in // a / use / instead. / bookmark)
➡ _____

28 (is / it / bookmark / a / can / that / your / save / books. // kind / be / your / to / books.)
➡ _____

29 (more / the / love / you / books, / your / happier / the / books / your / be. / will // about / how / own? / your / making)
➡ _____

30 (That / Facts / Fake / Sound)
➡ _____

31 (1. / 7% / about / all / of / who / people / ever / have / are / lived / living / the / on / today. / Earth)
➡ _____

32 (108,200 / about / people / million / ever / have / born / been / the / in / of / history / world. / the // about / and / million / 7,442 / living / are / the / on / today. / Earth)
➡ _____

33 (2. / has / Bangladesh / more / than / people / Russia.)
➡ _____

18 평화는 우리 모두의 내면에 있다. 우리는 단지 그것을 공유할 필요가 있을 뿐이다. – 장재희

19 웃읍시다

20 하루에 사과 한 개

21 Jake가 아빠를 보러 들어왔다. "아빠!" 그는 "하루에 사과 한 개가 의사를 멀리하게 만든다는 것이 사실이에요?"라고 말했다.

22 "사람들이 그렇게 말하지." 아빠가 말했다.

23 "자, 저에게 빨리 사과 한 개를 주세요! 제가 방금 의사 선생님의 유리창을 깨뜨렸어요!"

24 책들을 친절하게 대해 주세요!

25 여러분은 책들이 무엇을 싫어하는지 아나요? 그들은 물, 햇빛, 그리고 강아지 귀를 싫어합니다. 왜 강아지 귀일까요?

26 물은 마녀와 책에 해롭다! / 햇빛도 책을 누렇게 뜨게 한다. / 강아지 귀처럼 책을 접지 마라! 책갈피를 사용해라! / 책들을 친절하게 대해 주세요!

27 강아지 귀 모양으로 책을 접는 것을 멈춰 주세요. 대신에 책갈피를 이용하세요.

28 여러분의 책을 구해 주는 것은 바로 책갈피입니다. 여러분의 책들을 친절하게 대해 주세요.

29 여러분이 책을 더 많이 사랑하면 할수록 여러분의 책들은 더 행복해질 겁니다. 여러분 자신의 책갈피를 만들어 보는 게 어떨까요?

30 가짜 같은 사실

31 1 지금까지 살아온 모든 사람의 약 7%가 오늘날 지구상에 살고 있다.

32 세계 역사에서 약 1천8십2억 명의 사람들이 지금까지 태어났다. 그리고 약 7십4억 4천2백만 명이 오늘날 지구상에 살고 있다.

33 2 방글라데시는 러시아보다 인구가 더 많다.

34 (is / Russia / world's / the / country, / largest / tiny / but / has / Bangladesh / 166.3 / people / million / 2018 / in // has / Russia / million / 143.9 / people.)

➡ _____

_____

35 (3. / banyan / a / near / tree / India, / Kolkata, / is / than / bigger / average / the / Walmart.)

➡ _____

36 (average / the / store / Walmart / covers / 104,000 / about / feet. / square // Great / The / Banyan / in / Tree / India, / Kolkata, / about / is / the / of / size / forest, / a / 155,000 / covering / feet. / square)

➡ _____

_____

37 (4. / carrots / baby / invented / were / 1986. / in)

➡ _____

38 (carrots / baby / not / are / baby / actually / carrots. // ugly / big / are / carrots / into / cut / pieces / small / have / that / shape / the / a / of / carrot. / baby // Mike / Farmer / Yurosek / them / invented / 1986 / in / a / as / to / way / ugly / use / that / carrots / sold. / weren't)

➡ _____

_____

_____

39 (in / Jobs / Movies / the)

➡ _____

40 ((2016) / Zootopia // the / it's / movie / greatest / ever!)

➡ _____

41 (is / Flash / a / officer. / public // is / he / very / but / slow / hard. / works // will / you / surprised / be / see / to / he / what / does / free / in / time. / his // driving / it's / race / a / car!)

➡ _____

_____

42 (is / Nick / fox / a / with / mouth / big / a // Judy, / helping / gets / he / to / closer / her. // later / he / becomes / police / a / officer / Judy. / like)

➡ _____

_____

43 (is / Judy / a / rabbit, / small / she's / but / strong. / and / smart // a / after / of / lot / effort, / becomes / she / police / a / officer / solves / and / cases. / many)

➡ _____

_____

44 ((2007) / Ratatouille // will / everyone / this / love / movie.)

➡ _____

45 (Ego / Anton / a / is / critic. / food // he / after / the / eats / food / cooked, / Remy / realizes / he / that / can / anyone / cook.)

➡ _____

_____

34 러시아는 세계에서 가장 큰 나라이지만, 아주 작은 방글라데시에는 2018년 기준으로 1억 6천6백3십만 명의 인구가 있다. 러시아는 1억 4천3백9십만 명의 인구가 있다.

35 3 인도 Kolkata 부근의 한 바니안(banyan) 나무는 평균적인 월마트보다 크다.

36 평균적인 월마트 상점은 약 10만4천 평방피트의 넓이이다. 인도 Kolkata에 있는 그레이트 바니안 나무는 대략 숲 하나의 크기로 15만5천 평방피트를 차지한다.

37 4 베이비 당근은 1986년 발명되었다.

38 베이비 당근은 실제로 아기처럼 작은 당근이 아니다. 크고 못생긴 당근들이 베이비 당근 모양을 가진 작은 조각으로 잘린다. 농부 Mike Yurosek이 팔리지 않는 못생긴 당근을 사용할 하나의 방편으로 1986년에 그것을 발명하였다.

39 영화 속 직업들

40 주토피아(2016) 그것은 이제까지 가장 대단한 영화이다!

41 Flash는 공무원이다. 그는 아주 느리지만 열심히 일한다. 여러분은 그가 여가 시간에 무엇을 하는지 알게 되면 놀랄 것이다. 그것은 경주용 자동차를 운전하는 것이다!

42 Nick은 커다란 입을 가진 여우이다. Judy를 도우면서 그녀와 가까워진다. 나중에 Judy처럼 경찰관이 된다.

43 Judy는 작은 토끼지만, 영리하고 강하다. 많은 노력을 한 후에, 그녀는 경찰관이 되었고 많은 사건을 해결한다.

44 라따뚜이(2007) 누구라도 이 영화를 사랑할 것이다.

45 Anton Ego는 음식 비평가이다. Remy가 요리한 음식을 먹은 후에, 그는 "누구라도 요리할 수 있다."라는 것을 깨닫는다.

46 (a / Remy / little / mouse, / of / dreams / a / becoming / cook. // goes / he / a / into / restaurant / and / a / meets / named / boy / Linguini. // Linguini, / controlling / makes / he / food / delicious / and / up / ends / a / becoming / cook. / great)

➡ _____

_____

47 (It / Say / Emojis / with)

➡ _____

48 (you / do / what / know / emojis / these / mean?)

➡ _____

49 (two / killing / with / birds / stone. / one // apple / the / your / of / eyes. // play / don't / with / games / fire. // in / once / blue / a / moon. // call / let's / a / it / day. // does / money / grow / not / trees. / on // raining / it's / dogs. / and / cats // piece / a / cake. / of)

➡ _____

_____

_____

50 (Song / Emoji)

➡ _____

51 (let's / now, / sing / Christmas / a / together! / song // louder, / the / happier! / the)

➡ _____

52 (Messages / Secret)

➡ _____

53 (you / imagine / send / can / messages / your / to / that / friend / no / else / one / read! / can // not / it's / difficult / so / you / for / learn / to / to / how / read / and / your / write / own / messages. / secret)

➡ _____

_____

_____

54 (1. / Backward / Read)

➡ _____

55 (is / this / to / easy / solve. // read / just / words / the / backward! // seems / it / once / simple / know / the / you / secret, / it / but / be / can / one / hard / a / when / don't / you)

➡ _____

_____

56 (2. / Every / Read / Letter / Second)

➡ _____

57 (every / read / letter / second / with / starting / first / the / letter, / and / you / when / finish, / again / start / the / on / letters / missed. / you)

➡ _____

58 (Pig-pen / 3.)

➡ _____

59 (Pig-pen / the / easier / is / it / than / looks. // lines / the / each / around / letter / the / mean / letter / the / inside / lines.)

➡ _____

_____

60 (create / now / own / your / of / set / letters / secret / and / secret / write / messages / send / to / your / to / friends. // sure / make / send / you / along / key / a / so / friends / your / can / your / understand / messages!)

➡ _____

_____

_____

46 작은 쥐 Remy는 요리사가 되기를 꿈꾼다. 그는 식당에 들어가서 Linguini라는 이름의 소년을 만난다. Linguini를 통제하면서 그는 맛있는 음식을 만들고 결국에는 훌륭한 요리사가 된다.

47 이모지로 말하자

48 이 이모지들이 무엇을 의미하는지 아니?

49 돌 하나로 새 두 마리 잡기. (일석이조.) / 당신이 가장 사랑하는 사람. (눈에 넣어도 안 아플 사람.) / 불을 가지고 장난치지 마라. / 극히 드물게. / 오늘은 이만하자. / 돈이 나무에서 자라는 것은 아니다. (돈이 그냥 생기는 건 아니다.) / 비가 억수같이 온다. / 케이크 한 조각. (누워서 떡 먹기.)

50 이모지 노래

51 자, 함께 크리스마스 노래를 불러 봅시다! 더 크게 부를수록, 더 행복해집니다!

52 비밀 메시지

53 다른 어떤 사람도 읽을 수 없는 메시지를 친구에게 보낼 수 있다고 상상해 봐라! 여러분 자신의 비밀 메시지를 읽고 쓰는 법을 배우는 것이 그렇게 어렵지는 않다.

54 1. 거꾸로 읽어라

55 이것은 풀기 쉽다 – 그냥 단어들을 거꾸로 읽어라! 일단 여러분이 비밀을 알면 간단하지만, 그렇지 못하면 어려울 수 있다.

56 2. 두 번째 글자마다 읽어라

57 첫 번째 글자에서 시작해서 두 번째 글자마다 읽어라. 그리고 끝나면 여러분이 빠뜨린 글자로 다시 시작하라.

58 3. 피그펜

59 피그펜(돼지우리)은 보기보다 쉽다. 각 글자 주변의 선들은 그 선들 안에 있는 글자를 의미한다.

60 이제 여러분은 자신만의 비밀 문자 세트를 만들어서 친구들에게 보낼 비밀 메시지를 써 보아라. 친구들이 메시지를 이해할 수 있도록 해결의 열쇠도 함께 보내도록 해라.

※ 다음 우리말을 영어로 쓰시오.

1 십대들의 잡지
➡ _____

2 마을을 더 좋게 만드는 방법들
➡ _____

3 이웃들을 위해 뭔가 좋은 일을 하면 여러분의 마을을 변화시킬 수 있다. 작은 것부터 시작하라. 여기 몇 가지 도움말이 있다.
➡ _____

4 1. 이웃들에게 인사를 하고 미소를 지어라.
➡ _____

5 2. 잊지 말고 "고맙습니다."라고 말해라.
➡ _____

6 3. 비 오는 날에 당신의 우산을 함께 써라.
➡ _____

7 4. 이웃이 농담하면 크게 소리 내어 웃어라.
➡ _____

8 5. 이웃들을 위해 뭔가를 만들어라.
➡ _____

9 6. 뒤에 오는 사람을 위해 문을 잡아 줘라.
➡ _____

10 7. 이웃을 당신의 파티에 초대해라.
➡ _____

11 만약 당신이 매일 한 가지씩 하기만 하면, 당신의 마을을 더 좋게 만들 수 있다.
➡ _____

12 평화 메시지
➡ _____

13 우리는 세계 평화의 날에 게시판에 평화 메시지를 붙였다.
➡ _____

14 평화는 세상 어디에서나 친구가 있다는 것을 의미한다. – 김지민
➡ _____

15 나는 지구의 조각들을 갖느니 지구 위의 평화를 갖겠다. – 서은지

16 항상 싸우거나 소리치는 누군가가 있으므로 나는 내가 가는 모든 곳에서 평화를 원한다. – 박한솔
➡ _____

17 평화는 모든 사람을 미소 짓게 만든다. – 양미란
➡ _____

18 평화는 우리 모두의 내면에 있다. 우리는 단지 그것을 공유할 필요가 있을 뿐이다. – 장재희
➡ _____

19 웃읍시다
➡ _____

20 하루에 사과 한 개
➡ _____

21 ▸ Jake가 아빠를 보러 들어왔다. "아빠!" 그는 "하루에 사과 한 개가 의사를 멀리하게 만든다는 것이 사실이에요?"라고 말했다.
　　➡ _____

22 ▸ "사람들이 그렇게 말하지," 아빠가 말했다.
　　➡ _____

23 ▸ "자, 저에게 빨리 사과 한 개를 주세요! 제가 방금 의사 선생님의 유리창을 깨뜨렸어요!"
　　➡ _____

24 ▸ 책들을 친절하게 대해 주세요!
　　➡ _____

25 ▸ 여러분은 책들이 무엇을 싫어하는지 아나요? 그들은 물, 햇빛, 그리고 강아지 귀를 싫어합니다. 왜 강아지 귀일까요?
　　➡ _____

26 ▸ 물은 마녀와 책에 해롭다! / 햇빛도 책을 누렇게 뜨게 한다. / 강아지 귀처럼 책을 접지 마라! 책갈피를 사용해라! / 책들을 친절하게 대해 주세요!
　　➡ _____

27 ▸ 강아지 귀 모양으로 책을 접는 것을 멈춰 주세요. 대신에 책갈피를 이용하세요.
　　➡ _____

28 ▸ 여러분의 책을 구해 주는 것은 바로 책갈피입니다. 여러분의 책들을 친절하게 대해 주세요.
　　➡ _____

29 ▸ 여러분이 책을 더 많이 사랑하면 할수록 여러분의 책들은 더 행복해질 겁니다. 여러분 자신의 책갈피를 만들어 보는 게 어떨까요?
　　➡ _____

30 ▸ 가짜 같은 사실
　　➡ _____

31 ▸ 1. 지금까지 살아온 모든 사람의 약 7%가 오늘날 지구상에 살고 있다.
　　➡ _____

32 ▸ 세계 역사에서 약 1천8십2억 명의 사람들이 지금까지 태어났다. 그리고 약 7십4억 4천2백만 명이 오늘날 지구상에 살고 있다.
　　➡ _____

33 ▸ 2. 방글라데시는 러시아보다 인구가 더 많다.
　　➡ _____

34 ▸ 러시아는 세계에서 가장 큰 나라이지만, 아주 작은 방글라데시에는 2018년 기준으로 1억 6천6백3십만 명의 인구가 있다. 러시아는 1억 4천3백9십만 명의 인구가 있다.
　　➡ _____

35 ▸ 3. 인도 Kolkata 부근의 한 바니안(banyan) 나무는 평균적인 월마트보다 크다.
　　➡ _____

36 ▸ 평균적인 월마트 상점은 약 10만4천 평방피트의 넓이이다. 인도 Kolkata에 있는 그레이트 바니안 나무는 대략 숲 하나의 크기로 15만5천 평방피트를 차지한다.
　　➡ _____

37 ▸ 4. 베이비 당근은 1986년 발명되었다.
　　➡ _____

38 ▸ 베이비 당근은 실제로 아기처럼 작은 당근이 아니다. 크고 못생긴 당근들이 베이비 당근 모양을 가진 작은 조각으로 잘린다. 농부 Mike Yurosek이 팔리지 않는 못생긴 당근을 사용할 하나의 방편으로 1986년에 그것을 발명하였다.
　　➡ _____

39 ▸ 영화 속 직업들
　　➡ _____

40 ▸ 주토피아(2016) 그것은 이제까지 가장 대단한 영화이다!
　　➡ _____

41 Flash는 공무원이다. 그는 아주 느리지만 열심히 일한다. 여러분은 그가 여가 시간에 무엇을 하는지 알게 되면 놀랄 것이다. 그것은 경주용 자동차를 운전하는 것이다!
➡ _____

42 Nick은 커다란 입을 가진 여우이다. Judy를 도우면서 그녀와 가까워진다. 나중에 Judy처럼 경찰관이 된다.
➡ _____

43 Judy는 작은 토끼지만, 영리하고 강하다. 많은 노력을 한 후에, 그녀는 경찰관이 되었고 많은 사건을 해결한다.
➡ _____

44 라따뚜이(2007) 누구라도 이 영화를 사랑할 것이다.

45 Anton Ego는 음식 비평가이다. Remy가 요리한 음식을 먹은 후에, 그는 "누구라도 요리할 수 있다." 라는 것을 깨닫는다.

46 작은 쥐 Remy는 요리사가 되기를 꿈꾼다. 그는 식당에 들어가서 Linguini라는 이름의 소년을 만난다. Linguini를 통제하면서 그는 맛있는 음식을 만들고 결국에는 훌륭한 요리사가 된다.
➡ _____

47 이모지로 말하자
➡ _____

48 이 이모지들이 무엇을 의미하는지 아니?
➡ _____

49 돌 하나로 새 두 마리 잡기. (일석이조.) / 당신이 가장 사랑하는 사람. (눈에 넣어도 안 아플 사람.) / 불을 가지고 장난치지 마라. / 극히 드물게. / 오늘은 이만하자. / 돈이 나무에서 자라는 것은 아니다. (돈이 그냥 생기는 건 아니다.) / 비가 억수같이 온다. / 케이크 한 조각. (누워서 떡 먹기.)
➡ _____
_____

50 이모지 노래

51 자, 함께 크리스마스 노래를 불러 봅시다! 더 크게 부를수록, 더 행복해집니다!

52 비밀 메시지

53 다른 어떤 사람도 읽을 수 없는 메시지를 친구에게 보낼 수 있다고 상상해 봐라! 여러분 자신의 비밀 메시지를 읽고 쓰는 법을 배우는 것이 그렇게 어렵지는 않다.
➡ _____

54 1. 거꾸로 읽어라
➡ _____

55 이것은 풀기 쉽다 – 그냥 단어들을 거꾸로 읽어라! 일단 여러분이 비밀을 알면 간단하지만, 그렇지 못하면 어려울 수 있다.
➡ _____

56 2. 두 번째 글자마다 읽어라
➡ _____

57 첫 번째 글자에서 시작해서 두 번째 글자마다 읽어라. 그리고 끝나면 여러분이 빠뜨린 글자로 다시 시작하라.
➡ _____

58 3. 피그펜
➡ _____

59 피그펜(돼지우리)은 보기보다 쉽다. 각 글자 주변의 선들은 그 선들 안에 있는 글자를 의미한다.

60 이제 여러분은 자신만의 비밀 문자 세트를 만들어서 친구들에게 보낼 비밀 메시지를 써 보아라. 친구들이 메시지를 이해할 수 있도록 해결의 열쇠도 함께 보내도록 해라.
➡ _____
_____

MEMO

영어 기출 문제집

적중 100

영어 기출 문제집

2학기

정답 및 해설

천재 | 정사열

중 **3**

적중 100

Lesson 5

Pictures Speak a Thousand Words

시험대비 실력평가   p.08

01 (c)urious   02 ②   03 ⑤   04 ④
05 be covered with   06 ③   07 close

01 '무언가에 대하여 알거나 배우기를 원하는'의 뜻인 'curious(호기심 많은, 궁금한)'가 적절하다.

02 'letter'는 '편지', '글자, 문자'의 의미를 지닌다. • 전통적인 편지(mail)는 어떤 사람이 손으로 쓴 편지(letter)이기 때문에 특별한 의미를 포함합니다. • 오래 전에, 우리는 우리 자신의 글자(letter)를 가지고 있지 않았습니다.

03 '어떤 후보자에 대하여 선호를 표시하다'라는 의미로 '투표하다(vote)'가 적절하다.

04 '당신의 애정이나 우정을 보여주기 위하여 양팔로 다른 사람을 안는 행위'의 뜻으로 '포용(hug)'이 적절하다.

05 '~로 덮이다'는 'be covered with'를 사용한다.

06 (A) 나이아가라 폭포는 정말로 멋진 광경이다. (B) 그는 배우로서 그의 숨겨진 재능을 보여주었다.

07 1. crossing 2. lit 3. oil 4. son 5. except

서술형 시험대비   p.09

01 (1) lots of   (2) wait for   (3) except for
    (4) look after
02 Braille
03 (1) hire   (2) misunderstanding   (3) rather
04 (1) ring, 반지   (2) discover, 발견하다   (3) oil, 기름
    (4) translate, 번역하다
05 (A) (f)oreign   (B) (h)unters   (C) (s)oldier

01 (1) 이 가게에는 많은 멋진 신발이 있다. 'lot'을 이용하여 '많은'의 의미를 나타낼 때는 'lots of'가 적절하다. (2) 우리는 식당에서 20분 동안 그를 기다려야 했다. '~를 기다리다'는 'wait for'를 사용한다. (3) 나는 잘 지내고 있고, 미세먼지를 제외하면 날씨도 좋아. '~을 제외하고'는 'except for'를 사용한다. (4) 이웃이 고양이를 돌보아 달라고 부탁했다. '~를 돌보다'는 'look after'가 적절하다.

02 '시각 장애인들이 만져서 읽는 돋우어진 패턴을 사용하는 인쇄 체계'로 '점자(Braille)'가 적절하다.

03 (1) hire: 고용하다 (2) misunderstanding: 오해 (3) rather: 다소

04 (1) 손가락에 끼는 둥근 형태의 보석 (2) 전에 알지 못하던 것을 찾아내다 (3) 요리를 위하여 사용되는 식물이나 동물로부터 만들어진 걸쭉한 액체 (4) 구어 또는 문어를 다른 언어로 바꾸다

05 (A) 한국 사람들은 인구가 더 많은 다른 외국들보다도 더 많은 물을 쓰고 있습니다. (B) 인간은 가장 위대한 사냥꾼이고 항상 고기를 먹어왔다. (C) 그는 제복을 입고 있기 때문에 군인임에 틀림없다.

 교과서
Conversation

핵심 Check   p.10~11

1 ②
2 It means an enemy is coming close to the border.

교과서 대화문 익히기

Check(√) True or False   p.12

1 T   2 F   3 T   4 T

교과서 확인학습   p.14~15

(1) curious about, is it / a kind of, tells, batteries, powerful
(2) m curious about / traffic sign, means, enter
(3) dots for, m curious about / Braille, blind / guess, mean
(4) curious, balloon, hanging / ad, product, powerful

Start Off – Listen & Talk A

1. soldiers, chimneys / messages, by using, chimneys / m curious about, system / smoking chimneys / What, mean
2. enemy, smoke at all, do / Smoke, chimney / rising, What does, mean / It means, close, border

is crossing, border, dark, soldiers going to do, messages, about / light, chimneys / light, chimneys / It means, battle

시험대비 기본평가   p.16

01 It means, not enter   02 ④
03 ③   04 ⑤

01 'It means ~.'는 '그것은 ~을 의미한다.'라는 의미로 정의를 내리는 표현이다. 조동사 must의 부정은 뒤에 not을 사용하고 동사원형 enter를 쓴다.

02 궁금증을 표현하는 말로 'I am curious about ~', 'I'm curious if/whether 주어+동사 ~', 'I would like/want to know ~', 'I'd be very interested to know ~', 'Can you tell me about ~?' 등이 있다.

03 'I'm curious ~.' 등으로 상대방이 궁금증을 표현하거나 의미를 물어보면 'This/It means ~.(그것은 ~을 의미한다.)' 또는 'It is ~.(그것은 ~이다.)' 등의 표현을 사용하여 상대방이 궁금해하거나 알고 싶어 하는 것의 의미나 정의를 설명하는 표현을 쓰는 것이 적절하다.

04 'I'm curious about ~'은 '나는 ~이 궁금해'라는 의미로 궁금증을 표현하는 것이다.

시험대비 실력평가   p.17~18

01 ③, ⑤   02 (d) / Other → The other[Another]
03 ④   04 ②   05 ⑤   06 ④
07 batteries   08 ②   09 for   10 ③
11 this painting

01 빈칸 앞의 대화가 '그것은 "그것을 꺼."를 의미해.'라고 궁금증을 설명해주는 말을 하고, 그 말에 대해 '정말?'이라고 놀라움을 표현하고 있기 때문에 그 말을 한 이유를 물어보는 것이 타당하다.

02 'other'는 뒤에 복수명사가 온다. 단수명사 'hunter'와 함께 사용될 수 있는 단어는 'the other' 또는 'another'이다.

03 '메시지를 보내기 위해서 병사들은 무슨 일을 할까?'라는 물음 뒤에 그것에 관한 궁금함을 표현하는 말이 오는 것이 자연스럽다.

04 빈칸 (B) 다음의 말이 '그것은 전투가 시작되었음을 의미해.'라는 것으로 보아 빈칸은 의미를 묻는 말이 오는 것이 자연스럽다.

05 적이 없을 때 연기를 피운다고 했으므로 글의 흐름상 굴뚝 한 곳에서 나오는 연기는 'No enemy.(적이 없음.)'를 나타낸다.

06 '그들은 연기를 전혀 피우지 않아, 그렇지?'라는 부정의문문으로 'Yes'는 '아니'로 해석한다.

07 라디오, 장난감, 자동차와 같은 것에 전기를 공급하는 물체

08 나머지는 모두 궁금증을 표현하는 말이고, ②번은 놀라움을 나타낼 때 사용하는 표현이다.

09 (a)는 '~은 무엇을 위한 거니?'라는 의미로 'What ~ for?' 구문이고, (b)는 의미상 '시각장애인을 위한'의 의미로 전치사 'for'가 적절하다.

10 그림에 숨겨진 또 다른 비밀에 관한 말로 보기 (C) 앞의 "Okay."와 뒤의 "I don't understand."가 부자연스럽기 때문에 (C)에 들어가는 것이 적절하다.

11 it은 인칭대명사로 주어인 This painting을 가리킨다.

서술형 시험대비   p.19

01 They mean "Jan van Eyck was here. 1434."
02 (A) I'm curious about them.   (B) It means
03 What makes you think so?
04 They mean they just saw an enemy.
05 They are sending messages to the king by using the chimneys.

01 질문: 여자아이가 찾은 글자는 무엇을 의미하는가?

02 (A) 궁금증을 나타내는 표현으로 'be curious about'을 사용하고 'secrets'는 복수형이므로 복수대명사 'them'을 사용한다. (B) 'It means ~.(그것은 ~을 의미한다.)'라는 의미로 정의를 표현하는 말이다.

03 'Why do you think so?'와 같은 의미로 'What makes you think so?'를 사용할 수 있다.

04 'They mean+주어+동사' 어순을 이용한다.

교과서
Grammar

핵심 Check   p.20~21

1 (1) were   (2) would
2 (1) whose   (2) whose   (3) enjoy

01 (1) If I were[was] a duck
　　(2) What would you do
　　(3) whose dog is carrying a doll
　　(4) whose dog wants a hot dog
02 (1) If I had wings, I would fly in the sky.
　　(2) What would you do if you were a fish?
　　(3) Koko is the boy whose bag is on a big cat.
　　(4) The girl whose cat is dancing is Didi.
03 (1) If I had a lot of money, I could travel around
　　　the world.
　　(2) If I were[was] tall, I could be a basketball
　　　player.

01 (1), (2) 현재 사실에 대한 가정은 'If+주어+동사 과거형, 주
　어+조동사 과거형(would/should/could/might)+동사원형'
　의 형태로 쓴다. (3) 'Bubu is the boy.' 문장에서 선행사 the
　boy 뒤에 소유격 관계대명사 문장을 이어 쓴다. (4) 'Lala is
　the girl.' 문장에서 선행사 the girl 뒤에 소유격 관계대명사 문
　장을 이어 쓴다.
02 (1) 가정법 과거 문장은 주절에 조동사의 과거형을 쓴다. (2) 가
　정법 과거 문장은 If절에 과거동사를 쓴다. (3) 선행사가 사람일
　때 소유격 관계대명사는 of which를 쓰지 않고 whose를 쓴다.
　(4) 사람이 선행사이므로 소유격 관계대명사는 whose를 쓴다.
03 (1), (2) 현재 사실에 대한 가정은 'If+주어+동사 과거형, 주어
　+조동사 과거형(would/should/could/might)+동사원형'의
　형태로 쓴다.

01 ④　　　　　　02 ①
03 There was a queen whose daughter was cursed
　　by an evil fairy.
04 ①　　　　05 ③　　　　06 ②
07 Miso is a girl whose dog is jumping rope.
08 If I had a lot of money, I could buy that car.
09 ③, ⑤
10 (1) If I had a monkey, I could play with it.
　　　또는 If I have a monkey, I can play with it.
　　(2) The boys whose mom is a lawyer live next
　　　door.
11 ⑤
12 (1) would build　(2) knew　(3) whose　(4) who
　　(5) whose
13 ④
14 If I were[was] a bird, I would fly over the
　　mountain.

15 The animal whose name begins with z is a zebra.
16 ④　　　　17 ④　　　　18 ⑤
19 If I met the President, I would shake hands with
　　him[her].
20 (1) would / would　(2) were / were[was]
21 she doesn't work with him, is not[isn't] very
　　disappointed with him

01 선행사가 사물일 때 소유격 관계대명사로 whose와 of which
　둘 중의 하나를 쓴다. 이때 whose는 무관사의 명사를 써야 하
　므로 the+명사가 있는 경우는 of which를 쓴다.
02 선행사가 사물일 때 소유격 관계대명사로 whose와 of which
　둘 중의 하나를 쓴다. 이때 whose는 무관사의 명사를 써야 하
　고, the+명사가 있는 경우는 of which를 쓴다.
03 두 문장에서 a queen과 소유격 Her는 동일 인물이므로 소유격
　관계사 whose로 연결하여 쓴다.
04 ② drove → drive ③ can → could ④ wins → won ⑤
　will → would
05 ③ 건강 상태가 좋아서, 나는 너와 운동할 수 있다. ①, ②, ④,
　⑤ 건강 상태가 좋다면, 나는 너와 운동할 텐데. (건강 상태가
　좋지 않아서, 나는 너와 운동할 수 없다.)
06 '내가 너라면'이 적절하므로 둘 다 'were'를 쓴다.
07 선행사 a girl 뒤에 소유격 관계대명사를 이어서 쓴다.
08 가정법과거는 현재 사실과 반대되므로 직설법 부정은 가정법 긍
　정으로 쓰고, 동사는 과거시제로 쓴다.
09 우리는 충분한 시간이 없기 때문에 더 오래 머무를 수 없다. =
　우리가 충분한 시간이 있다면, 더 오래 머무를 텐데. (가정법과
　거) *with: ~이 있다면, without: ~이 없다면 (if절을 대신할
　수 있다.)
10 (1) 가정법 과거형 또는 조건절의 형태로 주절과 if절을 맞추어
　쓴다. (2) 동사 lives의 주어는 The boys이므로 live로 쓴다.
　또는 The boy whose mom is a lawyer lives next door.
　로 고쳐도 좋다.
11 가정법 과거의 주절은 '조동사의 과거형+동사원형'으로 쓴다.
　lent → would lend
12 (1) 가정법 과거의 주절은 '조동사의 과거형+동사원형'으로 쓴
　다. (2) 가정법 과거 문장은 If절에 과거동사를 쓴다. (3) 관계대
　명사의 선행사 'a friend'가 family를 소유하는 것이 자연스럽
　다. (4) 관계대명사 다음에 동사가 이어지는 것은 주격 관계대명
　사 문장이다. (5) 관계대명사의 선행사 animals가 명사 lives
　를 소유하는 것이 자연스럽다.
13 현재 사실에 대한 가정은 'If+주어+동사 과거형, 주어+조동사
　과거형(would/should/could/might)+동사원형'의 형태로 쓴
　다.
14 현재 사실에 대한 가정은 'If+주어+동사 과거형, 주어+조동사
　과거형(would/should/could/might)+동사원형'의 형태로 쓴
　다.

15 The animal is a zebra 문장에서, 선행사 The animal 뒤에 소유격 관계대명사 whose를 사용하여 문장을 이어 쓰고 술부 is a zebra를 쓴다.

16 현재 사실에 대한 가정은 'If+주어+동사 과거형, 주어+조동사 과거형(would/should/could/might)+동사원형'의 형태로 쓴다.

17 두 문장에서 A girl과 소유격 Her는 동일 인물이므로 소유격 관계사 whose로 연결하여 쓴다.

18 첫 번째 문장은 'They taste like apples.'에서 주어 They로 관계대명사를 만들었기 때문에 which 또는 that을 쓴다. 두 번째 문장은 'Its smell is so sweet.'에서 소유격 Its로 관계대명사를 만들었기 때문에 whose를 쓴다.

19 현재 사실에 대한 가정은 'If+주어+동사 과거형, 주어+조동사 과거형(would/should/could/might)+동사원형'의 형태로 쓴다.

20 (1) 주절에 조동사의 과거형을 쓴다. (2) '네가 오리라면', '내가 오리라면'의 뜻에는 were가 적절하다.

21 가정법과거의 문장은 현재 사실에 대한 반대를 가정한 문장이므로, 가정법 문장이 부정이면 직설법 문장은 긍정으로, 가정법이 과거시제이면 직설법은 현재시제로 쓴다.

🦉 **서술형 시험대비**   p.26~27

01 (1) I have a friend whose brother enjoys skateboarding.

(2) The boy who[that] is dancing on the floor is my brother.

(3) He wants to ride a bike which[that] I bought yesterday.

(4) Do you like the house whose roof looks like a hat? 또는 Do you like the house of which the roof[the roof of which] looks like a hat?

(5) The boy whose cat is spinning a hula hoop is Jeje.

02 (1) If I had strong arms, I could climb trees.

(2) If I had a long nose, I could use it to take a shower.

(3) If I had a beautiful voice, I would sing on the tree.

03 (1) If I were[was] an English teacher, I would play word games every day.

(2) If I were[was] on the moon, I could jump much higher.

04 (1) Were he rich, he could travel to Europe.

(2) The boy who[that] is talking to Mary is my cousin.

(3) He lent me the book which[that] I want to read.

(4) I stayed at the house whose walls are white. 또는 I stayed at the house of which the walls[the walls of which] are white.

(5) If I were you, I would take a swimming lesson.

05 (1) would give   (2) would dance with them

(3) would get my feet

06 were[was], could sing and dance

07 (1) he doesn't talk to her. (또는 he won't talk to her)

(2) Were he at home

08 (1) The boy whose cell phone is ringing loudly doesn't understand the man's gesture.

(2) The girl whose feet are in the water doesn't understand the man's gesture.

(3) The boy whose hand the woman is pulling doesn't understand her gesture.

(4) The boy whose bag the monkey is pulling doesn't understand its gesture.

01 (1) 두 문장에서 a friend와 소유격 His는 동일 인물이므로 소유격 관계대명사 whose로 연결하여 쓴다. (2) 두 문장에서 The boy와 주어 He가 동일 인물이므로 주격관계대명사 who 또는 that으로 연결하여 쓴다. (3) 두 문장에서 a bike와 목적어 it이 동일하므로 목적격 관계대명사 which 또는 that으로 연결하여 쓴다. (4) 두 문장에서 a house와 소유격 whose가 동일하므로 소유격 관계대명사 whose로 연결하여 쓴다. (5) 두 문장에서 The boy와 소유격 His는 동일 인물이므로 소유격 관계대명사 whose로 연결하여 쓴다.

02 현재 사실에 대한 가정은 'If+주어+동사 과거형, 주어+조동사 과거형(would/should/could/might)+동사원형'의 형태로 쓴다.

03 가정법 과거는 현재 사실과 반대되므로 직설법 부정은 가정법 긍정으로 쓰고, 동사는 과거시제로 쓴다.

04 (1) rich는 형용사이므로 be동사 were로 가정법 문장을 쓴다. (2) 관계대명사가 주어 역할을 하는 문장이므로 소유격이 아닌 주격 관계대명사를 쓴다. (3) 관계대명사가 목적어 역할을 하는 문장이므로 소유격이 아닌 목적격 관계대명사를 쓴다. (4) 선행사 the house가 walls를 소유하는 문장이므로 소유격 관계대명사 whose나 of which를 쓴다. (5) 가정법 과거의 주절은 '조동사의 과거형+동사원형'으로 쓴다.

05 가정법 과거의 주절은 '조동사의 과거형+동사원형'으로 쓴다.

06 현재 사실에 대한 가정은 'If+주어+동사 과거형, 주어+조동사 과거형(would/should/could/might)+동사원형'의 형태로 쓴다.

07 (1) 가정법 과거는 현재 사실과 반대되므로 직설법 문장으로 표

현할 때 긍정은 부정문으로, 과거시제는 현재시제로 쓴다. (2) 'If 주어 were ~'로 표현한 가정법은 if를 생략하고 were를 문두로 도치할 수 있다.

08 (1) 두 문장에서 The boy와 소유격 His는 동일 인물이므로 소유격 관계사 whose로 연결하여 쓴다. (2) 두 문장에서 The girl과 소유격 Her는 동일 인물이므로 소유격 관계사 whose로 연결하여 쓴다. (3) 두 문장에서 The boy와 소유격 his hand의 his는 동일 인물이므로 소유격 관계사 whose로 연결하여 쓴다. (4) 두 문장에서 The boy와 소유격 his bag의 his는 동일 인물이므로 소유격 관계사 whose로 연결하여 쓴다.

Reading

확인문제 p.28

1 T 2 F 3 T 4 F 5 T 6 F

확인문제 p.29

1 T 2 F 3 T 4 F 5 T 6 F

교과서 확인학습 A p.30~31

01 A Picture Letter	02 Speaking, is rather
03 that easy	04 waited for, for weeks
05 couldn't read or write	06 got over
07 whose, far away	08 in Germany
09 more than 5%, one of them	
10 was discovered by	11 translated, into
12 reach, out	13 all in good health, one
14 not seriously	15 there was no reply
16 got, would be	17 fell ill
18 while, looks after	19 had, prepare, plant
20 voted for	21 so, that
22 whether one or the other	
23 Nothing changes	24 will work again
25 picked, from	26 hired, whose
27 knocked, down, picking, up	
28 paid, for	29 spent, for
30 enough, to fill, one	31 at a price of
32 as	33 would be, were
34 miss	35 a big hug
36 dear love	37 joined, as

교과서 확인학습 B p.32~33

1 A Picture Letter from a Mother of Three

2 Speaking to family members or friends in a foreign country is rather easy and simple today.

3 But before the days of phones and the Internet, it was not that easy.

4 People just sent a letter and waited for a reply for weeks.

5 And it was a lot harder if they couldn't read or write.

6 This letter shows how people got over these difficulties.

7 It was written in 1973 by a woman whose husband was far away.

8 She lived in Sicily, an Italian island, while her husband worked in Germany.

9 At the time, more than 5% of the people in Italy could not read or write, and she was one of them.

10 This letter was discovered by Sicilian writer Gesualdo Bufalino.

11 Here's how he translated the pictures into words.

12 My dear love, I miss you so much, and I reach my arms out toward you, together with our three kids.

13 We are all in good health except for the little one.

14 He's a little sick, but not seriously.

15 I already sent you a letter, but there was no reply, so I am sad about it.

16 If I got a letter from you, I would be very happy.

17 Your mother fell ill, and I'm going to visit her in the hospital with some money and food.

18 I'll go there with our middle son while the oldest looks after the youngest.

19 I had two workers prepare our field and plant seeds for 150,000 lire.

20 I voted for the DC.

21 The PCI lost so many seats that it almost seems dead.

22 But whether one or the other wins, it's the same.

23 Nothing changes for us poor people.

24 We worked yesterday, and we will work again tomorrow.

25 We picked lots of olives from our olive trees this year.

26 I hired a man whose sons are good workers.

27 He knocked the olives down, and his two sons helped him, picking them up from the ground.

28 I paid him 27,000 lire for the work.

29 I spent 12,000 more for the olive press.

30 I got enough oil to fill a large pot and a small one.

31 I can sell it at a price of 1,300 lire a liter.

32 My love, my heart thinks of you as Christmas is coming.

33 I would be so happy if you were with me.

34 We all miss you so much.

35 I'm sending you a big hug from me and our three little kids.

36 Goodbye, dear love.

37 My heart is yours, joined to you as our two rings are.

시험대비 실력평가 p.34~37

01 ②, ④, ⑤   02 ④   03 ⑤   04 hired
05 일꾼이 올리브를 쳐서 떨어뜨리면 그의 두 아들이 땅에서 올리브를 주우면서 그를 도와주는 일
06 per   07 ②   08 ①   09 ⑤
10 ①   11 ⓑ so ⓒ that
12 one hundred (and) fifty thousand   13 ④
14 (A) missed   (B) three kids
15 joined   16 ②   17 joined
18 As[Because, Since] I don't get a letter from you, I'm not very happy. 또는 I don't get a letter from you, so I'm not very happy.
19 ①, ③
20 (A) nothing   (B) worked   (C) will work
21 ②   22 there was no reply
23 If I got a letter from you, I would be very happy.
24 ④   25 ②, ④   26 ⑤

01 ⓐ와 ②, ④, ⑤: 동명사, ①, ③: 현재분사

02 이 글은 '전화와 인터넷 시대 이전에 외국에 있는 가족이나 친구와 대화하는 것이 그렇게 쉽지 않았다'는 내용의 글이므로, 제목으로는 ④번 '예전에 해외에 있는 사람들에게 말하는 것의 어려움'이 적절하다.

03 ⑤ 이 글만 읽고서는 읽거나 쓸 수 없는 사람들이 외국에 있는 사람들과 어떻게 대화했는지는 대답할 수 없다. ① No, it is rather easy and simple today. ② No, it was not that easy. ③ They just sent a letter and waited for a reply for weeks. ④ It took weeks.

04 hire: 고용하다

05 일꾼과 그의 두 아들이 한 일을 쓰는 것이 적절하다.

06 ⓒ의 a는 '(가격·양·비율을 나타내어) ~당'이라는 뜻으로, 'per(~당[마다])'로 바꿔 쓸 수 있다.

07 ⓐ by: ~가 한(수동형 문장에서 행위자, 창작자 등을 나타냄), ⓑ translate A into B: A를 B로 번역하다, 해석하다

08 주어진 문장의 It에 주목한다. ①번 앞 문장의 This letter를 받고 있으므로 ①번이 적절하다.

09 Gesualdo Bufalino는 그녀의 '그림들'을 '글'로 번역했다. ② illiterate: 글을 (읽거나 쓸 줄) 모르는, 문맹의

10 have+사람+동사원형

11 so ... that ~ = so ... as to ~: 너무 …해서 ~하다

12 보통 3자리씩 끊어서 읽고, 천의 자리에 thousand를 붙여서 읽는 것이 적절하다. one hundred (and) fifty thousands(X)

13 '세 아이와 함께 당신을 향해 내 팔을 쭉 뻗고 있어요. 막내를 제외하고는 우리 모두 건강해요.'라는 내용을 나타내는 그림으로는 ④번이 적절하다.

14 한 여성이 멀리 떨어져 있는 남편을 '그리워하며' 그녀와 그들의 '세 아이'가 어떻게 지내고 있는지를 알려주는 편지를 썼다.

15 "I join my heart to you"의 수동태 형태로 '(my heart is) joined to you'로 쓰인 것이다. 분사구문의 형태로 볼 수 있다. joined: 연결된 채로

16 '나와 우리 세 아이의 큰 포옹을 보내요. 내 마음은 당신의 것이에요, 우리들의 두 반지처럼 당신과 연결된 채로요'라는 내용을 나타내는 그림으로는 ②번이 적절하다.

17 are 뒤에 'joined'가 생략되었다.

18 가정법 과거 문장은 현재 사실과 반대되는 상상이나 가정을 나타내는 것이므로, 직설법으로 고칠 때는 현재시제를 사용하는 것이 적절하다.

19 look after = take care of = care for: ~을 돌보다, ② ~을 닮다, ④ ~을 찾다, 구하다, ⑤ ~의 안부를 묻다, 문안하다

20 가난한 사람들에게는 '아무 것도 바뀌지 않고' 그들은 어제도 '일했고', 내일도 다시 '일할' 것이기 때문이다.

21 ⓐ와 ②: 그리워[아쉬워]하다, ① (치거나 잡거나 닿지 못하고) 놓치다[빗나가다], ③ (식사 등을) 거르다, ④ (기회를) 놓치다, ⑤ (어디에 참석하지 않아서 그 일을) 놓치다

22 '(편지를 보냈는데) 답장이 없는 것'을 가리킨다.

23 현재 사실과 반대되는 상상이나 가정을 나타내는 가정법 과거 문장으로 쓰는 것이 적절하다.

24 ⓐ [교환] ~에 대하여, ~의 금액[값]으로, ⓑ at a price of: ~의 가격으로

25 ⓒ와 ②, ④: (가격·양·비율을 나타내어) ~당, ① (사람의 이름 앞에 쓰여) ~라는 사람, ③ 단수 명사 앞에 쓰여 그 부류를 통칭함, ⑤ 글 속에 처음 언급되는 단수형 명사 앞에 쓰임.

26 글쓴이가 올리브 기름(올리브유)을 팔아 얼마를 벌었는지는 알 수 없다. ① Yes. ② A man whose sons are good workers. ③ 27,000 lire. ④ The writer got enough oil to fill a large pot and a small one.

01 This letter shows how people got over these difficulties.

02 Sicilian writer Gesualdo Bufalino discovered this letter.

03 (A) her husband (B) in Germany

04 stretch   05 We are all in good health

06 kid   07 (A) 27,000 (B) 12,000 (C) 1,300

08 the olives   09 She spent 39,000 lire.

10 I already sent a letter to you

11 will → would

12 (A) fell ill (B) some money and food

13 for   14 to prepare   15 as

16 As[Because, Since] you are not with me, I'm not so happy. 또는 You are not with me, so I'm not so happy.

---

01 shows의 목적어를 간접의문문의 순서(how+주어+동사)로 쓰는 것이 적절하다.

02 Sicilian writer Gesualdo Bufalino를 주어로 해서 능동태로 고치는 것이 적절하다.

03 '독일'에서 일하는 '그녀의 남편'에게 편지를 썼다.

04 reach ~ out = stretch ~ out: (손 등을) 내밀다, 뻗다

05 be in good health: 건강 상태가 좋다

06 세 아이(three kids) 중 막내'아이'를 가리킨다.

07 그림 편지의 '일꾼이 올리브를 쳐서 떨어뜨리면 그의 두 아들이 땅에서 올리브를 주우면서 그를 도와주는 것을' 나타내는 가운데 그림을 참조하여 (A)에는 '27,000'을, '올리브 압착'을 나타내는 오른쪽 그림을 참조하여 (B)에는 '12,000'을, '큰 항아리 하나와 작은 항아리 하나를 채울 만큼의 충분한 기름'을 나타내는 왼쪽 그림을 참조하여 (C)에는 '1,300'을 쓰는 것이 적절하다.

08 '올리브'를 가리킨다.

09 올리브나무에서 올리브를 따는 비용 27,000리라+올리브를 압착하는 비용 12,000리라 = 39,000리라

10 send는 to를 사용하여 3형식으로 고친다.

11 가정법 과거 문장이므로, 주절의 시제를 'would'+동사원형으로 고치는 것이 적절하다.

12 그녀의 시어머니께서 '병이 드셔서' 병원에 계시기 때문에, 그녀는 '약간의 돈과 음식'을 가지고 병원을 방문할 예정이다. mother-in-law: 시어머니

13 ⓐ [교환] ~의 금액[값]으로, ⓑ vote for: ~에 (찬성) 투표를 하다

14 have+사람+동사원형 = get+사람+to부정사

15 ⓐ as Christmas is coming: 크리스마스가 다가오면서, ⓑ ~처럼

16 가정법 과거 문장은 현재 사실과 반대되는 상상이나 가정을 나타내는 것이므로, 직설법으로 고칠 때는 현재시제를 사용하는 것이 적절하다.

---

01 hug   02 ②   03 ⑤   04 ①

05 expression   06 ③

07 (a) board → border   08 ④   09 ②

10 ③   11 ⑤   12 ⑤

13 (1) I didn't know the singer, I couldn't shake hands with him

(2) he were[was] smart, he would prepare for the game in advance

14 ①   15 ⓓdon't → didn't   16 ③

17 ③   18 could see, were[was] taller

19 (1) would use kites to send my messages

(2) whose face looks like a mountain

(3) whose bag is full of fruit

20 ②

21 more than 5% of the people in Italy who could not read or write

22 ③   23 ⑤   24 reply   25 ③

26 ①   27 picking them up from the ground

28 were[was]   29 its gesture

---

01 유의어 관계이다. 고용하다 – 포용하다, 안다

02 (a): 당신은 추위를 극복하기 위한 당신만의 방법을 갖고 있나요? (b): 이것이 존경할 만한 정치인을 뽑는 것이 중요한 이유이다.

03 한 여자가 결혼한 남자

04 '위원회, 법정 등의 구성원으로서의 지위'의 뜻으로 'seat(의석)'이 적절하다.

05 '특별한 의미를 가지는 단어들의 그룹'의 의미를 가지는 'expression(표현)'이 적절하다.

06 'whether'는 부사절 접속사로 사용되면 '~이든 아니든'의 의미가 된다. 명사절 접속사일 때는 '~인지 아닌지'로 해석한다.

07 board: 판, 위원회, border: 국경

08 그 당시의 사람들이 어떤 종류의 개를 기르고 싶어했는지는 알 수가 없다.

09 위 대화는 Jan van Eyck의 그림 속에 숨겨진 비밀을 발견하여 그림을 통해 화가가 전달하고자 하는 메시지를 파악할 수 있는지에 관한 내용이다.

10 (C) '이 점들이 무엇을 위한 거니?'라고 궁금증을 표현하는 말이 오고 → (B) 궁금증에 대한 설명이 오고, Braille의 용도를 이야기해 준다. (A) 마지막으로 알았다는 대답이 오는 것이 자연스럽다.

11 '난 수화가 궁금해'라는 A의 말에 대해, B가 '수화가 뭐니? 내가 표현 하나를 알려줄게.'라고 말하는 것은 어색하다.

12 가정법 과거의 문장이 '만일 그가 춤을 잘 춘다면'이므로 직설법 문장은 '그는 춤을 못 추기 때문에'로 쓰는 것이 적절하다. 'not poor'를 'poor' 또는 'not good'으로 쓴다.

13 가정법 과거는 현재 사실과 반대되므로 직설법 문장을 가정법으로 표현할 때 긍정은 부정문으로, 부정은 긍정문으로 쓰고, 현재 시제는 과거시제로 쓴다.

14 ①은 두 문장을 연결하는 접속사와 주어 역할을 하는 주격 관계대명사가 필요하므로 which 또는 that을 쓴다. ②, ③, ④, ⑤는 소유격 관계대명사 whose를 쓴다.

15 가정법 과거 문장이므로 if절의 동사를 과거시제로 쓴다.

16 ③은 의문사 whose이다. ①, ②, ④, ⑤는 소유격 관계대명사 whose이다.

17 c. have → had d. won't → wouldn't e. will → would

18 현재 사실에 대한 가정은 'If+주어+동사 과거형, 주어+조동사 과거형(would/should/could/might)+동사원형'의 형태로 쓴다.

19 (1) 가정법 과거의 주절은 '조동사의 과거형+동사원형'으로 쓴다. (2) 선행사 a kite가 명사 face를 소유하는 것이 자연스러우므로 whose를 쓴다. (3) 선행사 The boy가 명사 bag을 소유하는 것이 자연스러우므로 whose를 쓴다.

20 선행사가 사물인 경우에는 소유격을 whose나 of which로 쓸 수 있지만, 사람인 경우에는 of which로 쓸 수 없다. ① overcome: 극복하다, ③ over: ~ 이상, ④ the Italians: 이탈리아 사람들, ⑤ 관계부사 'how'를 'the way'로 바꿔 쓸 수 있다. 그러나 'the way how'와 같이 선행사와 관계부사를 함께 쓸 수는 없다.

21 '읽거나 쓸 수 없었던 5% 이상의 이탈리아 사람들'을 가리킨다.

22 글의 마지막에서 '그가 그림들을 어떻게 글로 번역했는지는 다음과 같다.'고 했으므로, 뒤에 올 내용으로는 'Gesualdo Bufalino가 그림 편지들을 글로 번역한 내용'이 가장 적절하다.

23 ⓐ와 ⑤: 부정대명사로 가산 명사를 반복하는 것을 피하기 위해 쓰임. ① 하나(의), ② (과거·미래의) 어느 한, ③ 같은, ④ 일반 사람, 누구나

24 ⓑ의 letter는 '편지'를 가리킨다.

25 글쓴이는 남편에게 이미 편지를 보냈지만, 답장이 없어서 슬프다고 했으므로, 처음으로 편지를 보내고 있다는 ③번은 옳지 않다. ④ mother-in-law: 시어머니.

26 ①번 다음 문장의 He에 주목한다. 주어진 문장의 a man을 받고 있으므로 ①번이 적절하다.

27 이어동사 picking: '주우면서'라는 의미로 동시 동작을 표현한다. 이어동사 picking up의 목적어가 인칭대명사 them이므로 picking과 up 사이에 them을 쓰는 것이 적절하다.

28 가정법 과거이므로 'were'로 쓰는 것이 적절하다. if절에 쓰이는 be동사의 과거형은 보통 'were'를 사용하지만, 구어체에서는

주어가 'I' 또는 3인칭 단수인 경우 'was'를 쓰기도 한다.

29 '원숭이의 몸짓'을 가리킨다.

단원별 예상문제 p.46~49

01 (a)live 02 ②
03 It means "Do not[Don't] enter." 또는 It means (that) you must not enter here.
04 (C) – (A) – (B) – (D)
05 They are for sending messages to the king.
06 ③ 07 ② 08 ④ 09 ⑤
10 ③ 11 ①
12 (1) Is there any student whose name was not called?
(2) Mike is the boy whose hair is very short.
(3) The house whose windows are very big is my uncle's.
(4) My sister is the girl whose cat is eating a fish.
(5) Do you know the old man whose shoes are red and blue?
13 (1) I know a boy whose mother grows bananas.
(2) The boy whose dog is barking is my cousin.
(3) The girl whose hat is covered with flowers is a great dancer.
(4) If you were with me(또는 Were you with me), I could show you my painting.
(5) If I were a fish, I could swim in the water.
14 Speaking to family members or friends in a foreign country
15 ② 16 ④ 17 ① 18 out
19 ③ 20 don't → doesn't
21 ②, ③, ⑤

01 반의어 관계다. 아픈-건강한 : 죽은-살아 있는

02 '어떤 것을 사용할 준비가 되도록 하다'라는 의미로 'prepare(준비하다)'가 적절하다.

03 그림은 진입 금지를 나타내는 표지판이다.

04 '병사들이 5개의 굴뚝으로 무엇을 하고 있니?'라는 물음에 → (C) 왕에게 메시지를 보내고 있다는 답을 하고 → (A) '정말?'이라고 놀라움을 표현한 다음, 그 체계에 대한 궁금증을 표현하며, 좀 더 말해달라고 부탁을 하는 말에 대해 → (B) '연기 나는 굴뚝 두 개가 보이지?'라는 물음을 통해 그 체계에 대한 질문을 하고 마지막으로 → (D) 긍정의 답을 하며 그것이 무엇을 의미하는지 묻고, 소녀의 마지막 말이 오는 것이 적절하다.

05 질문: 그 굴뚝들은 무엇을 위한 것이라고 생각하는가?

06 G의 빈칸 다음 말에서 굴뚝 하나에서 연기가 나오면 적이 없다는 것을 의미한다고 했으므로, '만약 적이 없다면, 그들은 연기

9

를 전혀 피우지 않아, 그렇지?'라는 B의 물음에 대해 '아니, 연기를 피워.'라는 대답이 적절하다.

07 주어진 문장은 '그것은 "Jan van Eyck가 여기 있었다. 1434."를 의미해.'라는 뜻으로 (B)에 오는 것이 적절하다.

08 남자의 마지막 말에 '그 여자는 연못을 가리키고 있어.'라고 말하는 것으로 보아 ④번이 자연스럽다.

09 ⑤번은 '이 집은 수 천 개의 비밀을 가진 것으로 유명해.'라는 말에 대해 '정말? 그것은 네가 비밀을 찾아야 하는 것을 의미해.'라고 말하는 것은 자연스럽지 않다.

10 빈칸 다음에 '그럼 그 소년은 과일을 얻기 위해 닭을 한 마리 가져와야 하는구나, 맞지?'라고 말하는 것으로 보아 ③이 적절하다.

11 선행사 The house 뒤에 its doors의 관계이므로 whose doors로 쓴다.

12 (1) 두 문장에서 any student와 소유격 His는 동일 인물이므로 소유격 관계사 whose로 연결하여 쓴다. (2) 두 문장에서 The boy와 소유격 His는 동일 인물이므로 소유격 관계사 whose로 연결하여 쓴다. (3) 두 문장에서 The house와 소유격 Its가 동일하므로 소유격 관계사 whose로 연결하여 쓴다. (4) 두 문장에서 the girl과 소유격 Her는 동일 인물이므로 소유격 관계사 whose로 연결하여 쓴다. (5) 두 문장에서 the old man과 소유격 His는 동일 인물이므로 소유격 관계사 whose로 연결하여 쓴다.

13 (1) 선행사 a boy가 mother를 소유하는 문장이므로 주격이 아닌 소유격 관계대명사 whose를 쓴다. (2) 선행사가 사람일 때는 소유격 관계대명사로 of which가 아닌 whose를 쓴다. (3) 선행사 The girl이 문장의 주어이므로 동사는 are가 아닌 is를 쓴다. (4) 한 문장에 두 개의 절이 있을 때 접속사가 필요하므로 If you were with me, 또는 if를 생략한 도치문장 Were you with me로 쓴다. (5) 가정법 과거의 주절은 '조동사의 과거형+동사원형'으로 쓴다.

14 '외국에 있는 가족이나 친구와 대화하는 것'을 가리킨다.

15 ⓑ와 ①, ⑤: 지시부사('그렇게'), ②, ④: 지시형용사, ③: 접속사

16 ④ a lot(much/even/still/far): 비교급을 강조하는 부사('훨씬'), ④ rather: 다소, 약간.

17 주어진 문장의 We에 주목한다. ①번 앞 문장의 'I'와 'our three kids'를 받고 있으므로 ①번이 적절하다.

18 reach ~ out: (손 등을) 내밀다, 뻗다,' 목적어가 명사일 경우에는 목적어를 out 다음에 쓰는 것도 가능하다.

19 그녀의 남편으로부터 왜 답장이 없었는지는 알 수 없다. ① There were three kids. ② No. ④ She will visit the hospital with her middle son. ⑤ The oldest will look after the youngest.

20 The boy가 주어이므로 don't를 doesn't로 고치는 것이 적절하다.

21 right away = right now = at once = immediately: 즉시, ① 머뭇거리며, 망설이며, ④ 순차적으로

서술형 실전문제   p.50~51

01 It tells people their batteries are very powerful.
02 Pictures speak a thousand words
03 hidden secrets, Latin, means, the rich, rich
04 (1) ㉠ → was created   (2) ㉡ → (to) use
    (3) ㉢ → couldn't
05 (1) If I didn't have any money, I couldn't buy the new shoes.
    (2) If Suji were[was] here, I could tell her the story.
06 (1) If I were you, I would set the alarm clock.
    (2) If I were you, I would write it by hand.
    (3) If I were you, I would search it on the Internet.
07 picking up them → picking them up
08 olive oil   **09** whose
10 (A) is   (B) while   (C) how
11 it was a lot harder if they couldn't read or write.

01 'tell+간접목적어(people)+직접목적어(their batteries are ~)' 어순으로 쓴다.

02 그림을 통해 여러 가지 숨겨진 사실들을 알 수 있다는 내용이므로 'Pictures speak a thousand words(그림이 천 마디 말을 하지.)'가 적절하다.

04 (1) 주어 Hangeul과 동사 'create'는 수동 관계이므로 수동태를 쓴다. (2) help의 목적보어는 원형부정사 또는 to부정사를 쓴다. (3) 가정법 과거를 써야 하므로 조동사를 과거형으로 쓴다.

05 가정법 과거는 현재 사실과 반대되므로 직설법 문장을 가정법으로 표현할 때, 긍정은 부정문으로, 부정은 긍정문으로 쓰고, 현재시제는 과거시제로 쓴다.

06 현재 사실에 대한 가정은 'If+주어+동사 과거형, 주어+조동사 과거형(would/should/could/might)+동사원형'의 형태로 쓴다.

07 picking up의 목적어가 인칭대명사 them이므로 picking과 up 사이에 them을 쓰는 것이 적절하다.

08 '올리브기름(올리브유)'을 가리킨다.

09 소유격 관계대명사 'whose'가 적절하다.

10 (A) 동명사 Speaking이 문장의 주어이므로 is가 적절하다. (B) 뒤에 '주어+동사'가 있으므로 while이 적절하다. during+기간을 나타내는 명사, while+주어+동사, (C) 뒤에 완전한 문장이 이어지고 있으므로 관계부사 how가 적절하다.

11 'Speaking to family members or friends in a foreign country'를 가리키는 'it'을 주어로 해서 쓰는 것이 적절하다.

|모범답안|

01 (1) A: What does this sign mean?

     B: It means you must not ride a bike here.

   (2) A: What does this sign mean?

     B: It means you must drive slowly here.

02 (1) I would see a doctor

   (2) I wouldn't wait for him anymore

   (3) I wouldn't hurry

   (4) I wouldn't quit the job

03 (A) in the pond   (B) gesture

   (C) Step back from the pond

01 ④   **02** border   **03** ④   **04** ⑤

05 ②   **06** No enemy   **07** ①   **08** ③

09 Because only the rich could have that kind of dog at that time.

10 (A) They mean they just saw an enemy.

   (B) Now the enemy is crossing the border in the dark.

   (C) It means the battle has started.

11 ②   **12** ⑤   **13** ②   **14** ②

15 I have a brother whose job is a fire fighter.

16 (1) If I were[was] God   (2) If I traveled to the past

17 ④

18 (A) a foreign country

   (B) phones and the Internet

19 the way how → the way 또는 how   **20** ②

21 ⓑ twenty-seven thousand   ⓒ twelve thousand

   ⓓ one thousand three hundred

22 ②   **23** ③

24 (A) a letter   (B) the hospital

25 oldest → middle   **26** ③   **27** pot

01 ④번은 '당신을 걱정하게 만들 만큼 나쁘거나 위험한 방법으로'를 의미하는 'seriously'에 대한 설명이다. 'ill'에 대한 설명은 'suffering from an illness or disease'이다.

02 유의어 관계이다. 궁금한 : 경계, 국경

03 '지구의 표면'의 의미로 'ground(땅, 지면)'가 적절하다.

04 ⑤: 이 글자가 무엇을 의미하는지 묻는 말에 이 편지가 파란 잉크로 쓰였다고 말하는 것은 어색하다.

05 '메시지를 보내기 위해서 병사들은 무슨 일을 할까?'라는 물음에 대한 답으로 ②번이 적절하다.

06 대화의 흐름상 굴뚝 한 곳에서 연기가 나오면 적이 없다는 것을 의미한다.

07 '~에 대해 궁금해 하다'는 'be curious about'을 사용한다.

08 G의 첫 번째 대화에서 '그 비밀들은 어디에 있니?'라고 묻는 것으로 보아 그림 속에 비밀이 숨겨져 있다는 것을 알 수 있다.

09 질문: 왜 사람들은 사진 속의 남자가 매우 부자였다고 생각하는가?

10 봉수대의 연기는 적이 성에 접근하는 위치에 따라 굴뚝의 연기 개수가 많아진다는 것을 알 수 있다.

11 이 남자의 몸짓은 무엇을 의미하는지 묻는 말 다음에 궁금증을 표현하는 말이 적절하다.

12 ①~④: were ⑤ had

13 'The man is good at playing soccer.' 문장에서, 선행사 'The man' 뒤에 소유격 관계대명사 whose를 사용하여 문장을 이어 쓰고 술부 'is good at playing soccer'를 쓴다.

14 현재 사실에 대한 가정은 'If+주어+동사 과거형, 주어+조동사 과거형(would/should/could/might)+동사원형'의 형태로 쓴다. *fall in love with: ~와 사랑에 빠지다 (수동형으로 쓰지 않는다.)

15 'I have a brother.'의 문장을 쓰고, 선행사 a brother 뒤에 소유격 관계대명사 문장을 이어 쓴다.

16 현재 사실에 대한 가정은 'If+주어+동사 과거형'으로 쓴다.

17 이 글은 '읽거나 쓸 줄 모르는 한 여자가 독일에서 일하는 남편에게 그림으로 쓴 편지를 시실리의 작가 Gesualdo Bufalino가 글로 번역했다'는 내용의 글이므로, 주제로는 ④번 '읽거나 쓸 줄 모르는 한 여자가 외국에 있는 남편에게 보낸 그림 편지'가 적절하다. ② illiterate: 글을 (읽거나 쓸 줄) 모르는, 문맹의, ③ illiteracy rate:문맹률

18 사람들, 특히 문맹인 사람들이 '전화와 인터넷' 시대 이전에 '외국'에 있는 가족이나 친구와 대화하려고 노력할 때 겪었던 어려움들을 의미한다.

19 관계부사 'how'를 'the way'로 바꿔 쓸 수 있지만, 'the way how'와 같이 선행사와 관계부사를 함께 쓸 수는 없다.

20 ⓐ와 ①, ②, ④: 현재분사, ③, ⑤: 동명사

21 천의 자리에서 끊어서 읽으면서, 그 자리에 thousand를 붙여서 읽는 것이 적절하다. ⓑ 십 단위와 단 단위 사이에 보통 하이픈으로 연결하는 것이 적절하다. twenty-seven thousands(×), ⓒ twelve thousands(×), ⓓ one thousand three hundreds(×)

22 땅에서 올리브를 주운 것은 '일꾼'이 아니라 그의 '두 아들'이다. 본문의 picking은 분사구문으로 행위자가 his two sons이고, ②번의 pick은 helped의 목적격보어로서 행위자가 목적어인 him이 된다.

23 ⓐ in good health: 건강하여, ⓑ look after: ~을 돌보다

24 그림 편지의 '편지 봉투' 문양을 참조하여 (A)에는 a letter를, '십자가 문양의 병원 표시'를 참조하여 (B)에는 the hospital을 쓰는 것이 적절하다.

25 글쓴이는 '둘째' 아들과 시어머니를 방문할 것이다.

26 ⓐ와 ①, ③, ④: 형용사적 용법, enough+명사+to부정사: 형용사적 용법, enough+형용사/부사+to부정사: 부사적 용법, ②: 부사적 용법, ⑤: 명사적 용법

27 '항아리'를 가리킨다.

Lesson 6

We Are All Makers

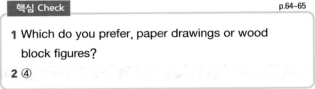

시험대비 실력평가   p.62

01 cloth   02 ③   03 ⑤   04 ①
05 gave away   06 ④   07 ⑤   08 ②

01 '대부분의 커튼은 천으로 만들어진다. <영어 설명> 옷과 같은 것을 만드는 데 사용되는 재료

02 figure는 '① (사람, 동물의) 상, 모형 ② 모양 ③ 숫자'의 의미를 지닌다. • 그는 말 청동상을 만들었다. • 그 수치는 OECD 평균 6,741 달러보다 낮은 것이다.

03 '공식적인 명단에 누군가 또는 무엇인가의 이름을 올리다'라는 의미로 '등록하다(register)'가 적절하다.

04 '액체나 기체에서 원치 않는 물질을 제거하다'라는 뜻으로 '~을 거르다, 여과하다(filter)'가 적절하다.

05 '남에게 주다, 나누어 주다'는 'give away'를 사용한다.

06 (A) 그는 중병에 걸려 병원에 입원했다. (B) 그녀는 그녀의 엄마를 친구로 생각한다.

07 나머지는 모두 '명사-형용사' 관계이고, ⑤번은 '동사-명사'관계이다.

08 공공의, 대중의: 한 나라의 모든 사람과 관련된. '우리는 밖에 있을 때, 공중 화장실을 사용해야 한다.

서술형 시험대비   p.63

01 (1) drinkable (2) report (3) necessary (4) tore
02 prefer
03 (1) (c)heerful (2) (a)ctually (3) both (4) (p)rovide
04 (1) bookstore, 서점 (2) leave, 남겨두다
    (3) pour, 붓다, 따르다
05 thought of[looked upon, regard], as

01 (1) 이 물은 마실 수 있나요? be동사 다음에 '마실 수 있는'의 뜻으로 형용사 'drinkable'이 적절하다. (2) 그는 대형 기사를 보도한 최초의 기자였다. (3) 음식과 물은 인간이 살기 위해 필요하다. (4) 내 고양이가 어제 그 책의 페이지를 찢었다. 'tear'의 과거형 'tore'가 적절하다.

02 '또 다른 사람이나 물건보다 어떤 사람이나 물건을 더 좋아하다'라는 의미로 '선호하다(prefer)'가 적절하다.

03 (1) cheerful: 유쾌한 (2) actually: 실제로, 사실상 (3) both: 둘 다 (4) provide: 제공하다

04 (1) 책을 파는 상점 (2) 어떤 것을 어떤 장소 특히 그것이 머무

를 장소에 두다 (3) 용기 밖으로 액체가 흘러가도록 만들다

05 그는 초창기 때부터 이 회사를 위해 일해서, 모든 사람들은 그를 실질적인 사장으로 여기고 있었다. '…을 ~로 생각하다[여기다]'는 'regard A as B = think of A as B = look upon A as B = consider A (as) B' 등으로 표현할 수 있다.

[교과서]
Conversation

핵심 Check   p.64~65

1 Which do you prefer, paper drawings or wood block figures?

2 ④

교과서 대화문 익히기

Check(√) True or False   p.66

1 T   2 F   3 F   4 T

교과서 확인학습   p.68~69

Get Ready 2
(1) Which, better, cloth, artwork / better, Actually
(2) Which do you prefer, drawings, wood / prefer, figures / Let's, some of them
(3) Which, prefer, folding, clothes / folding paper, to realx

Start Off – Listen & Talk A
1. Why don't we, pockets / What shall we / Which, board, holder / prefer, holder, to make, spending, making / Let's, together
2. Why don't we / What kind, to make / prefer / hate holding, in / Let's make

Start Off - Listen & Talk B
with jeans / for / draw / Which do you prefer / prefer, lovely / draw / I can't wait for

Start Off – Speak Up
Sure, Which, prefer, or / prefer, making / introduce, to

Start Off - Your Turn
Which, taking, taking / prefer taking, hate taking

away / proud that, collected, interesting, to give away / prepare, any / making / Let's / Which, prefer, writing / writing / No problem, cheerful messages / sure, bookmarks

Express Yourself A

1. flying, flying drones / flying / working, machines
2. Which, making, making / both, it, that, prefer / something delicious

---

시험대비 기본평가　　　　　　　　p.70

01 ④　　　　02 ②　　　　03 ⑤

01 전자책을 더 좋아한다는 말 다음의 Actually는 문장을 강조하는 표현으로 ④번이 어울린다.
02 푸드 아트 만들기를 좋아하는 이유를 묻는 말에 대해 '맛있는 것을 만들기를 좋아해'라는 말이 가장 자연스럽다.
03 'I hate ~(나는 ~하기를 싫어한다)'는 자신이 하기 싫어하는 것을 강하게 표현하는 말이다.

시험대비 실력평가　　　　　　　　p.71~72

01 ④　　　02 to draw → draw　　　03 ③
04 ②　　　05 the book club day is just one week away　　　06 prepare　　07 ⑤　　08 ③
09 ④　　　10 ①　　　11 or

01 빈칸은 선호를 묻는 표현이 적절하다. ④번은 판다를 더 좋아하는 이유를 묻는 표현으로 어색하다.
02 'let+목적어+목적보어(동사원형)' 형태가 적절하다.
03 빈칸은 '우리 낡은 청바지로 가방을 하나 만드는 게 어떨까?'라는 제안의 표현이 자연스럽다.
04 어깨에 메는 가방이 더 좋다고 말하고 있기 때문에 빈칸에는 손에 물건을 드는 것을 몹시 싫어한다는 표현이 오는 것이 적절하다.
05 '한 주 남았다'는 의미로 'one week away'를 사용한다.
06 '앞으로 일어날 일에 대한 계획을 하거나 준비를 하다'라는 의미로 '준비하다(prepare)'가 적절하다.
07 밑줄 친 (e) 다음 문장에서 '나는 책갈피를 만들고 싶어.'라고 말하고 있으므로 글쓰기를 좋아한다는 말은 어색하다. 'love'를 'hate'로 바꾸는 것이 적절하다.
08 대화의 흐름상 빈칸에는 무엇을 만들지 물어보는 말이 자연스럽다.
09 빈칸 앞에 '만들기가 더 쉬워'라고 말하고 있으므로 시간이 많이 걸리는 것은 싫어한다는 말이 오는 것이 자연스럽다.
10 빈칸은 둘 중에 무엇을 더 선호하는지를 묻는 표현이 적절하다.
11 A와 B 중에서 선택을 할 때 사용하는 접속사 'or'가 적절하다.

서술형 시험대비　　　　　　　　p.73

01 Which do you prefer, making the bookmarks or writing the messages?
02 She is going to make bookmarks.
03 I love making something delicious.
04 Why don't we make something with jean pockets?
05 I hate spending too much time making things.

01 상대방의 선호를 물을 때는 'prefer(더 좋아하다)'를 사용하여 'Which do you prefer, A or B?'를 쓴다.
02 질문: 민지는 방문객들에게 무엇을 만들어 줄 것인가?
03 좋아하는 표현은 'I love+동명사'를 사용하고, something은 형용사가 뒤에서 수식을 한다.
04 'Why don't we+동사원형 ~?'을 이용하여 '~하는 게 어때?'라는 제안의 표현을 쓸 수 있다.
05 hate는 동명사를 목적어로 취할 수 있고, 'spend+시간+-ing' 구문을 이용한다.

교과서
Grammar

핵심 Check　　　　　　　　　p.74~75

1 (1) happier　(2) better
2 (1) was my mother that[who]
　(2) was a chocolate cake that[which]

시험대비 기본평가　　　　　　　　p.76

01 (1) The more books we share
　 (2) the darker it gets
　 (3) the farther we see
　 (4) It was last Sunday that
02 (1) The longer I waited, the angrier I became.
　 (2) The harder you exercise, the stronger you will become.
　 (3) The earlier you register, the better seat you will get.
　 (4) The more books you read, the wiser you become.
03 (1) It is Paris that
　 (2) It is Minji that

01 'the+비교급, the+비교급'은 '…하면 할수록, 더 ~하다'라는 의미이다. (1) many books의 비교급을 the more books로 쓰고 '주어+동사'의 어순으로 쓴다. (2) dark의 비교급을 the darker로 쓰고 '주어+동사'의 어순으로 쓴다. (3) far의 비교급으로 farther(더 멀리)와 further(더 나아가)가 있다. 보통 farther는 거리를 나타내고, further는 정도를 나타내므로 여기서는 farther를 쓰는 것이 더 좋다. 그러나 further를 써도 틀리는 것은 아니다. (4) 'It is[was]+강조할 부분(last Sunday)+that+문장의 나머지 부분'으로 쓴다.

02 (1) angry의 비교급은 angrier이다. (2) 'the+비교급, the+비교급'의 형태로 써야 한다. (3) '더 좋은 자리'의 의미로 형용사 better와 명사 seat을 함께 써야 한다. (4) wiser가 이미 비교급이므로 more를 쓰지 않는다. (4) 사람이 선행사이므로 소유격 관계대명사는 whose를 쓴다.

03 'It is[was]+강조할 부분(Paris, Minji)+that+문장의 나머지 부분'으로 쓴다.

시험대비 실력평가
p.77~79

01 ⑤　　**02** ④　　**03** ①, ④
04 ⑤　　**05** ④
06 (1) It is Linda that[who] doesn't like cheese cake.
　　(2) It is this old computer that gives me a headache.
07 The more mistakes you make　　**08** ③
09 The higher the wave rose, the faster we swam.
10 The earlier you leave, the sooner you will arrive.
11 (1) shines brighter, I feel happier
　　(2) waited longer, I became angrier
　　(3) you read more books, you will know more things
12 ③
13 It is this beautiful garden that will make people feel better.
14 the more birds will come
15 ①　　**16** ④　　**17** ⑤　　**18** ③
19 (1) It was Makers' Camp that[which] we went to.
　　(2) It was Chagall that[who] painted *I and the Village*.
20 ③

---

01 'the+비교급, the+비교급'은 '…하면 할수록, 더 ~하다'라는 의미이다. happy의 비교급을 more happy로 쓰는 것은 옳지 않다.

02 'the+비교급, the+비교급'은 '…하면 할수록, 더 ~하다'라는 의미이다. the best는 최상급이므로 적절하지 않다.

03 Junha를 강조하는 'It was ~ that' 강조구문이다. 사람을 강조할 때 that 대신 who를 쓸 수 있다.

04 ⑤의 that은 진주어를 이끄는 접속사 that이다. 해석: 스마트폰이

학생들이 새로운 것을 배우는 것을 도와준다는 것은 분명하다.

05 Canadian team이 Team Kim을 이긴 것이 아니라 Team Kim이 Canadian team을 이긴 것이므로, It was the Canadian team that Team Kim beat in Gangneung in 2018.으로 쓰는 것이 적절하다. ③ Team Kim이 경기를 이긴 것은 바로 2점차이다.

06 (1) 'It ... that' 강조구문으로 강조하는 부분이 사람이므로 which가 아닌 that이나 who를 쓴다. (2) 'It is[was]+강조할 부분+that+문장의 나머지 부분'으로 쓸 때 강조 부분이 문장의 주어이면 that 뒤의 동사의 수는 그 주어에 일치시켜야 하므로 give는 gives로 쓰는 것이 적절하다.

07 'the+비교급, the+비교급' 문장을 쓸 때 비교급의 형용사가 명사를 수식하는 명사면, 'the+비교급 형용사(the more)+명사(mistakes)'로 쓴다.

08 'the+비교급, the+비교급'은 '…하면 할수록, 더 ~하다'라는 의미이다. difficult의 비교급은 more difficult이고, hard의 비교급은 harder이다.

09 '파도가 높아질수록 우리는 더 빨리 수영했다.'의 뜻으로 'the+비교급+주어+동사, the+비교급+주어+동사'로 완성한다.

10 'the+비교급+주어+동사, the+비교급+주어+동사' 형태로 쓴다.

11 (1), (2), (3) 'the+비교급, the+비교급' 구문은 접속사 'as' 또는 'if' 등을 사용하여, '접속사+주어+동사+비교급, 주어+동사+비교급'의 형태로 같은 의미의 문장을 쓸 수 있다.

12 'It ... that' 강조구문으로 'It is[was]+강조할 부분+that+문장의 나머지 부분'으로 쓰며, It was 다음에 강조할 부분인 the chocolate cake을 쓴 후 ③에 that을 쓰는 것이 적절하다.

13 'It is[was]+강조할 부분(this beautiful garden)+that+문장의 나머지 부분'으로 쓸 때, make를 사용한 5형식 문장(목적어+원형부정사) 형태로 쓴다.

14 'the+비교급, the+비교급' 문장을 쓸 때 비교급의 형용사가 명사를 수식하는 명사면, 'the+비교급 형용사+명사'로 쓴다.

15 disappointed의 비교급은 more disappointed이다. 'The more you want, the more disappointed you will be.'로 쓴다. 해석: 더 많이 원할수록, 너는 더 실망하게 된다.

16 첫 번째 문장은 'It ~ that' 강조구문이고 강조하는 부분이 사람이므로 that이나 who를 쓸 수 있다. 두 번째 문장은 주격 관계대명사를 계속적 용법으로 써야 하므로 who를 쓰는 것이 적절하다. 그러므로 공통으로 들어갈 단어는 'who'이다.

17 첫 번째의 빈칸은 'It ... that' 강조구문으로 강조부분이 주어이므로 동사는 그에 맞게 makes를 쓰는 것이 적절하다. 두 번째 문장은 'the+비교급, the+비교급' 구문이고, pretty의 비교급은 prettier이므로 the prettier를 쓰는 것이 적절하다.

18 faster가 이미 비교급의 형태이므로 more를 쓰지 않는 것이 적절하다.

19 A의 질문에 사용된 단어를 활용하여 'It was+강조할 부분(Makers' Camp, Chagall)+that+문장의 나머지 부분'으로

쓴다.

20 b. It was on the Internet that she bought her shirts.
c. It is Kiyoung that loves to write poems. d. The higher I climbed the mountain, the darker the sky was getting.

01 (1) The harder you practice, the faster you can type.
(2) The more they tried, the better they did.
(3) The colder it gets, the more clothes we need.
(4) The closer he got to the fire, the warmer he felt.
(5) The earlier you get up, the more time you can spend on makeup.

02 (1) the smell of lemons that[which] cats hate
(2) my grandmother that[who] made me banana cakes
(3) It was my grandfather that[who] told me the story.
(4) It is this Friday that[when] we will attend a conference.
(5) It was in front of the MBC building that[where] we saw the statue.

03 (1) It was five copies of the same books that he bought at the bookstore.
(2) It is the class field trip that I won't forget.
(3) It is this experience that deeply connected all of us.

04 (1) a light drone, lighter
(2) the facial design, more

05 (1) It is tomorrow that she will sing the song.
(2) It is Joan that cheers me up all the time.

06 the more worse → the worse

07 (1) It is her teddy bear that Cathy likes the best.
(2) It was from Junsu that I first heard the news.
(3) It was Minji that went to visit her aunt last Thursday.
(4) It is the star watching experience in Yeongwol that Minjun can't forget.
(5) It was at the bookstore that my dad first met my mom.

01 (1), (2), (4) 접속사를 뺀 후 'the+비교급+주어+동사, the+비교급+주어+동사' 형태로 쓴다. (3), (5) 'the+비교급, the+비교급' 문장을 쓸 때 비교급의 형용사가 명사를 수식하는 명사면, 'the 비교급 형용사+명사'로 쓴다. (3) the more clothes, (5)

the more time

02 'It is[was]+강조할 부분(last Sunday)+that+문장의 나머지 부분'으로 쓴다. 이때 문장의 시제에 따라 is와 was를 구분해서 쓴다. 또한 that 대신에 강조하는 것이 사람이면 who, 사물이면 which, 시간이면 when, 장소면 where를 쓸 수 있다.

03 'It is[was]+강조할 부분(five copies of the same books, the class field trip, this experience)+that+문장의 나머지 부분'으로 쓴다.

04 (1), (2) 첫 번째 빈칸은 'It ... that' 강조구문으로 빈칸에 강조하고자 하는 말을 쓴다. 두 번째 빈칸은 'the+비교급, the+비교급'이므로 형용사 light의 비교급인 lighter와 popular의 비교급인 more popular를 쓴다.

05 (1) 과거시제가 현재시제로 바뀌어야 하므로 동사의 시제를 모두 현재로 바꾼다. (2) 'It is[was]+강조할 부분+that+문장의 나머지 부분'으로 쓸 때 강조할 부분이 문장의 주어이면 that 뒤의 동사의 수는 그 주어에 맞추어야 한다. 복수 주어를 단수 주어로 바꾸면서 동사에 -s를 붙이는 것이 적절하다.

06 worse는 bad의 비교급이므로 more를 붙이지 않는다.

07 (1) that절의 시제가 현재이므로 강조구문의 동사를 was가 아닌 is를 쓴다. (2) 강조하는 부분이 사람이 아닌 장소(from Junsu)이므로 who가 아닌 that을 쓴다. (3) that절의 시제가 과거이므로 강조구문의 동사를 is가 아닌 was를 쓴다. (4) 강조하는 부분이 목적어이므로 that절에 목적어를 쓰지 않는다. (5) that절에 장소가 와야 하므로 강조하는 부분에 전치사를 넣어 장소로 쓴다.

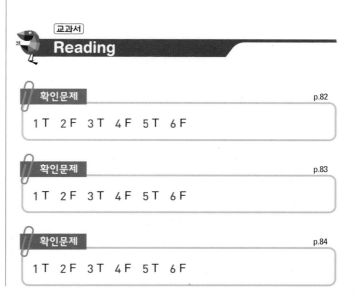

교과서
Reading

확인문제   p.82

1 T   2 F   3 T   4 F   5 T   6 F

확인문제   p.83

1 T   2 F   3 T   4 F   5 T   6 F

확인문제   p.84

1 T   2 F   3 T   4 F   5 T   6 F

01 Amazing
02 traditional paper books
03 unique
04 a few
05 Travel
06 found
07 read, Free
08 Take me home
09 ID number, was registered
10 had traveled, had read
11 How
12 book-sharing project
13 register, get
14 leave it
15 reports back, where your book is
16 a big library
17 The more books, the more
18 Drinkable
19 This tiny book
20 both the information and the tools
21 is called
22 as a filter
23 tear out, pour, on
24 As, changes into
25 It is, that
26 special filter paper
27 amazing, saves, from, diseases
28 Tree-Book-Tree Project
29 the most amazing book
30 reading, plant, water
31 growing
32 a copy of, producing
33 has seeds
34 these tiny seeds
35 was made by
36 not, anymore, think
37 just a few
38 What other unique books
39 would, like to do
40 The bigger, the more wonderful

1 This Book Is Amazing!

2 Most people think of books as traditional paper books to read.

3 However, there are many unique books around you.

4 Let's learn about a few of these books.

5 Books Travel!

6 I found this old book on a park bench yesterday.

7 A note on the cover read, "Free Book!

8 Take me home and read me!"

9 Actually, this book had an ID number and was registered on a website.

10 When I entered the number online, I found out that the book had traveled to many countries and that a number of readers in different countries had read it before me.

11 How was that possible?

12 There is a book-sharing project.

13 First, register your book online and get an ID number.

14 Next, leave it in a public place.

15 When the next reader finds your book and reports back to the website, you can check where your book is.

16 This way, the whole world can become a big library.

17 The more books we share, the more we learn.

18 The Drinkable Book

19 This tiny book is really important to people in my town.

20 It provides both the information and the tools necessary to make clean drinking water.

21 It is called the Drinkable Book.

22 You cannot actually drink the book, but you can use it as a filter.

23 Simply tear out a page and pour dirty water on it.

24 As the water goes through the page, it changes into clean drinking water.

25 It is this filtered water that you can drink.

26 This is possible because the book is made of special filter paper.

27 This amazing book saves the lives of many children from diseases that come from dirty water.

28 The Tree-Book-Tree Project

29 This is the most amazing book that I have ever seen.

30 After you finish reading this book, plant it and water it.

31 You will see new leaves growing on the book.

32 In some bookstores in my town, you can see a copy of this book producing new leaves.

33 The secret is that the book has seeds in each page.

34 It is these tiny seeds that change the book into a tree.

35 This book was made by a small children's book publisher in Argentina.

36 Though the company does not print this book anymore, this special project makes us think about where books come from.

37 These are just a few of the unique books you can find.

38 What other unique books do you want to make?

39 What special project would you like to do with the books?

시험대비 실력평가
p.91~95

01 ④	02 ①, ⑤	03 ②	04 ②
05 many	06 ⑤	07 (A) register (B) get	
08 private → public	09 ④	10 ④	

11 As the water goes through the page, it changes into clean drinking water.

12 ④	13 ①, ③	14 to read → reading	
15 ②	16 ⑤	17 ⑤	18 ④
19 ③	20 ④	21 ⑤	22 ②
23 the (dirty) water		24 ⑤	

25 (A) It is (B) think (C) to do　　26 ③

27 where books come from 28 ⑤　　29 ②

30 the bigger → bigger
the more wonderful → more wonderful

01 앞에 나오는 내용과 상반되는 내용이 뒤에 이어지므로 However가 가장 적절하다. ① 즉[말하자면], ② 그러므로, ③ 그 결과

02 (A)와 ①, ⑤: 형용사적 용법, ②, ④: 부사적 용법, ③: 명사적 용법

03 '여러분 주변에는 독특한 책이 많이 있습니다. 이러한 책 중 몇 가지에 대해 배워 봅시다.'라고 했으므로, 위 글의 뒤에 올 내용으로는 '몇 가지 독특한 책에 대한 설명'이 적절하다.

04 ⓐ on a park bench: 공원 벤치 위에서, ⓑ A note on the cover: 표지 위의 쪽지, ⓒ on a website: 웹사이트에

05 a number of = many

06 글쓴이는 그 책이 많은 나라를 여행하고 '다른 나라의 많은 독자가 자신보다 앞서 이 책을 읽었다'는 것을 알아냈으므로 최초의 독자라는 것은 사실이 아니다.

07 책을 공유하는 프로젝트의 첫 단계는 온라인에 여러분의 책을 '등록하고' ID 번호를 '얻는 것'이다.

08 다음 독자가 여러분의 책을 발견하도록 책을 '공공'장소에 놓아 두라고 하는 것이 적절하므로, private를 public으로 고치는 것이 적절하다. private: 사적인

09 이 글은 '책을 공유하는 프로젝트'에 관한 글이므로, 주제로는 ④번 '책을 공유하기 위한 프로젝트'가 적절하다. ③ report back on something to somebody: (~에 대한 정보를 …에게) 보고하다[알리다]

10 ⓐ와 ①, ②, ③, ⑤: 동명사, 목적, 용도를 나타낼 때: 동명사. ⑤ hearing aid: 보청기, ④ 진행, 상태를 나타낼 때: 현재분사

11 as: ~하면서, go through: ~을 통과하다, change into: ~로

변하다

12 선행사에 형용사의 최상급이 있을 때는 보통 관계대명사 that을 쓴다.

13 ⓑ와 ①, ③: 경험 용법, ②, ⑤: 완료 용법, ④ 계속 용법

14 finish는 동명사를 목적어로 취하는 동사이다.

15 report back to somebody: (…에게) 보고하다[알리다]

16 책을 공유하는 프로젝트를 통해 여러 독자들이 책을 빌려서 읽게 되는 것이므로, 전 세계가 하나의 큰 '도서관'이 될 수 있다고 하는 것이 적절하다. ② 출판사

17 (A)와 ③: 남겨 두다, 놓아두다, ① (관리, 처리 등을) 맡기다, ② (사람, 장소에서) 떠나다[출발하다], ④ (정기 또는 특별 사유에 의한) 휴가(명사), take a month's paid leave: 한 달간의 유급 휴가를 갖다, ⑤ (어떤 상태에 계속) 있게 하다

18 다음 독자가 여러분의 책을 발견하는 데 보통 얼마가 걸리는지는 대답할 수 없다. ① First, we should register our book online and get an ID number. ② We should leave it in a public place. ③ The next reader should report back to the website. ⑤ We can check where our book is when the next reader finds our book and reports back to the website.

19 이 글은 '책이 많은 나라를 여행하고 다른 나라의 많은 독자가 그 책을 읽는다.'는 내용의 글이므로, 제목으로는 ③번 '책이 여행합니다!'가 적절하다.

20 think of A as B = regard A as B = look upon A as B = consider A as B = see A as B = view A as B: A를 B로 생각하다

21 주어진 문장의 that에 주목한다. ⑤번 앞 문장의 내용을 받고 있으므로 ⑤번이 적절하다.

22 ⓐ와 ②: [역할·자격·기능·성질 따위를 나타내어] ~으로(전치사), ① ~일 때(접속사), ③ [비례] ~함에 따라, ~할수록(접속사), ④ [보통 as ~ as …로 형용사·부사 앞에서] …와 같은 정도로, (as ~ as …에서, 앞의 as가 지시부사, 뒤의 as는 접속사), ⑤ [상태] ~하는대로 (접속사)

23 '더러운 물'을 가리킨다.

24 이 글은 '특별한 여과지로 만들어진 책(the Drinkable Book: 마실 수 있는 책)을 필터로 사용해서 더러운 물을 깨끗한 마실 물로 바꾸는 것'에 관한 글이므로, 주제로는 '깨끗한 마실 물을 만드는 데 필요한 도구를 제공하는 책'이 적절하다.

25 (A) 'These tiny seeds change the book into a tree.'에서 주어 'These tiny seeds'를 강조하기 위한 'It … that ~' 강조 구문 문장이므로 It is가 적절하다. (B) 사역동사 makes의 목적격보어이므로 think가 적절하다. (C) would like는 to부정사를 목적어로 취한다.

26 이 책이 맨 처음 언제 출판되었는지는 대답할 수 없다. ① It

has seeds. ② A small children's book publisher in Argentina did. ④ No, it isn't. ⑤ We can think about where books come from.

27 전치사 'about'의 목적어 역할을 하는 간접의문문(의문사+주어+동사)의 어순으로 쓰는 것이 적절하다.

28 그 출판사는 더 이상 이 책을 발행하지 않는다.

29 글의 첫 부분에 '이것들은 여러분이 찾을 수 있는 독특한 책 중의 단지 몇 가지입니다.'라고 되어 있으므로, 앞에 올 내용으로는 '여러분이 찾을 수 있는 몇 가지 독특한 책에 대한 설명'이 적절하다.

30 The+비교급+주어+동사 …, the+비교급+주어+동사 ~: = As+주어+동사+비교급, 주어+동사+비교급: …하면 할수록, 더 ~하다

서술형 시험대비 p.96~97

01 (A) Most   (B) unique   (C) a

02 the book had traveled to many countries and a number of readers in different countries had read it before the writer

03 (A) an ID number   (B) on a website   (C) free

04 register   05 more books, more

06 (A) an ID number   (B) a public place
   (C) the website   (D) where

07 can not only → cannot actually

08 It is this filtered water that you can drink.

09 dirty water

10 producing 또는 produce

11 no more

12 It's that the book has seeds in each page.

---

01 (A) '대부분의' 사람이라고 해야 하므로 Most가 적절하다. almost: 거의, most: 대부분의, (B) '독특한' 책이 많이 있다고 해야 하므로 unique가 적절하다. ordinary: 보통의, unique: 독특한, (C) '많은' 독자라고 해야 하므로 a가 적절하다. a number of: 많은, the number of: ~의 수

02 '그 책이 많은 나라를 여행하고 다른 나라의 많은 독자가 글쓴이보다 앞서 이 책을 읽었다는 것'을 가리킨다.

03 글쓴이는 어제 공원 벤치에서 발견한 낡은 책은 'ID 번호'가 있고 '웹사이트'에 등록되어 있었다. 그 책은 '공짜' 책이기 때문에, 그 책을 발견한 사람은 누구라도 그것을 집으로 가져가서 읽을 수 있었다.

04 register: 등록하다, 어떤 것을 하기 위해서 혹은 서비스를 받기 위해서 공식적인 목록에 이름을 올리다

05 The+비교급+주어+동사 …, the+비교급+주어+동사 ~: = As+주어+동사+비교급, 주어+동사+비교급: …하면 할수록,

---

더 ~하다

06 (A) 여러분의 책을 등록하고 'ID 번호'를 얻으세요. (B) 그것을 '공공장소' 어디에라도 놓아두세요. (C) 누군가가 여러분의 책을 집어 들고 '웹사이트'에 알립니다. (D) 여러분의 책이 '어디' 있는지 그리고 누가 그것을 읽는지 확인하십시오.

07 여러분은 '실제로 그 책을 마실 수는 없지만', 그것을 필터로 사용할 수 있습니다.

08 'You can drink this filtered water.'에서 'this filtered water'를 강조하는 강조구문으로 쓰는 것이 적절하다.

09 the Drinkable Book(마실 수 있는 책) 덕분에, 많은 어린이들이 '더러운 물'로 생기는 질병으로부터 스스로를 보호할 수 있다.

10 지각동사 'see'의 목적격보어에 해당하므로 현재분사 producing으로 쓰는 것이 적절하다. produce도 가능하다.

11 not ~ anymore = no more

12 새잎이 자라는 책의 비밀은 '책이 각 페이지 안에 씨앗을 갖고 있다'는 것이다.

영역별 핵심문제 p.99~103

01 provide   02 ②   03 ⑤   04 ①

05 introduce   06 ⑤   07 (b) and → or

08 ③   09 ③   10 ④   11 ②

12 ⑤   13 (a) longer   (b) better

14 ②   15 ⑤

16 (1) The closer we got to the fire, the warmer we felt.
   (2) It was the lost key that[which] I found under the bed.
   (3) It was on the wall that[where] the baby drew the rabbit.

17 ④   18 ③   19 ④   20 ③

21 ③   22 the Drinkable Book(마실 수 있는 책)의 한 페이지를 떼어 내서 그 위에 더러운 물을 부으면, 물이 그 페이지를 통과하면서 깨끗한 마실 물로 바뀌게 되는 것.

23 ④   24 the more your books will become wonderful → the more wonderful your books will become   25 you can check where your book is

26 ⑤

---

01 유의어 관계다. 병, 질병 – 제공하다

02 (a) 친구에게 게임의 점수를 알아봐 달라고 부탁할 것이다. (b) 작은 개미들은 잎을 들어올리기 위해 함께 일했다.

03 '기계를 이용해서 종이 위에 단어, 그림, 숫자 등을 생성하다'라는 뜻으로 '인쇄하다(print)'가 적절하다.

04 '잡아 찢거나 작은 조각으로 뜯어내다'라는 뜻으로 '~을 찢다, 뜯어내다(tear)'가 적절하다.

05 처음 만났을 때 누군가에게 또 다른 사람의 이름을 말하다:소개

---

06 'register'는 '등록하다'라는 뜻이다.

07 'A와 B 중에서 어떤 것을 더 좋아하니?'를 묻는 선택의문문에서는 'Which do you prefer, A or B?'의 형태를 사용한다.

08 (C) 가면 만들기와 푸드 아트 만들기 중에서 어떤 것을 더 좋아하는지 묻고 → (B) 둘 다 좋아하는데 푸드 아트 만들기를 더 좋아한다고 대답하고 → (D) 그 이유를 묻는 말이 온다. 마지막으로 → (A) 이유를 설명하는 말이 온다.

09 등산을 하는 것과 해변에 가는 것 중에서 무엇을 더 좋아하니?'라는 물음에 '등반을 더 좋아해. 사실 해변에 가는 것을 가장 좋아해.'라고 말하는 것은 자연스럽지 못하다.

10 어깨에 메는 가방과 손에 드는 가방 중에서 무엇을 만들지에 대해 나누는 대화로, G가 손에 물건을 드는 것을 싫어한다고 말하고, B가 Okay라고 긍정의 대답을 하는 것으로 보아 어깨에 메는 가방을 만들자는 ④가 가장 적절하다.

11 첫 문장에 독서 동아리의 날이 일주일 남았다고 말하고 있고 이것을 준비하기 위해 할 일에 대해 이야기하고 있으므로 ②가 적절하다.

12 'It is[was]+강조할 부분+that+문장의 나머지 부분'으로 쓸 때 강조할 부분이 문장의 주어이면 that 뒤의 동사의 수는 그 주어에 맞추어야 한다. 그러므로 ⑤의 동사 go는 goes로 쓰는 것이 적절하다.

13 'the+비교급, the+비교급' 문장이므로, (a)는 명사 length의 형용사형인 long의 비교급 longer를, (b)는 부사 well의 비교급인 better를 넣는 것이 적절하다.

14 'the+비교급(the happier)+주어+동사, the+비교급(the more likely+주어+동사'로 쓴다.

15 a. 강조하는 부분이 주어이므로 that절에 주어를 쓰지 말아야 한다. It was Jack that broke the vase. c. 주절의 시제에 맞게 강조구문의 동사를 현재로 쓴다. It is Jessica that likes Korean dramas. d. 'the+비교급, the+비교급'의 형태가 되도록 쓴다. The more information you provide, the better we can help you. e. 비교급의 형용사가 명사를 수식하는 명사면, 'the+비교급 형용사+명사'로 쓴다. The more money you make, the more things you will buy. f. 'the+비교급, the+비교급'의 비교급 자리에는 형용사와 부사 모두 올 수 있고, 뒤에 이어지는 동사에 따라 달라진다. The harder he practiced, the more beautifully he got to dance.

16 (1) 'the+비교급, the+비교급'은 '…하면 할수록, 더 ~하다'라는 의미이다. 뒤에 주어 동사를 쓸 때 시제에 유의한다. (2), (3) 'It … that' 강조구문으로 'It is[was]+강조할 부분(the lost key, on the wall)+that+문장의 나머지 부분'으로 쓰며, '~하는 것은 바로 …이다'라고 해석한다.

17 앞에 나오는 내용과 상반되는 내용을 연결하는 However로 문장이 시작하고 있으므로, 대부분의 사람은 책을 읽기 위한 '전통적인 종이책'으로만 생각하지만 여러분 주변에는 '독특한

(unique) 책'이 많이 있다고 하는 것이 적절하다. ① 보통의, ② 보통의, 정상적인, ③ 일상의, 정기적인, ⑤ 전형적인

18 ⓑ와 ③: (이름·숫자·내용 등을) 적어 넣다[기입하다/입력하다], ① 들어가다[오다], ② (생각 따위가 머리에) 떠오르다(occur to), ④ (활동·상황 등을[에]) 시작하다[접어들다/진입하다], ⑤ (대회 등에) 출전[참가]하다

19 그 책의 ID 번호는 알 수 없다. ① On a park bench. ② Yesterday. ③ "Free Book! Take me home and read me!" ⑤ The writer found out that the book had traveled to many countries and that a number of readers in different countries had read it before him/her.

20 이 글은 '특별한 여과지로 만들어진 책(the Drinkable Book: 마실 수 있는 책)을 필터로 사용해서 더러운 물을 깨끗한 마실 물로 바꾸는 것'에 관한 글이므로, 제목으로는 ③번 '마실 수 있는 책'이 적절하다.

21 ⓑ와 ②, ⑤: 부사적 용법, ①, ④: 명사적 용법, ③: 형용사적 용법

22 책이 특별한 여과지로 만들어졌기 때문에 책을 필터로 사용하여 더러운 물을 사람들이 마실 수 있는 깨끗한 마실 물로 바꾸는 것을 가리킨다.

23 수동태의 행위자를 나타내는 'by'가 적절하다.

24 the+비교급+주어+동사 …, the+비교급+주어+동사 ~(…하면 할수록, 더 ~하다) 구문이므로, wonderful의 비교급 more wonderful 앞에 the를 같이 붙여 쓰는 것이 적절하다.

25 check의 목적어로 간접의문문(의문사+주어+동사)의 순서로 쓰는 것이 적절하다.

26 책을 공유하는 프로젝트를 통해 전 세계가 하나의 큰 도서관이 될 수 있고, '우리가 더 많은 책을 공유할수록, 우리는 더 많이 배운다'고 했다. ④ locate: ~의 정확한 위치를 찾아내다

단원별 예상문제   p.104~107

01 connection   02 ②

03 I hate working with a plan.

04 (C) – (A) – (B) – (D)

05 They are going to make a shoulder bag.   06 ②

07 ③   08 ④   09 ①   10 ⑤

11 ② looks like ③ The larger   12 ②

13 (1) It is the size that influences the time of your print

    (2) the longer you will have to wait

14 ②   15 (A) seeds   (B) a tree   16 ⑤

17 ②   18 ③, ④   19 ③   20 ①

21 special filter paper

22 A small children's book publisher in Argentina

made this book.

23 It makes us think about where books come from.

01 동사-명사의 관계이다. 모으다-수집 : 연결하다-연결

02 '해 놓은 어떤 것이나 갖고 있는 어떤 것에 대해 즐거움을 느끼는'이라는 뜻으로 '자랑으로 여기는(proud)'이 적절하다.

03 싫어하는 것을 말할 때는 'I hate+동명사'를 사용한다.

04 낡은 청바지로 가방을 하나 만들자는 제안에 → (C) 어떤 종류의 가방을 만들지 묻자 → (A) 어깨에 메는 가방과 손에 드는 가방 중에서 어떤 것을 더 좋아하는지 묻는다. → (B) 어깨에 메는 가방이 더 좋다는 말을 하고 사실, 손에 물건을 드는 것을 몹시 싫어한다는 강조의 말을 한다. → (D) 어깨에 메는 가방을 함께 만들자는 말이 오는 것이 적절하다.

05 질문: 대화자들은 무엇을 만들 것인가?

06 'Which do you prefer, A or B?(너는 A와 B 중에서 어느 것을 더 좋아하니?)'에서 A와 B는 문법적으로 병렬관계가 되어야 한다. 'taking the bus or taking the subway'가 되어야 한다.

07 둘 중 무엇을 더 좋아하는지 선호를 묻는 표현으로 적절한 것을 묻는 문제다.

08 주어진 문장의 It은 'a cell phone holder'를 가리키고, 물건을 만드는 데 많은 시간이 드는 것을 싫어한다는 말 앞에 오는 것이 적절하다.

09 선택의문문에서 접속사 'or'를 사용한다.

10 빈칸 다음의 말이 '고양이를 더 좋아해.'라고 말하고 있으므로 ⑤번이 적절하다.

11 ② look 다음에 명사가 올 때는 look like로 쓰는 것이 적절하다. ③ 'the+비교급, the+비교급'의 형태로 쓰는 것이 적절하다.

12 ②의 It은 가주어이다. ①, ③, ④, ⑤의 It은 강조구문의 It이다.

13 (1) 'It is[was]+강조할 부분(the size)+that+문장의 나머지 부분'으로 쓴다. (2) 'the+비교급, the+비교급' 문장이므로 형용사 long을 the longer로 쓰고 뒤에 주어와 동사를 쓴다.

14 이 글은 '책을 다 읽은 후에, 그것을 심고 물을 주면 책에서 새 잎이 자라게 되는 프로젝트'에 관한 글이므로, 제목으로는 ②번 '나무-책-나무 프로젝트'가 적절하다.

15 이 책은 각 페이지 안에 '씨앗'을 갖고 있어서, 만약 여러분이 이 책을 심고 물을 주면 이 아주 작은 씨앗들이 책을 '나무'로 변화시키게 된다.

16 ⑤는 '글쓴이'를 가리키고, 나머지는 다 글쓴이가 어제 공원 벤치에서 발견한 '낡은 책'을 가리킨다.

17 ⓐ와 ②: 'read'는 자동사로서 '~라고 쓰여 있다, ~로 해석되다'라는 의미이다. 그 표지판에는 '입장 금지'라고 적혀 있었다. ①, ④: (글,기호 등을) 읽다[판독하다], ③ (계기를) 확인[검침]하다, ⑤ 읽어 주다

18 actually: 사실, 실제로 (= in reality, in fact, as a matter of fact), ③, ④ especially = in particular: 특히

19 ⓐ change into: ~으로 바뀌다, ⓑ save A from B: B로부터 A를 구하다

20 주어진 문장의 the book에 주목한다. ①번 앞 문장의 the Drinkable Book을 받고 있으므로 ①번이 적절하다.

21 the Drinkable Book(마실 수 있는 책)이 '특별한 여과지'로 만들어졌기 때문에, 단지 그 책에서 떼어낸 페이지 위에 더러운 물을 부음으로써 깨끗한 마실 물을 만드는 것이 가능하다.

22 A small children's book publisher in Argentina를 주어로 해서 고치는 것이 적절하다.

23 the Tree-Book-Tree Project(나무-책-나무 프로젝트)는 우리에게 '책이 어디에서 오는지에 대해 생각하게' 해준다.

서술형 실전문제 p.108~109

01 It's because a cell phone holder will be easier to make. And he hates spending too much time making things.

02 it is making food art that[which] I prefer.

03 He is going to write cheerful messages on the bookmarks.

04 (1) called → is called
(2) it was difficult → difficult it was
(3) which → that[who]

05 (1) It was I that waited for him for a long time.
(2) The bigger my son grew, the more worried I got.

06 (1) it was the *Mona Lisa* that[which] Leonardo da Vinci painted
(2) the better you can speak

07 Most people think of books as traditional paper books to read.

08 many unique books around you

09 read → had read

10 People call it the Drinkable Book.

11 (A) filtered (B) of (C) amazing

12 (A) the tools (B) tear out (C) pour (D) clean

01 소년은 '만들기가 더 쉬울 거야. 그리고 나는 뭔가를 만드는 데 시간을 너무 많이 들이는 걸 몹시 싫어해.'라고 하고 있다.

02 강조구문은 'It is ~ that ...' 구문을 사용하고, 주어인 making food art를 강조하는 말을 쓴다.

03 질문: Seho는 책갈피를 만드는 것에 관해 무엇을 할 것인가?

04 (1) called 다음 목적어가 없고 목적보어만 있으므로 This를 주어로 수동으로 쓰는 것이 적절하다. (2) The larger와 상응하는 the 비교급을 쓸 때, difficult의 비교급은 the more difficult이고 분리해서 쓰지 않는다. (3) potter가 사람이므로 that이나 who로 써야 한다.

05 (1) 'It was+강조할 부분(I)+that+문장의 나머지 부분'으로 쓴다. (2) '아들이 더 커감에 따라 나는 점점 더 걱정이 되었다'라는 문장이므로 'the+비교급, the+비교급'을 사용하여 문장을 쓴다.

06 (1) 'It … that' 강조구문으로 'It is[was]+강조할 부분(the Mona Lisa)+that+문장의 나머지 부분'으로 쓰며, '~하는 것은 바로 …이다'라고 해석한다. (2) 'the+비교급, the+비교급'은 '…하면 할수록, 더 ~하다'라는 의미이다. 부사 well의 비교급을 the better로 쓰고 '주어(you)+동사(speak)'의 어순으로 쓴다.

07 think of A as B: A를 B로 생각하다, 'to read'가 to부정사의 형용사적 용법으로 앞의 'books'를 수식하도록 쓰는 것이 적절하다.

08 '여러분 주변의 많은 독특한 책들'을 가리킨다.

09 'I'가 '알아냈다'고 한 시점 이전에 사람들이 그 책을 읽었으므로 과거완료 'had read'로 쓰는 것이 적절하다.

10 People를 주어로 해서 고치는 것이 적절하다.

11 (A) '여과된 물'이라고 해야 하므로 filtered가 적절하다. (B) 종이로 책을 만든 것이므로 of가 적절하다. be made of: 물리적 변화, be made from: 화학적 변화, (C) 이 '놀라운' 책이라고 해야 하므로 amazing이 적절하다.

12 the Drinkable Book(마실 수 있는 책)은 깨끗한 마실 물을 만드는 데 필요한 '도구'를 제공합니다. 여러분이 그 책의 한 페이지를 '떼어 내서' 그 위에 더러운 물을 '부을' 때, 그 물이 '깨끗한' 마실 물로 바뀝니다.

창의사고력 서술형 문제 | p.110

|모범답안|

01 (1) A: Which do you prefer, working with a plan or working without a plan?
   B: I prefer working without a plan. Actually I hate working with a plan.
   (2) A: Which do you prefer, working with numbers and texts or working with pictures and music?
   B: I prefer working with pictures and music. Actually, I hate working with numbers and texts.

02 (1) it is in Pisa that I can visit the Leaning Tower
   (2) it was radium that the Curies discovered
   (3) it is English that is spoken all over the world

03 (A) a kite (B) the length (C) the better

단원별 모의고사 | p.111~114

01 ④   02 (d)islike   03 ③   04 ②

05 It is working with machines that I hate. 06 ③

07 I can't wait for it!

08 (A) Do you have any good ideas?
   (B) Which do you prefer, making the bookmarks or writing the messages?
   (C) I hate writing.

09 They have collected so many interesting books to give away.

10 ④   11 ③   12 ③

13 (1) was in 2017 that[when] he became President
   (2) was Dash that[who] chose what to eat at dinner

14 (1) The less sugar I use, the healthier the cookies are.
   (2) It is these healthy cookies that will make everyone healthy.

15 had traveled   16 ③   17 ②

18 The more books we share, the more we learn.

19 ⑤   20 ⑤   21 amazing   22 ⑤

---

01 ④번은 '매우 작은'의 의미로 'tiny'를 설명한 말이다.

02 반의어 관계이다. 필요한 - 불필요한 : 좋아하다 - 싫어하다

03 '책을 출판하는 사람 또는 회사'의 의미로 'publisher(출판업자, 출판사)'가 적절하다.

04 지하철 타는 것을 선호한다고 말한 다음 '사실(Actually)'이라고 말하고 있으므로 ②번이 자연스럽다.

05 'It is ~ that …' 강조구문은 강조하고자 하는 말을 It is와 that 사이에 넣어 쓰면 된다.

06 시간이 오래 걸리는 것을 싫어한다고 했기 때문에 만들기에 쉽다는 내용이 오는 것이 적절하다.

07 기대를 나타내는 표현으로 'can't wait for+명사[대명사]'를 사용한다.

09 Seho가 '나는 우리가 나눠 줄 재미있는 책을 많이 모아서 자랑스러워.'라고 하고 있다.

10 ④ 'the+비교급, the+비교급' 비교급 자리에는 형용사, 부사 모두 올 수 있고, 뒤에 이어지는 동사에 따라 달라진다. The more foolish you are, the more easily you believe what others say.

11 접속사를 뺀 후 'the+비교급+주어+동사, the+비교급+주어+동사' 형태로 쓴다.

12 문장의 시제가 과거이므로 'It was+강조할 부분+that+문장의 나머지 부분'으로 문장을 쓴다. 강조하는 부분이 사람이 아니므로 that 대신 who를 쓰지 않는다.

13 'It is[was]+강조할 부분+that+문장의 나머지 부분'으로 쓴다.

14 (1) 'the+비교급, the+비교급'은 '…하면 할수록, 더 ~하다'라는 의미이다. little sugar의 비교급을 the less sugar로 쓰고,

21

healthy의 비교급은 the healthier로 쓴 다음 각각 그 뒤에 '주어+동사'를 쓴다. (2) 'It is[was]+강조할 부분(these healthy cookies)+that+문장의 나머지 부분'으로 쓴다.

15 과거의 특정 시점 이전에 일어난 일은 과거완료(had+과거분사)로 표현한다. 'I'가 '알아냈다(found out)'고 한 시점 이전에 책이 여행하였으므로 과거완료 'had traveled'로 쓰는것이 적절하다.

16 (A)와 ③: 무료의, 공짜의, ① 사용 중이 아닌, ② (유해하거나 불쾌한 것이) 없는, live free from care: 걱정 없는 생활을 하다, ④: 사용 중이 아닌, 이 자리에 사람 없나요? ⑤ 자유로운, 자기 하고 싶은 대로 하는

17 이 글은 'ID 번호가 있고 웹사이트에 등록되어 있어 발견한 사람이 자신의 집으로 가져가 읽을 수 있는 공짜 책'에 관한 글이므로, 주제로는 ②번 '여러분 주변의 독특한 책'이 적절하다. ① typical: 전형적인

18 The+비교급+주어+동사 …, the+비교급+주어+동사 ~: …하면 할수록, 더 ~하다

19 독자가 여러분의 책을 발견한 다음, 독자 자신이 직접 그 웹사이트에 다시 알려야 한다.

20 ⑤는 the Drinkable Book(마실 수 있는 책)에서 떼어낸 한 페이지를 가리키고, 나머지는 다 the Drinkable Book(마실 수 있는 책)을 가리킨다.

21 책이 사람을 놀라게 하는 것이므로 현재분사형의 형용사가 알맞다.

22 ⑤ the Drinkable Book(마실 수 있는 책)은 '더러운 물'로 생기는 질병으로부터 많은 어린이의 생명을 구한다. malnutrition: 영양실조

22 정답 및 해설

Lesson 7

Fact, Opinion or Fake

시험대비 실력평가
p.118

01 opinion 02 ④ 03 ⑤ 04 ②
05 ③ 06 ① 07 turned out
08 false

01 내 생각에 영어는 가장 어려운 과목이다. <영어 설명> 사물 또는 사람에 대한 생각이나 믿음

02 'appear'는 '~처럼 보이다', '나타나다'의 의미를 가지고 있다.
• 이 새로운 추세는 한 동안 계속될 것으로 보인다. • 도쿄의 한 지하철역에 새로운 자판기가 등장할 것이다.

03 (A) 내 숙제가 완벽하지(complete) 않아서 선생님은 화가 나셨다. (B) 우리는 우선 정보의 출처(source)를 찾아야 한다. critical: 비평의, 비판적인, complex: 복잡한, 착잡한, resource: 자원, 역량

04 '물리적인 폭력을 사용하여 어떤 사람이나 어떤 것을 다치게 하거나 손상을 주려고 하다'의 의미로 'attack(공격하다)'이 적절하다.

05 '서커스에서 우스운 옷을 입고 밝은 화장을 하고 사람들을 웃게 하려고 어리석은 행동을 하는 공연자'란 의미로 'clown(광대)'이 적절하다. 'crown'은 '왕관'이다.

06 나머지는 모두 '명사-형용사' 관계이고, ①번은 '동사-명사'관계이다.

07 '~로 밝혀지다'는 'turn out'을 이용하여 과거형 turned를 쓰는 것이 적절하다.

08 유의어 관계다. 증거 : 거짓의

서술형 시험대비
p.119

01 (1) spread (2) critically (3) scared (4) sink
02 touching
03 (1) (c)omfortable (2) (b)oring
   (3) (m)ajor (4) (S)low
04 (1) support, 지지하다 (2) spread, 퍼지다
   (3) sink, 가라앉다 (4) octopus, 문어
05 (1) pay attention to (2) tell, from (3) made up

01 (1) '그 이야기는 빠르게 모든 사람에게 퍼졌다.' 'spread'의 과거형은 'spread'다. (2) '노동자들은 문제를 해결하기 위해 비판적으로 생각해야 한다.' 동사를 수식하기 위해 부사 'critically'로 바꾸어야 한다. (3) '그 어린 소년은 괴물을 무서워한다.'

'scare'는 동사로 be동사 뒤에 사용되기 위해 과거분사 형태로 바뀌어야 한다. (4) '만약 배에 구멍이 생기면, 배는 가라앉을 것이다.'

02 '연민, 동정, 슬픔 등을 느끼게 하는'의 의미로 'touching(감동적인)'이 적절하다.

03 (1) comfortable: 편안한 (2) boring: 지루한 (3) major: 주요한 (4) slow down: 속도를 줄이다

04 (1) 어떤 사람에게 도움, 동의, 위로, 격려 등을 주다 (2) 한 장소나 표면 위에 펼치거나 배열하다 (3) 수면 아래로 사라지다 (4) 여덟 개의 긴 다리를 가진 연한 바다 생물

05 (1) 학생들은 선생님에게 집중해야 한다. (2) 그의 부모님은 그에게 옳고 그른 것을 구별하는 법을 가르쳐 주셨다. (3) 분홍 말에 관한 이야기는 꾸며낸 것이었다.

[교과서] Conversation

핵심 Check p.120~121

1 How do you feel about them?　　　2 ③

교과서 대화문 익히기

Check(√) True or False p.122

1 T　2 F　3 T　4 T

교과서 확인학습

p.124~125

Get Ready 2

(1) like, I think, fake / agree, kind, real

(2) sharp teeth, What do you think of, real / search, check

(3) What / look like, strange / too

(4) This, real / Let's, fact

Start Off – Listen & Talk A

1. How do you feel about / light, comfortable / to buy, school field trip

2. is wearing / agree with, Actually, much heavier / believe

Start Off - Listen & Talk B

How, feel / touching, gave up, to save / Why / seem

real, a little boring

Start Off – Speak Up

How, about, ad / shows / should not

Step Up – Real-life Scene

cool, How do you feel about / that / makes, laugh, loud / octopus / make sense / when, climbing, lying / agree with, fake, out of

Express Yourself A

1. How, about / get along, with / these two, enjoying, together

2. By the way / guess / prefer / with, better than, In fact / to help

3. feel about / anything special / were made, uniform / passed away / touching

p.126

01 What, think of[about]　02 ④　03 ③
04 ②

01 'What do you think of[about] ~?'는 '~에 대하여 어떻게 생각하니?'라는 표현이다.

02 상대방에게 어떤 대상에 대한 의견을 물을 때 사용하는 표현으로 'How do you feel about ~?', 'What do you think about ~?(~에 대하여 어떻게 생각하니?)', 'What's your opinion about ~?(~에 대한 의견이 무엇이니?)', 'What do you say about ~?(~에 대하여 어떻게 생각하십니까?)' 등을 사용할 수 있다. ④번의 'What do you know about ~?'은 '~에 대해 무엇을 알고 있어?'라는 뜻으로 특정 대상에 대해 무엇을 알고 있는지 물을 때 사용하는 표현이다.

03 ④번의 'I couldn't agree more.'는 '전적으로 동의해.'라는 표현이다.

04 'I don't agree with you.(나는 동의하지 않아요.)'는 상대와 의견이 달라서 동의하지 않고 상대의 의견에 이의를 제기하는 말이다.

시험대비 실력평가

p.127~128

01 ④	02 (a) touching (b) boring	03 ⑤
04 ③	05 ③	06 ②
07 get along, with		08 ⑤	09 ④
10 ①	11 ③	

01 B의 '이 드라마가 올해 최고의 드라마다.'라는 말에 대해 G가 '그것은 좋은 드라마가 아니다.'라고 말하고 있으므로 ④가 적절하다. 나머지는 모두 동의하는 표현이다.

02 ⓐ는 '감동적인'의 뜻을 가지는 'touching'이 적절하고, ⓑ는 '지루한'의 뜻을 가진 'boring'이 적절하다.

03 Alex가 문어에 대해 많이 알고 있는지는 알 수 없다.

04 나머지는 'An octopus'를 가리키고, ⓒ는 앞 문장의 '문어가 나무에 사는 것'을 가리킨다.

05 빈칸 앞의 동의하지 않는다는 말에 대해 더 구체적으로 '강조, 첨가'하는 표현을 가진 'Actually(사실)'가 적절하다.

06 비교급을 강조하는 말은 'much, even, still, far, a lot'이다. 'very'는 원급(형용사나 부사)을 강조하는 말이다.

07 '사이좋게 지내다'라는 의미로 'get along (well) with'를 사용한다.

08 (A)는 상대방의 의견을 묻는 표현으로 'What do you think about ~?(~에 대하여 어떻게 생각하니?)', 'What's your opinion about ~?(~에 대한 의견이 무엇이니?)', 'What do you say about ~?(~에 대하여 어떻게 생각하십니까?)' 등으로 바꾸어 말할 수 있다.

09 대화에서 Fact에 해당하는 내용은 '아이가 아픈 아이들을 돕기 위해 머리를 잘랐다'는 것이다. 나머지는 '의견'이나 '거짓' 정보에 해당한다. ① 의견 ② 의견 ③ 거짓 정보 ⑤ 거짓 정보

10 상대방에게 어떤 대상에 대한 의견을 물을 때 사용하는 표현으로 '~에 대해 어떻게 생각하니?'라고 묻는 ①이 적절하다.

11 ⓐ는 이상한 동물을 보고 '진짜일까?' 또는 '가짜일까?'라고 물을 수 있다. ⓑ는 다리가 없고 뱀처럼 보이지는 않는 동물을 보고 '이것은 매우 이상해.'라고 말하는 것이 자연스럽다.

서술형 시험대비   p.129

01 (A) How do you feel about it?

   (B) I don't agree with you.

02 Because he always makes him laugh out loud.

03 (A) What do you think about

   (B) I think cats don't get along well with dogs

04 I don't agree with you

---

01 (A) 'How do you feel about ~?'은 '~을[~에 대해] 어떻게 생각해?'라는 의미로 상대방에게 어떤 대상에 대한 의견을 물을 때 사용하는 표현이다. (B) 'I don't agree with you.(나는 동의하지 않아요.)'는 상대와 의견이 달라서 동의하지 않고 상대의 의견에 이의를 제기하는 말이다.

02 질문: 왜 Alex는 Mr. Big Mouth를 좋아하는가?

03 (A) 'What do you think about ~?(~에 대하여 어떻게 생각하니?)', (B) 'I think+주어+동사 ~' 어순으로 쓴다.

04 G가 코트가 따뜻하고 가벼울 것 같아서 마음에 든다는 말에 대해 B가 '그렇게 따뜻하지도 않고 보기보다 훨씬 더 무거워.'라고 말하는 것으로 보아 G의 말에 동의하지 않는 표현이 들어가는 것이 적절하다.

교과서
Grammar

핵심 Check   p.130~131

1 (1) told   (2) was

2 (1) Whether   (2) whether

시험대비 기본평가   p.132

01 (1) he is very tall

   (2) she was very happy to meet him

   (3) she was not crying

   (4) she looked great

02 (1) I wonder if[whether] she will like my present.

   (2) I don't know if he will give me flowers or not.

   (3) I want to know if he will throw the ball.

   (4) The question is whether they believe what I said or not.

---

01 전달동사가 과거이므로 따옴표 안의 현재시제는 과거시제로 바꾸고 따옴표 속 'I'는 문장의 주어, 따옴표 속 'you'는 듣는 이로 바꾼다. (1)은 키가 큰 것이 현재의 사실이므로 시제의 일치 원칙에 적용되지 않는다.

02 (1) 동사 wonder의 목적절로는 if 또는 whether절이 적절하다. (2) 'if'는 'or not'을 함께 사용할 때 문장 끝에만 사용 가능하며, 'whether'는 바로 다음이나 문장 끝에 'or not'을 붙여 쓸 수도 있다. (3) 접속사 if 다음에 '주어+동사'의 어순으로 쓴다. (4) 'whether'는 주어, 보어, 동사의 목적어, 전치사의 목적어 자리에 모두 쓰일 수 있지만, 'if'는 동사의 목적어 자리에 주로 쓰인다. 이 글에서는 명사절이 보어로 쓰이고 있으므로 if가 아닌 whether를 쓰는 것이 적절하다.

시험대비 실력평가   p.133~135

01 ④   02 I wonder if he will catch my ball.

03 ⑤   04 ④   05 ④

06 (1) I told Amy that I wanted to play with her then.

   (2) Mom asked me if I was finished with my homework.

07 ③   08 ①   09 ③

10 I am not sure if I do well on the test.   11 ③

12 I'm not sure if[whether] they will give me a big hand.

13 My sister doubts if I cheated on the test (or not).

14 ②   15 ⑤   16 ⑤   17 ②

18 ③   19 (1) asked (2) says (3) if (4) felt (5) is

01 ④ 전달동사가 과거일 경우, 시제의 일치 법칙에 맞게 따옴표(" ") 안의 동사가 과거시제라면 과거완료로 바꾸어야 한다. (has eaten → had eaten)

02 wonder가 원형이므로 주절의 주어는 he가 아닌 I로 하고, 동사 wonder의 목적절로 'if+주어+동사+목적어'로 한다.

03 ①~④는 동사의 목적어로 쓰인 명사절의 접속사 if이고, ⑤는 조건을 나타내는 부사절의 접속사이다. 해석: 그 동물이 기분이 좋다면, 너는 그것을 볼 수 있을 거야.

04 ④ 전달동사(said)와 that절의 내용이 과거(would be)이므로, tomorrow를 the next day로 쓰는 것이 적절하다.

05 동사 asked의 목적어 자리에 질문을 나타내는 명사절의 접속사이면서 or not과 함께 쓸 수 있는 접속사는 whether이다.

06 (1) 부사를 전달자의 관점에 맞게 고쳐야 하므로 now는 then으로 쓰는 것이 적절하다. (2) 따옴표 안의 내용이 의문문인 화법전환은 전달동사를 ask로 바꾸어 쓴다.

07 ③은 목적절이 질문이 아닌 주어가 알고 있는 내용이므로, 명사절의 접속사 'that'이 적절하다. ①, ④는 조건을 나타내는 접속사 if가 적절하고 ②, ⑤는 목적어가 되는 명사절의 접속사 if를 쓰는 것이 적절하다.

08 의문문을 간접화법으로 전환할 때 전달동사 say 또는 say to를 ask로 바꿔야 한다.

09 첫 번째 문장은 동사 wonder의 목적절로 내용상 if 또는 whether가 적절하고, 두 번째 문장은 be동사의 보어절로 접속사 if는 쓸 수 없고 whether를 쓰는 것이 적절하다. 단, 두 문장 모두 질문하는 내용이므로 접속사 that의 사용은 어색하다.

10 am not sure(확실하지 않다)의 목적어 자리에 명사절의 접속사 if를 사용하여 목적절을 넣는다.

11 전달동사 said to는 told로 바꾼다. 직접화법을 간접화법으로 바꿀 때 따옴표 속 'I'는 문장의 주어로 바꾸고 따옴표 속 'you'는 듣는 이로 바꾼다. 전달동사가 과거이므로, 시제의 일치 법칙에 맞게 따옴표(" ") 안의 현재시제 동사는 과거시제로 바꾼다.

12 I'm not sure의 목적어 자리에 의문문을 넣어야 하므로, 명사절의 접속사 if 또는 whether를 넣어 연결한다. 이때, 이 의문문은 평서문의 어순으로 바꾸어 쓴다.

13 문장의 주어에 맞게 동사 doubt를 3인칭 단수형으로 쓰고 목적절로 if절을 쓴다. 단, 목적절의 내용이 과거이므로 if절의 동사 cheat는 과거시제로 쓴다.

14 ② 시제의 일치의 법칙에 맞게 My sister told me that she had met Tom by chance the day before.로 쓴다.

15 첫 번째 문장은 주어로 쓰인 명사절의 접속사이면서 or not과 함께 쓸 수 있는 whether가 적절하고, 두 번째 문장에서는 find out의 의미상 단정적 내용의 접속사 that이 아닌, 의문의 내용을 위한 접속사 if 또는 whether가 적절하다.

16 to keep과 함께 쓸 수 있는 전달동사로 made는 사용할 수 없다. 해석: 그 할머니는 나에게 그녀의 개를 지켜보라고 요청했다[말했다, 명령했다].

17 '내가 ~할게'의 의미로 'let me+동사원형'을 쓰고 동사 check의 목적절로 '~인지 아닌지'의 if절을 쓰는 것이 적절하다. 단, 접속사 if 바로 뒤에 or not을 쓰지 않고 문장 맨 끝에 써야 한다.

18 b. 듣는 이가 없으므로 전달동사를 told가 아닌 said로 쓴다. c. 전달동사를 said가 아닌 told로 쓴다. d. 명령문을 간접화법으로 쓸 때 부정명령문은 to not이 아닌 not to 동사원형으로 쓴다.

19 (1) 의문문을 간접화법으로 쓸 때 전달동사는 asked가 적절하다. (2) 듣는 이가 없으므로 전달동사는 says가 적절하다. (3) 목적절에 질문하는 내용이 적절하므로 접속사 if를 쓴다. (4) 전달하는 내용이 과거이므로 felt가 적절하다. (5) 전달동사는 과거나 명사절의 내용이 과학적 사실이므로 현재시제를 쓴다.

서술형 시험대비 p.136~137

01 (1) I wonder if[whether] the plane arrived on time.
   (2) I asked if[whether] she was married.
   (3) The question is whether the meeting is ready.
   (4) I think that he is very honest.
   (5) Whether she will attend the audition depends on her physical condition.

02 (1) He told me (that) he really appreciated my help.
   (2) My roommate told me (that) she[he] would be late that night.

03 (1) he knew   (2) I want   (3) he would help me

04 (1) John said to Mary, "I love you."
   (2) She told him that she was sorry.
   (3) I told my dad that I would call him later.
   (4) Mr. Brown told me that he wanted me to study more.
   (5) My mom said that dish tasted good.

05 He asked her what the weather was like in New York that day.

06 (1) I understand that you don't want to talk about it.
   (2) Whether you are a boy or a girl makes no difference to me.
   (3) Whether you will succeed or not depends on your efforts.
   (4) I am not sure if[whether] there is life on other planets.
   (5) Tell me if[whether] you have any plans for your future.

07 (1) whether we have enough money to buy the new car
   (2) that he had lied to his family
   (3) if she would have a garage sale in her backyard

08 (1) was hungry, why she looked angry
   (2) was very cute, if she liked that food

01 (1), (2) 의문사가 없는 의문문을 목적절로 만들어야 하므로 접속사 if 또는 whether를 사용한다. (3) 의문문을 보어로 만들어야 하므로 접속사 if는 사용할 수 없고 whether를 사용한다. (4) 평서문을 목적절로 만들 때는 접속사 that을 사용한다. (5) 의문문을 주절로 만들어야 하므로 접속사 if는 사용할 수 없고 whether를 사용한다.

02 (1) 간접화법을 쓸 때 전달동사가 과거라면, 시제의 일치 법칙에 맞게 따옴표(" ") 안의 현재동사를 과거시제로 바꾼다. 또한 따옴표 속 'I'는 문장의 주어로 바꾸고, 따옴표 속 'you'는 듣는 이로 바꾼다. (2) 부사 tonight는 시제에 맞게 that night으로 바꾼다.

03 (1) 직접화법을 간접화법으로 바꿀 때 따옴표 속 'I'는 문장의 주어로 바꾸고, 전달동사가 과거라면, 시제의 일치 법칙에 맞게 따옴표(" ") 안의 동사가 현재시제라면 과거시제로 바꾼다. (2) 주절의 주어와 that절의 주어가 같다면 직접화법에서 'I'가 되고 본동사의 시제와 that절의 시제가 과거로 같으므로 따옴표(" ") 안에서는 현재시제로 쓰는 것이 적절하다. (3) 직접화법을 간접화법으로 바꿀 때 따옴표 속 'I'는 문장의 주어로 바꾸고 따옴표 속 'you'는 듣는 이로 바꾼다.

04 (1) 직접화법의 전달동사는 듣는 이가 있을 때 said to로 쓴다. (2) 전달동사가 과거이므로 that절의 동사 is는 was로 쓴다. (3) 주어가 아버지에게 말한 내용이므로 that절의 you는 him으로 쓴다. (4) 간접화법의 전달동사는 듣는 이가 있을 때 told로 쓴다. (5) 간접화법이므로 지시형용사 this는 that으로 쓴다.

05 의문문을 간접화법으로 전환할 때 전달동사 said to를 asked로 바꿔야 한다. 전달동사가 과거이므로, 시제의 일치 법칙에 맞게 따옴표(" ") 안의 현재동사를 과거시제로 바꾼다. 이때 부사 today는 의미상 적절하게 that day로 쓴다.

06 (1) 동사 understand의 목적어로는 질문을 나타내는 if는 적절하지 않으므로 접속사 that을 쓴다. (2) 명사절이 주어일 때 단수로 취급하므로 동사 make를 makes로 쓴다. (3) if절은 주어로 쓰이지 않으므로 whether를 쓰는 것이 적절하다. (4) I am not sure(나는 확실하지 않다)와 어울리는 접속사는 질문의 의미를 가진 if나 whether가 적절하다. (5) 동사 Tell의 목적어로 if 또는 whether절을 쓰는 것이 적절하다.

07 (1) 문장의 보어 자리이고 내용상 질문이므로 접속사 whether를 쓴다. (2) 동사 admit와 어울리는 접속사는 that이다. (3) 동사 ask의 목적절로 질문을 나타내는 if를 쓰는 것이 적절하다. 해석: 나는 할머니에게 그녀의 뒷마당에서 중고물품 판매를 할 것인지 물었다.

08 (1) 전달동사가 과거이므로 그림 속 대화의 현재는 과거시제로 질문은 간접의문문으로 바꾼다. (2) 지시형용사를 적절히 바꾼다. (this → that)

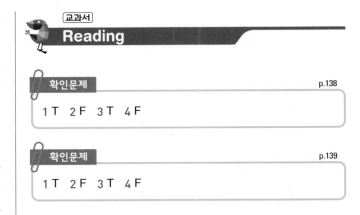

확인문제   p.138

1 T   2 F   3 T   4 F

확인문제   p.139

1 T   2 F   3 T   4 F

교과서 확인학습 A   p.140~141

01 Smart News Reader
02 shook schools, didn't believe, a bit
03 getting scared   04 checked up on
05 were actually made   06 no hard evidence
07 turned out to be   08 just look at one thing
09 to look at the right sources, what is real, what is fake
10 Like, to think critically, on the Internet
11 getting more important   12 how to tell, from
13 One of the first steps   14 too good to be true
15 what the writer says   16 coming from
17 how to tell, from   18 if, are based on
19 a smart news reader   20 appears to provide
21 along with   22 like, made up
23 once more carefully, question everything

교과서 확인학습 B   p.142~143

1 How to Be a Smart News Reader
2 In October 2016, stories about scary clowns shook schools across the Washington area, but Danina Garcia-Fuller's students didn't believe them a bit.
3 "Some people were getting scared because they saw things on social media," said Patricia Visoso, one of Garcia-Fuller's students.
4 "But they never checked up on who was saying this."
5 The stories were actually made by teenagers, not by major newspapers or TV stations.
6 They offered no hard evidence that clowns really were trying to attack students.
7 The story turned out to be a complete lie.
8 "I think a lot of people just look at one thing and believe it's true," Patricia's classmate Ivy-Brooks

9 "It's really important to look at the right sources and to pay attention to what is real and what is fake."

10 Like Garcia-Fuller's students, many teenagers in America are learning to think critically about information they're seeing in the news and on the Internet.

11 This skill is getting more important these days as stories can spread very fast, and anyone can make a website full of false information.

12 Garcia-Fuller said she was teaching her students how to tell fake news from real news.

13 "One of the first steps is to slow down.

14 If a story or a photo seems too good to be true, stop and think.

15 Is there any evidence that supports what the writer says?

16 And where is this coming from?"

17 Garcia-Fuller's students also learn how to tell fact from opinion in the news.

18 "Opinions are good to read," said 15-year-old McKenzie Campbell, "but you also have to check if they are based on facts."

19 Garcia-Fuller also said sometimes it can be very hard to be a smart news reader.

20 She tests her students with a website that appears to provide information on an animal called a tree octopus.

21 The site is full of information on this animal, along with a few unclear photos of octopuses in trees.

22 But like the story of scary clowns, it's totally made up.

23 The lesson, Garcia-Fuller tells her students, is to "check the information you're seeing once more carefully" and to "question everything, even things that I say."

시험대비 실력평가
p.144~147

01 ⑤   02 The stories 03 ④   04 ④

05 (A) sources (B) Like (C) false

06 look at everything → just look at one thing

07 is appeared → appears   08 together with

09 ⑤   10 ①, ④   11 ②, ⑤   12 ③

13 which[that] is   14 ⑤

15 Is there any evidence that supports what the

writer says?

16 opinions   17 ②   18 ①, ③   19 ③

20 called   21 ②

01 ⓐ on social media: 소셜 미디어에 올라온, ⓑ check up on: ~을 확인하다

02 '그 이야기들'을 가리킨다.

03 무서운 광대들에 관한 이야기들은 실제로 '주요 신문사나 TV 방송국'이 아닌 '10대들'이 지어냈다.

04 올바른 출처를 살펴보고, 무엇이 진짜이고 무엇이 가짜인지에 주의를 기울이는 것이 정말 중요하다고 생각하는 Garcia-Fuller의 학생들처럼, 많은 미국의 10대들은 '비판적으로' 생각하는 것을 배워 나가고 있다고 하는 것이 적절하다. ① 무비판적으로, ② 순응하여, ③ 적응하여, 순응하여, ⑤ 무조건적으로, 절대적으로

05 (A) 올바른 '출처'를 살펴보라고 해야 하므로 sources가 적절하다. source: 자료, 출처 resource: 자원, (B) Garcia-Fuller의 학생들'처럼'이라고 해야 하므로 Like가 적절하다. alike: [명사 앞에는 안 씀] (아주) 비슷한, like: ~와 비슷한, ~ 같은(전치사), (C) 누구나 '허위' 정보로 가득 찬 웹사이트를 만들어 낼 수 있기 때문에 이 기능이 최근 더 중요해지고 있다고 해야 하므로 false가 적절하다.

06 Patricia의 반 친구인 Ivy-Brooks는 많은 사람이 '단지 한 가지만을 보고' 그것이 사실이라고 믿는 것 같다고 했다.

07 appear는 수동태로 쓸 수 없기 때문에, is appeared를 appears로 고치는 것이 적절하다.

08 along with = together with: ~와 함께

09 누가 '나무 문어'에 대한 정보를 꾸며냈는지는 알 수 없다. ① Sometimes it can be very hard to be a smart news reader. ② No. ③ Information on an animal called a tree octopus. ④ Information on the animal called a tree octopus, along with a few unclear photos of octopuses in trees.

10 ⓐ와 ①, ④ tell(know/distinguish) A from B: A와 B를 구분하다

11 ⓑ와 ②, ⑤: 주격 관계대명사, ① so ... that ~: 너무 …해서 ~하다(접속사), ③ 동격의 접속사, ④ 목적어를 이끄는 접속사

12 이 글은 'Garcia-Fuller가 자신의 학생들에게 가짜 뉴스를 진짜 뉴스로부터 구분하는 방법과 뉴스에서 사실을 의견과 구분하는 방법에 대해서 가르치는' 내용의 글이므로, 주제로는 ③번 '가짜 뉴스와 진짜 뉴스를, 그리고 뉴스에서 사실을 의견과 구분하는 방법'이 적절하다.

13 주격 관계대명사 which[that]와 be동사인 is가 생략되어 있다.

14 '사람들이 왜 허위 정보로 가득 찬 웹사이트를 만드는지'는 대답

할 수 없다. ① They just look at one thing. ② They are learning to think critically about information they're seeing in the news and on the Internet. ③ They're seeing it in the news and on the Internet. ④ Yes.

15 주격 관계대명사 'that'이 선행사 'any evidence'를 수식하도록 하고, 선행사를 포함한 관계대명사 'what'이 이끄는 명사절이 동사 'supports'의 목적어가 되도록 쓰는 것이 적절하다.

16 '의견들'을 가리킨다.

17 주어진 문장의 they에 주목한다. ②번 앞 문장의 Some people을 받고 있으므로 ②번이 적절하다.

18 ⓐ와 ①, ③: 동격절을 이끄는 접속사, ② 목적절을 이끄는 접속사, ④ 주절을 이끄는 접속사, ⑤ 보어절을 이끄는 접속사

19 이 글은 '몇몇 사람들은 명백한 증거를 하나도 제공하지 못한 완벽한 거짓말로 드러난 무서운 광대들에 관한 이야기를 누가 말하고 있는지 전혀 확인하지도 않고 단지 소셜 미디어에 올라온 것만을 보고 무서워했지만, Danina Garcia-Fuller의 학생들은 조금도 그 이야기들을 믿지 않았다'는 내용의 글이므로, 제목으로는 ③번 '이봐, 소셜 미디어에 올라온 것들을 믿을 때는 신중해야 해!'가 적절하다.

20 '나무 문어'라고 불리는 동물이라고 해야 하므로 과거분사 called로 쓰는 것이 적절하다.

21 ⓑ와 ②: 교훈, ①, ④, ⑤: 수업[교습/교육] (시간), ③ (교과서의) 과(課)

서술형 시험대비
p.148~149

01 student → students   02 not, but

03 It turned out that the story was a complete lie.

04 (A) on social media   (B) a complete lie

05 to think critically about information they're seeing in the news and on the Internet

06 filled with

07 It is really important to look at the right sources and to pay attention to what is real and what is fake.

08 (A) I am   (B) my

09 (A) is   (B) too good   (C) supports

10 they should

11 (A) slow down   (B) stop   (C) any evidence

12 a tree octopus   13 what

14 (A) once more carefully   (B) question everything

01 one+of+소유격+복수명사: ~ 중의 하나

02 B, not A = not A but B: A가 아니라 B

03 the story를 that절의 주어로 바꾸고, to be를 was로 바꾸는

것이 적절하다.

04 몇몇 사람들은 그들이 '소셜 미디어에 올라온' 것들을 봤기 때문에 무서운 광대들에 관한 이야기를 무서워했지만 그들은 누가 그 이야기를 말하고 있는지를 전혀 확인하지 않았는데, 그 이야기는 결국 완벽한 거짓말인 것으로 드러났다.

05 '뉴스에서 그리고 인터넷상에서 보고 있는 정보에 관해 비판적으로 생각하는 것'을 가리킨다.

06 be full of = be filled with: ~로 가득 차 있다. full of 앞에 which[that] is가 생략되어 있다.

07 올바른 출처를 살펴보고, 무엇이 진짜이고 무엇이 가짜인지에 주의를 기울이는 것이 정말 중요하다.

08 직접화법으로 고치면 'she was'를 'I am'으로, 'her' students를 'my' students로 고치는 것이 적절하다.

09 (A) 주어가 One이므로 is가 적절하다. (B) '만약 어떤 이야기나 어떤 사진이 진짜라고 하기엔 너무 좋아 보인다면'이라고 해야 하므로 too good이 적절하다. too+형용사/부사+to부정사: '너무 …해서 ~할 수 없다', 형용사/부사+enough to부정사: ~할 만큼 충분히 …한, (C) 글쓴이가 말하고 있는 것을 '뒷받침하는' 어떠한 증거라도 있는가라고 해야 하므로 supports가 적절하다. deny: (무엇이) 사실이 아니라고 말하다, 부인[부정]하다

10 의문사+to부정사 = 의문사+주어+should+동사원형

11 첫 단계 중 하나는 '속도를 늦추는 것'이다. 만약 어떤 이야기나 어떤 사진이 진짜라고 하기엔 너무 좋아 보일 때, '멈춰서' 글쓴이의 말을 뒷받침하는 '어떠한 증거'라도 있는지와 이 정보의 출처에 대해 생각해야 한다.

12 '나무 문어'를 가리킨다.

13 선행사를 포함하는 관계대명사 'what'으로 바꿔 쓸 수 있다.

14 Garcia-Fuller가 그녀의 학생들에게 말하는 교훈은 당신이 보고 있는 정보를 '한 번 더 신중하게' 확인해 보라는 것과 '모든 것', 심지어 그녀가 말하는 것에도 '의문을 가져 보라'는 것이다.

영역별 핵심문제
p.151~155

01 attack   02 ③   03 ④   04 ④

05 ①   06 fake   07 comfortable

08 ③   09 ⑤   10 ④   11 ②

12 ④   13 ②   14 ①that → if[whether]

15 ④   16 ④   17 ③

18 (1) He said to her, "What are you doing here?"
   (2) She said to him, "I met my sister yesterday."
   (3) She said, "I am very happy now."

19 ②   20 무서운 광대들에 관한 이야기

21 They offered no hard evidence that clowns really were trying to attack students.

22 ④   23 ②   24 ③

25 invented   26 ⑤   27 ④

01 반의어 관계다. 지루한-흥미로운 : 방어하다-공격하다

02 ⓐ 이 책은 실화에 바탕을 둔다. '~에 근거하다'는 'be based on'을 사용한다. ⓑ 분홍 말에 관한 이야기는 꾸며낸 것이었다. '꾸며낸'은 'made up'을 사용한다.

03 ④번의 'complete'는 형용사로 '완전한'의 의미이다. 'complete'가 '완료하다'라는 의미의 동사로 사용되려면 'wasn't completed'의 수동형이 되는 것이 적절하다.

04 '당신이 어떤 것이 사실이라고 믿도록 만드는 어떤 것'의 의미로 'evidence(증거)'가 적절하다.

05 '불찬성을 표현하는 방식으로'의 의미로 'critically(비판적으로)'가 적절하다.

06 '진짜가 아니지만 진짜처럼 보이도록 만들어진'의 의미로 4글자 단어인 'fake(가짜의)'가 적절하다.

07 look의 보어로 comfort의 형용사형이 와야 한다.

08 G가 그것이 가짜라고 한 말에 대해 동의하지 않는다고 말하고 있고, TV에서 저런 종류의 원숭이를 봤다고 했으므로 빈칸에는 'real'이 적절하다.

09 ⑤번은 '이 광고에 대해 어떻게 생각해?'라는 A의 물음에 대해 B가 '훌륭하다고 생각해.'라고 말한 다음 '우리는 모든 광고를 다 믿으면 안 된다'고 말하는 것은 어색하다.

10 '문어가 나무에서 산다고 Mr. Big Mouth가 말했어.'라는 Alex의 말에 대해 Somi는 '말도 안 돼.'라고 말하는 것이 자연스럽다. 'It doesn't make sense.'로 바꾸어야 한다.

11 위 대화는 Big Mouth's Show에서 보여준 사진이 사실인지 아닌지에 대한 대화이다.

12 Alex는 나무를 오르는 문어 사진이 사실이라고 생각하고 있다.

13 주어진 문장은 동사 'tells'의 목적절로 '~인지 아닌지'이다. ② '~인지 아닌지' ①, ③, ④, ⑤ 조건절. '만일 ~라면'

14 동사 'don't know'와 어울리는 접속사는 의문을 의미하는 'if'이다.

15 의문사가 주어이므로 문장의 어순은 바뀌지 않는다. 전달동사가 과거이므로 의문문의 과거동사는 과거완료로, 지시형용사 this는 that으로 바꾼다. 해석: 그는 나에게 누가 저 도마뱀붙이를 집으로 가져왔는지 물었다. *gecko: 도마뱀붙이

16 a. Do you know if it will be rainy tomorrow? b. I am not sure if he can finish his project. d. Tell me if[whether] you have the time. e. He asked me if I wanted something to eat.

17 전달동사가 과거이므로, 시제의 일치 법칙에 맞게 따옴표(" ") 안의 현재동사를 과거시제로 바꾸고 부사 tomorrow는 의미상 적절하게 the following day로 바꾼다. 또한 따옴표 속 'I'는 문장의 주어로 바꾸고 따옴표 속 'you'는 듣는 이로 바꾼다.

18 (1) 따옴표 안에서 의문문의 형태인 '의문사+동사+주어'의 어순이어야 한다. (2) 간접화법에서 과거완료시제이고, 전달동사

는 과거이므로 따옴표 안에서 과거시제로 써야 한다. (3) 간접화법에서 then은 직접화법에서 내용이 현재시제이므로 now로 쓰는 것이 적절하다.

19 그 이야기들은 10대들이 지어낸 것이고 광대들이 정말로 학생들을 공격하려고 한다는 명백한 증거를 하나도 제공하지 않았다고 했으므로, 그 이야기는 결국 '완벽한 거짓말'인 것으로 드러났다고 하는 것이 적절하다. ① 근거 있는 소문, ③ valid: 타당한, ⑤ suspicious: 의심스러운, column: 칼럼

20 'the story about scary clowns'를 가리킨다.

21 동격의 접속사 'that' 이하가 'evidence'와 동격을 이루도록 쓰는 것이 적절하다.

22 ⓐ와 ④: 이유를 나타내는 접속사, ① ~하는 대로(접속사), ② ~하다시피[~이듯이](접속사), ③ [비례] ~함에 따라, ~할수록(접속사), ⑤ ~하고 있을 때(접속사)

23 이 글은 '이야기들은 아주 빠른 속도로 퍼져 나갈 수 있고 누구나 허위 정보로 가득 찬 웹사이트를 만들어 낼 수 있기 때문에, 뉴스에서 그리고 인터넷상에서 보고 있는 정보에 관해 비판적으로 생각하는 것이 최근 더 중요해지고 있다'는 내용의 글이므로, 주제로는 ②번 '뉴스에서 그리고 인터넷상에서 보고 있는 정보에 관해 비판적으로 생각하는 것의 중요성'이 적절하다.

24 많은 미국의 10대들은 '뉴스에서 그리고 인터넷상에서' 보고 있는 정보에 관해 비판적으로 생각하는 것을 배워 나가고 있다.

25 make up: (특히 남을 속이거나 즐겁게 하기 위해 이야기 등을) 지어[만들어] 내다, be made up: ~로 꾸며지다, invent: (사실이 아닌 것을) 지어내다[날조하다]

26 이 글은 'Garcia-Fuller가 또한 때로 현명한 뉴스 독자가 되는 것이 아주 어려울 수도 있다고 말하면서 그녀의 학생들에게 여러분이 보고 있는 정보를 한 번만 더 신중하게 확인해 보고 모든 것, 심지어 그녀가 말하는 것에도 의문을 가져 보라는 교훈을 말하는' 내용의 글이므로, 제목으로는 ⑤번 '정보를 신중하게 확인하고 모든 것에 의문을 가져라'가 적절하다.

27 앞에 나오는 내용과 상반되는 내용이 뒤에 이어지므로 However가 적절하다. ② 게다가, ③ 다시 말해서, ⑤ 그러므로

28 이어동사의 목적어가 인칭대명사일 때는 목적어를 동사와 부사 사이에 쓰는 것이 적절하다.

단원별 예상문제 p.156~159

01 preform   02 ⑤

03 They were made out of a police officer's uniform., This police officer made them for the kids.

04 Is there anything special about them?

05 ②   06 ④   07 ③   08 ②, ⑤

09 (1) the answer of that question

(2) had been in trouble

(3) my new house now

(4) said to

(5) Are you hungry now

10 (1) Don't go out during class

　(2) told[asked, ordered] students not to go out during class

11 I wonder if[whether] they will show us the fan dance.

12 (1) I am so tired now　(2) I was right

13 ④　　　　14 proved

15 They were made by teenagers.　　16 ②

17 many teenagers in America　　18 ①

19 ②, ③, ⑤　20 ④　　21 while → during

22 ①, ④　　23 best

01 '명사-동사'의 관계이다. 정보 - 알리다 : 공연 - 공연하다

02 '매우 중요하고 진지한'의 의미로 'major(주된, 주요한)'가 적절하다.

03 대화에서 'Teddy Bears'에 관해 알 수 있는 'Fact'는 '한 경찰관의 제복으로 만들어졌다.'는 것과 '이 경찰이 아이들을 위해 그것들을 만들어 줬다'는 두 가지다.

04 '~가 있니?'라는 의문문으로 'Is there+주어 ~?'로 시작하고, anything은 형용사가 뒤에서 수식해야 하므로 anything special로 쓴다.

05 '그것이 가짜라고 생각해.'라는 G의 말에 B가 '저런 종류의 원숭이를 TV에서 본 적이 있어.'라고 말하고 있으므로 G의 말에 동의하지 않는다는 것을 알 수 있다.

06 요새 여자아이들은 짧은 머리를 더 좋아한다는 말에 대해 '그것에 동의하지 않아.'라는 말을 한 다음 주어진 문장이 들어가는 것이 자연스럽다.

07 (a) '매우 예쁘다고 생각해.'라는 말 다음에 머리를 왜 잘랐는지 화제를 바꾸어 말하고 있으므로 'By the way'가 적절하다. (b) '여기 이 아이는 여자아이가 아니야.'라는 말 다음에 '강조, 첨가'하는 표현으로 '사실'의 의미를 가지는 'In fact'가 적절하다.

08 debate의 목적절이고 의문의 내용이므로 빈칸에 접속사 if 또는 whether를 쓴다. 해석: 팀 A와 팀 B는 십대들이 파트타임을 해야 할지에 관해 토론할 것이다.

09 (1) 직접화법에서 this는 간접화법에서 that으로 쓴다. (2) 전달동사가 과거이고 직접화법의 시제가 과거이면 간접화법에서 과거완료시제로 쓴다. (3) 간접화법에서 that절의 주어와 주절의 주어가 같다면 직접화법에서 일인칭으로 쓰고, then은 now로 쓴다. (4) 간접화법에서 전달동사 tell은 듣는 이가 있다면 직접화법에서 say to로 쓴다. (5) 간접화법에서의 듣는 이와 종속절의 주어가 같다면, 직접화법에서 you로 쓰고, 전달동사의 시제와 종속절의 시제가 과거로 같다면 직접화법에서 따옴표 안에서 현재시제로 쓴다. 부사 then은 now로 바꾸어 쓴다.

10 (1) 부정의 명령문 'Don't+동사원형'의 형태로 문장을 쓴다.

(2) 명령문으로 간접화법을 쓸 때, 전달동사는 의미에 따라 tell, ask, order 등을 쓸 수 있고, 부정의 명령문은 not to로 바꾸어 쓴다.

11 동사 wonder의 목적어 자리에 의미상 의문문을 넣어야 하므로, 명사절의 접속사 if 또는 whether를 넣어 목적절을 완성한다.

12 (1) that절의 주어와 주절의 주어가 같으면 따옴표 속에서 'I'로 쓰고, that절과 주절의 시제가 과거로 같으므로 따옴표 속에서 현재시제로 쓴다. 부사 then은 따옴표 속에서 now로 쓴다. (2) 직접화법을 간접화법으로 바꿀 때 전달동사가 과거라면 따옴표 속 현재시제는 과거로 바꾸고, 'you'는 듣는 이로 바꾼다.

13 ⓐ와 ④: 명백한(형용사), ① 단단한, 굳은(형용사), ② 열심히, 힘껏(부사), ③ (이해하거나 답하기) 어려운(형용사), ⑤ 열심히 하는(형용사)

14 turn out = prove: ~로 드러나다

15 무서운 광대들에 관한 이야기는 '10대들에 의해 지어졌다.'

16 ⓐ와 ②, ⑤: 명사적 용법, ①, ④: 부사적 용법, ③: 형용사적 용법

17 '많은 미국의 10대들'을 가리킨다.

18 주어진 문장의 the first steps에 주목한다. ①번 앞 문장의 '가짜 뉴스를 진짜 뉴스로부터 구분하는 방법'의 첫 단계를 말하는 것이므로 ①번이 적절하다.

19 ⓐ와 ①, ④: 부사적 용법, ②: 형용사적 용법, ③, ⑤: 명사적 용법

20 "의견들은 '읽을 만한' 가치가 있다."라고 15살인 McKenzie Campbell이 말했다.

21 during+기간을 나타내는 명사, while+주어+동사

22 ⓑ와 ①, ④: '~인지 아닌지'라는 뜻의 명사절을 이끄는 접속사, = whether, ②, ③, ⑤: '만약 ~한다면'이라는 조건의 의미를 지니는 부사절을 이끄는 접속사

23 비교급+than+any+other+단수명사: 최상급의 뜻

🦉 서술형 실전문제　　p.160~161

01 Because an octopus can't live out of the sea.

02 (1) if these shoes fit his feet

　(2) that the baby is crying now

　(3) Whether this kid is a girl or a boy

03 (1) she liked Tony

　(2) he wanted some water

　(3) his sister looked happy

04 (1) I was living then

　(2) if I liked to study in that library

05 he had seen the cat the day before[the previous day], if she had an owner

06 about information they're seeing in the news and on the Internet

07 fake

08 (A) the right sources   (B) what is real

09 so, that, can't   10 that → if[whether]

11 We have to check if[whether] they are based on facts.

---

stadium at 7

(3) how long his training hours had been that day

(4) it had taken 5 hours and had been really hard

(5) what he would do in his spare time that day

(6) after that interview, he would go swimming or watch a movie

---

01 질문: 왜 소미는 그것이 가짜 사진이라 말했는가?

02 (1) 동사 wonder의 목적절로 접속사 if절이 적절하다. (2) 확신하는 내용이므로 목적절로 접속사 that절이 적절하다. (3) 의문의 내용이고 주절이 필요하므로 접속사 whether절이 적절하다.

03 (1), (2), (3) 직접화법을 간접화법으로 바꿀 때 따옴표 속 'I'는 문장의 주어로 바꾼다. 또한 전달동사가 과거라면, 시제의 일치 법칙에 맞게 따옴표(" ") 안의 동사가 현재시제라면 과거시제로 바꾼다.

04 의문문을 직접화법에서 간접화법으로 바꿀 때, 간접의문문의 형태로 바꾸고, 따옴표 속 'I'는 문장의 주어로, 따옴표 속 'you'는 듣는 이로 바꾼다. 전달동사가 과거라면, 시제의 일치 법칙에 맞게 따옴표(" ") 안의 동사가 현재시제라면 과거시제로 바꾼다. 지시대명사와 부사를 전달자의 입장에 맞게 바꾼다. now는 then으로, this는 that으로 바꾼다.

05 전달동사가 과거이므로 그림 속 대화의 현재는 과거시제, 과거는 과거완료시제로 바꾸고, 질문은 간접의문문으로 바꾼다. 이때, 부사를 적절히 바꾼다. (yesterday → the day before 또는 the previous day)

06 'information'과 'they're' 사이에는 목적격 관계대명사 'that[which]'이 생략되어 있다.

07 fake: 가짜의, 거짓된, 진짜가 아닌; 진짜인 물건의 모조품이

08 Patricia의 반 친구인 Ivy-Brooks에 따르면, '올바른 출처들'을 살펴보고, '무엇이 진짜이고' 무엇이 가짜인지에 주의를 기울이는 것이 정말 중요하다.

09 too ~ to = so ~ that ... can't

10 접속사 'if'는 명사절을 이끌어 '~인지 아닌지'라는 뜻이다. 'whether'로 교체할 수 있다.

11 그것들이 사실에 기반을 둔 것인지를 확인해 보아야 한다.

창의사고력 서술형 문제   p.162

|모범답안|

01 (1) A: How do you feel about persimmons?
    B: I like them.

   (2) A: How do you feel about cucumbers?
    B: I hate them.

   (3) A: How do you feel about pears?
    B: I don't like them.

02 (1) if he could tell her about his day

   (2) he always gets up at 6 and goes to the

단원별 모의고사   p.163~167

01 ②   02 (p)rovide   03 ⑤   04 ④

05 ③   06 it doesn't seem real, it's a little boring

07 ③   08 Look at those shoes the girl is wearing.

09 (1) fact   (2) uniform   (3) if[whether]

10 It is climbing a tree.   11 ②   12 ①

13 Mr. Kim asked his daughter if[whether] he could ask her a few questions.

14 (1) He says to her, "Where do you work now?"

   (2) She told me that she hadn't been at school the day before.

15 ③

16 (1) I wonder if she will like my present.

   (2) Do you know if she is married?

17 (A) scary   (B) scared   (C) offered

18 stories about scary clowns

19 ③   20 ⑤

21 opinion in the news → real news
   또는 fake news → fact

22 ① 글쓴이가 말하고 있는 것을 뒷받침하는 어떠한 증거라도 있는가?
   ② 이 정보가 어디서 온 것인가?

23 ③   24 ④

---

01 ②번은 '무엇에 관하여 생각하거나 믿고 있는 것'의 의미로 'opinion(의견)'에 관한 설명이다. 'fact'는 'something that is known to have happened or to exist, especially something for which proof exists, or about which there is information'으로 '어떤 일이 일어났거나 존재한다고 알려진 것, 특히 증거가 존재하거나 정보가 있는 것'이다.

02 유의어 관계이다. 찾다, 조사하다 : 제공하다

03 '한 도시, 국가 또는 세계의 특정 부분'의 의미로 'area(지역)'가

적절하다.

04 상대방의 의견을 묻는 질문에 '나는 동의하지 않아.'라고 말하는 것은 어색하다.

05 빈칸 뒤에서 '소년이 그의 여동생을 구하기 위해 자신의 생명을 포기했잖아.'라고 하고 있으므로 '감동적이라고 생각한다'는 말이 적절하다.

06 질문: 여학생은 왜 그것이 좋은 드라마가 아니라고 생각하는가?

07 요즘 여자아이들은 짧은 머리를 더 좋아한다는 B의 의견에 대해 '대부분의 여자아이는 짧은 머리보다 긴 머리를 좋아해.'라고 말하고 있으므로 (3)은 'I don't agree with that.'이 되어야 한다.

08 명령문이므로 동사원형으로 문장을 시작한다. '저 여자애가 신고 있는'에 해당하는 말이 'shoes'를 수식하는 역할을 한다.

09 (1) 경찰관이 아이들에게 곰 인형을 사주었다는 말 다음에 'However'가 이어지므로, 앞 문장에 대한 역접의 의미가 온다는 것을 알 수 있다. (2) 경찰관 제복으로 인형을 만들어 주었다. (3) 기자가 그들을 직접 만났는지 어떤지 궁금하다는 의미로 접속사 'if나 whether'가 적절하다.

10 질문: 사진 속의 문어는 무엇을 하고 있는가?

11 보기와 ② 'that'은 형용사를 수식하는 '지시부사'다. ① 지시형용사, ③ 접속사, ④ It ~ that ... 강조구문에 사용된 접속사, ⑤ 지시대명사

12 ① 동사 discuss의 목적절로 '~인지 아닌지'의 의미이다. ②~⑤ 조건의 접속사로 '만일 ~라면'의 의미이다.

13 의문문을 간접화법으로 전환할 때 전달동사 said to를 asked로 바꾸고 접속사 if 또는 whether를 쓴다. 전달동사가 과거이므로, 시제의 일치 법칙에 맞게 따옴표(" ") 안의 현재동사를 과거시제로 바꾼다. 또한 따옴표 속 'I'는 문장의 주어로 바꾸고 따옴표 속 'you'는 듣는 이로 바꾼다.

14 (1) 듣는 이가 있을 때 직접화법의 전달동사는 say to를 쓴다. (2) 전달동사가 과거이므로 that절의 시제는 과거 또는 과거완료시제를 쓴다. 내용상 전달하기 이전의 내용이므로 과거완료시제로 쓰는 것이 적절하다.

15 의문사가 없는 의문문을 명사절로 바꿀 때 접속사 if는 사용할 수 없고, whether를 쓴다.

16 (1) 동사 wonder의 목적절로 if절을 쓴다. 이때 명사절인 if절에서는 will을 사용하는 것이 가능하다. (2) 의문문 'Do you know'의 목적절로 if절을 쓴다. 결혼한 상태를 나타내는 표현은 be married이다.

17 (A) '무서운 광대들'이라고 해야 하므로 scary가 적절하다. scary: 무서운, scared: 무서워하는, (B) '무서워했다'고 해야 하므로 scared가 적절하다. (C) They가 '그 이야기들'을 가리키고 있고, '그 이야기들은 증거를 하나도 제공하지 않았다'고 해야 하므로 능동태인 offered가 적절하다.

18 '무서운 광대들에 관한 이야기'를 가리킨다.

19 ⓐ pay attention to: ~에 주목하다, 유의하다, ⓑ on the Internet: 인터넷상에서

20 (A)와 ⑤: ~처럼(전치사), ① 비슷한(형용사), ② (예를 들어) ~과 같은(= such as)(전치사), ③ ~을 좋아하다(동사), ④ 비

숫한 것(명사)

21 Garcia-Fuller는 자신의 학생들에게 가짜 뉴스를 '진짜 뉴스'로부터 구분하는 방법과 또한 뉴스에서 '사실'을 의견과 구분하는 방법을 가르치고 있다

22 ① Is there any evidence that supports what the writer says? ② Where is this coming from?

23 주어진 문장의 The site에 주목한다. ③번 앞 문장의 a website를 받고 있으므로 ③번이 적절하다.

24 무서운 광대들의 이야기와 마찬가지로 '나무 문어'에 대한 정보는 완전히 꾸며진 것이다.

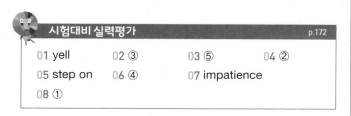

Make Peace with Others

시험대비 실력평가   p.172

01 yell   02 ③   03 ⑤   04 ②
05 step on   06 ④   07 impatience
08 ①

01 비록 누군가가 여러분에게 소리를 친다고 해도, 똑같이 반응해 서는 안 됩니다. <영어 설명> 큰 소리로 고함지르다

02 'general'은 형용사로 '일반적인', 명사로 '장군'의 의미를 가지 고 있다. • 첼로는 일반 대중에게는 여전히 낯선 악기로 여겨지 고 있습니다. • 김유신은 한국 역사상 훌륭한 장군이었습니다.

03 '특히 옛날에 존재하던 매우 용감하고 싸움에 숙련된 군인 또는 투사'의 의미로 'warrior(전사)'가 적절하다.

04 '어떤 사실을 알게 되거나 이해하다'란 의미로 'realize(깨닫다)' 가 적절하다.

05 '~을 밟다'는 'step on'을 사용한다.

06 (1) 이들 유권자들은 그들이 살고 있는 사회를 바꾸려고 노력하 는 것에 관하여 열정적이기 때문에, 그들은 수 시간 동안 줄을 서 있다. (2) 그것은 그에게는 쉽지 않은 일이었지만, 그는 포기 하지 않았습니다.

07 반의어 관계. 전쟁-평화 : 인내심-성급함

08 나머지는 '동사 – 명사' 관계로 '사람'을 나타내고, ①번은 '동사 – 명사' 관계로 '요리하다 – 요리기구'를 의미한다. 'cook'이 명 사로 사용될 때 '요리사'라는 뜻을 갖는다.

서술형 시험대비   p.173

01 (1) above   (2) army   (3) set, free   (4) reasons
02 (1) weapon   (2) pole
03 (1) look   (2) situation   (3) Palace
04 (1) powerful, 강력한   (2) wise, 현명한
    (3) injured, 부상당한   (4) push, 밀다
05 (1) decreasing   (2) pass by   (3) Sooner or later

01 (1) 그의 사진은 책상 위 선반에 놓여 있었다. (2) 내 동생은 작 년에 군대에 입대했다. (3) 왕은 부하들에게 죄수를 풀어주라 고 명령했다. '~을 석방하다'는 'set ~ free'다. (4) 내가 의사가 되기를 원하는 두 가지 이유가 있다. two와 어울리는 복수명사 'reasons'를 사용한다.

02 (1) 사람들은 비행기에 칼이나 총과 같은 어떤 무기도 가지고 와 서는 안 됩니다. (2) 우리는 장대의 꼭대기에 있는 그 나라의 깃발

을 보았다. 영영 풀이: 길고 얇은 나무나 금속 조각

03 (1) look: 표정 (2) situation: 상황 (3) palace: 궁전, 궁궐

04 (1) 사람과 사건을 통제할 수 있는 많은 힘을 갖고 있는 (2) 무 엇이 진실인지 또는 옳은지 제대로 판단할 수 있는 힘을 갖고 있 는 (3) 신체 일부분에 물리적인 상처를 입은 (4) 손으로 누름으 로써 누군가나 또는 무엇인가가 움직이게 하다

05 (1) 초등학생의 수가 계속해서 줄어들고 있다. '계속 ~하다'는 'keep -ing'를 사용한다. (2) 당신이 뭔가를 하든지 하지 않든 지 방학은 시작되고, 지나갈 것이다. (3) 조만간, 그는 그녀가 정 말로 그를 사랑했다는 것을 깨닫게 될 것이다.

교과서 Conversation

핵심 Check   p.174~175

1 ④   2 ④

교과서 대화문 익히기

Check(√) True or False   p.176

1 F   2 T   3 T   4 F

교과서 확인학습   p.178~179

Get Ready 2

(1) ve waited / Calm, almost
(2) What, hate, in line / Calm down
(3) wait in line / Calm down
(4) behind, keeps pushing, can't stand / Calm down, just

Start Off – Listen & Talk A

1. noise / fixing, heaters / focus on, at all, can't stand it
2. can't find, seen / put / gone, upset / Calm, find

Start Off – Listen & Talk B

on, foot / okay / third, did that, can't stand / Calm down, wearing, glasses / happened / broke, during / should have been

Start Off – Speak Up

can't stand, crowded / Calm down, festival, enjoy

시험대비 기본평가   p.180

01 can't stand, crowded   02 ④   03 ③
04 ④

01 '~을 참을 수 없다'는 'I can't stand ~'를 사용하고, '붐비는'은 'crowded'를 쓴다.

02 화가 난 상대방에게 응대할 때, 'Calm down!(진정해!)'이라는 표현을 쓸 수 있다. 이와 같은 표현으로는 'Relax.', 'Take it easy.', 'It's going to be okay. Take a deep breath and try to relax.', 'Chill out!', 'Don't stress yourself.', 'Control yourself.' 등이 있다.

03 화난 감정을 표현하는 문장으로 'I can't stand it.(참을 수 없어.)'을 사용할 수 있다. 이외에도 'I'm very angry.', 'I'm very upset.', 'I'm very annoyed.', 'How irritating!' 등이 있다.

04 화낸 상대방에게 응대할 때, 'Calm down!(진정해!)'이라는 표현을 쓸 수 있다.

시험대비 실력평가   p.181~182

01 ③   02 stepped on his, three   03 ③
04 ②   05 set, free
06 I can't spend a hundred days doing nothing.   07 ④
08 ⑤   09 ①   10 ④
11 The boy behind me keeps pushing me.

01 대화의 흐름상 '그 애는 더 조심했어야 했어.'라는 내용이 적절하다. '~했어야 했다'라는 과거의 유감을 나타내는 표현으로 'should have+과거분사'를 사용한다.

02 대화 속의 남자 아이가 Ben의 발을 세 번이나 밟았기 때문에 화가 났다.

03 대화의 흐름상 B가 화내는 말에 대해 '곧 끝날 거야.'라고 말하고 있는 것으로 보아 진정시키는 표현이 적절하다.

04 B가 '진정해! 이 뜨거운 우유를 마셔 봐.'라고 말하는 것으로 보아 ②번이 가장 적절하다.

05 '누군가 감옥에서 나가도록 허락하다'라는 의미로 'set+목적어+free'를 사용한다.

06 '~하면서 시간을 보내다'라는 표현으로 'spend+시간+V-ing' 구문을 이용한다.

07 대화에서 It은 'Waiting there for 100 days(100일을 거기서 기다리는 것)'를 가리키는 대명사이다.

08 민수의 누나가 가장 좋아하는 과목이 무엇인지는 대화에서 언급되어 있지 않다.

09 'forget+동명사'는 '~한 것을 잊다'라는 의미로 대화의 '설거지 할 것을 잊었다'라는 내용으로 'forgot to do'가 되어야 한다.

10 ④번의 'Chill out!'은 '침착해'라는 뜻으로 화난 상대방에게 해주는 말이다.

11 주어인 'The boy' 뒤에서 '전치사+명사(behind me)'가 주어를 꾸며주고, 주어가 단수 명사이므로 동사는 'keeps'를 사용한다. '계속 ~하다'라는 의미로 'keep+V-ing'를 사용한다.

서술형 시험대비   p.183

01 He will do the dishes after he finishes his homework.
02 to do the dishes, what he has to do, difficult, help with, after
03 I can't stand it / Calm down
04 (t)ie me up, (s)et me free / can't (s)tand / (C)alm down

01 질문: 민수는 설거지를 언제 할 것인가?

02 민수와 민수의 누나는 민수가 설거지하는 것을 잊어버린 것에 대해 이야기를 나누고 있다. 민수의 누나는 그가 해야 하는 것을 항상 잊어버리기 때문에 화가 나 있다. 민수가 설거지를 하지 않은 것은 과학 숙제가 어려워서라고 변명한다. 그의 누나는 그가 숙제를 하는 것을 도와주고, 그는 숙제를 끝낸 후 설거지를 할 것이다.

03 화난 감정을 표현하는 문장으로 'I can't stand it.(참을 수 없어.)'을 사용할 수 있다. 이외에도 'I'm very angry.', 'I'm very upset.', 'I'm very annoyed.', 'How irritating!' 등을 대신 사용할 수 있다. 화낸 상대방을 진정시킬 때는, 'Calm down!(진정해!)'이라는 표현을 쓸 수 있다. 이와 같은 표현으로는 'Relax.', 'Take it easy.', 'Chill out!', 'Don't stress yourself.', 'Control yourself.' 등이 있다.

04 M1: 저를 왜 여기에 묶어 두셨습니까? 저를 풀어 주십시오.
M2: 어떻게 풀려날 수 있겠느냐? 생각해 보아라.

M1: 저는 이 푯말을 참을 수가 없습니다. 저는 위험하지도 나쁘지도 않습니다.

M2: 진정하거라. 나는 네가 방법을 찾을 것이라고 확신한다.

교과서 Grammar

1 (1) the other　(2) the others　(3) some
2 (1) to be　(2) to go　(3) told

시험대비 기본평가　　　　　　　　　　p.186

01 (1) others are playing at snowballs
　(2) the other is sitting on the tree
　(3) the dog to get the ball
　(4) the boy to be careful
02 (1) another → the other
　(2) 첫 번째 the others → others
　(3) tell → to tell
　(4) studying → to study
03 (1) the others are dancing
　(2) the others are waving their hands to the singer

01 (1) 불특정한 다수의 일정하지 않은 몇몇과 다른 몇몇을 나타낼 때 some, others를 쓴다. (2) 두 개의 사람이나 사물 중 하나와 그 나머지 하나는 one, the other를 쓴다. (3), (4) 'order'와 'tell'은 목적격보어 자리에 to부정사가 오는 동사이다.

02 (1) 불특정한 두 사람이나 사물 중 하나와 나머지 하나를 나타낼 때 one, the other를 쓴다. (2) 불특정한 다수의 일정하지 않은 몇몇과 다른 몇몇을 나타낼 때 some, others를 쓰고 나머지 전체를 말할 때는 the others를 쓴다. (3), (4) 'want'와 'advise'는 목적격보어 자리에 to부정사가 오는 동사이다.

03 (1), (2) 불특정한 다수의 사람, 사물 중 하나와 그 나머지를 알 수 있을 때 one, the others를 쓴다.

시험대비 실력평가　　　　　　　　　　p.187~189

01 ⑤　　**02** ④　　**03** ④　　**04** ⑤
05 ③　　**06** ③
07 Peace tells us to help each other.　**08** ③
09 (1) He ordered his robot to do his homework.
　(2) She told him to lock the door.
10 to get up　**11** ②
12 (1) the other　(2) the others　(3) the others

---

　(4) the other　(5) Some
13 Some (shapes) are stars
14 I want him to know the truth.　　**15** ③
16 (1) Can you force your brothers to stop fighting?
　(2) My parents let me buy a new tablet PC.
17 ①　　　　　**18** Mom allowed me to go camping.
19 ①　　　　　**20** ④

01 'ask, tell, order, want'는 목적격보어 자리에 'to부정사'가 오는 동사이고, 'make'는 목적격보어로 원형부정사를 쓴다.

02 'advise'는 목적격보어 자리에 to부정사가 오는 동사이다. '주어+동사+목적어+to부정사'의 어순으로 과거시제로 문장을 완성한다.

03 불특정한 다수의 일정하지 않은 수량을 나타낼 때 두 번째 언급하는 경우 one은 쓰지 않는다. other는 단독으로 쓰지 않고 'other+복수명사' 혹은 others로 써야 하고 마지막에 나머지를 나타내는 the others가 있으므로 빈칸에 또 the others를 쓸 수 없다. 그러므로 정답은 others가 적절하다.

04 'ask'는 목적격보어 자리에 to부정사가 오는 동사이다.

05 'allow, tell, order, advise'는 목적격보어 자리에 to부정사가 오는 동사이다. 'keep'은 현재분사를 목적격보어로 쓴다. ③은 'going'이 적절하다.

06 'want'는 목적격보어 자리에 to부정사가 오는 동사이다.

07 'tell'은 목적격보어 자리에 to부정사가 오는 동사이다. '주어+동사+목적어+to부정사'의 어순으로 문장을 완성한다.

08 불특정한 둘 중 하나와 나머지 하나는 one, the other로 나타내고, 불특정한 다수의 일정하지 않은 몇몇과 다른 몇몇을 나타낼 때 some, others를 쓴다.

09 (1), (2) 'order'와 'tell'은 목적격보어 자리에 to부정사가 오는 동사이다.

10 'tell'은 목적격보어 자리에 to부정사가 오는 동사이다.

11 'tell, ask, want, encourage'는 목적격보어 자리에 to부정사가 오는 동사이다. 'see'는 목적격보어 자리에 원형부정사 또는 현재분사가 오는 동사이다.

12 (1), (4) 불특정한 두 명 중 한 명과 나머지 한 명은 one, the other로 나타낸다. (2) 불특정한 다수의 사람 중 처음 여럿과 그 나머지를 알 수 있을 때 some, the others를 쓴다. (3) 불특정한 다수의 사람 중 하나와 그 나머지를 알 수 있을 때 one, the others를 쓴다. (5) 불특정한 다수의 일정하지 않은 수량을 나타내고 나머지가 불확실 할 때는 some, others를 쓴다.

13 불특정한 다수의 사람, 사물 중 일부와 그 나머지를 알 수 있을 때 some, the others를 쓴다.

14 'want'는 목적격보어 자리에 to부정사가 오는 동사이다. '주어+동사+목적어+to부정사'의 어순으로 문장을 완성한다.

15 'allow'와 'let'은 5형식 동사로 '~하는 것을 허락하다'라는 뜻이다. 'let'은 목적격보어 자리에 원형부정사가, 'allow'는 목적격보어 자리에 to부정사가 오는 동사이다.

16 (1) 'make'는 목적격보어로 원형부정사를 취하는 동사이고 'force'는 목적격보어로 to부정사가 온다. (2) 'allow'는 목적격보어로 to부정사가 오는 동사이지만, 'let'은 목적격보어로 원형부정사를 취한다.

17 불특정한 두 가지 것 중 하나와 나머지 하나는 one, the other로 나타낸다. 또한 불특정한 다수 중 두 번째 다른 하나는 another로 나타낸다.

18 'allow'는 목적격보어 자리에 to부정사가 오는 동사이다. '주어+동사+목적어+to부정사'의 어순으로 과거시제 문장을 완성한다.

19 'have'와 'get'은 둘 다 '~에게 하도록 시키다'라는 뜻이지만, 'have'는 목적격보어로 원형부정사를, 'get'은 목적격보어로 to부정사를 취한다.

20 'want', 'ask', 'get'은 목적격보어 자리에 to부정사가 오는 동사이고, 'let'은 원형부정사를, 'see'는 원형부정사 또는 현재분사를 목적격보어로 취한다.

서술형 시험대비   p.190~191

01 (1) Here are two birds. One is flying, and the other is sitting on the tree.
  (2) The woman told the boy to be careful.
  (3) She has a lot of pens. Some are yellow, and others are red.
  (4) Jane asks me to teach math.
  (5) The farmer wanted me to feed the pigs.

02 (1) My mother told me to get up early.
  (2) I don't want you to tell anybody this secret.
  (3) My father allowed my uncle to use his car.

03 (1) Mr. Kim allowed us to bring what we wanted to eat.
  (2) Dr. Wang saw her patients work[working] out regularly during the day.

04 (1) the other has curly hair
  (2) the others are boys
  (3) another is rolling the snow

05 (1) The man allowed the boy to enter the grass.
  (2) She has three sons. One is a singer and the others are dancers.

06 (1) He asked his people to fight peacefully.
  (2) The police officer ordered the man to come out.
  (3) The girl asked the boy to help her.
  (4) The teacher told the boy to study hard.

07 (1) I want everyone to come here.
  (2) I'd like you to listen carefully.
  (3) They allow people to fish here.
  (4) I advise you not to walk home alone.

  (5) The dentist told Daniel to give up eating sweets.

08 (1) One (2) Some (3) the others

01 (1) 불특정한 두 개 중 하나와 나머지 하나는 one, the other로 나타낸다. (2), (4), (5) 'tell, ask, want'는 목적격보어 자리에 to부정사가 오는 동사이다. (3) 불특정한 다수의 일정하지 않은 수량을 나타내고 나머지가 불확실할 때는 some, others를 쓴다.

02 (1), (2), (3) 'tell, want, allow'는 목적격보어 자리에 to부정사가 오는 동사이다. '주어+동사+목적어+to부정사'의 어순으로 문장을 완성한다.

03 (1) 'let'은 목적격보어 자리에 원형부정사가 오는 동사이고, 'allow'는 목적격보어로 to부정사를 쓴다. (2) 'advise'는 목적격보어 자리에 to부정사가 오는 동사이고, 'see'는 목적격보어로 원형부정사 또는 현재분사를 쓸 수 있다.

04 (1) 불특정한 두 명 중 한 명과 나머지 한 명은 one, the other로 나타낸다. (2) 불특정한 다수의 사람, 사물 중 일부와 그 나머지를 알 수 있을 때 some, the others를 쓴다. (3) 불특정한 세 명 중 한 명과 또 다른 한 명, 그리고 나머지 한 명은 one, another, the other로 나타낸다.

05 (1) 'allow'는 목적격보어 자리에 to부정사가 오는 동사이다. '주어+동사+목적어+to부정사'의 어순으로 과거시제로 문장을 완성한다. (2) 셋 중 한 명과 나머지 두 명은 one, the others로 나타낸다.

06 'ask', 'order', 'tell'은 목적격보어 자리에 to부정사가 오는 동사이다. '주어+동사+목적어+to부정사'의 어순으로 문장을 완성한다.

07 (1), (2), (3) 'want, would like, allow'는 목적격보어 자리에 to부정사가 오는 동사이다. (4) to부정사의 부정은 'not to 동사원형'의 형태로 쓴다. (5) 목적어 Daniel과 목적격보어 give up은 능동 관계이므로 목적격보어로 과거분사가 아닌 to부정사를 쓰는 것이 적절하다.

08 (1) 불특정한 다수의 사람, 사물 중 하나와 그 나머지를 알 수 있을 때 one, the others를 쓴다. (2) 불특정한 다수의 일정하지 않은 몇몇을 나타낼 때 some을 쓴다. (3) 불특정한 다수의 사람, 사물 중 하나와 그 나머지를 알 수 있을 때 one, the others를 쓴다.

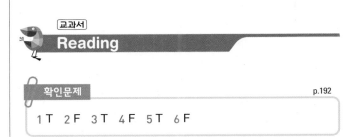

교과서
Reading

확인문제   p.192

1 T 2 F 3 T 4 F 5 T 6 F

1 T　2 F　3 T　4 F　5 T　6 F

1 T　2 F　3 T　4 F　5 T　6 F

교과서 확인학습 A　　　　　　　p.195~197

01 the Best Warrior
02 brave young
03 strongest, have much to learn
04 to go
05 In a hundred days
06 got angry
07 might be a reason
08 On the hundred and first day
09 first weapon, patience
10 to win a war
11 stand against
12 tied, to
13 that read
14 passed by
15 Some, others
16 shouted back
17 Set me free, or
18 made, worse
19 another
20 softly
21 not, but
22 kept saying
23 let him go
24 the most powerful weapon
25 stronger than
26 took, to
27 had passed
28 The first one to
29 the others
30 pushed, pulled
31 harder and harder
32 anymore
33 the injured
34 even harder
35 As
36 took good care of
37 except, following
38 to sit in it
39 standing with
40 all alone
41 the real winner
42 At that moment, my favorite
43 Sooner or later
44 returned to
45 approach, knowing, What's up

교과서 확인학습 B　　　　　　　p.198~200

1 Corky, the Best Warrior
2 Corky was a brave young man.
3 He wanted to be a general, but the king said, "You're the strongest man in my army, but you have much to learn."
4 He ordered Corky to go to a famous military school.
5 "Wait there. In a hundred days, your training will start," a voice said from inside the school gate.
6 Corky got angry.
7 But then he thought there might be a reason, so he waited.
8 On the hundred and first day, the gate opened.
9 An old man said, "You have learned to use your first weapon: patience.
10 Patience is the most important thing to win a war."
11 Then, the teacher told Corky to stand against a pole.
12 Suddenly, he tied Corky to the pole.
13 Above his head, he put a sign that read "Dangerous and Bad."
14 Many people passed by.
15 Some gave Corky angry looks, and others shouted at him.
16 Corky shouted back.
17 He yelled, "Set me free, or you all will be in big trouble!"
18 That made the situation worse.
19 "I need to try another way," he thought.
20 Then, Corky began to speak softly.
21 He said he was not dangerous or bad but was a good man.
22 He kept saying this in all possible ways.
23 Finally, the people let him go.
24 "Now you control the most powerful weapon: words.
25 Soft words are stronger than sharp swords," said the teacher.
26 Next, the teacher took Corky to a large hall with a chair in the middle.
27 There were 19 other warriors who had passed their tests.
28 "The first one to sit in the chair will be the winner," the teacher said.
29 Corky and the others began fighting.
30 They pushed, pulled, ran, and jumped.
31 They fought harder and harder, so Corky became tired.
32 Finally, he said, "I will not fight anymore.
33 Instead, I will take care of the injured."
34 The other warriors saw this and fought even harder.
35 As they fought, more warriors became tired and hurt.
36 Corky took good care of them, so they followed

him.

37 Soon, all the warriors except Thunder were following Corky.

38 Thunder walked toward the chair to sit in it.

39 Then, he saw Corky standing with his 18 followers.

40 Thunder realized he was all alone.

41 "I give up. You're the real winner," Thunder said to Corky.

42 At that moment, the teacher appeared and said. "Of all the great weapons, peace is my favorite.

43 Sooner or later, everyone wants to stand on the side of peace."

44 Corky returned to the palace after his training ended.

45 When the king saw him approach, he gave Corky a wise and knowing smile and said, "What's up, General?"

시험대비 실력평가
p.201~205

01 ②　　02 ①, ③, ⑤　　03 ④　　04 ②

05 Soft words are stronger than sharp swords

06 ④　　07 ②　　08 ③

09 처음에는 나머지 전사들과 격렬히 싸웠다. → 더는 싸움을 하지 않고 부상당한 자들을 돌보았다.

10 ①　　11 ⑤　　12 saying　　13 ④

14 Corky는 사람들에게 "나를 풀어 줘. 그렇지 않으면 모두 혼쭐날 줄 알아!"라고 소리를 질렀다. / Corky는 자신이 위험하거나 나쁘지 않고 좋은 사람이라고 계속해서 부드럽게 말하기 시작했다.

15 19 other warriors (who had passed their tests)

16 injured people[warriors]　　17 ⑤

18 to stand → standing 또는 stand

19 Sooner or later, everyone wants to stand on the side of peace.

20 ②　　21 ③　　22 you should[must]

23 ②　　24 that[which]　25 better → worse

26 ④　　27 ①, ④　　28 ④

01 ②는 왕을 가리키고, 나머지는 다 Corky를 가리킨다.

02 ⓐ와 ①, ③, ⑤: 형용사적 용법, ②: 부사적 용법, ④: 명사적 용법

03 '101일째 되던 날(On the hundred and first day)', 문이 열렸다.

04 ② let(사역동사)+목적어+동사원형(목적격보어), 나머지는 다 목적격보어 자리에 to부정사를 써야 하는 동사들이다.

05 stronger than: ~보다 강한

06 Corky가 얼마나 오래 기둥에 묶여져 있었는지는 대답할 수 없다. ① He told Corky to stand against a pole. ② Some gave Corky angry looks, and others shouted at him. ③ At first, he shouted back, but he realized that it made the situation worse. So he decided to try another way. ⑤ He came to control the most powerful weapon: words. come to+동사원형: ~하게 되다

07 더는 싸움을 하지 않는 '대신에' 부상당한 자들을 돌볼 것이라고 해야 하므로, Instead가 적절하다. ① 아직(도), ③ 사실, ⑤ 그러므로

08 even/much/still/far/a lot: 훨씬(비교급을 강조)

09 Corky도 처음에는 나머지 전사들과 격렬히 싸웠지만, 지치게 된 다음에는 더는 싸움을 하지 않고 부상당한 자들을 돌보았다.

10 ①은 Thunder를 가리키고, 나머지는 다 Corky를 가리킨다.

11 이 글은 'Corky가 마지막 무기인 평화를 얻고 진정한 승자가 되는' 내용의 글이므로, 교훈으로는 ⑤번 '모든 사람은 평화의 편에 서기를 원한다.'가 적절하다.

12 keep ~ing: 계속해서 ~하다

13 (A)와 ④: ~라고 적혀 있다[쓰여 있다](자동사), ① 읽다, 읽어서 알다, ② (특정한 방식으로) 이해하다, ③ (계기를) 확인[검침]하다, ⑤ (컴퓨터나 사용자가 디스크의 정보를) 읽다, 판독하다

14 Corky는 첫 번째 반응이 상황을 더 악화시키자, '다른 방법을 써야겠어.'라고 생각하며 부드럽게 말하기 시작했다.

15 '(시험에 통과한) 19명의 다른 전사들'을 가리킨다.

16 the+형용사 = 복수 보통명사

17 이 글은 '의자에 가장 먼저 앉는 사람이 승자가 될 것이라는 스승의 시험에 Corky도 처음에는 나머지 전사들과 격렬히 싸웠지만, 나중에는 더는 싸움을 하지 않고 부상당한 자들을 돌봐주었고, 그 결과 Thunder를 제외한 모든 전사들이 Corky를 따르게 되었다'는 내용의 글이므로, 주제로는 ⑤번 'Corky는 부상당한 자들을 돌봐줌으로써 많은 추종자들을 얻었다.'가 적절하다.

18 지각동사+목적어+현재분사/동사원형(목적격보어): …가 ~하는 것을 보다

19 sooner or later 조만간, 머잖아

20 이 글은 'Corky가 마지막 무기인 평화를 얻고 진정한 승자가 되어 성으로 돌아가 장군이 되는' 내용의 글이므로, 제목으로는 ②번 '진정한 승자인 Corky가 마지막 무기인 '평화'를 얻다'가 적절하다.

21 ⓐ in: (시간의 경과를 나타내어) ~ 후에[~ 만에/~ 있으면], In a hundred days: 100일 '후에', ⓑ on: (요일, 날짜, 때를 나타내어) ~에, On the hundred and first day: 101일째 되던 날

22 'to learn'은 앞에 나오는 'much'를 수식해 주는 형용사적 용법의 to부정사로, 'have much to learn'은 '배울 것이 많다'라는

뜻이다.

23 ②번 다음 문장의 he에 주목한다. 주어진 문장의 Corky를 받고 있으므로 ②번이 적절하다.

24 관계대명사 that[which]이 적절하다.

25 Corky가 "나를 풀어 줘. 그렇지 않으면 모두 혼쭐날 줄 알아!"라고 외친 것이 상황을 '더 악화시켰다'고 하는 것이 적절하다.

26 immediately: 즉시, 즉각, finally/at last/in the end/after all/eventually: 결국, 마침내

27 take care of = look after = care for: 돌보다, ② 이륙하다, ③ (특정한 상품을) 취급[거래]하다, ⑤ 찾다

28 '전사들이 얼마나 오래 싸웠는지'는 알 수 없다. ① To a large hall with a chair in the middle. ② There were 19 other warriors. ③ The first one to sit in the chair. ⑤ Because Corky took good care of them.

서술형 시험대비 p.206~207

01 (A) the strongest man (B) to learn
02 (A) wait here (B) a hundred
03 (A) in front of (B) patience
04 (1) If you don't (2) Unless you
05 (1) 부드럽게 말하는 것
   (2) 자신이 위험하거나 나쁘지 않고 좋은 사람이라고 계속해서 말하는 것
06 The first one to sit in the chair will be the winner
07 (A) tired (B) injured (C) following
08 (A) taking care of (B) fighting
09 he gave a wise and knowing smile to Corky
10 It was 'peace'.
11 (A) real winner (B) weapon

01 비록 Corky가 그의 군대에서 '가장 강한 전사'이지만 그는 아직도 '배울 게' 많다고 생각했기 때문이다.

02 'a reason' 뒤에는 문맥상 '그를 그곳에서 100일 동안 기다리도록 하는 것에 대한(for making him wait there for a hundred days)'이 생략되어 있다.

03 (A) "거기서 기다려라."라고 군사 학교 안에서 외치는 목소리가 들렸다고 했으므로, Corky가 기다린 곳은 군사 학교의 문 '앞'이었다고 하는 것이 적절하다. (B) Corky의 첫 번째 무기는 '인내'이다. Corky는 유명한 군사 학교에 갔지만 그 문 앞에서 100일 동안 기다려야 했다. 101일째 되던 날 한 노인이 Corky가 지난 100일 동안 그의 첫 번째 무기인 '인내'를 사용하는 법을 배운 것이라고 말했다.

04 '명령문, or'는 'If you don't'나 'Unless you'를 사용하여 고치는 것이 적절하다. 명령문+접속사 'or': …해라. 그렇지 않으면 ~할 것이다.

---

05 뒤에 이어지는 내용을 쓰는 것이 적절하다.

06 형용사적 용법의 to부정사 to sit이 The first one을 수식하도록 하는 것이 적절하다.

07 (A) Corky는 '지쳤다'고 해야 하므로 tired가 적절하다. tired: 피곤한, 지친, tiring: 피곤하게 만드는, (B) '부상당한 자들'을 돌볼 것이라고 해야 하므로 injured가 적절하다. the+과거분사 = 복수 보통명사, victims: 피해자들, (C) 전사들이 Corky를 '따르고 있었다'라고 해야 하므로 following이 적절하다.

08 Corky는 다른 전사들과 '싸우는' 대신에 부상당한 자들을 '돌봐줌으로써' 많은 추종자들을 얻었다.

09 give는 전치사 'to'를 사용하여 3형식으로 고치는 것이 적절하다.

10 Corky가 얻은 마지막 무기는 '평화'였다.

11 Thunder는 Corky가 '진정한 승자'라고 말했다. 마침내 Corky는 그의 스승이 가장 좋아하는 무기이기도 한 마지막 '무기'를 얻었다. Corky는 모든 훈련을 마친 후 궁으로 돌아가 장군이 되었다.

영역별 핵심문제 p.209~213

01 injured   02 ④   03 ①   04 ②
05 Calm down   06 ④   07 ⑤
08 ②   09 ④   10 ④
11 he should have been more careful   12 ③
13 ①, ②   14 ③   15 ③
16 ④ be → to be
17 (1) We need two things for peace. One is love and the other is hope.
   (2) We ask you to join us for peace.
   (3) I want you to stop fighting.
18 ⑤   19 ③   20 ②
21 should go
22 Patience is the most important thing to win a war.
23 ③   24 ④   25 ②   26 ①
27 he was not dangerous or bad but was a good man
28 ⑤   24 the other   25 ①, ③

01 유의어 관계이다. 전사 : 부상당한

02 (a) '조만간 당신은 결정을 내려야 할 것이다.'라는 의미로 '조만간'은 'sooner or later'를 사용한다. 'in all possible ways'는 '모든 가능한 방법으로'라는 뜻이다. (b) '그녀는 조국으로 돌아가기를 바랐다.'라는 의미로 '~로 돌아가다'는 'return to'를 사용한다.

03 '어떤 일을 하라고 누군가에게 말하다'의 의미로 'order(명령하다)'가 적절하다.

04 '경쟁에서 이기는 사람'의 의미로 'winner(우승자)'가 적절하다.

05 '화나거나, 기분 나쁘거나, 흥분을 느끼지 않게 하다'라는 의미로

39

'calm down(진정하다)'이 적절하다.

06 ④번의 'look'은 명사로 '표정'이라는 뜻이다.

07 문맥상 빈칸에는 '너무 붐빈다'를 나타내는 말이 적절하다.

08 (B) 밖의 소음이 무엇인지 묻자 → (C) 히터를 고치고 있다는 대답이 나오고 → (A) 공부에 집중할 수 없어 참을 수가 없다고 화내는 표현이 나오고 → (D) 화냄에 대해 '진정해'라는 답이 나오는 것이 자연스럽다.

09 ④번은 '가수들이 무엇을 하고 있니?'라는 A의 물음에 한 명은 노래를 하고 있고 '나머지 모두(the others)'는 춤을 추고 있다가 적절하다. 'another'는 '또 다른 한 명'을 뜻하고 단수 취급한다.

10 '오늘 안경을 쓰고 있지 않다'고 했으므로 잘 볼 수 '없다'는 말이 적절하다. 'can see'를 'can't see'로 바꾸어야 한다.

11 '과거의 유감이나 후회'를 나타내는 표현으로 '~했어야 했는데' 의 의미를 가지는 'should have p.p.'가 적절하다.

12 A가 '내 뒤에 있는 남자아이가 자꾸 밀어. 참을 수가 없어.'라고 화를 내는 말에 대해 '진정해. 그는 아직 어린아이야.'라는 대답이 자연스럽다.

13 'make'는 목적격보어로 원형부정사를 취하고, 'help'는 목적격보어로 원형부정사와 to부정사를 취한다. 'keep', 'leave'는 목적격보어로 현재분사를 쓰고, 'allow'는 to부정사를 쓰는 것이 적절하다.

14 b. 불특정한 두 가지 것 중 하나와 나머지 하나는 one, the other 로 나타낸다. c. hear의 목적격보어는 원형부정사 또는 현재분사를 쓴다. (talk 또는 talking) f. 불특정한 다수의 사람 중 하나와 그 나머지 모두를 알 수 있을 때 one, the others를 쓴다.

15 (A) 불특정한 두 가지[사람] 중 하나와 나머지 하나는 one, the other로 나타내고, (B) 'tell'은 목적격보어로 to부정사를 취한다.

16 'tell'은 목적격보어로 to부정사를 취한다.

17 (1) 불특정한 두 가지 것 중 하나와 나머지 하나는 one, the other로 나타낸다. (2), (3) 'want'와 'ask'는 목적격보어 자리에 to부정사가 오는 동사이다. '주어+동사+목적어+to부정사'의 어순으로 문장을 완성한다. *stop 동명사: ~하는 것을 멈추다.

18 'had'는 목적격보어로 원형부정사를 취한다.

19 c. 복수형 others로 쓴다. d. 나머지를 알 수 있으므로 the others로 표현한다. e. 불특정한 다수 중 또 다른 하나는 another로 쓴다.

20 (B)의 he가 주어진 글의 the teacher를 가리키므로 제일 먼저 오고 (A)의 another way가 (B)에서 말한 방법이 아닌 다른 방법을 말하는 것이므로 (B) 다음에 (A)가 이어지고 (C)에서 가장 강력한 무기인 '말'을 통제하게 된 것은 (A)에서 Corky가 자신이 위험하거나 나쁘지 않고 좋은 사람이라고 계속해서 말한 결과 마침내 사람들이 그를 풀어 준 것을 보고 스승이 하는 말이므로 (A) 다음에 (C)가 와야 한다. 그러므로 (B)-(A)-(C)의 순서가 적절하다.

21 명령을 나타내는 동사 뒤에 '당위성을 나타내는 조동사 should+동사원형'으로 고치는 것이 적절하다. 이때 should는

22 to win a war: '전쟁에서 이기기 위해', 부사적 용법(목적)

23 이 글은 '훈련은 100일 후에 시작할 것이라는 말을 듣고 100일 동안 군사 학교 문 앞에서 기다린 후에, 마침내 Corky가 자신의 첫 번째 무기인 '인내'를 사용하는 법을 배우게 되는' 내용의 글이므로, 제목으로는 ③번 '마침내 Corky는 첫 번째 무기인 '인내'를 얻다!'가 적절하다.

24 주어진 문장의 them에 주목한다. ④번 앞 문장의 more warriors를 받고 있으므로 ④번이 적절하다.

25 ⓐ와 ②: (비교급을 강조하여) 훨씬(부사), ① 짝수의(형용사), ③ 평평한, 반반한(형용사), ④ (예상 밖이나 놀라운 일을 나타내어) ~도[조차](부사), ⑤ (무엇의 양, 득점 등이) 균등한, 동일한(형용사)

26 ⓐ tie A to B: A를 B에 묶다, ⓑ be in trouble: 어려움에 처하다

27 '자신이 위험하거나 나쁘지 않고 좋은 사람이라는 것'을 가리킨다.

28 가장 '강력한(powerful)' 무기는 '말'이다.

29 두 사람 중에 나머지 한 명을 가리키므로 'the other'가 적절하다.

30 ⓑ와 ①, ③: 현재분사, ②, ④, ⑤: 동명사

01 untie   02 ⑤   03 ③
04 This is the third time he did that today.
05 ③   06 ③   07 ④
08 You always forget what you have to do.
09 ④   10 ⑤
11 told her students to listen to the dialog
12 (1) She told him to lock the door.
   (2) She wouldn't allow him to use her phone.
   (3) The grapes on the dish look very delicious.
      Some are green, and the others are purple.
   (4) Many children are big fans of animals. Some
      like monkeys, and others like lions.
   (5) I bought two pens. One is for me, and the
      other is for you.
13 He asked his people to fight peacefully against
England.
14 On the hundred and first day, the gate opened.
15 ②
16 Patience is the most important thing to win a war.
17 ⑤   18 ③   19 (A) control (B) words
20 ①, ②, ⑤
21 Corky가 더 이상 싸움을 하지 않고 대신 부상당한
   사람들을 돌볼 것이라고 말한 것

01 반의어 관계다. 밀다 - 당기다 : 묶다 - 풀다

02 '어떤 일이 왜 일어나는지 설명하는 사실이나 상황'이라는 의미로 'reason(이유)'이 적절하다.

03 빈칸 다음의 G의 말이 (A)의 물음에 대한 답이므로 안경이 어떻게 되었는지 묻는 말이 적절하다.

04 주어는 'This(이번)'가 되고 'he did that today'가 'time'을 수식하는 구조다.

05 필통이 사라졌다는 말로 보아 빈칸에는 화내는 표현이 적절하다. ③번은 '상쾌하다'라는 의미로 적절하지 않다.

06 '저 사람은 여기서 일하는 사람이야.'라는 B의 답으로 보아 불만을 표시하는 내용 중 ③번이 가장 적절하다.

07 그의 머리가 계속 내 어깨에 부딪힌다는 A의 말에 '진정해. 그는 나이가 들어서 잘 들을 수 없어.'라고 말하는 것은 자연스럽지 못하다.

08 빈도부사 'always'는 일반동사 앞에 위치하고 동사 'forget'의 목적어 자리에 'what+주어+동사' 어순을 사용한다.

09 Minsu는 과학 숙제가 그에게 어렵다고 생각한다.

10 불특정한 다수의 사람 중 하나와 그 나머지 모두를 알 수 있을 때 one, the others를 쓴다.

11 'tell'은 목적격보어 자리에 to부정사가 오는 동사이다. '주어+동사+목적어+to부정사'의 어순으로 과거시제로 문장을 완성한다. 동사 listen은 전치사 to와 함께 쓴다.

12 (1), (2) 'tell'과 'allow'는 목적격보어 자리에 to부정사가 오는 동사이다. (3) 불특정한 다수의 사물 중 일부와 그 나머지를 알 수 있을 때 some, the others를 쓴다. (4) 불특정한 다수의 일정하지 않은 수량을 나타내고 나머지가 불확실 할 때는 some, others를 쓴다. (5) 불특정한 두 사물 중 처음 하나와 나머지 하나는 one, the other로 나타낸다.

13 'ask'는 목적격보어 자리에 to부정사가 오는 동사이다. '주어+동사+목적어+to부정사'의 어순으로 배열한다.

14 on: (요일, 날짜, 때를 나타내어) ~에, on the hundred and first day: 101일째 되던 날

15 위 글은 '단편 소설'이라고 하는 것이 적절하다. ① 수필, ③ (신문, 잡지의) 글, 기사, ④ (책, 연극, 영화 등에 대한) 논평[비평], 감상문, ⑤ 독후감

16 '인내'가 전쟁에서 이기기 위해 가장 중요한 것이다.

17 주어진 문장의 That에 주목한다. ⑤번 앞 문장의 내용을 받고 있으므로 ⑤번이 적절하다.

18 이 글은 'Corky가 갑자기 기둥에 묶이고 그의 머리 위에 '위험하고 나쁨'이라는 푯말이 붙여진 상황에 대처하는 과정을 통해 가장 강력한 무기인 '말'을 통제하게 되는' 내용이다. 따라서, 주제로는 ③번 'Corky는 가장 강력한 무기인 '말'을 통제하게 되었다.'가 적절하다.

19 스승은 Corky에게 가장 강력한 무기인 '말'을 '통제하는 법'을 가르치기 위하여 Corky를 기둥에 묶고 그의 머리 위에는 '위험하고 나쁨'이라는 푯말을 붙였다.

20 ⓐ와 ③, ④: 형용사적 용법, ①, ⑤: 부사적 용법, ②: 명사적 용법

21 Corky가 "I will not fight anymore. Instead, I will take care of the injured."라고 말한 것을 가리킨다.

서술형 실전문제
p.218~219

01 (A) I can't stand it.   (B) Take it easy.

02 he should have been more careful

03 he was busy doing his homework

04 (1) Three of six people came to the party. The others didn't.
   (2) Amy wants Brian to tell her about his problem.

05 (1) Some of them are red
   (2) If you want me to stay

06 (1) He ordered his dog to get down on the ground.
   (2) She told him not to close the door.
   (3) My mom won't allow me to go there.

07 (A) Some   (B) others   (C) another

08 He yelled, "Set me free, or you all will be in big trouble!"

09 (A) worse   (B) told them   (C) free   (D) weapon

01 (A) 늦었다는 말 다음에 화냄을 표현하는 말이 자연스럽다. (B)는 화내는 상대방에게 진정하라고 말하는 표현이 적절하다.

02 '과거의 유감이나 후회'를 나타내는 표현으로 '~했어야 했는데'의 의미를 가지는 'should have p.p.'가 적절하다.

03 설거지 할 것을 잊어버린 것에 대한 민수의 변명은 무엇인가?

04 (1) 나머지가 모두 3명이므로, 'The others'로 쓴다. (2) 'want'는 목적격보어 자리에 to부정사가 오는 동사이다.

05 (1) 불특정한 다수의 일정하지 않은 몇몇과 다른 몇몇을 나타낼 때 some, others를 쓴다. (2) 'want'는 목적격보어 자리에 to부정사가 오는 동사이다. '주어+동사+목적어+to부정사'의 어순으로 문장을 완성한다.

06 (1), (3) 'order'와 'tell'은 목적격보어 자리에 to부정사가 오는 동사이다. '주어+동사+목적어+to부정사'의 어순으로 문장을 완성한다. (2) to부정사의 부정은 'not to 동사원형'으로 쓴다.

07 (A) 지나가는 많은 사람들 중 '몇몇은'이라고 해야 하므로 Some이 적절하다. 'Some'은 불특정 다수의 여러 사람 중 '몇몇 사람들'이라는 뜻, (B) 지나가는 많은 사람들 중 '다른 몇몇은'이라고 해야 하므로 others가 적절하다. 'others'는 '(그 밖의) 다른 사람들', the other: 둘 중 나머지 하나, (C) 여러 방법들 중 '또 다른' 방법이라고 해야 하므로 another가 적절하다. the other: 둘 중 나머지 하나

08 앞 문장 전체를 가리킨다.

09 (A) 그는 "나를 풀어 줘. 그렇지 않으면 모두 혼쭐날 줄 알아!"

41

라고 외침으로써 상황을 더 '악화'시켰다. (B) Corky가 자신이 위험하거나 나쁘지 않고 좋은 사람이라고 '말했을 때' 그는 풀려났다.

창의사고력 서술형 문제
p.220

|모범답안|

01 (1) A: She is talking too loudly on the phone. I can't stand it.
　　 B: Calm down! She is talking to her baby.
　 (2) A: His head keeps hitting me on my shoulder. I can't stand it.
　　 B: Calm down! He must be very tired.
　 (3) A: She is eating something. I can't stand it.
　　 B: Calm down! She looks so hungry.
　 (4) A: Children are running around. I can't stand it.
　　 B: Calm down! They are just kids.

02 (A) warriors　(B) the teacher　(C) standing
　 (D) to sit in the chair

단원별 모의고사
p.221~224

01 ③　　　　02 powerful　　03 ①　　　04 ⑤
05 (n)oise / (f)ixing / (f)ocus on / (s)tand it / (C)alm down
06 ④　　　　07 ⑤
08 I hate standing in line in cold weather.
09 (A) to do　(B) doing
10 (that) Minsu always forgets what he has to do
11 ②　　　12 ②　　　13 ②　　　14 ①
15 (1) Mina to use his pen
　 (2) the man not to say anything to the police
16 (1) Some (friends) are kind
　 (2) the other is brown
17 유명한 군사 학교 문 앞에서　18 ③
19 Set me free, or you all will be in big trouble
20 not as[so] strong as
21 had passed　　　　　22 ④

01 ③번은 '화내지 않고 침착하게 있을 수 있는 것'의 의미로 'patience(인내심)'에 관한 설명이다. 'impatience'는 '성급함'이란 뜻이다.
02 유의어 관계이다. 지나가다 : 강력한
03 '울타리나 벽 밖에 있는 문'의 의미로 'gate(정문, 대문)'가 적절하다.
04 ⑤번은 상대방이 화를 내는 말에 대해 'That's great!'라고 답하는 것은 어색하다.
06 '~ 동안'의 의미로 전치사 'for'는 뒤에 숫자가 있는 기간이 나올

때 사용 가능하다.
07 100일 뒤에 문이 열리기 때문에 기다리는 것이 이 학교에 들어가는 중요한 규칙이라는 내용의 대화. ⑤의 '하지만, 어떻게 풀려날 수 있겠느냐? 생각해 보아라.'는 글의 흐름에 어울리지 않는 문장이다.
08 동사 'hate'의 목적어 자리에 동명사 standing을 사용하고, '줄을 서다'는 'stand in line'을 사용한다.
09 (A): '~할 것을 잊다'라는 의미로 'forget to+동사원형'을 사용한다. (B): '~하느라 바쁘다'라는 의미로 'be busy+-ing'를 사용한다.
10 질문: 민수의 누나는 민수에게 왜 화가 났는가?
11 (C)와 ②는 '나머지'라는 뜻이고 ①, ④, ⑤는 '휴식', ③은 '휴식하다'라는 뜻이다.
12 (A) 불특정한 여럿 중 처음 하나는 one으로 나타내고, (B) 또다른 하나는 another로 나타낸다. (C) 나머지가 무엇인지 알 수 있고 복수일 때 the others를 쓴다.
13 'ask'는 목적격보어 자리에 to부정사가 오는 동사이다.
14 'tell'은 목적격보어 자리에 to부정사가 오는 동사이고, 'make'는 목적격보어 자리에 원형부정사가 오는 동사이다.
15 (1) 'allow'는 목적격보어 자리에 to부정사가 오는 동사이다.
　 (2) to부정사의 부정은 'not to 동사원형'으로 쓴다.
16 (1) 불특정한 다수의 일정하지 않은 몇몇과 다른 몇몇을 나타낼 때 some, others를 쓴다. (2) 불특정한 두 사물 중 처음 하나와 나머지 하나는 one, the other로 나타낸다.
17 'in front of a famous military school'을 가리킨다.
18 ⓑ와 ①, ④: 명사적 용법, ②, ⑤: 부사적 용법, ③: 형용사적 용법
19 or를 보충하면 된다. 명령문+접속사 'or': …해라, 그렇지 않으면 ~할 것이다.
20 A 비교급 than B를 'B not as[so] 원급 as A'를 사용하여 바꿔 쓰는 것이 적절하다.
21 '시험에 통과한' 것이 먼저 일어난 일이므로, 과거완료 시제인 'had passed'로 쓰는 것이 적절하다.
22 ⓐ와 ④: ~함에 따라(접속사), ① (자격·기능 등이) ~로(서)(전치사), ② ~한 대로(접속사), ③ ~이기 때문에(접속사), ⑤ ~하다시피[~이듯이](접속사)

Teen's Magazine

교과서 확인학습 A
p.232~234

01 Teens'	02 Make, Better
03 something nice	04 Say hello to
05 to say	06 on a rainy day
07 Laugh out loud	08 for
09 behind you	10 Invite, to
11 make, better	12 Peace
13 put, on	14 having friends
15 I'd rather	16 fighting, shouting
17 smile	18 inside
19 LAUGH	20 a day
21 keeps, away	22 what they say
23 just broke	24 Be Kind
25 what books hate, Why	26 bookmark
27 folding	28 It is, that
29 The more, the happier, How about	
30 Facts, Fake	31 have ever lived
32 have ever been born	33 more, than
34 largest	35 bigger than
36 covers, the size of, covering	
37 were invented	38 are cut into, pieces
39 Jobs	40 the greatest movie
41 what he does	42 with, Helping Judy
43 solves many cases	44 Everyone
45 anyone	
46 named, Controlling, ends up becoming	
47 with	
48 what these emojis mean	
49 Once in a, A piece of	
51 The louder, the happier	52 Secret
53 no one else can read	54 Backward
55 easy to solve, backward	56 Every
57 starting with	59 easier than it looks
60 to send to, Make sure, send along	

교과서 확인학습 B
p.235~237

1 Teens' Magazine

2 Ways to Make Your Town Better

3 Doing something nice for your neighbors can change your town. Start small. Here are some tips.

4 1. Say hello to your neighbors and smile.

5 2. Don't forget to say, "Thank you."

6 3. Share your umbrella on a rainy day.

7 4. Laugh out loud when your neighbor tells a joke.

8 5. Make something for your neighbors.

9 6. Hold the door for the person behind you.

10 7. Invite your neighbors to your party.

11 If you just do one thing each day, you can make your town better.

12 Messages for Peace

13 On World Peace Day, we put our peace messages on the board.

14 Peace means having friends around the world. - Kim Jimin

15 I'd rather have peace on Earth than pieces of Earth. - Seo Eunji

16 I want peace every place I go because there is always someone fighting or shouting. - Park Hansol

17 Peace makes everyone smile.- Yang Miran

18 Peace is inside all of us. We just need to share it. - Jang Jaehee

19 LET'S LAUGH

20 An apple a day

21 Jake came in to see his dad. "Dad!" he said, "Is it true that an apple a day keeps the doctor away?"

22 "That's what they say," said his dad.

23 "Well, give me an apple quickly! I just broke the doctor's window!"

24 Be Kind to Books!

25 Do you know what books hate? They hate water, the sun, and dog ears. Why dog ears?

26 Water is bad for WITCHES and BOOKS! / The SUN also TURNs Books YELLOW / Don't DOG-EAR! Use a bookmark! / Be Kind to Books!

27 Stop folding dog ears in books. Use a bookmark instead.

28 It is a bookmark that can save your books. Be kind to your books.

29 The more you love your books, the happier your books will be. How about making your own?

30 Facts That Sound Fake

31 1. About 7% of all people who have ever lived are living on the Earth today.

32 About 108,200 million people have ever been born in the history of the world. And about 7,442 million are living on the Earth today.

33 2. Bangladesh has more people than Russia.

34 Russia is the world's largest country, but tiny Bangladesh has 166.3 million people in 2018. Russia has 143.9 million people.

35 3. A banyan tree near Kolkata, India, is bigger than the average Walmart.

36 The average Walmart store covers about 104,000 square feet. The Great Banyan Tree in Kolkata, India, is about the size of a forest, covering 155,000 square feet.

37 4. Baby carrots were invented in 1986.

38 Baby carrots are not actually baby carrots. Big ugly carrots are cut into small pieces that have the shape of a baby carrot. Farmer Mike Yurosek invented them in 1986 as a way to use ugly carrots that weren't sold.

39 Jobs in the Movies

40 Zootopia (2016) It's the greatest movie ever!

41 Flash is a public officer. He is very slow but works hard. You will be surprised to see what he does in his free time. It's driving a race car!

42 Nick is a fox with a big mouth. Helping Judy, he gets closer to her. He later becomes a police officer like Judy.

43 Judy is a small rabbit, but she's smart and strong. After a lot of effort, she becomes a police officer and solves many cases.

44 Ratatouille (2007) Everyone will love this movie.

45 Anton Ego is a food critic. After he eats the food Remy cooked, he realizes that anyone can cook.

46 Remy, a little mouse, dreams of becoming a cook. He goes into a restaurant and meets a boy named Linguini. Controlling Linguini, he makes delicious food and ends up becoming a great cook.

47 Say It with Emojis

48 Do you know what these emojis mean?

49 Killing two birds with one stone. / The apple of your eyes. / Don't play games with fire. / Once in a blue moon. / Let's call it a day. / Money does not grow on trees. / It's raining cats and dogs. / A piece of cake.

50 Emoji Song

51 Now, let's sing a Christmas song together! The louder, the happier!

52 Secret Messages

53 Imagine you can send messages to your friend that no one else can read! It's not so difficult for you to learn how to read and write your own secret messages.

54 1. Read Backward

55 This is easy to solve. Just read the words backward! It seems simple once you know the secret, but it can be a hard one when you don't.

56 2. Read Every Second Letter

57 Read every second letter starting with the first letter, and when you finish, start again on the letters you missed.

58 3. Pig-pen

59 The Pig-pen is easier than it looks. The lines around each letter mean the letter inside the lines.

60 Now create your own set of secret letters and write secret messages to send to your friends. Make sure you send along a key so your friends can understand your messages!

서술형 실전문제   p.238~239

01 (1) case   (2) case

02 (1) had better   (2) keeps, away   (3) making sure

03 (1) end up arguing   (2) stop hiccupping
   (3) rained cats and dogs

04 (1) said (that) he had just broken the doctor's window
   (2) told his dad to give him an apple quickly

05 You will be surprised to see what he does in his free time.

06 (1) cut → are cut / Big ugly carrots가 작은 조각으로 잘리는 것이므로 수동태로 쓰는 것이 적절하다.
   (2) has → have / 주격 관계대명사 다음의 동사는 선행사에 수를 맞춘다. 선행사가 small pieces 이므로 동사는 have로 쓰는 것이 적절하다.

07 Why do books hate dog ears?

08 to fold → folding

09 more, happier

10 YOU LOOK GREAT TODAY.

11 every second letter

12 WHEN SHALL WE MEET? – LET'S MEET AT FIVE.

01 (1) 어떤 경우에는 사람들이 예약을 하기 위해 몇 주를 기다려야 했다. (2) 경찰이 그 사건 수사를 재개하기로 결정했다.

02 (1) 너는 외출하기 전에 설거지를 하는 것이 좋겠다. had better+동사원형: ~하는 게 낫다 (2) 하루에 사과 한 알이면 의사가 필요 없다. '~을 멀리하게 하다'라는 의미로 'keep+목적어+away'를 사용한다. 주어가 'an apple'로 3인칭 단수이므로 'keeps'를 사용한다. (3) 학교는 학생들이 배우고 있는 것을 확실히 하는 데에 집중해야 합니다. '~을 확실히 하다'라는 의미로 'make sure'를 사용하고, 전치사 on 뒤에는 '동명사'가 적절하므로 'make'를 'making'으로 바꾸어 준다.

03 (1) '결국 ~가 되다'라는 의미로 'end up –ing'를 사용한다. (2) '~을 멈추다'는 'stop+V-ing'를 사용한다. (3) '비가 억수같이 내리다'는 'It rains cats and dogs.'를 사용하고 시제가 과거이므로 'rained'를 쓴다. 여기서 'it'은 날씨를 나타내는 비인칭 주어이다.

04 (1) 전달동사가 과거이므로, 시제의 일치 법칙에 맞게 따옴표(" ") 안의 과거동사를 과거완료로 바꾼다. (just broke → had just broken), 또한 따옴표 속 'I'는 문장의 주어로 바꾼다. (I → he) (2) 전달동사 'said to'는 'told'로 바꿔야 하고 명령문의 간접화법이므로 명령문의 동사원형을 to부정사로 쓴다. 또한 따옴표 속 'me'는 문장의 주어인 'him'으로 바꾼다.

05 'What does he do in his free time?'이 간접의문문으로 이어지면서 '의문사+주어+동사'의 순으로 쓴다.

06 (1) Big ugly carrots가 작은 조각으로 잘리는 것이므로 수동태를 쓰는 것이 적절하다. (2) 주격 관계대명사 다음의 동사는 선행사에 수를 맞춘다. 선행사가 small pieces이므로 동사는 그에 맞게 have로 쓰는 것이 적절하다.

07 '왜 책들이 강아지 귀를 싫어할까요?'라고 해야 하므로 Why 다음에 'do books hate'가 생략되어 있다.

08 '강아지 귀 모양으로 책을 접는 것을 멈춰 주세요.'라고 해야 하므로 동명사로 고치는 것이 적절하다, stop+~ing: ~을 그만 두다, stop+to부정사: ~을 하기 위해 멈추다

09 'the+비교급 …, the+비교급 ~' 구문을 접속사 As를 사용하여 고칠 때는, 비교급 앞의 the를 생략한 다음에 비교급을 As 뒤의 적절한 자리를 찾아 옮겨 쓰는 것이 적절하다. the+비교급 …, the+비교급 ~: …하면 할수록, 더 ~하다

10 첫 번째 글자에서 시작해서 매 두 번째 글자를 읽고, 끝나면 여러분이 빠뜨린 글자로 다시 시작하라고 했으므로, 비밀 메시지의 내용은 'YOU LOOK GREAT TODAY.(너는 오늘 멋져 보인다.)'이다.

11 every second letter: 매 두 번째 글자

12 각 글자 주변의 선들은 그 선들 안에 있는 글자를 의미한다고 했으므로, 비밀 메시지의 내용은 'WHEN SHALL WE MEET? -

LET'S MEET AT FIVE.(우리 언제 만날까? – 5시에 만나자.)' 이다.

단원별 예상문제　　　　　　p.240~244

01 ③　　02 shout　　03 ①　　04 realize

05 I would rather stay home than go there.

06 ④　　07 ⑤

08 (1) instead, 대신에 (2) share, 공유하다
(3) fold, 접다 (4) realize, 깨닫다

09 ⑤

10 (1) The more you love your books, the happier your books will be.
(2) The more you work out, the harder you can study.
(3) The hotter it gets, the shorter our pants get.

11 ②　　12 ④　　13 ③, ⑤　　14 ③

15 ⑤　　16 becoming　17 critic　　18 Remy

19 ④　　20 saying → to say　　21 ①

22 It is a bookmark that can save your books.

23 ①, ③, ⑤　　24 ②

25 Imagine you can send messages to your friend that no one else can read! 또는 Imagine you can send messages that no one else can read to your friend!

26 COME TO MY HOUSE AT TEN.　　27 ②

28 What he does in his free time

29 ①, ②, ④　　30 ②, ⑤

01 ③번은 '책, 연극, 영화 등에 대한 의견을 말하는 것이 직업인 사람'의 뜻을 가지고 있는 'critic(비평가)'에 대한 설명이다. 'playwriter'는 '극작가'로 영어 풀이는 'a person who writes plays'가 적절하다.

02 유의어 관계이다. 구하다 : 외치다, 소리치다

03 '누군가에게 당신의 집이나 파티에 오라고 부탁하다'라는 의미로 '초대하다'가 적절하다.

04 • 나는 오늘 처음으로 에너지의 소중함을 깨달았어. • 그는 최근에 그의 꿈을 실현했습니다.

05 would rather A(동사원형) than B(동사원형) = prefer A(동명사/명사) to B(동명사/명사) = prefer A(to V) rather than B(to V): B보다 A하는 게 낫다

06 • 많은 배우들이 뉴욕의 브로드웨이 무대에서 공연하기를 꿈꿉니다. '~에 관해 꿈꾸다'는 'dream of'를 사용한다. • 저는 친구들과 더욱 많은 대화를 할 수 있고 그들에게 더욱 가까이 다가갈 수 있습니다. '~에 다가가다'는 'get closer to'를 사용한다.

• 그러니, 누가 알겠어? 너는 놀랄만한 요리사가 될 수도 있어! '결국 ~가 되다'는 'end up -ing'를 사용한다.

07 모두 반의어 관계이고, ⑤번은 '상상하다'는 유의어 관계다.

08 (1) 다른 사람 또는 다른 어떤 것을 대신하여 (2) 다른 사람과 동시에 무언가를 가지거나 사용하는 것 (3) 어떤 것의 일부분이 다른 부분 위에 평평하게 놓이도록 어떤 것을 구부리다 (4) 이전에는 알아차리지 못하거나 이해하지 못했던 것을 알아차리거나 이해하다

09 ①~④는 'It ~ that ...' 강조구문이다. ⑤는 원인과 결과를 나타내는 'so ~ that' 구문이다.

10 '…하면 할수록 더 ~하다'라는 의미로 'The+비교급+주어+동사, the+비교급+주어+동사' 구문으로 문장을 쓴다.

11 'Do you know' 뒤에 목적어로 의문문 'what do books hate?'를 간접의문문으로 바꾸어 '의문사+주어+동사'의 순으로 나옴에 유의한다. 동사 'know'는 의문사를 문장 맨 앞에 쓰지 않는다.

12 ④ '의문사+to부정사'를 써야 하므로 'to read'로 쓰는 것이 적절하다. ① be동사의 보어가 필요하므로 형용사를 쓴다. ② 부정사의 의미상 주어에 of를 쓸 때는 술부에 사람의 성격을 나타내는 단어가 쓰일 때이다. ③ 가주어, 진주어 구문이므로 'to동사원형'을 쓴다. ⑤ 뒤에 명사가 이어지므로 소유대명사가 아닌 소유격을 쓴다.

13 '…하면 할수록 더 ~하다'라는 의미로 'The+비교급+주어+동사, the+비교급+주어+동사' 구문으로 문장을 쓰고, 이 문장을 'As 주어+동사+비교급, 주어+동사+비교급'으로도 쓸 수 있다. 이때 비교급은 동사에 맞게 형용사와 부사를 골라서 쓴다.

14 ①. ②. ④. ⑤는 가주어이고, ③은 비인칭 주어이다.

15 ①~④는 '열쇠도 함께 보낼 것을 명심하라.'는 뜻으로 앞으로 할 일을 나타낸다. ⑤ remember의 동명사 목적어는 이미 한 일을 나타내므로 '열쇠도 함께 보낸 것을 기억하라.'는 뜻이 되므로 나머지 문장과 다른 뜻이 된다.

16 end up ~ing: 결국 ~하게 되다

17 critic: 비평가, 책, 영화, 음악, 또는 예술과 같은 것들에 대해 글을 쓰거나 의견을 표현하는 사람

18 '작은 쥐 Remy'를 가리킨다.

19 ⓐ for: ~을 위해, ⓑ invite A to B: A를 B에 초대하다

20 '잊지 말고 말해라'라고 해야 하므로 to부정사로 고치는 것이 적절하다. forget+~ing: (과거에) ~한 것을 잊다, forget+to부정사: (미래에) ~해야 할 것을 잊다

21 '작은' 것부터 시작하라고 했다.

22 'A bookmark can save your books'에서 주어인 'A bookmark'를 강조하기 위해 'It is ... that ~' 강조 구문으로 영작하는 것이 적절하다.

23 ⓑ와 ①, ③, ⑤: ~하는 게 어때?, ② How do you like ~?: ~은 어떻습니까?, ~이 마음에 드십니까?, ④ Why don't we ~?: 우리 ~하는 게 어때?

24 '강아지 귀 모양으로 책을 접는 것' 대신에 '책갈피'를 이용해야 한다.

25 선행사 'messages'를 수식하는 관계대명사절은 'your friend' 다음에 써도 상관없다.

26 그냥 단어들을 거꾸로 읽으라고 했으므로, 비밀 메시지의 내용은 'COME TO MY HOUSE AT TEN.(10시에 우리 집에 오세요.)'이다.

27 ⓒ와 ②, ⑤: 부사적 용법, ①: 형용사적 용법, ③, ④: 명사적 용법

28 '그가 여가 시간에 하는 것'을 가리킨다.

29 ⓑ와 ①, ②, ④: 동명사, ③, ⑤ 현재분사

30 'Helping Judy'는 동시동작을 나타내는 분사구문으로 'Judy를 도우면서'의 뜻이다. 동시동작을 나타내는 분사구문은 접속사 As나 While을 사용하여 고치는 것이 적절하다. He helps Judy, and (he) gets closer to her.

교과서 파헤치기

Lesson 5

1 dead, 죽은   2 toward, ~을 향하여   3 reply, 답장
4 foreign, 외국의   5 ground, 땅, 지면   6 hire, 고용하다
7 husband, 남편   8 ill, 아픈, 병든   9 prepare, 준비하다
10 seat, 의석   11 vote, 투표하다, 선출하다   12 oil, 기름
13 ring, 반지   14 translate, 번역하다, 해석하다
15 discover, 발견하다   16 hug, 포옹

단어 TEST Step 1   p.02

01 근사한, 멋진, 엄청난, 어마어마한	02 전쟁, 전투
03 땅, 지면 04 ~을 향하여	05 교통
06 굴뚝 07 광고	08 강한, 강력한
09 가까이, 근접하여 10 번역하다, 해석하다	
11 준비하다 12 호기심이 많은, 궁금한	
13 다소, 약간 14 답장	15 남편
16 죽은, 쓸모없는 17 치다, 두드리다	18 발견하다
19 숨은, 숨겨진 20 포옹; 포옹하다	21 오해
22 진지하게, 심각하게	
23 큰 소리로, 시끄럽게	24 ~처럼 보이다
25 적군, 적대자 26 좌석, 의석	27 군인
28 정확하게 29 투표하다, 선출하다	
30 국경, 경계 31 점자	32 표현
33 고용하다 34 상품, 제품	
35 이겨내다, 극복하다	36 ~을 돌보다
37 ~로 덮이다 38 ~의 가격으로	39 ~을 제외하고
40 ~에 (찬성하는) 투표를 하다	41 ~에 조심하다
42 즉시, 당장 43 ~ 대신에	

단어 TEST Step 2   p.03

01 traffic	02 awesome	03 letter
04 battle	05 translate	06 dead
07 enemy	08 discover	09 light
10 loudly	11 exactly	12 curious
13 expression	14 husband	15 toward
16 chimney	17 seriously	18 rather
19 prepare	20 hidden	21 soldier
22 border	23 product	24 sign language
25 hire	26 misunderstanding	
27 hug	28 knock	29 seat
30 pond	31 foreign	32 gesture
33 pull	34 vote	35 instead of
36 except for	37 look after	38 be careful with
39 step back	40 right away	
41 be covered with		42 at a price of
43 get over		

대화문 TEST Step 1   p.05~06

Get Ready 2

(1) curious about, is it standing / a kind of, tells, batteries, powerful
(2) m curious about / traffic sign, means, enter
(3) dots for, m curious about / Braille, blind / guess what, mean
(4) curious, balloon, hanging / ad, product, powerful

Start Off – Listen & Talk A

1. soldiers, with, chimneys / messages, by using, chimneys / m curious about, system / smoking chimneys / What, mean / saw, enemy
2. enemy, smoke at all, do / Smoke, chimney, enemy / rising, What does, mean / It means, close, border

Start Off B

is crossing, border, dark, soldiers going to do, messages, curious about / light, chimneys / light, chimneys / It means, battle, started

Start Off – Speak Up

m curious about, language / Let, show, expression / What, mean / It means

Step Up – Real-life Scene

hidden secrets / curious about, secrets / Find, yourself / Let's see, letters / one, means, Latin / awesome, Any other secrets / tells, rich / understand / spend lots of, to buy, kind at that time / the rich, that kind, right / Exactly, speak a thousand

Express Yourself A

1. gesture, curious about / it means, into, pond / Why, think so / lots of bees, pointing, pond
2. So, gesture mean / It means, chicken / should bring, to get, right / I think so
3. What, gesture mean, curious about / Turn it off / What makes, so / The other hunter, close / see

Get Ready 2

(1) G: I'm curious about that robot. Why is it standing there?

B: It's a kind of ad. It tells people their batteries are very powerful.

(2) G: What's this? I'm curious about it.

B: It's a traffic sign. It means "Do not enter."

G: Oh, I see.

(3) G: What are these dots for? I'm curious about them.

B: Oh, they are Braille. They are for blind people.

G: I see. Now I can guess what they mean.

(4) G: I'm curious about that balloon. Why is it hanging there?

B: Oh, that. It's an ad. It says the product is very powerful.

Start Off – Listen & Talk A

1. B: What are the soldiers doing with the five chimneys on TV?

G: They are sending messages to the king by using the chimneys.

B: Really? I'm curious about the system. Can you tell me more?

G: Well, do you see the two smoking chimneys?

B: Yes. What do they mean?

G: They mean they just saw an enemy.

2. B: If there's no enemy, they don't smoke at all, do they?

G: Yes, they do. Smoke from one chimney means "No enemy."

B: Now smoke is rising from three chimneys. What does that mean?

G: It means an enemy is coming close to the border.

Start Off B

B: Now the enemy is crossing the border in the dark. What are the soldiers going to do to send messages? I'm curious about that.

G: They will light four chimneys.

B: When they light all five of the chimneys, what does that mean?

G: It means the battle has started.

Start Off – Speak Up

B: I'm curious about sign language.

G: Are you? Let me show you one expression. Look.

B: What does it mean?

G: It means "Hello."

Step Up – Real-life Scene

B: This painting has some hidden secrets in it.

G: Really? I'm curious about them. Where are the secrets?

B: Find one yourself.

G: Let's see. ... Oh, I see some letters here.

B: You found one! It means "Jan van Eyck was here. 1434." It's Latin.

G: That's awesome! Any other secrets?

B: Okay. This dog tells us the man here was very rich.

G: I don't understand.

B: They had to spend lots of money to buy a dog of that kind at that time.

G: I see. Only the rich could have that kind of dog, right?

B: Exactly. Pictures speak a thousand words, you know.

Express Yourself A

1. W: What does this woman's gesture mean? I'm curious about it.

M: I think it means "Jump into the pond."

W: Why do you think so?

M: The boy has lots of bees on his head. And the woman is pointing at the pond.

2. W: This woman doesn't want a dollar. So what does her gesture mean?

M: It means she wants a chicken.

W: Then the boy should bring a chicken to get the fruit, right?

M: I think so.

3. W: What does this man's gesture mean? I'm curious about it.

M: It means "Turn it off."

W: Really? What makes you think so?

M: The other hunter there is coming close to an animal.

W: Oh, I see.

01 Picture Letter from, of

02 Speaking, foreign, rather, simple

03 before, days, that easy

04 sent, waited for, reply

05 lot harder, couldn't, write

06 how, got over, difficulties

07 by, whose, far away

08 island, while, worked in

09 more than, one of

10 was discovered by, writer

11 how, translated, into words

12 miss, reach, out toward   13 in, expect for, little

14 little sick, not seriously   15 sent, there, reply so

16 got, from, would be   17 fell ill, going, with

18 with, while, looks, youngest

19 had, prepare, plant seeds

20 voted for   21 so, that, almost seems

22 whether, other wins, same

23 Nothing changes, poor

24 worked, will work again   25 picked lots, from, this

26 hired, whose, workers

27 knocked, down, picking, up

28 paid, for, work   29 spent, for, press

30 enough, to fill, pot   31 sell, at, price, lire

32 heart, of, as, coming   33 would be, if, were

34 all miss, so   35 sending, big hug, little

36 dear love   37 heart, yours, joined, as

---

28 paid, for   29 spent, for, press

30 enough, to fill, one   31 at a price of

32 as   33 would be, were with

34 miss   35 a big hug, little kids

36 dear love   37 joined, as

---

1 세 아이의 엄마가 보낸 그림 편지

2 오늘날 외국에 있는 가족이나 친구와 대화하는 것은 다소 쉽고 간단하다.

3 하지만 전화와 인터넷 시대 이전에는 그것이 그렇게 쉽지 않았다.

4 사람들은 단지 편지를 보내고 답장을 몇 주 동안 기다렸다.

5 그리고 그들이 읽거나 쓸 수 없었다면 그건 훨씬 더 힘들었다.

6 이 편지는 사람들이 이런 어려움을 어떻게 극복했는지 보여 준다.

7 그것은 남편이 멀리 떨어져 살았던 한 여자에 의해 1973년에 쓰여졌다.

8 그녀의 남편은 독일에서 일한 반면, 그녀는 이탈리아의 섬인 시실리에서 살았다.

9 그 당시에는 5% 이상의 이탈리아 사람들이 읽거나 쓸 수 없었고, 그녀도 그들 중 한 명이었다.

10 이 편지는 시실리의 작가 Gesualdo Bufalino가 발견하였다.

11 그가 그림들을 어떻게 글로 번역했는지는 다음과 같다.

12 사랑하는 여보, 난 당신이 정말 그립고, 우리 세 아이와 함께 당신을 향해 내 팔을 쭉 뻗고 있어요.

13 막내를 제외하고는 우리 모두 건강해요.

14 그 아이는 약간 아프지만 심각하진 않아요.

15 난 당신에게 이미 편지를 보냈지만, 답장이 없어서 그것 때문에 나는 슬퍼요.

16 당신에게서 편지를 받는다면, 나는 정말 행복할 거예요.

17 당신의 어머니께서는 병이 드셨고, 나는 약간의 돈과 음식을 가지고 병원에 있는 어머니를 방문할 예정이에요.

18 큰애가 막내를 돌보는 동안 둘째와 함께 그곳에 갈 거예요.

19 나는 150,000리라에 두 일꾼을 시켜 우리 밭을 준비하고 씨앗을 심게 했어요.

20 나는 DC에 투표했어요.

21 PCI는 매우 많은 의석을 잃어서 거의 죽은 것처럼 보여요.

22 하지만 이쪽이 이기건 저쪽이 이기건, 상황은 똑같아요.

23 우리 가난한 사람들에게는 아무 것도 바뀌지 않지요.

24 우리는 어제도 일했고, 내일도 다시 일할 거예요.

25 우리는 올해 올리브나무에서 올리브를 많이 땄어요.

26 나는 아들들이 훌륭한 일꾼인 한 남자를 고용했어요.

27 그가 올리브를 쳐서 떨어뜨리면 그의 두 아들이 땅에서 올리브를 주우면서 그를 도왔어요.

---

01 A Picture Letter

02 Speaking, foregin country is rather, simple

03 before, that easy

04 sent, waited for, for weeks

05 a lot harder, couldn't read or write

06 got over

07 was written in, whose, far away

08 while, worked in Germany

09 more than 5%, one of them

10 was discovered by, writer

11 how, translated, into

12 miss, reach, out toward

13 all in good health except for, one

14 a little, not seriously

15 already, there was no reply

16 got, would be   17 fell ill, with

18 while, looks after, youngest

19 had, prepare, plant seeds

20 voted for   21 so, that

22 whether one or the other, the same

23 Nothing changes   24 will work again

25 picked, from   26 hired, whose, workers

27 knocked, down, picking, up from

28 나는 그 일을 위해 그에게 27,000리라를 지급했어요.

29 올리브 압착을 위해 12,000리라를 더 썼어요.

30 나는 큰 항아리 하나와 작은 항아리 하나를 채울 만큼 충분한 기름을 얻었어요.

31 리터당 1,300리라의 가격으로 팔 수 있을 것 같아요.

32 여보, 크리스마스가 다가오면서 내 마음은 당신을 떠올려요.

33 당신이 나와 함께 있다면 난 정말 행복할 거예요.

34 우리는 모두 당신을 매우 많이 그리워해요.

35 나와 우리 세 아이의 큰 포옹을 보내요.

36 잘 있어요, 여보.

37 내 마음은 당신의 것이에요, 우리들의 두 반지처럼 당신과 연결된 채로요.

본문 TEST Step 4·Step 5　　p.15~18

1 A Picture Letter from a Mother of Three

2 Speaking to family members or friends in a foreign country is rather easy and simple today.

3 But before the days of phones and the Internet, it was not that easy.

4 People just sent a letter and waited for a reply for weeks.

5 And it was a lot harder if they couldn't read or write.

6 This letter shows how people got over these difficulties.

7 It was written in 1973 by a woman whose husband was far away.

8 She lived in Sicily, an Italian island, while her husband worked in Germany.

9 At the time, more than 5% of the people in Italy could not read or write, and she was one of them.

10 This letter was discovered by Sicilian writer Gesualdo Bufalino.

11 Here's how he translated the pictures into words.

12 My dear love, I miss you so much, and I reach my arms out toward you, together with our three kids.

13 We are all in good health except for the little one.

14 He's a little sick, but not seriously.

15 I already sent you a letter, but there was no reply, so I am sad about it.

16 If I got a letter from you, I would be very happy.

17 Your mother fell ill, and I'm going to visit her in the hospital with some money and food.

18 I'll go there with our middle son while the oldest looks after the youngest.

19 I had two workers prepare our field and plant seeds for 150,000 lire.

20 I voted for the DC.

21 The PCI lost so many seats that it almost seems dead.

22 But whether one or the other wins, it's the same.

23 Nothing changes for us poor people.

24 We worked yesterday, and we will work again tomorrow.

25 We picked lots of olives from our olive trees this year.

26 I hired a man whose sons are good workers.

27 He knocked the olives down, and his two sons helped him, picking them up from the ground.

28 I paid him 27,000 lire for the work.

29 I spent 12,000 more for the olive press.

30 I got enough oil to fill a large pot and a small one.

31 I can sell it at a price of 1,300 lire a liter.

32 My love, my heart thinks of you as Christmas is coming.

33 I would be so happy if you were with me.

34 We all miss you so much.

35 I'm sending you a big hug from me and our three little kids.

36 Goodbye, dear love.

37 My heart is yours, joined to you as our two rings are.

구석구석지문 TEST Step 1　　p.19

Express Yourself C1

1. whose, is covered with, doesn't understand

2. means, Jump into

3. were, would jump into, right away

Project Do It Yourself

1. Climb up

2. had, would so kites to send

3. would fly, whose, looks like, make the soldiers climb

Link to the World

1. was created by

2. At first, didn't want to use, writing system

3. However, tried hard to help, use

4. Thanks to, can express anything with

5. didn't know, could not express ourselves

Express Yourself C1

1. The boy whose head is covered with bees doesn't understand the woman's gesture.
2. I think it means "Jump into the pond."
3. If I were the boy, I would jump into the pond right away.

Project Do It Yourself

1. "Climb up the mountain."
2. If I had soldiers to lead, I would so kites to send my messages.
3. For example, I would fly a kite whose face looks like a mountain to make the soldiers climb up the mountain.

Link to the World

1. Hangeul was created by King Sejong.
2. At first, many people didn't want to use this new writing system.
3. However, King Sejong tried hard to help people use Hangeul.
4. Thanks to him, we can express anything with Hangeul now.
5. If we didn't know Hangeul, we could not express ourselves easily.

01 생산하다, 산출하다	02 이용할 수 있는
03 ~을 거르다, 여과하다; 여과 장치	04 질병, 질환
05 얼굴의 06 예술품, 공예품	07 공공의, 공중의
08 도공, 옹기장이, 도예가	09 연결하다
10 출판업자, 출판사 11 예술적인	12 등록하다
13 사실, 실제로 14 (마음의) 긴장을 풀다	
15 3차원 인쇄를 하다 16 모으다	17 전통적인
18 제공하다 19 무게, 중량	20 화려한
21 회사 22 씨앗	23 길이
24 ~을 찢다, 뜯어내다	25 아주 작은
26 유쾌한, 기분 좋은 27 전시, 진열; 전시하다, 진열하다	
28 마실 수 있는 29 자랑으로 여기는	30 물리치다
31 (사람, 동물의) 상, 모양, 숫자	32 불가능한
33 필요한 34 물체	35 손으로
36 찢다 37 집어들다	38 목욕하다
39 알아내다 40 A와 B 둘 다	
41 남에게 주다, 나누어 주다	42 더 이상 ~ 않다
43 …을 ~으로 생각하다	

01 traditional	02 available	03 produce
04 artistic	05 beat	06 collect
07 tear	08 relax	09 colorful
10 proud	11 connect	12 disease
13 company	14 weight	15 provide
16 actually	17 cheerful	18 display
19 public	20 drinkable	21 figure
22 filter	23 facial	24 artwork
25 possible	26 pour	27 publisher
28 register	29 necessary	30 object
31 length	32 seed	33 3D print
34 tiny	35 find out	36 pick up
37 tear out	38 by hand	39 take a bath
40 think of ... as ~		41 both A and B
42 give away	43 not ~ anymore	

1 tiny, 아주 작은   2 bookstore, 서점
3 drinkable, 마실 수 있는   4 public, 공공의, 공중의
5 length, 길이   6 pour, 붓다, 따르다

7 tear, ~을 찢다, 뜯어내다   8 filter, ~을 거르다, 여과하다
9 publisher, 출판업자, 출판사   10 potter, 옹기장이, 도공
11 register, 등록하다   12 weight, 무게, 중량
13 leave, 남겨 두다   14 display, 전시하다
15 seed, 씨앗   16 print, 인쇄하다, 출판하다

대화문 TEST Step 1 p.24~25

Get Ready 2

(1) Which, better, cloth, artwork / better, Actually

(2) Which do you prefer, drawings, wood, figures / prefer, figures / Let's, some of them

(3) Which, prefer, folding, clothes / prefer folding paper, way to realx

Start Off – Listen & Talk A

1. Why don't we, pockets / What shall we / Which, board, holder / prefer, holder, to make, hate spending, making / Let's, together

2. Why don't we, with / What kind, to make / Which, prefer / Actually, hate holding, in / Let's make, together

Start Off - Listen & Talk B

with jeans / pencil case for / going to draw / Which do you prefer / prefer, lovely / draw, lovely / I can't wait for

Start Off – Speak Up

join / Sure. Which, prefer, or / prefer, making / Let, introduce, to

Start Off - Your Turn

Which, taking, taking / prefer taking the subway, hate taking

Step Up – Real-life Scene

just, away / proud that, collected, interesting, to give away / let's prepare, any / making bookmarks / Let's / Which, prefer, writing / Actually, writing / No problem, cheerful messages / sure, bookmarks

Express Yourself A

1. flying, flying drones / prefer flying / working, machines

2. Which, making, making / both, it, making, that, prefer / something delicious

대화문 TEST Step 2 p.26~27

Get Ready 2

(1) G: Which do you like better, cloth dolls or digital artwork?

B: I like digital artwork better. Actually, I don't like dolls much.

(2) G: Which do you prefer, paper drawings or wood block figures?

B: I prefer wood block figures.

G: Me, too. Let's go to look at some of them.

(3) G: Which do you prefer, folding paper or making clothes?

B: I prefer folding paper. It's fun and a great way to relax.

Start Off – Listen & Talk A

1. G: Why don't we make something with jean pockets?

B: Great! What shall we make?

G: Which do you prefer, a pocket board or a cell phone holder?

B: I prefer a cell phone holder. It'll be easier to make. And I hate spending too much time making things.

G: Okay. Let's make a cute cell phone holder together.

2. B: Why don't we make a bag with old jeans?

G: Great! What kind of bag are we going to make?

B: Which do you prefer, a shoulder bag or a hand bag?

G: I prefer a shoulder bag. Actually, I hate holding things in my hands.

B: Okay. Let's make a shoulder bag together.

Start Off - Listen & Talk B

G: Junha, what are you doing with jeans?

B: I'm making a pencil case for you.

G: That's great! What are you going to draw on it?

B: Which do you prefer, pandas or cats?

G: I prefer cats. They're lovely.

B: Okay. Let me draw a lovely cat on this pencil case.

G: Thanks! I can't wait for it!

Start Off – Speak Up

A: Can I join your book-making project?

B: Sure. Which do you prefer, paper books or digital books?

A: I prefer digital books. Actually, I hate making paper books.

B: Okay. Let me introduce you to the digital book team.

Start Off - Your Turn

A: Which do you prefer, taking the bus or taking the

subway?

B: I prefer taking the subway. Actually, I hate taking the bus.

Step Up – Real-life Scene

Minji: Seho, the book club day is just one week away.

Seho: Right, Minji. I'm proud that we've collected so many interesting books to give away.

Minji: Now, let's prepare some gifts for visitors. Do you have any good ideas?

Seho: How about making bookmarks?

Minji: Great idea! Let's write cheerful messages on them, too.

Seho: Okay. Which do you prefer, making the bookmarks or writing the messages?

Minji: Actually, I hate writing. I'd like to make the bookmarks.

Seho: No problem. I'll write the cheerful messages.

Minji: I'm sure they will love our bookmarks.

Express Yourself A

1. G: Which do you prefer, flying kites or flying drones?

   B: I prefer flying kites.

   G: Why is that?

   B: I hate working with machines.

2. B: Which do you prefer, making masks or making food art?

   G: I like both, but it is making food art that I prefer.

   B: Why is that?

   G: I love making something delicious.

본문 TEST Step 1   p.28~30

01 This, Amazing
02 think, traditional, books, read
03 However, there, unique, around
04 Let's learn, a few   05 Books Travel
06 found, old, on   07 note, read, Free
08 Take me home
09 Actually, had, was registered
10 out, traveled, number, different
11 How, that possible
12 There, book-sharing project
13 register, online, get
14 leave, public place
15 reader, reports back, check
16 way, whole, become, library

17 more, share, the, learn   18 Drinkable Book
19 tiny, important, in, town
20 provides both, information, tools
21 is called, Drinkable   22 actually, use, as, filter
23 tear out, pour, on
24 As, through, changes into
25 It, filtered, that, drink
26 possible because, made, special
27 amazing, saves, from diseases
28 Tree-Book-Tree Project
29 most amazing, have, seen
30 finish reading, plant, water
31 see new leaves growing
32 some, copy, producing, leaves
33 secret, has seeds, each
34 tiny seeds, change, into
35 made by, children's, publisher
36 not, anymore, think, from
37 just a few, unique
38 What other unique books
39 would, like to do
40 bigger, imagination, more wonderful

본문 TEST Step 2   p.31~33

01 This, Amazing
02 think of, as traditional paper books
03 are, unique, around   04 Let's, a few
05 Travel   06 found, old book
07 note, read, Free   08 Take me home
09 Actually, ID number, was registered
10 found out, had traveled, had read
11 How, possible   12 book-sharing project
13 register, get   14 leave it, public place
15 reports back, where your book is
16 whole world, a big library
17 The more books, the more
18 Drinkable   19 This tiny book
20 both the information and the tools necessary to make
21 is called, Drinkable   22 as a filter
23 tear out, pour, on
24 As, goes through, changes into
25 It is, that
26 is made of special filter paper
27 amazing, saves, from diseases, come from
28 Tree-Book-Tree Project
29 the most amazing book, seen

53

30 reading, plant, water
31 see new leaves growing
32 a copy of, producing new leaves
33 has seeds
34 these tiny seeds, change, into
35 was made by, publisher
36 Though, not, anymore, makes, think
37 just a few, unique books
38 What other unique books
39 would, like to do with
40 The bigger, imagination, the more wonderful

28 나무-책-나무 프로젝트
29 이것은 제가 지금까지 본 것 중에서 가장 놀라운 책입니다.
30 여러분이 이 책을 다 읽은 후에, 그것을 심고 물을 주세요.
31 여러분은 책에서 새잎이 자라는 것을 보게 될 거예요.
32 우리 마을의 몇몇 서점에서, 여러분은 이 책 한 권이 새잎을 내는 것을 볼 수 있습니다.
33 비밀은 책이 각 페이지 안에 씨앗을 갖고 있다는 것입니다.
34 책을 나무로 변화시키는 것은 이 아주 작은 씨앗들이에요.
35 이 책은 아르헨티나에 있는 한 작은 아동 도서 출판사에 의해 만들어졌습니다.
36 그 회사가 더는 이 책을 발행하지는 않지만, 이 특별한 프로젝트는 우리에게 책이 어디에서 오는지에 대해 생각하게 해 줍니다.
37 이것들은 여러분이 찾을 수 있는 독특한 책 중의 단지 몇 가지입니다.
38 여러분은 어떤 다른 독특한 책을 만들기 원하나요?
39 여러분은 책으로 어떤 특별한 프로젝트를 하고 싶나요?
40 여러분의 상상이 크면 클수록, 여러분의 책은 더 훌륭해질 것입니다.

본문 TEST Step 3   p.34~36

1 이 책은 놀라워요!
2 대부분의 사람은 책을 읽기 위한 전통적인 종이책으로 생각합니다.
3 하지만, 여러분 주변에는 독특한 책이 많이 있습니다.
4 이러한 책 중 몇 가지에 대해 배워 봅시다.
5 책이 여행합니다!
6 저는 어제 공원 벤치에서 이 낡은 책을 발견했습니다.
7 표지 위의 쪽지에 "공짜 책이에요!
8 저를 집으로 데려가서 읽어 주세요!"라고 쓰여 있었습니다.
9 사실, 이 책은 ID 번호가 있고 웹사이트에 등록되어 있었어요.
10 제가 온라인으로 그 번호를 입력했을 때, 저는 그 책이 많은 나라를 여행하고 다른 나라의 많은 독자가 저보다 앞서 이 책을 읽었다는 것을 알아냈습니다.
11 그게 어떻게 가능했을까요?
12 책을 공유하는 프로젝트가 있습니다.
13 우선, 온라인에 여러분의 책을 등록하고 ID 번호를 얻으세요.
14 그다음, 그것을 공공장소에 놓아두세요.
15 다음 독자가 여러분의 책을 발견해서 그 웹사이트에 다시 알릴 때, 여러분은 책이 어디 있는지 확인할 수 있습니다.
16 이런 식으로, 전 세계가 하나의 큰 도서관이 될 수 있습니다.
17 우리가 더 많은 책을 공유할수록, 우리는 더 많이 배웁니다.
18 마실 수 있는 책
19 이 작은 책은 우리 마을 사람들에게는 정말로 중요합니다.
20 그것은 깨끗한 마실 물을 만드는 데 필요한 정보와 도구 둘 다를 제공합니다.
21 그것은 '마실 수 있는 책'이라고 불립니다.
22 여러분은 실제로 그 책을 마실 수는 없지만, 그것을 필터로 사용할 수 있습니다.
23 그냥 한 페이지를 떼어 내서 그 위에 더러운 물을 부으세요.
24 물이 그 페이지를 통과하면서, 깨끗한 마실 물로 바뀝니다.
25 여러분이 마실 수 있는 것은 이 여과된 물입니다.
26 책이 특별한 여과지로 만들어졌기 때문에 이것이 가능합니다.
27 이 놀라운 책은 더러운 물로 생기는 질병으로부터 많은 어린이의 생명을 구합니다.

본문 TEST Step 4- Step 5   p.37~42

1 This Book Is Amazing!
2 Most people think of books as traditional paper books to read.
3 However, there are many unique books around you.
4 Let's learn about a few of these books.
5 Books Travel!
6 I found this old book on a park bench yesterday.
7 A note on the cover read, "Free Book!
8 Take me home and read me!"
9 Actually, this book had an ID number and was registered on a website.
10 When I entered the number online, I found out that the book had traveled to many countries and that a number of readers in different countries had read it before me.
11 How was that possible?
12 There is a book-sharing project.
13 First, register your book online and get an ID number.
14 Next, leave it in a public place.
15 When the next reader finds your book and reports back to the website, you can check where your book is.
16 This way, the whole world can become a big

library.

17 The more books we share, the more we learn.

18 The Drinkable Book

19 This tiny book is really important to people in my town.

20 It provides both the information and the tools necessary to make clean drinking water.

21 It is called the Drinkable Book.

22 You cannot actually drink the book, but you can use it as a filter.

23 Simply tear out a page and pour dirty water on it.

24 As the water goes through the page, it changes into clean drinking water.

25 It is this filtered water that you can drink.

26 This is possible because the book is made of special filter paper.

27 This amazing book saves the lives of many children from diseases that come from dirty water.

28 The Tree-Book-Tree Project

29 This is the most amazing book that I have ever seen.

30 After you finish reading this book, plant it and water it.

31 You will see new leaves growing on the book.

32 In some bookstores in my town, you can see a copy of this book producing new leaves.

33 The secret is that the book has seeds in each page.

34 It is these tiny seeds that change the book into a tree.

35 This book was made by a small children's book publisher in Argentina.

36 Though the company does not print this book anymore, this special project makes us think about where books come from.

37 These are just a few of the unique books you can find.

38 What other unique books do you want to make?

39 What special project would you like to do with the books?

40 The bigger your imagination is, the more wonderful your books will become.

Express Yourself C

1. making, flying, its weight

2. light drone, long battery life

3. The lighter, the longer

Link to the World

1. is called, because, looks like a full moon

2. it, impossible to make, by hand

3. The larger, the more difficult

4. It, a potter that

5. put, to make this moon jar

Learning Diary – Listen & Speak 2

1. Which, prefer, or

2. prefer going camping, hate going swimming

3. prefer going swimming

Express Yourself C

1. In making and flying a drone, its weight is important.

2. It is a light drone that has a long battery life.

3. The lighter the drone is, the longer it flies.

Link to the World

1. This is called Dalhang-ari, a moon jar, because it looks like a full moon.

2. In the past, it was impossible to make this large round jar by hand.

3. The larger a jar was, the more difficult it was to make.

4. It was a potter that solved this problem.

5. A smart potter put two large bowls together to make this moon jar.

Learning Diary – Listen & Speak 2

1. A: Which do you prefer, going camping or going swimming?

2. B: I prefer going camping. Actually, I hate going swimming. How about you?

3. A: Well, I prefer going swimming.

13 spread, 퍼지다　14 attack, 공격하다
15 support, 지지하다　16 clown, 광대

단어 TEST Step 1　p.45

01 제공하다　02 최근에　03 건강한
04 찾다, 검색하다　05 증거　06 거짓의, 잘못된
07 근원, 출처　08 실제로, 사실　09 예술 작품
10 지지하다, 후원하다　11 ~인 것 같다
12 전적으로　13 가라앉다　14 비판적으로
15 우스운　16 가벼운　17 주요한, 주된
18 문어　19 감동적인　20 장소
21 공격하다　22 광대　23 제공하다
24 독특한　25 편안한　26 사실이 아닌
27 세제, 청소기　28 완벽한　29 공연, 수행
30 퍼진; 퍼지다　31 불확실한　32 완전한
33 뱀　34 선호하다　35 판명되다
36 포기하다　37 A와 B를 구별하다
38 의미가 통하다　39 ~에 바탕을 두다
40 돌아가시다　41 ~에 주의를 기울이다
42 꾸며낸, 지어낸　43 큰 소리로 웃다

단어 TEST Step 2　p.46

01 save　02 perfect　03 sink
04 prefer　05 cleaner　06 critically
07 attack　08 recently　09 false
10 performance　11 comfortable　12 actually
13 totally　14 source　15 evidence
16 support　17 complete　18 provide
19 scary　20 site　21 clown
22 spread　23 healthy　24 cheer
25 untrue　26 light　27 major
28 touching　29 octopus　30 artwork
31 unique　32 wear　33 boring
34 search　35 give up　36 pass away
37 be based on　38 make sense　39 laugh out loud
40 be made out of　41 turn out
42 pay attention to　43 tell A from B

단어 TEST Step 3　p.47

1 totally, 전적으로　2 lie, 거짓말　3 touching, 감동적인
4 major, 주된, 주요한　5 false, 거짓의, 잘못된
6 cheer, 환호하다　7 opinion, 의견　8 provide, 제공하다
9 critically, 비판적으로　10 sink, 가라앉다
11 octopus, 문어　12 evidence, 증거

대화문 TEST Step 1　p.48~49

Get Ready 2
(1) like, I think, fake / agree, kind, real
(2) sharp teeth. What do you think of, real / let's search, check
(3) What, think of / look like, strange / too
(4) This, real / Let's, fact sites, check, together

Start Off – Listen & Talk A
1. How do you feel about / light, comfortable / to buy, school field trip
2. is wearing, warm, light / agree with, Actually, much heavier / believe

Start Off - Listen & Talk B
How, feel / touching, gave up, to save, the best drama / don't agree / Why, think so / seem real, a little boring

Start Off – Speak Up
How, about, ad / shows / should not believe

Step Up – Real-life Scene
cool, How do you feel about / that / makes, laugh out loud / everything, says / octopus / make sense / when, climbing, lying / agree with, fake, out of

Express Yourself A
1. How, feel about / get along, with / these two, enjoying, together
2. How, feel / By the way / guess / prefer / with, better than, In fact / to help
3. feel about / anything special / were made out, uniform / passed away recently / touching

대화문 TEST Step 2　p.50~51

Get Ready 2
(1) G: There's no monkey like this in the world. Its nose is too big. I think it's fake.
B: I don't agree. I saw that kind of monkey on TV. It's real.
(2) G: This animal has a long nose and two long, sharp teeth. What do you think of it? Is it real?
B: Well, let's search the Internet and check it together.
G: That's a good idea.

(3) B: What do you think of this animal?

G: It doesn't have legs, but it doesn't look like a snake. It's very strange.

B: I think so, too.

(4) B: This monkey is very small. Is it real?

G: I don't know. Let's visit some animal fact sites and check it together.

B: That's a good idea.

Start Off – Listen & Talk A

1. G: Look at those shoes the girl is wearing. I think they're great. How do you feel about them?

B: I think they look light and comfortable.

G: Right. I want to buy them for the school field trip.

2. G: I like the coat the boy is wearing. I think it's warm and light.

B: Well, I don't agree with you. Actually, I bought one last week. It's not so warm, and it's much heavier than it looks.

G: Really? I don't believe it.

Start Off - Listen & Talk B

G: How do you feel about this drama?

B: I think it's very touching. The boy gave up his life to save his sister. It's the best drama of this year.

G: I don't agree. It's not a good drama.

B: Come on. Why do you think so?

G: It doesn't seem real. And it's a little boring.

Start Off – Speak Up

A: How do you feel about this ad?

B: I think it's great. It shows the phone is strong.

A: I don't agree. We should not believe every ad.

Step Up – Real-life Scene

Alex: Big Mouth's show is really cool. How do you feel about it?

Somi: Well, I don't think it's that great.

Alex: Come on. I love Mr. Big Mouth. He always makes me laugh out loud.

Somi: He's funny, but don't believe everything he says.

Alex: All right. Oh, look at his photo of an octopus. He said it lives in a tree.

Somi: It doesn't make sense.

Alex: He took the photo when it was climbing the tree. I don't think he's lying. It's a great photo.

Somi: I don't agree with you. It's a fake photo. An octopus can't live out of the sea.

Express Yourself A

1. G: How do you feel about these animals?

B: They are very cute, but I think cats don't get along well with dogs.

G: I don't agree. And these two are good friends. They are enjoying the trip together.

2. G: How do you feel about this kid here?

B: I think she is very pretty. By the way, why did she cut her hair?

G: Can you guess?

B: Well, girls these days prefer short hair.

G: I don't agree with that. Most girls like long hair better than short hair. And this kid here is not a girl. In fact, he is a boy.

B: Really?

G: Yes. He grew his hair to help sick children.

3. G: How do you feel about the teddy bears?

B: They are cute. Is there anything special about them?

G: They were made out of a police officer's uniform.

B: Oh, I see.

G: This police officer made them for the kids. Their dad was a police officer, and he passed away recently.

B: That's very touching.

본문 TEST Step 1   p.52~53

01 Smart News Reader

02 scary, shook, across, bit

03 getting scared, things, one

04 checked up on, saying

05 actually made by, stations

06 hard evidence, trying, attack

07 turned out, complete lie

08 lot, at, thing, true

09 right sources, real, fake

10 Like, teenagers, think critically

11 getting, spread, full, false

12 how to tell, from

13 One, steps, slow down   14 too, to, true, think

15 evidence, supports what, says

16 where, coming from

17 tell fact from opinion   18 check, based on facts

19 hard, smart news reader

20 appears, provide, called, octopus

21 site, full, along, unclear

22 scary clowns, made up

23 once, carefully, everything, even

---

01 How to, Smart News Reader
02 shook schools across, didn't believe, a bit
03 getting scared, one of
04 checked up on, was saying
05 were actually made by, major newspapers
06 no hard evidence, trying to attack
07 turned out to be, complete lie
08 just look at one thing
09 to look at the right sources, pay attention to what is real, what is fake
10 Like, to think critically, on the Internet
11 getting more important, spread, full of false information
12 how to tell, from real news
13 One of the first steps, slow down
14 too good to be true
15 evidence, what the writer says
16 coming from   17 how to tell, from
18 have to, if, are based on facts
19 a smart news reader   20 appears to provide
21 is full of, along with, unclear photos
22 like, scary clowns, made up
23 once more carefully, question everything

1 현명한 뉴스 독자가 되는 방법
2 2016년 10월, 무서운 광대들에 관한 이야기가 워싱턴 지역 전역의 학교에 충격을 안겼지만, Danina Garcia-Fuller의 학생들은 조금도 그 이야기들을 믿지 않았다.
3 "몇몇 사람들은 그들이 소셜 미디어에 올라온 것들을 봤기 때문에 무서워했어요."라고 Garcia-Fuller의 학생 중 한 명인 Patricia Visoso가 말했다.
4 "하지만 그들은 이것을 누가 말하고 있는지를 전혀 확인하지 않았어요."
5 그 이야기들은 실제로 주요 신문사나 TV 방송국이 아닌 10대들이 지어냈다.
6 그들은 광대들이 정말로 학생들을 공격하려고 한다는 명백한 증거를 하나도 제공하지 않았다.
7 그 이야기는 결국 완벽한 거짓말인 것으로 드러났다.
8 "많은 사람이 단지 한 가지만을 보고 그것이 사실이라고 믿는 것 같아요."라고 Patricia의 반 친구인 Ivy-Brooks가 말했다.
9 올바른 출처를 살펴보고, 무엇이 진짜이고 무엇이 가짜인지에 주의를 기울이는 것은 정말 중요해요."
10 Garcia-Fuller의 학생들처럼, 많은 미국의 10대들은 뉴스 속 그리고 인터넷상에서 보고 있는 정보에 관해 비판적으로

생각하는 것을 배워 나가고 있다.
11 이 기능은 최근 더 중요해지고 있는데, 이야기들은 아주 빠른 속도로 퍼져 나갈 수 있고 누구나 허위 정보로 가득 찬 웹사이트를 만들어 낼 수 있기 때문이다.
12 Garcia-Fuller는 그녀가 자신의 학생들에게 가짜 뉴스를 진짜 뉴스로부터 구분하는 방법을 가르치고 있다고 말했다.
13 "첫 단계 중 하나는 속도를 늦추는 것(천천히 생각하는 것)입니다.
14 만약 어떤 이야기나 어떤 사진이 진짜라고 하기엔 너무 좋아 보인다면, 멈춰서 생각해 보세요.
15 글쓴이가 말하고 있는 것을 뒷받침하는 어떠한 증거라도 있나요?
16 그리고 이 정보가 어디서 온 것인가요?"
17 Garcia-Fuller의 학생들은 또한 뉴스에서 사실을 의견과 구분하는 방법에 대해서도 배운다.
18 "의견들은 읽을 만한 가치가 있습니다."라고 15살인 McKenzie Campbell이 말했다. "하지만 여러분은 그것들이 사실에 기반을 둔 것인지를 확인해 보아야 합니다."
19 Garcia-Fuller는 또한 때때로 현명한 뉴스 독자가 되는 것이 아주 어려울 수도 있다고 말했다.
20 그녀는 자신의 학생들을 '나무 문어'라는 이름의 동물에 대한 정보를 제공하는 것처럼 보이는 웹사이트로 시험한다.
21 그 사이트는 나무 위에 있는 문어들의 몇몇 불확실한 사진과 함께, 이 동물에 대한 정보로 가득 차 있다.
22 하지만 무서운 광대들의 이야기와 마찬가지로, 그것은 완전히 꾸며진 것이다.
23 Garcia-Fuller가 그녀의 학생에게 말하는 교훈은 '당신이 보고 있는 정보를 한 번만 더 신중하게 확인해 보라'는 것과 '모든 것, 심지어 내가 말하는 것에도 의문을 가져 보라'는 것이다.

1 How to Be a Smart News Reader
2 In October 2016, stories about scary clowns shook schools across the Washington area, but Danina Garcia-Fuller's students didn't believe them a bit.
3 "Some people were getting scared because they saw things on social media," said Patricia Visoso, one of Garcia-Fuller's students.
4 "But they never checked up on who was saying this."
5 The stories were actually made by teenagers, not by major newspapers or TV stations.
6 They offered no hard evidence that clowns really were trying to attack students.
7 The story turned out to be a complete lie.
8 "I think a lot of people just look at one thing and

believe it's true," Patricia's classmate Ivy-Brooks said.

9 "It's really important to look at the right sources and to pay attention to what is real and what is fake."

10 Like Garcia-Fuller's students, many teenagers in America are learning to think critically about information they're seeing in the news and on the Internet.

11 This skill is getting more important these days as stories can spread very fast, and anyone can make a website full of false information.

12 Garcia-Fuller said she was teaching her students how to tell fake news from real news.

13 "One of the first steps is to slow down.

14 If a story or a photo seems too good to be true, stop and think.

15 Is there any evidence that supports what the writer says?

16 And where is this coming from?"

17 Garcia-Fuller's students also learn how to tell fact from opinion in the news.

18 "Opinions are good to read," said 15-year-old McKenzie Campbell, "but you also have to check if they are based on facts."

19 Garcia-Fuller also said sometimes it can be very hard to be a smart news reader.

20 She tests her students with a website that appears to provide information on an animal called a tree octopus.

21 The site is full of information on this animal, along with a few unclear photos of octopuses in trees.

22 But like the story of scary clowns, it's totally made up.

23 The lesson, Garcia-Fuller tells her students, is to "check the information you're seeing once more carefully" and to "question everything, even things that I say."

After You Read A

1. shook, across the Washington area
2. how to tell fact from opinion
3. is full of, along with, unclear photos of octopuses

Do It Yourself

1. danced on the stage during

2. wondered if, would like their dancing
3. much better than any other
4. stood up, cheered loudly
5. the performance of the year

Link to the World

1. one of Picasso's works
2. drew, with, against a white background
3. if, brave, looks very tired, hungry
4. needs some food, water
5. artwork shows the most interesting part

After You Read A

1. In October 2016, stories about scary clowns shook schools across the Washington area.
2. Garcia-Fuller's students also learn how to tell fact from opinion in the news.
3. The site is full of information on this animal, along with a few unclear photos of octopuses in trees.

Do It Yourself

1. Team NW danced on the stage during the school festival.
2. They wondered if the students and teachers would like their dancing.
3. But they performed much better than any other team.
4. A lot of students stood up and cheered loudly when the team danced.
5. Ms. Yu, the P.E. teacher, said it was the performance of the year.

Link to the World

1. This drawing, *Don Quixote*, is one of Picasso's works.
2. Picasso drew it in 1955 with black lines against a white background.
3. I don't know if the man on the horse is brave, but he looks very tired and hungry.
4. I think he needs some food and water.
5. I think this artwork shows the most interesting part of Cervantes' novel *Don Quixote*.

14 look, 표정   15 reason, 이유   16 warrior, 전사

단어 TEST Step 1 p.64

01 기둥, 막대, 장대   02 수리하다   03 무기
04 이유   05 상황   06 대신에
07 다 안다는 듯한   08 다가가다   09 군대; 군대의
10 전사   11 부상당한
12 (사람들이 조직적으로 벌이는) 운동   13 인내심, 참을성
14 따르다, 따라가다   15 참다, 견디다   16 갑자기
17 장군   18 ~보다 위에   19 더 이상
20 일어나다, 발생하다   21 소리 지르다
22 표정   23 난방기, 히터   24 명령하다
25 궁, 궁전   26 군대, 육군   27 (개가) 짖다
28 강력한   29 정문, 대문   30 밀다
31 검, 칼   32 묶다   33 마침내
34 소음   35 포기하다   36 ~에 기대다
37 ~을 풀어주다, 석방하다   38 ~에 집중하다
39 진정하다   40 조만간, 머지않아   41 줄을 서다
42 그 순간에   43 모든 가능한 방법으로

단어 TEST Step 2 p.65

01 gate   02 military   03 above
04 sword   05 patience   06 fix
07 situation   08 order   09 finally
10 anymore   11 injured   12 general
13 pole   14 happen   15 instead
16 approach   17 stand   18 fast
19 follow   20 warrior   21 army
22 palace   23 bark   24 knowing
25 look   26 winner   27 reason
28 movement   29 noise   30 weapon
31 yell   32 powerful   33 suddenly
34 tie   35 be in trouble   36 focus on
37 sooner or later   38 let ~ go   39 at that moment
40 calm down   41 give up   42 take care of
43 on the side of

단어 TEST Step 3 p.66

1 yell, 소리 지르다   2 fix, 수리하다   3 general, 장군
4 fast, 단식하다   5 military, 군대   6 finally, 결국, 마침내
7 order, 명령하다   8 realize, 깨닫다   9 injured, 부상당한
10 patience, 인내심   11 powerful, 강력한
12 winner, 승리자, 우승자   13 bark, (개가) 짖다

대화문 TEST Step 1 p.67~68

Get Ready 2

(1) ve waited for more than / Calm, almost
(2) What, hate, in line, cold weather / Calm down, hot milk
(3) wait in line / Calm down, works
(4) behind, keeps pushing, can't stand / Calm down, just

Start Off – Listen & Talk A

1. noise outside / fixing, heaters / focus on, at all, can't stand it / down
2. can't find, seen / haven't, put / gone, upset / Calm, find

Start Off - Listen & Talk B

stepped on, foot / okay / third, did that, can't stand / Calm down, wearing, glasses / happened to / broke, during / should have been

Start Off – Speak Up

can't stand, crowded / Calm down, festival, enjoy

Step Up – Real-life Scene

I can use. Why didn't you, dishes / forgot to do / what, have to do, I can't stand, cleaned / busy doing / Do, dishes / finish, too difficult / m good at, Let me help / right now, the rest, after finishing

Express Yourself A

1. sent / in, hundred / spend, doing nothing, can't stand it / Calm down, It, rule to get
2. tie me up, set me free / get free / can't stand, sign, dangerous / I'm sure, way

Check yourself

noise outside / barking / can't focus on, stand it / Calm down, quiet

대화문 TEST Step 2 p.69~70

Get Ready 2

(1) M: We've waited for more than one hour, and we're still waiting.
   W: Calm down! We're almost there.
(2) G: Brrr.... What a cold day! I hate standing in line in cold weather.
   B: Calm down! Drink this hot milk.
   G: Oh, thank you so much.

(3) G: Look! That man didn't wait in line! I'm very angry.

   B: Calm down! He works here.

(4) B: The boy behind me keeps pushing me. I can't stand it.

   G: Calm down. He's just a child.

Start Off – Listen & Talk A

1. B: What's that noise outside?

   G: They're fixing the heaters.

   B: I can't focus on my studies at all. I can't stand it.

   G: Calm down! They will finish it soon.

2. G: I can't find my pencil case. Have you seen it?

   B: No, I haven't. Where did you put it?

   G: I put it on my desk, but now it's gone. I'm really upset.

   B: Calm down! I'll help you find it.

Start Off - Listen & Talk B

B: Ouch! He stepped on my foot again.

G: Are you okay?

B: No. This is the third time he did that today. I can't stand it. I'll go and talk to him.

G: Calm down! He's not wearing his glasses today, so he can't see well.

B: What happened to his glasses?

G: He broke his glasses during a soccer game this morning.

B: I see, but he should have been more careful.

Start Off – Speak Up

A: I can't stand this place. It's too crowded.

B: Calm down! We're at the festival. Let's enjoy it.

Step Up – Real-life Scene

Minji: Minsu, there is no cup I can use. Why didn't you do the dishes?

Minho: Sorry, but I forgot to do them.

Minji: What? You always forget what you have to do. I can't stand it. I cleaned the living room all morning.

Minho: Calm down! I'm busy doing my homework.

Minji: Do the dishes first, and then do your homework.

Minho: I can't. I don't think I can finish my homework today. Science is too difficult for me.

Minji: Science? You know I'm goot at science. Let me help you.

Minho: Great. Thanks. I'll wash your cup right now and I'll do the rest of the dishes after finishing this.

Express Yourself A

1. M1: The king sent me here. Open the door.

   M2: Wait there. The door will open in a hundred days.

   M1: What? A hundred days? I can't spend a hundred days doing nothing. I can't stand it.

   M2: Calm down! It is an important rule to get in this school.

2. M1: Why did you tie me up here? Please set me free.

   M2: How can you get free? Think.

   M1: I can't stand this sign. I'm not dangerous or bad.

   M2: Calm down. I'm sure you'll find a way.

Check yourself

G: What's that noise outside?

B: A dog is barking.

G: I can't focus on my studies at all. I can't stand it.

B: Calm down! He will be quiet soon.

본문 TEST Step 1   p.71~73

01 the Best Warrior   02 brave young man

03 general, strongest, army, much

04 ordered, to, famous military

05 hundred, training, voice, gate

06 got angry

07 thought, might, reason, waited

08 hundred, first, gate opened

09 learned, use, weapon, patience

10 Patience, most, thing, win

11 Then, stand against, pole

12 Suddenly, tied, to, pole

13 Above, put, read, Dangerous

14 passed by

15 Some, looks, others shouted

16 shouted back

17 yelled, Set, free, trouble 18 made, situation worse

19 try another way, thought

20 Then, speak softly

21 not dangerous, bad but

22 kept saying, possible ways

23 let him go

24 the most powerful weapon

25 words, stronger than, swords

26 took, to, with, middle

27 other warriors, had passed

28 first one to sit　　29 the others, fighting
30 pushed, pulled, jumped
31 fought, harder, became tired
32 Finally, fight anymore
33 Instead, take care, injured
34 other warriors, even harder
35 As, fought, warriors, hurt
36 care of, so, followed
37 all, warriors except, following
38 walked toward, sit in
39 saw, standing with, followers
40 realized, all alone　　41 give up, real winner
42 moment, appeared, weapons, favorite
43 Sooner, later, side, peace
44 returned, palace, training ended
45 approach, wise, knowing, up

35 As, became tired, hurt　　36 took good care of
37 except, following
38 walked toward, to sit in it
39 standing with　　40 all alone
41 give up, the real winner
42 At that moment, appeared, my favorite
43 Sooner or later, on the side of
44 returned to
45 approach, knowing, What's up

01 the Best Warrior　　02 brave young man
03 strongest, the strongest man, have much to learn
04 ordered, to go
05 In a hundred days, voice said
06 got angry
07 might be a reason so, waited
08 On the hundred and first day
09 have learned, first weapon, patience
10 to win a war　　11 to stand against
12 Suddenly, tied, to　　13 Above, that read
14 passed by
15 Some, angry looks, others
16 shouted back
17 Set me free, or, in big trouble
18 made, worse　　19 another, thought
20 began to speak softly　　21 not, but
22 kept saying, all possible ways
23 Finally, let him go
24 the most powerful weapon
25 stronger than sharp swords
26 took, to, in the middle　　27 other, had passed
28 The first one to, winner
29 the others began fighting
30 pushed, pulled, jumped
31 harder and harder, became tired
32 anymore
33 take care of the injured
34 other warriors, even harder

1 최고의 전사, Corky
2 Corky는 용감한 청년이었다.
3 그는 장군이 되기를 원했지만 왕은 이렇게 말했다. "자네는 우리 군대에서 가장 강한 전사이네. 하지만 자네는 아직도 배울 게 많아."
4 왕은 Corky에게 유명한 군사 학교에 갈 것을 명령했다.
5 "거기서 기다려라. 훈련은 100일 후에 시작할 것이다." 군사 학교 안에서 이렇게 외치는 목소리가 들렸다.
6 Corky는 화가 났다.
7 하지만 이유가 있을 것으로 생각하고 기다렸다.
8 101일째 되던 날, 문이 열렸다.
9 한 노인이 이렇게 말했다. "너는 첫 번째 무기인 '인내'를 사용하는 법을 배운 것이다.
10 인내는 전쟁에서 이기기 위해 가장 중요한 것이다."
11 그리고 난 뒤, 스승은 Corky에게 기둥 앞에 서라고 말했다.
12 갑자기 그는 Corky를 기둥에 묶었다.
13 그의 머리 위에는 '위험하고 나쁨'이라는 푯말을 붙였다.
14 많은 사람이 지나갔다.
15 몇몇은 Corky를 화난 표정으로 쳐다봤고, 다른 몇몇은 그에게 소리를 질렀다.
16 Corky도 그들에게 소리를 질렀다.
17 그는 "나를 풀어 줘. 그러지 않으면 모두 혼쭐날 줄 알아!"라고 외쳤다.
18 그것은 상황을 더 악화시켰다.
19 그는 '다른 방법을 써야겠어.'라고 생각했다.
20 그리고 나서 Corky는 부드럽게 말하기 시작했다.
21 그는 자신이 위험하거나 나쁘지 않고 좋은 사람이라고 말했다.
22 그는 모든 방법을 동원해 계속해서 이렇게 말했다.
23 마침내 사람들은 그를 풀어 주었다.
24 "이제 너는 가장 강력한 무기인 '말'을 통제하게 되었다.
25 부드러운 말은 날카로운 칼보다 강하니라."라고 스승은 말했다.
26 다음 단계로 스승은 Corky를 중앙에 의자가 놓여 있는 커다란 홀로 데리고 갔다.
27 그곳에는 시험에 통과한 19명의 다른 전사들이 있었다.
28 "저 의자에 가장 먼저 앉는 사람이 승자가 될 것이다."라고 스승이 말했다.

29 Corky와 나머지 전사들은 싸우기 시작했다.

30 그들은 밀고 당기고 달리고 뛰어올랐다.

31 그들은 점점 더 격렬히 싸웠고, Corky는 지쳤다.

32 마침내 그가 말했다. "나는 더는 싸움을 하지 않겠다.

33 대신에 부상당한 자들을 돌볼 것이다."

34 나머지 전사들은 이것을 보고 더 심하게 싸움을 했다.

35 그들이 싸움을 할수록 더 많은 전사들이 지치고 다쳤다.

36 Corky는 그들을 잘 돌봐 주었고, 그들은 Corky를 따르게 되었다.

37 곧 Thunder를 제외한 모든 전사들이 Corky를 따르고 있었다.

38 Thunder는 의자로 걸어가 그곳에 앉으려 했다.

39 그러다 그는 Corky가 18명의 추종자들과 함께 서 있는 것을 봤다.

40 Thunder는 자신이 혼자라는 사실을 깨달았다.

41 "나는 포기하겠다. 네가 진정한 승자다."라고 Thunder가 Corky에게 말했다.

42 그때 스승이 나타나 말했다. "모든 훌륭한 무기 중에서 평화는 내가 가장 좋아하는 것이다.

43 조만간 모든 사람은 평화의 편에 서기를 원한다."

44 Corky는 훈련을 마친 후 성으로 돌아갔다.

45 Corky가 다가오는 것을 본 왕은 그에게 이미 모든 것을 알고 있다는 듯한 현명한 미소를 띠며 말했다. "안녕하시오, 장군?"

1 Corky, the Best Warrior

2 Corky was a brave young man.

3 He wanted to be a general, but the king said, "You're the strongest man in my army, but you have much to learn."

4 He ordered Corky to go to a famous military school.

5 "Wait there. In a hundred days, your training will start," a voice said from inside the school gate.

6 Corky got angry.

7 But then he thought there might be a reason, so he waited.

8 On the hundred and first day, the gate opened.

9 An old man said, "You have learned to use your first weapon: patience.

10 Patience is the most important thing to win a war."

11 Then, the teacher told Corky to stand against a pole.

12 Suddenly, he tied Corky to the pole.

13 Above his head, he put a sign that read "Dangerous

and Bad."

14 Many people passed by.

15 Some gave Corky angry looks, and others shouted at him.

16 Corky shouted back.

17 He yelled, "Set me free, or you all will be in big trouble!"

18 That made the situation worse.

19 "I need to try another way," he thought.

20 Then, Corky began to speak softly.

21 He said he was not dangerous or bad but was a good man.

22 He kept saying this in all possible ways.

23 Finally, the people let him go.

24 "Now you control the most powerful weapon: words.

25 Soft words are stronger than sharp swords," said the teacher.

26 Next, the teacher took Corky to a large hall with a chair in the middle.

27 There were 19 other warriors who had passed their tests.

28 "The first one to sit in the chair will be the winner," the teacher said.

29 Corky and the others began fighting.

30 They pushed, pulled, ran, and jumped.

31 They fought harder and harder, so Corky became tired.

32 Finally, he said, "I will not fight anymore.

33 Instead, I will take care of the injured."

34 The other warriors saw this and fought even harder.

35 As they fought, more warriors became tired and hurt.

36 Corky took good care of them, so they followed him.

37 Soon, all the warriors except Thunder were following Corky.

38 Thunder walked toward the chair to sit in it.

39 Then, he saw Corky standing with his 18 followers.

40 Thunder realized he was all alone.

41 "I give up. You're the real winner," Thunder said to Corky.

42 At that moment, the teacher appeared and said, "Of all the great weapons, peace is my favorite.

43 Sooner or later, everyone wants to stand on the side of peace."

44 Corky returned to the palace after his training

ended.

45 When the king saw him approach, he gave Corky a wise and knowing smile and said, "What's up, General?"

After You Read A

1. wanted to be a general
2. the military school, for a hundred days
3. kept saying, dangerous[bad], set, free
4. stopped fighting, the injured

Inside the Story

1. are talking, One, the other
2. orders, to go to the military school
3. One, the others are listening
4. tells Corky to be quiet, stay
5. One, sword, the other is holding a stick
6. The man holding a sword, to wait
7. Some, the others are kneeling
8. to keep fighting to sit in

Link to the World

1. peaceful movement to free India
2. asked, to fight peacefully against
3. fasted, instead of fighting
4. An eye for an eye, make, blind

After You Read A

1. Corky wanted to be a general in the army.
2. Corky went to the military school and waited for a hundred days.
3. Corky kept saying he was not dangerous[bad], so people finally set him free.
4. Corky stopped fighting and took care of the injured.

Inside the Story

1. Two people are talking in the hall. One is the king, and the other is Corky.
2. The king orders Corky to go to the military school.
3. Many people are standing around Corky. One is talking to Corky, the others are listening.
4. The teacher tells Corky to be quiet and stay there.
5. Two men are standing inside the gate. One is holding a sword, and the other is holding a stick.
6. The man holding a sword tells Corky to wait there for 100 days.

7. Many warriors are listening to the teacher. Some are standing, and the others are kneeling.
8. The teacher wants them to keep fighting to sit in the chair.

Link to the World

1. Mahatma Gandhi led a peaceful movement to free India.
2. He asked his people to fight peacefully against England.
3. He fasted for a long time instead of fighting with weapons.
4. "An eye for an eye will only make the whole world blind," he said.

단어 TEST Step 1   p.88

01 대신에	02 평균; 평균의	03 통제하다, 조종하다
04 조언, 도움말	05 비평가	06 노력
07 공공의	08 깨닫다	09 대략
10 가짜의	11 접다	12 숲
13 모양, 형태	14 백만	
15 뒤에서부터, 역방향으로		16 사건
17 잡다	18 상상하다	19 공유하다, 나누다
20 작은	21 농담	22 이웃, 옆집 사람
23 소리치다	24 일단 ~하기만 하면	
25 (주로 소유격 뒤에서) ~ 자신의		26 평화
27 공무원	28 구하다	29 싫어하다
30 책갈피	31 관리, 관료	32 조각
33 해결하다	34 경주용 차	35 결국 ~가 되다
36 B하느니 A하겠다	37 ~와 가까워지다	38 ~를 멀리하게 하다
39 큰 소리로 웃다	40 ~를 잘게 썰다	41 ~하는 것을 멈추다
42 ~에게 인사하다	43 비가 억수같이 오다	

단어 TEST Step 2   p.89

01 critic	02 effort	03 average
04 fake	05 tip	06 fold
07 control	08 share	09 about
10 joke	11 public	12 forest
13 solve	14 once	15 race car
16 realize	17 save	18 shout
19 tiny	20 backward	21 own
22 peace	23 case	24 million
25 create	26 shape	27 bookmark
28 public officer	29 hold	30 neighbor
31 officer	32 instead	33 piece
34 imagine	35 laugh out loud	36 stop+-ing
37 make sure	28 would rather A than B	
39 end up -ing	40 get closer to	41 keep ~ away
42 say hello to	43 rain cats and dogs	

단어 TEST Step 3   p.90

1 effort, 노력   2 neighbor, 이웃 사람

3 backward, 뒤에서부터   4 delicious, 맛있는

5 forest, 숲   6 rain cats and dogs, 비가 억수같이 오다

7 instead, 대신에   8 invite, 초대하다

9 imagine, 상상하다   10 peace, 평화

11 share, 공유하다   12 fold, 접다   13 save, 구하다

14 critic, 비평가   15 realize, 깨닫다

16 make sure, 틀림없이 ~하다

본문 TEST Step 1   p.91~94

01 Teens' Magazine   02 Ways, Make, Better

03 something nice, change, tips

04 Say hello, neighbors, smile

05 forget to say   06 on a rainy day

07 Laugh out loud, joke

08 something for, neighbors

09 Hold, door, person behind

10 Invite, neighbors to

11 each, make, town better 12 Messages. Peace

13 put, messages on, board

14 having friends around

15 rather, peace, than pieces

16 place, because, fighting, shouting

17 makes everyone smile   18 inside, need to share

19 LET'S LAUGH   20 An, a day

21 true that, keeps, away 22 what they say

23 apple, just broke, window

24 Be Kind to

25 what books hate, Why

26 bad, WITCHES, TURNs, bookmark

27 Stop folding, bookmark instead

28 It, that, save, Be

29 more, happier, How about

30 Facts, Fake   31 About, have ever lived

32 have ever been born   33 has more people than

34 largest country, tiny, in

35 near, bigger than, average

36 covers, square, size, covering

37 were invented in

38 into, pieces, shape, sold

39 Jobs in, Movies

40 the greatest movie ever

41 public, surprised, what, free

42 with, gets closer, later

43 lot, effort, solves, cases 44 will love this

45 critic, cooked, realizes, anyone

46 named, Controlling, ends, becoming

47 Say It with

48 what these emojis mean

49 stone, grow, cats, piece 50 Emoji Song

51 let's sing, louder, happier

52 Secret Messages

53 Imagine, else, difficult, secret

54 Read Backward

55 solve, backward, simple, hard

56 Every Second Letter

57 every, starting, finish, missed

59 easier, looks, around, inside

60 Make sure, send along

49 Once in a, cats, dogs, A piece of

51 let's sing, The louder, the happier

52 Secret   53 no one else can read

54 Backward

55 easy to solve, backward, once

56 Every   57 starting with, missed

59 easier than it looks, each letter

60 secret letters, to send to, Make sure, send along

본문 TEST Step 2   p.95~97

01 Teens'   02 Ways to Make, Better

03 something nice, some tips

04 Say hello to, smile   05 forget to say

06 on a rainy day   07 Laugh out loud

08 for   09 Hold, behind you

10 Invite, to

11 each day, make, better   12 Peace

13 put, on   14 having friends

15 I'd rather, than pieces

16 every place, fighting, shouting

17 makes, smile   18 inside

19 LAUGH   20 a day

21 it, that, keeps, away   22 what they say

23 just broke   24 Be Kind

25 what books hate, Why

26 WITCHES, TURNs, Don't, bookmark, Be Kind

27 folding, instead   28 It is, that can save

29 The more, the happier, How about, your own

30 Facts, Sound Fake

31 have ever lived, living on

32 have ever been born, about

33 more, than   34 largest

35 bigger than, average

36 covers, the size of, covering

37 were invented in

38 are cut into, pieces, way to use, weren't sold

39 Jobs   40 the greatest movie

41 public officer, surprised to see what he does

42 with, Helping Judy, later

43 a lot of effort, solves many cases

44 Everyone will love

45 food critic, realizes, anyone

46 dreams of becoming, named, Controlling, ends
   up becoming

47 with

48 what these emojis mean

본문 TEST Step 3   p.98~100

1 십대들의 잡지

2 마을을 더 좋게 만드는 방법들

3 이웃들을 위해 뭔가 좋은 일을 하면 여러분의 마을을 변화시킬
  수 있다. 작은 것부터 시작하라. 여기 몇 가지 도움말이 있다.

4 1. 이웃들에게 인사를 하고 미소를 지어라.

5 2. 잊지 말고 "고맙습니다."라고 말해라.

6 3. 비 오는 날에 당신의 우산을 함께 써라.

7 4. 이웃이 농담하면 크게 소리 내어 웃어라.

8 5. 이웃들을 위해 뭔가를 만들어라.

9 6. 뒤에 오는 사람을 위해 문을 잡아 줘라.

10 7. 이웃을 당신의 파티에 초대해라.

11 만약 당신이 매일 한 가지씩 하기만 하면, 당신의 마을을 더
   좋게 만들 수 있다.

12 평화 메시지

13 우리는 세계 평화의 날에 게시판에 평화 메시지를 붙였다.

14 평화는 세상 어디에서나 친구가 있다는 것을 의미한다. −
   김지민

15 나는 지구의 조각들을 갖느니 지구 위의 평화를 갖겠다. −
   서은지

16 항상 싸우거나 소리치는 누군가가 있으므로 나는 내가 가는
   모든 곳에서 평화를 원한다. − 박한솔

17 평화는 모든 사람을 미소 짓게 만든다. − 양미란

18 평화는 우리 모두의 내면에 있다. 우리는 단지 그것을 공유할
   필요가 있을 뿐이다. − 장재희

19 웃읍시다

20 하루에 사과 한 개

21 Jake가 아빠를 보러 들어왔다. "아빠!" 그는 "하루에 사과 한
   개가 의사를 멀리하게 만든다는 것이 사실이에요?"라고
   말했다.

22 "사람들이 그렇게 말하지," 아빠가 말했다.

23 "자, 저에게 빨리 사과 한 개를 주세요! 제가 방금 의사
   선생님의 유리창을 깨뜨렸어요!"

24 책들을 친절하게 대해 주세요!

25 여러분은 책들이 무엇을 싫어하는지 아나요? 그들은 물, 햇빛,
   그리고 강아지 귀를 싫어합니다. 왜 강아지 귀일까요?

26 물은 마녀와 책에 해롭다! / 햇빛도 책을 누렇게 뜨게 한다. /

강아지 귀처럼 책을 접지 마라! 책갈피를 사용해라! / 책들을 친절하게 대해 주세요!

27 강아지 귀 모양으로 책을 접는 것을 멈춰 주세요. 대신에 책갈피를 이용하세요.

28 여러분의 책을 구해 주는 것은 바로 책갈피입니다. 여러분의 책들을 친절하게 대해 주세요.

29 여러분이 책을 더 많이 사랑하면 할수록 여러분의 책들은 더 행복해질 겁니다. 여러분 자신의 책갈피를 만들어 보는 게 어떨까요?

30 가짜 같은 사실

31 1. 지금까지 살아온 모든 사람의 약 7%가 오늘날 지구상에 살고 있다.

32 세계 역사에서 약 1천8십2억 명의 사람들이 지금까지 태어났다. 그리고 약 7십4억 4천2백만 명이 오늘날 지구상에 살고 있다.

33 2. 방글라데시는 러시아보다 인구가 더 많다.

34 러시아는 세계에서 가장 큰 나라이지만, 아주 작은 방글라데시에는 2018년 기준으로 1억 6천6백3십만 명의 인구가 있다. 러시아는 1억 4천3백9십만 명의 인구가 있다.

35 3. 인도 Kolkata 부근의 한 바니안(banyan) 나무는 평균적인 월마트보다 크다.

36 평균적인 월마트 상점은 약 10만4천 평방피트의 넓이이다. 인도 Kolkata에 있는 그레이트 바니안 나무는 대략 숲 하나의 크기로 15만5천 평방피트를 차지한다.

37 4. 베이비 당근은 1986년 발명되었다.

38 베이비 당근은 실제로 아기처럼 작은 당근이 아니다. 크고 못생긴 당근들이 베이비 당근 모양을 가진 작은 조각으로 잘린다. 농부 Mike Yurosek이 팔리지 않는 못생긴 당근을 사용할 하나의 방편으로 1986년에 그것을 발명하였다.

39 영화 속 직업들

40 주토피아(2016) 그것은 이제까지 가장 대단한 영화이다!

41 Flash는 공무원이다. 그는 아주 느리지만 열심히 일한다. 여러분은 그가 여가 시간에 무엇을 하는지 알게 되면 놀랄 것이다. 그것은 경주용 자동차를 운전하는 것이다!

42 Nick은 커다란 입을 가진 여우이다. Judy를 도우면서 그녀와 가까워진다. 나중에 Judy처럼 경찰관이 된다.

43 Judy는 작은 토끼지만, 영리하고 강하다. 많은 노력을 한 후에, 그녀는 경찰관이 되었고 많은 사건을 해결한다.

44 라따뚜이(2007) 누구라도 이 영화를 사랑할 것이다.

45 Anton Ego는 음식 비평가이다. Remy가 요리한 음식을 먹은 후에, 그는 "누구라도 요리할 수 있다."라는 것을 깨닫는다.

46 작은 쥐 Remy는 요리사가 되기를 꿈꾼다. 그는 식당에 들어가서 Linguini라는 이름의 소년을 만난다. Linguini를 통제하면서 그는 맛있는 음식을 만들고 결국에는 훌륭한 요리사가 된다.

47 이모지로 말하자

48 이 이모지들이 무엇을 의미하는지 아니?

49 돌 하나로 새 두 마리 잡기. (일석이조.) / 당신이 가장 사랑하는

사람. (눈에 넣어도 안 아플 사람.) / 불을 가지고 장난치지 마라. / 극히 드물게. / 오늘은 이만하자. / 돈이 나무에서 자라는 것은 아니다. (돈이 그냥 생기는 건 아니다.) / 비가 억수같이 온다. / 케이크 한 조각. (누워서 떡 먹기.)

50 이모지 노래

51 자, 함께 크리스마스 노래를 불러 봅시다! 더 크게 부를수록, 더 행복해집니다!

52 비밀 메시지

53 다른 어떤 사람도 읽을 수 없는 메시지를 친구에게 보낼 수 있다고 상상해 봐! 여러분 자신의 비밀 메시지를 읽고 쓰는 법을 배우는 것이 그렇게 어렵지는 않다.

54 1. 거꾸로 읽어라

55 이것은 풀기 쉽다 – 그냥 단어들을 거꾸로 읽어라! 일단 여러분이 비밀을 알면 간단하지만, 그렇지 못하면 어려울 수 있다.

56 2. 두 번째 글자마다 읽어라

57 첫 번째 글자에서 시작해서 두 번째 글자마다 읽어라. 그리고 끝나면 여러분이 빠뜨린 글자로 다시 시작하라.

58 3. 피그펜

59 피그펜(돼지우리)은 보기보다 쉽다. 각 글자 주변의 선들은 그 선들 안에 있는 글자를 의미한다.

60 이제 여러분은 자신만의 비밀 문자 세트를 만들어서 친구들에게 보낼 비밀 메시지를 써 보아라. 친구들이 메시지를 이해할 수 있도록 해결의 열쇠도 함께 보내도록 해라.

1 Teens' Magazine

2 Ways to Make Your Town Better

3 Doing something nice for your neighbors can change your town. Start small. Here are some tips.

4 1. Say hello to your neighbors and smile.

5 2. Don't forget to say, "Thank you."

6 3. Share your umbrella on a rainy day.

7 4. Laugh out loud when your neighbor tells a joke.

8 5. Make something for your neighbors.

9 6. Hold the door for the person behind you.

10 7. Invite your neighbors to your party.

11 If you just do one thing each day, you can make your town better.

12 Messages for Peace

13 On World Peace Day, we put our peace messages on the board.

14 Peace means having friends around the world. - Kim Jimin

15 I'd rather have peace on Earth than pieces of Earth. - Seo Eunji

16 I want peace every place I go because there is always someone fighting or shouting. - Park Hansol

17 Peace makes everyone smile.- Yang Miran

18 Peace is inside all of us. We just need to share it. - Jang Jaehee

19 LET'S LAUGH

20 An apple a day

21 Jake came in to see his dad. "Dad!" he said, "Is it true that an apple a day keeps the doctor away?"

22 "That's what they say," said his dad.

23 "Well, give me an apple quickly! I just broke the doctor's window!"

24 Be Kind to Books!

25 Do you know what books hate? They hate water, the sun, and dog ears. Why dog ears?

26 Water is bad for WITCHES and BOOKS! / The SUN also TURNs Books YELLOW / Don't DOG-EAR! Use a bookmark! / Be Kind to Books!

27 Stop folding dog ears in books. Use a bookmark instead.

28 It is a bookmark that can save your books. Be kind to your books.

29 The more you love your books, the happier your books will be. How about making your own?

30 Facts That Sound Fake

31 1. About 7% of all people who have ever lived are living on the Earth today.

32 About 108,200 million people have ever been born in the history of the world. And about 7,442 million are living on the Earth today.

33 2. Bangladesh has more people than Russia.

34 Russia is the world's largest country, but tiny Bangladesh has 166.3 million people in 2018. Russia has 143.9 million people.

35 3. A banyan tree near Kolkata, India, is bigger than the average Walmart.

36 The average Walmart store covers about 104,000 square feet. The Great Banyan Tree in Kolkata, India, is about the size of a forest, covering 155,000 square feet.

37 4. Baby carrots were invented in 1986.

38 Baby carrots are not actually baby carrots. Big ugly carrots are cut into small pieces that have the shape of a baby carrot. Farmer Mike Yurosek invented them in 1986 as a way to use ugly carrots that weren't sold.

39 Jobs in the Movies

40 Zootopia (2016) It's the greatest movie ever!

41 Flash is a public officer. He is very slow but works hard. You will be surprised to see what he does in his free time. It's driving a race car!

42 Nick is a fox with a big mouth. Helping Judy, he gets closer to her. He later becomes a police officer like Judy.

43 Judy is a small rabbit, but she's smart and strong. After a lot of effort, she becomes a police officer and solves many cases.

44 Ratatouille (2007) Everyone will love this movie.

45 Anton Ego is a food critic. After he eats the food Remy cooked, he realizes that anyone can cook.

46 Remy, a little mouse, dreams of becoming a cook. He goes into a restaurant and meets a boy named Linguini. Controlling Linguini, he makes delicious food and ends up becoming a great cook.

47 Say It with Emojis

48 Do you know what these emojis mean?

49 Killing two birds with one stone. / The apple of your eyes. / Don't play games with fire. / Once in a blue moon. / Let's call it a day. / Money does not grow on trees. / It's raining cats and dogs. / A piece of cake.

50 Emoji Song

51 Now, let's sing a Christmas song together! The louder, the happier!

52 Secret Messages

53 Imagine you can send messages to your friend that no one else can read! It's not so difficult for you to learn how to read and write your own secret messages.

54 1. Read Backward

55 This is easy to solve. Just read the words backward! It seems simple once you know the secret, but it can be a hard one when you don't.

56 2. Read Every Second Letter

57 Read every second letter starting with the first letter, and when you finish, start again on the letters you missed.

58 3. Pig-pen

59 The Pig-pen is easier than it looks. The lines around each letter mean the letter inside the lines.

60 Now create your own set of secret letters and write secret messages to send to your friends. Make sure you send along a key so your friends can understand your messages!

MEMO

MEMO

2학기 전과정

적중 100 plus

영어 기출 문제집

정답 및 해설

천재 | 정사열

적중 **100** + 특별부록

Plan B

우리학교 최신기출

천재 · 정사열 교과서를 배우는

학교 시험문제 분석 · 모음 · 해설집

전국단위 학교 시험문제 수집 및 분석
출제 빈도가 높은 문제 위주로 선별
문제 풀이에 필요한 상세한 해설

중3-2
영어

천재 · 정사열

적중 100 + 특별부록

Plan B
우리학교 최신기출

중3-2
영어

천재 · 정사열

◎ 선택형 문항의 답안은 컴퓨터용 수정 싸인펜을 사용하여 OMR 답안지에 바르게 표기하시오.
◎ 서술형 문제는 답을 답안지에 반드시 검정 볼펜으로 쓰시오.
◎ 총 30문항 100점 만점입니다. 문항별 배점은 각 문항에 표시되어 있습니다.

[충북 ○○중]

[1~2] 다음 대화를 읽고 물음에 답하시오.

Boy: What are the soldiers doing with the five chimneys on TV?
Girl: ⓐThey are sending messages to the king by using the chimneys.
Boy: ⓑReally? Can you tell me more about the system, *bongsudae*?
Girl: Well, do you see the two smoking chimneys?
Boy: Yes. ⓒWhat do they mean?
Girl: They mean they just saw an enemy.
Boy: If there's no enemy, they don't smoke at all, do they?
Girl: ⓓNo, they don't. Smoke from one chimney means "No enemy."
Boy: Now smoke is rising from three chimneys. What does that mean?
Girl: ⓔIt means an enemy is coming close to the border.

01 위 대화의 밑줄 친 ⓐ~ⓔ 중 흐름상 가장 어색한 것은? (3점)

① ⓐ ② ⓑ ③ ⓒ ④ ⓓ ⑤ ⓔ

02 위 대화의 내용과 일치하는 것은? (3점)

① 왕은 *bongsudae*를 이용하여 군사들에게 메시지를 보내고 있다.
② 한 개의 굴뚝에서 연기가 나는 것은 적이 없음을 의미한다.
③ 세 개의 굴뚝에서 연기가 나는 것은 방금 적을 봤다는 것을 의미한다.
④ 소녀는 *bongsudae* 신호에 대해 알지 못한다.
⑤ 소년이 소녀에게 *bongsudae* 신호에 대해 설명하고 있다.

[충북 ○○중]

03 다음 대화의 내용과 일치하지 <u>않는</u> 것은? (4점)

B: Jan van Eyck's painting has some hidden secrets in it.
G: Really? I'm curious about them. Where are the secrets?
B: Find one yourself.
G: Let's see. ... Oh, I see some letters here.
B: You found one! It means "Jan van Eyck was here. 1434." It's Latin.
G: That's awesome! Any other secrets?
B: Okay. This dog tells us the man here was very rich.
G: I don't understand.
B: They had to spend lots of money to buy a dog of that kind at that time.
G: I see. Only the rich could have that kind of dog, right?
B: Exactly. Pictures speak a thousand words, you know.

*B: Boy G: Girl

① There are some hidden secrets in the picture.
② The picture was painted by Jan van Eyck.
③ The girl found some letters in the picture.
④ The man in the picture was very rich because he could have that kind of dog.
⑤ The letters in the picture are English.

[전북 ○○중]

04 다음 두 문장을 관계대명사를 이용하여 한 문장으로 만드시오. (4점)

• The girl is Tami.
• Her dog is dancing.

→ _____

05 다음 두 사람의 대화가 옳지 <u>않은</u> 것은? (2점)

① A: Which do you prefer, eating rice or eating bread?
　B: I prefer eating bread.
② A: Why don't we make a bag with old jeans?
　B: Great! What kind of bag are we going to make?
③ A: Can I join your book-making project?
　B: Sure.
④ A: What are you doing with old jeans?
　B: I'm making a pencil case for you.
⑤ A: What does your name mean?
　B: I like the meaning of your name.

06 다음 글의 밑줄 친 부분 중 어법의 쓰임이 적절하지 <u>않은</u> 것은? (3점)

Speaking to family members or friends in a foreign country ⓐ<u>is</u> rather easy and simple today. But before the days of phones and the Internet, it was not that easy. People just sent a letter and waited for a reply for weeks. And it was ⓑ<u>much</u> harder if they couldn't read or write.
This letter shows ⓒ<u>the way</u> people got over these difficulties. It was written in 1973 by a woman ⓓ<u>whom</u> husband was far away. She lived in Sicily, an Italian island, ⓔ<u>while</u> her husband worked in Germany. At the time, more than 5% of the people in Italy could not read or write, and she was one of them. This letter was discovered by Sicilian writer Gesualdo Bufalino.
Here's how he translated the pictures into words.

① ⓐ　② ⓑ　③ ⓒ　④ ⓓ　⑤ ⓔ

[7~8] 다음 글을 읽고 물음에 답하시오.

Speaking to family members or friends in a foreign country is rather easy and simple today. But before the days of phones and the Internet, ⓐ<u>it</u> was not that easy. People just sent a letter and waited for a reply for weeks. And ⓑ<u>it</u> was a lot harder if they couldn't read or write.
This letter shows ⓒ<u>how</u> people got over these difficulties. It was written in 1973 by a woman whose husband was far away.

07 위 글에서 밑줄 친 ⓐ와 ⓑ가 공통으로 가리키는 것을 찾아 10 단어로 쓰시오. (4점)

→ _____

08 위 글의 밑줄 친 ⓒhow와 용법이 같은 것은? (3점)

① <u>How</u> are you?
② <u>How</u> old are you?
③ <u>How</u> beautiful the flower is!
④ <u>How</u> many sisters do you have?
⑤ He doesn't know <u>how</u> he fixes the car.

09 다음 두 문장을 관계대명사를 이용하여 한 문장으로 바꿔 쓰시오. (4점)

・The girl doesn't understand the sign.
・Her dog wants to eat a hot dog.

→ _____

[10~14] 다음 글을 읽고 물음에 답하시오.

My dear love, I miss you so much, and I reach my arms out ⓐ_____ you, together with our three kids. We are all in good health except for the little ⓑone. He's a little sick, but not seriously. I already sent you a letter, but there was no reply, so I am sad about it. ⓒAs I don't get a letter from you, I am not very happy. Your mother fell ill, and I'm going to visit her in the hospital with some money and food. I'll go there with our middle son while the oldest looks ⓓ_____ the youngest.

10 위 글의 내용과 일치하지 <u>않는</u> 것은?　(4점)

① 글쓴이의 자녀는 3명이다.
② 글쓴이의 남편의 엄마가 아프다.
③ 글쓴이가 보낸 첫 번째 편지이다.
④ 글쓴이는 병문안을 갈 예정이다.
⑤ 글쓴이의 막내 아들이 아프다.

11 위 글의 밑줄 친 문장 ⓒ를 가정법으로 올바르게 바꾼 것은?　(4점)

① If I didn't get a letter from you, I would be very happy.
② If I get a letter from you, I would be very happy.
③ If I got a letter from you, I will be very happy.
④ If I got a letter from you, I would not be very happy.
⑤ If I got a letter from you, I would be very happy.

12 위 글의 빈칸 ⓐ와 ⓓ에 알맞은 말이 순서대로 짝지어진 것은?　(3점)

① for – after　② to – for
③ after – toward　④ toward – after
⑤ toward – for

13 위 글에서 밑줄 친 ⓑone과 바꿔 쓸 수 있는 한 단어를 찾아 쓰시오.　(3점)

→ _____

14 위 글에서 편지를 쓴 사람과 받는 사람의 관계는?　(2점)

① wife – husband　② son – mom
③ teacher – student　④ daughter – mom
⑤ husband – mother-in-law

15 다음 글의 빈칸 (A), (B)에 들어갈 말이 가장 알맞게 짝지어진 것은?　(4점)

We picked lots of olives from our olive trees this year. I hired a man (A)_____ sons are good workers. He knocked the olives down, and his two sons helped him, picking them up from the ground. I paid him 27,000 lire for the work. I spent 12,000 more for the olive press. I got (B)_____ oil to fill a large pot and a small one. I can sell it at a price of 1,300 lire a liter.

	(A)	(B)
①	who	much
②	which	enough
③	whose	enough
④	whose	little
⑤	of which	too

18 위 글의 밑줄 친 (A)~(E)를 바르게 설명하지 <u>않은</u> 것은? (3점)

① (A): '시대'라는 의미로 쓰임
② (B): 문장의 어떤 부분을 강조할 때 씀
③ (C): '몇 주 동안'의 의미로 쓰임
④ (D): 소유격 관계대명사임
⑤ (E): '~가 여기에 있다'라는 의미임

[16~18] 다음 글을 읽고 물음에 답하시오.

Speaking to family members or friends in a foreign country ⓐis rather easy and simple today. But before the (A)days of phones and the Internet, (B)it was not that easy. People just ⓑsent a letter and waited for a reply (C)for weeks. And it was ⓒ a lot harder if they couldn't read or write.
This letter shows how people got over ⓓthese difficulties. It was written in 1973 by a woman (D)whose husband was far away. She lived in Sicily, an Italian island, while her husband worked in Germany. At the time, more than 5% of the people in Italy could not read or write, and she was one of them. This letter ⓔdiscovered by Sicilian writer Gesualdo Bufalino.
(E)Here's how he translated the pictures into words.

16 위 글의 밑줄 친 ⓐ~ⓔ 중 어법상 <u>어색한</u> 것은? (3점)

① ⓐ   ② ⓑ   ③ ⓒ   ④ ⓓ   ⑤ ⓔ

19 다음 글의 밑줄 친 부분 중 어법상 <u>어색한</u> 것은 몇 개인가? (4점)

I had two workers <u>prepare</u> our field and <u>to plant</u> seeds for 150,000 lire. I voted for the DC. The PCI lost so many seats that it almost seems <u>dead</u>. But whether one or <u>another</u> wins, it's the same. Nothing changes for us poor people. We worked yesterday, and we will work again tomorrow. We picked <u>much</u> olives from our olive trees this year.

① 1개   ② 2개   ③ 3개
④ 4개   ⑤ 5개

17 위 글의 내용과 일치하는 것은? (4점)

① 인터넷 시대 이전에 외국에 있는 가족이나 친구와 대화하는 것은 쉽고 간단했다.
② 위 글 속 편지는 아내와 멀리 떨어져 살았던 남편에 의해 쓰여진 것이다
③ 이탈리아에 살았던 사람들 중 5% 이상이 읽거나 쓸 수 없었다.
④ 위 글 속의 편지를 발견한 사람은 독일인 작가 Gesualdo Bufalino이다.
⑤ Gesualdo Bufalino는 발견된 편지 속의 글을 그림으로 바꾸었다.

20 다음 글에서 화자의 심경으로 가장 알맞은 것은? (3점)

I hired a man whose sons are good workers. He knocked the olives down, and his two sons helped him, picking them up from the ground. I paid him 27,000 lire for the work. I spent 12,000 more for the olive press. I got enough oil to fill a large pot and a small one. I can sell it at a price of 1,300 lire a liter. I and three kids could go through this winter without worry.

① bored   ② relieved   ③ anxious
④ surprised   ⑤ depressed

[21~24] 다음 글을 읽고 물음에 답하시오.

I had two workers prepare our field and plant seeds for 150,000 lire. I voted for the DC. The PCI lost so many seats that it almost seems dead. But whether one or the other wins, it's the same. Nothing changes for us poor people. We worked yesterday, and we will work again tomorrow. We ⓐ_____ lots of olives from our olive trees this year. I hired a man whose sons are good workers. He knocked the olives down, and his two sons helped him, ⓑ_____ them up from the ground. I paid him 27,000 lire for the work. I spent 12,000 more for the olive press. I got enough oil to fill a large pot and a small one. I can sell it at a price of 1,300 lire a liter.

21 위 글에서 그녀가 밭을 준비하고 씨앗을 심도록 하기 위해 두 명의 일꾼에게 준 돈은 얼마인가? (2점)

① 150,000 lire ② 27,000 lire
③ 12,000 lire ④ 13,000 lire
⑤ nothing

22 위 글의 빈칸 ⓐ와 ⓑ에 들어갈 단어 pick의 올바른 형태는? (4점)

① pick – pick
② picked – picking
③ pick – picked
④ picked – picked
⑤ picking – picking

23 위 글의 내용과 <u>다른</u> 것은? (3점)

① 글쓴이는 씨앗을 심기 위해 일꾼을 고용했다.
② 글쓴이는 투표를 했다.
③ 글쓴이는 작년에 올리브나무에서 많은 올리브를 수확했다.
④ 글쓴이는 올리브 압착을 위해 돈을 지불했다.
⑤ 글쓴이는 큰 항아리와 작은 항아리를 채울 만큼 충분한 양의 기름을 얻었다.

24 주어진 글에서 위 글의 내용과 <u>다른</u> 부분 2곳을 찾아 바르게 고쳐 문장을 다시 쓰시오. (3점)

> • I voted for the PCI. The PCI won many seats.

→ _____

25 다음 글의 밑줄 친 부분을 가정법으로 가장 적절하게 바꾼 것은? (4점)

I already sent you a letter, but there was no reply, so I am sad about it. <u>Because I don't get a letter from you, I am not happy.</u> Your mother is ill, and I will visit her in the hospital with some money and food. I will go there with our middle son while the oldest looks after the youngest.

① If I get a letter from you, I will be happy.
② If I got a letter from you, I would be happy.
③ If I will get a letter from you, I will be happy.
④ When I get a letter from you, I would be happy.
⑤ If I had gotten a letter from you, I have been happy.

26 다음 글의 밑줄 친 부분에서 주인공 'I'의 심정으로 가장 알맞은 것은? (3점)

> My love, my heart thinks of you as Christmas is coming. <u>I would be so happy if you were with me.</u> We all miss you so much. I'm sending you a big hug from me and our three little kids. Goodbye, dear love. My heart is yours, joined to you as our two rings are.

① angry　　② scared　　③ unhappy

④ excited　　⑤ pleased

[27~30] 다음 글을 읽고 물음에 답하시오.

> ⓐ<u>This letter</u> shows how people got over these difficulties. It was written in 1973 by a woman whose husband was far away. She lived in Sicily, an Italian island, while her husband worked in Germany. At the time, more than 5% of the people in Italy could not read or write, and she was one of them. (A) Here's how he translated the pictures into words. (B) My dear love, I miss you so much, and I reach my arms out toward you, together with our three kids. (C) We are all in good health except for the little one. He's a little sick, but not seriously. (D) I already sent you a letter, but there was no reply, so I am sad about it. ⓑ<u>If I got a letter from you, I would be very happy.</u> (E) Your mother fell ill, and I'm going to visit her in the hospital with some money and food. I'll go there with our middle son while the oldest looks after the youngest.

27 위 글의 (A)~(E) 중 다음 문장이 들어갈 곳으로 가장 알맞은 것은? (4점)

> This letter was discovered by Sicilian writer Gesualdo Bufalino.

① (A)　② (B)　③ (C)　④ (D)　⑤ (E)

28 위 글의 내용과 일치하는 것은? (3점)

① She doesn't have three children.

② The little kid is seriously sick.

③ Her mother falls ill and is in the hospital.

④ Her oldest kid takes care of the youngest kid.

⑤ She will visit the hospital with her middle daughter.

29 위 글의 밑줄 친 ⓐ에 관한 설명으로 가장 알맞은 것은? (4점)

① 독일 작가가 최초로 이 편지를 발견하였다.

② 이 편지를 쓴 사람은 글을 읽거나 쓸 수 없었다.

③ 이 편지를 쓴 사람의 남편은 이탈리아에서 일했다.

④ 이 편지는 남편과 사별한 한 여자에 의해 쓰여졌다.

⑤ 이 편지가 쓰여질 당시에 5% 이하의 이탈리아 사람들은 글을 읽거나 쓸 수 없었다.

30 위 글의 밑줄 친 ⓑ가 의미하는 것으로 가장 알맞은 것은? (3점)

① Though I get a letter from you, I am happy.

② Though I don't get a letter from you, I am not sad.

③ When I get a letter from you, I am not very happy.

④ Because I get a letter from you, I am not very happy.

⑤ As I don't get a letter from you, I'm not very happy.

3학년 영어 2학기 중간고사(5과) 2회

문항수 : 선택형(25문항) 서술형(3문항)

반		점수	
이름			

20 . . .

◎ 선택형 문항의 답안은 컴퓨터용 수정 싸인펜을 사용하여 OMR 답안지에 바르게 표기하시오.

◎ 서술형 문제는 답을 답안지에 반드시 검정 볼펜으로 쓰시오.

◎ 총 28문항 100점 만점입니다. 문항별 배점은 각 문항에 표시되어 있습니다.

[경기 ○○중]

01 다음 영어 설명에 알맞은 단어는? (3점)

to change spoken or written words into another language

① hire ② prepare ③ translate
④ hug ⑤ vote

[전북 ○○중]

02 다음 빈칸 (A), (B), (C)에 들어가기에 알맞은 말을 아래 〈보기〉에서 고르시오. (3점)

Tami: (A)_____ sign language.
Rinda: Are you? (B)_____ one expression. Look.
Tami: What does it mean?
Rinda: (C)_____ "You're welcome."

> 보기
> ⓐ It means
> ⓑ Let me show you
> ⓒ I'm curious about

→ (A) _____, (B) _____, (C) _____

[경기 ○○중]

03 다음 중 단어의 의미가 **잘못** 연결된 것은? (3점)

① look after – 뒤돌아보다
② prepare – 준비하다
③ except for – ~을 제외하고
④ foreign – 외국의
⑤ awesome – 멋진, 근사한

[서울 종로구 ○○중]

04 다음 두 문장을 한 문장으로 바꿔 쓸 때 빈칸에 들어갈 말로 가장 적절한 것은? (3점)

• The house is my father's.
• Its windows are very big.
→ The house _____ windows are very big is my father's.

① who ② what ③ which
④ whom ⑤ whose

[충북 ○○중]

05 다음 내용과 일치하는 것을 고르면? (4점)

B: What are the soldiers doing with the four chimneys on TV?
G: They are sending messages to the king by using the chimneys.
B: Really? I'm curious about the system. Can you tell me more?
G: Well, do you see the two smoking chimneys?
B: Yes. What do they mean?
G: They mean they just saw an enemy.
B: If there's no enemy, they don't smoke at all, do they?
G: Yes, they do. Smoke from one chimney means "No enemy."
B: Now smoke is rising from three chimneys. What does that mean?
G: It means an enemy is coming close to the border.

① TV 화면에 보이는 굴뚝의 수는 총 여섯 개다.
② 군인들은 굴뚝을 이용해서 그들의 장군에게 메시지를 보낸다.
③ 두 개의 굴뚝에서 연기가 나는 것은 적과 교전한다는 것을 의미한다.
④ 한 개의 굴뚝에서 연기가 나는 것은 적이 없다는 뜻이다.
⑤ 다섯 개의 굴뚝에서 연기가 나면 적이 국경선을 넘었다는 뜻이다.

06 다음 대화의 흐름상, 아래 주어진 말이 들어갈 위치로 가장 적절한 곳은? (4점)

I'm curious about the system.

A: What are the soldiers doing with the five chimneys on TV?
B: (A) They are sending messages to the king by using the chimneys.
A: Really? (B) Can you tell me more?
B: Well, do you see the two smoking chimneys? (C)
A: Yes. (D) What do they mean?
B: (E) They mean they just saw an enemy.

① (A)　② (B)　③ (C)　④ (D)　⑤ (E)

07 다음 주어진 Seho의 말 다음에 이어질 대화의 순서로 가장 적절한 것은? (4점)

Seho: Now the enemy is crossing the border in the night. What are the soldiers going to do to send messages? I'm curious about that.

(A) It means the battle has started.
(B) When they light all five of the chimneys, what does that mean?
(C) They will light four chimneys.

① (A) - (B) - (C)　② (B) - (A) - (C)
③ (B) - (C) - (A)　④ (C) - (A) - (B)
⑤ (C) - (B) - (A)

[8~10] 다음 대화를 읽고 물음에 답하시오.

A: This painting has some hidden secrets in it.
B: Really? I'm curious about them. Where are the secrets?
A: Find one yourself.
B: Let's see.... Oh, I see some letters here.
A: You found one! It means "Jan van Eyck was here. 1434." It's Latin.
B: That's awesome! Any other secrets?
A: Okay. This dog tells us the man here was very rich.
B: I don't understand.
A: They had to spend lots of money to buy a dog of that kind at that time.
B: I see. Only the rich could have that kind of dog, right?
A: Exactly. Pictures speak a thousand words, you know.

08 Where are A and B having this conversation? (3점)

① at school　② in an art museum
③ in the park　④ at a hospital
⑤ at the airport

09 위 대화를 읽고 답할 수 없는 질문은? (4점)

① Where was the painting discovered?
② What do the letters A found mean?
③ Are the letters A found English?
④ What makes people think the man in the picture was very rich?
⑤ Who could have that kind of dog at that time?

10 What are A and B talking about? (3점)

① an artist　② drawing skills
③ art history　④ pet dogs
⑤ an artwork

11 다음 빈칸에 들어갈 관계대명사가 바르게 짝지어진 것은?

(4점)

1. Lala is the girl (A)_____ dog wants water.
2. Jack is the owner of the farm, (B)_____ makes me surprised.
3. The guy (C)_____ is wearing a red bag is my friend.

	(A)	(B)	(C)
①	who	that	which
②	who	which	whose
③	whose	which	who
④	whose	which	whom
⑤	whose	that	who

12 다음 빈칸 (A), (B), (C)에 들어갈 말이 바르게 연결된 것은?

(4점)

- If I (A)_____ a fish, I would swim in the pond.
- If I had enough money, I (B)_____ the bike.
- Koko is the boy (C)_____ bag is by a big cat.

	(A)	(B)	(C)
①	were	would buy	whose
②	were	would buy	who
③	were	will buy	whose
④	am	will buy	who
⑤	am	will buy	whose

13 다음 〈보기〉에서 밑줄 친 부분이 어법상 옳은 것을 있는 대로 고른 것은?

(4점)

> 보기
>
> (A) He has a sister whose eyes <u>are</u> brown.
> (B) The girl <u>of which</u> dog is dancing is Didi.
> (C) Look at the book <u>whose</u> price is expensive.
> (D) This is the hotel <u>whose</u> windows were broken.

① (A), (B)   ② (A), (C)   ③ (B), (D)

④ (A), (C), (D)   ⑤ (B), (C), (D)

14 다음 우리말을 영어로 바꾸어 쓴 것으로 옳은 것은?

(3점)

- 내가 만약 그라면, 그 가방을 살 텐데.

① If I were him, I bought the bag.
② Were I him, I would buy the bag.
③ If were I him, I would buy the bag.
④ If I am him, I would bought the bag.
⑤ If I were him, I would bought the bag.

15 다음 짝지어진 두 문장의 밑줄 친 단어의 용법이 서로 같은 것은?

(3점)

① A: Mike is the boy <u>whose</u> cat is brown.
　 B: She asked me <u>whose</u> bag that is.
② A: I think <u>that</u> she is the best teacher.
　 B: I found out <u>that</u> the man was standing there.
③ A: She <u>lives</u> in Seoul with her two friends.
　 B: We need to save the <u>lives</u> of wild animals.
④ A: Be ready to <u>light</u> up the candles.
　 B: I need some <u>light</u> here to see inside.
⑤ A: The lady <u>leaves</u> the book on the desk.
　 B: There are many fallen <u>leaves</u>.

[16~17] 다음 글을 읽고 물음에 답하시오.

> Dear my love,
>
> I already sent you a letter, but there was no reply, so I am sad about it. ⓐ<u>As I don't get a letter from you, I'm not very happy.</u> Your mother fell ill and I'm going to visit her in the hospital with some money and food. I'll go there with our middle son while the oldest looks after the youngest. I miss you so much, and I reach my arms out toward you, together with our three sons.
>
> Your truly,
> Jane

16 위 글에 관한 질문의 답으로 알맞은 것은?　　(4점)

> Q: With whom will the writer visit the hospital?
> A: With _____.

① the writer's middle son
② the youngest son
③ the writer's mother
④ three sons
⑤ the writer's oldest son

17 위 글의 밑줄 친 ⓐ와 의미가 통하도록 if를 이용하여 완성하시오.　　(4점)

> ⓐ<u>As I don't get a letter from you,</u> I'm not very happy.

→ _____, I would be very happy.

18 다음 글의 밑줄 친 ⓐ가 가리키는 것으로 가장 알맞은 것은?
　　(4점)

> Speaking to family members or friends in a foreign country is rather easy and simple today. But before the days of phones and the Internet, ⓐ<u>it</u> was not that easy. People just sent a letter and waited for a reply for weeks. And it was a lot harder if they couldn't read or write.

① Using phones or the Internet
② Meeting friends or family members
③ Sending an e-mail to friends or family members
④ Waiting for a reply from friends or family members
⑤ Speaking to family members or friends in a foreign country

19 다음 글의 빈칸 (A), (B)에 들어갈 연결사로 가장 바르게 짝지어진 것은?　　(3점)

> Speaking to family members or friends in a foreign country is rather easy and simple today. (A)_____ before the days of phones and the Internet, it was not that easy. People just sent a letter and waited for a reply for weeks. (B)_____ it was a lot harder if they couldn't read or write.

	(A)	(B)
①	So	And
②	So	But
③	And	So
④	But	So
⑤	But	And

[20~22] 다음 글을 읽고 물음에 답하시오.

My dear love, I miss you so much, and I reach my arms out toward you, together with our kids. We are all in good health except for the little one. He's a little sick, but not seriously.

I already sent you a letter, but there was no reply, so I am sad about it. If I got a letter from you, I would be very happy. Your mother ⓐ<u>fell</u> ill, and I'm going to visit her in the hospital with some money and food. I'll go there with our middle son while the oldest looks after the youngest.

I ⓑ<u>had</u> two workers prepare our field and plant seeds for 150,000 lire. I voted for the DC. The PCI lost so many seats that it almost seems ⓒ <u>alive</u>. But whether one or the other wins, it's the same. Nothing changes for us poor people. We worked yesterday, and we will work again tomorrow.

We picked lots of olives from our olive trees this year. I ⓓ<u>hired</u> a man whose sons are good workers. He knocked the olives down, and his two sons helped him, picking them up from the ground. I paid him 27,000 lire for the work. I spent 12,000 more for the olive press. I got enough oil to fill a large pot and a small one. I can sell it at a price of 1,300 lire a liter.

My love, my heart thinks of you as Christmas is coming. (A)<u>As you are not with me, I'm not so happy.</u> We all miss you so much.

I'm sending you a big hug from me and our three little kids. Goodbye, dear love. My heart is yours, joined to you as our two rings are ⓔ<u>joined</u>.

20 위 글의 밑줄 친 ⓐ~ⓔ 중, 문맥상 단어의 쓰임이 적절하지 않은 것은? (3점)

① ⓐ fell   ② ⓑ had
③ ⓒ alive   ④ ⓓ hired
⑤ ⓔ joined

21 위 글의 내용을 바르게 이해한 학생은? (4점)

① Tom: There were only two kids in the family.
② Sam: The wife received the letter from the husband.
③ John: It cost 1,300 lire per a liter for pressing the olives.
④ Mary: The man hired by the wife got paid 12,000 lire for the work.
⑤ Jack: The wife thought her life would be the same whether the DC or the PCI would win.

22 위 글의 밑줄 친 (A)를 if절을 사용하여 표현하시오. (단, 〈조건〉에 맞게 작성할 것.) (4점)

> **조건**
> • 반드시 if절을 사용할 것.
> • 단어의 형태를 적절히 변형할 것.

→ _____

23 다음 글의 흐름으로 보아, 주어진 문장이 들어가기에 가장 적절한 곳은? (4점)

> It was written in 1973 by a woman whose husband was far away.

This letter shows how people got over these difficulties. (A) She lived in Sicily, an Italian island, while her husband worked in Germany. (B) At the time, more than 5% of the people in Italy could not read or write, and she was one of them. (C) This letter was discovered by Sicilian writer Gesualdo Bufalino. (D) Here's how he translated the pictures into words. (E)

① (A)   ② (B)   ③ (C)   ④ (D)   ⑤ (E)

[24~25] 다음 글을 읽고 물음에 답하시오.

Speaking to family members or friends in a foreign country is rather easy and simple today. But before the days of phones and the Internet, it was not that easy. People just sent a letter and waited for a reply for weeks. And it was a lot harder if they couldn't read or write.
This letter shows how people got over these difficulties. It was written in 1973 by a woman whose husband was far away. She lived in Sicily, an Italian island, while her husband worked in Germany. At the time, more than 5% of the people in Italy could not read or write and she was one of them. This letter was discovered by Sicilian writer Gesualdo Bufalino.
Here's how he translated the pictures into words.

24 Which question CAN'T you answer from the passage above? (4점)

① Is it easy to get in touch with family members in a foreign country today?

② What was a lot harder if people couldn't read or write?

③ When was the letter written by the woman?

④ How long didn't the woman see her husband?

⑤ Who translated the pictures into words?

25 위 글의 밑줄 친 'a lot' 대신 쓸 수 없는 것은? (3점)

① still　　② even　　③ very

④ far　　⑤ much

[26~27] 다음 글을 읽고 물음에 답하시오.

My love, my heart thinks of you as Christmas is coming. As you are not with me, I'm not so happy. We all miss you so much.
I'm sending you big hug from me and our three little kids. Goodbye, dear love. My heart is yours, joined to you as our two rings are.

26 위 글의 밑줄 친 부분과 뜻이 같은 문장은? (4점)

① If you are with me, I am so happy.

② If you are with me, I will be so happy.

③ If you are with me, I would be so happy.

④ If you were with me, I would be so happy.

⑤ If you were with me, I will be so happy.

27 위 글에 드러난 'I'의 심경으로 가장 적절한 것은? (3점)

① disappointed　② sad　　③ angry

④ nervous　　⑤ bored

28 다음 글을 읽고 답할 수 없는 질문은? (4점)

I had two workers prepare our field and plant seeds for 150,000 lire. I voted for the DC. The PCI lost so many seats that it almost seems dead. But whether one or the other wins, it's the same. Nothing changes for us poor people. We worked yesterday, and we will work again tomorrow.

① 왜 PCI는 죽은 것처럼 보였을까?

② 글쓴이는 어느 정당에 투표했을까?

③ 글쓴이는 몇 명의 일꾼을 시켰는가?

④ DC는 얼마나 많은 의석을 확보했는가?

⑤ 글쓴이가 얼마나 많은 돈을 일꾼에게 지불했을까?

◎ 선택형 문항의 답안은 컴퓨터용 수정 싸인펜을 사용하여 OMR 답안지에 바르게 표기하시오.
◎ 서술형 문제는 답을 답안지에 반드시 검정 볼펜으로 쓰시오.
◎ 총 30문항 100점 만점입니다. 문항별 배점은 각 문항에 표시되어 있습니다.

[경기 ○○중]

01 다음 영어 사전의 뜻풀이가 의미하는 단어로 가장 적절한 것은? (3점)

> <English Dictionary>
> ⓐ _____
> needed in order to do something

① complete ② false
③ necessary ④ possible
⑤ public

[전북 ○○중]

[2~3] 다음 대화를 읽고 물음에 답하시오.

A: Seho, the book club day is ⓐjust one week away.
B: Right, Minji. I'm proud that we've collected so ⓑmany interesting books to give away.
A: Now, let's prepare some gifts for visitors. Do you have any good ideas?
B: ⓒHow about making bookmarks?
A: Great idea! Let's write cheerful messages on them, too.
B: Okay, ⓓwhich do you prefer, making the bookmarks or writing the messages?
A: Actually, ⓔI love writing. I'd like to make the bookmarks.
B: No problem. I'll write the cheerful messages.
A: I'm sure they will love our bookmarks.

02 위 대화의 ⓐ~ⓔ 중 흐름상 어색한 것은? (3점)

① ⓐ ② ⓑ ③ ⓒ ④ ⓓ ⑤ ⓔ

03 위 대화에서 세호가 만들려고 하는 것은? (2점)

① 기분 좋은 메시지
② 화사한 꽃무늬 책갈피
③ 독서의 날 준비 메시지
④ 사랑에 관한 글귀
⑤ 음료 무료 쿠폰

[충북 ○○중]

[4~5] 다음 대화를 읽고 물음에 답하시오.

G: Junha, what are you doing with jeans?
B: I'm making a pencil case for you.
G: That's great! What are you going to draw on it?
B: Sujin, which do you (A)_____, pandas or cats?
G: I (A)_____ cats. They're lovely.
B: Okay. Let me draw a lovely cat on this pencil case.
G: Thanks! I can't wait for it!

*G: Sujin B: Junha

04 위 대화의 내용과 일치하는 것은? (4점)

① Junha is using old shirts to make something.
② Junha's gift is for his father.
③ Sujin likes cats better than pandas.
④ Sujin is going to draw a cat on the pencil case.
⑤ Sujin is not very interested in Junha's gift.

05 위 대화의 빈칸 (A)에 공통으로 들어갈 단어로 가장 적절한 것은? (2점)

① introduce ② make ③ find
④ raise ⑤ prefer

06 다음 대화의 내용과 일치하지 <u>않는</u> 것을 고르면? (3점)

> G: Why don't we make something with jean pockets?
>
> B: Great! What shall we make?
>
> G: Which do you prefer, a pocket board or a cell phone holder?
>
> B: I prefer a cell phone holder. It'll be easier to make. And I hate spending too much time making things.
>
> G: Okay. Let's make a cute cell phone holder together.
>
> * G: 소녀, B: 소년

① 소녀는 청바지 주머니로 어떤 것을 만들고 싶어 한다.

② 소년은 핸드폰 주머니를 만들고 싶어 한다.

③ 소년은 만들기 쉬운 것을 제작하고 싶어 한다.

④ 소년은 많은 시간을 들여서 뭔가를 만드는 것을 좋아한다.

⑤ 소녀는 소년의 말에 동의하고 같이 핸드폰 주머니를 만들기로 한다.

07 다음 중 <u>어색한</u> 대화를 고르면? (2점)

① G: Which do you like better, cloth dolls or digital artwork?

　B: I like digital artwork better. Actually, I do like dolls much.

② G: Which do you prefer, paper drawings or wood block figures?

　B: I prefer wood block figures.

　G: Me, too. Let's go look at some of them.

③ G: Which do you prefer, folding paper or making clothes?

　B: I prefer folding paper. It's fun and a great way to relax.

④ G: Junha, what are you doing with these jeans?

　B: I'm making a pencil case for you.

　G: That's great!

⑤ G: Hey! What are you going to draw on the case?

　B: Which do you prefer, pandas or cats?

　G: I prefer cats. They're lovely.

　B: Okay. Let me draw a lovely cat on this case.

08 다음 문장 중 어법상 <u>잘못된</u> 것은? (4점)

① The more books we share, the more we learn.

② The deeper we go under the sea, the darker it gets.

③ The faster we go down, the more excited we get.

④ The much money we have, the much money we want.

⑤ The harder you exercise, the stronger you become.

09 다음 밑줄 친 부분 중 나머지 넷과 그 쓰임이 <u>다른</u> 것은? (3점)

① I remember <u>flying</u> kites in my childhood.

② My brother loves <u>shopping</u> for clothes.

③ <u>Working</u> mothers worry about their children.

④ <u>Working</u> too much made me sad and stressed.

⑤ Grandparents enjoy <u>buying</u> presents for their grandchildren.

10 다음 중 대화의 흐름이 <u>어색한</u> 것은? (3점)

① A: Alice met David last Friday.

　B: No. It was yesterday that Alice met David.

② A: Seho likes New York the most.

　B: No. It is Paris that Seho likes the most.

③ A: Junha walks to school every day.

　B: No. It is Minji that walks to school every day.

④ A: My sister made me a chocolate cake.

　B: No. It was your brother that made you a chocolate cake.

⑤ A: Minho met Tony in the shopping mall.

　B: No. It was Minho that met Tony in the shopping mall.

11 다음 문장을 〈보기〉와 같이 바꿔 쓰시오. (4점)

> 보기
> • If you practice harder, you can run faster.
> → The harder you practice, the faster you can run.

> • If you act more kindly, you can have more friends.

→ ＿＿＿＿＿＿＿＿＿＿＿＿＿＿＿＿

12 다음 밑줄 친 as의 쓰임과 같은 것은? (4점)

> • Most people think of books <u>as</u> traditional paper books.

① Do <u>as</u> we do.

② I respect him <u>as</u> a doctor.

③ He told us stories <u>as</u> we went along.

④ I don't like her <u>as</u> she always tells lies.

⑤ She became more silent <u>as</u> she got older.

13 다음 주어진 문장을 'It ~ that 강조 구문'을 이용하여 밑줄 친 부분(a ring)을 강조하는 문장으로 바꿔 쓰시오. (4점)

> • Sam gave <u>a ring</u> to her yesterday.

→ ＿＿＿＿＿＿＿＿＿＿＿＿＿＿＿＿

14 다음 〈보기〉와 같이 옳은 답을 강조하는 문장을 완성하시오. (4점)

> 보기
> A: Edison invented the telephone, right?
> B: No, it was Bell that invented the telephone.

A: Nick teaches French in Daesung Middle School, right?

B: No, it is ＿＿＿＿＿＿＿＿＿＿＿＿＿.

15 다음 문장을 원형부정사를 사용하여 주어진 우리말 표현을 영어로 옮기시오. (5점)

(1) 나는 그에게 내 자전거를 타는 것을 허락했다.

　(let)

→ I ＿＿＿＿＿＿＿＿＿＿＿＿＿＿＿.

(2) 그는 그들에게 구명조끼를 입도록 했다.

　(make, life jackets)

→ He ＿＿＿＿＿＿＿＿＿＿＿＿＿＿.

[16~17] 다음 글을 읽고 물음에 답하시오.

This tiny book is really important to people in my town. It provides both the information and the tools necessary to make clean drinking water.
It is called the Drinkable Book. You cannot actually drink the book, but you can use it as a filter. Simply tear out a page and pour dirty water on it. As the water goes through the page, it changes into clean drinking water. ⓐIt is the filtered water that you can drink.
Thanks to this amazing book, we can (A)_____ many children (B)_____ from diseases caused by poor and dirty water. Clean water is (C)_____ for the survival and development of children.

16 위 글의 빈칸 (A)~(C)에 들어갈 말이 순서대로 나열된 것은?
(4점)

	(A)	(B)	(C)
①	save	dying	indifferent
②	have	dying	essential
③	save	dying	essential
④	have	dyeing	basic
⑤	save	dyeing	important

17 위 글의 밑줄 친 ⓐ 부분과 어법상 쓰임이 같은 것은? (3점)

① It is true that he loves Jane.

② It is certain that he will pass the test.

③ It was you that helped me at that time.

④ It was strange that he didn't attend the meeting.

⑤ It was clear that she was talented in many ways.

[18~20] 다음 글을 읽고 물음에 답하시오.

This is the most amazing book that I have ever seen. After you finish reading this book, ⓐplant it and ⓑwater it. You will see new leaves Ⓐgrow on the book. In some bookstores in my town, you can see a copy of this book Ⓑproduce new leaves.
The secret is that the book has ⓒseeds in each page. (A)These tiny seeds change the book into a tree. This book was made by a small children's book publisher in Argentina. Though the ⓓcompany does not print this book ⓔanymore, this special project makes us think about where books come from.

18 위 글의 밑줄 친 Ⓐ와 Ⓑ의 형태로 알맞은 것은? (3점)

① grow – to produce

② to grow – to produce

③ growing – to produce

④ growing – producing

⑤ to grow – producing

19 위 글의 밑줄 친 단어 ⓐ~ⓔ의 우리말 뜻이 올바르게 짝지어진 것은? (2점)

① ⓐplant – 식물   ② ⓑwater – 물

③ ⓒseeds – 씨앗   ④ ⓓcompany – 친구

⑤ ⓔanymore – 언젠가

20 위 글의 밑줄 친 문장 (A)를 조건에 맞게 바꿔 쓰시오. (4점)

> **조건**
> • These tiny seeds를 강조하는 문장으로 만드시오.

→ _____

[21~23] 다음 글을 읽고 물음에 답하시오.

The Tree-Book-Tree Project
This is the most amazing book that I have ever seen. After you finish reading this book, plant it and water it. You will see new leaves ⓐgrowing on the book. In some bookstores in my town, you can see a copy of this book producing new leaves. The secret is ⓑthat the book has seeds in each page. (A)These tiny seeds change the book into a tree. This book was made by a small children's book publisher in Argentina. Though the company does not print this book anymore, this special project makes us think about ⓒwhere books come from.
These are just a few of the unique books you can find. ⓓWhat other unique do you want books to make? What special project would you like to do with the books? The bigger your imagination is, ⓔ the more wonderful your books will become.

21 위 글의 ⓐ~ⓔ 중, 문장 내 어법의 쓰임이 적절하지 않은 것은? (3점)

① ⓐ ② ⓑ ③ ⓒ ④ ⓓ ⑤ ⓔ

22 위 글의 내용과 일치하지 않는 것은? (4점)

① People can grow plants using the book.
② There are some seeds in each page of the book.
③ The book was made by a small children's book publisher.
④ As the book is popular worldwide, the publisher still prints more books.
⑤ The book helps us think of trees, the origin of books.

23 위 글의 밑줄 친 (A)를 아래 〈보기〉의 의미가 되도록 변형하시오. (단, 〈조건〉에 맞게 작성할 것.) (4점)

┌─ 보기 ──────────────────────┐
│ • 책을 나무로 변화시키는 것은 바로 이 아주 작│
│   은 씨앗들이다. │
└────────────────────────────┘

┌─ 조건 ──────────────────────┐
│ • 반드시 단어를 추가할 것. │
└────────────────────────────┘

→ _____

[24~26] 다음 글을 읽고 물음에 답하시오.

This tiny book is really important to people in my town. It provides ⓐ_____ the information and the tools necessary to make clean drinking water.
It is called ⓑ_____. You cannot actually drink the book, but you can use it as a filter. Simply tear out a page and pour dirty water on it. As the water goes through the page, it changes into clean drinking water. It is this filtered water ⓒ_____ you can drink. This is possible because the book is made of special filter paper. This amazing book saves the lives of many children from diseases ⓓ_____ come from dirty water.

24 위 글의 빈칸 ⓐ에 들어갈 적절한 단어는? (3점)

① whether ② both ③ either
④ neither ⑤ not only

25 위 글의 빈칸 ⓑ에 들어갈 적절한 표현은? (3점)

① books travel
② the drinkable book
③ the tree-book-tree project
④ the book-sharing project
⑤ the unique book

26 위 글의 빈칸 ⓒ와 ⓓ에 공통으로 들어갈 한 단어를 쓰시오.

(2점)

→ _____

[강원 ㅇㅇ중]

[27~29] 다음 글을 읽고 물음에 답하시오.

I found this old book on a park bench yesterday. A note on the cover read, "Free Book! Take me home and read me!" Actually, this book had an ID number and was registered on a website. When I entered the number online, I found out that the book had traveled to many countries and that a number of readers in different countries had read it before me. How was that possible?

There is a book-sharing project. First, register your book online and get an ID number. Next, leave it in a public place. When the next reader finds your book and reports back to the website, you can check where your book is. This way, the whole world can become a big library. The more books we _____, the more we _____.

27 위 글의 제목으로 가장 알맞은 것은?

(3점)

① Free Book!　　② Books Travel!

③ Lost Books!　　④ A Big Library!

⑤ Imagine Books!

28 위 글의 내용과 일치하지 <u>않는</u> 것은?

(4점)

① 글쓴이가 공원 벤치에서 발견한 것은 낡은 책이었다.

② 글쓴이가 발견한 책에는 ID 번호가 있었다.

③ 글쓴이가 발견한 책은 많은 나라를 여행하고 있었다.

④ 도서관에서 책을 등록하고 ID 번호를 얻을 수 있다.

⑤ 책을 공유하는 프로젝트로 전 세계가 하나의 큰 도서관이 될 수 있다.

29 위 글의 빈칸에 들어갈 알맞은 말로 짝지어진 것은?　　(4점)

The more books we (A)_____, the more we (B)_____.

	(A)	(B)
①	share	learn
②	read	think
③	register	travel
④	buy	learn
⑤	find	think

[충북 ㅇㅇ중]

30 다음 'A book-sharing project'에 관한 내용과 일치하지 <u>않는</u> 것은?　　(4점)

Let your book travel
with a book-sharing project!

First, register your book online and get an ID number. Next, leave it in a public place. When the next reader finds your book and reports back to the website, you can check where your book is. This way, the whole world can become a big library.

① As your book is registered, it has an ID number.

② Your book is left anywhere that you want.

③ Someone picks up your book and reports to the website.

④ You can locate your book after next reader reports back to the website.

⑤ The world can be a huge place to read through this project.

◎ 선택형 문항의 답안은 컴퓨터용 수정 싸인펜을 사용
하여 OMR 답안지에 바르게 표기하시오.
◎ 서술형 문제는 답을 답안지에 반드시 검정 볼펜으
로 쓰시오.
◎ 총 26문항 100점 만점입니다. 문항별 배점은 각
문항에 표시되어 있습니다.

① Preparing for Book Club Day
② Making Plans for the Visitors
③ Good Messages for the Bookmarks
④ How to Make Bookmarks
⑤ Some Ideas for the Club Day

[경기 ○○중]

01 다음 중 단어의 영영 풀이가 <u>어색한</u> 것은?   (3점)

① produce: to make or grow something
② disease: an illness that affects people and animals
③ tool: the ability to think of new things in your mind
④ necessary: needed in order to achieve a particular result
⑤ register: to put information, especially your name, into an official list or record

[경기 ○○중]

03 다음 대화의 밑줄 친 부분과 바꾸어 쓸 수 있는 것은?   (3점)

A: <u>Which do you prefer</u>, a pocket board or a cell phone holder?
B: I prefer a cell phone holder. It'll be easier to make.

① Do you have
② Do you mean
③ What do you see
④ What do you think
⑤ Which do you like better

[광주 ○○중]

02 Which one is the best title for this conversation?   (4점)

A: Seho, the book club day is just one week away.
B: Right, Minji. I'm proud that we've collected so many interesting books to give away.
A: Now, let's prepare some gifts for visitors. Do you have any good ideas?
B: How about making bookmarks?
A: Great idea! Let's write cheerful messages on them, too.
B: Okay. Which do you prefer, making the bookmarks or writing the messages?
A: Actually, I hate writing. I'd like to make the bookmarks.
B: No problem. I'll write the cheerful messages.
A: I'm sure they will love our bookmarks.

광주 ○○중

04 What are A and B going to do after this conversation?   (3점)

A: Why don't we make something with jean pockets?
B: Great! What shall we make?
A: Which do you prefer, a pocket board or a cell phone holder?
B: I prefer a cell phone holder. It'll be easier to make. And I hate spending too much time making things.
A: Okay. Let's make a cute cell phone holder.

① buy a new cell phone for them
② make a shoulder bag with old jeans
③ draw some pictures on the cell phone
④ collect some old cell phones
⑤ make a cell phone holder

05 다음 문장이 자연스러운 대화가 되도록 ⓐ~ⓔ를 바르게 배열한 것은? (4점)

ⓐ Great! What kind of bag are we going to make?
ⓑ Why don't we make a bag with old jeans?
ⓒ Okay. Let's make a shoulder bag together.
ⓓ I prefer a shoulder bag. Actually, I hate holding things in my hands.
ⓔ Which do you prefer, a shoulder bag or a hand bag?

① ⓑ - ⓐ - ⓓ - ⓒ - ⓔ
② ⓑ - ⓐ - ⓔ - ⓓ - ⓒ
③ ⓑ - ⓐ - ⓔ - ⓒ - ⓓ
④ ⓔ - ⓓ - ⓒ - ⓑ - ⓐ
⑤ ⓔ - ⓓ - ⓒ - ⓐ - ⓑ

06 다음 대화의 빈칸에 들어가기에 적절하지 <u>않은</u> 것은? (3점)

A: Which do you prefer, making masks or making food art?
B: I like both, but it is making food art that I prefer.
A: Why is that?
B: _____

① I like to draw something.
② I love making something delicious.
③ Making masks takes too much time.
④ I am interested in making funny masks.
⑤ I already made some cute masks last week.

07 다음 우리말에 맞게, 주어진 어구를 이용하여 영작하시오. (6점)

> **조건**
> • v-ing 구문을 사용할 것.

(1) 밤에 오토바이를 타는 것은 위험하다. (at night, a motorcycle, ride)

→ _____

(2) 온라인으로 쇼핑하는 사람들의 수가 늘어나고 있다. (is growing, the number of, shop online, people)

→ _____

08 다음 대화의 흐름에 맞게 (A)~(E)를 알맞은 순서로 배열한 것은? (4점)

A: Junha, what are you doing with jeans?
B: _____
A: _____
B: _____
A: _____
B: _____
A: Thanks. I can't wait for it!

(A) Okay, let me draw a lovely cat on it.
(B) I'm making a pencil case for you.
(C) I prefer cats. They are lovely.
(D) That's great! What are you going to draw on it?
(E) Which do you prefer, pandas or cats?

① (D)-(B)-(E)-(C)-(A)
② (B)-(C)-(E)-(A)-(D)
③ (B)-(D)-(E)-(C)-(A)
④ (D)-(B)-(E)-(A)-(C)
⑤ (B)-(A)-(E)-(C)-(D)

09 다음 글의 밑줄 친 부분을 영어로 가장 알맞게 바꾼 것은?

(4점)

> These are just a few of the unique books you can find. What other unique books do you want to make? What special project would you like to do with the books? 여러분의 상상이 크면 클수록, 여러분의 책은 더 훌륭해질 것입니다.

① When your imagination is big, your books will become wonderful.

② The bigger your imagination is, your books will become wonderful.

③ The bigger your imagination is, the more wonderful your books will become.

④ If your imagination is the bigger, your books will become the more wonderful.

⑤ As your imagination is the bigger, your books will become the more wonderful.

10 다음 밑줄 친 동사의 쓰임과 어법상 같은 것은?

(3점)

> • Though the company does not print this book anymore, this special project <u>makes</u> us think about where books come from.

① He <u>made</u> us a meal.

② She <u>made</u> me feel happy.

③ He <u>made</u> her a new dress.

④ I <u>made</u> myself a cup of tea.

⑤ She has <u>made</u> several movies.

11 다음 중 어법상 <u>어색한</u> 부분이 있는 것은?

(4점)

① The higher we go up, the farther we see.

② The faster we go down, the more excited we get.

③ The harder you exercise, the stronger you become.

④ The much money we have, the much money we want.

⑤ The deeper we go under the sea, the darker it gets.

12 다음 빈칸 (A), (B)에 들어갈 말이 바르게 짝지어진 것은? (4점)

> • The more books you read, (A)_____.
> • (B)_____, the darker it gets.

① (A): the wiser you become

   (B): The deeper we go under the sea

② (A): the wiser you become

   (B): The deepest we go under the sea

③ (A): you become the wiser

   (B): The lower we go under the sea

④ (A): the less wiser you become

   (B): The deeper we go under the sea

⑤ (A): the less wiser you become

   (B): The lower we go under the sea

13 다음 중 어법상 옳지 <u>않은</u> 것은?

(4점)

① It is pizza that Jack likes the most.

② It is walk that Tom and John to school.

③ It is at the library that they read books.

④ It is David that goes deep under the sea.

⑤ It is in the morning that he will meet her.

[14~15] 다음 글을 읽고 물음에 답하시오.

I found this old book on a park bench yesterday. A note on the cover read, "Free Book! @Take me home and ⓑread me!" Actually, this book had an ID number and ©registered on a website. When I entered the number online, I found out that the book ⓓhad traveled to many countries and that a number of readers in different countries ⓔhad read it before me. How was that possible?

14 위 글의 밑줄 친 @~ⓔ의 동사 중 어법상 잘못 쓰인 것은?
(3점)

① @   ② ⓑ   ③ ©   ④ ⓓ   ⑤ ⓔ

15 위 글의 바로 뒤에 연결될 내용으로 알맞은 것은? (4점)

① 책이 여행하는 과정
② 세계의 여러 가지 책
③ 책이 만들어지는 과정
④ 책 만들기 프로젝트에 관한 내용
⑤ 책의 역사

16 다음 글을 읽고 빈칸에 들어갈 말로 가장 적당한 것은? (4점)

This is the most amazing book that I have ever seen. After you finish reading this book, plant it and water it. You will see new leaves growing on the book. In some bookstores in my town, you can see a copy of this book producing new leaves.

The secret is that the book has seeds in each page. It is these tiny seeds that change the book into a tree. This special project gives _____ back to us.

① sun   ② soil   ③ light
④ trees   ⑤ smoke

[17~18] 다음 글을 읽고 물음에 답하시오.

I found this old book on a park bench yesterday. (A) A note on the cover read, "Free Book! Take me home and read me!" (B) Actually, this book had an ID number and was registered on a website. (C) When I entered the number online, I found out that the book had traveled to many countries and that a number of readers in different countries had read it before me. How was that possible?
(D) There is a book-sharing project. First, register your book online and get an ID number. (E) When the next reader finds your book and reports back to the website, you can check where your book is. This way, the whole world can become a big library.

17 위 글의 (A)~(E) 중 다음의 문장이 들어갈 곳으로 가장 알맞은 것은? (4점)

Next, leave it in a public place.

① (A)   ② (B)   ③ (C)   ④ (D)   ⑤ (E)

18 위 글을 읽고 질문에 답할 수 없는 것은? (4점)

① Where does the next reader live in?
② Where did the writer find the old book?
③ Where can we check the location of our book?
④ What was the message on a note on the book cover?
⑤ What should we do first to join the book-sharing project?

[19~20] 다음 글을 읽고 물음에 답하시오.

This is the most amazing book that I have ever seen. (A) After you finish ⓐread this book, plant it and water it. (B) You will see new leaves growing on the book. (C) The secret is that the book has seeds in each page. (D) This book was ⓑmake by a small children's book publisher in Argentina. (E) Though the company does not print this book anymore, this special project makes us ⓒthink about where books come from.

19 위 글의 흐름으로 보아, 다음 주어진 문장이 들어가기에 가장 적절한 곳은? (4점)

> These tiny seeds change the book into a tree.

① (A)　② (B)　③ (C)　④ (D)　⑤ (E)

20 위 글의 밑줄 친 ⓐ~ⓒ에 들어갈 단어의 형태가 적절한 것으로 짝지어진 것은? (4점)

	ⓐ	ⓑ	ⓒ
①	reading	made	think
②	reading	made	thinking
③	reading	making	thinking
④	to read	made	think
⑤	to read	making	thinking

[21~22] 다음 글을 읽고 물음에 답하시오.

This tiny book is really important to people in my town. It provides both the information and the tools necessary to make clean drinking water. It is called the Drinkable Book. You cannot actually drink the book, but you can use it as a filter. Simply tear out a page and ⓐpour dirty water on it. As the water goes through the page, it changes into ⓑclean drinking water. It is this filtered water that you can drink. This is ⓒpossible because the book is made of special filter paper. This amazing book ⓓtakes the lives of many children from diseases that come from ⓔdirty water.

21 위 글의 제목으로 가장 적절한 것은? (4점)

① How to Get Energy by Using a Book
② A Unique Book Used Not Just for Reading
③ The Ways to Read Books Wisely
④ The Process of Making Clean Water
⑤ The Effects of Dirty Water on Our Body

22 위 글의 밑줄 친 ⓐ~ⓔ 중에서 문맥상 낱말의 쓰임이 적절하지 <u>않은</u> 것은? (4점)

① ⓐ　② ⓑ　③ ⓒ　④ ⓓ　⑤ ⓔ

[23~24] 다음 글을 읽고 물음에 답하시오.

The Drinkable Book
This tiny book is really important to people in my town. ⓐIt provides both the information and the tools (A)[necessary / necessarily] to make clean drinking water.
ⓑIt is called the Drinkable Book. You cannot actually drink the book, but you can use ⓒit as a filter. Simply tear out a page of ⓓthe book and pour dirty water on ⓔit. As the water goes through the pages, it (B)[changes into / changes dirty water into] clean drinking water. It is this filtered water that you can drink. This is possible because the book is made of special filter paper. This amazing book saves the lives of many children from diseases that (C)[come from / comes from] dirty water.

23 위 글의 밑줄 친 ⓐ~ⓔ 중 가리키는 대상이 <u>다른</u> 하나는? (4점)

① ⓐ ② ⓑ ③ ⓒ ④ ⓓ ⑤ ⓔ

24 위 글의 괄호 (A), (B), (C) 안에서 어법에 맞는 어구로 적절한 것은? (4점)

   (A)   (B)   (C)

① necessary – changes into – come from

② necessary – changes into – comes from

③ necessary – changes dirty water into – come from

④ necessarily – changes into – comes from

⑤ necessarily – changes dirty water into – comes from

25 다음 글의 빈칸에 들어갈 말로 가장 적절한 것은? (4점)

Books Travel!
I found this old book on a park bench yesterday. A note on the cover read, "Free Book! Take me home and read me!" Actually, this book had an ID number and was registered on a website. When I entered the number online, I found out that the book had traveled to many countries and that a number of readers in different countries had read it before me. How was that possible?
There is a book-sharing project. First, register your book online and get an ID number. Next, leave it in a public place. When the next reader finds your book and reports back to the website, you can check where your book is. This way, _____.
The more books we share, the more we learn.

① you can read more books

② the whole world can become a big library

③ the online book market gets bigger and wider

④ the whole world can communicate more easily

⑤ all the people in the world want to have more books

26 다음 문장을 〈보기〉와 같이 바꿔 쓰시오. (4점)

보기
• If you practice harder, you can type faster.
→ The harder you practice, the faster you can type.

• If it gets hotter, we need more water.

→ _____

3학년 영어 2학기 기말고사(7과) 1회

문항수 : 선택형(22문항) 서술형(3문항) | 20 . . .

◎ 선택형 문항의 답안은 컴퓨터용 수정 싸인펜을 사용하여 OMR 답안지에 바르게 표기하시오.
◎ 서술형 문제는 답을 답안지에 반드시 검정 볼펜으로 쓰시오.
◎ 총 25문항 100점 만점입니다. 문항별 배점은 각 문항에 표시되어 있습니다.

[경기 ○○중]

01 다음 영어 사전의 뜻풀이가 의미하는 단어로 가장 적절한 것은? (4점)

> <English Dictionary>
> ⓥ_____
> to make sure that someone is doing what they should do

① check up on   ② get over
③ give away   ④ make sense
⑤ slow down

[전북 ○○중]

[2~4] 다음 대화를 읽고 물음에 답하시오.

Alex: Big Mouth's Show is really cool. How do you feel about it?
Somi: Well, I don't think it's that great.
Alex: Come on. I love Mr. Big Mouth. He always makes me laugh out loud.
Somi: He's funny, but don't believe everything he says.
Alex: All right. Oh, look at his photo of an octopus. He said it lives in a tree.
Somi: (A)_____
Alex: He took the photo when it was climbing the tree. I don't think he's lying. It's a great photo.
Somi: I don't agree with you. It's a (B)_____ photo. An octopus can't live out of the sea.

02 위 대화의 빈칸 (A)에 들어갈 적절한 표현은? (3점)

① I agree with you.
② That's a great idea.
③ I think so.
④ Have you ever heard about it?
⑤ It doesn't make sense.

03 위 대화의 내용과 일치하지 <u>않는</u> 것은? (3점)

① Alex는 Big Mouth 쇼가 멋지다고 생각한다.
② Somi도 Big Mouth 쇼가 훌륭하다고 생각한다.
③ Alex와 Somi는 Mr. Big Mouth가 웃긴다고 생각한다.
④ Alex는 문어 사진을 보고 있는 중이다.
⑤ Alex는 문어가 나무에서 살 수 있다고 생각한다.

04 위 대화의 빈칸 (B)에 들어갈 적절한 단어는? (3점)

① fake   ② real   ③ nice
④ old   ⑤ great

[충북 ○○중]

05 자연스러운 대화가 되도록 ⓐ~ⓔ를 바르게 배열한 것은? (4점)

> ⓐ: I think it's very touching. It's the best drama of this year, I think.
> ⓑ: Come on. Why do you think so?
> ⓒ: I don't agree. It's not a good drama.
> ⓓ: How do you feel about the drama?
> ⓔ: It doesn't seem real.

① ⓓ-ⓔ-ⓐ-ⓑ-ⓒ   ② ⓓ-ⓔ-ⓑ-ⓐ-ⓒ
③ ⓓ-ⓔ-ⓑ-ⓒ-ⓐ   ④ ⓓ-ⓐ-ⓒ-ⓑ-ⓔ
⑤ ⓓ-ⓐ-ⓑ-ⓒ-ⓔ

06 다음 대화를 읽고 내용의 흐름상 빈칸에 Somi가 할 말로 가장 적절한 것은? (4점)

> Alex: Big Mouth's Show is really cool. How do you feel about it?
> Somi: Well, I don't think it's that great.
> Alex: Come on. I love Mr. Big Mouth. He always makes me laugh out loud.
> Somi: He's funny, but don't believe everything he says.
> Alex: All right. Oh, look at his photo of a Spaghetti Tree. He said noodles can grow on a tree.
> Somi: It doesn't make sense.
> Alex: He really took the photo. I don't think he's lying. It's a great photo.
> Somi: I don't agree with you. It's a fake photo. Noodles can't grow on any trees. Let's search for _____ _____.

① the evidence that a Spaghetti Tree is fake

② the recipe for making spaghetti

③ the place we can buy the tree

④ the way we can grow the tree

⑤ the photos which include as many Spaghetti Trees as possible

07 다음 중 빈칸에 들어갈 어휘가 같은 것끼리 짝지어진 것은? (5점)

> ⓐ: We'll go on a field trip _____ this situation gets better.
> ⓑ: It makes no difference _____ you are a boy or a girl.
> ⓒ: I understand _____ you don't want to talk about the event.
> ⓓ: I'm not sure _____ or not I will do well on the final exam.

① ⓐ, ⓒ, ⓓ   ② ⓐ, ⓑ   ③ ⓑ, ⓓ
④ ⓒ, ⓓ   ⑤ ⓐ, ⓑ, ⓒ

08 다음 문장을 간접화법으로 바꾸어 쓰시오. (단, 9 단어를 이용해 빈칸을 완성하여 쓰시오.) (5점)

> I will meet your sister tomorrow.   Where are you going to meet her?

> • Kate said to Tom, "I will meet your sister tomorrow."

→ Kate told Tom _____.

09 다음 문장들을 간접화법으로 잘못 바꾼 것은? (4점)

① He said, "I'm waiting for Tami."
　→ He said that he was waiting for Tami.

② She said, "I am very depressed now."
　→ She said that she was very depressed then.

③ She said to me, "My grandma died three years ago."
　→ She told me that my grandma died three years before.

④ He said to me, "The early bird catches the worm."
　→ He told me the early bird catches the worm.

⑤ She said, "I saw Tami here yesterday."
　→ She said she had seen Tami there the day before.

[10~12] 다음 글을 읽고 물음에 답하시오.

In October 2016, stories about scary clowns shook schools across the Washington area, but Danina Garcia-Fuller's students didn't believe them a bit.

"Some people were getting scared because they saw things on social media," said Patricia Visoso, one of Garcia-Fuller's students. "But they never checked up on who was saying this." The stories were actually made by teenagers, not by major newspapers or TV stations. They offered no hard evidence that clowns really were trying to attack students. The story turned out to be a complete lie.

"I think a lot of people just look at one thing and believe it's true," Patricia's classmate Ivy-Brooks said. "It's really important to look at the right sources and (A)[paying / to pay] attention to what is real and what is fake."

Like Garcia-Fuller's students, many teenagers in America are learning to think critically about information they're seeing in the news and on the Internet. This skill is getting more important these days as stories can spread very fast, and anyone can make a website full of false information.

Garcia-Fuller said she was teaching her students how to tell fake news from real news.
"One of the first steps is to slow down. If a story or a photo seems too good to be true, stop and think: Is there any evidence that supports (B)[what the writer says / what does the writer say]? And where is this coming from?"

Garcia-Fuller's students also learn how to tell fact from opinion in the news. "Opinions are good to read," said 15-year-old McKenzie Campbell, "but you also have to check if they are based on facts."

Garcia-Fuller also said sometimes it can be very hard to be a smart news reader. She tests her students with a website that (C)[appears with / appears to] provide information on an animal called a tree octopus. The site is full of information on this animal, along with a few unclear photos of octopuses in trees. But like the story of scary clowns, it's totally made up.

The lesson, Garcia-Fuller tells her students, is to "check the information you're seeing once more carefully" and to "question everything, even things that I say."

10 위 글에 관한 질문의 답으로 어색한 것은? (4점)

> Q: What do you need to be a smart news reader?
> A: _____

① To find out hard evidence.

② To deny the whole things that your teacher says all the time.

③ To think critically.

④ To find out what is real and what is fake.

⑤ To check if the news is based on facts.

11 위 글의 괄호 (A), (B), (C) 안에서 알맞은 말이 바르게 짝지어진 것은? (4점)

(A)　　　　　(B)　　　　　(C)

① to pay – what does the writer say – appears with

② to pay – what the writer says – appears with

③ to pay – what the writer says – appears to

④ paying – what the writer says – appears with

⑤ paying – what does the writer say – appears to

12 위 글의 내용과 일치하지 <u>않는</u> 것은? (5점)

① Garcia-Fuller said that it is not easy to be a smart news reader.

② If a story seems too good to be true, we can believe that.

③ It is important to search for the right source for news.

④ To tell fake news from real ones, we need to slow down.

⑤ Both the scary clowns and the tree octopuses were fake.

[전북 ○○중]

[13~16] 다음 글을 읽고 물음에 답하시오.

Like Garcia-Fuller's students, many teenagers in America are learning to think ⓐcritical about information they're seeing in the news and on the Internet.

(A) "One of the first steps is to slow down. If a story or a photo seems too good to be true, stop and think: Is there any evidence that supports what the writer says? And where is this coming from?"

(B) This skill is getting more important these days ⓑas stories can spread very fast, and anyone can make a website full of ⓒ_____ information.

(C) Garcia-Fuller said she was teaching her students how to tell fake news from ⓓ_____ news.

13 위 글의 밑줄 친 ⓐcritical을 올바른 형태로 바꾸시오. (3점)

→ _____

14 위 글의 ⓑas와 바꿔 쓸 수 있는 접속사는? (3점)

① when ② while ③ because

④ after ⑤ before

15 위 글의 빈칸 ⓒ와 ⓓ에 들어갈 알맞은 단어는? (4점)

① false - fake ② true - false

③ false - good ④ true - fake

⑤ false - real

16 위 글이 자연스럽게 이어지도록 (A)~(C)를 바르게 배열한 것은? (4점)

① (A)-(B)-(C) ② (A)-(C)-(B) ③ (B)-(A)-(C)

④ (B)-(C)-(A) ⑤ (C)-(A)-(B)

[충북 ○○중]

17 다음 글의 빈칸에 들어갈 말로 가장 적절한 것은? (4점)

Like Garcia-Fuller's students, many teenagers in America are learning to think critically about information they're seeing in the news and on the Internet. This skill is getting more important these days as stories can spread very fast, and anyone _____ _____.

① can write lots of beautiful stories

② can make a website full of fake news

③ can make a website full of useful information

④ can send countless messages without any permission

⑤ can make a website which can check the source of the information

[18~19] 다음 글을 읽고 물음에 답하시오.

In October 2016, stories about scary clowns shook schools across the Washington area, but Danina Garcia-Fuller's students didn't believe them a bit. "Some people were getting scared because they saw things on social media," said Patricia Visoso, one of Garcia-Fuller's students. "But they never checked up on who was saying this." The stories were actually made by teenagers, not by major newspapers or TV stations. They offered no hard evidence that clowns really were trying to attack students. The story turned out to be a complete lie. "I think a lot of people just look at one thing and believe it's true." Patricia's classmate Ivy Brooks said. "It's really important to look at the right sources and to pay attention to what is real and what is fake."

Like Garcia-Fuller's students, many teenagers in America are learning to think critically about information they're seeing in the news and on the Internet. This skill is getting more important these days as stories can spread very fast, and anyone can make a website full of false information.

18 위 글의 제목으로 가장 적절한 것은? (4점)

① The Urban Legend: Scary Clown Stories
② The Rise of Social Media: Is It Helpful or Not?
③ The Advantage and Weakness of Critical Thinking
④ The Lack of Evidence that Clowns Attacked Students
⑤ Critical Thinking: the Most Important Skill to Find Real Information

19 위 글의 내용과 일치하지 <u>않는</u> 것은? (5점)

① The students of Garcia-Fuller didn't believe the scary clown stories.
② Though they were made up by teenagers, the scary clown stories had the evidence that clowns actually attacked students.
③ It turned out that the scary clown story was a complete lie.
④ Ivy-Brooks thinks that it is important to think critically about the information on the Internet.
⑤ Stories or rumors can spread very fast these days due to the development of Internet.

20 다음 글의 밑줄 친 부분과 용법이 같은 것을 모두 찾아 바르게 짝지어진 것을 고르면? (4점)

"I think a lot of people just look at one thing and believe it's true," Patricia's classmate Ivy-Brooks said. "<u>It</u>'s really important to look at the right sources and to pay attention to what is real and what is fake."

ⓐ <u>It</u> is difficult to master a foreign language in a year.
ⓑ <u>It</u> is not natural to earn money for nothing.
ⓒ <u>It</u> was very windy at the beach last weekend.
ⓓ <u>It</u> is important to find the necessary tool for the work.
ⓔ I enjoyed the book, and <u>it</u> was very interesting.

① ⓐ, ⓑ   ② ⓐ, ⓑ, ⓒ
③ ⓑ, ⓒ, ⓓ   ④ ⓒ, ⓓ, ⓔ
⑤ ⓐ, ⓑ, ⓓ

[21~22] 다음 글을 읽고 물음에 답하시오.

"Some people ⓐwere getting scared because they saw things on social media," said Patricia Visoso, one of Garcia-Fuller's students. "But they never checked up on ⓑwho this was saying." The stories ⓒwere actually made by teenagers, not by major newspapers or TV stations. They offered no hard evidence (A)that clowns really were trying to attack students. The story ⓓturned out to be a complete lie.

"I think a lot of people just look at one thing and believe it's true," Patricia's classmate Ivy-Brooks said. "It's really important to look at the right sources and to pay attention to ⓔwhat is real and what is fake."

21 위 글의 밑줄 친 (A)that과 같은 용법으로 쓰인 것은? (4점)

① I heard the news that he was badly injured.

② I don't think the news is that great.

③ I think that he is a really good teacher.

④ Look at the boy that I met yesterday.

⑤ Look at that lady!

22 위 글의 밑줄 친 ⓐ~ⓔ 중 어법상 잘못된 것은? (4점)

① ⓐ　　② ⓑ　　③ ⓒ　　④ ⓓ　　⑤ ⓔ

[23~25] 다음 글을 읽고 물음에 답하시오.

Garcia-Fuller said she was teaching her students how to tell fake news from real news.

"One of the first steps is to slow down. If a story or a photo seems too good to be true, stop and think: Is there any evidence that ⓐsupports what the writer says? And where is this coming from?"
Garcia-Fuller's students also learn how to tell fact from opinion in the news. "Opinions are good ⓑto read," said 15-year-old McKenzie Campbell, "but you also have to check ⓒwhether they are based on facts."

Garcia-Fuller also said that sometimes it can be very hard ⓓto be a smart news reader. She tests her students with a website that appears to provide information on an animal ⓔcalling a tree octopus. The site is full of information on this animal, along with (A)a few unclear photos of octopuses in trees. But like the story of scary clowns, it's totally made up.

(B)She said to her students "You have to check the information and question everything, even things that I say."

23 위 글의 ⓐ~ⓔ 중 어법상 쓰임이 적절하지 않은 것은? (3점)

① ⓐ　　② ⓑ　　③ ⓒ　　④ ⓓ　　⑤ ⓔ

24 위 글의 (A)에 대한 이유로 가장 적절한 것은? (4점)

① 거짓 정보라서 실제의 사진이 아니기 때문에

② 그 웹사이트에 여러 재미있는 이야기가 많기 때문에

③ 선명했던 사진이 누군가에 의해 훼손됐기 때문에

④ 사진 기술이 발달하기 전에 촬영된 사진이기 때문에

⑤ 육지에서 생존하기 위해 나무 문어는 보호색을 띠기 때문에

25 위 글의 밑줄 친 (B)를 간접화법으로 바꿔 쓰시오. (단, 〈조건〉에 맞게 작성할 것.) (6점)

조건
• 필요하면 단어의 형태를 변형할 것.

→ _____

◎ 선택형 문항의 답안은 컴퓨터용 수정 싸인펜을 사용하여 OMR 답안지에 바르게 표기하시오.
◎ 서술형 문제는 답을 답안지에 반드시 검정 볼펜으로 쓰시오.
◎ 총 27문항 100점 만점입니다. 문항별 배점은 각 문항에 표시되어 있습니다.

① So do I.
② That's right.
③ I agree with you.
④ I don't agree with you.
⑤ You can say that again.

[경기 ○○중]

01 다음 영영 풀이에 해당하는 단어의 반의어는?   (3점)

> made to look like a real material or object in order to deceive people

① fake   ② genius   ③ final
④ genuine   ⑤ false

[경기 ○○중]

02 다음 중 영영 풀이가 적절하지 <u>않은</u> 것은?   (4점)

① connect: to join two or more things together
② spread: to fasten things together using a piece of string, rope, etc.
③ artwork: paintings and other objects produced by artists
④ sink: to go down below the surface of water, mud, etc.
⑤ source: a thing, place, activity, etc. that you get something from

[경기 ○○중]

04 다음 대화의 밑줄 친 ⓐ~ⓔ 중 흐름상 어색한 것은?   (4점)

> Big Mouth's Show
> Alex: Big Mouth's Show is really cool. How do you feel about it?
> Somi: ⓐWell, I don't think it's that great.
> Alex: Come on. I love Mr. Big Mouth. He always makes me laugh out loud.
> Somi: ⓑHe's funny, but don't believe everything he says.
> Alex: All right. Oh, look at his photo of an octopus. ⓒHe said it lives in a tree.
> Somi: ⓓI think it's a good idea.
> Alex: He took the photo when it was climbing the tree. I don't think he's lying. It's a great photo.
> Somi: ⓔI don't agree with you. It's a fake photo. An octopus can't live out of the sea.

① ⓐ   ② ⓑ   ③ ⓒ   ④ ⓓ   ⑤ ⓔ

[서울 영등포구 ○○중]

03 다음 대화의 흐름상 빈칸에 들어갈 가장 알맞은 것은?   (3점)

> G: I like the coat the boy is wearing. I think it's warm and light.
> B: Well, _____ Actually, I bought one last week. It's not so warm, and it's much heavier than it looks.
> G: Really? I don't believe it.

[경기 ○○중]

05 다음 빈칸에 공통으로 들어갈 말로 적절한 것은?   (3점)

> • Promise that you won't _____ him about it.
> • Can you _____ Tom from his twin brother?

① say   ② ask   ③ tell
④ turn   ⑤ express

06 다음 대화의 (A)~(E) 중 밑줄 친 문장이 들어갈 위치로 가장 알맞은 곳은? (4점)

Most girls like long hair better than short hair.

A: How do you feel about this kid here?
B: I think she is very pretty. By the way, why did she cut her hair?
A: Can you guess? (A)
B: Well, girls these days prefer short hair. (B)
A: I don't agree with that. (C) And this kid here is not a girl. In fact, he is a boy. (D)
B: Really? (E)
A: Yes. He grew his hair to help sick children.

① (A) ② (B) ③ (C) ④ (D) ⑤ (E)

08 다음 대화의 빈칸에 들어갈 말로 적절하지 <u>않은</u> 것은? (4점)

A: Look at those shoes the girl is wearing. I think they're great. _____
B: I think they look light and comfortable.
A: Right. I want to buy them for the school field trip.

① What do you think of them?
② How do you feel about them?
③ What do you say about them?
④ Why do you agree with them?
⑤ What's your opinion about them?

07 다음 대화의 두 사람에 대해 알 수 있는 것은? (3점)

G: How do you feel about this drama?
B: I think it's very touching. The boy gave up his life to save his sister. It's the best drama of this year.
G: I don't agree. It's not a good drama.
B: Come on. Why do you think so?
G: It doesn't seem real. And it's a little boring.

① They are drama writers.
② They were touched by the drama.
③ They have different opinions about the drama.
④ They think the drama is the best of this year.
⑤ They think the drama is based on the true story.

09 다음 대화의 밑줄 친 (A)~(E) 중에서 흐름상 <u>어색한</u> 문장은? (4점)

Alex: Big Mouth's Show is really cool. How do you feel about it?
Somi: (A)<u>Well, I don't think it's that great.</u>
Alex: Come on. I love Mr. Big Mouth. He always makes me laugh out loud.
Somi: (B)<u>He's funny, but don't believe everything he says.</u>
Alex: All right. Oh, look at his photo of an octopus. He said it lives in a tree.
Somi: (C)<u>It makes sense.</u>
Alex: He took the photo when it was climbing the tree. (D)<u>I don't think he's lying. It's a great photo.</u>
Somi: (E)<u>I don't agree with you.</u> It's a fake photo. An octopus can't live out of the sea.

① (A) ② (B) ③ (C) ④ (D) ⑤ (E)

10 다음 두 문장의 빈칸에 공통으로 들어갈 단어를 쓰시오. (대 · 소문자 무시) (3점)

> • _____ it rains tomorrow, I will stay at home.
> • I'm not sure _____ it will rain tomorrow.

→ _____

11 다음 문장 중 어법상 올바른 것을 2개 고르면? (4점)

① I wonder if will he like that food.

② If you are rich or not doesn't matter.

③ Tell me whether she will come to school.

④ I don't know if or not you will like my present.

⑤ The problem is whether they believe what I said or not.

12 밑줄 친 부분의 쓰임이 다른 하나는? (3점)

① It is very necessary to study English.

② It is very important to do the project.

③ It was last month that they helped the poor.

④ It was very hard to be a smart news reader.

⑤ It is very important that they should help each other.

13 다음 중 두 문장이 의미가 같도록 바르게 전환된 것을 2개 고르면? (4점)

① He said to me, "You look tired today."
→ He told me that you looked tired today.

② Jane said, "I want to be a teacher."
→ Jane said that I wanted to be a teacher.

③ He said to me, "Do you like her?"
→ He asked me whether you liked her.

④ He said to me, "I will help you tomorrow."
→ He told me that he would help me the next day.

⑤ She said to me, "What do you want to buy now?"
→ She asked me what I wanted to buy then.

14 다음 중 A를 B로 바꿀 때 어법에 맞게 쓴 것은? (4점)

① A: Mike said to her, "What are you doing here?"
→ B: Mike asked her what was she doing there.

② A: Mary said, "I'm living in Seoul now."
→ B: Mary said that she was living in Seoul now.

③ A: I said to my dad, "I'll call you later."
→ B: I said to my dad that I would call him later.

④ A: Amy said to her brother, "Today you are late again."
→ B: Amy told her brother that that day he is late again.

⑤ A: She said to him, "I met your sister yesterday."
→ B: She told him that she had met his sister the day before.

[15~18] 다음 글을 읽고 물음에 답하시오.

In October 2016, stories about scary clowns shook schools across the Washington area, but Danina Garcia-Fuller's students didn't believe them a bit. "Some people were getting scared because they saw things on social media," said Patricia Visoso, one of Garcia-Fuller's students. "But they never checked up on who was saying ⓐthis." The stories were actually made by teenagers, not by major newspapers or TV stations. They offered no ⓑhard evidence that clowns really were trying to attack students. The story (A)[turned out / turned out to be] a complete lie.

"I think a lot of people just look at one thing and believe it's true," Patricia's classmate Ivy Brooks said. "It's really important to look at the right (B)[resources / sources] and to pay attention to what is real and what is fake."

Like Garcia-Fuller's students, many teenagers in America are learning to think (C)[creatively / critically] about information they're seeing in the news and on the Internet. This skill is getting more important these days as stories can spread very fast, and anyone can make a website full of false information.

15 위 글의 밑줄 친 ⓐthis가 가리키는 것은? (4점)

① social media
② a story about scary clowns
③ one of Garcia-Fuller's students
④ evidence that clowns attacked students
⑤ a school across the Washington area

16 위 글의 문맥상 ⓑhard와 바꿔 쓸 수 있는 단어는? (4점)

① clear   ② tough   ③ false
④ difficult   ⑤ powerful

17 위 글의 괄호 (A), (B), (C) 안에서 어법에 맞는 표현으로 가장 적절한 것은? (4점)

	(A)	(B)	(C)
①	turned out	resources	creatively
②	turned out to be	resources	critically
③	turned out	sources	creatively
④	turned out to be	sources	critically
⑤	turned out to be	sources	creatively

18 위 글의 내용과 일치하는 것을 2개 고르면? (4점)

① Patricia's classmate Ivy-Brooks thinks many people look at everything and believe it's true.
② Not only teenagers but also TV stations spread stories of scary clowns.
③ The story about scary clowns proved to be a false one completely.
④ Stories about scary clowns didn't make Garcia-Fuller's students nervous.
⑤ Garcia-Fuller's students as well as many teenagers in America are learning how to make stories spread fast on a website.

19 다음 중 밑줄 친 단어의 쓰임이 나머지 넷과 <u>다른</u> 것은? (3점)

① I am not sure <u>if</u> she will come here.
② I can't tell <u>if</u> that kid is a boy or a girl.
③ I wonder <u>if</u> this soup is delicious or not.
④ I want to know <u>if</u> he will throw the ball.
⑤ You'll be healthier <u>if</u> you exercise every day.

[20~21] 다음 글을 읽고 물음에 답하시오.

Garcia-Fuller said she was teaching her students how to tell fake news from real news.
"One of the first steps is to slow down. (A)만약 어떤 이야기나 어떤 사진이 진짜라고 하기엔 너무 좋아 보인다면, stop and think: Is there any evidence that supports what the writer says? And where is this coming from?"
Garcia-Fuller's students also learn how to tell fact from opinion in the news. "Opinions are good to read," said 15-year-old McKenzie Campbell, "but you also have to check if they are based on facts."

20 위 글의 밑줄 친 (A)의 우리말을 문맥에 맞도록 가장 바르게 영작한 것을 2개 고르면? (4점)

① If a story or a photo seems too good to be true,

② If a story or a photo seems true enough to be good,

③ If a story or a photo seems so good that it can't be true,

④ If a story or a photo seems too true to be good,

⑤ If a story or a photo seems too good not to be true,

21 위 글에 나오는 단어의 영영 풀이가 아닌 것은? (4점)

① a piece of information that is known to be true

② your ideas or beliefs about a particular subject

③ facts or signs that show clearly that something exists or is true

④ to say that you agree with an idea, group, or person, and usually to help them because you want them to succeed

⑤ the area that is behind the main thing that you are looking at, especially in a picture

22 다음 글의 빈칸 (A), (B)에 들어갈 말로 가장 바르게 짝지어진 것은? (4점)

Garcia-Fuller tests her students with a website that appears to provide information on an animal called a tree octopus. The site is full of information on this animal, along with a few unclear photos of octopuses in trees. But like the story of scary clowns, it's totally made up. The lesson, Garcia-Fuller tells her students, is to "(A)_____ the information you're seeing once more carefully" and to "(B)_____ everything, even things that I say."

	(A)	(B)
①	believe	accept
②	believe	trust
③	choose	question
④	check	trust
⑤	check	question

23 다음 빈칸에 들어갈 단어의 뜻풀이로 가장 적절한 것은? (4점)

• The little boy is _____ of monsters.

① difficult to do or solve

② having all necessary parts

③ frightened of something

④ very important and serious

⑤ incorrect, untrue, or mistaken

[24~25] 다음 글을 읽고 물음에 답하시오.

In October (A)2016, stories about scary clowns shook schools across the Washington area, but Danina Garcia-Fuller's students didn't believe them a bit.

"Some people were getting scared because they saw things on social media," said Patricia Visoso, one of Garcia-Fuller's students. "But they never checked up on who was saying this." The stories were actually made by teenagers, not by major newspapers or TV stations. They offered no hard evidence that clowns really were trying to attack students. (B)The story turned out to be a complete lie.

24 위 글의 밑줄 친 (A)와 같은 연도를 영어로 <u>어색하게</u> 표현한 것은? (3점)

① 2016: twenty sixteen

② 1620: sixteen twenty

③ 1435: fourteen thirty-five

④ 2025: twenty twenty-five

⑤ 1500: one thousand five hundred

25 위 글의 밑줄 친 (B)의 문장을 가장 적절하게 바꾼 것은? (4점)

① It turns out that the story is a complete lie.

② It turns out that the story had a complete lie.

③ It turned out that the story is a complete lie.

④ It turned out that the story has a complete lie.

⑤ It turned out that the story was a complete lie.

26 다음 글을 읽고 요약문의 밑줄 친 ⓐ~ⓔ 중 적절하지 <u>않은</u> 것은? (4점)

Like Garcia-Fuller's students, many teenagers in America are learning to think critically about information they're seeing in the news and on the Internet. This skill is getting more important these days as stories can spread very fast, and anyone can make a website full of false information. Garcia-Fuller said she was teaching her students how to tell fake news from real news. Garcia-Fuller's students also learn how to tell fact from opinion in the news. "Opinions are good to read," said 15-year-old McKenzie Campbell.

<요약문>
Many teenagers in America are learning to think ⓐcritically about information in the news and on the ⓑInternet.
Garcia-Fuller teaches her students how to ⓒ distinguish fake news from real news and ⓓ talk fact from ⓔopinion in the news.

① ⓐ ② ⓑ ③ ⓒ ④ ⓓ ⑤ ⓔ

27 다음 글의 밑줄 친 ⓐ~ⓔ 중에서 지칭하는 바가 <u>다른</u> 하나는? (4점)

In October 2016, ⓐstories about scary clowns shook schools across the Washington area, but Danina Garcia-Fuller's students didn't believe ⓑthem a bit. "Some people were getting scared because ⓒthey saw things on social media," said Patricia Visoso, one of Garcia-Fuller's students. "But they never checked up on who was saying this." The stories were actually made by teenagers, not by major newspapers or TV stations. ⓓ They didn't have any hard evidence that clowns really were trying to attack students. ⓔThey turned out to be a complete lie.

① ⓐ ② ⓑ ③ ⓒ ④ ⓓ ⑤ ⓔ

3학년 영어 2학기 기말고사(8과) 1회

문항수 : 선택형(21문항) 서술형(5문항) | 20 . . .

◎ 선택형 문항의 답안은 컴퓨터용 수정 싸인펜을 사용하여 OMR 답안지에 바르게 표기하시오.
◎ 서술형 문제는 답을 답안지에 반드시 검정 볼펜으로 쓰시오.
◎ 총 26문항 100점 만점입니다. 문항별 배점은 각 문항에 표시되어 있습니다.

[전북 ○○중]

01 다음 문장의 밑줄 친 단어가 잘못 쓰인 것은? (3점)

① The couple <u>approached</u> the woman to ask her a question.

② The <u>injuring</u> soccer player could not play in the big game.

③ I am not sure, but Jane <u>might</u> be studying in her room.

④ The members of the <u>team</u> must exercise often and stay healthy.

⑤ The two princes lifted their <u>head</u> to start the fight.

[서울 영등포구 ○○중]

02 다음 중 문맥상 빈칸에 사용되지 <u>않는</u> 것은? (4점)

- Have you met him _____?
- It's a false rumor, which is totally _____.
- Reporters _____ the woman to ask her a question.
- Mahatma Gandhi asked his people to fight peacefully _____ England.
- He _____ for a long time to lose weight.

① appeared ② made up ③ against
④ fasted ⑤ recently

[전북 ○○중]

[3~5] 다음 대화를 읽고 물음에 답하시오.

A: Minsu, there's no cup I can use. Why didn't you do the dishes?
B: Sorry, but I forgot @<u>do</u> them.
A: What? You always forget what you have to do. ⓑ<u>나는 참을 수가 없어</u>. I cleaned the living room all morning.
B: Calm down! ⓒ<u>나는 숙제를 하느라 바빠</u>.
A: Do the dishes first, and then do your homework.
B: I can't! I don't think I can finish my homework today. Science is too difficult for me.
A: Science? You know I'm good at science. Let me help you.
B: Great. Thanks. I'll wash your cup right now and I'll do the rest of the dishes after finishing this.

03 위 대화의 밑줄 친 @do의 알맞은 형태는? (4점)

① do ② doing ③ did
④ to do ⑤ done

04 위 대화의 우리말 ⓑ에 적절한 표현을 아래 단어를 이용하여 4단어로 쓰시오. (4점)

stand

→ _____ _____ _____ _____.

05 위 대화의 밑줄 친 우리말 ⓒ를 영작하시오. (4점)

→ _____ _____ _____ _____
_____ _____.

06 다음 중 짝지어진 대화가 가장 자연스러운 것은? (4점)

① A: If there's no enemy, they don't smoke at all, do they?

B: No, they don't. Smoke from one chimney means "No enemy."

A: Now smoke is rising from three chimneys.

B: It means an enemy is coming close to the border.

② A: How do you feel about this drama?

B: I think it's very touching. The boy gave up his life to save his sister. I think it's the best drama of this year.

A: So do I. I can't wait to watch it one more time.

③ A: Which do you prefer, a shoulder bag or a hand bag?

B: I prefer a hand bag. Actually, I hate holding things in my hands.

④ A: The teddy bears were made out of a police officer's uniform.

B: Oh, I see.

A: This police officer made them for the kids. Their dad was a police officer, and he passed away recently.

B: They must be glad to hear that their dad passed the test and became a police officer.

⑤ A: Look! That man didn't wait in line! I'm very angry. I can't stand it.

B: Try one more time to stand upright, or your back will get hurt.

07 다음 빈칸에 알맞은 말이 순서대로 짝지어진 것은? (4점)

• Many teenagers are big fans of BTS. _____ like their beautiful songs, and _____ like their powerful dancing.

① One - another

② Some - others

③ Another - one

④ The former - the latter

⑤ This - that

08 다음 밑줄 친 문장에서 잘못 쓰인 곳을 찾아 바르게 고쳐 문장을 다시 쓰시오. (4점)

• Next, the teacher took Corky to a large hall with a chair in the middle. <u>There were 19 other warriors who pass their tests.</u>

→ _____

09 다음 중 문맥이나 어법상 밑줄 친 부분이 바른 것을 2개 고르면? (4점)

① I have two books. <u>One</u> is for you, and <u>the second</u> is for me.

② Ten students like to play sports in their free time. <u>Some</u> like to play soccer. <u>Others</u> like to play baseball. <u>The others</u> like to go swimming.

③ Students in the classroom are taking a test. <u>Some</u> are finished, but <u>the others</u> are not yet.

④ He has five sons. <u>Some</u> is a police officer, and <u>the others</u> are fire fighters.

⑤ Two girls on the stage are dancing. <u>One</u> is dancing well, <u>other</u> is not.

[10~14] 다음 글을 읽고 물음에 답하시오.

Then, the teacher told Corky to ⓐ<u>stand against</u> a pole. Suddenly, he tied Corky to the pole. ⓑ<u>Above his head</u>, he put a sign that read "Dangerous and Bad." Many people ⓒ<u>passed on</u>. Some gave Corky angry looks, and others ⓓ<u>shouted at</u> him. Corky ⓔ<u>shouted back</u>. He yelled, "Set me free, (A)_____ you all will be in big trouble!" That made the situation worse.

"I need to try another way," he thought. Then, Corky began to speak softly. He said he was not dangerous or bad but was a good man. He kept saying this in all possible ways. Finally, the people let him go.

"Now you control the most powerful weapon: (B)_____. Soft (B)_____ are stronger than sharp (C)_____," said the teacher.

10 위 글의 밑줄 친 ⓐ~ⓔ 중 쓰임이 잘못된 것은?　(3점)

　① ⓐ　　② ⓑ　　③ ⓒ　　④ ⓓ　　⑤ ⓔ

11 위 글의 빈칸 (A)에 적절한 접속사는?　(2점)

　① and　　② but　　③ so
　④ nor　　⑤ or

12 위 글의 내용과 일치하지 않는 것은?　(4점)

　① 선생님은 Corky를 학교 문 앞에 묶었다.
　② Corky의 머리 위에는 '위험하고 나쁨'이라고 쓰인 푯말을 붙였다.
　③ 지나가는 몇몇 사람들의 Corky에게 소리를 질렀다.
　④ Corky는 부드러운 목소리로 말하기 시작했다.
　⑤ 마침내 사람들이 Corky를 풀어 주었다.

13 위 글의 첫 단락에 나타난 Corky의 심경은?　(4점)

　① happy　　② excited　　③ upset
　④ worried　　⑤ surprised

14 위 글의 빈칸 (B), (C)에 들어갈 알맞은 단어를 쓰시오.　(5점)

　(B) _____　(C) _____

15 다음 글의 ⓐ~ⓔ 중 어법상 쓰임이 적절하지 않은 것은?　(5점)

Young, brave Corky wanted to be a general, but he was ordered ⓐ<u>to go</u> to a military school by the king. Corky went to the school but had to wait in front of the gate for a hundred days. He got the first weapon, patience. Then, the teacher made Corky ⓑ<u>stand</u> against a pole. Corky was tied to the pole under a sign ⓒ<u>saying</u> "Dangerous and Bad." He ⓓ<u>was set free</u> after persuading people that he was a good man. He got the second weapon, words.

Then, Corky had to fight against the other warriors to sit in a chair. Suddenly, he decided to stop fighting and took care of the injured. ⓔ<u>Impressing</u> by this, all the warriors followed Corky. Finally, he got the last weapon, peace.

　① ⓐ　　② ⓑ　　③ ⓒ　　④ ⓓ　　⑤ ⓔ

[16~18] 다음 글을 읽고 물음에 답하시오.

Next, the teacher took Corky to a large hall with a chair in the middle. There were 19 other warriors who (A)[passed / had passed] their tests.

"The first one to sit in the chair will be the winner," the teacher said.

Corky and (B)[the other / the others] began fighting. They pushed, pulled, ran, and jumped. They fought harder and harder, so Corky became tired.

Finally, he said, "I will not fight anymore. Instead, I will take care of the injured." The other warriors saw this and fought even harder. As they fought, more warriors became tired and hurt. Corky took good care of them, so they followed him. Soon, all the warriors except Thunder (C)[was / were] following Corky.

Thunder walked toward the chair to sit in it. Then, he saw Corky standing with his 18 followers. Thunder realized he was all alone. "I give up. ⓐ You're the real winner," Thunder said to Corky.

At that moment, the teacher appeared and said. "Of all the great weapons, peace is my favorite. Sooner or later, everyone wants to stand on the side of peace."

Corky returned to the palace after his training ended. When the king saw him approach, he gave Corky a wise and knowing smile and said, ⓑ "What's up, General?"

16 위 글의 밑줄 친 ⓐ의 의미로 가장 적절한 것은? (4점)

① Corky and Thunder fought each other harder and harder.

② Corky beat the 19 other warriors and became the winner.

③ Corky decided to continue fighting and all the warriors followed him.

④ Corky made injured warriors support him by taking care of them.

⑤ To be the first one to sit in the chair, Corky led other warriors to beat Thunder and he made it.

17 위 글의 밑줄 친 ⓑ를 다르게 표현한 것으로 가장 적절한 것은? (5점)

① Corky, how're you doing today?

② I finally recognize you as a general.

③ Something has happened and I need you as a general.

④ I know that you've come a long way to become a general but it's not enough.

⑤ I acknowledge you as the most powerful man in my country, but there is no vacancy for the general right now.

18 위 글의 괄호 (A), (B), (C) 안에서 어법에 맞는 것으로 가장 적절한 것은? (4점)

	(A)	(B)	(C)
①	passed	the other	was
②	passed	the others	were
③	had passed	the other	was
④	had passed	the others	was
⑤	had passed	the others	were

[19~20] 다음 글을 읽고 물음에 답하시오.

Corky was a brave young man. He wanted to be a general, but the king said, "You're the strongest man in my army, but you have ⓐ<u>little</u> to learn." He ordered Corky to go to a famous military school.

"Wait there. In a hundred days, your training will start," a voice said from inside the school gate. Corky got ⓑ<u>upset</u>. But then he thought there might be a reason, so he waited. On the hundred and first day, the gate opened. An old man said, "You have learned to use your first weapon: patience. Patience is the most ⓒ<u>important</u> thing to win a war."

Then, the teacher told Corky to stand against a pole. Suddenly, he tied Corky to the pole. Above his head, he put a sign that read "Dangerous and Bad." Many people passed by. Some gave Corky ⓓ<u>angry</u> looks, and others shouted at him. Corky shouted back. He yelled, "Set me free, or you all will be in big trouble!" That made the situation ⓔ <u>worse</u>.

19 위 글에 드러난 Corky의 심경 변화로 가장 적절한 것은? (4점)

① calm → annoyed

② comfortable → disappointed

③ angry → hopeful

④ frustrated → excited

⑤ confused → bored

20 위 글의 밑줄 친 ⓐ~ⓔ 중 문맥상 단어의 쓰임이 적절하지 않은 것은? (3점)

① ⓐ little　　　② ⓑ upset

③ ⓒ important　④ ⓓ angry

⑤ ⓔ worse

[21~23] 다음 글을 읽고 물음에 답하시오.

Corky was a brave young man. He wanted to be a general, but the king said, "You're the strongest man in my army, but you have much to learn."
(A)<u>Corky / he / go / to a famous military school / ordered / to.</u>

"Wait there. In a hundred days, your training will start," a voice said from inside the school gate. Corky got angry. But then he thought there might be a reason, so he waited. On the hundred and first day, the gate opened. An old man said, "You have learned to use your first weapon: (B)_____.
(B)_____ is the most important thing to win a war."

21 위 글에서 Corky의 꿈은 무엇인가? (2점)

① 장군　　　② 교사

③ 의사　　　④ 군인

⑤ 연예인

22 위 글의 밑줄 친 (A)의 단어들을 바르게 배열하시오. (4점)

→ _____

23 위 글의 빈칸 (B)에 들어갈 알맞은 단어는? (대 · 소문자 무시) (3점)

① swords　　② words

③ peace　　　④ patience

⑤ friendship

[24~26] 다음 글을 읽고 물음에 답하시오.

Corky was a brave young man. He wanted to be a general, but the king said, "You're the strongest man in my army, but you have much to learn." He ordered Corky to go to a famous military school. "Wait there. In a hundred days, your training will start," a voice said from inside the school gate. Corky got angry. But then he thought there might be a reason, so he waited. On the hundred and first day, the gate opened. An old man said, "You have learned to use your first weapon: patience. Patience is the most important thing to win a war." Then, the teacher told Corky to stand against a pole. Suddenly, he tied Corky to the pole. Above his head, he put a sign that read "Dangerous and Bad." Many people passed by. (A) Some gave Corky angry looks, and others shouted at him. Corky shouted back. (B) He yelled, "Set me free, or you all will be in big trouble!" That made the situation worse. (C)

"I need to try another way," he thought. (D) He kept saying this in all possible ways. (E) Finally, the people let him go. "Now you control the most powerful weapon: words. Soft words are stronger than sharp swords," said the teacher.

24 위 글의 제목으로 가장 알맞은 것은? (4점)

① Corky, a Brave Young Man

② Patience or Words, Which One Is Better?

③ Weapons Corky Finally Got: Patience and Words

④ Corky, the Strongest Warrior in the Army

⑤ How to Control Patience and Strong Words

25 위 글의 (A)~(E) 중 다음 문장이 들어갈 위치로 가장 알맞은 곳은? (4점)

Then, Corky began to speak softly. He said he was not dangerous or bad but was a good man.

① (A)　② (B)　③ (C)　④ (D)　⑤ (E)

26 Which is true about Corky? (5점)

① A voice from inside the school gate told Corky to train for a hundred days.

② Corky was the strongest man in the army, so he became a general.

③ It was on the hundred and first day that the military school let Corky in.

④ The reason why Corky was tied to the pole was that he was against his teacher.

⑤ Corky shouted back, which made him get sharp swords.

정답 및 해설

Lesson 5 (중간) 〔1회〕

01 ④ 02 ② 03 ⑤
04 The girl whose dog is dancing is Tami. 05 ⑤ 06 ④
07 Speaking to family members or friends in a foreign country
08 ⑤
09 The girl whose dog wants to eat a hot dog doesn't understand the sign.
10 ③ 11 ⑤ 12 ④ 13 kid 14 ① 15 ③ 16 ⑤
17 ③ 18 ② 19 ③ 20 ② 21 ① 22 ② 23 ③
24 I voted for the DC. The PCI lost (so) many seats.
25 ② 26 ③ 27 ① 28 ④ 29 ② 30 ⑤

---

01 뒤에서 'Smoke from one chimney means "No enemy."'라고 했으므로 'Yes, they do.'가 적절하다. 부정의 질문이라도 긍정의 의미로 답하는 경우에는 'Yes'를 쓰는 것에 유의한다.

02 'Smoke from one chimney means "No enemy."'라고 했다.

03 'It means "Jan van Eyck was here. 1434." It's Latin.'이라고 했다.

04 'Her'가 'The girl'을 가리키므로 소유격 관계대명사 whose로 바꾸어 'whose dog is dancing'으로 관계대명사절을 쓴다.

05 '이름이 어떤 의미인지' 묻는 질문에 '네 이름의 의미가 마음에 든다.'는 대답은 어색하다.

06 'a woman'을 수식하며 뒤에 '주어와 동사'가 나오므로 소유격 관계대명사 whose가 적절하다.

07 'it'은 앞에서 언급한 'Speaking to family members or friends in a foreign country'를 가리킨다.

08 ⓒ의 how는 관계부사이며 'the way'로 바꿔 쓸 수 있다. 'the way how'와 같이 'the way'와 'how'를 함께 쓸 수 없다는 것에 주의한다. ①, ②, ④ 의문 부사 ③ 감탄문에 쓰인 의문사 ⑤ 관계부사

09 'Her'가 'The girl'을 가리키므로 소유격 관계대명사 whose로 바꾸어 'whose dog wants to eat a hot dog'로 관계대명사절을 쓴다.

10 'I already sent you a letter, but there was no reply'라고 했다.

11 가정법과거는 현재 사실과 반대되는 상상이나 가정을 나타내어 '만약 …한다면 ~할 텐데'의 의미를 가지며, 'If+주어+동사 과거

형(be동사의 경우 were) …, 주어+would/should/could/might+동사원형 ~.'으로 쓴다.

12 ⓐ reach ... out toward ~: ~을 향해 (손 등을) 내밀다[뻗다]
ⓓ look after: ~을 돌보다

13 one은 'kid'를 가리킨다.

14 'my love'는 부부간의 호칭으로 '여보, 당신'을 뜻한다.

15 (A) a man을 수식하며 뒤에 '주어와 동사'가 나오므로 소유격 관계대명사 whose가 적절하다.
(B) enough ... to ~: ~할 만큼 충분한 …

16 This letter가 발견한 것이 아니라 '발견된' 것이므로 수동태(was discovered)로 써야 한다.

17 'At the time, more than 5% of the people in Italy could not read or write'라고 했다.

18 (B)의 'it'은 문장의 어떤 부분을 강조하는 것이 아니라 앞에서 언급한 'Speaking to family members or friends in a foreign country'를 가리킨다.

19 to plant → plant, another → the other, much → many

20 'I and three kids could go through this winter without worry.'라고 했으므로 'relieved(안심한, 안도한)'가 적절하다.
① bored: 지루한 ③ anxious: 염려하는 ⑤ depressed: 우울한

21 'I had two workers prepare our field and plant seeds for 150,000 lire.'라고 했다.

22 ⓐ 금년에 올리브를 따서 올리브 기름을 얻은 것을 언급하고 있으므로 과거시제로 쓰는 것이 적절하다.
ⓑ 접속사 없이 연결되고 있으므로 분사구문으로 쓰는 것이 적절하다.

23 'We picked lots of olives from our olive trees this year.'라고 했다.

24 'I voted for the DC. The PCI lost so many seats'라고 했다.

25 가정법과거는 현재 사실과 반대되는 상상이나 가정을 나타내어 '만약 …한다면 ~할 텐데'의 의미를 가지며, 'If+주어+동사 과거형(be동사의 경우 were) …, 주어+would/should/could/might+동사원형 ~.'으로 쓴다.

26 현재 사실과 반대되는 상상이나 가정을 나타내는 '가정법과거' 문장이므로 'unhappy'가 적절하다.

27 (A) 다음의 'the pictures'가 주어진 문장의 'This letter'를 의미하고 이어서 편지의 내용이 나오므로 (A)가 적절하다.

28 'while the oldest looks after the youngest'라고 했다.

29 'At the time, more than 5% of the people in Italy could not read or write, and she was one of them.'이라고 했다.

30 'If+주어+동사 과거형(be동사의 경우 were) …, 주어+would/should/could/might+동사원형 ~.'으로 쓰여진 가정법과거 문장으로 '현재 사실과 반대되는 상상이나 가정'을 나타낸다.

Lesson 5 (중간) 2회

01 ③ 02 (A) ⓒ, (B) ⓑ, (C) ⓐ 03 ① 04 ⑤ 05 ④
06 ② 07 ② 08 ② 09 ① 10 ④ 11 ③ 12 ① 13 ④
14 ② 15 ② 16 ① 17 If I got a letter from you 18 ⑤
19 ⑤ 20 ③ 21 ⑤
22 If you were with me, I would be so happy.
23 ① 24 ④ 25 ③ 26 ④ 27 ② 28 ④

01 '말해진 것이나 쓰여진 것을 다른 언어로 바꾸다'는 'translate(번역하다)'이다.

02 (A) 뒤에서 'Are you?'라고 했으므로 be동사가 있는 ⓒ, (B) 뒤에서 'What does it mean?'이라고 묻고 있으므로 ⓑ, (C) 의미를 설명하는 것이 자연스러우므로 ⓐ가 적절하다.

03 look after는 '돌보다'라는 뜻이다.

04 접속사와 소유격 Its를 대신하는 관계대명사 whose가 적절하다.

05 'Smoke from one chimney means "No enemy."'라고 했다.

06 주어진 문장의 'the system'이 (B) 앞에 나온 'sending messages to the king by using the chimneys'를 가리키므로 (B)가 적절하다.

07 병사들이 무슨 일을 할지 궁금해하는 말에 이어 (C)에서 굴뚝 4개에 불을 밝히고 (B)에서 5개 굴뚝 모두에 불을 피웠을 때, 그것은 무엇을 의미하는지 묻자 (A)에서 전투가 시작되었음을 의미한다고 답하는 순서가 적절하다.

08 This painting has some hidden secrets in it.'이라고 했으므로 ②번이 적절하다.

09 그림이 어디서 발견되었는지는 알 수 없다.

10 'This painting has some hidden secrets in it.'이라고 했다.

11 (A) 'the girl'을 수식하며 뒤에 '주어와 동사'가 나오므로 소유격 관계대명사 whose가 적절하다. (B) 앞 문장 전체가 선행사로 앞에 콤마(,)가 있는 계속적 용법이므로 which가 적절하다. (C) 'The guy'가 선행사이므로 who가 적절하다.

12 (A), (B) 가정법과거로 'If+주어+동사의 과거형(be동사의 경우 were) ..., 주어+would/should/could/might+동사원형 ~.'으로 쓴다. (C) 뒤에 명사가 이어지고 소유격이 필요하므로 whose가 적절하다.

13 (B)는 사람인 'The girl'이 주어이므로 'of which'를 'whose'로 바꾸어야 한다.

14 가정법과거에서 If를 생략하면 'Were+주어+ …, 주어+would/should/could/might+동사원형 ~.'의 형태로 쓴다.

15 ① A: 관계대명사 B: 의문사, ② A, B: 접속사, ③ A: 동사 B: 명사 ④ A: 동사 B: 명사 ⑤ A: 동사 B: 명사

16 'I'll go there with our middle son'이라고 했다.

17 가정법과거는 현재 사실과 반대되는 상상이나 가정을 나타내어 '만약 …한다면 ~할 텐데'의 의미를 가지며, 'If+주어+동사의 과거형(be동사의 경우 were) …, 주어+would/should/could/might+동사원형 ~.'으로 쓴다.

18 'it'은 앞에서 언급한 'Speaking to family members or friends in a foreign country'를 가리킨다.

19 (A) 서로 상반되는 내용이 이어지고 있으므로 'But', (B) 비슷한 내용이 추가되고 있으므로 'And'가 적절하다.

20 앞에서 'The PCI lost so many seats'라고 했으므로 'alive'가 아니라 'dead' 정도가 적절하다.

21 'But whether one or the other wins, it's the same. Nothing changes for us poor people.'이라고 했다.

22 가정법과거는 현재 사실과 반대되는 상상이나 가정을 나타내어 '만약 …한다면 ~할 텐데'의 의미를 가지며, 'If+주어+동사의 과거형(be동사의 경우 were) …, 주어+would/should/could/might+동사원형 ~.'으로 쓴다.

23 주어진 문장의 'It'이 (A) 앞의 'letter'를 가리키고, (A) 다음의 'She'가 주어진 문장의 'a woman'이므로 (A)가 적절하다.

24 얼마나 오랫동안 여자가 남편을 못 보았는지는 알 수 없다.

25 밑줄 친 'a lot'은 비교급을 강조하는 표현이다. very는 비교급을 강조하는 데 쓰이지 않는다.

26 'If+주어+동사의 과거형(be동사의 경우 were) …, 주어+would/should/could/might+동사원형 ~.'으로 쓰여진 가정법과거 문장으로 바꿔 쓸 수 있다.

27 'As you are not with me, I'm not so happy. We all miss you so much.'라고 했다.

28 DC가 얼마나 많은 의석을 확보했는지는 알 수 없다.

Lesson 6 (중간) 1회

01 ③ 02 ⑤ 03 ① 04 ③ 05 ⑤ 06 ④ 07 ① 08 ④
09 ③ 10 ⑤
11 The more kindly you act, the more friends you can have.
12 ② 13 It was a ring that Sam gave to her yesterday.
14 No, it is Frank that teaches French in Daesung Middle School.
15 (1) I let him ride my bicycle[bike].
  (2) He made them wear life jackets.
16 ③ 17 ③ 18 ④ 19 ③
20 It is these tiny seeds that change the book into a tree.
21 ④ 22 ④
23 It is these tiny seeds that change the book into a tree.
24 ② 25 ② 26 that 27 ② 28 ④ 29 ① 30 ②

01 '무언가를 하기 위해 필요한'은 'necessary(필요한)'이다.

02 뒤에서 'I'd like to make the bookmarks.'라고 했으므로 ⓔ의 'I love writing.'을 'I hate writing.' 정도로 고치는 것이 적절하다.

03 B가 Seho이며 'B: No problem. I'll write the cheerful messages.'라고 했다.

04 'I prefer cats. They're lovely.'라고 했다.

05 'Which do you prefer, A or B?'로 선호하는 것에 대해 물을 수 있다.

06 소년은 'And I hate spending too much time making things'라고 했다.

07 선호를 묻는 질문에 'I like digital artwork better.'라고 한 후에 'Actually, I do like dolls much.'라고 하는 것은 어색하다.

08 The+비교급+주어+동사 …, the+비교급+주어+동사 ~: …하면 할수록, 더 ~하다

09 ③번은 '현재분사'이지만 나머지는 '동명사'이다.

10 'Minho met Tony ~'에서 'No'라고 했으므로 'It was Minsu that met Tony ~'처럼 'Minho' 이외의 사람이 나와야 한다.

11 'The+비교급+주어+동사 …, the+비교급+주어+동사 ~' 구문은 '…하면 할수록, 더 ~하다'라는 의미로 'If+주어+동사+비교급 …, 주어+동사+비교급 ~'으로 바꿔 쓸 수 있다.

12 주어진 문장의 as와 ②는 '전치사'이지만 나머지는 '접속사'이다.

13 'It ~ that 강조 구문'은 'It is[was]+강조할 부분+that+문장의 나머지 부분'으로 쓰며, '…하는 것은 바로 ~이다'라고 해석한다.

14 'It ~ that 강조 구문'은 'It is[was]+강조할 부분+that+문장의 나머지 부분'으로 쓰며, '…하는 것은 바로 ~이다'라고 해석한다.

15 사역동사는 목적격보어로 원형부정사를 받는다.
(1) let: ~하도록 허락하다 = allow+목적어+to부정사
(2) make: ~하도록 하게 하다

16 (A) 아이들을 구하는 것이므로 save가 적절하다.
(B) 아이들이 질병으로 죽어가는 것이므로 dying이 적절하다. dyeing: 염색(법)
(C) 깨끗한 물은 아이들의 생존과 발달에 '중요하다'는 문맥이 자연스러우므로 important나 essential이 적절하다. indifferent: 무관심한

17 ⓐ와 ③은 'It ~ that 강조 구문'이지만 나머지는 '가주어 ~ 진주어' 구문이다.

18 지각동사 see의 목적격보어로 동사원형이나 현재분사가 와야 한다.

19 ⓐ plant – 심다 ⓑ water – 물을 주다 ⓓ company – 회사 ⓔ anymore – 더 이상(흔히 부정문이나 의문문 끝에 쓰여 any longer의 뜻을 나타냄)

20 'It ~ that 강조 구문'은 'It is[was]+강조할 부분+that+문장의 나머

21 의문사 What이 other unique books를 수식하는 것이므로 한 덩어리로 함께 쓰여야 한다. 'What other unique books do you want to make?'가 되어야 한다.

22 'Though the company does not print this book anymore, this special project makes us think about where books come from.'이라고 했다.

23 'It is[was] ~ that 강조 구문'을 이용하여 'It is+these tiny seeds+that+change the book into a tree.'로 쓴다.

24 both A and B: A와 B 둘 다

25 앞에서 'necessary to make clean drinking water'라고 했으므로 ②번이 적절하다.

26 ⓒ It ~ that 강조 구문의 that ⓓ diseases를 수식하는 관계대명사 that이 적절하다.

27 책을 공유하는 프로젝트를 통해서 전 세계가 하나의 큰 도서관이 될 수 있다는 내용의 글이므로 ②번 Books Travel!(책이 여행합니다!)이 가장 적절하다.

28 'First, register your book online and get an ID number.'라고 했다.

29 책을 공유하는 프로젝트를 통해서 전 세계가 하나의 큰 도서관이 될 수 있다는 내용의 글이므로 (A)에는 share가, (B)에는 learn이 적절하다.

30 'Next, leave it in a public place.'라고 했다. 네가 원하는 아무 데나 두어서는 안 될 것이다.

Lesson 6 (중간)   2회

01 ③	**02** ①	**03** ⑤	**04** ⑤	**05** ②	**06** ②

07 (1) Riding a motorcycle at night is dangerous.
(2) The number of people shopping online is growing.

08 ③	**09** ③	**10** ②	**11** ④	**12** ①	**13** ②	**14** ③	**15** ①
16 ④	**17** ⑤	**18** ①	**19** ④	**20** ①	**21** ②	**22** ④	**23** ⑤
24 ①	**25** ②	**26** The hotter it gets, the more water we need.					

01 tool: something (such as a hammer, saw, shovel, etc.) that you hold in your hand and use for a particular task

02 독서 동아리의 날이 한 주 남았다며 책갈피를 준비하자는 내용이다.

03 "Which do you prefer, A or B?"는 두 가지 중에서 어느 것을 더 좋아하는지 물을 때 쓰는 표현이다. 여기서 prefer는 '더 좋아하다'라는 말로 'like better'와 같은 의미이다.

04 대화 마지막에 'Let's make a cute cell phone holder.'라고 했다.

05 ⓑ에서 낡은 청바지로 가방을 만들자고 하고, ⓐ에서 좋다며 어떤 종류의 가방을 만들 건지 묻자, ⓔ에서 어깨에 메는 가방과 손에 드는 가방 중에서 어떤 것을 더 좋아하는지 묻고, ⓓ에서 어깨에 메는 가방이 더 좋다고 하자 ⓒ에서 어깨에 메는 가방을 함께 만들자고 하는 순서가 적절하다.

06 'Why is that?'으로 이유를 묻고 있으므로 적절한 답은 ②번이다.

07 (1) 동명사 Riding을 주어로 하여 영작한다.
(2) 현재분사 shopping이 people을 수식하도록 영작한다.

08 청바지로 뭐 하는지 묻자, (B)에서 필통을 만들고 있다고 답하고, (D)에서 멋지다며 그 위에 뭘 그릴지 묻자, (E)에서 판다랑 고양이 중에서 어떤 것을 더 좋아하는지 묻고, (C)에서 고양이를 더 좋아한다고 하자, (A)에서 고양이를 그려 주겠다는 순서가 적절하다.

09 The+비교급+주어+동사 …, the+비교급+주어+동사 ~: …하면 할수록, 더 ~하다

10 주어진 문장의 makes와 ②: 5형식을 이끄는 사역동사 ①, ③, ④: 수여동사 ⑤: 3형식 동사

11 'The+비교급+주어+동사 …, the+비교급+주어+동사 ~' 구문은 '…하면 할수록, 더 ~하다'라는 의미이다.

12 'The+비교급+주어+동사 …, the+비교급+주어+동사 ~'는 '…하면 할수록, 더 ~하다'라는 의미이며, 문맥상 (A)에는 'the wiser', (B)에는 'The deeper'가 나와야 한다.

13 'It ~ that 강조 구문'은 'It is[was]+강조할 부분+that+문장의 나머지 부분'으로 쓰며, 동사를 강조할 수는 없다.

14 책이 등록을 하는 것이 아니라 등록되는 것이므로 수동태로 써야 한다.

15 글의 마지막에 'How was that(그 책이 많은 나라를 여행하고 다른 나라의 많은 독자가 나보다 앞서 이 책을 읽었다는 것) possible?'이라고 했으므로 ①번이 적절하다.

16 책을 심어 물을 주면 나무로 자라므로 '책'이 적절하다.

17 책을 등록하고 공공장소에 놓아두어야 다음 독자가 책을 읽을 수 있을 것이므로 (E)가 적절하다.

18 다음 독자가 어디에 사는지는 알 수 없다.

19 주어진 문장의 'These tiny seeds'가 (D) 앞의 'seeds in each page'를 가리키므로 (D)가 적절하다.

20 ⓐ finish의 목적어로 동명사 ⓑ 책이 만들어지는 것이므로 수동태 ⓒ 사역동사 make의 목적격보어로 동사원형이 적절하다.

21 책이 독서만을 위한 것이 아니라 식수용 필터로도 사용된다는 내용이므로 ②번이 적절하다.

22 ⓓ의 takes는 saves로 고쳐야 한다. 'take the life of ~'는 '~을 죽이다'라는 뜻이다.

23 ⓔ는 'a page of the book'을 가리키지만 나머지는 모두

'book'을 가리킨다.

24 (A) which are가 생략된 형태로 the information and the tools를 수식하는 형용사 necessary가 적절하다.
(B) it이 'the water'를 가리키므로 'changes into'가 적절하다.
(C) diseases가 선행사이므로 come from이 적절하다.

25 책을 읽은 후, 웹사이트에 등록하고 공공장소에 두면 그것을 발견한 사람이 웹사이트에 정보를 입력하고 나서 또 다른 전달자가 되어 책을 같은 방식으로 다른 사람에게 전달하는 책을 공유하는 프로젝트를 언급하는 글로 이렇게 되면 '전 세계가 하나의 큰 도서관이 될 수 있다.'는 것이 적절하다.

26 The+비교급+주어+동사 …, the+비교급+주어+동사 ~' 구문은 '…하면 할수록, 더 ~하다'라는 의미로 'If+주어+동사+비교급 …, 주어+동사+비교급 ~'으로 바꿔 쓸 수 있다.

Lesson 7 (기말) 1회

01 ① **02** ⑤ **03** ② **04** ① **05** ④ **06** ① **07** ③
08 that she would meet his sister the next[following] day
09 ③ **10** ② **11** ③ **12** ② **13** critically **14** ③ **15** ⑤
16 ④ **17** ② **18** ⑤ **19** ② **20** ⑤ **21** ① **22** ② **23** ⑤
24 ①
25 She told her students that they had to check the information and question everything, even things that she said.

01 '누군가가 해야 할 일을 하고 있는지 확인하다'는 '확인하다'이다. check up on: ~을 확인하다

02 Somi가 뒤에서 'I don't agree with you.'라고 했으므로 'It doesn't make sense.(말도 안 돼.)'가 적절하다.

03 Somi는 'Well, I don't think it's that great.'라고 했다.

04 뒤에서 'An octopus can't live out of the sea.'라고 했으므로 'fake(가짜)'가 적절하다.

05 ⓓ 드라마에 대해 어떻게 생각하는지 묻자 ⓐ 감동적이라고 답하고 ⓒ 동의하지 않는다며 좋은 드라마가 아니라고 하자 ⓑ 왜 그렇게 생각하는지 묻고 ⓔ 진짜 같지 않다고 이유를 말하는 순서가 적절하다.

06 'Noodles can't grow on any trees.'라고 했으므로 'the evidence that a Spaghetti Tree is fake'가 적절하다.

07 ⓐ, ⓒ: if ⓑ, ⓓ: whether

08 'said to'를 told로 바꾸고, 인용부호를 없애고 그 내용을 that절로 해서 인칭과 시제 및 부사(I → she, will meet → would meet, your sister → his sister, tomorrow → the next[following] day) 등을 알맞게 바꿔야 한다.

09 She told me that her grandma had died three years before. 'said to'를 told로 바꾸고, 인용부호를 없애고 그 내용을 that절로 해서 인칭과 시제 및 부사(My grandma, → her grandma, died → had died, three years ago → three years before) 등을 알맞게 바꿔야 한다.

10 '현명한 뉴스 독자가 되기 위해 필요한 것'이 무엇인지 묻는 질문에 대한 답으로 '선생님이 말씀하시는 모든 것을 늘 부정하기'는 적절하지 않다.

11 (A) 'to look'과 병렬로 진주어가 되는 'to pay'
(B) supports의 목적어로 간접의문문이 나오므로 'what the writer says(의문사+주어+동사)'
(C) appear to+동사원형: ~인 것 같다

12 'If a story or a photo seems too good to be true, stop and think: Is there any evidence that supports what the writer says?'라고 했다.

13 'think'를 수식하고 있으므로 부사 critically가 적절하다.

14 ⓑ의 as는 '이유'를 나타내고 있다.

15 ⓒ '누구나 '허위' 정보로 가득 찬 웹사이트를 만들어 낼 수 있기 때문'이라고 해야 하므로 'false'가 적절하다.
ⓓ '가짜' 뉴스를 '진짜' 뉴스로부터 구분하는 것이므로 'real'이 적절하다. tell A from B: A와 B를 구별하다

16 (B)의 This skill이 주어진 문장의 내용이므로 먼저 나오고 (A)의 'One of the first steps'가 (C)의 'how to tell fake news from real news'의 '첫 단계 중 하나'이므로 (C) 다음에 (A)가 이어진다. 그러므로 (B)-(C)-(A)가 적절하다.

17 빈칸의 내용으로 비판적으로 생각하는 것이 점점 중요해지는 이유가 나와야 하므로 ②번이 적절하다.

18 10대들이 지어낸 완벽한 거짓말을 확인하지 않고 믿어서 워싱턴 지역 전역의 학교에 충격을 안겼다면서 이야기들은 아주 빠른 속도로 퍼져 나갈 수 있고 누구나 허위 정보로 가득 찬 웹사이트를 만들어 낼 수 있기 때문에 뉴스 속 그리고 인터넷상에서 보고 있는 정보에 관해 비판적으로 생각하는 것을 배워야 한다는 글이므로 ⑤번 '비판적 사고: 진짜 정보를 찾는 중요한 기술'이 적절하다.

19 'The story turned out to be a complete lie.'라고 했다.

20 밑줄 친 'It'과 ⓐ, ⓑ, ⓓ는 '가주어'이다. ⓒ 비인칭 주어 ⓔ 인칭대명사

21 (A)와 ①: 동격의 접속사 ② 지시부사 ③ 명사절을 이끄는 접속사 ④ 관계대명사 ⑤ 지시형용사

22 간접의문문으로 의문사 'who'가 주어로 쓰였으므로 'who was saying this'로 '의문사(주어)+동사+목적어'의 어순이 된다.

23 'an animal'이 'a tree octopus'라고 불리는 것이므로 과거분사 'called'가 되어야 한다.

24 'But like the story of scary clowns, it's totally made up.'

25 'said to'를 told로 바꾸고, 인용부호를 없애고 그 내용을 that절로 해서 인칭과 시제(You → they, have to → had to, I say → she said) 등을 알맞게 바꿔야 한다.

Lesson 7 (기말)

 2회

01 ④	02 ②	03 ④	04 ④	05 ③	06 ③	07 ③	08 ④
09 ③	10 if	11 ③, ⑤		12 ③	13 ④, ⑤		14 ⑤
15 ②	16 ①	17 ④	18 ③, ④		19 ⑤	20 ①, ③	
21 ⑤	22 ⑤	23 ③	24 ⑤	25 ⑤	26 ④	27 ③	

01 '사람들을 속이기 위해 진짜 재료나 물체처럼 보이게 만들어진'은 fake이며 이것의 반의어는 'genuine'이다.

02 spread: to open, arrange, or place (something) over a large area

03 뒤에서 G와 반대되는 내용을 언급하고 있으므로 ④번이 적절하다.

04 ⓓ는 It doesn't make sense. 정도가 적절하다.

05 tell: 말하다, 구별[식별]하다

06 주어진 문장은 (B) 앞의 내용과 상반되는 내용이며 (C) 앞에서 동의하지 않는다고 했으므로 (C)에 들어가는 것이 적절하다.

07 I don't agree.'로 보아 ③번이 적절하다.

08 ④번은 '왜 동의를 하느냐?'라는 뜻이고 나머지는 '어떻게 생각하느냐?'라고 의견을 묻는 표현이다.

09 (C)는 It doesn't make sense.가 적절하다.

10 'If[if] 조건'의 부사절과 목적어로 쓰이는 '~인지 아닌지'라는 뜻의 '명사절'을 이끌 수 있는 것은 'if'이다.

11 ① I wonder if he will like that food.
② Whether you are rich or not doesn't matter.
④ I don't know if you will like my present or not.

12 ③번은 강조 용법에 쓰인 것이지만 나머지는 모두 가주어로 쓰였다.

13 ① He told me that I looked tired that day.
② Jane said that she wanted to be a teacher.
③ He asked me whether I liked her.

14 ① Mike asked her what she was doing there.
② Mary said that she was living in Seoul then.
③ I told my dad that I would call him later.
④ Amy told her brother that that day he was late again.

15 ⓐ의 this는 앞에서 언급된 'a story about scary clowns'를 말한다.

16 ⓑ의 hard는 '명백한, 엄연한'이라는 뜻이다.

17 (A) turn out to be: ~인 것으로 드러나다

(B) resource: 자원, 재원 source: 자료, 출처

(C) creatively: 창조적[독창적]으로 critically: 비평[비판]적으로

18 'The story turned out to be a complete lie.', 'stories about scary clowns shook schools across the Washington area, but Danina Garcia-Fuller's students didn't believe them a bit.'이라고 했다.

19 ⑤번은 부사절을 이끌고 있지만 나머지는 명사절을 이끌고 있다.

20 'too+형용사/부사+to부정사: 너무 …해서 ~할 수 없다'는 'so+형용사/부사+that+주어+can't ~'로 바꿔 쓸 수 있다.

21 각각 ① fact ② opinion ③ evidence ④ support ⑤ background의 풀이이다.

22 '학생들을 '나무 문어'라는 이름의 동물에 대한 정보를 제공하는 것처럼 보이는 웹사이트로 시험한다.'고 했으므로 (A)에는 check(확인하다), (B)에는 question(의문을 가지다)이 적절하다.

23 빈칸에는 scared가 들어간다. ③번이 적절하다.

24 1500년은 'fifteen hundred'로 읽는다.

25 The story turned out to be a complete lie.를 It을 주어로 쓰면 to부정사 부분을 절로 고쳐서 that the story was a complete lie로 쓴다.

26 ⓓ는 talk가 아니라 tell이 되어야 한다.

27 ⓒ는 'Some people'을, 나머지는 'stories'를 지칭한다.

Lesson 8 (기말)

> **01** ② **02** ① **03** ④ **04** I can't stand it.
> **05** I am busy doing my homework. **06** ② **07** ②
> **08** There were 19 other warriors who had passed their tests.
> **09** ②, ③ **10** ③ **11** ⑤ **12** ① **13** ③
> **14** (B) words (C) swords **15** ⑤ **16** ④ **17** ② **18** ⑤
> **19** ① **20** ① **21** ①
> **22** He ordered Corky to go to a famous military school.
> **23** ④ **24** ③ **25** ④ **26** ③

01 injuring → injured

02 순서대로 • recently • made up • approached • against • fasted가 들어간다.

03 forget to ~: ~할 것을 잊다, forget ~ing: ~한 것을 잊다

04 뒤에서 'I cleaned the living room all morning.'이라고 하자 'Calm down!'이라고 했으므로 'I can't stand it.(참을 수가 없어.)'이 적절하다.

05 be busy -ing: ~하느라 바쁘다

06 드라마에 대한 느낌을 묻자 감동적이라고 답하며 여동생을 위해 삶을 포기했다면서 금년 최고의 드라마라고 하자 자기도 그렇다며 빨리 한 번 더 보고 싶다고 하는 ②가 자연스러운 대화이다.

07 'Some'은 불특정 다수의 여러 사람 중 '몇몇 사람들'이라는 뜻이고, 'others'는 '(그 밖의) 다른 사람들'이라는 뜻이다.

08 19명의 다른 전사들이 홀에 있는 시점(were: 과거)보다 시험에 통과한 시점이 앞서므로 과거완료로 쓰는 것이 적절하다. pass → had passed

09 ① the second → the other ④ Some → One
⑤ other → the other

10 pass by: 옆을 지나가다

11 명령문+or: …해라, 그러지 않으면 ~할 것이다

12 'Then, the teacher told Corky to stand against a pole. Suddenly, he tied Corky to the pole.'이라고 했다.

13 'Corky shouted back. He yelled, "Set me free, or you all will be in big trouble!"'로 보아 'upset(당황한, 화가 난)'이 적절하다.

14 (B) Corky가 부드럽게 말하기 시작해서 마침내 사람들은 그를 풀어 주었으므로 'words(말)'가 적절하다.
(C) 앞에서 '강력한 무기'가 나오므로 'swords(칼)'가 적절하다.

15 'Impressing'은 능동의 의미로 '~을 감동시키다'라는 의미이므로 '감동을 받은'의 뜻을 갖는 Impressed로 고치는 것이 적절하다.

16 '네가 진정한 승자다.'라는 말은 Corky가 부상당한 전사들을 돌봐 주어 18명이 따르게 된 것을 의미한다.

17 왕이 "안녕하시오, 장군?"이라고 한 것은 Corky가 장군임을 인정한 것이다.

18 (A) 19명의 다른 전사들이 홀에 있는 시점(were: 과거)보다 시험에 통과한 시점이 앞서므로 과거완료가 적절하다.
(B) the others: 나머지 사람들
(C) 주어가 'all the warriors except Thunder'이므로 were가 적절하다.

19 첫 번째 단락에서 'there might be a reason'이라고 생각하며 '100일'을 기다린 것으로 보아 'calm(침착한, 냉정한)'이 적절하다. 두 번째 단락에서 'Corky shouted back. He yelled, "Set me free, or you all will be in big trouble!"'로 보아 'annoyed(화가 난)'가 적절하다.

20 'little'은 '거의 없는'이라는 뜻이므로 'much' 정도로 바꿔야 한다.

21 'He wanted to be a general'이라고 했다.

22 'ordered'의 목적어로 Corky를 쓰고 목적격보어로 'to go'를 쓴다. order+목적어+to부정사(목적격 보어): …에게 ~하라고 명령

하다

23 앞에서 100일을 기다렸으므로 'patience(인내)'가 적절하다.

24 Corky가 군사 학교에 가서 '인내'와 '말'을 통제하는 법을 배웠다는 내용의 글이므로 ③번이 적절하다.

25 (D) 다음의 this가 주어진 문장의 내용을 가리키므로 (D)가 적절하다.

26 'On the hundred and first day, the gate opened.'라고 했다.